IRISH TAX REPORTS

2001 Cases,
Cumulative Tables
and Index (1922-2001)

Butterworths
A Member of the LexisNexis Group

IRISH TAX REPORTS

2001 Cases,
Cumulative Tables
and Index (1922-2001)

Edited by

B H Giblin BA BL

and

David Hession BCL, Solicitor

Butterworths
A Member of the LexisNexis Group

Members of LexisNexis Group worldwide:

Ireland	Butterworth (Ireland) Ltd, 24-26 Upper Ormond Quay, DUBLIN 7
Argentina	Abeledo Perrot, Jurisprudencia Argentina and Depalma, BUENOS AIRES
Australia	Butterworths, a Division of Reed International Books Australia Pty Ltd, CHATSWOOD, New South Wales
Austria	ARD Betriebsdienst and Verlag Orac, VIENNA
Canada	Butterworths Canada Ltd, MARKHAM, Ontario
Chile	Publitecsa and Conosur Ltda, SANTIAGO DE CHILE
Czech Republic	Orac sro, PRAGUE
France	Editions du Juris-Classeur SA, PARIS
Hong Kong	Butterworths Asia (Hong Kong), HONG KONG
Hungary	Hvg Orac, BUDAPEST
India	Butterworths India, NEW DELHI
Italy	Giuffré, MILAN
Malaysia	Malayan Law Journal Sdn Bhd, KUALA LUMPUR
New Zealand	Butterworths of New Zealand, WELLINGTON
Poland	Wydawnictwa Prawnicze PWN, WARSAW
Singapore	Butterworths Asia, SINGAPORE
South Africa	Butterworths Publishers (Pty) Ltd, DURBAN
Switzerland	Stämpfli Verlag AG, BERNE
United Kingdom	Butterworths Tolley, a Division of Reed Elsevier (UK) Ltd, Halsbury House, 35 Chancery Lane, LONDON, WC2A 1EL, and 4 Hill Street, EDINBURGH EH2 3JZ
USA	LexisNexis, DAYTON, Ohio

© Butterworth Ireland Ltd 2002

All rights reserved. No part of this publication may be reproduced or transmitted in any form or by any means, including photocopying and recording, without the written permission of the copyright holder, application for which should be addressed to the publisher. Such written permission must also be obtained before any part of this publication is stored in a retrieval system of any nature.

A CIP Catalogue record for this book is available from the British Library.

These reports should be cited thus:

[Year] (Volume) ITR (Page)

ISBN for complete set: 1 85475 7008

ISBN for this book: 1 85475 2170

Typeset by Marlex Editorial Services Ltd, Dublin, Ireland
Printed by Antony Rowe, Chippenham, Wiltshire
Visit us at our website: http//www.butterworths.ie

Introduction

This book contains the tax cases in 2001. As with previous editions of this book it also serves as a cumulative tables and index volume for the five volumes of Irish tax reports and the 1998/2000 cases volumes. These tables and index should ensure that the required cases are easily and quickly relocated. If you have any comments or suggestions for improvements please contact the editor.

1. **Contents 2001** vii
   This outlines cases and determinations contained in the 2001 volume.

2. **Contents 1922-2001** 1
   This is a complete *chronological* list of all the cases reported in the entire set which also shows key words relating to each case and references indicating where the case was previously reported.

3. **Cases 2001** 57
   These are all the relevant cases heard since the 2000 publication.

4. **Cases reported** 169
   This is an *alphabetical* list of the cases reported.

5. **Cases reported and considered** 179
   This is an *alphabetical* list of the cases reported, however, this table is extended to include cases referred to in judgments or cases cited in the cases reported in full. The cases reported in full are shown in italics.

6. **Statutes considered** 225
   This table lists in *alphabetical and numerical* sequence the statutory provisions considered by the courts.

7. **Destination table (Taxes Consolidation Act 1997)** 247
   This table enables the reader to trace the present *location* of legislation between 1967 and 1997.

8. **Index** 341
   This is an *alphabetical* subject index which sets out the subject matter of each case in the five volumes.

David Hession
Editor
March 2002

Contents 2001

Simple Imports Limited and Another v Revenue Commissioners and Others 57
Cyril Forbes v John Tobin And Janet Tobin 71
In the Matter of Millhouse Taverns Ltd and the Companies Act 1963-1999 77
Patrick J O'Connell (Inspector of Taxes) v Tara Mines Ltd 79
Beverly Cooper-Flynn v RTE, Charlie Bird and James Howard 97
Patrick J O'Connell (Inspector of Taxes) v Thomas Keleghan 103
Seán MacAonghusa (Inspector of Taxes) v Ringmahon Company 117
Francis Griffin v Minister for Social, Community and Family Affairs 125
John Gilligan v Criminal Assets Bureau, Revenue Commissioners & Others 135

Contents

Arthur Guinness Son & Co Ltd v Commissioners of Inland Revenue
1 ITC 1, [1923] 2 IR 186 .... Vol I p 1

Income tax and excess profits duty - liability in respect of transactions under DORA requisition orders - trade or business - ITA Sch D - FA 1915 (No 2) s 38.

McCall (Deceased) v Commissioners of Inland Revenue
1 ITC 31 .... Vol I p 28

Excess profits duty - purchase of whiskey in bond by a publican - whiskey in bond could be sold to best advantage - whether sale at cost plus interest constituted a trade - whether an investment with capital gains - whether a trade is carried on as a question of law and fact - whether facts found by Special Commissioners can be reopened.

Boland's Ltd v Commissioners of Inland Revenue
1 ITC 42 .... Vol I p 34

Excess profits duty - whether profits to be ascertained by actual profits or a percentage standard - percentage standard based on 6 per cent of company's net capital - whether proper deduction for wear and tear and capital expenditure on replacements of capital items - whether assessment can be reopened - doctrines of res judicata and equitable estoppel - whether inspector entitled to recompute percentage basis - whether appellants precluded from introducing new grounds of appeal.

Evans & Co v Phillips (Inspector of Taxes)
1 ITC 38 .... Vol I p 43

Income tax - Schedule D - obsolescence of assets - ITA 1918 Sch D Cases I & II rule 7.

Irish Provident Assurance Co Ltd (In Liquidation) v Kavanagh (Inspector of Taxes)
1 ITC 52, [1930] IR 231 .... Vol I p 45

Income tax - Schedule D - interest on money - ITA 1918 Sch D Case III.

The King (Harris Stein) v The Special Commissioners
1 ITC 71 .... Vol I p 62

Confirmation of assessment - request for case stated by taxpayer - allowance of expenses where assessment has been confirmed

Phillips (Inspector of Taxes) v Keane
I ITC 69, [1925] 2 IR 48 .... Vol I p 64

Income tax - Schedule E - deduction - travelling expenses - ITA 1918 (8 & (Geo V, Ch 40)), Sch E, rule 9.

Phillips (Inspector of Taxes) v Limerick County Council
1 ITC 96, [1925] 2 IR 139 .... Vol I p 66

Income tax - Sch D Case III - interest - deduction.

Commissioners of Inland Revenue v The Governor & Company of The Bank of Ireland
1 ITC 74, [1925] 2 IR 90..Vol I p 70

Corporation profits tax - the Governor and Company of the Bank of Ireland incorporated by letter patent - Act of Irish Parliament 1783 - whether a company within the meaning of FA 1920 s 52(3) - unpaid debts of bank - whether personal liability of members unlimited.

Boland's Ltd v Davis (Inspector of Taxes)
1 ITC 91, [1925] ILTR 73 ....Vol I p 86

Income tax - Schedule D - discontinuance - distance trades - set-off for losses - ITA 1918 Sch D Cases I and II and miscellaneous rules.

Fitzgerald v Commissioners of Inland Revenue
1 ITC 100, [1926] IR 182, 585..Vol I p 91

Excess profits duty - deductions - expenditure on temporary premises - restoration of destroyed premises under covenant to repair.

The Alliance & Dublin Consumers' Gas Co v Davis (Inspector of Taxes)
1 ITC 114, [1926] IR 372..Vol I p 104

Income tax - Schedule D - profits of trade - deduction - capital loss - ITA 1918 Sch D, Cases I & II, rule 3.

The City of Dublin Steampacket Co v The Revenue Commissioners
1 ITC 118, [1926] IR 436..Vol I p 108

Corporation profits tax - company formed mainly for purpose of trading by use of steam vessels - cargo business and carriage of mails between Dun Laoghaire and Liverpool and Holyhead - cargo business ceased 1919 - mails contract terminated 1920 - whether running down of business constituted a trade or business - whether collection of debts a business undertaking - periodic payments on foot of an earlier debt and acquisition of profits - whether carrying on a business.

Donovan (Inspector of Taxes) v Crofts
1 ITC 214, [1926] IR 477..Vol I p 115

Income tax - husband and wife living apart - "married woman living with her husband" - ITA 1918 rule 16 of general rules.

Commissioners of Inland Revenue v The Dublin and Kingstown Railway Co
1 ITC 285, [1930] IR 317..Vol I p 119

Corporation profits tax - The Dublin and Kingston Railway Co was incorporated in 1831 to make and maintain a railway between Dublin and Kingston - railway lines leased to another company at an annual rent - all the property of owning company (except offices) passed to lessee company - whether collection of rents and dividends and distribution of profits thereout to shareholders constituted a trade or business - whether company has a corporate existence.

Green & Co (Cork) Ltd v The Revenue Commissioners
1 ITC 142, [1927] IR 240 .... Vol I p 130

Excess profits duty - stock relief claim - "trading stock in hand" - FA 1921, Sch 2 Pt II, rule 1.

Wing v O'Connell (Inspector of Taxes)
1 ITC 170, [1927] IR 84 .... Vol I p 155

Income tax - Schedule E - vocation - professional jockey - whether present from employer taxable emolument or gift.

The Executors and Trustees of A C Ferguson (Deceased) v Donovan (Inspector of Taxes)
1 ITC 214, [1927] ILTR 49, [1929] IR 489 .... Vol I p 183

Income tax - Sch D Case 1 - business carried on abroad - control by trustees.

Hayes (Inspector of Taxes) v Duggan
1 ITC 269, [1929] IR 406 .... Vol I p 195

Income tax - Schedule D - profits on sweepstakes - illegal trades not assessable to tax - ITA 1918 Sch D Cases II & VI.

The Alliance and Dublin Consumers' Gas Co v McWilliams (Inspector of Taxes)
1 ITC 199, [1928] IR 1 .... Vol I p 207

Income tax - profits of trade - compulsory detention of ships by government - compensation payment - capital or trading receipt - ITA 1918.

MacKeown (Inspector of Taxes) v Roe
1 ITC 206, [1928] IR 195 .... Vol I p 214

Income tax - public office or employment of profit - solicitor to local authority - ITA 1918 Sch E, rules 1 & 5 - profits not received in the year of assessment.

The King (Evelyn Spain) v The Special Commissioners
1 ITC 227, [1934] IR 27 .... Vol I p 221

Mandamus - finality of Special Commissioners' decision on claim for relief -income tax - income accumulated for minor - benefit taken by way of capital - ITA 1918 ss 25 & 202.

Conyngham v The Revenue Commissioners
1 ITC 259, [1928] ILTR 57, 136.. Vol I p 231

Super tax - total income - trust deed - trust for expenditure of moneys upon property beneficially occupied by life tenant - ITA 1918 s 5.

The Revenue Commissioners v Latchford & Sons Ltd
1 ITC 238 .... Vol I p 240

Excess profits duty - loss in trade - forward purchase contracts - fall in market value of goods before delivery - FA 1915 (No 2) Fourth Schedule Pt I rule I.

Prior-Wandesforde v The Revenue Commissioners
1 ITC 248 ....Vol I p 249

Income tax - Schedule D - domicile and ordinary residence - foreign possessions - ITA 1918 Case V rule 3, FA 1925 Sch D (No 28) s 12.

Earl of Iveagh v The Revenue Commissioners
1 ITC 316, [1930] IR 386, 431..Vol I p 259

Income tax - Schedule D - super tax - domicile and ordinary residence, foreign securities and possessions - ITA 1918 Sch D Case IV rule 2(a) & Case V rule 3(a) - FA 1925 (No 28) s 12.

Kennedy (Inspector of Taxes) v The Rattoo Co-operative Dairy Society Ltd
1 ITC 282 ....Vol I p 315

Corporation profits tax - The Rattoo Co-operative Dairy Society Ltd - registered under the Industrial and Provident Societies Act 1893 - milk supplied by members and non-members - whether monthly surpluses retained by the society arose from trading - whether surpluses arose from trading with its own members - whether exemption under FA 1921 s 53 applied.

The City of Dublin Steampacket Co (In Liquidation) v The Revenue Commissioners
1 ITC 285, [1930] IR 217..Vol I p 318

Corporation profits tax - company's contract to carry mails between Ireland and England terminated in 1920 - petition to wind up the company filed on 11 August 1924 - income from company's investments continued after winding up application - business - whether during a period of winding up a company may earn income - whether winding up order prevents carrying on business for tax purposes.

The Cunard Steam Ship Co Ltd v Herlihy (Inspector of Taxes), and
The Cunard Steam Ship Co Ltd v Revenue Commissioners
1 ITC 373, [1931] IR 287, 307..Vol I p 330

Income tax - Schedule D - non-resident company - exercise of trade within Saorstat Eireann - ITA 1918 Sch D, rule 1(a)(iii).

The Great Southern Railways Co v The Revenue Commissioners
1 ITC 298, [1930] IR 299..Vol I p 359

Corporation profits tax - The Great Southern Railways Co - Railways Act 1924 - absorbed the Dublin and Kingston Railway Co - lessor of railway line - whether a railway undertaking - whether precluded from charging any higher price or distributing any higher rate of dividend - whether lessor company carries on a railway undertaking - whether prices under control of lessee company.

McGarry (Inspector of Taxes) v Limerick Gas Committee
1 ITC 405, [1932] IR 125..Vol I p 375

Income tax - deduction - expenses of promoting bill in Parliament - ITA 1918 (8 & 9 Geo V, Ch 40), Sch D, Cases I & II, rule 3.

Beirne (Inspector of Taxes) v St Vincent De Paul Society (Wexford Conference)
1 ITC 413 .... Vol I p 383

Income tax - exemption - trading by charity - work done by beneficiaries - FA 1921 (11 & 12 Geo V, Ch 32) s 30(1)(c).

Davis (Inspector of Taxes) v The Superioress, Mater Misericordiae Hospital, Dublin
2 ITC 1, [1933] IR 480, 503 .... Vol I p 387

Income tax - Schedule D - Hospital - whether carrying on a trade - profits derived from associated private nursing home - ITA 1918 Sch D.

Hughes (Inspector of Taxes) v Smyth and Others
1 ITC 418, [1933] IR 253 .... Vol I p 411

Income tax - disposition of income - deed of trust in favour of charitable objects with provision for re-vesting of income in settlor in certain contingencies - FA 1922 (12 & 13 Geo V c 17) s 20(1)(c).

Robinson T/A James Pim & Son v Dolan (Inspector of Taxes)
2 ITC 25, [1935] IR 509 .... Vol I p 427

Income tax - Sch D Case 1 - ex gratia payment by British government - recommendation by Irish Grants Committee - whether income of appellant assessable to income tax.

Howth Estate Co v Davis (Inspector of Taxes)
2 ITC 74, [1936] ILTR 79 .... Vol I p 447

Income tax - family estate company - claim for relief in respect of expenses of management - "company whose business consists mainly in the making of investments, and the principal part of whose income is derived therefrom" - ITA 1918 s 33(1).

The Agricultural Credit Corporation Ltd v Vale (Inspector of Taxes)
2 ITC 46, [1935] IR 681 .... Vol I p 474

Income tax - Schedule D - profits on realisation of investments - whether trading profits.

Estate of Teresa Downing (Owner)
2 ITC 103, [1936] IR 164 .... Vol I p 487

Income tax - Land Purchase Acts - arrears of jointure - ITA 1918 rule 21 of general rules.

Cloghran Stud Farm v A G Birch (Inspector of Taxes)
2 ITC 65, [1936] IR 1 .... Vol I p 496

Income tax - Schedule D - profits from stallion fees.

Davis (Inspector of Taxes) v Hibernian Bank Ltd
2 ITC 111 .... Vol I p 503

Income tax - Schedule D - banking company - change effected by Railways Act 1933, in company's holdings of railway stock - whether equivalent to sale or realisation.

Birch (Inspector of Taxes) v Delaney
2 ITC 127, [1936] IR 517, 531 ....Vol I p 515

Income tax - Schedule D - builder's profits - whether fines and capitalised value of ground rents are assessable to tax.

The Trustees of The Ward Union Hunt Races v Hughes (Inspector of Taxes)
2 ITC 152 ....Vol I p 538

Income tax - exemption - Agricultural Society - FA 1925 s 4.

The Pharmaceutical Society of Ireland v The Revenue Commissioners
2 ITC 157, [1938] IR 202 ....Vol I p 542

Income tax - exemption - charitable purposes - ITA 1918 s 37(1)(b) - FA 1921 s 30(1)(a) - trade - ITA 1918 s 237.

Mulvey (Inspector of Taxes) v Kieran
2 ITC 179, [1938] IR 87 ....Vol I p 563

Income tax - husband and wife living together - husband's income from securities - additional assessment on husband in respect of first year of wife's income from securities etc - ITA 1918 General Rule 16 - FA 1929 ss 10 & 11 and Sch 1 Pt.

The State (at the prosecution of Patrick J Whelan) v Smidic (Special Commissioners of Income Tax)
2 ITC 188, [1938] IR 626 ....Vol I p 571

Income tax - Schedule D - assessment of builder's profits - ruling of Special Commissioner on question of discontinuance - variation of ruling before figures agreed upon or fixed - determination of an appeal - ITA 1918 (8 & 9 Geo 5, c 40) ss 133, 137 & 149, FA 1929 (No 32 of 1929) s 5.

Connolly v Birch (Inspector of Taxes)
2 ITC 201, [1939] IR 534 ....Vol I p 583

Income tax, FA 1935 Sch D s 6 - assessment of builders profits - inclusion in 1935-36 assessment of amounts received in respect of fines and capitalised value of surplus ground rents created prior to the coming into operation of the section.

O'Reilly v Casey (Inspector of Taxes)
2 ITC 220, [1942] IR 378 ....Vol I p 601

Income tax - provisions in codicil to a will charging the rents of the testator's real and leasehold property with the payment of 10 per cent, thereof to a named son so long as that son continued to manage the property - whether such payment was remuneration chargeable upon the recipient under ITA 1918 Sch E - ITA 1918 Sch E - Charging Rule: FA 1922 s 18.

Mulvey (Inspector of Taxes) v Coffey
2 ITC 239, [1942] IR 277 ....Vol I p 618

Income tax - Schedule E - emolument of office - grant to a President of a college on retirement - whether chargeable to income tax - ITA 1918 Sch E rule 1 - FA 1929 s 17.

O'Dwyer (Inspector of Taxes) and The Revenue Commissioners v Irish Exporters and Importers Ltd (In Liquidation)
2 ITC 251, [1943] IR 176 .... Vol I p 629

Income tax and corporation profits tax - whether or not a sum of money payable and paid to a limited liability company under a prior agreement by the Minister for Agriculture in the event of his having terminated, within a prescribed period, a supply of the raw material of the trade of another company, (promoted by the first company at the request of said Minister), is or is not a receipt of the first company's trade - ITA 1918 Sch D Case 1 - FA 1920 s 53.

Kealy (Inspector of Taxes) v O'Mara (Limerick) Ltd
2 ITC 265, [1942] IR 616 .... Vol I p 642

Income tax - deductions - whether expenses preliminary to, and in connection with, the formation of a "holding company" were admissible as part of trading expenses of a bacon manufacturing company - ITA 1918 ss 100(2), 209 and Sch D, rule applicable to Case I, and rules 1(1) & 3 of Cases I & II.

Dolan (Inspector of Taxes) v "K" National School Teacher
2 ITC 280, [1944] IR 470 .... Vol I p 656

Income tax - Schedule E - professed nun employed as national school teacher but bound by constitutions of her order to hand over all her earnings to the order - whether or not assessable Schedule E as having earned or exercising an office or employment, as national school teacher - ITA 1918 Sch E rule 1.

McGarry (Inspector of Taxes) v Spencer
2 ITC 297, [1946] IR 11 .... Vol II p 1

Nurseries and market gardens - ITA 1918 Sch B rule 8 ss 186 & 187 - whether rule 8 applies in Eire, that is, whether the income is chargeable with reference to annual value or upon profits estimated according to the rules of Schedule D.

Gilbert Hewson v Kealy (Inspector of Taxes)
2 ITC 286 .... Vol II p 15

Income tax - Sch D Case III - interest and income from securities and possessions - execution of document under seal in the Isle of Man - contention that beneficial interest in the said securities and possessions had been transferred - original document not produced - secondary evidence of its terms not admissible.

The Revenue Commissioners v Switzer Ltd
2 ITC 290, [1945] IR 378 .... Vol II p 19

Excess corporation profits tax - company on "substituted standard" - portion of issue of debenture stock bought back by company - whether in computing substituted standard such portion of the issue should be taken into account - FA 1941 s 39 as amended by FA 1942 s 16.

Property Loan & Investment Co Ltd v The Revenue Commissioners
2 ITC 312, [1946] IR 159... Vol II p 25

Corporation profits tax - company incorporated under the Companies Acts 1908 to 1917 - business consisting of the advancement of moneys to persons not members of the company for the purpose of enabling them to acquire dwelling-houses - whether company carries on "the business of a building society" - FA 1929 s 33(1)(d), as amended.

Vale (Inspector of Taxes) v Martin Mahony & Brothers Ltd
2 ITC 331, [1947] IR 30, 41.. Vol II p 32

Income tax - Schedule D - deduction - expenditure upon mill sanitation.

Davis (Inspector of Taxes) v X Ltd
2 ITC 320, [1946] ILTR 57, [1947] ILTR 157.. Vol II p 45

Income tax - Schedule D - profits of trade - deductions - new factory in course of erection - interference with rights as regards light and air claimed by tenants of adjoining houses - settlement of action - sums paid to tenants as compensation and for legal costs.

AB v Mulvey (Inspector of Taxes)
2 ITC 345, [1947] IR 121... Vol II p 55

Income tax - Schedule D - business carried on by sole trader - partner admitted at beginning of year - business sold later in year to private company - whether assessment on sole trader for the previous year can be reviewed - ITA 1918 Sch D Cases I & II rule 11 - FA 1929 s 12.

A and B v Davis (Inspector of Taxes) 2 ITC 350.. Vol II p 60

Income tax, Schedule D - appeal to High Court by way of case stated from decision of Circuit Judge - failure of appellants to send to respondent, at or before the required date, notice in writing of fact that case had been stated etc - ITA 1918 s 149(1)(e).

O'Sullivan (Inspector of Taxes) v O'Connor, as Administratrix of O'Brien, (Deceased)
2 ITC 352, [1947] IR 416... Vol II p 61

Income tax - Schedule D - compulsory sale to Minister for Finance, in return for sterling equivalents, of dollar balances consisting of income from securities, etc, in the USA - whether moneys so received assessable - FA 1929 Sch 1 Pt II.

Tipping (Inspector of Taxes) v Jeancard
2 ITC 360, [1948] IR 233... Vol II p 68

Income tax - Schedule E - office of profit within the State - director, resident abroad, of a company incorporated in the State but managed and controlled abroad.

Ua Clothasaigh (Inspector of Taxes) v McCartan
2 ITC 367, [1948] IR 219... Vol II p 75

Income tax - husband and wife- "married woman living with her husband" - ITA 1918 general rule 16.

O'Dwyer (Inspector of Taxes) v Cafolla & Co
2 ITC 374, [1949] IR 210 ....Vol II p 82

Income tax - dispositions of income - father taking his elder children and his mother-in-law into partnership - subsequent assignment of mother-in-law's interest to his younger children - whether income of children to be deemed to be income of father - FA 1922 s 20 - FA 1937 s 2.

The Attorney-General v Irish Steel Ltd and Crowley
2 ITC 402 ....Vol II p 108

Income tax and corporation profits tax - company in hands of a receiver - preferential claim - Companies (Consolidation) Act 1908 ss 107 and 209.

O'Dwyer (Inspector of Taxes) v The Dublin United Transport Co Ltd
2 ITC 437, [1949] IR 295 ....Vol II p 115

Income tax - Schedule D - cessation - deduction of corporation profits tax and excess corporation profits tax in computing profits for income tax purposes - ITA 1918 Sch D, Cases I & II, rule 4 - FA 1929 s 12.

The Revenue Commissioners v R Hilliard & Sons Ltd
2 ITC 410 ....Vol II p 130

Corporation profits tax (including excess corporation profits tax) - accounting period - accounts made up half-yearly - yearly account for general meeting prepared from half-yearly accounts - whether Revenue Commissioners required to determine the accounting period - FA 1920 s 54(1).

CD v O'Sullivan (Inspector of Taxes)
2 ITC 422, [1949] IR 264 ....Vol II p 140

Income tax - Schedule D - bad debts - executor carrying on trade - recovery by executor of debts allowed as bad debts in lifetime of deceased - whether a trading receipt.

O'Loan (Inspector of Taxes) v Noone & Co
2 ITC 430, [1949] IR 171 ....Vol II p 146

Income tax - Schedule D - fuel merchants - whether a new trade of coal mining set up or commenced - FA 1929 ss 8(1) & 9(2).

Moville District Board of Conservators v Ua Clothasaigh (Inspector of Taxes)
3 ITC 1, [1950] IR 301 ....Vol II p 154

Income tax - Schedule D - surplus revenue of Board of Conservators - whether annual profits or gains - ITA 1918 Case VI.

Corr (Inspector of Taxes) v Larkin
3 ITC 13, [1949] IR 399 ....Vol II p 164

Income tax - Schedule D - sum recovered under loss of profits policy - whether a profit or gain arising from the trade - year in which assessable.

Associated Properties Ltd v The Revenue Commissioners
3 ITC 25, [1951] IR 140 .... Vol II p 175

Corporation profits tax -"the shareholders" - whether a "post-appointed day company" was a subsidiary of the appellant company - whether appellant company director-controlled and, if so, whether its managing director was the beneficial owner of, or able to control more than 5 per cent of its ordinary shares - FA 1944 s 14 - FA 1941 s 36(4).

The Revenue Commissioners v Y Ltd
3 ITC 49 .... Vol II p 195

Corporation profits tax (including excess corporation profit tax) - Industrial and Provident Societies - society trading with its own members and with non-members - investments and property purchased out of trading profits - whether the dividends and rents form part of the profits or surplus arising from the trade - additional assessments - FA 1920 s 53(2)(h) - FA 1921 s 53 - FA 1946 s 24.

The Veterinary Council v Corr (Inspector of Taxes)
3 ITC 59, [1953] IR 12 .... Vol II p 204

Income tax - body corporate performing statutory functions - surplus of receipts over expenditure - whether annual profits or gains - ITA 1918 Sch D Case VI.

The Exported Live Stock (Insurance) Board v Carroll (Inspector of Taxes)
3 ITC 67, [1951] IR 286 .... Vol II p 211

Income tax - Sch D Case 1 - statutory body set up to carry into effect a compulsory insurance scheme - whether statutory body was carrying on a trade within the meaning of Sch D Case I and whether the surpluses arising from the carrying on of its statutory activities were taxable as profits of such a trade - ITA 1918 Sch D Case I.

Flynn (Inspector of Taxes) v John Noone Ltd, and
Flynn (Inspector of Taxes) v Blackwood & Co (Sligo) Ltd
3 ITC 79 .... Vol II p 222

Income tax, Schedule D - capital or revenue - lump sum paid on execution of lease - whether capital payment and receipt or rent paid in advance - ITA 1918 Sch D Case III rule 5 and Cases I & II, rule 3(a).

L v McGarry (Inspector of Taxes)
3 ITC 111 .... Vol II p 241

Income tax - Schedule B - whether rule 8 applicable where the lands occupied as gardens for the sale of produce comprise part only of a unit of valuation - power to apportion valuation and land purchase annuity - ITA 1918 ss 186 & 187 and Sch B rule 8.

McGarry (Inspector of Taxes) v E F
3 ITC 103, [1954] IR 64 .... Vol II p 261

Income tax - general manager of company "Y" - professional services rendered to company "X" without agreement as regards remuneration - payment made by company "X" on termination of services - whether chargeable as income - ITA 1918 Sch E rule 7 and Sch D Case VI.

Hodgins (Inspector of Taxes) v Plunder & Pollak (Ireland) Ltd
3 ITC 135, [1957] IR 58 .... Vol II p 267

Income tax - Schedule D - deduction in computing profits - cost of replacement of weighbridge house - ITA 1918 Sch D Cases I & II, rule 3(d) and (g).

The Revenue Commissioners v L & Co
3 ITC 205 .... Vol II p 281

Corporation profits tax - foreign company trading in this country - expenditure attributable to Irish trading not transferred from company's Irish resources to head office in the USA - devaluation of sterling - deduction from profits.

Collins and Byrne and Power v Mulvey (Inspector of Taxes)
3 ITC 151, [1956] IR 233 .... Vol II p 291

Income tax - Schedule D - profits from illegal trade - admissibility of evidence of illegality - ITA 1918 Sch D Case I.

O'Conaill (Inspector of Taxes) v R
3 ITC 167, [1956] IR 97 .... Vol II p 304

Income tax - Schedule D - trade carried on wholly in England - basis of assessment under Case III - "single source" - ITA 1918 Sch D Case III rule 2 (FA 1922 s 17) - FA 1926 Sch 1 Pt II s 2(2) & 1(3) - FA 1929 ss 10, 11 & 18 and Sch 2 para 3.

Mac Giolla Riogh (Inspector of Taxes) v G Ltd
3 ITC 181, [1957] IR 90 .... Vol II p 315

Income tax - Schedule D - company trading in bloodstock - animal bought in course of trade, sent to stud after successful racing career and subsequently sold to a syndicate - whether amount realised on syndication a trading receipt - ITA 1918 Sch D Case I and FA 1939 Sch B s 7.

The Revenue Commissioners v Orwell Ltd
3 ITC 193 .... Vol II p 326

Corporation profits tax and excess corporation profits tax - whether excess corporation profits tax is exigible for accounting periods in respect of which no corporation profits tax (other than excess corporation profits tax) is payable - FA 1941 s 37.

Colclough v Colclough
[1965] IR 668 .... Vol II p 332

Income tax-funds in court - (a) whether rules 19 and 21 of the general rules applicable to ITA 1918 Sch A, B, C, D and E apply to the court when paying interest on debts out of funds in court and - (b) whether tax deductible from income accrued to funds in court for years prior to 1922/23.

EG v Mac Shamhrain (Inspector of Taxes)
3 ITC 217, [1958] IR 288.. Vol II p 352

Income tax - Sch D Case III - Settlement of income - deed of appointment by parent in favour of child - power of revocation - FA 1922 s 20(1), FA 1937 s 2(1) - rule 16, general rules applicable to all Schedules.

Curtin (Inspector of Taxes) v M Ltd
3 ITC 227, [1960] IR 59... Vol II p 360

Income tax - Schedule D - profits of trade - deduction - expenditure on rebuilding of business premises - whether portion thereof deductible in computing profits.

O'Broin (Inspector of Taxes) v Mac Giolla Meidhre
O'Broin (Inspector of Taxes) v Pigott
3 ITC 235, [1959] IR 98... Vol II p 366

Income tax - Schedule E - deductions - expenses - ITA 1918 Sch E rule 9.

Bourke (Inspector of Taxes) v Lyster & Sons Ltd
3 ITC 247 .... Vol II p 374

Income tax - Schedule D - profits of a trade - sum received in part payment of a debt previously treated as bad-res judicata - jurisdiction of Circuit Court Judge when hearing on appeal against an assessment.

Milverton Quarries Ltd v The Revenue Commissioners
3 ITC 279, [1960] IR 224... Vol II p 382

Corporation profits tax - deduction from profits - expenses of removing top soil from surface of quarry - whether capital or revenue expenditure - ITA 1918 Sch D Cases I & II rule 2 - FA 1920 s 53.

McHugh (Inspector of Taxes) v A
3 ITC 257, [1958] IR 142, [1959] ILTR 125 .... Vol II p 393

Income tax - Schedule D - pension, annuity or other annual payment - payments made by a British company to a person resident in the State - whether income from a foreign possession - ITA 1918 Sch D Case III, FA 1922 s 18, FA 1929 s 11, FA 1932 s 4.

The Revenue Commissioners v Associated Properties Ltd
3 ITC 293 .... Vol II p 412

Corporation profits tax - Interest paid to a person having controlling interest - FA 1920 s 53(2)(b).

AB Ltd v Mac Giolla Riogh (Inspector of Taxes)
3 ITC 301 .... Vol II p 419

Income tax - Schedule D - finance company dealing in stocks and shares - whether investments should be valued at cost or market value.

Casey (Inspector of Taxes) v The Monteagle Estate Co
3 ITC 313, [1962] IR 106 ....Vol II p 429

Income tax - estate company - claim for relief in respect of expenses of management - "company whose business consists mainly in the making of investments and the principal part of whose income is derived therefrom" - ITA 1918 s 33(1).

Connolly (Inspector of Taxes) v McNamara
3 ITC 341 ....Vol II p 452

Income tax - Schedule E - emolument of employment - rent paid by employing company for house occupied voluntarily by employee - ITA 1918 Sch E, FA 1922 s 18.

Kelly (Inspector of Taxes) v H
3 ITC 351, [1964] IR 488 ....Vol II p 460

Income tax - Schedule E - deductions - expenses - ITA 1918 Sch E rule 9.

O'Sullivan (Inspector of Taxes) v P Ltd
3 ITC 355 ....Vol II p 464

Income tax - Schedule D - payment in advance on the signing of a lease - whether a capital receipt (ie a fine or premium) or rent paid in advance assessable to income tax - ITA 1918 Sch D Case III, FA 1929 s 11 and Sch 1 Pt II.

Swaine (Inspector of Taxes) v VE
3 ITC 387, [1964] IR 423, 100 ILTR 21 ....Vol II p 472

Income tax - Schedule D - builder's profits - whether fines and capitalised value of ground rents are assessable to tax.

Molmac Ltd v MacGiolla Riogh (Inspector of Taxes)
3 ITC 376, [1965] IR 201, 101 ILTR 114 ....Vol II p 482

Income tax Schedule D - carry forward of losses - managing of "six following years of assessment" - FA 1929 s 14.

Forbes (Inspector of Taxes) v GHD
3 ITC 365, [1964] IR 447 ....Vol II p 491

Income tax - Schedule D - pensions payable under the British National Insurance Act 1946, as amended or extended, to persons resident in the State - whether income from foreign possessions - ITA 1918 Sch D Case III, FA 1926 Sch 1 Pt II, FA 1929 s 11.

Casey (Inspector of Taxes) v AB Ltd
[1965] IR 575 ....Vol II p 500

Income tax - Schedule D - legal costs in defending action in High Court for balance alleged to be due to a building contractor in respect of the construction of cinema - whether the costs were incurred in earning the profits assessed, and whether they were capital or revenue expenditure - ITA 1918 Sch D Case I.

Dolan (Inspector of Taxes) v AB Co Ltd
[1969] IR 282, 104 ILTR 101 .... Vol II p 515

Income tax - Schedule D - petrol marketing company-whether expenditure incurred under exclusivity agreements with retailers deductible - ITA 1918 s 209 and Sch D Cases I & II rule 3 - FA 1929 s 9.

Bedford (Collector-General) v H
[1968] IR 320 .... Vol II p 588

Aggregate of monthly payments made in year on account of remunerations less than tax-free allowances-no tax deducted under PAYE - balance of remuneration for year voted and paid in following year - tax deducted under PAYE - assessment made in respect of full remuneration for earlier year - whether tax so deducted under PAYE from balance of remuneration in following year should be treated as covering tax charged in assessment - FA (No 2) 1959 s 13(1) (ITA 1967 s 133(1)), IT(E)R 1960 clause 45(1) (SI 28/1960).

Cronin (Inspector of Taxes) v C
TL 106 .... Vol II p 592

Income tax - Schedule D - personal pension and other assets assigned to company - pension continued to be paid to pensioner - whether pensioner ceased to receive pension as a source of income for himself beneficially - ITA 1918 Sch D, Case III of miscellaneous rules applicable to Schedule D and FA 1929 s 10

Pairceir (Inspector of Taxes) v EM
[Not previously reported] .... Vol II p 596

Income tax - Schedule D - income from the leasing of premises - whether such activity constitutes a "trade" the income from which would qualify for earned income relief - FA 1920 s 16 - replaced by FA(No 2) 1959 s16 - amended by FA 1961 s 3.

S Ltd v O'Sullivan
[Not previously reported] .... Vol II p 602

Income tax - Schedule D - payments made under an agreement for the supply of technical information.

HH v Forbes (Inspector of Taxes)
[Not previously reported] .... Vol II p 614

Income tax - whether profits of a bookmaker from certain transactions in Irish Hospital Sweepstakes tickets should be included as receipts for purposes of assessment to tax under Schedule D.

W Ltd v Wilson (Inspector of Taxes)
[Not previously reported] .... Vol II p 627

Income tax - Schedule D and corporation profits tax, FA 1920 - whether the inspector of taxes had made a "discovery" on finding that inadmissible deductions had been allowed in the computation of the company's tax liability for certain years and whether he was entitled to raise additional assessments for those years - ITA 1967 s 186.

O Conaill (Inspector of Taxes) v Z Ltd
[Not previously reported] .... Vol II p 636

Income tax - whether the appellant company was in occupation of lands, forming part of a military establishment, for the purposes of ITA 1918 Sch B or ITA 1967.

S W Ltd v McDermott (Inspector of Taxes)
[Not previously reported] .... Vol II p 661

Income tax - whether the capital allowances to be apportioned in accordance with the provisions of ITA 1967 s 220(5), in computing the appellant's liability under Sch D Case I were to be confined to the allowances outlined in Part XVI of that Act.

Mara (Inspector of Taxes) v GG (Hummingbird) Ltd
[1982] ILRM 421 .... Vol II p 667

Income tax - Sch D Case I - whether the surplus arising to the company from the sale of certain property was profit of a trade of dealing in or developing land, or the profit of a business which was deemed by F(MP)A 1968 s 17, to be such a trade.

MacDaibheid (Inspector of Taxes) v SD
[Not previously reported] .... Vol III p 1

Income tax - whether a deduction should be allowed under ITA 1967 Sch 2(3) in respect of incidental expenses.

O hArgain (Inspector of Taxes) v B Ltd
[1979] ILRM 56 .... Vol III p 9

Property company - income tax - trade - trading stock - farm land - company letting land to partners on conacre - area zoned for development - land transferred to new company - whether land trading stock of company - F(MP)A 1968 (No 7) s 17.

De Brun (Inspector of Taxes) v Kiernan
[1981] IR 117, [1982] ILRM 13 .... Vol III p 19

Income tax - whether the taxpayer was a "dealer in cattle" within the meaning of ITA 1918 Sch D Case III rule 4 and ITA 1967 s 78.

Revenue v ORMG
[1984] ILRM 406 .... Vol III p 28

Club to promote athletics or amateur games or sports - whether legitimate avoidance of payment of tax - funds provided by one person - total control in two trustees - whether bona fide club - whether established for sole purpose of "promoting sport" - whether two persons can constitute a "body of person" - ITA 1967 ss (1), 349.

MacDermott (Inspector of Taxes) v BC
[Not previously reported] .... Vol III p 43

Income tax - Schedule E - whether the taxpayer was engaged under a contract of service or a contract for services - ITA 1967 s 110.

O'Laoghaire (Inspector of Taxes) v CD Ltd
[Not previously reported] .... Vol III p 51

Corporation profits tax - company engaged in manufacture and erection of prefabricated buildings - deposit of 15 per cent of total cost paid on execution of contract - whether a payment on account in respect of trading stock - whether security for contracts - whether value of stock for stock relief be reduced - FA 1975 s 31.

K Co v Hogan (Inspector of Taxes)
[1985] ILRM 200 .... Vol III p 56

Appellant unlimited investment company - whether dividends arising from sales of capital assets liable to corporation profits tax - whether profits shall be profits and gains determined on the same principles as those on which the profits and gains of a trade are determined - whether company carrying on a trade - whether similar distributions previously charged to corporation profits tax - whether statutory provision can become obsolete on the basis of past practice - whether FA 1920 s 53(2) ambiguous in meaning - whether words of a taxing statute must be clear and unambiguous - whether s (2) is purely for purpose of determining profits for income tax purposes - whether question of distinguishing capital and income arises - whether proceeds of sale of capital assets may be capital in hands of companies selling the assets and income in the hands of the shareholders to whom paid in the form of dividends.

O'Conaill (Inspector of Taxes) v JJ Ltd
[Not previously reported] .... Vol III p 65

Income tax - whether a building which housed offices, a showroom, a canteen, computer department and utilities qualified for industrial building allowance under ITA 1967 s 255.

Doyle & Others v An Taoiseach & Others
[1986] ILRM 522 .... Vol III p 73

Excise duty - levy of 2 per cent of value of bovine animals imposed on the farmer producer - whether ultra vires the enabling provisions of FA 1986 - imposed on proprietors of slaughter houses and exporters of live animals - whether levy operated arbitrarily and unreasonably - whether levy passed on to the prime producer - whether end result untargeted indiscriminate and unfair - FA 1966 - SI 152/1970 and 160/1979 - Treaty of Rome Article 177 - FA 1980 s 79.

GH (Stephen Court) Ltd v Browne (Inspector of Taxes)
[1984] ILRM 231 .... Vol III p 95

Income tax - whether letting fees and legal expenses incurred by the company in respect of first lettings of property qualified as deductions under ITA 1967 s 81(5)(d).

BKJ v The Revenue Commissioners
[Not previously reported] .... Vol III p 104

Family settlement dated 22 December 1955 - discretionary trust - income to beneficiary on attaining thirty years of age until 31 December 1985 and thereafter to the beneficiary absolutely - whether beneficiary took an absolute interest on attaining thirty years of age - whether vested interest subject to contingency of favour of children and remoter issue -

appointment dated 4 April 1978 in favour of beneficiary - whether gift of a contingent interest - whether liable to gift tax - CATA 1976 ss 2, 4, 5, 6.

Breathnach (Inspector of Taxes) v McCann
[1984] IR 340 .... Vol III p 113

Income tax - Sch D Case II - profession - capital allowances - whether barrister's books are plant.

In Re HT Ltd (In Liquidation) and Others
[1984] ILRM 583 .... Vol III p 120

Income tax - corporation profits tax - corporation tax - court liquidation - whether deposit interest earned on monies held by the official liquidator liable to tax - whether tax payable a "necessary disbursement" under court winding-up rules - whether tax payable ranks as a preferential payment or an unsecured debt - Companies Act 1963 ss 244, 285 - FA 1983 s 56, Winding Up Rules 1966 r 129.

The State (FIC Ltd) v O'Ceallaigh
[Not previously reported] .... Vol III p 124

Capital gains tax clearance certificate on sale of bonds - whether statutory requirements satisfied - whether applicant is the person making the disposal - whether applicant is the owner of the property and ordinarily resident in the state - whether statutory provision mandatory - whether inspector of taxes is entitled to investigate applicant's title to the property - whether applicant as owner and ordinarily resident in the state is entitled to a clearance certificate.

Madigan v The Attorney General, The Revenue Commissioners and Others
[1986] ILRM 136 .... Vol III p 127

Residential property tax - whether unconstitutional - whether unjust attack on property and family rights - whether invidious discrimination - whether unreasonable or arbitrary - whether taxation statutes presumed to be unconstitutional - locus standi - FA 1983 - Constitution of Ireland 1937 Articles 40(1), 40(3), 41, 43.

JB O'C v PCD and A Bank
[1985] IR 265 .... Vol III p 153

Income tax - particulars of taxpayers bank accounts - bond of confidentiality between banks and customers - strict compliance with statutory provisions - whether reasonable grounds for court application - discretion of court - particulars of accounts - dealings in accounts - name(s), nature of account and dates of opening and closing - whether costs of bank to be borne by Revenue - FA 1983 s 18.

The State (Multiprint Label Systems Ltd) v Neylon
[1984] ILRM 545 .... Vol III p 159

Practice - Revenue case - statutory provision requiring person to express dissatisfaction with the determination of a point of law "immediately after the determination" - whether "immediately" to be interpreted strictly - whether provision directory or mandatory - ITA(No 6) 1967 ss 428, 430.

O'Cleirigh (Inspector of Taxes) v Jacobs International Ltd Incorporated
[1985] ILRM 651 .... Vol III p 165

Corporation tax - whether a training grant paid to the company was a capital or revenue receipt.

McElligott & Sons Ltd v Duigenan (Inspector of Taxes)
[1985] ILRM 210 .... Vol III p 178

Stock relief - whether the company was carrying on a single trade, or several different trades, for the purposes of a claim under FA 1975 s 31 (as amended by FA 1977 s 43).

Muckley v Ireland, The Attorney General and The Revenue Commissioners
[1985] IR 472, [1986] ILRM 364 .... Vol III p 188

Constitution validity of taxing statute - personal rights of citizens - unauthorised exactions - married persons - statute with retrospective effect - enacted in consequence of decision that portion of income tax legislation unconstitutional - whether lawful for the State to collect arrears of tax due under the unconstitutional provisions - FA 1980 s 21 - Constitution of Ireland 1937, Articles 40.1, 40.3, 41

Cronin (Inspector of Taxes) v Cork & County Property Co Ltd
[1986] IR 559 .... Vol III p 198

Corporation tax - property company dealing in land - interest in land acquired and disposed of within one accounting period - whether ordinary principles of commercial accounting apply - whether artificial method of valuation pursuant to F(MP)A 1968 s 18(2) prevails.

Mac Giolla Mhaith (Inspector of Taxes) v Cronin & Associates Ltd
[Not previously reported] .... Vol III p 211

Corporation tax - advertising agency - whether its business consisted of or included the carrying on of a profession or the provision of professional services for the purposes of the corporation tax surcharge provided for in CTA 1976 s 162

O'Srianain (Inspector of Taxes) v Lakeview Ltd
[Not previously reported] .... Vol III p 219

Capital allowances - machinery and plant - whether applicable to the provision of a deep pit poultry house.

Cronin (Inspector of Taxes) v Youghal Carpets (Yarns) Ltd
[1985] IR 312, [1985] ILRM 666 .... Vol III p 229

Corporation tax - whether the expression "total income brought into charge to corporation tax" for the purposes of CTA 1976 s 58(3) meant income before or after the deduction of group relief.

The Revenue Commissioners v HI
[Not previously reported] .... Vol III p 242

Income tax - whether an individual was entitled to repayment of tax deducted from payments made under an indenture of covenant pursuant to ITA 1967 s 439(1)(iv).

Murphy (Inspector of Taxes) v Asahi Synthetic Fibres (Ireland) Ltd
[1985] IR 509, [1986] IR 777 .... Vol III p 246

Irish subsidiary company and Japanese parent company - interest on loan by parent company - whether tax chargeable under Schedule D or Schedule F - Double Taxation Relief (Taxes on Income)(Japan) Order 1974 SI 259/1974, CTA 1976 ss 83/84.

MacCarthaigh (Inspector of Taxes) v Daly
[1985] IR 73, [1986] ILRM 24, 116 .... Vol III p 253

Income tax - whether the taxpayer was entitled to claim a share of capital allowances on the basis of a leasing transaction, involving a purported limited partnership, against his personal income tax liability.

The Attorney General v Sun Alliance and London Insurance Ltd
[1985] ILRM 522 .... Vol III p 265

Excise duty - deed of bond - principal and surety - payment of excise duty deferred - whether creditor to resort to securities received by creditor from principal before proceeding against surety - Excise Collection and Management Act 1841 (4 & 5 Vict c 20) s 24.

O'Connlain (Inspector of Taxes) v Belvedere Estates Ltd
[1985] IR 22 .... Vol III p 271

Trading company dealing in and developing - tax avoidance scheme - series of transactions with associated companies - aggregate of costs of stock in trade - artificial method of valuation under F(MP)A 1968 s 18 - legal consequences of transaction - whether s 18 can be construed to alter legal consequences.

The State (Melbarian Enterprises Ltd) v The Revenue Commissioners
[1985] IR 706 .... Vol III p 290

State side - mandamus - requirement of tax clearance certificate with tenders for Government contracts - refusal to issue by Collector General - whether Revenue Commissioners can have regard to tax default of previous "connected" company - whether Collector General's decision amenable to judicial review - duty to act judicially - requirement not based on statutory provisions.

Heron and Others v The Minister For Communications
[1985] IR 623 .... Vol III p 298

Liability for capital gains tax - compulsory acquisition - tax arising on disposal - compensation determined without regard to the liability of landowner for tax on chargeable gain - Acquisition of Land (Assessment of Compensation) Act 1919 s 2.

McCann Ltd v O'Culachain (Inspector of Taxes)
[1985] IR 298, [1986] IR 196 .... Vol III p 304

Corporation tax - exports sales relief - whether process of ripening bananas constituted manufacturing - no statutory definition of word manufacture - interpretation of taxation statute - ordinary meaning or strict construction - scheme and purpose of statute - test to be applied - matter of degree - CTA 1976 s 54 and Pt IV.

Knockhall Piggeries v Kerrane (Inspector of Taxes)
[1985] ILRM 655 .... Vol III p 319

Income tax - whether the activity of intensive pig rearing constituted farming for the purposes of FA 1974 s 13(1).

Maye v The Revenue Commissioners
[1986] ILRM 377 .... Vol III p 332

Value added tax - installation of fixtures subject to low rate of value added tax - whether or not television aerials attached to roof of a house are fixtures - test based on mode and object of annexation - VATA 1972 s 10(8).

Belville Holdings Ltd (In Receivership and Liquidation) v Cronin (Inspector of Taxes)
[1985] IR 465 .... Vol III p 340

Corporation tax - case stated on question of losses incurred by a holding company, whether notional management fees deductible - whether evidence required to determine the amount of such fees - whether Appeal Commissioner in error - whether a High Court order can be subsequently amended by a further High Court order - whether High Court has jurisdiction to amend order - whether jurisdiction limited to Order 28 rule 11 of Superior Court rules and judgments incorrectly drawn up - whether certainty of administration of law can be breached - whether discretion under ITA 1967 s 428 applied by judge - whether discretion "implicit" in judgment - whether application of s 428(b) an additional remedy - whether amending order be set aside.

Warnock and Others practising as Stokes Kennedy Crowley & Co v The Revenue Commissioners
[1985] IR 663, [1986] ILRM 37 .... Vol III p 356

Income tax - tax avoidance - transfer of assets to offshore tax havens - statutory notice requesting information - whether from of accountants could be requested to furnish relevant particulars in respect of all their clients - ten named territories over a six year period - whether a limit to extent of particulars sought - whether cost of compliance excessive - whether notice ultra vires the section - FA 1974 s 59.

Cronin (Inspector of Taxes) v Lunham Brothers Ltd
[1986] ILRM 415 .... Vol III p 363

Corporation tax - relief - losses forward - cessation of company's trade - major change in nature of conduct of trade - change of ownership - CTA 1976 ss 16(1), 27(1), 182 184.

Guinness & Mahon Ltd v Browne (Inspector of Taxes)
[Not previously reported] .... Vol III p 373

Corporation tax - whether a sum which arose to the company on the liquidation of a wholly owned subsidiary was part of its trading profits.

McLoughlin and Tuite v The Revenue Commissioners and The Attorney General
[1986] IR 235, [1986] ILRM 304, [1990] IR 83 .... Vol III p 387

Income tax returns - whether penalties for failure to make returns are punitive - whether proceedings for recovery of penalties are criminal trials - whether unconstitutional - ITA 1967 s 500 - Constitution of Ireland Act 1937 s 34.

Navan Carpets Ltd v O'Culachain (Inspector of Taxes)
[1988] IR 164... Vol III p 403

Corporation tax - interest on repayment of tax - no provision for interest in Taxes Act - whether or not award on interest applicable under Courts Act 1981.

Curtis and Geough v The Attorney General and The Revenue Commissioners
[1986] ILRM 428 .... Vol III p 419

Customs duties - locus standi evasion of customs duties on specified goods - whether District Court authorised to determine value of goods - criminal case - whether disputed issue of fact a matter for jury - whether statutory provisions unconstitutional - whether unappealable finding unjust - FA 1963 ss 34(4)(d)(i), 34(4)(d)(iii) - Constitution of Ireland 1937, Articles 34.3.4, 38.1, 38.2, 38.

Williams Group Tullamore Ltd v Companies Act 1963 - 1983
[Not previously reported].. Vol III p 423

Petition under Companies Act 1963 s 205 - oppression of ordinary minority shareholders - voting and non voting shares - whether preference shareholders entitled to receive a portion of issue of new ordinary shares - whether preference shareholders entitled to participate in capital distribution - whether proposal burdensome harsh and wrongful - whether isolated transaction can give rise to relief - whether for benefit of company as a whole - whether in disregard of interests of ordinary shareholders.

Bairead (Inspector of Taxes) v Maxwells of Donegal Ltd
[1986] ILRM 508 .... Vol III p 430

Corporation tax - whether a company, resident and trading in Northern Ireland was an associated company of a company resident and trading in the State for the purposes of CTA 1976 s 28.

Kinghan v The Minister for Social Welfare
[Not previously reported].. Vol III p 436

Social welfare - benefits - whether entitled to old age contributory pension - whether issue open to appeal - true construction of statute - jurisdiction of High Court - meaning of entry into insurance - definition of contribution year - Social Welfare (Consolidation Act 1951 s 299).

Cronin (Inspector of Taxes) v Strand Dairy Ltd
[Not previously reported].. Vol III p 441

Corporation tax - whether the processing of and sale of milk in plastic bottles produced by the company constituted the manufacture of goods for the purposes of the reduction in corporation tax provided for in FA 1980 Pt I Ch VI.

Cronin (Inspector of Taxes) v IMP Midleton Ltd
[Not previously reported].. Vol III p 452

Corporation profits tax - export sales relief - sale of meat into intervention within the EEC - conditional contracts - when does property in goods pass - sold in course of trade - exporter need not be owner at time of export - F(MP)A 1956 s 13(3).

Director of Public Prosecutions v McLoughlin
[1986] IR 355, [1986] ILRM 493 .... Vol III p 467

Income tax (PAYE) and Social Welfare (PRSI) regulations - whether contract for services between skipper of fishing vessel and crew members - whether a partnership existed - no wages - rights to share of profits and to decide on division of profits but not to share in losses.

Moloney (Inspector of Taxes) v Allied Irish Banks Ltd as Executors of the Estate of Doherty, Deceased
[1986] IR 67 .... Vol III p 477

Income tax - liability of personal representatives - income on estate in course of administration - trustees under Succession Act 1965 - ITA 1967 s 105.

O'Coindealbhain (Inspector of Taxes) v Gannon
[1986] IR 154 .... Vol III p 484

Income tax - fees due to a barrister prior to his appointment to the bench - fees refused but could be paid to a family company if solicitors so wished - whether or not received within the meaning of FA 1970 s 20 - interpretation of taxing act.

Healy v Breathnach (Inspector of Taxes)
[1986] IR 105 .... Vol III p 496

Income tax - exemption of earnings from original and creative works of artistic or cultural merit - whether newspaper articles and journalism qualify - tests for exemption - grounds for setting aside a Circuit Court decision on a Revenue case stated - FA 1969 s 2.

The Minister for Labour v PMPA Insurance Co Ltd (Under Administration)
[1990] IR 284 .... Vol III p 505

Contract of service or contract for services - temporary employee engaged through employment agency - agreement between employee and agency - agreement between agency and defendant hirer - whether defendant liable for employee's holiday pay - nature of contractual relationship between employee and defendant - whether a contract of service between employee and agency - Holidays (Employees) Act 1973.

The Companies Act 1963-1983 v Castlemahon Poultry Products Ltd
[1986] IR 750, [1987] ILRM 222 .... Vol III p 509

Social Welfare Acts - employer's contribution in respect of "reckonable earnings" of employees - when payable - liability of liquidator - preferential status under Companies Act 1963 s 285.

Rahinstown Estates Co v Hughes (Inspector of Taxes)
[1987] ILRM 599 .... Vol III p 517

Corporation tax - surcharge on undistributed income of close company - extension of period for making distribution of dividends - shorter period allowed for making distributions of share capital in a winding up - whether distinction absurd or unjust. CTA 1976 ss 84(1), 100 & 101.

Noyek & Sons Ltd (In Voluntary Liquidation) v Hearne (Inspector of Taxes)
[1988] IR 772 .... Vol III p 523

Voluntary liquidator - interest earned on deposit interest after date of liquidation - whether corporation tax on such interest is a charge within the meaning of Companies Act 1963 s 281 - whether liability of voluntary liquidator is different to that of court liquidator.

Orr (Kilternan) Ltd v The Companies Act 1963-1983, and
Thornberry Construction (Irl) Ltd v The Companies Act 1963-1983
[1986] IR 273 .... Vol III p 530

Liquidation - High Court fees on funds realised by liquidator in course of liquidation - whether applicable to monies payable to secured creditors or to proceeds of sale of property subject to a fixed charge - Supreme Court and High Court (Fees) Order 1984 (SI 19/1984 as amended by SI 36/1985).

Deighan v Hearne (Inspector of Taxes), Fitzgerald, Murphy, Ireland, The Attorney General and The Minister for Finance
[1986] IR 603, [1990] IR 499 .... Vol III p 533

Income Tax Acts - constitutionality -estimated assessments - incorrect description of taxpayer - material enactments and statutory instruments not available - invalid seizure of goods - exercise of judicial function - Courts bypassed - personal rights of citizen violated - constitutional right to have recourse to High Court denied - ITA 1967 as amended.

Masser Ltd (In Receivership) and Others v The Revenue Commissioners
[Not previously reported] .... Vol III p 548

Charge on book debts by deed of mortgage - whether a fixed or floating charge - essential distinction - when is charge effected - test is whether unrestricted use of property is permitted - conflict in terms of deed - determining restriction in prevention of charging, assigning or otherwise disposing of book debts and other debts.

Wayte (Holdings) Ltd (In Receivership) v Hearne (Inspector of Taxes)
[1986] IR 448 .... Vol III p 553

Liability of receiver appointed by a debenture holder to corporation tax provisions of CTA 1976 - company is chargeable and tax assessed on company - whether provisions of ITA 1967 are adopted into corporation tax code - role of company secretary - adoption heavily qualified - whether permissible to adopt paying provision while ignoring charging provisions.

Murphy (Inspector of Taxes) v The Borden Co Ltd
[Not previously reported] .... Vol III p 559

Case stated - whether a dividend declared on 11 December 1980 was received by related company not later than 12 December 1980 - whether payment of cheque required - whether payment through inter-company account was sufficient evidence of actual payment - whether making of journal entries after 23 December 1980 material evidence - whether making of accounting entry a mere record of underlying transaction.

Cronin (Inspector of Taxes) v C
[1968] IR 148 .... Vol III p 568

Income tax - Schedule D - Personal Pension and other assets assigned to company - pension continued to be paid to pensioner - whether pensioner ceased to receive pension as a source of income for himself beneficially - ITA 1918 Sch D Case III, rule of miscellaneous rules applicable to Schedule D and FA 1929 s 10.

Rowan, (Deceased) v Rowan and Others
[1988] ILRM 65 .... Vol III p 572

Domicile - Irish domicile of origin - tests for acquisition of domicile of choice - whether determined by Irish law - whether domicile of origin restored - whether intention without residence sufficient.

The State (Calcul International Ltd and Solatrex International Ltd) v The Appeal Commissioners and The Revenue Commissioners
[Not previously reported] .... Vol III p 577

Corporation/income/value added tax - concurrent determination of tax liability by High Court and Appeal Commissioners - whether mutually exclusive - conditional order of prohibition against Appeal Commissioners - application to make order absolute - tax code only permissible procedure - Appeal Commissioners powers and functions unconstitutional - nature of powers - limited or unlimited - ITA 1967 Pt XXVI and s 488. Articles 34 and 37 of the constitution.

Kennedy v Hearne, The Attorney General and Others
[1987] IR 120, [1988] IR 481, [1988] ILRM 53, 531 .... Vol III p 590

PAYE regulations - whether procedures unfair and unconstitutional - whether Revenue Commissioners involved in administration of justice - enforcement order issue to city sheriff after payment of tax - whether defamatory of plaintiff - question of damages.

Irish Agricultural Machinery Ltd v O'Culachain (Inspector of Taxes)
[1987] IR 458, [1990] IR 535 .... Vol III p 611

Stock relief under FA 1975 s 31 - trade consisting of the manufacturing of goods or sale of machinery or plant to farmers - whether assembly of agricultural machinery constitutes manufacturing - raw materials manufactured goods - changes in appearance but assembly not understood as manufacturing by well informed laymen - whether sales operations constitute a trade under s 31 - sales must be direct to farmers.

Kerrane (Inspector of Taxes) v Hanlon (Ireland) Ltd
[1987] IR 259 .... Vol III p 633

Export sales relief - ambulances manufactured in the State and exported - payments in advance lodged in deposit account - income not "immediately derived" from a trade of business - income received on foot of an obligation with bank - CTA 1976 ss 58 and 59.

Director of Public Prosecutions v Downes
[1987] IR 139, [1987] ILRM 665 .... Vol III p 641

Prosecution for payment of a Revenue penalty - whether criminal or civil proceedings applicable - no indicia of a criminal offence - ITA 1967 ss 17, 127, 128 & 500.

Browne (Inspector of Taxes) v Bank of Ireland Finance Ltd
[1987] IR 346, [1991] 1 IR 431 .... Vol III p 644

Business of banking - government stocks purchased to comply with Central Bank requirements - whether carrying on trade of dealing in securities - whether liable as profits under Schedule D or exempt capital gains on Government stocks - tests to be applied in a case stated by High Court - whether true and only reasonable conclusion to be drawn - Corporation Tax Act.

Patrick Monahan (Drogheda) Ltd v O'Connell (Inspector of Taxes)
[Not previously reported].. Vol III p 661

Capital allowances - industrial building or structure for the purposes of a dock undertaking - whether bonded transit sheds qualify - nature of business -sheds used as clearing house and not for storage - meaning of undertaking - ancillary to business of dock undertaking - ITA 1967 s 255.

Pandion Haliaetus Ltd, Ospreycare Ltd, Osprey Systems Design Ltd v The Revenue Commissioners
[1987] IR 309, [1988] ILRM 419 .... Vol III p 670

Corporation income tax - hot car wash invention - whether income from patent rights disregarded for income tax purposes - where payable to a non-resident - effect of interpretation of FA 1973 s 34 as given by Revenue Commissioners - whether particular scheme disclosed - whether interpretation binding on Inspector of Taxes - tax avoidance scheme within Furniss v Dawson *principle - declaration by way of application for judicial review.*

The Diners Club Ltd v The Revenue Commissioners and The Minister for Finance
[1988] IR 158 .... Vol III p 680

Value added tax - interpretation of statutory instrument - charge card scheme - method of conducting business - purpose of a charge or credit cards - to facilitate sales by retailer to a purchaser - retailer paid by credit card or charge card company - described in statutory instrument as reimbursement - accepted as meaning paid for - whether debt due to retailer purchased - whether part of overall agreement between credit card company, retailer and purchaser - whether an individual transaction to be looked at in isolation.

McGrath and Others v McDermott (Inspector of Taxes)
[1988] IR 258, [1988] ILRM 181, 647 .... Vol III p 683

Capital gains tax - tax avoidance scheme - scheme technically valid - allowable loss - s 33 of Act plain and unambiguous meaning - whether provision to be disregarded unless a real loss - no equity in taxation - separation of powers - functions of courts and legislature - Superior Courts alone review court decisions - no general anti-avoidance legislation.

Kill Inn Motel Ltd (In Liquidation) v The Companies Acts 1963-1983
[Not previously reported].. Vol III p 706

Disposal of assets at an undervalue by a company - granting of a preferential mortgage - creditors prejudiced - application by liquidator - gifts made by a company - Fraudulent Conveyances Act 1634 (10 Charles 1).

O'Coindealbhain (Inspector of Taxes) v Price
[1988] IR 14 .... Vol IV p 1

Capital gain on sale of lands - absent landowner - proceeds of sale reinvested in acquisition of further lands - absent owner returns to take on active farming - whether rollover relief on transfer of a trade applies - FA 1974 ss 13, 15, 17 & 21, FA 1975 s 12 and CGTA 1975 s 28.

Murphy (Inspector of Taxes) v Dataproducts (Dublin) Ltd
[1988] IR 10 .... Vol IV p 12

Non resident company - carries on a manufacturing business through a branch in the State - tax free profits from Irish branch paid into a Swiss bank account - whether interest earned on Swiss bank account is chargeable to corporation tax on the Irish branch.

McNally v O'Maoldhomhniagh
[Not previously reported] .... Vol IV p 22

Income tax - capital allowance - plant and machinery used in a designated area - whether used exclusively in designated area - whether allowance extends to plant and machinery used under a hire contract - FA 1971 s 22.

O'Culachain (Inspector of Taxes) v Hunter Advertising Ltd
[Not previously reported] .... Vol IV p 35

Corporation tax - manufacturing relief - advertising company - production for sale of advertising materials such as TV videos - word manufacture not defined - creative concept formed into a film - printing and processing in UK - tangible physical product - whether manufacturing process applied by respondent - nature and complexity of process - view of ordinary man - test of change brought about by process - characteristics and value - chemical reaction - matter of degree - purpose of legislation - promotion of manufacturing industry.

O'Coindealbhain (Inspector of Taxes) v Mooney
[1990] IR 422 .... Vol IV p 45

Income tax - a contract of employment - whether a contract of service or a contract for services - branch manager of local employment office of Dept of Social Welfare - income tax assessed on PAYE basis - whether respondent a self employed independent contractor - whether Court should look beyond terms of written contract - tests to be applied, essential conditions of a contract of service.

Mooney v O'Coindealbhain and The Revenue Commissioners
[Not previously reported] .... Vol IV p 62

Income tax - whether interest recoverable on foot of overpaid income tax - whether basis of assessment under Schedule E or Schedule D - whether branch manager of employment exchange to be taxed as an employee or as a self employed person - whether interest recoverable under FA 1976 s 30 - whether appeal to nil assessments to tax rules out interest on overpayments on tax - whether appeal of assessments under wrong Schedule rules out interest on overpayments of tax - whether implied agreement applies between the parties in regard to years of assessment not appealed.

Dunnes Stores (Oakville) Ltd v Cronin (Inspector of Taxes)
[Not previously reported] .... Vol IV p 68

Capital allowance against corporation tax - plant - expenditure on installation of suspended ceiling in supermarket - whether suspended ceiling constitutes plant - nature of trade - functional test - question of degree - goods distinguished from services.

The Racing Board v O'Culachain
[Not previously reported] .... Vol IV p 73

Levies on course betting by bookmakers - whether an activity analogous to a trade - whether income taxable as profits - scheme of Act - development of horse breeding and racing, statutory body whether to Racing Board and Racecourse - Act 1945 ss 4, 15, 27(1) - ITA 1967 s 537.

The Companies Act 1963-1983 v M F N Construction Co Ltd (In Liquidation) on the application of Patrick Tuffy (Liquidator)
[Not previously reported] .... Vol IV p 82

PAYE/PRSI - company insolvent - Bank of Ireland a secured creditor and revenue debts due to collector general - winding up deferred by reason of scheme of arrangement approved by High Court - collector general agreed to deferral of revenue debt pending completion of contracts by company - unsecured creditors promised 40p in £1 and voted to accept scheme - a third party paid off the unsecured creditors by way of subrogation agreements - whether third party bound by terms of scheme of arrangement.

Cusack v O'Reilly and The Collector General
[Not previously reported] .... Vol IV p 86

This interpleader summons arose out of the seizure by the applicant in his role as Revenue sheriff of goods and chattels claimed to be the property of the claimant in the action. The sheriff on being challenged, issued the interpleader summons to have his claim determined by the court whether or not the chattels in question are:

Texaco Ireland Ltd v Murphy (Inspector of Taxes)
[1989] IR 496, [1991] 2 IR 449 .... Vol IV p 91

Corporation tax -whether petroleum exploration constitutes scientific research - whether such scientific research qualifies for tax relief by way of an allowance under ITA 1967 s 244 - whether proximate sections are relevant to the interpretation of the particular section - whether Act as a whole should be construed - whether proviso to s 244(3) applies - the principles of construction of taxing statutes - whether there is any equity about taxation, whether in imposition, exemption or manner of application - whether capital expenditure herein comes within the application of the proviso - whether the claim for relief comes within the express wording of the proviso.

United Bars Ltd (In Receivership), Walkinstown Inn Ltd (In Receivership) and Jackson v The Revenue Commissioners
[1991] IR 396 .... Vol IV p 107

Company - debentures creating fixed and floating charges - receiver appointed by debenture holder - fixed charges paid off leaving surplus - preferential creditors - priority -

whether surplus to be paid to preferential creditors or to company - Companies Act 1963 (No 33) s 98.

Hearne (Inspector of Taxes) v O'Cionna and Others T/A J A Kenny & Partners
[Not previously reported] .... Vol IV p 113

Employer's liability to deduct PAYE and PRSI from employee's emoluments - deductions to be paid to the collector general - loan arrangement between partnership and limited company - whether partnership liable for PAYE and PRSI of employees of company - special meaning of word employer under Income Tax Acts - no similar meaning under social welfare legislation - whether employer's liability different in respect of PRSI.

Bourke (Inspector of Taxes) v Bradley & Sons
[1990] IR 379 .... Vol IV p 117

Value added tax - service supplied by solicitor on instructions of Insurance underwriter - in relation to insured litigant - whether supplied to underwriter or to the defendant - services to a non-resident in the State but resident within EEC - no establishment in the state - where services are deemed to be supplied.

McMahon (Inspector of Taxes) v Murphy
[Not previously reported] .... Vol IV p 125

Capital gains tax - market value on 6 April 1974 of holding of 73 acres of land - agricultural land situate outside town of Macroom - appeal on value of land as determined in Circuit Court - whether subsequent planning permission for milk processing plant relevant - whether development potential attached to the lands on 6 April 1974 - whether agricultural value the sole determining factor.

Carroll Industries Plc v S O'Culachain (Inspector of Taxes)
[1988] IR 705 .... Vol IV p 135

Appellant company's accounts, based on current cost accounting convention (ie replacement cost) - whether acceptable for tax purposes as a basis for accountancy - whether historical cost accounting convention is the only method of commercial accountancy for tax purposes - Whimster *decision and its two "fundamental commonplaces" - true profits for tax purposes based on difference between receipts and expenditure laid out to earn those receipts and the accounts framed consistently with ordinary principles of commercial accounting - profits and gains for tax purposes not defined in Tax Acts - no particular basis of accountancy stipulated by statute - appropriate accounting method may not give "true profits" - whether provision for inflation applicable - stock relief allowed by Finance Acts - different methods of costing stock - basic premise that profits is the difference between receipts and expenditure laid out to earn those receipts.*

McDaid v Sheehy, The Director of Public Prosecutions and Others
[1991] IR 1 .... Vol IV p 162

Whether applicant validly convicted of an offence and fined for keeping in the fuel tank of his motor vehicle hydrocarbon oil on which custom or excise duty had not been paid - whether Imposition of Duties Act 1957 Constitutional - whether order empowering the government to impose, terminate or vary duties invalid - where delegation of powers is permissible - whether test of coming within principles and policies of Act applies - whether subsequent statutory provision validates order - whether reasonable interpretation to be applied.

Wiley v The Revenue Commissioners
[1989] IR 351 .... Vol IV p 170

Excise duty - what persons may be authorised by order of the Minister for Finance to import goods such as motor vehicles free of excise duties - to what extent must such persons be suffering from disability - whether such persons must be wholly without the use of each of his legs - doctrine of legitimate expectation - whether refunds of excise duty on two previous occasions constitutes a practice - whether expectation is a legitimate one - whether a regular practice can be discontinued or altered without notice.

Waterford Glass (Group Services) Ltd v The Revenue Commissioners
[1990] IR 334 .... Vol IV p 187

Stamp duty - agreement for sale granting immediate possession on payment of deposit followed by agreement for sale of residual interest - whether the transfer of the residual interest stampable on the value of the residual interest or on the value of the entire property - what constitutes a conveyance for sale under Stamp Act of 1891 - whether courts will look at legal effect and legal rights of a transaction - whether FA 1986 s 96(1) applies - whether a contract for sale of legal estate is a contract for sale of property - whether contract conferred a benefit within the meaning of F(1909-10)A 1910 s 74(5).

The Hammond Lane Metal Co Ltd v O'Culachain (Inspector of Taxes)
[1990] IR 560

Corporation tax - whether an agreement between the taxpayer and the inspector of taxes in relation to an assessment of tax under appeal is binding and conclusive - whether full disclosure - whether "discovery" applies - whether unappealed assessment and compromised appeal are subject to the same interpretation - whether discovery constitutes unfair procedure - whether tax avoidance scheme under ITA 1967 Ch VI tax effective - whether premium under lease allowable under ITA 1967 s 91 - whether election under s 83(6) alters lessee's entitlement to deduction for entire premium - whether lessee to be treated as paying an amount according to a formula - whether s 83 is dealing with actualities - whether general rules on deductions overruled.

Bank of Ireland Finance Ltd v The Revenue Commissioners
[Not previously reported] .... Vol IV p 217

Disposal of property by mortgagee - disposal as nominee for mortgagor - whether payment of capital gains tax by purchaser was in accordance with CGTA 1975 - whether absence of a clearance certificate entitled Revenue Commissioners to return the payment - whether mortgagee entitled to a refund of tax paid.

O'Coindealbhain (Inspector of Taxes) v O'Carroll
[1989] IR 229 .... Vol IV p 221

Garda Siochana Pensions Order 1981 - widows contributory pension and children'' contributory pensions granted - whether children's pension income of the widow or income of the children for income tax purposes - widow's pension payable to the widow whereas children's pension payable to widow for children - children's pension not mandatory when widow's pension not payable - rate of tax related to tax status of payee - whether children's pension the beneficial property of children in all circumstances.

Purcell v Attorney General
[Not previously reported] .... Vol IV p 229

Whether implementation of Farm Tax Act constituted unfair procedures - effect of repeal in budget statement in March 1987 - consequences of absence of amending legislation - locus standi of applicant - legislation based on will of Oireachtas - if legislation interfered unlawfully then what remains cannot be enforceable in the future or past.

O Cahill (Inspector of Taxes) v Harding and Others
[Not previously reported] .... Vol IV p 233

Income tax - whether lump sum payments to disabled employees exempt from income tax - closure of assembly works made most of work force redundant - compensation package agreed but no distinction between disabled and other employees - whether disabled employees whose jobs were lost because of redundancy were entitled to claim relief from income tax - whether a distinction to be made between disabled employees whose jobs continued and disabled employees whose jobs ceased.

Frederick Inns Ltd, The Rendezvous Ltd, The Graduate Ltd, Motels Ltd (In Liquidation) v The Companies Acts 1963-1983
[Not previously reported] .... Vol IV p 247

Recovery of outstanding taxes from a group of companies - whether Revenue Commissioners may appropriate payments between separate companies within the group - company law in regard to gratuitous alienation of assets by a company - whether insolvency of a company is relevant to gratuitous alienation of assets - whether Revenue disregarded rights of creditors of individual companies within the group.

O'Grady v Laragan Quarries Ltd
[1991] 1 IR 237 .... Vol IV p 269

Whether lorry owners carrying sand and gravel were engaged in the haulage for hire of materials within the meaning of FA 1970 s 17 - whether the payments to the lorry owners were for subcontracting under a construction contract - whether the lorry owners became the proprietors of the quarry materials - whether any ambiguity attached to the agreements - whether parties are free to enter into form of contract which is tax effective.

Murphy v District Justice Brendan Wallace and Others
[Not previously reported] .... Vol IV p 278

Excise duty - bookmaker convicted and fined in the District Court of offences under the Betting Acts - arising out of non-payment of fines distress warrants issued to Garda Superintendent to distrain against defaulter's goods - return of no goods - penal warrants for imprisonment of defaulter sought by Revenue Authorities under provisions of Excise Management Act 1827 s 90 (as amended) - discretion to Revenue under s 90 to release or retain defaulter in prison for six months - whether such power constitutional and whether s 90 invalid.

O'Culachain v McMullan Brothers
[1991] 1 IR 363 .... Vol IV p 284

Whether forecourt canopies at petrol filling stations constitute plant for tax purposes - competition between petrol companies has led to major changes in the design and facilities at petrol stations - whether a canopy is essential to provide advertising, brand image and attractive setting - whether canopies provide no more than shelter from rain and wind or play a part in carrying on the trade of selling petrol - market research has proven the sales effectiveness of canopies - principles upon which the court approaches a case stated in relation to findings of primary fact, conclusions or inferences and interpretation of the law - test to be applied in deciding whether disputed object is apparatus or not - whether canopy creates an ambience and has a function in the carrying on of the business.

Irish Nationwide Building Society v The Revenue Commissioners
[Not previously reported] .... Vol IV p 296

Whether a conveyance to a building society was exempt from stamp duty by virtue of the Building Societies Act of 1976 - certain categories of instruments relating to the internal affairs of a society were specifically exempted by the Act of 1976 - whether the general provision of the exempting provision contained in s 91 of the Act extended to a conveyance or transfer of a premises to a society for the purpose of conducting its business - ejusdem generis rule - intention of legislature - whether the internal affairs of a society are distinguishable from its commercial dealings.

Murnaghan Brothers Ltd v O'Maoldhomhnaigh
[1991] 1 IR 455 .... Vol IV p 304

Whether lands the subject matter of a contract for sale entered into during an accounting period constitute trading stock for the year ending in that accounting period - trading stock and trade as defined in the Finance Acts - appellant company carrying on trade of building contractors - whether absence of possession, conveyance of legal estate and planning permission fatal to taxpayer's claim for relief - whether inclusion of the lands in the accounts by accountant in accordance with good accounting procedure was the best evidence of the commercial reality of the transaction.

Phonographic Performance (Ireland) Ltd v Somers (Inspector of Taxes)
[1992] ILRM 657 .... Vol IV p 314

Value added tax - whether corporate body exploiting copyrights supplying service within meaning of the Value Added Tax Act - Copyright Act 1963 (No 10), ss 7(1), 7(3) & 17(4) - VATA 1972 (No 22) ss 2(1), 5.

Browne and Others v The Revenue Commissioners and Others
[1991] 2 IR 58 .... Vol IV p 323

Sales representative - motor car "a tool of his trade" - whether in position of tax on benefit accruing from private use of employer's motor car is constitutional - whether legislation impinges on individuals' right to earn a livelihood - whether an unjust attack on property rights in breach of Article 40 of the Constitution - whether legislation impinges on individuals' rights to be held equal before the law - whether any constitutional right infringed - whether tax limited to availability of car for private use - whether tax avoidable

- *Constitution of Ireland Art 40 - ITA 1967 ss 117, 118, 119, 120 - FA 1958 ss 23, 24, 25, 26 - FA 1982 s 4.*

Quigley (Inspector of Taxes) v Burke
[1991] 2 IR 169 .... Vol IV p 332

Whether the inspector of taxes is entitled to call for production of a taxpayer's nominal ledger - whether the inspector required the nominal ledger to satisfy himself on the adjustments made in the accounts and the reasons for such adjustments made in the accounts - whether the accountant was acting as agent to the taxpayer or as a professional person and client - whether the nominal ledger formed part of the accountant's working papers - whether the nominal ledger was "within the power or possession" of the taxpayer - whether a reasonable person could be satisfied on the income tax computation in the absence of the nominal ledger.

Crowe Engineering Ltd v Lynch and Others
In the Matter of The Trustee Act 1893 s 36
[Not previously reported] .... Vol IV p 340

Superannuation scheme - whether trustees have absolute discretion on the distribution of the fund following the death of a member - whether trustees are bound by a direction in the member's will - whether a separated wife, a common law wife and children are entitled as defendants or relatives to be considered as beneficiaries - whether renunciation under a separation deed rules out entitlement under the superannuation scheme - whether discretion of trustees is absolute - whether court can be called on for guidance.

Forde Decision by Appeal Commissioners
[Not previously reported] .... Vol IV p 348

This appeal was brought by Michael Forde against the refusal of the inspector of taxes to grant him exemption under FA 1969 s 2 in respect of the books written by him on the Constitutional law in Ireland, Company law in Ireland and Extradition law in Ireland. Section 2 grants an exemption from income tax in respect of original and creative works which are generally recognised as having cultural or artistic merit. Subsection 5(b) provides a right of appeal as if it were a right of appeal against an assessment subject to all the appeal provisions of ITA 1967.

Brosnan (Inspector of Taxes) v Cork Communications Ltd
[Not previously reported] .... Vol IV p 349

Cork Communications Ltd providing a cable television system - whether company supplying electricity - whether company transmitting TV and radio signals - whether liable to vat on sales to customers - whether company's system consists of immovable goods and exempt from value added tax.

O'Leary v The Revenue Commissioners
[Not previously reported] .... Vol IV p 357

This application for judicial review was made on the grounds that the interest and penalty provisions for stamp duties which were introduced by FA 1991 s 100 did not take effect until 1 November 1991 and that the previous provision for interest and penalties under Stamp Act 1891 s 15 was repealed on 29 May 1991, the date of the passing of FA 1991.

O'Laochdha (Inspector of Taxes) v Johnson & Johnson (Ireland) Ltd
[1991] 2 IR 287 .... Vol IV p 361

Corporation tax - case stated as to whether the production of J Cloths and nappy liners from bales of fabric is a manufacturing process - whether manufacturing relief under FA 1980 s 42 applies - whether use of a sophisticated and expensive machine constitutes manufacturing - whether absence of change in raw material is relevant - whether product is a commercially different product - what is manufacturing - whether appearance, utility, qualities and value are the characteristics of manufacturing - whether question is one of degree - whether use of expensive and sophisticated machinery is relevant - how product is perceived by an ordinary adequately informed person - whether quality of and product is commercially enhanced by process.

VIEK Investments Ltd v The Revenue Commissioners
[1991] 2 IR 520 .... Vol IV p 367

Stamp duty - proper amount of stamp duty chargeable on a deed of transfer - contracts and consideration structured to minimise stamp duty - substance of transactions - Stamp Act 1891 s 13.

The Minister for Social Welfare v Griffiths
[Not previously reported] .... Vol IV p 378

Whether a member of the crew of a fishing vessel can be an "employee" - whether Social Welfare (Consolidation) Act 1981 applies to self employed persons - whether Act is limited in its application to the traditional relationship of employer/employee - whether there can be an "employee" without there being a corresponding employer - whether scheme of Act and regulations is limited to employer/employee circumstances - whether Minister has unlimited power to make regulations enabling any person to be treated as an employee.

McCrystal Oil Co Ltd v The Revenue Commissioners and Others
[Not previously reported] .... Vol IV p 386

Customs duties - action for damages for retinue and conversion arising out of the seizure by the Revenue Commissioners of an oil tanker - marked gas oil found in one of the tanker's compartments - outlet from the compartment not indelibly marked as required by statutory regulations - tanker seized and gas oil sold - whether there was a breach of the statutory regulation - what constitutes a conveyance under the legislation - whether outlet distinguished from container - whether defendants' case confined to breach in respect of the outlet - whether regulations must be construed strictly - whether court restricted to consideration of the breach of the regulations as pleaded - issue of damages.

Louth & Others v Minister for Social Welfare
[Not previously reported] .... Vol IV p 391

Appeal on a point of law under the social welfare code - whether deepsea dockers working under a pooling arrangement have a right to sign on for social welfare benefit as being unemployed when they are not occupied in unloading ships - whether dockers had a contract of employment with their association - whether level of earnings material to question of employment - whether a contract of service or a contract for services - whether separate contracts with dockers on each occasion of their employment.

The Director of Public Prosecutions v Boyle
[Not previously reported] .... Vol IV p 395

Excise duty - case stated - complaints of non-payment of excise duty payable on bets entered into by the defendant as a registered bookmaker - whether recovery of an excise penalty a criminal matter - whether use of words guilty of an offence and summary conviction indicate a criminal matter - whether amount of penalty is relevant - what is a crime - whether a crime can be defined - whether the act is prohibited with legal consequences - what are the indicia of a crime - whether any words of prohibition - whether option of making a payment as alternative to compliance - whether words such as fine, offence, summary conviction disigrate a criminal offence.

The Revenue Commissioners v Arida Ltd
[Not previously reported] .... Vol IV p 401

Income tax - case stated by Circuit Court Judge pursuant to ITA 1967 ss 428 and 430 - whether or not a Circuit Court Judge hearing an appeal pursuant to ITA 1967 s 429 has jurisdiction to award costs -whether a tax appeal constitutes proceedings under the Circuit Court rules - whether the Circuit Court Judge's jurisdiction is limited to the powers and duties of the Appeal Commissioners - whether the principle "expressio unius exclusio alterius" applies - whether s 428(b) granting power to High Court to award costs is superfluous - whether exception to Circuit Court rule expressly or impliedly stated - extensive jurisdiction of Circuit Court - normal practice on costs.

O'Siochain (Inspector of Taxes) v Morrissey
[Not previously reported] .... Vol IV p 407

Eleanor Morrissey commenced employment with the Bank of Ireland 27 March 1972 - she married respondent 14 May 1977 and resigned employment 10 May 1985 - whether "marriage gratuity" received on resignation was a retirement payment under ITA 1967 s 114 or was a perquisite of her office under ITA 1967 s 110 - whether a conflict between agreement of March 1974 with bank officials and bank superannuation scheme - whether real issue of liability under s 100 considered by Circuit Court Judge.

In the matter of Stamp (Deceased) v Noel Redmond and Others
[Not previously reported] .... Vol IV p 415

Succession - construction of will - whether "issue" included adopted children - whether Adoption Acts changed scope and meaning of family to include adopted as well as legitimate children - whether court bound by words used in will - intention of testator - whether issue restricted to children of marriage - Adoption Act 1952 ss 4, 26(2).

Connolly v The Collector of Customs and Excise
[Not previously reported] .... Vol IV p 419

Excise duty - judicial review - publican's licence - whether new licence obtainable - whether application within six year period - meaning of year immediately preceding.

O'Grady (Inspector of Taxes) v Roscommon Race Committee
[Not previously reported] .... Vol IV p 425

Expenditure on racecourse stand - whether deductible repairs or non deductible capital expenditure or expenditure qualifying as plant - trade of promoting and organising horse races - long established stand used for viewing races - what is function of stand - provides shelter and creates atmosphere of excitement - categories of work carried out - whether works on retained part of stand constitutes repairs - whether new bar and extension to old bar non-deductible capital improvements - whether stand or racecourse is the entirety - whether expenditure on roof a repair - whether word done to walls a repair - whether re-design or lower terracing an improvement - whether stand as renewed and repaired is plant - agreed test - whether stand is part of the means by which trade is carried on or merely part of the place where at which trade is carried on.

JW v JW
[Not previously reported].. Vol IV p 437

Domicile - constitutional rights - whether common law rule of dependent domicile of a wife constitutional - recognition of foreign divorces - wife's separate domicile.

McGurrin (Inspector of Taxes) v The Champion Publications Ltd
[Not previously reported].. Vol IV p 466

Respondent is a newspaper publisher - newspapers are "goods" for the purpose of manufacturing relief from corporation tax - whether income from advertising qualifies for such relief - whether indirect income from advertising can be treated equally with direct income from newsagents - whether advertising income is receivable in respect of the sale in the course of the trade of goods - whether advertising income is from a separate trade or providing a service - whether the matter to be considered from aspect of commercial reality - whether proper construction of words of s 41 brought advertisements within definition of goods - whether advertising revenue is received in respect of the sale of newspapers.

Bairead v McDonald
[Not previously reported].. Vol IV p 475

Appeal against judgment for income tax and interest - what constitutes a proper return of income for the assessment of income tax - whether a return of income equalling income tax exemption limits a valid return - whether lack of records justifies such a return - whether taxpayer treated unfairly by the Revenue - whether practice of allowing late returns amounts to promissory estoppel - whether taxpayer has availed of opportunity to make later returns after assessments had become final - whether treated unfairly by the Revenue - whether adjournment be granted to allow taxpayer to make proper returns - whether counterclaim for damages for harassment untenable.

O'Callaghan v Clifford and Others
[Not previously reported].. Vol IV p 478

Income tax - appeal against a decision of the High Court to refuse on a judicial review application to quash three convictions with six months imprisonment for each offence imposed in the District Court on the appellant for failure to make income tax returns - inspector of taxes empowered to require of an individual by notice a return of income - civil offence rendered a criminal offence by FA 1983 s 94(2) - whether a certificate by the inspector of non compliance is sufficient proof - whether in absence of accused in court the certificate contains the necessary mens rea - whether refusal in District Court to grant an adjournment denied the appellant the opportunity to defend himself - whether such refusal was unconstitutional - whether limits to District Judge's discretion to refuse an adjournment - whether extra degree of caution called for a criminal matter - whether appellant's right to instruct his counsel denied - whether audi alteram partem *rule and fair administration of justice applies - whether absence of due process on foot of certificate.*

Manning v Shackleton and Cork County Council
[Not previously reported] .... Vol IV p 485

Capital gains tax compulsory acquisition of land - whether property arbitrator obliged to give details of his findings of facts and law and a breakdown of his award - whether applicant is unable to formulate an appeal without being given the reasons for the award - whether breakdown required for capital gains tax purposes - whether award could be justified on the evidence - whether any obligation imposed on arbitrator by the Acquisition of Land (Assessment of Compensation) Act 1919 - whether the giving of reasons necessary for the proper exercise of a judicial or administrative function - whether failure by applicant at the hearing to request an apportionment of the award under the several heads of claim or to request a case stated rules out any further relief - whether failure to advance further arguments of unfairness amounted to acceptance of the normal practice - whether undertakings affected the amount of the arbitrator's award.

Carbery Milk Products Ltd v The Minister for Agriculture and Others
[Not previously reported] .... Vol IV p 492

Classification of milk products - EC regulations - milk protein powder - whether a whey or skimmed milk product - whether export refunds on consignments from EC countries to non EC countries - whether Revenue Commissioners responsible for classification - whether Revenue Commissioners and state chemist negligent and in breach of duty - whether re-classification renders products liable for repayment of export refunds - whether principle of legitimate expectation applies - whether Minister for Agriculture agent for European Commission - whether Minister entitled to counterclaim against plaintiff - whether plaintiff entitled to indemnity against Revenue Commissioners - EEC Regulations 804/68 and 2682/72.

Bairead v Carr
[Not previously reported] .... Vol IV p 505

Summary summonses served on the defendant in respect of tax liabilities the subject matter of earlier appeals - whether dissatisfaction expressed at the Circuit Court appeal hearings - whether dissatisfaction must be expressed immediately after determination by the Circuit Court Judge - whether notice to county registrar must be lodged within 21 days together with the £20 fee - whether requirements are directory or mandatory - whether tax must be paid before the case stated is determined - whether time lapse after expression of dissatisfaction is fatal - whether payment of tax denies access to the courts - whether Circuit Court judge has discretion to accept late filing of notice and fee.

Keller v The Revenue Commissioners and Others
[Not previously reported] .... Vol IV p 512

Importation of used motor vehicles from a Member State - interpretation of excise duties payable under SI 422/1983 - applicant a German citizen residing with his family in Ireland for upwards of twenty years - a collector of vintage Mercedes Benz motor cars - whether his normal residence in Germany - whether requirements for normal residence in Germany satisfied - whether importation for temporary purpose and for transport for private use - interpretation of the expression "a new motor vehicle of a similar or corresponding type" - whether regulations provide guidance on the retail price as may be determined by the Revenue Commissioners - whether regulations contrary to Article 95 of Treaty of Rome - whether excise duties fall more unfairly on imported used cars than on used cars sold on the Irish market - whether credit of German value added tax allowable - whether onus of proof discharged - whether value added tax charged on value added tax contrary to Sixth Council Directive - whether penalty of seizure and forfeiture disproportionate to offence - whether legitimate expectation infringed.

Kelly (Inspector of Taxes) v Cobb Straffan Ireland Ltd
[Not previously reported] .... Vol IV p 526

Case stated on question of manufacturing relief - respondent company carries on business of producing day old chicks - whether day old chicks are goods within the meaning of FA 1980 - whether use of extensive plant machinery and skilled workers constitute a process of manufacturing - whether goods are required to be inanimate - whether question is one of degree - whether raw material in process was not the egg but twenty years of research - whether process is similar to fish farming which required a specific statutory exemption - whether respondent was producing as opposed to manufacturing day old chicks - whether chick is a product that could not be produced by a natural process - whether process constitutes manufacturing.

Hussey (Inspector of Taxes) v Gleeson & Co Ltd
[Not previously reported] .... Vol IV p 533

Case stated on question of manufacturing relief - respondent company a wholesaler of beers and stouts as part of its trade conditions bottled Guinness stout - whether conditioning of bottled Guinness constitutes manufacturing process - chemical change in contents, carbon dioxide added and alcohol level increased - whether plant and equipment sufficiently sophisticated - whether process no more than keeping the stout in an even temperature for fourteen days - whether process of such a degree as to be classified as manufacturing.

Pine Valley Developments Ltd, Healy & Others v The Revenue Commissioners
[Not previously reported] .... Vol IV p 543

Award by European Court of Human Rights for pecuniary and non-pecuniary damages and costs lodged in High Court on foot of a claim by the plaintiffs - part of the award amounting to £273,000 held pending determination of the tax liabilities of the third plaintiff - conceded that £209,250 out of the £273,000 was in respect of income tax on interest accruing in the year 1993/94 - income tax liability would not arise prior to January 1995 - consequently £209,250 released on consent - balance of £63,750 relates to capital gains tax - third plaintiff is resident in the State and entitled to tax clearance certificate from capital gains tax - whether the sum of £63,750 should be withheld.

Dilleen (Inspector of Taxes) v Kearns
[Not previously reported] .... Vol IV p 547

Abandonment of an option within the meaning of CGTA 1975 s 47(3) - tax avoidance scheme - respondent and his wife grant each other options over their separate shareholdings in a private company - series of transactions through a chain of companies including the abandonment by the respondent and his wife of their respective options for sums totalling £2,532,500 - whether abandonment of options for a cash consideration constitutes an abandonment of the option or a chargeable disposal of assets - what is true meaning of term abandonment of an option - whether it means non-exercise - whether ordinary meaning applies - whether the entire and the substance of the transaction to be considered - whether tax avoidance exercise relevant - whether substantial payment for non-exercise can be said to be an abandonment within the meaning of the Act.

Allied Irish Banks plc v Bolger
[Not previously reported] .... Vol V p 1

Stamp duty - mortgage deeds - whether property stamped - whether admissible in evidence - whether admissible on foot of undertaking - whether possession of a premises can be obtained by way of special summons or summary procedure - whether ejectment proceedings required - whether procedure question raised in course of hearing

Airspace Investments Ltd v Moore (Inspector of Taxes)
[Not previously reported] .... Vol V p 3

Corporation tax - whether company carrying on a trade - whether capital expenditure - series of agreements - whether a tax avoidance scheme - whether agreements to be viewed as a composite transaction - whether loan repayable - whether transactions can be considered with the benefit of hindsight.

Brosnan (Inspector of Taxes) v Leeside Nurseries Ltd
[Not previously reported] .... Vol V p 21

Corporation tax - case stated - manufacturing relief - dwarfed potted chrysanthemum plants - whether McCann v O'Culachain properly decided - whether sophisticated process of cultivation constitutes manufacturing - whether a question of change in appearance, quality and value - whether a question of degree - whether "goods" capable of being manufactured - whether goods are inanimate - whether growing plants can be manufactured - whether manufactured or cultivated

In the Matter of Davoren, (Deceased); O'Byrne v Davoren and Coughlan
[Not previously reported] .... Vol V p 36

Trust - Discretionary - interpretation of residuary bequest - whether a valid charitable gift trust for education of children at discretion of trustees - class consisting of children, grandchildren and descendants of specified persons - meaning of the term "descendants" - whether capital of fund to be preserved - whether rule against perpetuities - whether bequest failed for uncertainty.

The Governor & Co of the Bank of Ireland v Meeneghan & Others
[Not previously reported] .... Vol V p 44

Value added tax - UK liability - UK court order restraining the taxpayer from disposing of his assets - whether bank account in Ireland subject to court order - whether foreign revenue debt recoverable in Ireland - whether effect of UK court order prevents the taxpayer from withdrawing the monies - whether principle of international law relating to revenue debts applies - whether value added tax subject to laws of European Union

Travers v O'Siochain (Inspector of Taxes)
[Not previously reported] .... Vol V p 54

Income tax - case stated - appellant's wife employed as a nurse by a Health Board in Northern Ireland - wife's remuneration taxed in Northern Ireland - whether appellant entitled to double taxation relief in Ireland - whether Article 18(2) of Double Taxation Relief (Taxes on Income and Capital Gains) [UK] Order 1976 grants relief.

WLD Worldwide Leather Diffusion Ltd v The Revenue Commissioners
[Not previously reported] .... Vol V p 61

Value added tax - judicial review - non resident company registered in the State - single trading transaction - whether entitled to be registered for value added tax - whether Revenue Commissioners have discretion to refuse registration - whether applicant a taxable person - fiscal advantage - whether application bona fide - whether transaction a trading transaction.

Orange v The Revenue Commissioners
[Not previously reported] .... Vol V p 70

Judicial Review application - applicant dependent upon criminal legal aid work - all legal aid fees due by Minister for Justice attached by respondents pursuant to FA 1988 s 73 whether procedure constitutional - whether court order required - whether constitutional right to earn a livelihood infringed - whether an unfair attack on applicant's property rights - whether attachment of value added tax element of legal aid fees unconstitutional applicant offered reasonable terms of payment by respondents - whether attack on property rights to be viewed in the light of surrounding circumstances - whether legislation requires amendment.

Erin Executor and Trustee Co Ltd v The Revenue Commissioners
[Not previously reported] .... Vol V p 76

Value added tax - properties leased for ten or more years - VAT incurred on expenditure on leasehold properties - whether credits for VAT allowable - whether reversionary interest outside VAT net.

McAuliffe v The Minister for Social Welfare
[Not previously reported] .... Vol V p 94

Social welfare appeal - appeal as to whether a contract of services or a contract for services - wholesale distributor of newspapers - deliveries of newspapers subcontracted to two individuals - individuals own delivery vehicles and pay all overheads - provide relief drivers - accept liability for losses or delays - time and reliability essence of contracts - whether contracts contain distinctive features of contracts for services - whether differences with contracts of service.

The Revenue Commissioners v O'Loinsigh
[Not previously reported] .... Vol V p 98

Income tax - case stated - series of books known as "Pathways to History" whether original and creative - whether within the meaning of FA 1969 s 2

McCabe (Inspector of Taxes) v South City & County Investment Co Ltd
[Not previously reported] .... Vol V p 107

Corporation Tax - whether periodic payments subject to Corporation Tax - annuity contract - annual payments off £500 plus share of profits in return for capital sum - whether correctly described as annuities - whether income receipts - whether return of capital - whether case law overturns logic of transactions - interpretation of tax statutes and documents - whether content of agreement conforms with its purpose
Additional judgment 1998 p 183

Fennessy (Inspector of Taxes) v McConnellogue
[Not previously reported] .... Vol V p 129

Income tax - respondent resides with his wife in Northern Ireland - respondent employed in Co Donegal and chargeable to Irish tax in his salary - respondent's wife employed in Northern Ireland and because of her residence there her salary not chargeable to Irish tax - whether respondent entitled to a full married allowance and double rate income tax bands - whether allowances restricted to a single person's allowance and single rate bands.

O'Shea (Inspector of Taxes) v Mulqueen
[Not previously reported] .... Vol V p 134

Income tax - lump sum payment on retirement - whether liable to income tax - whether received on account of illness - whether a redundancy payment - whether payment made on grounds of retirement - whether payment made on grounds of ill health.

Brosnan (Inspector of Taxes) v Mutual Enterprises Ltd
[Not previously reported] .... Vol V p 138

Case Stated - Corporation Tax - purchase of trading premises financed by foreign borrowings - losses incurred annually by reason of fluctuations in currency rates - whether allowable against trading profits - whether losses a revenue or capital item - whether a means of fluctuating and temporary accommodation - whether conflicting views of UK courts to be distinguished - whether monies borrowed to be used for purchase of a capital asset - whether monies so used - whether repayable on demand - whether a question of fact or law - whether grounds for setting aside findings of primary facts.

Mooney (Inspector Of Taxes) v McSweeney
[Not previously reported] .... Vol V p 163

Capital Gains Tax - loan to company - loan agreement with right to convert loan into shares - whether a mere debt - whether a debt on a security - whether an allowable loss for Capital Gains Tax purposes - whether characteristics of a debt on a security exist - whether synonymous with secured debt - whether marketable - whether loan had potential to be released at a profit - whether difficulty in finding a purchaser relevant - whether right to repayment and right to convert can co-exist -whether right to convert distinguishing factor - whether proviso to s 46 of Capital Tax Act 1975 applies.

In re Cherry Court v The Revenue Commissioners
[Not previously reported] .... Vol V p 180

Stamp duty - deed of release - whether or not a sale - whether liable to ad valorem stamp duty - series of transactions - whether release of option constituted a sale - meaning of sale - reality of transaction - whether phrases used imply a transfer of property.

In re Private Motorists Provident Society Ltd (In Liquidation) and Horgan v Minister for Justice
[Not previously reported] .... Vol V p 186

Court fees payable by official liquidator - court liquidation fees prescribed by statutory instrument - whether monies received in realisation of assets of a company - meaning of assets - meaning of realisation - whether assets can be realised more than once - whether accrual of interest a realisation - whether assets vested in liquidator - whether monies received from associated companies in liquidation constitute a realisation - whether interpretation of realisations a matter of debate.

In re Hibernian Transport Companies Ltd
[Not previously reported] .... Vol V p 194

Court liquidation - fees payable by official liquidator - fees prescribed by statutory instrument - monies received in realisation of assets of a company - interest earned from monies on deposit - capital gains from disposals of exchequer bills - whether a realisation - whether an investment - rate of court duty - yearly accounts - whether rate in force for accounting period applicable - whether rate at date of certification applies.

O'Culachain (Inspector of Taxes) v McMullan Brothers Ltd
[Not previously reported] .... Vol V p 200

Corporation tax - principles to be applied in a case stated - whether canopies in forecourts of petrol filling stations constitute plant - whether part of the premises - whether part of setting in which business carried on - whether function is to provide shelter and light - whether function is to attract customers - whether view of law correct - whether correct tests applied - whether "setting" and "plant" mutually exclusive - whether conclusion is one which a reasonable judge could not have arrived at.

Irwin v Grimes
[Not previously reported] .... Vol V p 209

Income tax - summary summons issued on 4 October 1989 - whether certificates under Waiver of Certain Tax, Interest and Penalties Act 1993 apply - whether proceedings initiated prior to 1993 Act - whether defendant non resident in the State up to 1992 - whether defendant liable for any taxes.

Daly v The Revenue Commissioners & Ors
[Not previously reported] .... Vol V p 213

Income tax - judicial review - fees paid by Health Board - applicant a medical doctor - payments subject to withholding tax - scheme of withholding tax amended by FA 1990 - self employed taxed on profits and gains of actual year of assessment - windfall gain to established taxpayers - amendment to eliminate gain - effect on new entrants to system -

effect of interim refunds - financial hardship - property rights infringed - proportionality test - whether unconstitutional.

Revenue Commissioners v Arida Ltd
[Not previously reported] .... Vol V p 221

Circuit Court rehearing of tax appeal - whether Circuit Court judge has jurisdiction to award costs - whether a tax appeal constitutes "proceedings" - whether statutory authority required - whether court has inherent jurisdiction to award costs - whether award of costs ultra vires the rules of the Circuit Court - whether jurisdiction of Circuit Court to award costs extends to cases vested in the Circuit Court since the passing of the Courts of Justice Act 1961.

In re Sugar Distributors Ltd
[Not previously reported] .... Vol V p 225

High Court application - whether share issue invalid - whether meetings took place or resolutions passed - whether backdating of transactions invalid - whether acts of company binds company - whether consent of corporators sufficient - whether s 89 be given a liberal "just and equitable" meaning - whether discretion of court under s 89 restricted - whether underlying policy of s 89 to be considered - whether remedy limited to defective title to shares - whether any proprietary interest in shares acquired by "innocent" persons - whether remedy available without court assistance - whether court can accede to a fiction.

Henry Denny & Sons (Ireland) Ltd T/A Kerry Foods v Minister for Social Welfare
[Not previously reported] .... Vol V p 238

Social Welfare appeal - PRSI - whether demonstrator engaged under a contract of service or contract for service - whether on insurable person as an employee or insurable as a self-employed person - whether written contract the determining factor - whether facts and realities govern the relationship - whether Circuit Court decision relevant - whether decision of Appeals Officer incorrect in law - whether control the deciding factor - whether in business on one's own account decisive - whether written agreement the sole source of the relationship - whether agreement fully considered by Appeals Officer - whether each case to be considered on its particular facts - whether Appeals Officer was entitled to conclude that there was a contract of service.

Quigley (Inspector of Taxes) v Maurice Burke
[Not previously reported] .... Vol V p 265

Income tax - whether an accountant acting in the preparation of accounts and computations of taxable income on behalf of a taxpayer is acting as an agent of the taxpayer - whether the relationship is that of a professional person and client - whether nominal ledger drawn up by the accountant is a document within the possession or power of the taxpayer - whether nominal ledger is part of accountant's working papers - whether accountant acting as auditor or agent.

Lynch v Burke & AIB Banks plc
[Not previously reported] .... Vol V p 271

Succession - joint bank deposit account - whether survivor entitled - whether presumption of resulting trust - whether immediate gift to joint holder - whether true joint tenancy -

whether provider retained a life interest - whether intention in favour of survivor - whether trust on death in favour of survivor - whether a testamentary disposition - whether in contravention of Wills Act 1837.

Purcell v The Attorney General Ireland & The Minister for the Environment
[Not previously reported] .... Vol V p 288

Farm tax - Farm Tax Act 1985 repealed in March 1987 - whether legislation lawfully amended - whether application of Act resulted in prejudicial discrimination - whether Act validly imposed - whether tax imposed in disregard of the intention of the Oireachtas - whether classification of farms had first to be completed - whether Act intended to discriminate between farmers according to the acreage of their farms - whether provisions of Act open to more than one construction - whether constitutional construction to be upheld - whether Minister obliged to bring farm tax into operation in the year 1986 - whether statutory instrument made under powers conferred and for purposes authorised by the Oireachtas - whether statutory instrument ultra vires.

The Revenue Commissioners v Young
[Not previously reported] .... Vol V p 294

Case Stated - Capital acquisitions tax - valuation of shares in a private non trading investment company - whether method of valuation of shares governed by CATA 1976 s 17 - whether s 17 subject to the market value rules comprised in s 15 - whether artificial method governed by commercial reality - whether voting rights held by Ordinary Shares could be used to redeem the Preference Shares - whether the application of s 17 mandatory.

O'Grady (Inspector of Taxes) v Roscommon Race Committee
[Not previously reported] .... Vol V p 317

Case stated - whether a stand at Roscommon Racecourse was plant-trade of promoting and organising horse races at the racecourse for viewing by the public - raised stand gives better views and generates an atmosphere of excitement for patrons - provides shelter and a meeting place - work undertaken provides a new and enlarged stand giving shelter, additional viewing space and bars - test is whether the stand is part of the means whereby the trade is carried on or whether it is merely part of the place where the trade is carried on.

O'Rourke v The Revenue Commissioners
[Not previously reported] .... Vol V p 321

Income tax - repayment of overpaid PAYE tax - whether taxpayer entitled to interest - whether FA 1976 s 30 applied - whether requirements for assessments and appeals satisfied - whether implied agreement - whether constructive trust - whether statutory possession required - whether common law right to interest - appropriate rate of interest - Woolwich doctrine of common law rights - whether repayment of tax as a matter of right whether defendants unjustly enriched at expense of plaintiff - whether plaintiff acquiesced without protest in payment of tax - recovery of money paid in mistake of law - development of law of restitution - money paid without consideration - Murphy's case - whether fiscal problem for State - whether present case can be distinguished - small number of affected taxpayers and minimal fiscal consequences - whether taxpayer entitled as of right to interest - whether rate of interest under Courts Acts applicable.

In the Matter of G O'C & A O'C (Application of Liston (Inspector Taxes))
[Not previously reported] .... Vol V p 346

Income tax - appeal to Supreme Court - application by inspector of taxes for High Court order - order to bank to furnish particulars of accounts of taxpayers and their children - whether discrepancy between returns of income and assets owned by taxpayers - whether discovery of illegal export of £500,000 by taxpayers a matter for further investigation - whether inspector had reasonable grounds for application - whether pre-condition of a request to deliver a return of income satisfied - whether findings of High Court erroneous in point of law - whether taxpayers deemed to have made returns of income - whether deeming provision confined to ITA 1967 s 172(4) - whether unjust, anomalous or absurd result would follow.

McMahon and Others v Rt Hon Lord Mayor Alderman & Burgess of Dublin
[Not previously reported] .... Vol V p 357

Residential development - tax benefits for holiday cottages - planning permission for private residential purposes - whether holiday homes a change of use - whether use specified - purpose for which the homes designated - whether exempted development - complaints by permanent residents - appeal against the decision of An Bord Pleanala.

Kenny v The Revenue Commissioners, Goodman & Gemon Ltd (Notice Parties)
[Not previously reported] .... Vol V p 363

Stamp duty - judicial review - instruments incorrectly stamped - whether instrument a promissory note - whether an assignment of a debt fully stamped - whether Revenue adjudication correct - whether taxpayer is entitled to challenge administrative decisions relating to another taxpayer's affairs - defendant is entitled to question the stamping of documents in the course of court proceedings - whether judicial review is an appropriate remedy - whether court has jurisdiction to make declaratory orders against notice parties - whether court has jurisdiction to issue declaratory orders relating to admissibility of documents in proceedings in which the admissibility has been raised.

In Re Estates of Cummins: O'Dwyer & Charleton v Keegan & Ors
[Not previously reported] .... Vol V p 367

Capital Acquisitions Tax - Succession Act 1965 - legal right share - husband survived by wife twelve hours - no children - wife in a coma and unaware of husband's death - whether widow's estate acquired a half share in husband's estate - whether legal right share vests on death - whether legal right share has the same meaning as a share under a will or intestacy - whether intentions of deceased husband and surviving spouse frustrated - law should be certain

Saatchi & Saatchi Advertising Ltd v McGarry (Inspector of Taxes)
[Not previously reported] .... Vol V p 376

Corporation tax - case stated - manufacturing relief for film production - proper construction of FA 1990 s 41 - relief deemed to apply prior to FA 1990 where relief was sought - whether application for relief a pre-requisite - whether scheme and purpose of a statutory enactment relevant - whether procedure irrelevant to taxing statutes - whether equitable principles operate - whether principles of construction of taxing statutes must be applied.

In the Matter of Williams (Tallaght) (In Receivership) and Companies Act 1963-1990
[Not previously reported] .... Vol V p 388

Revenue debts - company in receivership - property subject to floating charge - Revenue as preferential creditors for PAYE and PRSI - company in liquidation - whether Revenue a preferential creditor for corporation tax liability of company - whether double preference claims precluded - no statutory authority to deny double preference claims - whether Revenue debt statute barred - six months limitation period - whether notified - whether known to liquidator - whether actual knowledge required - whether extended to include constructive knowledge - whether statutory time limit can be extended by court.

Action Aid Ltd v The Revenue Commissioners
[Not previously reported] .... Vol V p 392

Income tax - payments under deeds of covenant in favour of named children in Third World countries - whether entitled to exemption limits under FA 1980 s 1 - appellant a registered corporate charity in Ireland and a trustee for the named children - whether withdrawal of relief from 1984 onwards justified - whether payments applied for benefit of covenantees - whether payments made into fund for a group - whether payment must be made direct to covenantee - whether exemption restricted to persons aged over 65 years - whether exemption applies to non residents.

Taxback Limited v The Revenue Commissioners
[Not previously reported] .... Vol V p 412

Value Added Tax - judicial review - goods transported to a destination outside EC member states exempt from VAT - whether foreign tourists to Ireland can claim VAT refunds on goods purchased in Ireland - whether refunds obtainable through refunding agencies - whether accounts of refunding agency in order - whether Revenue justified in withholding refunds

Burke & Sons Ltd v The Revenue Commissioners, Ireland and the Attorney General
[Not previously reported] .... Vol V p 418

Value Added Tax - Judicial review - VAT scheme for retailers - interpretation of scheme - whether scheme based on sales or purchases - alcoholic liquors purchased out of bonded warehouse - whether payment of excise duty to be treated as zero rated - whether applicant's interpretation correct - whether scheme retrospectively altered - whether Revenue acted in breach of natural justice - whether Revenue bound by accepted applicant's interpretation over a period of years

Gilligan v Criminal Assets Bureau, Galvin, Lanigan and The Revenue Commissioners
[Not previously reported] .... Vol V p 424

Income Tax - husband and wife - joint assessment - whether husband is liable for tax on wife's income - whether wife is separately liable on her income - whether both living together for chargeable period - whether wife is obliged to make a return in respect of her own income - whether "Special Provisions" in relation to married couples prevail in all circumstances.

O'Siochain (Inspector of Taxes) v Neenan
[Not previously reported] .... Vol V p 472

Case Stated - Income Tax - increase in Widows Social Welfare Contributory Pension granted in respect of dependent children - whether the income of the widow or the child - whether beneficiary distinguished from qualified child - whether additions to pension for benefit of children - whether a residence relationship applies - whether rate of pension or entitlement attracts chargeability to tax - whether trust in favour of children read into Act - whether purposeful construction to be applied - whether additional payment 'travels' with child - whether payments to qualified children exempt from income tax

Proes v The Revenue Commissioners
[Not previously reported] .... Vol V p 481

Case Stated - Income Tax - domicile of appellant - Irish domicile of origin - English domicile of choice - holiday house in Ireland - death of appellant's husband - whether new domicile of choice acquired - whether existing domicile of choice abandoned - whether wrong test applied - when was domicile of choice abandoned - whether appellant's intention in regard to her permanent home retained.

Hibernian Insurance Company Limited v MacUimis (Inspector of Taxes)
[Not previously reported] .... Vol V p 495

Corporation tax - case stated - investment company - whether expenses of management tax deductible - interpretation of expenses of management - whether management implies regular expenditure - whether expenses of acquisition are capital expenditure - whether expenses of management and expenses by management can be distinguished - whether expenses an integral part of costs of purchaser - whether phrase expenses of management has a technical or special meaning.

Kearns v Dilleen (Inspector of Taxes)
[Not previously reported] .... Vol V p 514

Capital Gains Tax - tax avoidance scheme - options to purchase shares in the same company granted by husband to wife and by wife to husband - 98% of the purchase price paid for the option and 2% payable on the exercise of the option - commercial reality of transactions - meaning of word abandonment - substance of transactions - principles of construction of taxing statutes - whether rights and obligations of parties to the transaction to be considered - whether an abandonment when consideration is received - whether receipt of capital sum a separate taxable disposal

The Attorney General v Power and Others
[Not previously reported] .... Vol V p 525

Estate duty - FA 1894 (57 & 58 Vict c 30), s 5(3) - interest in possession - whether conveyancing form determines liability.

Smyth v The Revenue Commissioners
[Not previously reported] .... Vol V p 532

Estate duty - valuation of private company shares - restriction on transfer of shares - whether dividends paid represented profit earning capacity of the company - whether profit earning capacity is proper test of value of shares - whether remuneration of directors exceeded commercial level - return on monies invested by purchasers - whether a sale of entire shareholding.

The Revenue Commissioners v Doorley
[Not previously reported].. Vol V p 539

Legacy duty - charitable bequest - whether to be expended in Ireland - construction of will - interpretation of taxing statute - exemption from legacy duty - whether charitable bequest had to be expended in Ireland.

Byrne v The Revenue Commissioners
[Not previously reported].. Vol V p 560

Revenue - stamp duty - deed of conveyance - exemption from stamp duty - deed executed by grantors and delivered as escrow - subsequent execution by grantees - inadvertent stamping - repayment of duty - date of execution of deed - whether claim for repayment within two years of date of execution - Poor Relief (Ireland) Act 1838 (1 & 2 Vict c 56) s 96 - Stamp Duties Management Act 1891 (54 & 55 Vict c 38) s 10 - Revenue Act 1898 (61 & 62 Vict c 46) s 13.

In re Swan, (Deceased); Hibernian Bank Ltd v Frances Stewart Munro and Others
[Not previously reported].. Vol V p 565

Will - construction - annuity "free of income tax" - annuitant entitled to refunds in respect of tax borne by testator's estate - whether annuitant entitled to retain such refunds or bound to account for them to testator's estate - ITA 1918 (8 & 9 Geo, 5, c 40) ss 16 and 29, All Schedules Rules, r 19.

O'Sullivan v The Revenue Commissioners
[Not previously reported].. Vol V p 570

Stamp duty - case stated - whether a lease assessable as a conveyance or transfer on sale - money consideration in addition to rent - whether words and scheme of FA 1947 s 13 are appropriate to leases - whether doubt in a Stamp Act construed in favour of the taxpayer - whether a tax upon the citizen must be stated in clear language.

In re Estate of McNamee and Others v The Revenue Commissioners
[Not previously reported].. Vol V p 577

Estate duty - valuation of private company shares - minority shareholding - principles of valuation - profit earning capacity - preservation of assets - dividend policy - past sales - actual sale - imaginary open market.

The Revenue Commissioners v Moroney and Others
[Not previously reported].. Vol V p 589

Estate duty - whether receipt clause in a deed binding - whether stated consideration recoverable - whether extrinsic evidence admissible to contradict statement of consideration - whether doctrine of promissory estoppel applies - whether a question of mistake or rectification.

In Re the Estate of Urquhart, (Deceased) and The Revenue Commissioners v AIB Ltd
[Not previously reported] .... Vol V p 600

Revenue - Estate duty - legal right - whether surviving spouse competent to dispose of statutory share in estate - election - FA 1894 (57 & 58 Vict c 30) ss 2, 22 - Succession Act 1965 (No 27) ss 111, 115.

Murphy v The Attorney General
[Not previously reported] .... Vol V p 613

Income tax -incomes of husband and wife aggregated - tax payable by a married couple in excess of the amounts payable by a husband and wife if taxed as separate persons - whether in breach of constitutional rights - ITA 1967 ss 138, 192-198 - income tax - recovery of tax overpaid - tax improved by statute deceased to be invalid - whether money paid under mistake of law can be recovered.

Stephen Court Ltd v Browne (Inspector of Taxes)
[3 ITR 95] .... Vol V p 680

Corporation tax - auctioneer's commission and solicitor's costs - whether expenses of a revenue or capital nature - ITA 1967 ss 81(5)(d), 81(6)(a)(i) - FA 1969 s 22 - CTA 1976 s 15

AE v The Revenue Commissioners
[Not previously reported] .... Vol V p 686

Revenue - capital acquisitions tax - gift of farm to niece - whether niece worked substantially full-time on the farm - whether herding of cattle under a letting agreement constituted a business - meaning of business - CATA 1976 (No 8) 2nd Schedule, Pt 1, para 9.

Director of Public Prosecutions v Cunningham
[Not previously reported] .... Vol V p 691

Betting duty - whether Inland Revenue Regulation Act 1890 complied with - whether court proceedings preceded by order of the Revenue Commissioners - whether onus on prosecution to prove existence of order of the Commissioners.

McDaid v Sheehy and Others
[Not previously reported] .... Vol V p 696

Excise duties - judicial review - whether applicant entitled to an order of certiorari - whether order validated by confirmation and re-enactment in subsequent legislation - whether court should rule on constitutional validity of legislation when pronouncement of no benefit to applicant.

Re Coombe Importers Ltd (In Liq) and Re the Companies Acts 1963-1990
[Not previously reported] .... 1998 p 59

PAYE/PRSI – payments to employees without deduction of PAYE/PRSI – Company in examinership – estimated assessments by Inspector of Taxes – Company in liquidation – Revenue debt – whether super-preferential status – interpretation of s 120(2) Social Welfare Consolidation Act 1981 – whether Court obliged to look at things done or failing to be done s 301 Social Welfare (Consolidation) Act 1993.

The Revenue Commissioners v Sisters of Charity of the Incarnate Word
[Not previously reported] ....1998 p 65

Income Tax – Case stated – foreign charity with a branch in Ireland – whether Irish branch entitled to exemption from income tax on its profits – whether "established" in Ireland – interpretation of ss 333/334 Income Tax Act 1967 – whether geographical limitation contained in the statute – charitable activities in Ireland – whether facts distinguished from Camille case in UK – meaning of word established – whether a sufficient Irish establishment to justify exemption.

Byrne (John Oliver) v Noel Conroy
[Not previously reported] ....1998 p 75

Extradition Order - appeal on grounds of a revenue offence - Monetary Compensation Amounts - agricultural levies under EEC regulations - fraudulent charges - whether agricultural levies constitute a tax - question to be determined by Irish law - whether a tax in normal concept of taxes - whether part of revenue of any particular country.

Saatchi & Saatchi Advertising Limited v Kevin McGarry (Inspector of Taxes)
[Not previously reported] ....1998 p 99

Corporation Tax - case stated - manufacturing relief for film production - whether relief applies to short advertising films produced for use on television - retrospective application of s 41 Finance Act 1990 - whether claim for relief prior to assessment a pre-requisite - whether strict interpretation of a taxing statute prevails - whether scheme and purpose of a statute relevant.

Sean O'Siochain (Inspector of Taxes) v Bridget Neenan
[Not previously reported] ....1998 p 111

Income Tax – Case stated – social welfare benefits – increases in widow's contributory pension by reason of dependent children - whether liable to income tax – whether increases the property of the children or the widow – whether widow liable for income tax on the benefits for dependent children – proper interpretation Chapter II of Social Welfare (Consolidation) Act 1981.

Haughey and Others v Attorney General and Others
[Not previously reported] ....1998 p 119

Tribunal of Inquiry - jurisdiction of Oireachtas and Taoiseach - whether Tribunal of Inquiry Evidence Act 1921 applies - whether Tribunal constitutionally valid - whether powers of Tribunal unlimited - grounds of appeal - whether personal rights infringed - right to equality of treatment, privacy and fair procedures - whether powers of Tribunal exceeded

Parkes (Roberta) v David Parkes
[Not previously reported] ....1998 p 169

Stamp Duty – Husband purchasing property in wife's name – Presumption of advancement rebutted – whether resulting trust – Husband procuring wife to make false declaration in conveyance – Husband subsequently seeking court's aid to enforce trust – Whether husband entitled to relief in equity

In the matter of The Sunday Tribune Limited (in Liquidation)
[Not previously reported] .... 1998 p 177

Company - Winding up - Creditors - Preferential payments - Test applicable - Unpaid wages of employees or contractual payments Whether employee engaged under a contract of service or a contract for services journalists - Claimants entitled to be paid as creditors preferential - Companies Act 1963 s 285.

B McCabe (Inspector of Taxes) v South City & County Investment Co Ltd
[Vol V p 107] .... 1998 p 183

Corporation Tax - whether periodic payments subject to Corporation Tax - annuity contract - annual payments of £500 plus share of profits in return for capital sum - whether correctly described as annuities - whether income receipts - whether return of capital - whether case law overturns logic of transactions - interpretation of tax statutes and documents - whether content of agreement conforms with its purpose

Criminal Assets Bureau v Gerard Hutch
[Not previously reported] .... 1999 p 65

Income tax - appeal against judgment - assessment made in absence of income tax returns - tax appeal procedures - late appeal - assessment becoming final and conclusive - Collector General's certificate as proof of amount due

Patrick J O'Connell (Inspector of Taxes) v Fyffes Banana Processing Limited
[Not previously reported] .... 1999 p 71

Corporation Tax - Case Stated - company providing banana ripening services - process of maturation of foodstuffs - whether goods manufactured within the State - strict interpretation of taxing statutes - whether any doubt or ambiguity in the statutory provisions - services rendered deemed to be the manufacture of goods - goods manufactured within the State to be distinguished from services rendered in a process of manufacture of goods

Sean MacAonghusa (Inspector of Taxes) v Ringmahon Company
[Not previously reported] .... 1999 p 81

Corporation tax - case stated - whether loan interest was money wholly and exclusively expended for the purpose of trade of the company - company redeemed £6 million Redeemable Preference shares - company raised a loan of £6 million - whether loan for purpose of restricting share capital and paying off shareholders - whether loan a temporary and fluctuating borrowing - purposes of trade is to serve purposes of the trade - object in making the payment is based on the intentions of the taxpayer - whether incidental consequences - question of degree - whether Inspector can direct company on how to finance its business - whether loan needed to continue trade - whether company entitled to a deduction for annual loan interest - whether judge's determination properly within the evidence adduced before him

Derek Crilly v T & J Farrington Limited and John O'Connor
[not previously reported] .... 2000 p 63

Health Board charge - hospital maintenance charge - whether patient entitled to compensation or damages for personal injury - whether amount of the charge to be determined by the Minister for Health - whether amount of the charge to be a reasonable charge - method of determining a reasonable charge - whether method specified in statute - whether charge to be based on average daily costs of hospital - whether costs relate to overall costs of hospital or to costs of specialist section hospital - interpretation of statutes - which extracts from Dail Debates admissible - whether legislative history of statute admissible - whether legislative history of corresponding UK statute admissible - whether reference to parliamentary statements limited to ambiguous statutory provisions

Hibernian Insurance Company Limited v MacUimis (Inspector of Taxes)
[not previously reported] .... 2000 p 73

Corporation Tax - Case stated - investment company - expenses of management deductible - interpretation of expenses of management for corporation tax purposes - expenses incurred in respect of investment appraisals and advices with a view to acquisitions of investments - whether expenses incurred prior to the date on which a decision was made to acquire the particular investment - whether character of expenditure alters depending upon whether the investment was purchased or not - whether expenses were of a revenue or capital nature - Corporation Tax Act 1976, s 15

Michael Gayson v Allied Irish Banks Plc
[not previously reported] .... 2000 p 103

Income tax – Tax evasion – non-resident deposit accounts – tax amnesty– whether a bank customer given negligent advice – whether customer advised not to avail of amnesty – personal liability to and account for income tax – whether monies deposited on trust for customer's children – whether non resident address false – whether AIB implicated in tax evasion – whether customer aware of tax evasion – whether bank employee under a duty of care as agent of the bank – whether customer totally aware of tax and amnesty implications

Patrick J O'Connell (Inspector of Taxes) v Thomas Keleghan
[not previously reported] .... 2000 p 111

Capital gains tax/income tax - case stated - sale of shares - sale price in the form of loan notes - loan notes not transferable or assignable - "paper for paper" transaction - whether capital gains tax deferred pending redemption of loan notes - whether loan notes a simple debt or a debt on a security - whether CGT 1975 Sch 2 para 2 is based on "two fictions" - whether fictions are no more than rules of computing tax - "no disposal fiction" and "composite simple asset fiction" - whether marketability is the essence of a loan note - inducement payment to enter into service contract - whether payment liable to income tax - whether taxpayer ever took up employment on foot of the service contract

The Criminal Assets Bureau v Patrick A McSweeney .... 2000 p 213

Income tax – Mareva Injunction – freezing of defendant's assets prior to hearing of trial – application made ex parte – whether proceedings can be brought on a plenary summons – whether Revenue Commissioners empowered to sue by plenary summons - interpretation of TCA 1997 s 966 – whether undue delay unconstitutional – whether High Court authorised to grant Mareva injunctions – High Court practice and procedure

The Criminal Assets Bureau v John Kelly .... 2000 p 223

Income tax – assessments issued by Criminal Assets Bureau – whether time limit for appeal expired – whether assessments final and conclusive – whether assessment made in accordance with s 922 – whether valid appeal lodged – seizure of assets – denial to monies to fund appeal – whether unconstitutional – whether defendant failed to avail of statutory remedies – whether freezing order could have been varied – whether tax appeal could have been pursued – whether CAB entitled to judgment

Patrick J O'Connell (Inspector of Taxes) v Fyffes Banana Processing Limited
[1999 p 71] .... 2000 p 233

Corporation tax – case stated – company providing banana ripening services – process of maturation of foodstuffs – whether profits from manufacturing tax relief – strict interpretation of taxing statutes whether in the imposition of tax or relief from tax – whether intention of legislature to be considered – whether the word goods has the same meaning for all provisions of FA 1990 s 39 – FA 1980 s 41(2) relieving provision

BD O'Shea (Inspector of Taxes) v Colle Parkview Service Station Limited
[not previously reported] .... 2000 p 245

Value Added Tax – Case Stated – purchase of garage premises comprising a plot of land, four petrol pumps, and automatic car-wash and a compressor – VAT charged on transaction – whether respondent company entitled to an input credit in respect of VAT – whether transfer of ownership made in connection with transfer of business – whether business had ceased - whether findings of fact by Appeal Commissioners can be set aside – whether determination correct in law.

Dunnes Stores v Gerard Ryan and The Minister for Enterprise, Trade and Employment
[not previously reported] .... 2000 p 259

Judicial review - Companies Act 1990 s 19 - authorised officers appointed to examine books and records of companies - whether order invalid - whether conduct of company necessitates appointment of inspector - whether affairs of company conducted unlawfully or fraudulently - whether Minister acting unreasonably or irrationally - whether contrary to fundamental reason and common sense and ultra vires

Michael Hogan v Steele And Co Ltd and Electricity Supply Board
[not previously reported] .... 2000 p 267

Income Tax and PRSI - damages for personal injuries - undertaking by plaintiff to refund to ESB from the damages all advances made to him during his absence from work duties - income tax, PRSI, and pension contributions deducted from gross wages paid - whether payment of PAYE and PRSI a statutory duty - whether such payments gone forever as a matter of law

The Director of Public Prosecutions v George Redmond
[not previously reported] .... 2000 p 271

Income Tax – failure to deliver income tax returns – whether fines of £7,500 in respect of charges too lenient – whether taxpayer's arrest added to gravity of offences – whether DPP has satisfied onus of proof – whether an error in principle by judge - whether a gross departure from norm – whether settlement payment included penal interest – whether revenue penalty of punitive consequence to offender – whether fine or sentence additional to other penalties – whether a sentence of imprisonment sought – whether principle of proportionality applied.

Case C-358/97 Commission of the European Communities v Ireland
....2000 p 287

Value Added Tax - whether VAT chargeable on tolls for use of roads and bridges - East Link and West Link Bridges, Dublin - whether a supply of goods and services for consideration by a taxable person - whether person carrying on a economic activity - whether exploitation of a tangible asset - whether private operator acting as a public authority - whether operator governed by public law - whether tolls levied in exercise of public authority - whether an exempt activity - whether supply of infrastructure constitutes leasing - whether subject to collection of own resources in accordance with Sixth Directive.

Simple Imports Limited and Another v Revenue Commissioners and Others
[not previously reported]... 2001 p 57

Customs Law – Books or Documents, Transactions contravening customs laws – whether search warrants invalid – whether reasonable cause – whether exercise properly conveyed on face of warrant – whether exercise of warrant challenged – whether entry refused – whether within jurisdiction of district judge.

Cyril Forbes v John Tobin And Janet Tobin
[not previously reported]... 2001 p 71

Value Added Tax - specific performance - contract for sale of garage premises - whether sale of a business or a property - whether purchaser liable for Burmah-Castrol agreements - whether VAT chargeable - whether development property for VAT purposes - prior development expenditure - Revenue statement of practice on property transactions - whether 10% rule applied - whether 10% rule a statutory provision - whether parties ad idem - whether equitable remedy of specific performance applicable.

In the Matter of Millhouse Taverns Ltd and the Companies Act 1963-1999
[not previously reported]... 2001 p 77

VAT, PAYE and PRSI – unpaid taxes, interest and penalties – petition to wind up company – whether a substantial and reasonable defence to petition – whether company insolvent

Patrick J O'Connell (Inspector of Taxes) v Tara Mines Ltd
[not previously reported]... 2001 p 79

Corporation tax – case stated – mining company – whether carrying on mining operations – whether mining or manufacturing – whether a qualifying mine – whether entitled to export sales relief or capital allowances – whether findings of fact justified conclusions – whether findings can be set aside – whether ambiguity in findings – whether decisions based on findings

Beverly Cooper-Flynn v RTE, Charlie Bird and James Howard
[not previously reported]... 2001 p 97

Tax evasion- whether James Howard sought to evade his obligation to pay tax by not availing of the tax amnesty – whether he failed to return for tax his investment in the CMI

Personal Portfolio – whether Beverly Cooper-Flynn ('the plaintiff') had induced him and others to invest in the CMI Personal Portfolio for the purpose of evading tax – issue of costs – whether plaintiff's reputation had suffered – whether costs should follow the decision – whether special causes apply – whether plaintiff obtained something of value – whether inconsistencies in evidence of defendants amounted to a special cause.

Patrick J O'Connell (Inspector of Taxes) v Thomas Keleghan
[2000 p 111] .... 2001 p 103

Case stated – Income Tax (IT) – service contract of sale of shares – binding contract to serve as sale director of Siúcre Éireann ('the Purchaser') – inducement payment of £250,000 – whether taxpayer ever became an employee – whether Purchaser had an interest direct or indirect in the performance of the contract of employment – whether inference of acceptance of agreement – whether payment taxable under ITA 1967 s 110

Capital Gains Tax (CGT) – sale of shares in Gladebrook Ltd by shareholders in 1990 for a consideration in the form of loan notes – loan notes not transferable or assignable – whether CGT chargeable on redemption of loan notes for cash in 1993 – whether loan notes constitute debenture stock – 'paper for paper' transaction and exempt under CGTA 1975 Sch 2 para 4 – whether statutory fiction treats loan notes as shares – whether legislation so provides – whether exemption on disposal of a debt applies – whether loan notes a debt on a security – whether marketable and capable of increasing in value

Seán MacAonghusa (Inspector of Taxes) v Ringmahon Company
[1999 p 81] .... 2001 p 117

Corporation Tax – case stated – redeemable preference shares issued to satisfy borrowings- Ringmahon Company redeemed £6 million redeemable preference shares and raised a bank load for this purpose- whether the annual interest on the loan is a deductible expense- whether the loan was related to the capital restructuring of the company – whether the interest on such a loan was stamped with the character of capital expenditure and therefore was deductible – whether non deductibility an anomaly in tax code – whether interest on borrowings used for purposes of trade allowable.

Francis Griffin v Minister for Social, Community and Family Affairs
[not previously reported] .... 2001 p 125

PRSI – share fisherman – whether employed on a contract of service or engaged in a joint venture with boat owner – whether liable to PRSI as a self employed person – whether agreement whereby net proceeds of catch divisible between boat owner and crew constitutes a partnership – optimal social welfare scheme for self employed share fishermen – whether losses carried forward – whether leading Irish judgment disregarded – whether relationship between parties is one of employment or one of partnership – whether each voyage a separate venture – whether Minister has unlimited power to make regulations – whether High Court decisions are binding on Appeals Officer – whether tests of control, enterprise integration remuneration or economic reality apply – whether conclusions based on evidence – whether capital investment essential for a partnership – whether equality among partners required – whether same mistake of law made in decisions by both Appeals Officers

John Gilligan v Criminal Assets Bureau, Revenue Commissioners & Others
[not previously reported].. 2001 p 135

Proceeds of Crime Act 1996 – provisions relating to proceeds derived from criminal activities – non-constitutional and constitutional issues- whether defendants can be prohibited from disposing of a sum of £300,000 – whether defendants obliged to give details of all property and income therefrom in their possession or control over past 10 years – whether High Court has jurisdiction to impose orders of restraint and appropriation over property situate within and outside the State – whether plenary summons procedure seeking interim and interlocutory relief appropriate – whether provisions of Act retrospective – whether hearsay evidence sufficient to satisfy onus of proof on the balance of probabilities – whether provisions of Act formed part of the criminal law and not of the civil law – whether persons affected deprived of safeguards under criminal code – whether presumption of innocence ignored – whether standard of proof based on reasonable doubt rather than balance of probabilities – whether provision for trial by jury required – whether purposes and mens rea punitive and deterrent – whether forfeiture of property and mens rea indicative of crime – whether Revenue case precedents apply – whether delays under Act oppressive – whether provisions unfair and retrospective – whether in breach of European Convention on Human Rights.

Simple Imports Limited and Another v Revenue Commissioners and Others

Supreme Court
Keane J, Barron J
19 January 2000

Customs Law – Books or Documents, Transactions contravening customs laws – whether search warrants invalid – whether reasonable cause – whether exercise properly conveyed on face of warrant – whether exercise of warrant challenged – whether entry refused – whether within jurisdiction of district judge.

These proceedings have been brought for a declaration that the warrants grounding searches and seizures by Customs Officers were unlawful, void and of no effect and failed to show jurisdiction on their face for two reasons:

(i) they did not disclose that the Customs Officer had reasonable grounds for his suspicion that such goods were on the said premises and,

(ii) they did not disclose that the district judge had reasonable cause for believing that the Customs Officer had such suspicion

Facts

Customs officers entered the premises of Simple Imports Ltd. ('the Company') at Dublin, Limerick and Cork on 5 December 1996 pursuant to search warrants and in pursuance of the searches removed magazines, videos and documentation relating to the import export, sale and distribution of such goods. The warrants were issued under s 205 Customs Consolidation Act 1876 and s 5(1) Customs and Excise (Miscellaneous Provisions) Act 1988 in the appropriate District Courts.

The law

The statutory authority to issue the search warrant is unquestionably subject to two preconditions. First, the person applying for the warrant must have reasonable cause to suspect that there is material to be found on a particular premises and, secondly, the judge must be satisfied from information given on oath by the applicant that the applicant had that reasonable suspicion.

In the UK case of *IRC v Rossminster Ltd and Others* [1980] AC 952 in the House of Lords it was held by the majority that while it was reasonable it was not essential to state on the face of the warrant that the judge was satisfied as to the existence of reasonable suspicion.

Conclusion

There is sufficient evidence to show that the Customs Officer had reasonable cause for the suspicions and that the district judges were satisfied that they held such suspicions. Accordingly the decisions to issue the warrants were made within jurisdiction.

This leaves the question whether the exercise was properly conveyed by the words in the warrant. The warrants herein do not say on their face that the judges considered that there was reasonable cause to suspect. The absence of the word 'reasonable' does not affect its validity. Once the warrant had been signed by the judge expressly stating that it appeared to him that there was cause, it must be assumed that he acted reasonably and that the warrant must be valid.

The execution of the warrants was not challenged. If the appellant or its staff had not accepted the validity of the warrants they could have refused entry. The legal advice was that entry had to be allowed and was granted. In the circumstances herein the person who allows the search cannot subsequently object. The warrant itself is merely a document to assure against whom it is directed that the proposed search is a legal one.

Held by Barron J in dismissing the appeal that:

(i) The decisions to issue the searches were made within jurisdiction

(ii) The jurisdiction of the district judges was not invalidly exercised merely because the valid exercise was not indicated on the face of the warrant

(iii) The searches were legally authorised and were not challenged

---

Legislation:
Customs Consolidation Act 1876, s 205; Customs and Excise (Miscellaneous Provisions) Act 1988, s 5(1)

Cases referred to in judgement:
AG of Jamaica v Williams [1998] AC 357.
Berkeley v Edwards [1988] IR 219.
Byrne v Grey [1988] IR 31
IRC v Rossminster and Others [1980] AC 952.

Supreme Court - 19 January 2000

The factual and statutory background

Keane J, This case raises an issue which has concerned the courts on a number of occasions in recent years, ie the validity of certain search warrants. The warrants now under challenge were issued by the three District Judges named as respondents in the proceedings and purported to authorise officers of the first named respondent, the Revenue Commissioners, to enter premises owned by the applicants in Dublin, Cork and Limerick, to search for material said to be indecent, obscene or pornographic and, if found, to seize and remove such material. Another set of warrants purported to authorise the officers named to search for books or documents relating to transactions in contravention of the laws relating to customs and to seize and remove any such books or documents that might be found on the premises.

The first category of warrants was issued in purported exercise of a power conferred by s 205 of the Customs Consolidation Act 1876, which provides that:

> If any officer of Customs shall have reasonable cause to suspect that any uncustomed or prohibited goods are harboured kept or concealed in any house or other place either in the United Kingdom or the Channel Islands, and it shall be made to appear by information on oath before any justice of the peace in the United Kingdom or the Channel Islands, it shall be lawful for such justice, by special warrant under his hand, to authorise such officer to enter and search such house or other place, and to seize and carry away any such uncustomed or prohibited goods as may be found therein,: and it shall be lawful for such officer, and he is hereby authorised, in case of resistance, to break open any door, and to force and remove any other impediment or obstruction to such entry search or seizure as aforesaid: and such officer may if he sees fit avail himself of the service of any constable or police officer to aid and assist

in the execution of such warrant, and any constable or other police officer is hereby required when so called upon to aid and assist accordingly.

The second category of warrants was granted in purported exercise of the power conferred by s 5(1) of the Customs and Excise Miscellaneous Provisions) Act 1988, which is as follows:

> If a Justice of the District Court or a Peace Commissioner is satisfied by information on oath of an officer of Customs and Excise that there is reasonable ground for suspecting that any books or documents relating to transactions in contravention of the laws relating to customs are kept or concealed in any premises or place, such Justice or Commissioner may issue a search warrant under this section.

The reference in the 1876 Act to a 'justice of the peace' as adapted is a reference to a District Judge. Section 42 of that Act sets out a table of goods prohibited to be imported into the United Kingdom including:

> Indecent or obscene prints, paintings, photographs, books, cards, lithographic or other engravings, or any other indecent or obscene articles.

On foot of the warrants in question, officers of the Revenue Commissioners went to the premises of the applicants in Dublin, Cork and Limerick and seized a quantity of magazines, compact discs, videos and documents. On the 13 December 1996, the applicants were given leave by the High Court to apply for the following reliefs by way of judicial review:

(i) A declaration that the warrants were unlawful, void and of no legal effect;

(ii) An order of *certiorari* quashing the warrants;

(iii) An injunction directing the respondents to deliver up to the applicants all the goods seized on foot of the warrants;

(iv) Damages for trespass;

(v) An injunction preventing the respondents from dealing in any way with the goods seized on foot of the warrants.

The grounds upon which that relief was sought and which were pursued in the proceedings in the High Court and in this court were:

(1) That the warrants on their face showed a lack of jurisdiction;

(2) That there was not information on oath before the District Judges from which it could have appeared to them or which could have satisfied them that the officers had reasonable cause for suspecting that there were uncustomed or prohibited goods on the premises or that they had reasonable ground for suspecting that books or documents relating to such goods were on the premises.

A statement of opposition having been filed on behalf of the respondents, a notice of motion seeking the reliefs in question came on for hearing before the late Shanley J. In a judgment delivered on 12 June 1998, he dismissed the applicant's claim. From that decision, they now appeal to this court.

The warrants and informations

The warrants in each case were in a standard form, with the blank spaces being filled in with hand written entries. For the purposes of this judgment, it is sufficient to set out one warrant only in the case of each Act, since the warrants issued in Dublin, Cork and

Limerick were substantially similar. They are set out in photocopied form in the appendix to this judgment.

It will be seen that, in the case of the 1876 Act, the warrant recites that it appears to the District Judge by the information on oath of the officer Peter R Mooney) that:

> ... the said Peter R Mooney hath cause to suspect and doth suspect that certain goods to wit indecent and or obscene pornographic material the same being uncustomed or prohibited goods are harboured, kept or concealed in a certain place to wit ...

In the case of the 1988 Act, the warrant recites that it appears to the District Judge by the information on oath of the officer that:

> ... the said Peter R Mooney has cause to suspect and does suspect that certain Books or Documents relating to transactions in contravention of the laws relating to Customs are kept or concealed in a certain premises or place to wit ...

The affidavits filed in support of the statement of opposition exhibited the information on oath sworn by the officer concerned before the District Judge in each case. In addition, the affidavits set out what transpired in the course of the application for the issuing of the warrant.

In the Cork case, the officer, Mr Patrick G O'Regan, swore two informations. The first recited that he had reasonable cause to suspect and did suspect that uncustomed or prohibited goods, ie books magazines and video recorded tapes, were kept on the specified premises. In the information, he also stated that:

> I observed on the premises what appeared to be indecent or obscene material which I believe to be for sale. I believe this material was imported into the State.

The second information sworn by him was broadly to the same effect but directed to the requirements of the 1988 Act. In the case of each of these informations, there is appended a note initialled by the District Judge as follows:

> Oral evidence given.

In paragraph 5 of the Affidavit, Mr O'Riordan says:

> In the course of seeking the said Warrants, I advised District Judge Riordan that I had visited the premises and of the opinion I had formed and the basis therefor. District Judge Riordan questioned me and then issued the Warrant. I recall that he specifically raised a question as to the information being on a separate sheet and he requested that the basis for my suspicions, which I originally furnished on a separate sheet, should be shown on the information itself. This was complied with.

In the case of the Dublin premises, Mr Mooney, in his affidavit said that he had been informed by Mr Brendan Martin, a higher executive officer of the Investigation Bureau that he had visited the premises of the applicants and that indecent and/or obscene video tapes and magazines were on sale at the premises. Mr Mooney said that he was of the opinion that these were prohibited goods imported in breach of the provisions of the customs legislation. The information sworn to him was broadly in the same form as that in the Cork case, but included an additional written note as follows:

> From information I have obtained from Mr Brendan Martin, HEO, Customs and Excise Investigation Division, indecent and/or obscene pornographic material is being sold and stored in the premises at 164 Capel Street, Dublin. Therefore, I request this warrant to enable me to search the premises and remove any prohibited material found thereon.

In the case of the Limerick premises, the officer, Mr Gerard P Garrahy, said that he visited the premises on the 4 December 1996, and that:

> I saw magazines of an explicit nature displayed on shelves, together with video tapes and compact discs with explicit titles. I formed the opinion that these materials were prohibited goods, and had been imported into the State, which importation was prohibited.

The information again was in the same form as the Cork and Dublin case, but included an additional note as follows:

> I visited the premises of 'Utopia' at 7 Ellen Street, Limerick on 4.12.96. I saw magazines of an explicit nature displayed on shelves. I also saw video tapes and CDs with explicit titles.

Submissions of the parties

On behalf of the applicants, Mr Hardiman, SC submitted that it was clear on the face of each of the warrants that the District Judge had not satisfied himself that there was reasonable cause or grounds for the suspicion of the officer concerned that there were uncustomed or prohibited goods or documents relating to them in the premises. The warrants were thus bad on their face and should have been quashed on that ground alone. The opinion to the contrary of the majority of the House of Lords in *R v Inland Revenue Commissioners, ex p Rossminster* [1980] AC 952 should not be followed.

He further submitted that, in any event, it was clear that the District Judge in each of these cases had not satisfied himself, as was required by both the enabling provisions, that there were reasonable grounds for the suspicion of the officer concerned, but had simply accepted the averment of the officer that he (the officer) suspected that there were prohibited goods or documents relating to them on the premises, citing in support the decision of Hamilton P as he then was, in *Byrne v Grey & Anor* [1988] IR 31. He submitted that, in a case of this nature, where it would have been possible for the officers to buy the material which was on sale and produce it to the District Judge when applying for the warrant, the statutory preconditions for issuing the warrant could easily have been met but were not in fact met.

On behalf of the respondents, Mr Feichin McDonagh, SC, submitted that the evidence in the case demonstrated that the District Judges, when issuing the warrants, had not simply accepted a bald averment from the officers that they had reasonable cause or grounds for their suspicions: each of the officers concerned had given oral evidence on oath of their reasons for believing that there were uncustomed or prohibited goods on the premises.

In the case of the Cork and Limerick premises, that consisted of evidence that they had actually visited the premises and satisfied themselves that there was such material on display. In the case of the Dublin premises, the officer concerned had given oral evidence on oath that he had been informed by another officer that he had visited the premises and seen such material on display. He submitted that, in those circumstances, it was a matter for the District Judge to decide whether the evidence satisfied him that there were reasonable grounds for the officer's suspicion and had no basis for the contention that the statutory precondition had not been met. The onus was on the applicants to satisfy the High Court that there has been a want of or excess of jurisdiction in the issuing of the warrants and this they failed to do.

As to the submission that the warrants were bad on their face, Mr McDonagh submitted that it would be wrong to quash warrants which had been granted in a proper exercise by the District Judges of their jurisdiction under the relevant statutes because of what was alleged to be a defective statement of that jurisdiction on the face of the warrant. In such circumstances, the court was entitled to look behind the warrant in order to determine whether it was granted within jurisdiction. He submitted that the decision of the High Court in the present case was supported, not merely by the majority judgments of the House of Lords in *R v Inland Revenue Commissioner ex p Rossminster* [1980] AC 952 but also by the more recent decision of the Judicial Committee of the Privy Council in *AG of Jamaica v Williams and & Anor* [1998] AC 351.

Conclusions

Search warrants, such as those issued in the present case, entitle police and other officers to enter the dwellinghouse or other property of a citizen, carry out searches and (in the present case) remove material which they find on the premises and, in the course of so doing, use such force as is necessary to gain admission and carry out the search and seizure authorised by the warrant. These are powers which the police and other authorities must enjoy in defined circumstances for the protection of society, but since they authorise the forcible invasion of a person's property, the courts must always be concerned to ensure that the conditions imposed by the legislature before such powers can be validly exercised are strictly met.

That principle has been recognised from early times by the common law. In a passage cited by Lord Hoffman in *Attorney General of Jamaica v Williams & Anor* [1998] AC 351 at 355, Camden CJ said in *Entick v Carrington* (1765) 2Wils 275 at 291:

> (O)ur law holds the property of every man so sacred, that no man can set his foot upon his neighbour's close without his leave; if he does he is a trespasser, though be does no damage at all; if he will tread upon his neighbour's ground, he must justify it by law ...

Under the Constitution, this principle is expressly recognised, in Article 40.5, in the case of the dwelling of every citizen. Protection against unjustified searches and seizures is not, however, confined to the dwelling of the citizen: it extends to every person's private property.

Parliament, in stipulating that the power to issue the warrants now under consideration was to be vested in judges and could be exercised by them only provided certain preconditions were met, recognised that the citizen was entitled to such protection. It must be presumed that it was envisaged that the judges would, in no sense, permit themselves to be treated as ciphers, but would conscientiously satisfy themselves that the relevant preconditions had been satisfied.

In the case of the 1876 Act, the precondition was that:

> If any officer of Customs shall have reasonable cause to suspect ... and *it* shall be made to appear by information on oath before any [District Judge]..' [Emphasis added]

While the syntax is rather odd, the meaning is clear: the District Judge, before issuing the warrant, must have come to the conclusion, from the information on oath of the customs officer, not merely that he (the officer) suspects that there are uncustomed or prohibited goods on the particular premises but that his suspicion is 'reasonable'. The District Judge is no doubt performing a purely ministerial act in issuing the warrant. He or she does not purport to adjudicate on any lis in issuing the warrant. He or she would clearly be entitled to rely on material, such as hearsay, which would not be admissible in legal proceedings. It is to be presumed, moreover, that the District Judge, in issuing the warrant, will act in accordance with the requirements of the relevant legislation and the onus of establishing that he or she failed to do so rests on the person challenging the validity of the warrant.

That having been said, the fact remains that, if the District Judges in the present case issued the warrants because they were satisfied that the officers concerned simply had cause or a 'ground' for their suspicion, as the wording of the warrant indicates, the requirements of the legislation would not have been satisfied. It is plainly not sufficient that the officer considered he had cause to apply for the warrant: the District Judge must be satisfied, on the basis of the information provided by the officer, that, viewed objectively, the cause or ground relied on by the officer for his suspicion was reasonable.

What then is the consequence of a recital in the warrant which, if it correctly records the basis on which the warrant was issued, shows on its face that a statutory precondition for the exercise of the jurisdiction was not satisfied? To this difficult question, unfortunately, the authorities do not provide a wholly clear answer.

The decision of Hamilton P in *Byrne v Grey & Anor* [1988] IR 31 which was discussed in the course of the argument, is not, in my view, relevant to this specific issue. The challenge to the validity of the warrant in that case was not based upon any alleged defects in the wording of the warrant itself. The warrant had, however, been issued following the swearing of an information which said no more than that the member of the Garda Síochána concerned had reasonable grounds for suspecting that cannabis was being cultivated on the particular premises. The learned President took the view that the District Justice or Peace Commissioner issuing the warrant under the relevant legislation had to be himself satisfied that there were reasonable grounds for suspicion and was not entitled to rely solely on a mere averment by the Garda that he had reasonable grounds for suspicion.

Accordingly, the decision, although clearly relevant to the second ground upon which the applicants relied, is of no assistance to them on the first ground, ie that the warrants were bad on their face.

In contrast, in *R v Inland Revenue Commissioners, ex p Rossminster* [1980] AC 952 what was alleged to be a defect in the form of the warrant was relied on. That was a case in which searches were carried out on the respondent's offices by officers of the Inland Revenue under powers alleged to have been conferred by certain fiscal legislation. That authorised an 'appropriate judicial authority' to issue a warrant, if it was satisfied on information on oath given by an officer that there were reasonable grounds for suspecting that an offence involving any form of tax fraud had been committed and that evidence of it was to be found on the premises specified in the information. The warrants under challenge began with the following recital:

> Information on oath having been laid this day by Raymond Quinlan in accordance with the provision of section 20C of the Taxes Management Act 1970 stating that there is reasonable ground for suspecting that an offence involving fraud in connection with or in relation to tax has been committed and that evidence of it is to be found on the premises described in the second schedule annexed hereto ...

The warrant went on to authorise the named officer to enter the premises, search them and remove the evidence in question. So far as it went, accordingly, the recital in the warrant in that case did not positively misstate the statutory precondition for granting the warrant. It was attacked on a different ground, ie that, because it did not contain a statement that the judge himself was satisfied that there was reasonable ground for suspecting that a tax offence had been committed and that evidence of it was to be found on the premises, the warrant did not comply with the requirements of the section.

The majority of the Law Lords rejected that challenge, while conceding, with varying degrees of emphasis, that it would be desirable that the warrant should make clear the statutory basis for its being issued, ie the fact that the judge was satisfied as to the matters in question. They were of the view that there was no defect as such in the warrant and that it was to be presumed that the judge issuing it was satisfied that the preconditions had been met.

Thus, Lord Diplock said [at p 1009]:

> Section 20C(1) makes it a condition precedent to the issue of the warrant that the circuit judge should himself be satisfied by information on oath that facts exist which constitute reasonable ground for suspecting that an offence involving some form of fraud in connection with or in relation to tax has been committed, and also for suspecting that evidence of the offence is to be found on the premises in respect of which the warrant to search is sought. It is not, in my view, open to your Lordships to approach the instant case on the assumption that the Common Serjeant did not satisfy himself on both of these matters, or to imagine circumstances which might have led him to commit so grave a dereliction of his judicial duties. The presumption is that he acted lawfully arid properly; and it is only fair to him to say that, in my view, there is nothing in the evidence before your Lordships to suggest the contrary; nor, indeed, have the respondents themselves so contended.

Mr Hardiman urged that these remarks, and similar observations in the speech of Viscount Dilhorne, go further than our courts should be prepared to go in presuming, in the absence of evidence to the contrary, that judges will act in accordance with the terms of the statute which confers on them a specific jurisdiction. I am satisfied, however, that the Superior Courts in this jurisdiction are entitled to assume, unless the contrary is established, that judges of the District Court act in accordance with the Constitution and the law in discharging their functions. Different considerations arise, however, where, as here, the warrant itself, unlike the warrant in *Rossminster*, recites that the District Judge has purported to exercise the jurisdiction where the statutory preconditions for its exercise have not been met. It need hardly be said that the error was clearly unintentional and resulted from the use of a standard form which had obviously been in existence for some time.

It is indeed striking that, in the *Rossminster* case, Lord Salmon vigorously dissented and considered the warrant defective, even though, in contrast to the present case, there was no inaccuracy on its face. He said at p 1019:

> Section 20C makes a wide inroad into the citizen's basic human rights, the right to privacy in his own home and business premises and the right to keep what belongs to him. It allows the Inland Revenue the power to force its way into a man's home or offices and deprive him of his private papers and books. In my view, it provides only one real safeguard against an abuse of power. That safeguard is not that the Inland Revenue is satisfied that there is reasonable ground for suspecting that an offence involving fraud in relation to tax has been committed, but that the judge who issues the search warrant is so satisfied after he has been told on oath by the Inland Revenue full details of the facts which it has discovered. That is why I am inclined to the view that it is implicit in section 20C that a search warrant signed by the judge should state that he is so satisfied, ie that the warrant should always give the reason for its issue. In any event, I hope that in the future the practice will always be that such warrants state plainly that the judge who signed them is so satisfied.

> I am, however, convinced that search warrants like the present are invalid because they recite as the reason for their issue only that an officer of the Inland Revenue has stated on oath that there is reasonable ground for suspecting that offence involving fraud in relation to tax has been committed. If the judge gives that as his reason for issuing a warrant, it seems to me to follow that his reason for issuing it cannot be that he is so satisfied by the information given to him on oath By an officer of the Inland Revenue of the detailed facts which the officer has ascertained; but that the judge's reason for issuing the warrant was because the officer had stated on oath that there is reasonable ground to suspect, etc. I am afraid that I do not agree

that the warrants in the present case make it clear that they were issued by the judge pursuant to the powers conferred on him section 20C. Indeed, for the reasons I have given, I consider that the exact contrary is made clear by these warrants.

Lord Salmon was, accordingly, prepared to arrive at that conclusion although the warrants in that case on their face did not recite an erroneous ground for the exercise of the jurisdiction, but, at worst, were incomplete in not including a separate and additional recital that the judge himself was satisfied that there was reasonable ground to suspect etc. If there had been, as here, a recital that the judge was simply satisfied that the officer had a ground for suspecting etc, the opinions of the majority might well have been different.

In *AG of Jamaica v Williams* [1998] AC 351 a provision in virtually identical terms to s 205 of the 1876 Act was under consideration. In that case, the opening recital in the warrant was:

> To Arthur McNeish or any customs officer.
>
> Whereas the undersigned, one of Her Majesty's justices of the peace in and for the Parish of Kingston being satisfied upon written information on oath that there is good reason to believe that in a certain place, to wit ... is kept or concealed uncustomed goods ...

The warrant then went on to authorise the search and seizure. In that case, unlike the present, the Judicial Committee, like the courts in Jamaica from which the appeal was brought, had no information about what passed between the officer and the justice issuing the warrant. Having referred to the recitals in the warrant, Lord Hoffman, delivering the judgment of the Judicial Committee, went on at p 361:

> Prima facie, this statement must be accepted and their Lordships agree with both lower courts that if the justice was satisfied that there was 'good reason to believe' that uncustomed goods etc were on the premises, it must follow that he was satisfied that the officer had reasonable cause to suspect this to be the case.

Again, the position is not the same in this case. Here, the recital was to the effect that it appeared to the District Judge, or he was satisfied, that the officer had 'cause' or a 'ground' - not 'good reason' - to suspect that there were uncustomed goods on the premises.

I am satisfied that the submission on behalf of the respondents that, in a case where the warrant itself states that it is being issued by the District Judge on a basis which is not justified by the statute creating the power, the invalidity of the warrant can be cured by evidence that there was in fact before the District Judge evidence which entitled him to issue the warrant within the terms of the statute is not well founded. That proposition seems to me contrary to principle and unsupported by authority. Given the necessarily draconian nature of the powers conferred by the statute, a warrant cannot be regarded as valid which carries on its face a statement that it has been issued on a basis which is not authorised by the statute. It follows that the warrants were invalid and must be quashed.

We are not concerned in this case with an issue which arose in *Byrne v Grey* [1988] IR 31 her case decided by Hamilton P *Berkeley v Edwards* [1988] IR 217. In both cases, the court was of the view that the discretionary remedy of certiorari should be refused since the object in seeking it was to have excluded the evidence obtained on foot of the search warrant and the proper forum for the determination of the issue of the admissibility of the evidence was the forthcoming trial of the applicant. In the present case, there will not necessarily be any criminal proceedings arising out of the seizure of the goods alleged to be uncustomed or prohibited. The applicants are, accordingly, clearly entitled to the immediate return of the property which has been seized on foot of an invalid warrant and are not obliged to avail of the somewhat archaic procedure prescribed by s 207 of the 1876

Act enabling the person from whom the seizure is made to give notice in writing within a month that he claims the property, in which case the customs are required to take proceedings for the forfeiture and condemnation of the property. [Under s 267, even where the claimant is successful, but there was 'reasonable or probable cause' for the seizure, the damages to which he is entitled are limited to two old pence and he is not to recover any costs.]

That is sufficient to dispose of the appeal in the present case, but, had it been necessary so to decide I would have been satisfied that there was before the District Judges in each case sufficient evidence in the form of the informations on oath, accompanied in the Cork case by oral evidence, on which they would have been entitled to reach the conclusion that uncustomed or prohibited goods, and books and documents relating to them, were kept on the specified premises.

For the reasons I have already given, I would allow the appeal and substitute for the Order of the High Court an order of certiorari quashing the warrants and an injunction directing the respondents to deliver up to the applicants the goods seized on foot of the warrants. I would hear counsel on the question as to whether any of the other reliefs sought should be granted.

Barron J, On the 5 December 1996 Customs Officers entered the premises the applicants at 5 Capel Street, Dublin 164A Capel Street, Dublin, 7 Earl Street, Limerick and 1 Dean Street, Cork pursuant to search warrants issued by second, third and fourth named respondents respectively. In pursuance of their search they removed from the premises various magazines, videos and documentation relating to the import, export, sale and distribution of such goods. The present proceedings have been brought for a declaration that the warrants grounding the searches and seizures were unlawful, void and of no legal effect. It is submitted that there was no evidence before the district judges to justify the issue of the several warrants and that the warrants in any event failed to show jurisdiction on their face for two reasons:

(1) They did not disclose that the Customs Officer had reasonable grounds for his suspicion that such goods were on the said premises; and

(2) that they did not disclose that the district judge had reasonable cause for believing that the Customs Officer had such suspicion.

There were seven such warrants in all, two in respect of the premises in Limerick and Cork and 164A Capel Street and one in respect of the premises 5 Capel Street, Dublin. This latter search warrant was issued pursuant to the Provisions of s 5(1) of the Customs and Excise (Miscellaneous Provisions) Act 1988. In respect of the other premises the warrants were issued under this section and also under s 205 of the Customs Consolidation Act 1876.

The relevant provisions of s 5 of the 1988 Act are as follows:

> If a Justice of the District Court or a Peace Commissioner is satisfied by information on oath of an officer of Customs and Excise that there is reasonable ground for suspecting that any books or documents relating to transactions in contravention of the laws relating to customs are kept or concealed in any premises or place, such Justice or Commissioner may issue a search warrant under this section.

The relevant provisions of s 205 of the 1876 Act are as follows:

> If any officer of Customs shall have reasonable cause to suspect that any uncustomed or prohibited goods are harboured, kept, or concealed in any house or other place ..., it shall be made to appear by information on oath before any justice of the peace ..., it shall be lawful for

such justice, by special warrant under his hand, to authorise such officer to enter and search such house or other place, and to seize and carry away any such uncustomed or prohibited goods as may be found therein ...

The several warrants are in common form and each of them contains the following recital:

> Whereas it appears to me by the information on Oath of (naming the Customs Officer) an Officer of Customs and Excise that the said (officer) has cause to suspect and doth suspect that certain Books or Documents relating to transactions in contravention(s) of the laws relating to Customs are kept or concealed in a certain premises (which are then named).

This case must be approached upon the basis that there should be a clear authority validly given before an involuntary search of premises can be enforced. The first matter to be considered is the power to authorise the search; then whether that power has been validly exercised; and finally, whether that exercise has been properly conveyed to the person concerned.

In the present case, the statutory authority is clear. It is contained in the two sections. For the power to be validly exercised, there are the two preconditions.

First, the person applying for the warrant must have reasonable cause to suspect that there is relevant material to be found on a particular premises. Secondly, in this case, the judge must himself or herself have been satisfied from information on Oath given by the applicant that the applicant had that reasonable suspicion. In other words, the evidence before the judge must show that it is reasonable for the applicant to have the required suspicion, and it must also be shown that the judge was satisfied that this suspicion was reasonably held.

For the purpose of determining whether such exercise has been properly conveyed to the occupier of the premises concerned, it is necessary further to consider what the warrant itself should set out.

To answer these questions for the purposes of the present case, it is necessary to look to decided cases.

In *Byrne v Grey* [1988] IR 31, upon which the applicant relies, the search warrant had been issued by a peace commissioner on the strength of an information on Oath of a police officer that he had a reasonable suspicion. There was no evidence to show that the peace commissioner had made up his own mind as to whether they were grounds for the police officer to have such suspicion, rather he accepted such averment without questioning it.

Hamilton P, as he then was, held that the person issuing the warrant had himself to be satisfied that there was reasonable ground for suspicion.

He said at p. 40:

> It is quite clear that the District Justice or peace commissioner issuing the warrant must himself be satisfied that there is reasonable ground for suspicion. He is not entitled to rely on a mere averment by a member of the Garda Síochána that he, the member of the Garda Síochána, has reasonable grounds for suspicion.

In that case the relief of certiorari was refused because Hamilton P regarded the warrant as spent and the only matter at issue being whether or not the evidence obtained was admissible in the course of a subsequent criminal trial. He regarded this as a matter for a decision of the trial judge in those proceedings.

In *Berkeley v Edwards* [1988] IR 217 upon which the respondent relies a similar issue also came before Hamilton P, as he then was. In that case, however, he accepted that there was sufficient evidence before the district judge to justify him in being satisfied that the applicant for the warrant had a reasonable suspicion.

The sufficiency of the warrant itself has been considered in England in *Inland Revenue Commissioners and Another v Rossminster Limited and Others* [1980] AC 952. In that case the relevant warrants were issued to revenue officials. The relevant statutory authority empowered a judge if satisfied on information on Oath given by such officer that there was a reasonable ground for suspecting that an offence had been committed.

As in the instant case, the importance was stressed of the need for the judge to be satisfied as to the existence of the reasonable suspicion of the applicant for the warrant. The sufficiency of the material before the judge in that case to enable him to be so satisfied was not contested.

The substantial issue so far as the instant case is concerned was whether that fact should have been stated on the face of the warrant.

This was held by the majority not to have been necessary. Lord Wilberforce was of the view however that it would have been wise to have included such a statement on the warrant. Lord Dilhorne emphasised the need for the judge to be so satisfied, but did not accept that the absence of any reference to such fact on the face of the warrant implied that he had not been so satisfied. Lord Diplock took broadly the same view. Lord Scarman regarded it as desirable to include such a recital on the warrant. In his view, the issue of the warrant was a judicial act and that the case should be approached upon the basis that the judge did satisfy himself upon the matters which he was required to be satisfied before issuing the warrants. However, he was satisfied that the particular warrants contained sufficient information to enable the occupier of the premises to know under what authority they had been issued.

Lord Salmon was in the minority. In his view, this could not be implied because the warrant gave a different reason, that the revenue officer was so satisfied. The warrant in that case stated:

> Information, on oath having been laid this day by (naming file officer) in accordance with the provisions of (naming the section of the relevant Act) stating that there is reasonable ground for suspecting that an offence involving fraud ... has been committed and that evidence of it is to be found on the premises (referred to).

In his view, a warrant should also give the reason for its issue and when signed by a judge should state that he, the judge, was so satisfied.

Dealing with the particular search warrants he said at p 1019:

> I am, however, convinced that search warrants like the present are invalid because they recite as the reason for their issue only that an officer of the Inland Revenue has stated on oath that there is reasonable ground for suspecting that an offence involving fraud in relation to tax has been committed. If the judge gives that as his reason for issuing a warrant, it seems to me to follow that his reason for issuing it cannot be that he is so satisfied by the information given to him on oath by an officer of the Inland Revenue of the detailed facts which the officer has ascertained; but that the judge's reason for issuing the warrant was because the officer had stated on oath that there is reasonable ground to suspect, etc.

Similar issues arose in *Attorney-General of Jamaica v Williams* [19981 AC 351. In that case, the warrant stated on its face that the justice issuing it was satisfied upon written information on Oath that there was good reason to believe that uncustomed material was on the particular premises. The wording of the statute under which the warrant had been issued was very similar to s 205 of the 1876 Act. It provided, inter alia:

> If any officer shall have reasonable cause to suspect that any uncustomed or prohibited goods ... are harboured, kept or concealed in any house or other place in the island, and it shall be

made to appear by information on oath before any resident magistrate or justice in the island, it shall be lawful for such resident magistrate or justice by special warrant under his hand to authorise such officer to enter arid search such house ...

This case also upheld the proposition that it was insufficient for the revenue officer to have reasonable cause for suspicion, it had to appear to the Justice issuing the warrant that he had such reasonable cause.

In that case there was a sworn information in writing which would not on its own have been sufficient to enable the justice to form the requisite opinion. There was no evidence that any additional evidence had been given to him. The Privy Council held that the statement on the face of the warrant that the Justice himself was satisfied that the officer's suspicion was based upon reasonable cause was prima facie to be accepted.

These two latter cases are significantly different. In the former, the warrant was validly issued, but the warrant itself did not so indicate. In the latter, there was evidence that the warrant was not validly issued, while at the same time the warrant itself indicated the basis, being a legal basis, from which the warrant was issued.

Neither case is on all fours with the present. In my view, once the warrant is challenged in court, there should be an enquiry as to whether it was validly issued. Once that enquiry shows that it was - in this case that the officer had reasonable cause to suspect and that the judge was likewise so satisfied - then whatever is down on foot of the warrant cannot be unlawful on the ground that the warrant was not lawfully issued. However, if at the same time the warrant itself does not express this lawful authority, it will not be lawful to act on foot of it if it's validity is challenged.

Here, the evidence shows that the several judges were not satisfied to accept the common form informations. They asked questions and heard oral evidence. To that extent, it is unnecessary to consider whether to adopt the views expressed in *Attorney General of Jamaica v Williams* [1998] AC 351 whether the sworn informations would on their own have been insufficient. Here, I am satisfied that there is sufficient evidence to show that the Customs Officers had reasonable cause for their suspicions and that the judges were satisfied that they held such suspicions. I am satisfied that the decisions to issue the warrants were made within jurisdiction.

This leaves the question whether that exercise has been properly conveyed by the words in the warrant. This question leads to the further question, if it has not been properly conveyed, what is the legal effect of such omission?

The first of these issues is whether or not the warrants are good on their face.

All the members of the House of Lords in *Rossminster* were of the view that the warrant should state the legal reason for issuing the warrant although only Lord Salmon regarded it as being vital in the circumstances of that case. Even then, he did so because in his view the warrant gave an incorrect reason, that it was the Customs Officers alone who had the appropriate suspicion.

In the instant case, the warrants themselves indicate that it appeared to each District Judge that the Customs Officer had cause to suspect and did suspect the existence of uncustomed goods in the various premises. But what the warrants do not say on their face is that the district judges considered that there was reasonable cause to suspect.

In my view the absence of the word 'reasonable' on the face of the warrant does not affect its validity. First, there was no error within jurisdiction relating to the issue of the warrant. Secondly, once the warrant has been signed by the judge expressly stating that it appeared to him that there was cause, it must be assumed that he has acted responsibly and not frivolously and that the warrant must be valid.

Even if I am wrong in this view, the legal effect of the omission of the word 'reasonable' could not invalidate the authority under which it was issued.

In the ordinary course certiorari did not issue for errors made within jurisdiction. The jurisdiction to quash a record bad on its face was exercised not just because the record itself was bad on its face but because it was evidence that the decision itself was made in error. The quashing of the order was, accordingly, a declaration to this effect. However, where the order is made within jurisdiction but at the same time appears on its face not to say so it seems to me that it is more appropriate that it should be regarded as ineffective. This is particularly so in relation to a search warrant because until it is challenged it seems to me that when it has been issued within jurisdiction the only reason why it can be challenged is that it does not say so.

The execution of the warrants was not challenged. They were executed peacefully. If the appellant or his staff had not accepted the validity of the warrants they could have refused entry. In the instant case, their legal advice was that they were bound to allow entry and they did so.

The purpose of a warrant is to indicate to the person against whom it is to be executed that it has been issued under lawful authority. If on the face of the warrant it does not appear to be so then the person against whom it is directed can refuse to allow the entry to his premises. This does not, however, make the authority invalid in any way. The appropriate course in such circumstances would be for the Customs Officer to return to the district judge, to amend the warrant so that it does not show any error on its face or, alternatively, to obtain a fresh warrant without such error. In both cases, of course, the district judge would be required to again sign the warrant.

This view is supported by a passage in the judgment of the Privy Council given by Lord Hoffmann in *Attorney General of Jamaica v Williams* [1998] AC 351 at 364 where it was said:

> Their Lordships agree that it is highly desirable for a file warrant to contain an express statement of the statutory authority under which it was issued. If it does not, the householder might reasonably think that it was not based upon any authority and resist entry. But this does not mean that in a case in which a file warrant was in fact issued under proper authority and there was no resistance to entry, the warrant should be treated as invalid, particularly when ... it is clear from the terms of the warrant that it was issued under the [section.]

In my view the question which arises in the present case is as to the nature of the warrant itself. If it is merely a document which is provided to assure the person against whom it is directed that the proposed search is a legal one, then it seems to me that if the search is allowed to proceed then the person against whom it has been made cannot subsequently object.

However, if the purpose of the warrant is itself a legal statement, then it seems to me that if the statement is inaccurate its legality may be lost.

In my view the former is the more appropriate construction to be placed on the warrant and in those circumstances it seems to me that since the search was legally authorised the appellant cannot now complain that it was invalid. Nor is he entitled to say that the jurisdiction of the district judge was invalidly exercised merely because the valid exercise was not correspondingly indicated on the face of the warrant.

I would reject the appeal in this case.

Cyril Forbes v John Tobin And Janet Tobin

High Court
McCracken J
8 March 2001

Value Added Tax - specific performance - contract for sale of garage premises - whether sale of a business or a property - whether purchaser liable for Burmah-Castrol agreements - whether VAT chargeable - whether development property for VAT purposes - prior development expenditure - Revenue statement of practice on property transactions - whether 10% rule applied - whether 10% rule a statutory provision - whether parties ad idem - whether equitable remedy of specific performance applicable.

Cyril Forbes ('the plaintiff') sought an order for specific performance of a contract for sale dated 12 March 1998 whereby John Tobin and Janet Tobin ('the defendants') agreed to sell and the plaintiff agreed to purchase for £180,000 a garage premises at Inistioge, County Kilkenny in which a garage business was still in operation at the date of the contract.

A special condition in the standard Law Society Conditions of Sale was that the purchaser pay to the vendor Value Added Tax ('VAT') in accordance with the VAT Act 1972. A general condition was that, if the purchaser failed in any material respect to comply with any of the conditions of sale, the vendor became entitled to forfeit the deposit of £18,000 and to re-sell the property.

A serious dispute between the parties led to long and protracted correspondence as to whether (i) VAT was payable and (ii) the Burmah-Castrol agreements became the liability of the purchaser.

Eventually the misunderstandings between the parties were clarified. As regards VAT, the plaintiff had contended that the sale was of a property on which development expenditure of £3,000 had been incurred. A Revenue statement of practice on property transactions states that development expenditure of less than 10% of the sale price of a property can be ignored. Although the plaintiff relied on this statement of practice, McCracken J pointed out that this Revenue rule of thumb has no legal significance in the context of a statutory tax. Subsequent to the institution of proceedings it became known that the defendant's predecessors in title had incurred expenditure of £17,000 on the premises, notwithstanding that the defendants did not pay any VAT on their purchase of the premises and, on enquiry, the Revenue informed the defendants that VAT was chargeable on the current sale.

Since the contract did not contain the usual clauses for the sale of a business as a going concern, it was not a sale of a business.

Conclusion

The plaintiff is not entitled to an order for specific performance because of his refusal to pay VAT in accordance with the conditions of the contract. The defendants are not entitled to forfeit the deposit because of vacant possession with the removal of the Burmah-Castrol agreements and the equipment and effects thereunder.

Held by McCracken J in refusing the orders sought:
  (i)   it would be inequitable to grant the order sought either by the plaintiff and or by the defendants in the circumstances herein;
  (ii) an injunction was granted restraining the defendants from forfeiting the deposit;

(iii) an order was made for the re-payment of the deposit of £18,000 with interest at Courts Act rates of interest and

(iv) the Revenue 10% rule is not a legal provision and has no legal significance in the context of a statutory tax.

Legislation
VAT Act 1972

High Court - 8 March 2001

McCracken J, In these proceedings the plaintiff seeks specific performance of a contract for sale dated 12 March 1998 whereby the defendants agreed to sell and the plaintiff agreed to purchase for the sum of £180,000 certain premises described as:

> ALL THAT AND THOSE the lands and hereditaments being the garage premises at Inistioge situate in the barony of Gowran and County of Kilkenny and more particularly delineated on the map attached hereto and thereon outlined in red

At the time of signing the contract there was a business carried on in the premises of a filling station, a shop and a small workshop. The first defendant had entered into several agreements with Burmah-Castrol (Ireland) Limited in relation to the supply of motor fuels and the provision of equipment including a canopy, electric pumps, an over ground diesel tank and certain instruments which were clearly stated to remain the property of Burmah-Castrol (Ireland) Limited. The dealer supply agreement also contained certain provisions as to the procedures to be followed if the defendants sold the premises, which I will deal with later.

Special condition (7) in the contract provided:

> In addition to the purchase price, the purchaser shall pay to the vendor an amount equivalent to such value added tax as shall be exigible in relation to the sale, same to be calculated in accordance with the provisions of the Value Added Tax Act 1972 and to be paid on completion of the sale forthwith upon receipt by the purchaser of an appropriate invoice (whichever be the later).

The general conditions of sale were the standard 1995 edition of the Law Society of Ireland conditions, including the following:

> 40. Save where time is of the essence in respect of the closing date, the following provisions shall apply:
>
> (a) If the sale be not completed on or before the closing date either party may on or after that date (unless the sale shall first have been rescinded or become void) give to the other party notice to complete the sale in accordance with this condition, but such notice shall be effective only if the party giving it shall then either be able, ready and willing to complete the sale or is not so able, ready or willing by reason of the default or misconduct of the other party.
>
> (b) Upon service of such notice the party upon whom it shall have been served shall complete the sale within a period of 28 days after the date of such service (as defined in condition 49 and excluding the date of service), and in respect of such period time shall be of the essence of the contract but without prejudice to any intermediate right of recission by either party.
>
> (c) The recipient of any such notice shall give to the parties serving the same reasonable advice of his readiness to complete

(d) If the purchaser shall not comply with such a notice within the said period (or within any extension thereof which the vendor may agree) he shall be deemed to have failed to comply with these conditions in a material respect and the vendor may enforce against the purchaser, without further notice, such rights and remedies as may be available to the vendor at law or in equity, or (without prejudice to such rights and remedies) may invoke and impose the provisions of condition 41.

(e) The vendor shall not be deemed to be other than able, ready and willing to complete for the purposes of this condition:

...

(ii) By reason of being unable, not ready or unwilling at the date of service of such notice to deliver vacant possession of the subject property provided that (where it is a term of the sale that vacant possession thereof be given) the vendor is, upon being given reasonable advice of the other party's intention to close the sale on a date within the said period of 28 days or any extension thereof pursuant to condition 40(f), able, ready and willing to deliver vacant possession of the subject property on that date.

General condition 41 then provided that if the purchaser should fail in any material respect to comply with any of the conditions, the vendor should be entitled to forfeit the deposit and be at liberty to re-sell the property. A serious dispute arose between the solicitors for the respective parties as to whether value added tax was in fact exigible, and therefore as to whether the plaintiff was bound to pay value added tax to the defendants in addition to the purchase price. The plaintiff maintained that no value added tax was payable and actually put his solicitor in funds to complete the sale on the basis of the purchase price of £180,000. The defendant's solicitors refused to complete on this basis and initially served a completion notice pursuant to condition 40 on 26 January 1999. This was not acted upon, and a further notice was served dated 2 March 1999. This notice recites the contract and then continues:

TAKE NOTICE that the vendors being ready, willing and able to complete this sale hereby call upon the purchaser in accordance with general condition of the contract herein to complete the sale within 28 days from the date of service hereof.

AND TAKE FURTHER NOTICE that if the purchaser shall fail to so complete the sale within the said period the vendors intend to enforce against the purchaser such rights and remedies as may be available to the vendors at law or in equity and/or on foot of but not limited to, the provisions of the general conditions of the contract for sale herein.

AND TAKE FURTHER NOTICE that if the purchaser shall fail to so complete this sale within 28 days from the date of service in respect of which such period time shall be of the essence, the purchaser will be deemed to have failed to comply with the conditions as set out in the aforesaid contract for sale and the provisions of clause 41 of the general conditions of the said conditions of sale will apply accordingly and the deposit paid herein shall be absolutely forfeited and the remaining provisions of clause 41 aforesaid of the said conditions of sale shall apply.

The service of this notice was preceded by lengthy correspondence between the solicitors for the parties in which the defendant's solicitors maintained that the contract was for the sale, not only of the premises, but of the business being carried on therein by the defendants. On the other hand, the plaintiff's solicitor at all times maintained that this was purely a contract to purchase buildings, and that there never had been any question of a purchase of a business. This dispute as to the nature of the contract led to two demands being made by the defendant's solicitors. Firstly, they contended that value added tax was payable because this was the sale of a business, and secondly they contended that the plaintiff was also bound to take over the agreements between the defendants and Burmah-Castrol (Ireland) Limited. Both of these contentions continued to be maintained by the defendant's solicitors up to and after the date of the service of the completion notice.

The defendant's solicitor gave evidence that in a telephone conversation on 8 March 1999 he acknowledged to the plaintiff's solicitor that this was only a sale of property and not the sale of a business, but unfortunately in a letter dated 9 March the defendant's solicitors make no mention of this, but continue to demand payment of value added tax and also to contend that the plaintiff had verbally agreed to assume liability for the agreements with Burmah-Castrol (Ireland) Limited. This letter purported to enclose a copy letter of 2 March 1999 from the inspector of taxes in relation to the value added tax position, but in fact did not enclose that letter.

By letter of 11 March 1999 the plaintiff's solicitors contested the validity of the completion notice on the basis that:

> Our client is ready, willing and able to complete. It is your client who is refusing to complete under the terms of contract by:
>
> (a) Requiring VAT to be paid, when there is no liability on our client to do so;
>
> (b) Requiring our client to take over liability for the oil company agreements when there is no obligation on our client to do so;
>
> (c) Requiring interest on the purchase money when our client has no liability for same.

By letter of 19 March 1999 the vendor's solicitors continued to maintain that value added tax was payable, but stated for the first time that they were not requiring the plaintiff to take over the liability for the oil company agreements. This letter again makes no mention of withdrawing the claim that this was a sale of a business. By letter dated 22 March the plaintiff's solicitors state:

> Your client's claim that our client is liable for VAT rests entirely on your clients contention that the contract is one for the sale of the business as a going concern and therefore VAT is exigible. The contract is not one for the sale of the business as a going concern and therefore our client is not liable for VAT for that reason. If there is some other reason why the property carried a properly exigible VAT liability then please tell us what that is so that we can address the matter. To date no such reason has been advanced by your clients.

This letter also points out that there are still goods on the property belonging to Burmah-Castrol (Ireland) Limited and points out that they must be removed from the property so that vacant possession can be given.

By further letter of 30 March 1999 the defendant's solicitors state that the completion notice will expire on that day and, for the first time in correspondence with the plaintiff's solicitor, expressly state that they are no longer maintaining that VAT is chargeable by virtue of the fact that it is the sale of a business, but maintaining that VAT was still chargeable.

Unfortunately this rather lengthy correspondence which took place over several months could probably be described as a comedy of errors. The contract for sale on its face is clearly only a contract for the sale of property, and does not include any of the standard clauses which one would expect on the sale of a business as a going concern. This was pointed out to the defendant's solicitors on a number of occasions, but they refused to accept it. On the other hand, the plaintiff's solicitors appeared to have been operating under a totally mistaken apprehension as to liability for value added tax on the sale of property. Liability for value added tax does arise on the sale of a business as a going concern where the purchaser is not himself registered for value added tax, but it is also payable under certain circumstances where property has been developed in whole or in part after 31 October 1972, and this appears to have been ignored by the purchaser's solicitor until after the service of the completion notice. This may be understandable, because of the basis on which the vendor's solicitor were claiming value added tax, but the fact remains, and it now seems to be conceded, that value added tax is payable on the transfer of an interest in property where there has been a development of that property by or on behalf of the vendor subsequent to 31 October 1972 in circumstances where the vendor was entitled to recover any part of the value added tax chargeable to him on the purchase or redevelopment of the property.

The facts relating to the property in the present case are that the defendants expended some £3,000 on what would be a development of the property within the meaning of the Value Added Tax Act, that when the defendants purchased the property they did not pay any value added tax, that their predecessors in title had expended some £17,000 in the development of the property prior to its purchase by the defendants, and that the defendants, and presumably their predecessors, would have been in a position to obtain a refund of value added tax paid by them on the development of the property. The position has now been made even more clear by a letter from the Revenue Commissioners dated 6 February 2001 in which they restate their opinion that value added tax is payable.

It must be said in fairness to the plaintiff's solicitors that, while at some stage they became aware of the £3,000 expended by the defendant shortly after the service of the completion notice, they did not become aware of the expenditure of the £17,000 until after the completion notice had expired.

A further complication arises because there is a rule of thumb applied by the revenue authorities that if the amount expended on a development is less than 10% of the purchase price, they do not in fact seek to enforce a claim for value added tax. However, in my view this has no legal significance, as this is a statutory tax, and under the terms of the Value Added Tax Act the liability still exists, and in my view quite clearly the tax is 'exigible' within the meaning of clause 7 of the special conditions of sale. In any event, if one takes into account the £17,000 expended by the defendants predecessors, this clearly well exceeds 10% of the purchase price paid by the defendants.

Probably the last chapter in the comedy of errors is that the defendant's solicitors served completion notices on two occasions in both of which the plaintiff was called to complete within 28 days from the date of service of the notice, which is not in accordance with general condition 40, and is not sufficient notice under that provision.

The above facts give rise to a number of issues. Clearly the first of these is whether, when the plaintiff issued the proceedings, he himself was ready, willing and able to complete in accordance with the terms of the contract. He was refusing to pay the value added tax, and it now transpires the transaction is subject to value added tax, although not on the basis on which it was originally claimed by the defendants. Indeed, it is only in very recent times, and subsequent to the issue of these proceedings, that the question of the expenditure of the £17,000 on the property became known to the parties. However, at the time the proceedings were issued the plaintiff clearly was aware of the expenditure of the £3,000 by the defendants, but he relied on the 10% rule of thumb to excuse payment. As I said, this is merely a rule of thumb and is not a legal provision, and therefore technically there was a liability for value added tax at all times. Furthermore, the plaintiff was informed by the defendants that the revenue authorities had advised that value added tax was payable. The defendants were entitled to act on such advice, and of course assuming that advice was correct, the defendants would be liable to the revenue for the value added tax whether they recovered it from the plaintiff or not. There is, therefore, the very odd situation that the defendants appear to have been correct all along in requiring value added tax, but for all the wrong reasons. In my view, therefore, and with some reluctance, I must find that the plaintiff is not entitled to an order for specific performance, because his refusal to pay value added tax meant that he was not willing to close in accordance with the contract.

The second issue is the validity of the defendant's completion notice. I would be of the view that the error in dates in the completion notice is not fatal, as condition 40 does not require any specific length of notice to be stated, but simply requires a notice to be served and then provides that completion shall take place within 28 days after the service excluding the date of service. I also do not think that the notice could be condemned because there was property belonging to Burmah-Castrol (Ireland) Limited still on the premises which prevented vacant possession being handed over, as condition 40(g)(ii) appears to expressly envisage this situation.

On the other hand, the question must be asked as to whether, at the time of service of the notice, the vendors themselves were ready, willing or able to complete. The only basis upon which they were so willing was that the plaintiff should pay value added tax, should take over the oil suppliers agreement and should pay interest. While they may have been correct in relation to value added tax, for the wrong reasons, quite clearly there was no obligation on the plaintiff to take over the Burmah-Castrol (Ireland) Limited agreements, and in my view, as value added tax had been claimed on the wrong basis, there was probably no liability to interest. For this reason at the time of service of the completion notice the defendants were not willing and able to complete in accordance with the contract, and therefore it follows that condition 41 did not apply and the defendants were not entitled to forfeit the deposit of £18,000 paid on foot of the contract. The plaintiff has sought an injunction restraining the defendants from forfeiting the deposit, and it has also sought damages. As I have found that the contract was not properly rescinded by the defendants, and there was no right to forfeit the deposit, logically it must follow that the contract is still in existence. However, the granting of specific performance is an equitable remedy, and I certainly would not grant specific performance at this stage even if the plaintiff were prepared to pay the value added tax, as I would consider it inequitable to do so. However, the plaintiff has been at a loss of £18,000 for some two years and I think justice would be done between the parties if I make an order refusing specific performance, declaring the contract for sale now to be rescinded and granting an injunction restraining the defendants from forfeiting the deposit and ordering the repayment by the defendants to the plaintiff of the said deposit of £18,000 together with interest thereon at Courts Act rates from the date of the contract, which I understand to be 12 March 1998.

A number of authorities were open to me by counsel on both sides of this case, and I mean no disrespect to them by not citing such authorities. However, I feel that the facts of this case are so unusual as to make it extremely difficult to fit them within any of the recognised authorities.

In the Matter of Millhouse Taverns Ltd and the Companies Act 1963-1999

High Court
Finnegan J
3 April 2000

VAT, PAYE and PRSI – unpaid taxes, interest and penalties – petition to wind up company – whether a substantial and reasonable defence to petition – whether company insolvent

The Revenue Commissioners had presented a petition for the winding up of Millhouse Taverns Ltd based on an unpaid demand for £146,768.04 in respect of VAT, PAYE and PRSI together with interest pursuant to Companies Act 1963 ss 213(e) and 214.

The law

It is well settled that a petition should not be brought where the petitioner is well aware that the company has a substantial and reasonable defence to the petitioner's claim.

Held by Finnegan J in making an order that the company be wound up that:

(i) The affidavits filed on behalf of the company fall far short of showing that the company has a substantial and reasonable defence to the petitioner's claim, and

(ii) The company is deemed to be insolvent and unable to pay in debts in pursuance of the Companies Act 1963 s 214(c).

Legislation
Companies Act 1963, ss 231(e), 214

Cases referred to in judgment
Stonegate Securities Ltd v Gregory [1980] IR 241
In the Matter of Page Boy Couriers Ltd ILRM 510

High Court - 3 April 2000

Finnegan J, On the 30 November 1999 the Revenue Commissioners presented a petition for the winding up of Milhouse Taverns Limited. The Petitioner relied upon a demand dated 29 July 1999 made pursuant to the Companies Act 1963 s 214 for the sum of £146,768.04 in respect of VAT, PAYE and PRSI together with interest. The company neglected to pay the said sum or to secure or compound for it to the reasonable satisfaction of the Petitioner. Accordingly the company is deemed to be unable to pay it's debts and may be wound up by the Court pursuant to the Companies Act 1963 s 213(E).

On behalf of the company Patrick Harrisson an accountant swore an Affidavit on the 9 March 2000 in which he sets out the assets and liabilities of the company. Upon the basis of an offer of £405,000 being accepted for the company's premises it appears that a sum of £154,525 would be available to satisfy the Petitioner's demand. The company's indebtedness in the amount of the demand is not denied in the Affidavit.

In response to this an affidavit was sworn on behalf of the petitioner by Gerard Scanoll on the 10 March 2000. Mr Scanoll deposes to his belief that the company is insolvent and unable to meet it's debts. Having commenced trading in December, 1996 the company ceased trading in December, 1999. The only payment made to the Revenue Commissioners during the period of trading is a sum of £4,280 in respect of PAYE and PRSI for the years

1996/1997 and 1997/1998. No payment was made in respect of VAT and no returns were filed in respect of corporation tax. As a result of an audit carried out by the Revenue Commissioners the company was assessed for VAT for the period November/December 1996 to May/June 1998 together with interest and penalties in the amount of £199,366. No assessment for Value Added Tax for the period from July 1998 to December, 1999 has been made and no returns have been submitted by the company but the Revenue Commissioners estimate the company's liability for Value Added Tax for this period at £69,363. In addition for PAYE and PRSI estimated assessments for the years 1996/1997 and 1997/1998 were raised and the outstanding liability on foot of these is £60,666. While no assessments have been raised in respect of PAYE and PRSI for the years 1998/1999 and 1999/2000 and no returns have been submitted the Revenue Commissioners estimate the company's liability for these years at £56,345. The total liability of the company in respect of Value Added Tax, PAYE and PRSI together with interest and penalties is estimated at £381,522. The Affidavit exhibits a letter dated 13 January 2000 from Patrick Harrison which upon the basis of what he describes as very scanty information he suggests a liability for VAT, PAYE and PRSI of £156,301 this sum being exclusive of interest and penalties. The letter records an offer of £405,000 for the company's premises and upon the basis of this offer the sum of £156,301 would be available to satisfy the Revenue's claim. No account has been taken by Mr Harrison of liability for capital gains tax in estimating the amount which he calculates would be available. On the basis of this Affidavit I am satisfied that a sale of the company's present premises at £405,000 would not enable it to meet its liabilities.

It is material to note that an offer of £460,000 in respect of the company's premises was made on 2 March, 2000.

Finally a further Affidavit was sworn by Patrick Harrison on behalf of the company on the 2 March 2000 in which he calculates the capital gains tax payable upon a sale of the premises for £405,000 at £12,880 and upon a sale at that price estimates the amount which would be available to the Petitioner after satisfaction of the claim for capital gains tax at £141,645.29. An increased offer from the purchaser has been obtained in the amount of £426,200 and upon my calculation on the basis of this offer the amount available to the Revenue Commissioners to satisfy it's claim for all taxes other than capital gains tax would be £158,605.29. The company's accountant in his letter of the 13 January 2000 estimates the company's liability for all taxes excluding capital gains tax for the period December, 1996 to December, 1999 at £156,301; however this sum does not take into account interest and penalties. In these circumstances it is quite clear that a sale even at the enhanced price of £405,200 would not result in the company being in a position to discharge it's liability to the Petitioner upon the basis of it's own accountants computation.

It is well settled that a petition should not be brought were the person claiming as petitioning creditor is well aware that the company has a substantial and reasonable defence to the claim which it wishes to plead and on which it proposes to rely to defeat the entire claim brought against it; *Stonegate Securities Limited v Gregory* [1980] 1 IR 241 and *In The Matter of Pane Boy Couriers Limited* [1983] ILRM 510. The Affidavits filed on behalf of the company in this matter fall far short of showing that the company has a substantial and reasonable defence to the Petitioners claim which would enable it to defeat the entire of the claim brought against it. Further on the basis of the Affidavits filed in the matter I am satisfied that the company is deemed to be insolvent and unable to pay it's debts pursuant to the Companies Act 1963 s 214(c).

Accordingly I propose making an Order that the company be wound up pursuant to the provision of the Companies Act 1963-1990.

Patrick J O'Connell (Inspector of Taxes) v Tara Mines Ltd

High Court
Murphy J
4 April 2001

Corporation tax – case stated – mining company – whether carrying on mining operations – whether mining or manufacturing – whether a qualifying mine – whether entitled to export sales relief or capital allowances – whether findings of fact justified conclusions – whether findings can be set aside – whether ambiguity in findings – whether decisions based on findings

This appeal by the Inspector of Taxes is against the determination of the Appeal Commissioners who held that Tara Mines Ltd ('the company') was entitled to export sales relief pursuant to CTA 1976 Part IV. Pending the outcome of the appeal the company reserves its position in regard to a further determination by the Appeal Commissioners that the company was not entitled to a mining development allowance under the provisions of the Finance (Taxation of Profits of Certain Minerals) Act 1974 in respect of certain foreign exchange losses on its capital borrowings. These issues related to the accounting periods ending on 31 December 1988.

A preliminary determination by the Appeal Commissioners that the lead and zinc concentrates produced by the company constituted 'goods' within the meaning of CTA 1976 Part IV was accepted by the Inspector. CTA 1976 s 58(3) provides that export sales relief ('ESR') shall be granted to a company in respect of goods which in the course of trade are exported out of the State. CTA 1976 s 58(9) states that no reduction shall be made in respect of corporation tax ('CT') payable on income from mining operations. A capital allowance is available under the 1974 Act for development expenditure in relation to a qualifying mine.

Facts

The Appeal Commissioners made extensive findings of fact, 22 in all including 19 sub-findings under the headings of steps carried out in extracting ore and the status of processing. The company extracts lead and zinc ores from the earth which are then processed to produce the finished product of lead and zinc concentrates. The ore contains an average of 8% zinc and 2.5% lead. All the concentrates sold by the company during the accounting periods were exported out of the State.

The whole operation at Tara is divided into two divisions, the Mining Division and the Processing Division. There was conflicting evidence as to whether the term 'mining operation' as used in the mining industry included all of the company's activities or just the underground activities. However, in their general usage, terms such mining, mining activity, mining operations etc could depending upon the context encompass the type of activities carried on by the company.

Decisions of Appeal Commissioners

(1) The fact that the mining activity and the manufacturing activity are of equal scale rules out the concept of overall mining operations. Consequently the company cannot be said to have income from mining operations and is therefore entitled to ESR.

(2) While the company's trade included the working of a mine it could not be said that it was carrying on the trade of working a qualifying mine given the significance of the manufacturing activity and consequently the company is not entitled to allowances under the 1974 Act. If, however, the decision at (1) is set aside on appeal the claim for the capital allowances should be remitted to this tribunal for further consideration.

Submissions

The Inspector disputes the conclusion that mining operations end before the processing operation begins and contends that the findings of facts do not establish this conclusion. On behalf of the company it is argued that the findings of primary fact cannot be set aside by the Court unless there was no evidence whatsoever to support those findings.

Held by Murphy J in allowing the appeal that:

(i) There was ambiguity in the Appeal Commissioner's findings on the definition of mining and the output of concentrates from ore

(ii) The Court should consider the overall scheme of tax legislation relating to mining operations from 1956 onwards.

(iii) The conclusion that not all of the company's activities could be said to come within the meaning of 'mining operations' is not soundly based on the facts

(iv) There was not an express finding that the mining operations ceased after the extraction of the ore from the mine, and

(v) The decisions of the Appeal Commissioners do not accordingly sit firmly on the findings

---

Legislation
Finance (Miscellaneous Provisions) Act 1956; Finance (Taxation of Certain Mines) Act 1974, s 1; CTA 1976, Part IV, ss 54, 58

Cases referred to in judgment
de Brun (Inspector of Taxes) v Kiernan 3 ITR 19
Federal Commissioners of Taxation v Broken Hill Property Ltd
Federal Commissioners of Taxation v Utah Development (1996) 76 ATC 4119
Mara v Hummingbird Ltd [1982] ILRM 401
O'Culachain v McMullen Bros Ltd 5 ITR 2000

High Court - 4 April 2001

Issues

Murphy J, The issues in this case stated, under s 428 of the Income Tax Act 1967 are twofold:

(a) Is Tara Mines Limited entitled to export sales relief under the provisions of Part IV of the Corporation Tax Act 1976 in respect of ten accounting periods ending on 31 December 1988? Alternatively is Tara Mines Limited outside the terms of this relief by virtue of the words contained in s 58(9) of that Act?

(b) In computing its income for these accounting periods, is Tara Mines Limited entitled to mining development allowance under the provisions of the Finance (Taxation of Profits of Certain Mines) Act 1974 in respect of certain foreign exchange loses on its capital borrowings?

The Appeal Commissioners found in favour of Tara Mines Limited (the Company) on issue (a) and against the company on issue (b).

The Inspector of Taxes appeals by way of case stated against the decision on issue (a) The company reserves its position in relation to the decision on issue (b) pending the outcome of this appeal.

The question arose during the hearing before the Appeal Commissioners, which extended from January 1995 to July 1996, as to whether the concentrates produced by the company constitute 'goods' within the meaning of part four of the Corporation Tax Act 1976. The Inspector accepted that the concentrates are 'goods' within the meaning of that part.

Statutory provisions

Section 54 of the Act defines goods as follows:

> Goods manufactured within the State by the person who exports them or some of them and who in relation to the relevant accounting period is the company claiming relief under this part.

In relation to export tax relief s 58(3) of the 1976 Act provides that:

> Where a company claims and proves as respect a relevant accounting period -
>
> ....
>
> (b)   that, during the relevant accounting period, goods were in the course of trade, exported out of the State.'

Section 58(9) of the Act states that:

> A reduction shall not be made under this section in respect of Corporation Tax payable on income from any mining operations.

A capital allowance is available for development expenditure in relation to a qualifying mine under the 1974 Act referred to above. Development expenditure is defined in s 1 of that Act as:

Capital expenditure

(a)   on the development of a qualifying mine, or

(b)   on the construction of any works in connection with the qualifying mine which were of such a nature that, when the mine ceases to be operated, they are likely to have so diminished in value that their value would be little or nothing,

and includes interest on money borrowed to meet such expenditure, but does not include -

(c)   expenditure on the acquisition of the site or the mine or the site of any such works or of rights in or over any such site,

(d)   expenditure on the acquisition of a scheduled mineral asset, or

(e)   expenditure on works consisting wholly or mainly for subjecting the raw product of a mine to any process accept a process designed for preparing the raw product for use as such.

Findings of the Appeal Commissioners

The Commissioners made extensive findings - 22 in all - including many sub-findings under the heading of steps carried out in extracting the ore (7 sub-findings) and the status of processing (12 sub-findings).

This Court is, of course, bound by such findings.

These findings may be reduced to the following relevant findings on which submissions were made by the parties.

The company extracts lead and zinc ores from the earth... which are then processed to produce the finished product of lead and zinc concentrates. A major constituent (approximately 90%) of the concentrates are sphalerite and galena. Sphalerite is a naturally occurring substance containing zinc in the form of zinc sulphide. Galena is a naturally occurring substance containing lead in the form of lead sulphide. (Finding (b))

The ore contains an average of 8% zinc and 2.5% lead. All the concentrates sold by the company during the accounting periods were exported out of the State. (Finding (d))

The company's whole operation at Tara is divided into two major divisions under the management of the Production Manager and the divisions are entitled the Mining Division and the Processing Division respectively. (Each division has a separate manager who gave evidence before the Appeal Commissioners). (Finding (f)) In summary the Manager of the Mining Division is responsible for the exploration and development of the mine, together with the extraction of ore from the mine and its transportation to the storage tepee located on the surface. His responsibilities end at that point. The Manager of the Processing Division is responsible for all activities after the ore arrives in the tepee, including the manufacture of lead and zinc concentrates. (Finding (j)) This type of specialisation exists throughout the industry. Exploration is generally managed by Geologists, mining managed by Mineral Engineers and processing managed by Mineral or Chemical Engineers. There is some overlap, with the core professional capabilities of these specialities differing (Finding (k)) The personnel working in the Mining Division, with the exception of the Mobile Equipment Department personnel, work exclusively in that division. Likewise, Processing Division personnel do not work in the Mining Division. (Finding (m)) The steps carried out by the company in extracting the ore appear, from the further findings of the Appeal Commissioners, to extend from surface drilling, access tunnelling, blasting, excavating blasting of broken ore, crushing, back filling transferring to coarse or bin and from that to surface storage bin or tepee.

The main stages of processing appear from the three pages of findings of the Appeal Commissioners to be more complex. The first of these is as follows:

> (1) the coarse ore is subjected to a highly sophisticated process which is carried out at the company's on-site milling plant. The object of this process is to produce precisely calibrated lead and zinc concentrates suitable for sale in other European countries.

It would appear that this finding encompasses some or all of the eleven findings which follow, in relation to the detail of processing which would seem to involve further discreet activities:

> Comminution (the reduction to minute particulars by way of further dry crushing and wet grinding),

> Processing (separating galena and, then, sphalerite by way of a flotation process using organic and inorganic chemicals which react with and change the surface characteristics of the lead mineral (galena) making it water repellent.

> Following that the zinc mineral (sphalerite) is floated as described for galena. The zinc concentrate is reground to produce a zinc flotation concentrate. Further processing by acid leaching reduces the magnesium oxide content of the zinc concentrate to a level acceptable to smelters.

> Final treatment with sulphuric acid and magnesium together with processing in the reflotation plant upgrades the zinc concentrate to, typically, 56% zinc.

The findings also refer to the high degree of computer control and monitoring of reagent dosing rates and other control variables.

Two further findings are relevant.

> The process above ground was described by the various experts as a process to liberate, extract or separate the galena and sphalerite. The concentrates produced as the end product of the company are quite distinct from the ore. The chemical change occurs in the processing stages in that the chemical compound on the surface of the mineral changes during the flotation process and in the leaching process carbonates are converted to sulphates which are subsequently removed. (Emphasis added.) (Finding (s)).

The last finding is as follows:

> There was conflicting evidence as to whether the term 'mining operations' as used within the mining industry would include all the activities carried on by the company or just the underground activities. We did not find it necessary to make a finding of fact in this regard. However, in their general usage, terms such as 'mining', 'mining activity', 'mining operations', etc could, depending on the context in which they are used, encompass the type of activities carried on by the company. (Finding (v)) (emphasis added) The Appeal Commissioners summarise the contentions on behalf of the company and on behalf of the Inspector of Taxes, made reference to cases cited and other references and gave their decision in relation to export tax relief and in relation to the claim for capital allowances and whether that claim could cover foreign exchange losses incurred by the company.

Decision on export sales relief

It is necessary to refer in extenso to the Commissioners' reasoning in relation to the first issue:

> In relation to exports sales relief we had the task of deciding whether the company had '... income from any mining operations...' and was therefore debarred by virtue of s 58(9) of the Corporation Tax Act 1976, from claiming export sales relief in respect of that income for corporation tax purposes.

> The expert witnesses who gave evidence before us differed to some extent the meaning of 'mining operations'. In the Australian case *Federal Commissioners of Taxation v Utah Development Company* the same situation applied. We decided that, applying the principles of construction laid down by the Supreme Court in the case of *de Brun (Inspector of Taxes) v Kiernan*, we should give the words their ordinary meaning and should not adopt a technical approach to construing them: in any event the evidence of the experts clearly established that there was no specific widely accepted technical meaning of the phrase.

> We came broadly to the same conclusion as the Judges in the Australian High Court did in the *Utah* case: that while the company did carry out 'mining operations' on its land not all of the activities could be said to come within the meaning of that phrase.

> We decided that the company operates a mine and that it also carries out a separate activity subsequent to its mining activity: namely the processing of ore, the result of mining operations, to manufacture concentrates of lead and zinc. We also decided that the mining activity and the manufacturing activity were of similar scale and that neither was subsidiary or incidental to the other. In our opinion the manufacturing activity was, in the words of the judges in the *Broken Hill* case at page 4030 '... distinct from although connected with the tax payer's mining operations...' and clearly did not come within the meaning of the phrase 'mining operations'. While we did not have any difficulty in so deciding, we found support from our conclusion in the evidence of the expert witnesses the different branches of science are involved in the mining activity and in the manufacturing process, each branch of which requires separate training and education of its specialists.

We concluded that the company does not sell its mining output. It subjects that output to separate manufacturing process to produce concentrates of lead and zinc which it sells in the course of its trade. Therefore the company's income is derived from the sale of the said concentrates. It follows that the company cannot be said to have '... income from any mining operations ... within the meaning of s 58(9) of the Corporation Tax Act 1976, and that it is consequently entitled to export sales relief in respect of its trading income for the periods with which this appeal is concerned. A schedule of the assessments amended in accordance with their determination is detailed in the following paragraph.

While we believe we would have reached the same decision outlined above without the assistance of the decided cases to which we have referred (and which are obviously not in any way binding on it) we found the entire judgment of the Australian High Court in the *Utah* case (when read in conjunction with the Judgment of Newton J given in the Supreme Court of Victoria and approved by the High Court) to be of considerable reassurance.

There are many comments and conclusions in the *Utah* case and the *Broken Hill* case which are of some relevance to the issues which we had to consider. However, we have decided not to refer to specific passages and judgments but to repeat our conclusion that both judgments read in their entirety are consonant with the decisions which we have reached in this case.

Decision in relation to mining development allowance

In relation to the second issue before the Appeal Commissioners, that of the claim for certain capital allowances, the Appeal Commissioners decided as follows:

We heard arguments on behalf of the company and the inspector in relation to the company's claim for certain capital allowances under the Finance (Taxation of Profits of Certain Mines) Act 1974 and the issue of whether the claim should cover foreign exchange losses incurred by the company.

We found that while the company's trade did include the working of a mine it could not be said that it was carrying on the trade of working a qualifying mine given the significance of the further manufacturing activity carried on be the company. For this reason we determined that the company was not entitled to the allowance sought under the 1974 Act. We did not determine the merits of the arguments made on behalf of the company that it's claim to mining development allowances under the 1974 Act should take account of the foreign exchange losses incurred by it in the course of developing its mine at Navan.

In the event that our determination on the exports sales relief issue is upheld on appeal the question of the company's entitlement to the allowances in the 1974 Act becomes largely academic, since the company would in that case have no liability to corporation tax in respect of its tax adjusted trading profits whether or not these profits were reduced by allowances under the 1974 Act.

On the other hand, if our determinations on the export sales relief issue and the issue of the claim allowances under the 1974 Act are not upheld, it would appear appropriate that the company's claim under the 1974 Act should be remitted to this tribunal to enable the quantum of claim to be finalised.

A determination followed with regard to the assessment to taxation which does not concern this appeal.

Case stated to High Court

Immediately after the determination the Inspector of Taxes expressed dissatisfaction in relation to the determination regarding the export sales relief as being erroneous in law. The company and the Inspector of Taxes both expressed dissatisfaction in relation to the second issue, that is the claim for certain capital allowances, as also being erroneous in law. The company and the Inspector both asked for a case stated for the opinion of the High Court as to whether, on the foregoing facts and evidence, the Appeal Commissioners' decisions are correct in law.

Applicable law

The Court is not debarred from exercising its supervisory function where a decision of the Commissioners is unreasonable in the sense in which the term is used in Judicial Review applications. However, the Courts will not intervene unless there is no way in which a reasonable decision maker could have reached the same conclusion. In *Mara v Hummingbird Limited* (1982) ILRM 421 Kenny J delivering the judgment of the Supreme Court, held, at p 426, that findings of primary fact by Appeal Commissioners should not be interfered with unless there was no evidence whatever to support them. As to conclusions or inferences drawn from these primary facts which Kenny J referred to as mixed questions of fact and law, the Courts would not disturb them unless they were ones that no reasonable Commissioner could draw, or were based on a mistaken view of the law. The High Court, accordingly, declined to interfere with the decision of the Appeal Commissioners and followed the decision of the House of Lords in *Edwards v Bairstow* (1956) AC 14.

Lord Radcliffe stated, in relation to the law:

> When the case comes before the Court it is its duty to examine the determination having regard to its knowledge of the relevant law. If the case contains anything ex facie which is bad law and which bears on the determination, it is, obviously erroneous in point of law. But, without any such misconception appearing ex facie, it may be that the facts found are such that no person acting judicially and properly instructed as to the relevant law could come to the determination under appeal. In those circumstances, too, the Court must intervene. In *O'Culachain (Inspector of Taxes) v MacMullan Brothers Limited* [1995] (Vol 5) ITR 200 at 203 (SC), Blayney J held that, in determining whether a particular decision was correct in law, the Court is to consider the following five principles:
>
> (1) Findings of primary fact should not be disturbed unless there is no evidence to support them;
>
> (2) Inferences from primary facts are mixed questions of fact and law;
>
> (3) If the Judge's conclusions show that he has adopted a wrong view of the law, they should be set aside;
>
> (4) If his conclusions are not based on a mistaken view of the law, they should not be set aside unless the inferences with which he drew were ones which no reasonable Judge could draw;
>
> (5) where some evidence would point to one conclusion and other evidence to the opposite, these are essentially matters of degree and the Judge's conclusions should not be disturbed (even if the Court does not agree with them, for we are not retrying the case) unless they are such that a reasonable Judge could not have arrived at them or they are based on a mistaken view of the law.

In *Clark v British Telecom Pension Scheme Trustees* [2000] STC 222 at 230 Robert Walker LJ held that an error of law by the Special Commissioners on one issue did not affect a conclusion on another issue, If it 'had no real causal connection with the conclusion'.

Submissions on behalf of the appellant

The Inspector, in his appeal, relies on the findings that the company is engaged in the extraction of lead and zinc ores from the earth which are then processed to produce the finished products of lead and zinc concentrates. (Finding (b)) While the ore contains on average 8% zinc and 2.5% lead (finding (c)) the major constituent of the concentrates are sphalarite and galena (90% approximately) which is sold to smelters in other European countries.

It is disputed by the Inspector that the mining operations end before the processing operation begins as is the submission of the company. Mr Fitzsimmons SC, for the inspector outlined the legislative history of the Finance (Profits of certain Mines) (Temporary Relief from Taxation) Act 1956 as amended by s 9 of the Finance Act 1967 whereby profits from mining activities were exempt for the first four years and a 50% exemption for the subsequent four years which was (subsequently extended to the first twenty years by the 1967 Act).

In the same year the Finance (Miscellaneous Provisions) Act 1956 introduced exports sales reliefs in respect of profits from the export of manufactured goods. Section 15(1)(b) of the 1956 Act provided that reduction shall not be made –

(b) in respect of income tax or corporation profits tax payable on profits from any mining operations.

The 1956 Act was repealed and replaced with the Finance (Taxation of Profits of Certain Mines) Act 1974 which eliminated the tax exemption from mining of scheduled minerals and reimposed the normal rate of tax on mining profits. It did introduce a generous capital allowance regime for mining companies.

Section 15(1)(b) of the 1956 Act, which excluded reductions in respect of income tax or corporation profits tax payable on profits from any mining operations, was carried through in s 58(9) of the Corporation Tax Act 1976 which is the subject of interpretation in this case stated.

The term 'mining operation' is not defined in any of the legislative provisions cited above. This is the issue before the Court. What is also before the Court is whether the company is entitled to allowances under the 1974 Act and, if so, whether it is entitled to claim mining development allowances on foreign exchange borrowings.

The correct approach to the interpretation of taxing statutes is, in the Appellant's submission, three basic rules enunciated by Henchy J in *de Brun (Inspector of Taxes) v Kiernan* (3 ITR 19):

(a) Words are to be construed as having a particular trade meaning if the Act is passed with reference to that particular trade business or transaction, though it may differ from the common or ordinary meaning of the words. Otherwise the words should be given the meaning which an ordinary member of the public would intend it to have when ordinarily using it.

(b) Where a word or expression is used in the statute creating a penal or taxation liability, then if there is looseness or ambiguity attaching to it, it should be construed strictly so as to prevent the fresh imposition of liability from being created unfairly by the use of oblique or slack language.

(c) Where a word which requires to be given its natural and ordinary meaning is a simple word which has widespread and unambiguous currency, the Judge construing it should draw primarily on his own experience of its use.

Indeed the first decision of the Appeal Commissioners is in relation to the principle of construction laid down by that case given that the expert witnesses differed to some extent on the meaning of 'mining operations'. This was so because of finding (v) in relation to the term as used within the mining industry.

Mr Fitzsimons urges that where the company is seeking to bring itself within a relieving section it must fall within the section without any doubt or ambiguity. He referred to the decision of Keane CJ in *O'Connell v Fyffes Banana Processing Limited* (24 July 2000, unreported), Supreme Court at p 6:

> Relief of that nature must be given expressly and in clear and unambiguous terms

Where there is ambiguity the Court can consider the purpose and intention of the legislator to be inferred from other provisions of the statute involved, or even of other statutes expressed to be constructed with it (see Finlay CJ in *McGrath v McDermott* 3 ITR 683 at 703).

Henchy J in *de Brun v Kiernan*, cited above, stated at 26 that:

> A word or expression in a given statute must be given meaning and scope according to its immediate context in line with the scheme and purpose of a particular statutory pattern as a whole, and to an extent that will truly effectuate the particular legislation or a particular definition therein. [1981] IR 117 at 121.

The same line of reasoning is evident in the decision of McCarthy J in *McCann v O'Culachain* (1986) 3 ITR 304 at 318.

In the Inspector's submission the Appeal Commissioners found that in its general usage 'mining operations' could, depending on the context in which it is used, encompass all the activities carried on at Tara Mines (see finding (v)). The Commissioners did not examine the context any further. They would appear to have drawn a wholly artificial line through the company's activities. They failed to give proper weight of consideration to the integrated nature of the operation in which the company is engaged as described in the case stated.

The critical submission of the Inspector is that the phrase 'any mining operation', income in respect of which is excluded from the scope of s 58, would have no point if there were mining operations which could also be manufacturing operations. Section 58 is concerned with the granting of an exemption from tax for certain manufactured goods and denying that exemption to other manufactured goods such are those which are the result of mining operations.

The subsection in question 58(9) does not exclude income from manufactured goods arising from mining operations but income from any mining operations.

It is the appellant's submission, that as it is clear that what goes on underground is not manufacturing, the exclusion found in s 58(9) must be directed at the other kinds of works carried on namely the bulk reduction and concentration activities which are associated with mining in the case of minerals which occur in low concentrations.

Allowing export sales relief would render that subsection redundant. It was enacted to ensure that mining companies did not qualify for export sales relief. The scheme and purpose of the section was to encourage the creation of employment within the State. In its submission the contention that the section was intended to encourage the further processing of the run of mine ore in the State does not stand up to scrutiny as the Commissioners found, as a fact, that it would be uneconomic to transport this ore off site for processing. The processing would have to occur anyway as the value of the ore can only be extracted by processing it on site. The company sells only lead and zinc concentrates.

Mr Fitzsimons urges that the 1974/1976 Acts should be read together as there is a coherence between them in the sense that the two sets of provisions are interlinked. The

1974 Act provides a comprehensive code for the taxation of mining operations in respect of scheduled minerals. If the operations involved in this case fall to be dealt with under the framework of the 1974 Act then they should be regarded as mining operations and, accordingly, outside the scope of the legislation relating to export sales relief.

Development expenditure means capital expenditure on the development of a qualifying mine but excludes expenditure on works constructed wholly or mainly for subjecting the raw product of the mine to any process except a process designed for preparing the raw material for use as such (see p 3 above). It is submitted that the only possible interpretation of the exception is that it refers to processes that occur after the rock is brought to the surface. Processes designed for preparing the raw product for use 'as such' include processes which removes unwanted material in which the mineral is embedded thus completing the recovery of the mineral. Processes above ground are processes of bulk reduction allowing recovery in the form of concentrates. The processes merely prepare the raw product of the mine for use as such - sphalerite and galena embedded in rock. The rock is of no use and cannot be transported from the site for economic reasons. Therefore, as a matter of fact, the only product of the mine that is available for any use 'as such' is the concentrate which can be taken away from the mine. In the contention of the inspector, all of Tara Mines activities are mining operations.

In order to claim any capital allowances under the 1974 Act a company must carry on 'the trade of working a qualified mine' as defined in s 2 of the Act. It is not sufficient that the trade includes the work of a qualifying mine.

In disallowing the company's claim to capital allowances on exchange losses the appeal commissioners have accepted this exclusivity analysis and have found that, although the company operated a mine, it did not carry on the trade of working a qualifying mine. This submission is based on paragraph 9(b) of the decision of the commissioners (p 25 of the case stated) which is as follows:

> We found that while the company's trade did include the working of a mine it could not be said that it was carrying on the trade of working a qualifying mine giving the significance of the further manufacturing activity carried on by the company. For this reason we determined that the company was not entitled to the allowance sought under the 1974 Act.

The Inspector's submission is that this finding excludes the company not only (a) from claiming capital allowances on its exchange losses but also from (b) claiming any allowances at all under the 1974 Act in respect of all of its exploration expenditure and all of the underground workings that it undertook to gain access to the ore. This, it is submitted, makes a nonsense of the 1974 legislation.

However, the inspector agrees that the Appeal Commissioners in deciding that the Company is entitled to export sales relief under the 1976 Act and not capital allowances under the 1974 Act are consistent in their approach. But this very consistency highlights the fallacy of their findings in respect of the export sales relief claimed. The 1974 Act was intended to remove the exemption from tax for income derived from mining of scheduled materials and replacing it with a system of generous capital allowances. The Commissioners' decision renders ineffective the entire legislation. The inspector submits that the company does indeed carry on the trade of a working qualifying mine and is therefore entitled to mining development and other capital allowances under the 1974 Act but is not entitled to export sales relief under the 1976 Act.

However the inspector has accepted that the produce of the process are goods for the purpose of the legislation.

The inspector contends that the highly integrated trade, from rock face to mine gate makes it impossible to draw an artificial line, as the Appeal Commissioners have done, between operating a mine and carrying out a separate processing activity. The company's income derives from the trade of working a qualifying mine. This is consistent with the coherence of the 1974/1976 Acts.

The inspector submits that the Commissioners were heavily influenced by certain Australian case law. The context, scheme and purpose of Australian legislation cannot be substituted for that of the Irish provisions.

Subject to that proviso the inspector submits that when these cases are considered fully in the context of other Australian cases a number of general principles can be distilled which leads to the conclusion that the company's operation is a mining operation.

One of the reasons for the finding that the process of pelletisation in *Broken Hill* was not a mining operation was that it was not carried out for the purpose of separating out or liberating the minerals. The same principle applied in deciding the *Utah* case. In the former case the ore before that process was a saleable product.

However in *North West Iron* it was found that until pelletisation took place the concentrates were of no use to anybody. The process in that case was found to be a 'mining operation'.

In the light of the above arguments the inspector submits that the Court should determine the questions of law in the case stated by finding that the trade carried on by the company consisted of mining operations and that the income from that trade was 'income from any mining operations' within the meaning of s 58(9) and that the company is thereby excluded from the reliefs provided for under the export sales relief legislation.

In relation to the second issue the inspector submits that the Court should answer that the company is entitled to the allowances under the 1974 Act on the basis that it is carrying on the trade of working a qualifying mine and that, accordingly, the case be submitted to the Commissioners to finalise that claim.

Submissions on behalf of the company outline

The very extensive submissions of the company outline and supplemental written submissions (running to 46 pages) referred to the statutory provisions, to the determination of the Appeal Commissioners, to the jurisdiction of the court and to the grounds on which the company submits that the question be answered in the affirmative and the inspector's appeal dismissed.

The first two matters have been referred to in the inspector's submissions.

With regard to the determination of the Appeal Commissioners the company highlights the basic finding that the company operates a mine and that it also carries out a separate activity. The company further highlights the consequential finding that the company's income is derived from the sale of the concentrates which derive from that separate activity and it follows that the company cannot be said to have 'income from mining operations' within the meaning of s 58(9). Furthermore the company relies on the acceptance that the ultimate output are regarded as 'goods'.

Jurisdiction

The nature of the Courts jurisdiction is contained in s 428(6) of the Income Tax Act 1967 which provides that:

> The High Court shall hear and determine any question or questions of law arising on the case, and shall reverse, affirm or amend the determination in respect of which the case has been

stated, or shall remit the matter to the Commissioners with the opinion of the Court thereon, or may make such order in relation to the matter, and make such order as to costs as the Court may seem fit.

This section was referred to in *Hummingbird* (supra) and in *Bosnan v Mutual Enterprise Limited* [1997] 3 IR 257. In the latter case the section was considered, in relation to whether a loss arising from adverse currency movements in respect of a sterling loan were revenue or capital in nature, Murphy J then a Judge of the High Court, stated:

> To my mind the fact that the purpose of the borrowing was clearly identified and that the purpose was the acquisition of a capital asset and that it was implemented was a factor of very considerable importance. These relevant factors were obvious to the learned trial Judge (of the Circuit Court). It may be that he attached less weight to them than I would have done or that he attached greater weight to other factors, such as, the fact that the borrowing was repayable 'on demand'. All one can say is that there were a number of factors to be taken into account and I cannot say that no reasonable Judge of first instance could have concluded on the facts as a whole that the loans were a means of fluctuating and temporary accommodation. In the circumstances there are no grounds in which I would be justified interfering with the decision which he reached. (At p 266).

The Supreme Court (Hamilton CJ with whom Barrington and Lynch JJ agreed), stated:

> The learned trial Judge in the High Court held that the determination of this issue was a question of fact which had to be determined having regard to all the circumstances and I have held that he was correct in so holding.
>
> The Circuit Court Judge had held that the loan was temporary and fluctuating. Such finding by the Circuit Court Judge can only be disturbed if it was a finding in respect of which there was no evidence to support or which no Judge could reasonably have made on the basis of the facts proved or admitted before him. (At 283/284).

It is clear that there is no issue taken by either party as to the nature of the Courts jurisdiction.

Findings of primary fact made by the Appeal Commissioners cannot be set aside by the Court unless there was no evidence whatsoever to support those findings.

Conclusions or inferences drawn from findings of primary fact can only be disturbed if there was no evidence to support such conclusions or inferences were ones which no decision maker could reasonably have made on the basis of approved or admitted facts.

Where there is a mistake of law or misconstruction of documents, the Court can intervene. In that case the company contends that s 58(9) of the 1976 Act must be construed strictly.

Grounds submitted

While it is normally for the tax payer to show that he comes clearly within any exemption, where the inspector has accepted that the company manufactured and exported 'goods' within the meaning of Part IV of the 1976 Act then, in the company's submission, the onus is on the inspector.

The Commissioners established that the company had no income from mining operations. Before s 58(9) can have any application, the taxpayer must be in receipt of income from mining operations. It is not sufficient that the taxpayer be engaged in mining operations: those mining operations must be the source of the relevant income if the exclusion is to apply.

If the concentrates are 'goods' it necessarily follows that the production of the ore into the concentrates is a process of 'manufacture'. This is not disputed by the inspector.

Indeed the decision of the Commissioners at 9(a) at the end of p 23 is as follows:

> We decided that the company operates a mine and that it also carries out a separate activity subsequent to its mining activities; namely the processing of ore, the result of its mining operations, to manufacture concentrates of lead and zinc.

To say that the end products of the company's operations were concentrates and that therefore all of the antecedent operations ought to be characterised as mining operations is flawed by circular reasoning.

The distinction between mining and manufacturing operations is reflected in the wording of s 50(2) of the 1980 Act which, so far as it relates to corporation tax, is to be construed as one with the Corporation Tax Act 1996 (see s 96(2) of that Act). That subsection expressly provides for a situation where a company obtains a scheduled mineral etc which is not sold as such but instead forms whole or part of the materials used in the manufacture of goods or is, to any extent, incorporated in the goods in the course of the manufacture then:-

> Part of the income which, apart from this subsection, would be income from the sale of goods for the purpose of s 41 shall be deemed, for the purposes of subsection (1), to be income from such mining operations.

This subsection acknowledges that income from the sale of goods manufactured in whole or in part from minerals obtained from mining operations will not constitute income from mining operations. This section has to deem a portion of that income to be income from mining operations.

As s 58 of the 1976 Act does not contain any analogous deeming provision there is no grounds for treating any part of the company's relevant income from the sale of concentrates as though it were income from mining operations. Income from the sale of goods under s 58(4) of the 1976 Act must be construed narrowly that is income deriving directly or immediately from the sale of goods (see *JG Kerrane v O'Hanlon Limited* (1987) 3 ITR 633).

It is not the function of the Court to add or delete from expressed statutory provisions so as to achieve objectives which to the inspector or to the Court appears desirable in interpreting s 58(9).

In relation to the wider statutory scheme, the 1974 and 1976 Acts recognise a distinction between mining on the one hand, in respect of which mining development allowances are available in respect of certain capital expenditure, and processing on the other, in respect of which such development allowances are excluded because references to capital expenditure in both sections is expressly defined to exclude 'expenditure and works constructed wholly or mainly for subjecting the raw material of the mine to any process except a process designed for preparing the raw product for use as such.'

The products are, in the findings of the Appeal Commissioners, quite distinct from the ore (Finding (5)(s) of the case stated).

In relation to decisions from other jurisdictions, the company submits that the Appeal Commissioners' decision was not founded on those decisions.

Paragraph 9(a) of case stated is emphatic that the Commissioners believed that they would have reached the same decision without the assistance of such cases.

While the company acknowledges that decisions from other jurisdictions inevitably pose difficulties with regard to the scheme and context in which the statutory provisions operate, these decisions do indeed support the company's claim in the instant case.

In the *Utah* case, mined coal was converted into metallurgical coking coal. Under the relevant statutory provisions deductions against tax in respect of expenditure on plant to convert the coal into coke were allowable if the tax payer could establish the operations carried on in the plant were 'operations by means of which manufactured goods are derived from other goods' and that the plant was not 'plant for use in mining operations.'

Newton J held that the operations carried out in the plants were indeed 'operations by means of which manufactured goods are derived from other goods' and referred to the 'highly technical process, the use of which involves human labour and also numerous items of plant, equipment and machinery, some of which are very large, many of which are complicated and sophisticated, and all of which are housed in or situated near large factory like building'. (*Utah Development Company v Federal Commissioner of Taxation* (1995) 75 ATC 4103 at 4108.

On appeal from the Supreme Court to the High Court of Victoria (*Federal Commissioners of Taxation v Utah Development Company* (1996) 76 ATC 4119 the full High Court dismissed the appeal of the Commissioner Barwick CJ (with whom Gibbs and Steven JJ agreed) referring to the decision of the lower court stated:

> In my opinion, his honour was not in error in concluding that the treatment in the plants was a process of manufacture and that the product of the plants was manufactured goods within the operation of the section; in other words, that the coal already won by the mining operation was treated so as to be coking coal suitable for a specific purpose. That treatment, unlike the shearing and bailing operation in *MP Metals Pty Limited v FC of T* 117 CLR 631, did more than merely change the form of the recovered material for ease of its transport or its use.

The concentration of the coking coal elements and the recovered coal to produce homogenous coking coal did produce a product essentially different, in my opinion, from the recovered coal.

I am not persuaded that his Honour was in error in either of his conclusions. In my opinion he made no error of law in approaching what, in my opinion, was ultimately a question of fact nor did he overlook any factor or give undue weight to any factor, proper to be considered in reaching that ultimate conclusion. His conclusion is not disconformable to any decision of this Court in the relevant field.

It was, in my opinion, fully open to his Honour to consider that the mining operation finished with the extraction of coal from the ground and that the subsequent treatment of the mined substance to obtain therefrom homogeneous coking coal was not part of the mining operation, but on the contrary was, at least, the treatment of the mineral recovered for the better utilisation of that material, to use the language of the Judgment of the majority of this Court in the *FC of T v Broker' Hill Pty Limited*.

In the company's submission the concentrates are suitable for export, as the metallurgical coking coal in *Utah* simply did not exist in the mine. They are, as is correctly accepted by the Inspector, manufactured products.

The company also referred to *Marbridge Mines Limited v Minister for National Revenue* (1971) 71 DTC 5231 where the Exchequer Court of Canada accepted the distinction between 'mining operations' and subsequent processing activities where Gibson J at 5233 states that mining ends with the bringing of the mineral ore to the ground surface and that before that terminal point three stages of physical operations have been gone through namely: exploration, development and extradition.

Following the bringing of the materials to the surface. The physical operation that takes place is 'treatment' of the ore. Treatment consist of three stages of physical operation, namely: milling smelting and refining.

In the Company's submission the Appeal Commissioners followed the same distinction between mining and non mining.

Decision

Findings on primary fact should not be set aside by the Court unless there was no evidence whatsoever to support them. Kenny J in (*Inspector of Taxes) Mara v Hummingbird* [1982] ILRM 42 1 at 426; and Blayney J in *Revenue Commissioners v O'Loinsigh* [1994] Vol 5 ITR 98 at 106 and Hamilton CJ (with whom Barrington and Lynch JJ agreed) in *Brosnan v Mutual Enterprises Limited* [1997] 3 IR 257 at 284.

This appeal is by way of case stated which is necessarily restricted to points of Law only (see Tax Consolidation Act 1997, s 941). This Court cannot entertain an appeal insofar as it seeks to address issues of fact. The Court has, of course, an inherent jurisdiction to exercise a supervisory function by way of Judicial Review. It may, therefore, be open to impugn a decision of the Appeal Commissioners if that decision is unreasonable in the sense in which that term is used in administrative law (see *O'Keeffe v An Bord Pleanála* (1992) ILRM 69 and Hogan and Morgan, *Administrative Law in Ireland* (3rd edn), pp 617-690).

I accept the cogent arguments submitted by Mr Fitzsimons SC for the Inspector that the Court should relate the overall scheme of the legislation so the ambiguous finding of the Commissioners in relation (a) to the definition of mining and (b) to the output of concentrates from ore.

In interpreting s 58(9) of the 1976 Act, in relation to income from any mining operations, this Court should have regard to the findings of the Commissioners at (v) that, in general usage, terms such as 'mining', 'mining activity', 'mining operations', etc could, depending on the context in which they are used, encompass the type of activities carried on by the company. The Commissioners did not find it necessary to make a finding of fact as to whether the term 'mining operations' as used within the mining industry did include all of the activities carried on by the company or just the underground activities.

Moreover, finding (b) that the company extracts lead and zinc ores from the earth which are then processed to produce the finished product of zinc and lead concentrates is a finding that there are no new elements produced and, by definition, each of the concentrates is a naturally occurring substance and also a finding that there is a process of manufacturing. It goes someway to establishing that production and manufacturing are not mining activities.

That two major divisions of the company under the management of the Production Manager are the mining division and the processing division does not necessarily delimit mining output. The steps carried out by the company in extracting the ore - see finding (n) - as distinct from the main stages of processing (finding (a)) could both be mining operations.

The finding (e) that the company commenced commercial production of zinc and lead concentrates in or around 1978 pursuant to a state mining lease granted to the company in 1975 is a finding which leads to an inference that the object of the operation of mining is the commercial production of concentrates all of which were exported out of the State '(see finding (d)).

The company's reliance on findings that distinguish between extracting of ores and processing of concentrates (finding (b)) depend on a finding that the production of concentrates is a manufacturing process which is distinct from the exploration, development and extraction of ore and its transportation to the storage tepee located on the surface (see finding (j)), further depends on a definition of what mining is.

The steps taken by the company in extracting the ore (detailed in finding (n)) are distinct from the main stages in processing, detailed in finding (o) depends on a finding that the latter is a highly sophisticated process which is carried out at the milling plant which produces precisely calibrated concentrates suitable for sated smelters and also that the concentrates produced as the end product of the company are quite distinct from the ore.

The decision of the Commissioners was that while the company did carry out 'mining operations' on its land not all of its activities could be said to come within the meaning of that phrase. The company contends that this follows from the findings of the Commissioners, in particular finding (j) - the manufacture of concentrates as distinct from the extraction of ore from the mine - and (s): the concentrates produced as the end product of the company are quite distinct from the ore.

The Commissioners also decided that the company operates a mine and that it also carries out a separate activity subsequent to its activity; namely, the processing of ore, the result of its mining operations, to manufacture concentrates of lead and zinc. The company contends that that decision is based on findings (b) - extracts and then processes - (j) and (s) as above.

The decision of the Commissioners concluded that the company does not sell its mining output. It subjects that output to a separate manufacturing process to produce concentrates which it sells. Therefore the company's income is derived from the sale of the said concentrates. It follows that the company cannot be said to have 'income from any mining operations' within the meaning of s 58(9) of the 1976 Act. Consequently the company is entitled to export sales relief.

The conclusion that not all of the company's activities could be said to come within the meaning of 'mining operations' can however, have no basis given the finding that the term 'mining', depending on the context in which it and cognate terms are used, could encompass the type of activities carried out by the company. The conclusion is not a finding of paragraph (v) as the Commissioners did not deem it necessary to make a finding of fact specifically in regard to whether the term 'mining operations' as used within the mining industry would include all of the activities carried on by the company or just the underground activities.

The general observation implying that the activities carried on by the company were encompassed by the term was not a finding. The question arises whether a finding is necessary to support the decision. The company has urged that other findings, in particular (j) and (s) support the contention that not all of the company's activities are mining.

As a preliminary to their decision, the Commissioners decided that, applying the principles of construction laid down by the Supreme Court in the *Kiernan* case, they should give the words their ordinary meanings and should not adopt a technical approach to construing them. They observed that, in any event, the evidence of the experts clearly established that there was no specific widely accepted technical meaning of the term 'mining operations.' It was in that context that they decided that the company did carry on 'mining operations' but that not all of its activities could be said to come within the meaning of that phrase. This is, of course, to beg the question of what the meaning is which is pivotal to the further decisions that, for example, the company did not sell its mining output.

In the absence of a finding of what constitutes 'mining operations' it is at this stage that a concession made by the Inspector should be considered. The company contends that for the purpose of part IV of the Corporation Tax Act 1976, the concentrates represent 'goods'. This appears to have been conceded by the Inspector. The company argues that goods are necessarily manufactured. The term 'manufactured' is not defined in the Tax Acts. Accordingly, the normal meaning of the word must be applied. There is no doubt that the use of the word in finding (j) on the basis of the complexity of the process involved in the output of lead and zinc concentrates that the company is engaged in the manufacture of goods. The consideration of *Cronin v Strand Dairies Limited* [1985] 3 ITR 441, *Charles McCann v O'Culachain* [1985] IR 298 and (1986) IR 196; *McCausland v Ministry for Commerce* [1956] NI 367 and *Irish Agricultural Machinery Limited v O'Culachain* [1985] IR 458 and [1990] 1 IR 535 support a wide interpretation of the term manufactured.

Section 54 of the 1976 Act provides that 'goods' means goods manufactured within the State by the person who exports them.

Section 58(1) provides for relief for the export out of the State of goods in the course of trade.

The next subsections detail the said relief and subsection (9), which is central to the consideration of this appeal, provides that the reduction shall not be made under this section in respect of Corporation Tax payable on income from any mining operations.

The concession that the concentrates are 'goods' does not determine whether the output of the company's activities is manufacturing or mining, given the wide definition of each term.

What an analysis of the whole section does show, however, is that a reduction shall not be made in respect of income from any mining operations. Without definition of 'mining operations' and in the absence of a finding by the Commissioners other than the general observation that mining operations could encompass the activities of the company, 'any mining operations' must be interpreted in the broadest manner.

Moreover, the provisions of the Finance (Taxation of Profits of Certain Mines) Act 1974 (which, so far as it relates to income tax, is to be read and constructed together with the Income Taxes Acts and the Corporation Tax Acts) provides allowances for a company carrying on 'the trade of working on a qualifying mine'. There would not seem to be any distinction possible between such trade and 'mining operations'. It is clear that the definition of development expenditure in s 1 of the 1974 Act applies to all of the capital expenditure of the company. Expenditure on works constructed wholly or mainly for subjecting the raw product of the mine to any process except a process designed for preparing the raw product for use as such is excluded. It would seem that the 'manufacturing process' for preparing the raw product for use as such is applicable to the concentrates and is not restricted to the ores which, on the Commissioners findings, have no commercial value.

This would appear to be the effect both of the common construction but also of the policy inherent in the 1974 and 1976 Acts.

It seems, accordingly, that the basis for the Commissioners' decision requires an express finding that the mining operations cease after the extraction of the ore from the mine and its transportation to the storage tepee. It is not sufficient to rely on *Marsden* or *Utah* in this regard.

The general observation that mining operations could encompass the type of activities carried on by the company does restrain the Commissioners from making a clear finding in relation to mining operations. The finding that the concentrates produced as the end product of the company are quite distinct from the ore is not a finding that they are essentially different and do not derive from mining.

The decision of the Commissioners itself would appear to involve a finding which is not supported by facts as found by them. To come broadly to the same conclusion as the Australian Judges in the *Utah* case that, while the company did carry on 'mining operations' on its land not all of its activities could be said to come within the meaning of that phrase is, in my view, not soundly based on facts found.

The second decision would appear to be a finding which is perhaps closer to the facts as found. The Commissioners decided that the mining activity and the manufacturing activity were of similar scale and that neither was subsidiary or incidental to the other. It is the Commissioners' opinion that the manufacturing activity was, in the words of the Judges of the *Broken Hill* case, 'distinct from although connected with the taxpayers mining operations' and did not come within the meaning of the phrase 'mining operations.' They continue as follows:

> While we did not have difficulty in so deciding, we found support for our conclusion in the evidence of the expert witnesses that different branches of science are involved in the mining activity and the manufacturing process, each branch of which requires separate training and education of its specialist.

The finding that the Manager of the mining division's responsibilities end at that point and that the Manager of the processing division is responsible for all activities after the ore arrives in the tepe including the manufacture of lead and zinc concentrates does not, in my view, determine the beginning and end of mining operations, as experts would appear to be uncertain as to the extent of 'mining operations' and such term could encompass all the activities the company.

The decisions of the Commissioners do not accordingly sit firmly on the findings. It may be that, within the decision, there are further latent findings. These further findings seem in turn to be somewhat at variance with the extensive findings found by the Commissioners as such.

I would allow the appeal.

Beverly Cooper-Flynn v RTE, Charlie Bird and James Howard

High Court
Morris J
5 April 2001

Tax evasion- whether James Howard sought to evade his obligation to pay tax by not availing of the tax amnesty – whether he failed to return for tax his investment in the CMI Personal Portfolio – whether Beverly Cooper-Flynn ('the plaintiff') had induced him and others to invest in the CMI Personal Portfolio for the purpose of evading tax – issue of costs – whether plaintiff's reputation had suffered – whether costs should follow the decision – whether special causes apply – whether plaintiff obtained something of value – whether inconsistencies in evidence of defendants amounted to a special cause.

This action came before the High Court for determination of costs to be paid by the plaintiff. The libel trial before the jury lasted 28 days. The jury found that:

(i) the plaintiff did not induce James Howard to evade his lawful tax obligation by not availing of the tax amnesty.

(ii) the plaintiff had advised or encouraged other individuals to evade tax.

(iii) the plaintiff's reputation had not suffered as a result of the RTE publication and

(iv) awarded nil damages.

The plaintiff denied having any dealings with James Howard and because she was targeted by Charlie Bird and RTE she had little alternative but to institute libel proceedings. Although she obtained a favourable answer to question No 1 the Superior Court Rules provide that the costs shall be paid to the winning party unless the Court for special cause directs otherwise.

It is submitted on behalf of the plaintiff that there are special causes, firstly in the finding by the jury that the plaintiff did not speak the words alleged to James Howard and secondly the inconsistencies and frailties in the evidence of Charlie Bird.

The first cause might be considered to be 'something of value' but the finding in favour of the plaintiff is rendered valueless by the other finding that the plaintiff had advised and encouraged other individuals to evade their tax liabilities. The inconsistencies and frailties are not of such a grievous nature as to justify a departure from the general rule as to costs, particularly in view of the absence of damages.

The submission on behalf of the defendants is that a 'cause of action' only arises when defamatory matter is published causing damage to the plaintiff's character. The jury found that the plaintiff's character had suffered no material damage.

Held by Morris J in awarding the defendants their costs against the plaintiff that the general rule is that costs follow the event and there are no special causes to justify a departure from the general rule.

Legislation:
Rules of the Superior Courts 1986 (SI 1986/15), Order 99, rule 1

Cases referred to in judgement:
Reynolds v Times Newspapers & Others [1998] 3 All ER 961
Roache v Newsgroup Newspapers Ltd & Others [1998] EMLR 161

High Court – 5 April 2001

Morris J, This matter now comes before the court for a determination on the issue of costs.

The action was heard before a jury over a period of 28 days. The plaintiff claimed that she was libelled in a number of television and radio broadcasts in which it was alleged that she induced the Third Named defendant to evade his lawful obligations to pay tax by not availing of the tax amnesty and moreover declined to return an investment which he had made in the CMI Personal Portfolio to him for the purpose of paying the tax. It was also alleged that she had induced others to invest in the CMI Personal Portfolio and had pointed out to them in the course of doing so the advantages which the investment had for tax evasion.

The plaintiff denied ever having spoken to Mr Howard and in particular denied ever making the statements which he attributed to her. Moreover she denied ever advising or encouraging other persons to purchase the CMI Personal Portfolio for the purpose of evading tax.

The following questions were put to the jury at the end of the case:

> (1) Had the defendants proved that the plaintiff induced the Third Named defendant to evade his lawful obligation to pay tax by not availing of the tax amnesty. To this question the jury answered 'No.'

The questions went on: If the answer is 'No' proceed to question No 2. If the answer is 'Yes' proceed no further.

> (2) Have the defendants proved that the plaintiff advised or encouraged other persons being those referred to in the evidence to evade tax. To this the jury answered 'Yes'.

In view of this finding and the finding on question (3) namely that the plaintiff's reputation had not suffered as a result of the publication to Mr Howard's question (4) was not of relevance.

To question (5) the question as to damages, the jury answered 'Nil'.

It will be seen therefore that the first matter that was in contention between the Parties namely what conversation, if any, took place between the plaintiff and Mr Howard was answered in her favour. It is correct to say that it was the broadcasting of this alleged conversation on a number of occasions by RTE which brought this matter to a head. It is also correct to say that notwithstanding the plaintiff's repeated denials that any such conversation took place and notwithstanding her demands for a withdrawal and an apology RTE continued to broadcast this report both on radio and on television.

It is probably correct to say that it was because of the fact that the Second Named defendant, Mr Charlie Bird targeted the plaintiff and in his reports repeated the allegations that the plaintiff had little option since she is a member of Dáil Éireann and was a member of the Public Accounts Committee she was left with little alternative but to appropriately react to the allegations.

She instituted proceedings claiming damages for liable against RTE, Mr Bird and Mr Howard.

In determining the issue of costs Counsel for the plaintiff makes the case that by obtaining a favourable answer to question No 1 the plaintiff has been to a large extent successful in her action even though the jury have not awarded damages.

Order 99 Rule 1 of the Rules of the Superior Courts provides:

> Subject to the provisions of the Acts and any other Statutes relating to costs and accept as otherwise provided by these Rules (3) the costs of every action, question or issue tried by a Jury shall follow the event unless the court, for special cause to be mentioned in the Order, shall otherwise direct.

It is important, I believe, in considering the leading text book on this topic, *Gatley on Libel and Slander* to which I have been referred to appreciate that many of the clear statements of law contained on the section relating to costs are based upon the English Rules of Court. Having read the relevant Rules of Court which are referred to in the Judgment of Sir Thomas Bingham Master of the Rolls in *Roache v Newsgroup Newspapers Limited & Others* [1998] EMLR 161 I am satisfied that the English Rules of Court allow the Trial Judge a greater discretion on the question of costs than the Rules of the Superior Courts in this Jurisdiction. Here, as has been seen, it is provided that costs follow the event, that is to say that the Winning Party is to obtain an Order for costs to be paid by the other Party, unless the court for special cause otherwise directs.

Counsel for the plaintiff makes two submissions which he says constitute 'special cause' within the meaning of the Rule and therefore even if the court were to hold that the defendants had succeeded in the action there was justification for the court departing from the general rule. These special causes are as follows:

(a) It is submitted that a fundamental issue that developed during the hearing and is identified as such in that it is allocated a special question on the issue paper (question 1) is whether the plaintiff spoke the words alleged to Mr Howard. He submits that the plaintiff has succeeded in this issue and that the court is required to have regard to this and treat it as a 'special cause' within the Rule.

(b) The second basis upon which Counsel submits that there is 'special cause' in the case is, in a variety of ways, the conduct of the defendants both before and during the case and the manner in which the case was met in court. I shall deal with these matters later on.

With regard to Counsel's first submission:

I have been referred by Counsel to *Reynolds v Times Newspapers & Others* [1998] 3 All ER 961 where the Court of Appeal in England had to consider a situation similar to that which arises in this case. The plaintiff instituted proceedings claiming damages for an allegation which he alleged amounted to dishonesty on his part. At the hearing the question left to the jury was 'Is the allegation complained of by the plaintiff in substance true?' To this the jury answered 'No'. This represented a major success for the plaintiff however the Jury went on to award the plaintiff no damages.

Among the issues which went on appeal was the decision of the trial judge on the question of costs. He refused the defendants their costs of the action up to the date upon which they had made a lodgment in court. The basis upon which the trial judge founded that decision was that by obtaining a favourable verdict on the first question and notwithstanding the fact that the plaintiff had been awarded no damages he had nevertheless obtained 'something of value'.

This phrase 'something of value' had its origin in *Roache v Newsgroup Newspapers Limited*. In that case the plaintiff in a defamation action obtained a favourable verdict but only obtained the same award of damages as the amount lodged in court and the issue arose as to whether he had in fact obtained 'something of value' by the favourable verdict.

In *Reynolds v Times Newspapers* the Court of Appeal ordered a retrial of the plaintiff's action but had this to say in relation to the Judge's decision on costs.

> Since this Court is ordering a retrial, and the costs below will be at the discretion of the Judge at the retrial, it is not necessary for us to express a definite view on this cross appeal. However we are of the clear opinion that, had the Judge awarded the defendants the whole of their costs, it would not have been right to interfere with such an Order; and we are doubtful whether, in the light of the jurys' answers, the way in which the Judge actually exercised his discretion could be supported. The Judge did not give any subsidiary reasons relating to the conduct of the trial. The only reason which he gave, that the defendant did obtain 'something of value' from the jury's first question seems to be contradicted by Mr Reynolds' failure to obtain any real vindication.

While decisions in another jurisdiction are in no way binding on me as is the practice in all Jurisdictions regard is had to decisions in other jurisdictions and if they are found to be persuasive they are followed.

In the present case the issue which I have to consider is whether by obtaining a finding from the jury that she did not induce Mr Howard to evade paying his lawful taxes the plaintiff has obtained something of value.

It is beyond doubt that if this were the only issue in the case it would be of immeasurable value but coupled with the finding of the jury that she had in fact advised and encouraged other persons namely Mr Duff, Mr Rowe, Mrs Quigley and Ms Hawe to evade tax the finding is in my view valueless and accordingly does not constitute 'special cause' for the purposes of the Rule.

With regard to the second point raised by Counsel:

Counsel for the plaintiff points to a variety of ways in which he says the conduct of the defendants was such as to bring the case within the definition of 'special cause'. He points, for instance, to what he alleges was the failure of Mr Bird to check on the story before he broadcast it. He submits that an examination of the papers associated with the case would have shown the name of Patricia Roche on the papers and alert him to the likelihood that the story was false. He points to the fact that Mr Howard was in error in a number of the details which he provided in relation to the investment. He points to the fact that Mr Bird targeted Ms Cooper-Flynn by advertising in the local paper, circulating in the area in which Ms Cooper-Flynn did business. He points to what he describes as the information which he received from 'an anonymous source' and finally he points to what he submits are inconsistencies and frailties in Mr Bird's evidence which bring the matter within the definition of 'special cause' and asks the court to depart from the ordinary rule in these circumstances.

I am unable to identify anything in any of the criticisms referred to by Counsel, which may or may not be correct, which are of such a grievous nature as could cause me to depart from the general rule. In my view all of these matters would be of extreme relevance if in fact the jury were to address the issue of damages but in this way and in this way only are they of relevance. I accordingly reject Counsel's submissions that there should be a departure from the general rule.

Apart from the submissions advanced on behalf of the plaintiff by Counsel a number of other submissions have been made to me by Counsel on behalf of the defendants which in my view have merit. It is submitted by Counsel on behalf of the first and second named defendant that the resolution of the matters in contention in question No (1) in favour of the plaintiff is of no significance so long as the plaintiff's character has suffered no material damage. He submits that the 'cause of action' only arises when defamatory matter is published causing damage to the plaintiff's character. He submits that since it has been found by the jury that prior to the commencement of the proceedings the plaintiffs character was flawed, that the resolution of question No 1 in her favour is irrelevant. I believe this to be a correct statement of the legal principles involved.

Accordingly the Order that I make is that I enter judgment for the defendants and I award the defendants costs against the plaintiff. The costs will include all reserve costs.

Patrick J O'Connell (Inspector of Taxes) v Thomas Keleghan

Supreme Court
Murphy J
16 May 2001

Case stated – Income Tax (IT) – service contract of sale of shares – binding contract to serve as sale director of Siúcre Éireann ('the Purchaser') – inducement payment of £250,000 – whether taxpayer ever became an employee – whether Purchaser had an interest direct or indirect in the performance of the contract of employment – whether inference of acceptance of agreement – whether payment taxable under ITA 1967 s 110

Capital Gains Tax (CGT) – sale of shares in Gladebrook Ltd by shareholders in 1990 for a consideration in the form of loan notes – loan notes not transferable or assignable – whether CGT chargeable on redemption of loan notes for cash in 1993 – whether loan notes constitute debenture stock – 'paper for paper' transaction and exempt under CGTA 1975 Sch 2 para 4 – whether statutory fiction treats loan notes as shares – whether legislation so provides – whether exemption on disposal of a debt applies – whether loan notes a debt on a security – whether marketable and capable of increasing in value

This appeal by the Inspector of Taxes against the decision of the High Court concerns two issues. The first issue is whether an inducement payment of £250,000 to the taxpayer to take up employment with Siúcre Éireann Cpt ('the Purchaser') was subject to IT pursuant to ITA 1977 s 110. The second issue was whether the redemption of a loan note was subject to CGT in accordance with CGTA 1975 Sch 2 paras 2/4 or exempt as the disposal of a debt under CGTA 1975 s 46(1).

Facts

(i) Thomas Keleghan ('the taxpayer') together with the four other shareholders in Gladebrook Ltd entered into a share purchase agreement dated 8 February 1990 whereby he sold his shareholding for a consideration of £1,867,068 in the form of a loan note which he redeemed for cash in February 1993. This interest bearing loan note was not transferable or assignable.

(ii) On 8 February 1990 the taxpayer who was the sales director of Sugar Distributors (Holdings) Ltd in which Gladebrrok Ltd held a 49% interest entered into a service contract with Siúcre Eireann Cpt ('the company') whereby for a consideration of £250,000 he agreed to serve the company as sales director. He never became an employee of the company but remained as sales director of Sugar Distributors until his retirement in June 1991.

(iii) The above transactions incorporated tax avoidance measures.

The Law

Income tax

ITA 1967 s 110 is a wide ranging provision aimed at taxing all manner of payments to employees. The Appeal Commissioners made a finding of fact that the taxpayer never became an employee of the company and this finding was accepted by the High Court judge. Nevertheless Murphy J held that the Court must infer that Siúcre Éireann were satisfied to accept the continued service of the taxpayer with Sugar Distributors as compliance with his service agreement and hence the £250,000 was a taxable emolument.

Capital gains tax

The sale of the shares in Gladebrook Ltd in return for a loan note issued by the company Siúcre Éireann Cpt gave rise to a capital gain but that gain was not chargeable to CGT by virtue of the 'paper for paper' relieving provision of CGTA 1975 Sch 2 paras 2/4. On redemption of the loan note for cash the points in issue are:

(1) whether the redemption fell to be treated as a disposition of the original shares in Gladebrook and thereby taxable or

(2) whether the disposition fell to be treated as relating to the loan note itself and if so, whether the loan note constituted a debt on a security and thereby taxable.

The 'paper for paper' exemption is a statutory fiction. The contention that the purpose of the fiction is to permit the first transaction to escape tax on the footing that tax would be payable on a subsequent disposition as if no change had taken place in the shareholdings of the parties to the original transaction is not valid in the absence of a specific statutory provision.

There is no statutory definition of a debt on a security but the case law requirement is that such a debt be marketable and have the potential of increasing in value.

Held by Murphy J in allowing the appeal on the IT issue and dismissing the appeal on the CGT issue that:

(i) Notwithstanding the non-fulfilment of the service contract by the taxpayer, it must be inferred that Siúcre Éireann was satisfied to accept the continued service of the taxpayer with Sugar Distributors as compliance with the terms of his service contract.

(ii) Consequently the payment of £250,000 was a taxable emolument pursuant to ITA 1976 s 110.

(iii) The exemption from CGT on the disposal of the shares in Gladebrook Ltd for a loan note arose by virtue of a statutory fiction as provided for under the CGTA 1975 Sch paras 2/4.

(iv) The CGTA does not provide that the disposal of the loan note is to be treated as a disposal of the original shares in Gladebrook Ltd.

(v) There is no necessary requirement in law or in logic for the extension of the statutory fiction to the disposal of the loan notes so as to render the disposal of the loan note a chargeable disposition.

(vi) A debt on a security postulates marketability and a potential to appreciate in value.

(vii) Consequently the loan note herein did not constitute a debt on a security and thereby bring about a charge to CGT.

(viii) The appeal in regard to the IT issue is allowed and the appeal in regard to the CGT issue is dismissed.

Legislation
ITA 1967, ss 110, 428; CGTA 1975, s 46(1), Sch 2 paras 2/4

Cases referred to in judgment
Shilton v Wilmhurst [1991] STC 88
Aberdeen Construction Ltd v CIR 52 TC 281
CIR v Metrolands 54 TC 679
Cleveleys Investment Trust Co v CIR 47 TC 3000
Eastend Dwellings Co Ltd v Finsbury Borough Council [1953] AC 109
Holt v IRC [1953] 1 WLR 1492
McSweeney v Mooney [1997] 3 IR 424
Taylor Clark International Ltd v Lewis [1998] STC 1259
WT Ramsey Ltd v CIR 54 TC 101

Note

The statutory definition of a debt on a security was amended by FA 1996 s 61 (TCA 1997 s 541(7)) to provide that debentures or loan notes issued in exempted 'paper for paper' exchanges are treated as chargeable assets on subsequent disposals.

Supreme Court - 16 May 2001

Murphy J, The case stated under s 428 of the Income Tax Act 1968, by John O'Callaghan and Ronan Kelly, the Appeal Commissioners, on the 29th day of September, 1 999, for the opinion of the High Court sets out in detail the facts and findings in this matter and the issues which arise thereon. They may be summarised as follows.

A company called Gladebrook Limited held 49% of the share capital of Sugar Distributors (Holdings) Limited ('Holdings') which in turn held 100% of the share capital of Sugar Distributors Limited ('Distributors').

In 1990 the issued share capital in Gladebrook was £10,000 divided into 10,000 shares of £1 each which were held and registered in the name of five persons (hereinafter called the Vendors) of whom the above named Thomas Keleghan (Mr Keleghan) was one. Mr Keleghan was the registered owner of 2,151 of those shares. By an agreement in writing dated the 8th day of February 1990, the Vendors agreed with Siúcre Éireann (therein and hereinafter sometimes called 'the Purchaser') for the sale to the Purchaser of the issued share capital in Gladebrook for the sum of £8,680,000 to be paid to the Vendors in the proportions set out in the third column of Schedule I to that agreement and on the express terms that:

> The purchase consideration shall be satisfied by the issue by the Purchaser on completion of the Loan Notes to the Vendors.

The proportion of the purchase consideration to be paid to Mr Keleghan amounted to £1,867,068. The 'loan notes' were defined as being the loan notes set out in Schedule VIII to the agreement.

The loan notes took the form of a certificate to which an identifying number was ascribed and a particular amount inserted. The Certificate stated that the documentation was:

> Issued pursuant to a resolution of the Board of Directors of Siúcre Éireann having its registered office at Stephen's Green, Dublin 2 passed on the day of February 1990.

It then provides space for the name and address of the holder of the note followed by a statement in the following terms:

> This is to certify that the above named is/are the registered holder (S) of Irish pounds nominal amount of the loan notes of Siúcre Éireann Cpt. The holders of the loan notes are entitled to the benefit of and are subject to the conditions hereinafter contained.

There is then provision for the certificate to be sealed by Siúcre Éireann and dated. That is followed by the significant annotation:

> No loan note or any part thereof is transferable or assignable by any note holder.

The financial provisions contained in the conditions on which the notes were issued are simple. First, there is provision for the payment of interest on notes not redeemed on or after the 31 October 1991, secondly, for interest at a rate equal to the Dublin Inter Bank Offered Rate for six months funds (DIBOR) and, thirdly, there is provision that the note holders may elect at any time to have loan notes redeemed in whole or in part by Siúcre Éireann on 30 days notice: the earliest date for redemption being the 1 November 1991 and the latest date for redemption the 31 October 1997. All notes outstanding on the 31 October 1997, must then be redeemed in full. The conditions provide in considerable detail for the issue - and where necessary the replacement - of certificates to the holders of the loan notes. There is also provision for the maintenance of a register of holders of the loan notes and the details to be kept in that register. There is provision for transmission of the loan notes on the death or bankruptcy of a note holder but the conditions repeat in clause 8 the express prohibition on transfer in the following terms:

> Except in the case of the death of a note holder no loan note or any part thereof shall be transferable or assignable by any note holder.

Neither the certificate nor the conditions make any reference to conversion rights attaching to the loan notes. The share purchase agreement, however, expressly provides that in the event of a public floatation or a private placing of shares in the Purchaser the loan notes may be converted into ordinary shares of the Purchaser on the basis of £100 of note for every £100 of shares provided that the floatation or placing takes place after the 1 October 1991, but on the basis that a discounted value will be attributed to the loan notes in the event of the floatation or placing occurring between the date of the share purchase agreement and the 1 October 1991.

Superficially the loan notes and the conditions on which they were issued bear considerable similarity to debenture stock. The fact that the indebtedness secured by the loan notes is not charged on property of the Purchaser might be unusual in practice but unexceptional in principle. What is more surprising is the inclusion of the standard conditions dealing with the issue of certificates and the registration of owners, which are procedures ordinarily designed to facilitate marketability, coupled with an express prohibition on assignment and transfer. This apparent contradiction is not due to any error or oversight. I will return to this aspect of the matter later.

On the same date as the share purchase agreement, the 8 February 1990, Mr Keleghan executed a service agreement with the Purchaser as required by the provisions of the share purchase agreement. Under the service agreement Mr Keleghan was bound to serve the Purchaser for a term of 18 months expiring on the 30 June 1991, and thereafter until termination by either party giving three months notice to the other of them. Whilst the agreement provided that Mr Keleghan 'shall serve the company as sales director' at clause 2 (E) it was stated that:

> In pursuance of his duties hereunder [Mr Keleghan shall] perform such services for subsidiary companies or any parent company and (without further remuneration unless otherwise agreed)

accept and hold for the duration of this agreement such offices or appointments in such subsidiary companies as the general manager may from time to time reasonably require.

The service agreement does contain covenants in restraint of competition to which some importance was attached but those covenants do not differ significantly from those to which Mr Keleghan was committed under the share purchase agreement.

The final document to which reference must be made is the 'side letter' also dated the 5 February 1990, signed by Mr Keleghan. By that letter he expressly recognised that of the purchase price payable to him in respect of his share holding in Gladebrook £250,000 'was paid as an inducement for me to enter into the service contract (as defined in the share purchase agreement) and accordingly in the event of my not complying with the terms of the said service contract that portion of the £250,000 purchase consideration attributable to the sale of my shares in Gladebrook Limited will become repayable by me to Siúcre Éireann Cpt.

Apparently the transfer of the shares in Gladebrook to the Purchaser was completed in February 1990, and the loan notes issued to the Vendors on the same date. Mr Keleghan's loan note was ultimately redeemed for cash by the Purchaser in February 1993. The Appeal Commissioners expressly found that Mr Keleghan never became an employee of the Purchaser. Before signing the service agreement he had been sales director of Distributors and he remained in that capacity until his retirement in June 1991, when he attained the age of 65 years. Distributors were of course a wholly owned subsidiary of Holdings which in turn had become a wholly owned subsidiary of the Purchaser.

If Mr Keleghan had sold his shares in Gladebrook in 1990 for £1.8m in cash (whether payable immediately or at a later date) or, indeed, if he had exchanged his share holding for other assets, prima facie this would have constituted a disposal for the purposes of the Capital Gains Tax Act 1975, and rendered Mr Keleghan liable to tax on the difference between the sale price of his share holding and the cost of acquiring it. It is common case - agreed by both Mr Keleghan and the Revenue Authorities - that the exchange of the shares with the Purchaser was exempt from Capital Gains Tax on the grounds that the transaction fell within paragraph 4 of the Second Schedule to Act of 1975. That paragraph - so far as material - provides as follows:

> 4(1) Subject to paragraph 5, where a company issues shares or debentures to a person in exchange for shares in or debentures of another company, paragraph 2 shall apply with any necessary adaptations as if the two companies were the same company and the exchange were a reorganisation of its share capital.
>
> (2) This paragraph shall apply only where the company issuing the shares or debentures has or in consequence of the exchange will have control of the other company ...

Those parts of paragraph 2 which would appear to be relevant to the present proceedings are as follows:

> 2(1) This paragraph shall apply in relation to any reorganisation or reduction of a company's share capital, and in this paragraph –
>
> (a) references to a reorganisation of a company's share capital include -
>
>   (i) any case where persons are, whether for payment or not, allotted shares in or debentures of the company in respect of and in proportion to (or as nearly as may be in proportion to) their holdings of shares in the company or of any class of shares in the company; and
>
>   (ii) any case where there are more than one class of shares and the rights attached to shares of any class are altered; and

(b) 'original shares' means shares held before and concerned in the reorganisation or reduction of capital, and 'new holding' means, in relation to any original shares, the shares in and debentures of the company which as a result of the reorganisation or reduction of capital represent the original shares (including such, if any, of the original shares as remain).

(2) Subject to the following subparagraphs, a reorganisation or reduction of a company's share capital shall not be treated as involving any disposal of the original shares or any acquisition of the new holding or any part of it but the original shares (taken as a single asset) and the new holding (taken as a single asset) shall be treated as the same asset acquired as the original shares were acquired.

(3) ....

(4) ...

(5) Where, for the purpose of computing the gain or loss accruing to a person from the acquisition and disposal of any part of the new holding, it is necessary to apportion the cost of acquisition of any of the original shares between the part which is disposed of and the part which is retained, the apportionment shall be made by reference to market value at the date of the disposal (with such adjustment of the market value of any part of the new holding as may be required to offset any liability attaching thereto but forming part of the cost to be apportioned); and any corresponding apportionment for the purposes of subparagraph (4) shall be made in like manner.

(6) ...

(7) ...

(8) ...

(9) ...

It was conceded by the Revenue Authorities that the Loan Notes in the Purchaser constituted 'debentures' for the purposes of paragraph 4 aforesaid with the result that the exchange of the shares in Gladebrook (the original shares) for the Loan Notes (the new Holding) did not fall to be treated as involving any disposal of the original shares or the acquisition of the new Holding. The issue was whether the ultimate redemption of the new holding in 1993 was a disposal or whether it too was exempt this time by virtue of s 46 of the Act of 1975 which so far as material provides as follows:

46(1) Where a person incurs a debt to another (that is, the original creditor), whether in Irish currency or in some other currency, no chargeable gain shall accrue to that creditor or his personal representative or legatee on a disposal of the debt:

Provided that this subsection shall not apply in the case of the debt on a security as defined in paragraph 3 of Schedule 2 (conversion of securities).

(2) Subject to the provisions of the said paragraph 3 and of paragraph 4 of Schedule 2 (company amalgamations), and subject to the foregoing subsection, the satisfaction of a debt or part of it (including a debt on a security as defined in the said paragraph 3) shall be treated as a disposal of the debt or of that part by the creditor made at the time when the debt or that part is satisfied.

Notwithstanding the complex cross-references contained therein it seems reasonably clear that s 46 deems no chargeable gain to accrue on the disposition or satisfaction of debts generally but that exemption does not extend to the disposition or satisfaction of a 'debt on a security'. Unhappily the latter phrase is not defined in the Act although the word 'security' is defined in paragraph 3 of Schedule 2 as including:

Any loan stock or similar security whether of any government or of any public or local authority or of any company and whether secured or unsecured but excluding securities falling within section 19.

In those circumstances two questions arose in relation to Capital Gains Tax, namely,

1. Whether the redemption in 1993 of the Loan Notes fell to be treated as a disposition of the original shares, that is to say, the Gladebrook shares, in which CGT was clearly payable, or

2. Whether the disposition fell to be treated as relating to the Loan Notes themselves and, if so, whether the Notes constituted a 'debt on security' in which event - but only in that event - CGT was likewise payable.

The other issue which arose on the case stated was whether the sum of £250,000 which, as appears from the side letter, was paid to Mr Keleghan by the Purchaser as an inducement to influence him to join the employment of the Purchaser was taxable on him under s 110 of the Income Tax Act 1967.

Both questions were answered by McCracken J in favour of Mr Keleghan. From that decision the Inspector of Taxes has appealed to this Court.

Like the learned trial Judge I will deal first with the income tax issue.

It is common case that if the sum of £250,000 were to be liable to tax such a liability would arise under s 110 of the Income Tax Act 1967, (as amended) or not at all. Subsection 1(1) of that section reads as follows:

> Tax under Schedule E shall be annually charged on every person having or exercising an office or employment of profit mentioned in that Schedule, or to whom any annuity, pension or stipend, chargeable under that Schedule, is payable, in respect of all salaries, fees, wages, perquisites or profits whatsoever therefrom and shall be computed on the amount of all such salaries, fees, wages, perquisites or profits whatsoever therefrom for the year of assessment.

McCracken J dealt shortly and clearly with the application of Section to the facts of the present case in the following terms:

> This being a case stated, I am bound by the facts as found by the Appeal Commissioners, in particular I must accept that the respondent was never employed by the Purchaser. The section imposes the charge on persons having or exercising an office or employment of profit in respect of income of various kinds received by him 'therefrom', that is from the office or employment of profit. If he had no such office or employment, he could have received no income therefrom, and therefore could have no liability under schedule E.

It may be helpful to consider that conclusion in the context of the analysis made by the House of Lords in *Shilton v Wilmshurst* [1991] STC 88 of somewhat analogous problems of fact and law.

Mr Shilton was a well-known football player under contract to Nottingham Forest Football Club in 1982. With a view to raising money, Nottingham agreed to transfer Mr Shilton, subject to his consent, to Southampton Football Club. The manager of Nottingham informed Mr Shilton that they would pay him a sum of £75,000 if he consented to the transfer. The Inspector of Taxes assessed that sum of £75,000 under schedule E pursuant to s 181(1) of the UK Income and Corporation Taxes Act 1970 (which is similar to s 110 of the Irish Act of 1967). The General Commissioners upheld the assessment. In the High Court Morritt J allowed the tax payer's appeal and the Court of Appeal upheld the decision of Morritt J. The House of Lords allowed the appeal from the Court of Appeal and reinstated the decision of the General Commissioners. The issues in the *Shilton* case were not as complex as that legal history might suggest. In the High Court Morritt J having analysed the facts and the material authorities concluded (at p 877) that:

> A payment by a third party may nevertheless be an emolument from the employment where the payer has an interest direct or indirect in the performance of the contract of employment either in the past as in the case of tips or in the future as in the case of the *Pritchard v Arundale* case itself.

> But in this case Nottingham Forest were only concerned that the taxpayer should enter into a contract of employment with Southampton in order that Nottingham Forest should obtain the agreed transfer fee from Southampton. Thereafter Nottingham Forest had no concern or interest direct or indirect in performance of that contract.

> In my judgment, in those circumstances the payment by Nottingham Forest to the taxpayer was not as the Commissioners concluded 'an emolument flowing from that service which he was to render to Southampton', nor was it an emolument 'from' his employment by or with Southampton within the meaning of section 181(1) of the Income and Corporation Taxes Act 1970 ....

Whilst the Court of Appeal recognised that payments made by third parties to persons who were in the employment of another - such as tips to waiters or taxi drivers - were emoluments of the recipient taxable under Schedule E they endorsed the reasoning and conclusion of Morritt J.

The unanimous decision of the House of Lords was delivered in the speech of Lord Templeman who noted that the Court of Appeal had accepted that payments made to an employee by a person other than his employer might be liable to tax under Schedule E but subject to the qualification that such liability could only arise 'where the payer has an interest direct or indirect in the performance of the contract of employment'. The House of Lords rejected that qualification pointing out that there was nothing in s 181 of the UK legislation to justify that inference. I believe that the law so stated in the judgment of Lord Templeman in this respect is a correct statement of the law in this jurisdiction.

No doubt that there are many cases in which it would be important to ascertain why money is paid to an employee by a person who is not his employer. A question might arise as to whether the payment was a non taxable gift or a payment relating to some entirely different action or activity which might give rise to no liability to tax or alternatively to taxation on a different basis or with the benefit of particular allowances. However, the fact that it was a matter of indifference to Nottingham whether in playing for Southampton Peter Shilton never scored a goal or, more correctly, never saved one, did not affect the nature and purpose of the payment of the sum of £75,000. That sum was paid by Nottingham to induce Mr Shilton to play for Southampton and thus achieve the ulterior motive of Nottingham, if it may be so described, of obtaining a substantial transfer fee. The payment by Nottingham was nonetheless as much a payment to induce him to join Southampton as the signing-on fee paid by that club to Mr Shilton.

Of course Peter Shilton did play for Southampton whereas Mr Keleghan never took up employment with Siúcre Éireann. The Appeal Commissioners have found that as a fact and indeed there is no reason to believe that it was ever disputed that Mr Keleghan had been prior to the share exchange and until his ultimate retirement in June 1991, an employee of Distributors and never an employee of Siúcre Éireann. Nevertheless, regard must be had to the fact that he expressly and in writing agreed to enter into a service contract with Siúcre Éireann and for that was paid a sum of £250,000. There was also the provision for the repayment of that sum if the transaction was not consummated. Whilst there is no specific finding in relation to it, I understand that it is agreed that the payment of that sum was never sought or made. If it had been repaid the question of taxation would not arise. Whilst tax legislation frequently proceeds on the basis of legal fictions, as has already been noted, and legitimate tax avoidance arrangements may well demand the implementation of transactions which would not be justified on purely commercial considerations, I think that the Court must infer that Siúcre Éireann were satisfied to accept the continued service of Mr Keleghan with Distributors as compliance with the terms of his service agreement and in particular clause 2(e) thereof. The alternative interpretation would be to treat the payment as one made for a consideration which wholly failed or else as a gift the validity of which might be open to question. These alternatives are neither attractive nor compelling. In my view the payment of £250,000 by Siúcre Éireann or the treatment of that sum as having been so paid in accordance with the provisions of the side letter resulted in a taxable emolument in the hands of Mr Keleghan which is prima facie liable to tax under Schedule E. Accordingly I would allow the appeal in that regard. However, an issue as to whether the assessment was raised in relation to the correct year is recorded in the Case Stated. As that issue was not resolved in the judgment of the learned trial Judge it must now be remitted to the High Court for further consideration.

The issues in relation to Capital Gains Tax are even more complex. It is common case that the initial transaction by which the Gladebrook shares were exchanged for the Loan Notes did not give rise to a liability for CGT. By an exception or statutory fiction provided for in paragraph 2 of the second schedule to the Act of 1974 that exchange was deemed not to be a disposal for the purposes of the Act of 1974. The first issue between the parties in this connection was whether that statutory fiction extended to the transaction which occurred in February 1983. When Mr Keleghan was paid the redemption sum in February 1993 was he to be treated as disposing of shares in Gladebrook or Loan Notes in Siúcre Éireann? Mr Keleghan correctly points out that there is nothing in Schedule 2 expressly extending the statutory fiction to the ultimate disposition of the asset received in exchange for the original share holding whereas the Appellant argues it must be accepted that the statutory 'fiction'extends to or revives on the realisation of the asset received in exchange. It is agreed that if the realisation gave rise to a chargeable gain the amount thereof would have to be calculated by reference to the cost of acquisition of the Gladebrook shares. The issue was whether the statutory fiction requires the Loan Notes to be treated as retaining the character, and indeed the identity of the Gladebrook shares, as well as having been acquired at the same cost as those shares.

The Appellants drew attention to Lord Asquith's admonition in *Eastend Dwellings Company Lid v Finsbury Borough Council* [1952] AC 109 in the following terms:

> If you are bidden to treat an imaginary state of affairs as real, you must surely, unless prohibited from doing so, also imagine as real the consequences and incidents which, if the putative state of affairs had in fact existed, must inevitably have flowed from or accompanied it The statute says that you must imagine a state of affairs; it does not say that having done so, you must cause or permit your imagination to boggle when it comes to the inevitable corollaries of that state of affairs.

Having quoted that passage Nourse J in *CIR v Metrolands* 54 TC 679 went on to explain as follows:

> When considering the extent to which a deeming provision should be applied, the Court is entitled and bound to ascertain for what purpose and between what persons the statutory fiction is to be resorted to. It will not always be clear what those purposes are. If the application of the provision would lead to an unjust, anomalous or absurd result, then, unless

its application would clearly be within the purposes of the fiction, it should not be applied. If, on the other hand, its application would not lead to any such result then, unless that would clearly be outside the purposes of the fiction, it should be applied.

That legislation may and does from time to time deem acts or events to be what they are not is common particularly in legislation imposing taxation or seeking to prevent its avoidance.

There is no reason why the Courts would not enforce such legislative fictions as fully and faithfully as any other legislation or 'boggle when it comes to the inevitable corollaries' of the fiction. The Courts are not unaccustomed to dealing with notional or hypothetical situations or (in the words of Danckwert J in *Holt* (1953) 1 WLR 1488 at 1492) entering 'into a dim world peopled by the indeterminate spirits of fictitious or unborn sales'. If the second schedule to the Act of 1975 requires that the Loan Notes should be deemed to be or treated as if they were shares in Gladebrook Limited so be it. The difficulty from the Appellant's point of view is that the legislation does not so provide and the only justification for accepting that fiction would be the alleged purpose of the particular legislation. It was contended that the purpose of the fiction was to permit the first transaction to escape tax on the footing that tax would be payable on a subsequent disposition as if no change had taken place in the share holdings of the parties to the original transaction.

In my view the requirement to treat the disposal of the Loan Notes in February 1993, as a disposal in substance of shares in Gladebrook Limited is in no sense a consequence or a corollary of the original fiction which deemed the exchange not to be a disposition or of the further 'selective' fiction requiring the cost price of the Gladebrook shares to be that of the Loan Notes. There was no necessary requirement in law or in logic for the extension of the fiction. The Legislature might well have been content to impose tax by reference to the price which might be expected to be obtained for the asset received in exchange for the original share holding. In my view the learned trial Judge was correct in concluding that the asset realised by way of redemption in February 1993, was in law, as it was in fact, a disposition of the Loan Notes which had been issued to Mr Keleghan for his shares in Gladebrook Limited.

The remaining question is whether the Siúcre Éireann Loan Notes constituted a 'debt on a security' within the meaning of s 46(1) of the 1975 Act.

The learned trial Judge understandably lamented the absence of any statutory definition of that crucial phrase. He did recognise, correctly, in my view that as a debt on a security is treated differently from an ordinary debt it must have some distinctive feature or features. What constitutes a 'debt on a security' for the purposes of the Act of 1975 was considered by Morris J (as he then was) in *McSweeney v Mooney* [1997] 3 IR 424 and the same expression as used in virtually identical legislation was considered in a series of English cases of the highest persuasive authority including *Cleveleys Investment Trust Company v CIR* 47 TC 300; *Aberdeen Construction Group Ltd v CIR* 52 TC 281; *WT Ramsey Ltd v CIR* 54 TC 101 and *Taylor Clark International Ltd v Lewis* [1998] STC 1259. All of these cases demonstrate that the term does not admit of any fully satisfactory definition or explanation. Furthermore, there is the difficulty that it is not possible to pray in aid the principle that taxation should not be imposed in the absence of clear wording because the existence of a debt due on a security (as opposed to an ordinary debt) will in some cases impose a liability to tax and in others create a deductible allowance.

The decision of the Court of Appeal in *Taylor Clark International Ltd v Lewis* (above), contained in the judgment delivered in November 1998 by Peter Gibson LJ has the advantage that it reviews and seeks to reconcile the earlier English and Scottish authorities which had grappled with this problem. The learned Lord Justice analysed the variety of features which it had been contended were material in determining whether a debt would properly be described for the purposes of the Capital Gains Tax legislation as a 'debt on a security'.

Much of the judgment in *Taylor Clark* was devoted to a consideration of whether the existence of a charge on property or a guarantee (which were described as a proprietorial securities) was an essential ingredient of the statutory 'debt' on a security. Considerable debate had taken place in the earlier authorities as to whether the presence or absence of a proprietorial security was of decisive importance. Peter Gibson LJ, concluded on both precedent and principle that such a security had little or no significance in determining whether a particular transaction constituted a debt on a security. The relevance (or irrelevance) of a proprietorial security was dealt with by Peter Gibson LJ, in the concluding part of his judgment on that aspect of the matter (at p 1271) in the following terms:

> I agree with the submissions of Mr Henderson QC for the Crown that while the existence of proprietary security for a debt should increase the original lender's chances of avoiding a loss, that security does not of itself turn the loan into an asset which is in principle capable of being disposed of at a profit. As he said, Parliament could not have intended that the existence of any security, however inadequate, for any debt, however impermanent, should without any more turn the debt into a debt on a security.

In the Court of Appeal it was noted that the Judge of first instance had identified certain features of a debt on a security which Peter Gibson LJ, summarised (at page 1271) as follows:

> The judge ([1997] STC 499 at 520/521) identified three principal characteristics of a debt on a security which the courts have so far had to consider: (1) The indicia of loan stock, one irreducible minimum requirement being that the debt should be capable of being assigned so as to realise a gain for the original creditor; (2) The debt should bear interest; (3) A structure of permanence.

The learned Judge then turned to consider the terms of the particular loan made by *Taylor Clark* in the light of those characteristics which he clearly accepted as helpful if not necessarily decisive.

The loan made by *Taylor Clark* was, as counsel on their behalf emphasised, secured; it was evidenced in writing in the form of promissory note; it was assignable. The monies advanced were to be used for property development purposes. On the other hand counsel on behalf of the Revenue Authorities pointed out that the creditor or the debtor could bring the transaction to an end at any time.

As in earlier cases some doubt was cast upon the relevance of provisions dealing with the assignment of the debt in whole or in part. It was noted that equity would recognise an assignment of part of the benefit of the loan even though the express provisions for assignment did not extend to such an arrangement.

The features of the loan in the *Taylor Clark* case which might have pointed to the degree of marketability which would have qualified it as a debt on a security were, in the judgment of the Court of Appeal, wholly outweighed by the impermanence of the transaction which appears to have been the most important but not the only factor influencing the decision of the Court to reject the claim by the taxpayer.

Though the judgment of the Court of Appeal in *Taylor Clark* is helpful it does seem to me that the decision in *McSweeney v Mooney* [1997] 3 IR 424 provides clearer guidance as to what constitutes a debt on a security for the purposes of the Capital Gains Tax Act 1975.

Having analysed the UK cases and in particular the decision of the High Court in the *Taylor Clark* case Morris J (as he then was) he went on to say (at p 429):

> The essence of a loan on a security must be whether the additional 'bundle of rights' acquired with the granting of the loan, to use Lord Wilberforce's phrase, enhances the loan, so as to make it marketable and potentially more valuable than the value of the repaid loan upon repayment. This potential increase in value must not be illusory or theoretical. It must be realistic at the time of the loan and the rights are acquired by the lender.

The legal and logical justification for that approach had been dealt with in the previous page of the report in the following terms:

> In *WT Ramsay v Inland Revenue Commissioners* [1981] 2 WL.R 449, Lord Wilberforce referred at p.462 of the report to debts on a security as 'debts with added characteristics such as enable them to be realised, or dealt with at a profit' and in *Aberdeen Construction Group v IRC* [1978] AC 885 at 895, to be a debt which has 'such characteristics as enable it to be dealt in and, if necessary, converted into shares or other securities.
>
> In my view, these are the elements which identify a debt on a security. This, seems to be to be no more than common sense. The pure loan is exempt from capital gains tax because it can never exceed in value (sic). With the additional rights to be converted into stock, a debt on a security, may appreciate in value and can be marketed at a profit. This is a clear distinction between the two.

Whilst the right to assign a debt in whole or in part and the arrangements made to facilitate such an assignment may be material in determining whether a particular debt has the requisite characteristic of marketability the clear analysis provided by the President shows the decisive importance of the underlying commercial potential of the debt to appreciate in value if it is to qualify as a 'debt on a security' for Capital Gains Tax purposes.

In the present case the terms of the Loan Notes are in a sense contradictory. They adopt a number of clauses which would suggest that the company by which they were issued intended them to be marketable. These clauses are effectively negatived by the unequivocal prohibition on assignment. However, more significant are the commercial terms of the loan. The period of the loan is nearly six years and to that extent the transaction is distinguishable from the *Taylor Clark* case. The loan does carry interest but it is limited to DIBOR (now the Euribor) rate from time to time. Apart from the modest rate of such interest, the fact that it would fluctuate with public financial conditions suggests that there could be no capital appreciation on the debt over the period of the loan. Certainly no expert evidence was adduced at the hearing before the Appeal Commissioners which would suggest that there was any prospect of an increased value attaching to the Loan Notes though presumably there would have been confidence that the Vendor was of such substance that a reduction in value was unlikely. The extent to which the Loan Notes might have been converted into shares was extremely limited indeed. First of all the right did not attach by virtue of the Loan Notes but by virtue of the agreement to which Mr Keleghan and the other vendors were parties. No enforceable right arose on the public flotation and such a right as might have arisen in the case of a private placing seems to have been of questionable value. Certainly the share purchase agreement excluded the possibility of the Vendors enjoying any special discount in applying for such shares. In my view the conversion rights, such as they are, added nothing to the value or marketability of the debt.

The entire transaction was consciously and carefully designed so as to create a document or transaction which would qualify as a debenture for the purpose of the exchange which took place in February 1990, but yet fall short of a debt on a security when the repayment was made in 1993. No doubt this was a deliberate tax avoidance scheme. Many will resent the transaction on which the Vendors embarked. Others will envy it. The only function of this Court at this stage is to determine whether the Loan Notes possessed sufficient characteristics to elevate it above the status of a mere unsecured debt to one which would properly be described as 'a debt on a security' within the meaning of the Capital Gains Tax Act 1975.

In my view it did not achieve that status. Whether it even escaped the character of a mere unsecured debt is not for me to decide. I would dismiss the appeal in this regard.

Seán MacAonghusa (Inspector of Taxes) v Ringmahon Company

Supreme Court
Geoghegan J
29 May 2001

Corporation Tax – case stated – redeemable preference shares issued to satisfy borrowings- Ringmahon Company redeemed £6 million redeemable preference shares and raised a bank load for this purpose- whether the annual interest on the loan is a deductible expense- whether the loan was related to the capital restructuring of the company – whether the interest on such a loan was stamped with the character of capital expenditure and therefore was deductible – whether non deductibility an anomaly in tax code – whether interest on borrowings used for purposes of trade allowable.

This appeal by the Inspector of Taxes is against the decision of the High Court that the interest on a bank loan obtained for the purpose of redeeming £6m redeemable preference shares is allowable in computing the taxable profits of the company.

Facts

Ringmahon ('the company') purchased the H.Williams shops by way of a loan from Dunnes Stores Ireland Company ('DSIC') an on 4 January 1988, this loan was replaced by the issue of 11,500,000 redeemable preference shares. In 1991, the company decided to redeem 6 million of the redeemable preference shares and for that purpose negotiated a loan of £6m from Allied Irish Banks. The shares were redeemed on 2 May 1991.

The company is engaged in the trade of 'Retailing of food, clothing and other household goods'. The proposal to redeem the shares was in pursuance of the stated objective at the time that the company would trade as a separate company independent of the Dunne Group. The company had sole discretion in the decision to redeem all or part of the redeemable preference shares.

The law

ITA 1967 s 61 provides as follows:

> Subject to the provisions of this Act, in computing the amount of profits or gains to be charged, no sum shall be deducted in respect of:
>
> (a) any disbursements or expenses not being money wholly and exclusively laid out or expended for the purposes of the trade or profession.

Normally where a trading company has to pay interest to a bank, that interest is deductible for tax purposes because it will have been 'wholly and exclusively laid out or expended for the purposes of the trade.' Capital expenditure is not deductible and the Inspector's argument is that since the purpose of the loan was to redeem the preference shares, it was therefore related to the capital structure of the company and not the ongoing interest liability. On behalf of the company it was argued that had the company, at all times, financed its business by bank borrowings the interest payable would clearly have been allowable as a trading expense.

Geoghegan J referred to the large number of decided cases but considered that the only case in point was the Canadian case of *Trans-Prairie Pipelines Ltd v Minister for National Revenue* 70 DTC 6351. In that case the circumstances and borrowings were very similar to the instant case and the judgement by Jackett P held that the entire of the borrowed money was being used in its business for the purpose of earning income from the business notwithstanding that the major part of the borrowings was in fact paid on the redemption of preferred shares. Accordingly, on a true interpretation of the relevant Irish legislation it makes no sense to hold that because the loan was originally raised for the purposes of paying off the preference shareholders the interest thereon cannot ever thereafter be treated a 'wholly and exclusively laid out or expended for the purposes of a trade'.

Held by Geoghegan J in dismissing the appeal that:

(i) The bank loan as a matter of business common sense went to fill the hole left by the redemption of the preference shares.

(ii) Without the assistance of decided cases the argument on behalf of the company is far more convincing on the grounds that if the company had been financed, at all times, by bank borrowings the interest would have been allowable.

(iii) The only decided case in point is the Canadian case of *Trans-Prairie Pipelines Ltd v Minister for National Revenue* in which the facts are extraordinarily similar and in which it was held that since the entire of the borrowed money was used in the business for the purpose of earning income the interest thereon was allowable.

(iv) For the reasons given appeal dismissed.

Legislation
ITA 1967 s 61 (TCA 1997 s 86(i))

Cases referred to in judgement
Trans-Prairie Pipelines Ltd v Minister for National Revenue 70 DTC 6351
Archbold Thomson Black and Company v Betty 7TC 158
Strong and Company of Romsey Limited v Woodfield STC 215
Montreal Coke and Manufacturing Co v Minister for National Revenue [1944] 1 All ER 743

Supreme Court - 29 May 2001

Geoghegan J, The appellant is an inspector of taxes, and he has brought an appeal to this court from a decision of the High Court (Budd J) on a case stated from the Circuit Court (Judge Lynch) in which the learned Circuit Court judge sought the opinion of the High Court as to whether he was correct in holding that the respondent was entitled to a deduction of £435,764 in computing the amount of its profits under Case 1 of Schedule D. The High Court answered the question in the affirmative. The basic facts proved or admitted are well summarised in paragraph 4 of the case stated and they read as follows:

(a) Ringmahon, an unlimited company, is a wholly owned subsidiary of Ringmahon Holdings Limited, the ordinary shares of which are held by members of the Dunne family.

(b) In 1987 Ringmahon acquired some of the former H Williams supermarkets and began to trade from these stores under the Dunnes Stores brand name.

(c) Ringmahon is engaged in the trade of 'Retailing of food, clothing and other Household Goods'.

(d) The purchase of the H Williams shops was initially financed by way of loan from Dunnes Stores Ireland Company (hereinafter called 'DSIC'), but this finance was replaced by the issue by Ringmahon of 11, 500,000 redeemable preference shares of 5p at a premium of 95p per share to DSIC on the 4/1/1988. (DSIC is ultimately controlled

(e) In 1991 the Ringmahon Board decided to redeem 6 million of the redeemable preference shares held by DSIC. The company negotiated a loan of £6 m. with Allied Irish Banks for this stated purpose. The loan was drawn down by Ringmahon on the 30/4/1991, and on the 2/5/1991 Ringmahon issued a cheque for £6m to DSIC. The journal entries reflect a redemption of 6,000,000 redeemable preference shares in the accounts of Ringmahon for the period ended 28/12/1991.

(f) The proposal to redeem part of the preference share capital was in pursuance of the stated objective at the time that Ringmahon was set up that the company would be financed independently of the Dunne Family Trust (including the group companies owned by the Trust) and would stand alone as a separate operation.

(g) There was no obligation on Ringmahon to redeem the preference share capital. The Articles of Association provide that the company has sole discretion in the decision to redeem all or part of its redeemable preference shares.

(h) The issued ordinary share capital of Ringmahon at the date of the aforementioned redemption was two ordinary £1 shares fully paid up.

Following on the loan from Allied Irish Banks being applied for the redemption of the preference shares, there was a continuing ongoing liability on the part of the respondent to the bank for interest on the loan. Normally, where a trading company has to pay interest to a bank, that interest is deductible for tax purposes because it will have been 'wholly and exclusively laid out or expended for the purposes of the trade, profession, or vocation' of the taxpayer. In the case of non-capital expenditure that is the statutory test of whether it is deductible for tax purposes or not and that form of wording has been repeated from its original enactment to subsequent re-enactments in various Acts culminating in the Taxes Consolidation Act 1997. However, the relevant enactment in this case, which applied at the relevant time, was section 61 of the Income Tax Act 1967. The part of that section relevant to this case reads as follows:

> Subject to the provisions of this Act, in computing the amount of the profits or gains to be charged, no sum shall be deducted in respect of -
>
> (a) any disbursements or expenses, not being money wholly and exclusively laid out or expended for the purposes of the trade or profession; ...

The arguments of both sides can be summarised very shortly. The appellant argues that since the purpose of the loan was to redeem the preference shares and, therefore, was related to the capital structuring of the company and not the ordinary trading, ongoing interest liability in respect of that loan must be treated as stamped with the same character and, therefore, cannot be deducted against profits for tax purposes. The respondent, on the other hand, argues that although the loan was undoubtedly for the redemption of the shares and that there could be no question of the capital sum spent on the redemption being deductible, the ongoing annual interest is in quite a different position as it becomes merged in the ordinary ongoing liabilities of the company in its trading. Counsel for the respondent, at p 3 of his written submissions, puts it this way:

> From the point of view of the respondents this in effect means that the interest must have been 'wholly and exclusively' laid out for the purposes of the trade carried on by them. In the submission of the respondents it was so laid out - the basis of this submission is that the only way in which the trade could be carried on after the redeemable preference shares had been redeemed was by new share capital or by borrowings and the interest on those borrowings is

then wholly and exclusively laid out for the purposes of the trade. If the interest was not laid out for the purposes of the trade the question arises as to what it was laid out for - nothing in the case stated suggests that it was laid out for anything other than to enable the company to carry on the trade and while the principal was laid out to redeem the preference shares the interest in each year was laid out to retain the benefits of the borrowing so as to enable the company to carry on its trade.

Later on in the same written submission it is pointed out that

> the essence of interest is that it must be looked at in each year and is not, it is submitted necessarily coloured by the fact that the principal was used for a capital purpose - indeed it is not so coloured at all because if one builds a factory on borrowings, which is clearly a capital expenditure and the borrowings would not be an allowable deduction, nonetheless the interest is an allowable deduction as has been agreed with the Revenue. In the present case no new asset was acquired by the respondent- it extinguished share capital and continued its business by substituting bank borrowings on which it pays interest.

Without the assistance of any decided cases and simply upon the basis of interpreting the statutory provisions, I find the respondent's argument much more convincing. Indeed, if the respondent is not correct, there would be somewhat of an anomaly in the tax regime because as counsel for the respondent, Mr Thomas S McCann, SC points out in the written submissions at p 6 and as he further orally argued in court, if the respondent had, at all times, financed its business by bank borrowings the interest payable would clearly have been allowable as a trading expense and this could not have been disputed by the Revenue Commissioners. Yet if that is the case, it would seem strange if the position should be different, merely because there were no borrowings prior to the 1991 accounting period, the company having financed its business by redeemable share capital. The respondent submits that there is no distinction in principle between interest payable on the bank borrowings for the purposes of the redemption of the share capital and interest payable upon bank borrowings incurred in substitution for earlier borrowings from another bank. But even if this is no better than a debating point, I think that the respondent successfully demonstrates that the interest on an ongoing basis must be regarded as being laid out wholly or exclusively in earning of the profits of the particular accounting year.

I have already indicated that I arrive at that view as a matter of principle on the arguments put before the court and without recourse to case law. A large number of cases have in fact been cited in this court and in the court below. These have been accurately and exhaustively reviewed in the written judgment of Budd J. The general principles applicable have been considered in Irish, English, Scottish and Canadian cases. While in a very broad way each of them may be helpful, nevertheless with one single exception, I do not find any of them directly in point in relation to the particular application of the principles to the facts of this case. That single exception is the Canadian case of *Trans-Prairie Pipelines Limited v Minister of National Revenue* 70 DTC 6351. The facts of that case are extraordinarily similar to the facts of this case, and although the wording of the relevant statutory provision is different, I do not think that that difference is material to the points at issue in this case. Therefore, find very considerable support for the view which I have taken in the *Trans-Prairie* case. I think it useful to treat of that case at some length.

The *Trans-Prairie* case was an appeal from the Canadian Tax Appeal Board to the Exchequer Court of Canada. The appellant company had been incorporated to construct and operate a pipeline and its original issued capital had consisted of a number of 'common shares' (presumably the equivalent of ordinary shares' in our terminology) and 140,000 redeemable preferred shares ('preference shares' in our terminology), these preferred shares having a total par value of $700,000. Two years after incorporation the company issued $700,000 First Mortgage Bonds and used $400,000 of the amount thus borrowed (with $300,000 obtained by issuing additional common shares) to redeem the preferred shares. For the purposes of arriving at taxable income the company, in each of the subsequent years, deducted the interest paid on the bonds, but the Minister of National Revenue, who was the relevant authority for this purpose, allowed the company to deduct only three sevenths of the expenses claimed on the grounds that four sevenths or $400,000 of the money borrowed through the issue of the bonds was used by the company to redeem the preferred shares and was not used 'for the purpose of earning income from its business' which was the relevant requirement under the Canadian legislation. An appeal was taken from the Minister's decision to the Tax Appeal Board and the Minister's interpretation was upheld. A further appeal was then taken to the Exchequer Court of Canada. The appeal was heard by a single judge, Jackett P, and he delivered a written judgment allowing the appeal. In the course of that judgment he cited the relevant Canadian statutory provision in the following manner:

> 11.(1) Notwithstanding paragraphs (a), (b) and (h) of subsection (1) of section 12, the following amounts may be deducted in computing the income of a taxpayer for a taxation year:
>
> ...
>
> (c) An amount paid in the year or payable in respect of the year (depending upon the method regularly followed by the taxpayer in computing his income) pursuant to a legal obligation to pay interest on
>
> > (i) borrowed money used for the purpose of earning income from a business or property (other than borrowed money used to acquire property the income from which would be exempt) or
>
> ...
>
> a reasonable amount in respect thereof, whichever is the lesser;'

The learned judge then went on to observe as follows on the third page of his judgment:

> The respondent has disallowed the deduction of four-sevenths of the amount of such interest for each of the years in question on the ground that $400,000 out of the $700,000 borrowed by the bond issue was used to redeem the preferred shares and was not, therefore, used for the purpose of earning income 'from the business. In this conclusion, the respondent has been upheld by the Tax Appeal Board.
>
> The alternative view is that, prior to the transactions in question, the capital being used for the purpose of earning income from the appellant's business was the $700,000 subscribed by the preferred shareholders and the $140,006 subscribed by the common shareholders, and that, after those transactions, the money subscribed by the preferred shareholders had been withdrawn and what the appellant was using in its business to earn income was the $440,006 subscribed by common shareholders and the $700,000 of borrowed money. This, in my view, is a correct appreciation of the matter.
>
> It follows that, in my view, the whole of the $700,000 of borrowed money was being used by the appellant in its business for the purpose of earning income from the business; and that is my view even though, from another point of view, and in a different sense, some $400,000 of the $700,000 was in fact paid on the redemption of the preferred shares.

I cannot see any difference in principle between that case and this case, though of course, this court would be perfectly entitled to take a different view from the view taken by the Exchequer Court of Canada. But as is clear from the earlier part of this judgment, I am in complete agreement with the reasoning adopted in that case. Budd J, in the High Court, also found it persuasive.

The Canadian legislation, as cited above, contains the expression 'money used for the purpose of earning income from a business or property', whereas the wording in s. 61 of the Irish Income Tax Act 1967 is 'wholly and exclusively laid out or expended for the purposes of the trade'. But although it may well be that there could be cases in which that distinction would be relevant, it would not appear to be at all relevant in this case. Jackett P, in his analysis of what happened to the borrowings, was clearly expressing the view that they were wholly and exclusively laid out or expended for the purposes of the business.

In view of the understandably strong reliance being placed on this case by counsel for the respondent, it is interesting how little analysis there is of it in the written submissions of the appellant. Counsel for the appellant has effectively confined themselves to drawing attention to the acknowledgment by the learned trial judge that the wordings of the relevant legislation differed, and while admitting that the facts were similar they submitted 'that for those and other reasons it is of little assistance'. There is really no indication as to what those 'other reasons' were and nothing convincing emerged from the oral argument of the appeal. Furthermore, the reference to Budd J's acknowledgment of the differences in the legislative wording is somewhat misleading in that after a quite detailed resume of the Canadian case the learned trial judge expressed the view that assistance can be gleaned from that case 'even though the Canadian section is narrower in scope'. Budd J points out that under the Canadian statutory provision the loan could be drawn down and used for the purchase of a luxury yacht, a use of the money which would, obviously, not be for the purpose of earning income from the business, but if the yacht was then sold and the proceeds of the sale were used for the purposes of earning income from the business then the interest paid on the loan would become deductible. He then cites the argument of counsel for the respondent (I think with some implicit approval) that:

> under the Canadian section the interest on the loan should be deductible for the years in which the borrowed capital was employed in the business and he says that the same principle applies in the very similar situation in Ringmahon.

Returning to the judgment of Jackett P, I think it useful to cite a further sentence towards the end of his judgment where he said:

> Surely, what must have been intended by section 11(1)(c) was that the interest should be deductible for the years in which the borrowed capital was employed in the business rather than that it should be deductible for the life of the loan as long as its first use was in the business.

By the same token it makes no sense, in my view, to hold that on a true interpretation of the relevant Irish legislation that because the loan was originally raised for the purposes of paying off the preference shareholders, the interest thereon cannot ever thereafter be treated as 'wholly and exclusively laid out or expended for the purposes of a trade'. The final paragraph of the judgment of Jackett P in the *Trans-Prairie* case neatly illustrates the weakness of any alternative interpretation, and for the reasons which I have indicated would appear to be equally applicable to this case. It reads as follows:

> The facts of the present appeal provide an even more striking illustration of the inappropriateness of the meaning of the words 'money used for the purpose of earning income from a business' that is relied on by the respondent. Prior to the 1956 transactions, the appellant's capital used in its business consisted in part of $700,000 subscribed by preferred shareholders. As a result of those transactions the $700,000 had been repaid to those

shareholders and the appellant had borrowed $700,000 which as a practical matter of business common sense, went to fill the hole left by redemption of the $700,000 preferred. Yet, according to the view relied on by the respondent, for the purpose of this provision concerning interest on borrowed capital, $400,000 of the borrowed money cannot be regarded as being used to earn income from the business.

For the reasons given I would, therefore, dismiss the appeal. I have also explained why I am reluctant to delve into the many other authorities, which were cited because in the first place they are of little assistance in the application of the correct principles to this particular case, and secondly, they have been very fully reviewed by the learned trial judge in his judgment. I would, however, make clear in this connection that I have read and considered, in addition to the Trans-Prairie case, the cases listed in the appendix to this judgment. I will just briefly refer to a few of them. *Archbold Thomson, Black and Company v Batty* 7 TC 158 was a Scottish case relied on by the appellant. But the facts were wholly different. £300 had been spent in reducing the capital of the company and it was then claimed as an allowable deduction from the profits for income tax purposes. But there had been a finding of fact that the reduction of the share capital and, therefore, the expenditure of the money was for the purpose of giving a better dividend to the remaining shareholders and not for any purposes of the trade. The Second Division of the Inner House of the Court of Session being bound by that finding of fact held that as a matter of law it was not deductible. Who could argue with that result? But it is of no avail to the appellant in this case. In *Strong and Company of Romsey Limited v Woodifield* 5 TC 215, a brewing company which also owned licensed houses in which they carried on the business of innkeepers incurred damages and costs to the amount of £1,490 on account of injuries caused to a visitor staying at one of their houses by the falling in of a chimney. The House of Lords held that these once off payments were not deductible, that because although there may have been a connection with the trade they were not made for the purpose of enabling the carrying on and earning profits in the trade. That case is also clearly distinguishable. The remaining cases, in so far as they are really relevant at all, were decided on their own facts and by that I mean, there was a finding of fact as to the purpose of the payment and in the light of that finding of fact it was reasonably clear whether as a matter of law the payment was deductible or not. If, for instance, the purpose of the payment was the financing of the business rather than the earning of profits, the payment could not be deductible (see *Montreal Coke and Manufacturing Co v Minister of National Revenue* [1944] 1 All ER 743, a decision of the Privy Council. I have no doubt that, in this case, the learned Circuit Court judge took the view that the ongoing interest payments were necessarily part and parcel of the trading of the company and were clearly deductible. In my opinion the learned High Court judge was correct in upholding that view.

Appendix

1. *Strong and Company of Romsey Limited v Woodfield* 5 TC 215.
2. *Montreal Coke and Manufacturing Co v Minister of National Revenue* [1944] 1 All ER 743.
3. *Commissioners of Inland Revenue v Carron Company* 45 TC 18.
4. *Craddock v Zevo Finance Company Limited* 27 TC 267.
5. *Morgan v Tate and Lyle Limited* 35 TC 367.
6. *Atherton v British Insulated and Helsby Cables Limited* 10 TC 155.
7. *WS McGarry v The Limerick Gas Committee* 1 ITR 375.

8. *Mara v Hummingbird* 1982 ILRM 421.
9. *Commissioners of Inland Revenue v Coleman Car Company Limited* 35 TC 221.
10. *Trans-Prairie Pipelines Limited v Minister of National Revenue* 70 DTC 6351.
11. *McGrath v McDermott* 111 ITR 683.
12. *Archbold Thomson, Black and Company v Batty* 7 TC 158.
13. *Vodafone Cellular Limited v Shaw* 1997 [STC 734].
14. *MacNiven v Westmoreland Investments Limited* [1998] STC 1131.
15. *Boyle Brothers Drilling Company Limited v Minister of National Revenue* 51 DTC 70.

Francis Griffin v Minister for Social, Community and Family Affairs
William Deasy v The Minister for Social, Community and Family Affairs

High Court
Carroll J
2 October 2001

PRSI – share fisherman – whether employed on a contract of service or engaged in a joint venture with boat owner – whether liable to PRSI as a self employed person – whether agreement whereby net proceeds of catch divisible between boat owner and crew constitutes a partnership – optimal social welfare scheme for self employed share fishermen – whether losses carried forward – whether leading Irish judgment disregarded – whether relationship between parties is one of employment or one of partnership – whether each voyage a separate venture – whether Minister has unlimited power to make regulations – whether High Court decisions are binding on Appeals Officer – whether tests of control, enterprise integration remuneration or economic reality apply – whether conclusions based on evidence – whether capital investment essential for a partnership – whether equality among partners required – whether same mistake of law made in decisions by both Appeals Officers

This matter concerns two appeals to the High Court on a question of law against the determination of the Chief Appeals Officer under the Social Welfare Consolidation Act 1993. The net issue in each case is whether the share fisherman is employed on a contract of service or whether he is engaged in a joint venture with the boat owner.

The manner in which share fishing is operated is that the expenses of each voyage is deducted from the gross value of the catch and the net proceeds are divided in agreed shares between the owner of the fishing boat and the crew. In the Griffin case the net profit was divided into 13 shares, shares went to meet the expenses of the boat owner such as fishing gear, repairs, insurance and loan repayments, Mr Griffin's skipper got 26 shares and each of the five crew received 1 share. If the expenses exceed the value of the catch the loss is carried forward to the next trip. The boat is at sea 35-40 weeks in the year. For the remaining weeks the share fishermen receive no payment, no sick pay, no holiday pay and no contribution to a pension scheme. A crew member who is unable to make a voyage is expected to send a substitute. The skipper has control over the crew and ultimate control over the operation. The Revenue Commissioners treat share fishermen as self employed persons and allow deductions for expenses such as oilskins, knives and travelling expenses to and from the boat.

Mr Griffin was normally the skipper of his boat and on any occasion when he was not available Denis Coakley was the skipper. Denis Coakley applied to the Social Welfare office to be treated as an employee and was held to be an employee by the deciding officer. As an employee he could claim unemployment assistance when he was not working.

The leading Irish judgment on share fishermen, *DPP v McLoughlin* [1986] IR 358, was ignored by the Appeal Officer. In that case Costello J held that the relationship between the boat owner and crew was one of partnership and not of employment. In the subsequent case of *Minister for Social Welfare v John Griffiths* [1992] ILRM 667 it was held that the crew member was not an employee and that the Minister did not have unlimited power to make regulations whereby any person be treated as an employee in the absence of an employer/

employee relationship. Decisions of the High Court are binding on the Appeals Officer and the Chief Appeal Officer.

Where there is an appeal on a question of law the court does not go into the merits of the decision unless there are conclusions based on an identifiable error of law or an unsustainable finding of fact by a tribunal.

The Appeals Officer made no attempt to apply Irish law relating to share fishermen as set forth in the *McLoughlin* and *Griffith* cases. On the contrary, he applied American Law which says that workers who are obliged to work as a matter of economic reality are regarded as 'employees'. This is not in accordance with Irish Law which requires the relationship of employer/employee to exist.

The Appeals Officer's factual conclusion that the old tradition of one person providing a boat and the others labour was radically different in concept to this case and was not based on any evidence and there was no justification for such a conclusion. The finding that there were no examples of cases is unsustainable and contrary to the evidence given. It is also a mistake of law to conclude that an agreement to set off losses against the next fishing trip is not a commercial risk. The general statement that self employed persons have a degree of influence over the determination of their remuneration only applies if their services are in demand. If the market determines that their services have only a certain value they are no different to share fishermen and either accept the terms of try elsewhere. It is a mistake of law to hold that there must be an equal coming together of partners to be self employed.

The difference in the *Deasy* appeal was that Mr Deasy the boat owner did not skipper the boat. Trevor Byrne was the skipper and he was in control of how, when and where the boat would fish. Expenses came off the top and the net proceeds were divided on the share basis. Mr Deasy could dismiss Mr Byrne. The Appeals Officer finding that Mr Byrne was the manager who was employed to run a branch of Mr Deasy's business was not in accordance with the facts.

The Appeals Officer made the same mistake of law as in the Griffin case. He made no attempt to apply the law as laid down in the McLoughlin case. He applied tests of control and enterprise without reference to the Costello judgment.

The decisions of the Appeals Officers in both cases are set aside on the grounds of errors of law and unsustainable findings of fact.

Held by Carroll J in setting aside the decisions of the Appeals Officer that –

(i) The law as enunciated in the *McLoughlin* and *Griffith* judgments was not followed.

(ii) The test of economic reality as stated in the US case of *US v Silk* is not in accordance with Irish law.

(iii) The tests of control, enterprise, integration and remuneration were incorrectly applied.

(iv) The relationship between the fishing boat owner and the crew was that of a partnership.

(v) The status of the crew was that of self employment.

(vi) There were several findings of fact which were not in accordance with the evidence.

Legislation
Social Welfare Consolidation Act 1993 s 271
Social Welfare (No 2) 1993, Part III

Cases referred to in judgment
DPP v McLoughlin [1986] IR 355
Minister for Social Welfare v John Griffiths [1992] ILRM 667
Parke v Walker & Ors (1961) SLT 251
Mark Fishing Co v United Fishermen & Anor 24 DLR 585
Duncan v O'Driscoll [1997] ELR 38
Henry Denny & Sons Irl Ltd v Minister for Social Welfare [1998] 1 IR 34

High Court, 2 October 2001

Carroll J, This matter conceals two appeals to the High Court on a question of law under s 271 of the Social Welfare Consolidation Act 1993 against the determination of the Chief Appeals Officer dated 1 September 1999 in the Griffin case and 2 September 1999 in the *Deasy* case. Section 271 provides:

> Any person who is dissatisfied with
> (a) The decision of an Appeals Officer or:
> (b) The revised decision of the Chief Appeals Officer on any question ... may appeal that decision or the revised decision as the case may be to the High Court on any point of law.

The Chief Appeals Officer refused to revise the decisions of an Appeals Officer both dated the 24 June 1999 in these cases. The Appeals Officer in turn had disallowed appeals from the deciding officer dated the 18th February 1998 (*Griffiths*) and 12 June 1998 (*Deasy*). The deciding Officer, in circumstances where each of the plaintiffs owned a fishing boat, decided that a named share fisherman in each boat was insurable at PRSI class A when their share earnings were over a certain level per week. But it is the decisions of the Appeals Officer which were confirmed by the Chief Appeals Officer which fall to be analysed.

The net issue in each case is whether the share fisherman is employed on a contract of service or whether he is engaged in a joint venture with the boat owner.

The way in which the share fishing system operates is that the expenses of the voyage are deducted from the gross value of idle catch. The net value is divided in agreed shares between the owner of the boat and the crew. Up to 1952 share fishermen were considered by the Department of Social Welfare to come within PRSI class A (ie employees). Following the decision of the High Court in *DPP v Griffiths* [1992] ILRM 667, the Revenue Commissioners took the view that share fishermen were self employed and they changed over to PRSI class 3 (self employed).

Under Part III of the Social Welfare (No 2) Act, 1993 a special scheme was introduced with effect from 23 February 1994 for share fishermen to join an optional social insurance contribution scheme if earning more than £2,500 per annum. They were required to contribute as self employed persons (class S) 5% of reckonable earnings. They could opt to contribute up to 10%. The number joining the optional scheme was minimal (113 in 1994/95 and 70 in 1995/96). The boat owners were not liable for contributions for the crew and liability rested with each worker. One of the advantages in being treated as coming within PRSI class A contributors as distinct from self employed contributors, was that they would be entitled, during periods when they were not working, to unemployment assistance.

In Mr Griffin's case, he was the owner of MFV Naoimh Oileabhair from 1978 to 1999 and he was also normally the skipper. On any occasion when he was not the skipper Declan

Coakley was the skipper. Declan Coakley is the named fisherman seeking to be considered as an employee of Mr Griffin.

In his grounding affidavit Mr Griffin stated the expenses of each trip are deducted from the gross profit. These included food, ice, diesel, oil, transport, insurance for the crew (but not as named members) etc. The net profit is divided into thirteen shares. The boat gets six shares (to cover repayments of loan, fishing gear, necessary repairs and insurance for the boat). The skipper gets two shares and each of the five crew one share.

In the event that the expenses of the trip exceed the value of the catch the losses are canted forward to the next trip. Mr Griffin said he specifically said to the Appeals Officer that in the last few years at one stage there were five weeks consecutively without catching any fish. A share fisherman contributes to the value of the catch by the standard of gutting and packing the fish properly. The boat is at sea 35-40 weeks in the year. For the remaining weeks the share fishermen receive no remuneration. They receive no sick pay, no holiday pay and no contribution to a pension scheme. The weekly remuneration in the case of Mr Coakley varied from nil to £1,875.00. If a particular crew member was unable to make a voyage he is expected to send a substitute. The other crew and the skipper would have a right of veto over the substitute with the skipper having the final say. If a substitute makes a trip it is the substitute who gets the share. In the fishing industry the skipper is the person who has control over the crew and ultimate control over the operation. All the share fishermen treated by the Revenue Commissioners as self employed persons and entitled to deduct from their income, expenses such as knives, oilskins, travelling expenses to and from the boat. The size of the vessel dictates how many crew can be on board and members of the crew cannot employ someone to assist them in their task.

Mr Coakley applied 8 January 1998 to be treated as an employee of Mr Griffin. He completed two Social Welfare forms, one on the 8 January, 1998 and one specifically related to share fishermen on 16 January 1998. Mr Griffin completed neither. Following the decision of the deciding Officer (18 February 1998) that Mr Coakley was an employee, an oral hearing was held by the Appeals Officer on the 26 March 1999 at which Mr Griffin gave evidence. According to the notes taken by his solicitor the evidence he gave is substantially the same as in his Affidavit. The Appeals Officer gave his decision on the 24 June 1999 in which he held that Mr Coakley was employed by Mr Griffin from 14 February 1992 and was insurable at PRSI class A if earnings were over a certain amount otherwise at class J.

At the time this matter was considered by the Appeals Officer (and the Chief Appeals Officer) the leading Irish case on share fishermen was *DPP v McLoughlin* ([1986] 1 IR 355) where Costello J considered whether share fishermen were employed on a contract of service or on a contract for services. In that case the defendant engaged the crew before setting out on each fishing expedition. Crew members tended to turn up regularly but there was no contract to engage them again at the end of each fishing expedition. Generally crew members were consulted before a new crew member was taken on. The vessel went to sea on Monday at 11 am and came back to Howth on Wednesday at 5 am The catch was sent to the Dublin market. The cheque was sent to the defendant for distribution of proceeds; There was no agreement for wages. Remuneration was based on a sharing agreement and the size of the catch. The division was based upon custom and agreement. Expenses (oil, ice, food, rent of navigational aids, gas, water) were deducted from the gross proceeds. Where there were four crew members and the defendant acting as skipper, the net proceeds were divided into eleven parts, 5½ shares were allocated to the boat (to cover mortgage repayments, general maintenance, BIM insurance policy). The division of the crew's share was determined by the crew in consultation with the defendant. If there was an inexperienced young boy or a crew member sick they might get a half or a quarter share. If there was no profit the crew received no share. Members of the crew were not required to contribute to any loss that might be sustained on any voyage.

The learned trial judge said at p 358:

> There are of course a considerable number of judicial authorities both in this country and in England where the distinction between a contract of service and a contract for services is made and over the years a number of principles or tests have been established for the purpose of defining the two different contractual relationships. But these authorities are concerned with analysing contracts of employment and focus on such aspects of the parties agreement as the degree of control which the employer exercises on the alleged 'employee' or the role of the alleged 'employee' in the employer's organisation. They do not assist greatly when as here the point for determination is whether the relationship between the parties is one of employment or one of partnership.

He was referred (inter alia) to the Scottish case of *Parker v Walker and Others* [1961] SLT 251 where the share fisherman's legal relationship with the boat owner was held to lee that of joint adventure. He was also referred to the Canadian case of *Mark Fishing Company v United Fishermen and Allied Workers Union* 24 DLR 585 where one of the issues raised was whether the crew of the ship were employees of the ship owner or coadventurers with him. It was held that a partnership relationship existed. In both of these cases if a loss were sustained, the loss was carried forward or the members of the crew had to contribute their share.

Costello J held that the proper inference to be drawn from all the relevant factors was that a partnership relationship rather than an employer/employee one existed. He said:

> It is true that the defendant exercised a large measure of control over the manner in which each member of the crew performed his work but the right to do so arose as much from the nature of the operation being carried on as from the contractual relationship which existed and is a factor which is consistent both with the existence of a contract of service and an agreement of partnership. It is also true that the defendant engaged the other members of the crew for each voyage but again this is consistent both with an employer/employee relationship and an agreement in the nature of a partnership, that is one in which the defendant agreed to provide the vessel and its equipment for the voyage whilst each crew member agreed to provide his labour and skills.

The learned trial judge went on to find that the fact that the defendant dispersed the proceeds of sale making 'subs' in some cases (ie, advances where no profit was made) and that the crew bore no losses were out-weighed by the facts that each weekly voyage was a separate venture, that no crew member had a contract entitling him to take part in any subsequent voyage, that no wages were paid, only a share in the profits (if any) and that the defendant did not himself determine the rate of remuneration. This was determined partly by custom (50% of net profits to the boat) and partly by agreement between the crew in consultation with the defendant. Accordingly he found that the skipper and his crew were partners in the joint adventure undertaken each Monday morning.

In another case the *Minister for Social Welfare v John Griffiths* [1992] ILRM 667 the question for determination was whether the accused John Griffiths the owner of a fishing vessel was the employer of one Eugene Pepper. It was conceded that a partnership existed between them and that each voyage was a separate venture and a new partnership but it was argued that nevertheless Mr Griffiths was an 'employer' within the meaning of that term under the Social Welfare (Collection of Employment Contributions for Special

Contributors) Regulations 1989. It was held by Blayney J that Eugene Pepper was not employed in any one of the particular employments specified in Part I of the first Schedule to the Social Welfare (Consolidation) Act 1981. He was not employed by the accused or by anyone else. It was also held that the Minister for Social Welfare had no unlimited power entitling him to make regulations enabling any person to be treated as an employee for the purpose of the act. There must be an employer/employee relationship.

The legal position therefore was that share fishermen in the same or similar position to share fishermen in the *McLoughlin* case were legally partners on a joint venture with their respective boat owners. High Court decisions are binding on both the Appeals Officer and the Chief Appeal Officer. The two cases were followed by the Employment Appeals Tribunal in *Duncan v O'Driscoll* [1997] Employment Law Reports 38.

It is not disputed that in a case such as this, where there is an appeal on a question of law, the Court does not go into the merits of the decision. But as Hamilton CJ said in *Henry Denning and Sons Ireland Limited v Minister for Social Welfare* [1998] 1 IR 34:

> Where conclusions are based upon an identifiable error of law or an unsustainable finding of fact by a Tribunal such conclusion must be corrected.

The facts and conclusions which emerge from the *Griffiths* decision are as follows:

Re Control

1. (Fact) As a safety measure on board someone has to be in charge.
2. (Conclusion) The issue of control and direction is wider than that.
3. (Fact) The Appeals Officer did not accept Mr Griffin's rebuttal to replies of Mr Coakley to question 19 on INS 1 Form where Mr Coakley said (a) he must perform the work himself (b) cannot hire a person to assist him and (c) that he cannot send a substitute. The rebuttal on behalf of Mr Griffin was to agree with (a), to agree with (b) and explain that the size of the boat did not permit this and (c) to disagree saying Mr Coakley could send a substitute.
4. (Fact) That Mr Coakley was appointed to skipper the vessel on occasions.
5. (Conclusion) That this was indicative of overall control of the operation.
6. (Fact) That none of the other crew members had input into this decision.
7. (Fact) That Mr Coakley could send a substitute if temporarily incapacitated (this contradicts the finding of fact that he did not accept Mr Griffin's rebuttal of Mr Coakley's answer that he could not send a substitute (See 3 above).
8. (Fact) That the substitute is subject to Mr Griffin's veto.
9. (Fact) That Mr Coakley has to perform the work in the boat on a regular basis or his place may be given to someone else without his permission.
10. (Fact) That Mr Griffin said he could dismiss Mr Coakley.
11. (Fact) That Mr Coakley was engaged for his particular work expertise.
12. (Fact) That he could not nominate anyone to take his position on a permanent basis.

Re Enterprise Test

13. (Fact) That while it was argued that Mr Coakley invested his labour in the fishing venture, Mr Coakley was not an investor in the enterprise; he did not risk any capital; he had no investment in the boat; he was engaged to man or crew the vessel.
14. (Fact) That he worked for no one else since 1980.

15. (Conclusion) That the provision of oilskins and knives could not be regarded as an investment in the context of a venture which required very substantial capital (in excess of £10 million).
16. (Fact) While it was contended that Mr Coakley was liable to contribute to losses on a fishing trip there was no evidence of examples or frequency.
17. (Conclusion) Even if it did arise, it could not be equated with the loss sustained by the boat owner if the boat was tied up for a long period due to damage or bad weather.
18. (Conclusion) It did not constitute loss of any funds invested in the enterprise.
19. (Conclusion) The setting off of losses against the next trip is more part of 'the intrinsic nature of the terms on which crew are engaged rather thaw a commercial risk'.
20. (Conclusion) The provision of personal labour services does not provide conclusive evidence of investment in a business partnership or joint venture.
21. (Fact) The labour services provided by Mr Coakley although necessary along with other crew were dwarfed by Mr Griffin's investment.
22. (Fact) These labour services could be replaced with relative ease.
23. (Conclusion) The old tradition in a port of one person providing a boat and other persons labour is radically different in this case in scale and concept.

Integration Test

24. (Fact) Mr Coakley and his colleagues were engaged for their labour without which the boat could not operate. (Conclusion) Like skilled machinists in a clothing factory or qualified mechanics in a garage.
25. (Conclusion) Mr Coakley was employed as part of the business part of the workforce without which the business could not operate therefore he is an employee 'as a matter of economic reality'.
26. (Conclusion) Mr Coakley is not an accessory to the business.

Re Remuneration

27. (General Statement) Self employed persons have a degree of influence over the manner in which remuneration is determined. (Conclusion) which is not the case here.
28. (Fact) Mr Coakley was offered a berth with a predetermined share at the discretion of Mr Griffin with no flexibility to negotiate.
29. (Fact) The share remuneration system is effectively determined solely by boat owners.
30. (Conclusion) There is not an equal coming together of partners or any debate about the size of the share.
31. (Conclusion) Crew men either accept the terms or go elsewhere.
32. (Conclusion) The manner of calculating remuneration is grounded on the variability of income in fishing and the desire to limit liability on the part of boat owners.

The decision is expressed to be based on the evidence in the file, evidence at the oral hearing, written submissions, having regard to criteria emanating from various legal judgments on the nature of the employment relationship and in particular looking at the totality of the relationship.

The Appeals Officer quoted Denning LJ in *Stephenson Jordan and Harrison Limited v McDonald and Evans* 1952 ITR 191:

> Under a contract of service an employee's work is an integral part of the business while under a contract for services an individual's work while done for the business does not form an integral part of it.

He also referred to *US v Silk* 331 US 704 whether an individual is a employee as a matter of economic reality. In that case unloaders of coal who provided their own tools worked only when they wished and were paid an agreed price per ton to unload coal from railroad cars, were held to be employees within the meaning of the Social Security Act, 1935. The reference to employees of economic reality appears in the judgment of Mr Justice Reid at page 713:

> The word 'employee' we said, was not there used as a word of art and its content in its context was a federal problem to be construed 'in the light of the mischief to be corrected and the end to be attained', we concluded that since that end was the elimination of labour disputes and industrial strife 'employees' included workers who were such as a matter of economic reality.

The first observation is that nowhere did the Appeals Officer attempt to apply the *McLoughlin* case which together with the *Griffith* case represented Irish Law applicable to share fishermen in a similar situation. He applied American Law (*US v Silk*) which appears to say that workers who are obliged to work as a matter of economic reality were to be regarded as 'employees'. This is not in accordance with Irish Law which requires the relationship of employer/employee to exist.

While he referred to the judgment of Denning LJ which deals with contracts of service and contracts for service, he did not appear to appreciate the difference between contracts for service, where a person is paid an agreed amount (whether weekly, monthly or yearly) whether there is a profit or not and a joint venture where the partners share in profits and losses in agreed shares. This was adverted to by Costello J in *DPP v McLoughlin* where he said that focusing on the degree of control or the role of the employee in the employers organisation did not assist in determining if a partnership existed.

The Appeal Officer's conclusion (paragraph 23) that the old tradition of one person providing a boat and the others labour was radically different in concept to this case is not based on any evidence and there is no justification for it. The scale may be different from olden days but the concept is the same. Also the circumstances in the *McLoughlin* case which was heard in 1986 would not have been radically different in either scale or concept.

It was a mistake of law not to take the *McLoughlin* case for a starting point and determine whether there were factors in this case which distinguished it from that case. If he had applied the reasoning in the *McLoughlin* case he would not have concentrated on control. In any event his finding that Mr Coakley was in overall control of the operation (para 5) cannot refer to control exercised by the skipper as a safety measure (para 1). It can only mean that he decided who should skipper his boat. This is consistent with a joint venture ie, he supplies the boat and either skippers the boat himself or names the skipper. The joint venture is between himself as owner/skipper and the crew or between him as owner and his replacement skipper and crew. The finding that he did not find Mr Griffin's rebuttal to question 19 convincing (see para 3) is contradicted by the finding at para 7 that Mr Coakley could send a substitute.

The finding at para 12 that Mr Coakley could not nominate anyone to take his position on a permanent basis is not based on any evidence. There was no evidence that he had a permanent place.

The Appeals Officer took the view that Mr Coakley was not an investor in the enterprise because he did not risk any capital, that he had no investment in the boat (para 13) that the provision of oilskins and knives was not an investment (para 15) and that the provision of personal labour was not an investment (para 20). It is a mistake of law to conclude that there cannot be a joint enterprise/partnership unless there is a capital investment. It is also a mistake of law to conclude that the provision of labour in a joint enterprise is not sufficient to sustain that relationship. There are manly examples where one partner may provide premises and labour is provided by other partners (eg, firms of solicitors' accountants etc). In the *McLoughlin* case there was no question of the crew having been required to have a capital investment in the boat before they could be considered as part of a joint venture.

In relation to losses the finding at para 16 that there was no evidence of actual examples or frequency is unsubstantiated and is contrary to the evidence given. Mr Griffin gave evidence at the oral heading of five weeks in a row when no fish were caught.

Where the crew must contribute to losses sustained on a fishing trip, it is immaterial to compare their loss to the loss sustained by the owner if the boat is tied up due to damage or bad weather (para 17) and it was immaterial that for the crew it did not constitute the loss of funds invested (para 18).

It is a mistake of law to conclude that an agreement to set off losses against the next fishing trip is not a commercial risk (para 19). Every share fisherman must weigh the consequences of agreeing to carry forward losses incurred as against the possibility of sharing in a profitable catch.

There was no evidence to base the finding of fact (para 22) that the labour services (of the crew) could be replaced with relative ease.

The Appeals Officer did not advert to the observation of Costello J in *McLoughlin*'s case that the role of the employee in the employer's business did not assist in determining if a partnership existed. So his findings in paras 24, 25 and 26 that the business could not operate without the crew is equally consistent with the joint enterprise. There is no basis in law for finding that Mr Coakley is an employee 'as a matter of economic reality' (para 25). This concept does not exist in Irish Law.

The general statement that self employed persons have a degree of influence over the manner in which remuneration is determined only applies if their services are in demand. If the market determines that their services have only a certain value, they are no different to share fishermen and either accept the terms or try elsewhere.

It is a mistake of law to hold that there must be an equal coming together of partners in order to be self employed (para 30). There is nothing to prevent a joint venture being agreed where the partners are not equal as in share fishing. The boat owner is at risk of having his boat damaged or not earning enough to pay the mortgage. The share fishermen are at risk of working for no recompense if there are no profits.

For all the above reasons, mistakes of law and findings of unsustainable facts, the decision of the Appeals Officer and the decision of the Chief Appeals Officer which confirmed it, must be set aside.

In the *Deasy* case the Appeals Officer in his decision of the 24 June determined that Mr Trevor Byrne was employed by Mr William Deasy and insurable at PRSI class A from the 1 June 1993 provided his earnings were a certain amount otherwise at class J. He dealt with the matter under the same headings as the Griffin case and to a large measure the content is identical.

The difference in the *Deasy* case is that Mr Deasy, the boat owner, did not skipper the boat. Trevor Byrne was the skipper.

According to the note of evidence at the oral hearing Mr Deasy said that Mr Byrne decided when, where and how often the boat would fish. He found the crew were remunerated on a share basis. Expenses of the voyage came off the top. He decided how many shares each fisherman would get. Losses were rolled over to the next trip or until it made money. The division of shares depended on the number of crew. Mr Byrne decided where the catch would be sold. He lodged the money in Drogheda to a joint account in both names and paid the crew out of the account. He sent the remainder to Mr Deasy's bank in Skibereen. The bills for diesel, ice, food, fish boxes etc, were sent for payment to Mr Deasy who was registered for VAT but the amount of these items were taken into account in calculating the share of the crew. Mr Byrne could purchase a net (costing £3,000 to £4,000) without reference to Mr Deasy. Mr Byrne operated the boat from June 1993 to October 1997. On one occasion Mr Byrne supplied a replacement skipper and informed Mr Deasy. This was for insurance purposes.

There were some differences between the two cases in findings. The Appeals Officer found (Re Control) that Mr Byrne had a large degree of authority in day to day running of the boat but it was delegated authority and not uncircumscribed. His freedom to determine when the boat should put to sea was true only in a narrow sense and Mr Deasy could dismiss Mr Byrne. He concluded that the receipt of financial accounts, ordering of supplies in Mr Deasy's name, sending of bills to the accountant for payment, registration for VAT, suggested Mr Deasy was in ultimate control of affairs and Mr Byrne was only in charge on a day to day basis and had to account for his performance. The section on the enterprise test is almost identical with the Griffin decision, except that the Appeals Officer found that Mr Byrne was essentially a manager who was employed to run a branch of Mr Deasy's business. The sections on the integration test and remuneration are substantially the same as in the Griffin decision but shorter.

In dealing with the *Deasy* case, the Appeals Officer made the same mistake of law as in the Griffin case, in that he did not attempt to apply the *McLoughlin* case which represents the law on share fishermen in the same or similar condition. He applied control and enterprise tests without reference to Costello J's observation that they are not helpful when the issue is whether a partnership or joint venture exists. My observations on the detailed finding of facts and conclusion in the Griffin decision where they are repeated in the *Deasy* decision also apply here. For the same reasons the decision of the Appeals Officer and the decision of the Chief Appeals Officer which confirmed it, must be set aside.

Michael F Murphy v GM, DB, PC Ltd and GH
John Gilligan v Criminal Assets Bureau, Revenue Commissioners & Others

Supreme Court
Keane CJ
18 October 2001

Proceeds of Crime Act 1996 – provisions relating to proceeds derived from criminal activities – non-constitutional and constitutional issues- whether defendants can be prohibited from disposing of a sum of £300,000 – whether defendants obliged to give details of all property and income therefrom in their possession or control over past 10 years – whether High Court has jurisdiction to impose orders of restraint and appropriation over property situate within and outside the State – whether plenary summons procedure seeking interim and interlocutory relief appropriate – whether provisions of Act retrospective – whether hearsay evidence sufficient to satisfy onus of proof on the balance of probabilities – whether provisions of Act formed part of the criminal law and not of the civil law – whether persons affected deprived of safeguards under criminal code – whether presumption of innocence ignored – whether standard of proof based on reasonable doubt rather than balance of probabilities – whether provision for trial by jury required – whether purposes and mens rea punitive and deterrent – whether forfeiture of property and mens rea indicative of crime – whether Revenue case precedents apply – whether delays under Act oppressive – whether provisions unfair and retrospective – whether in breach of European Convention on Human Rights.

These appeals arose out of the application of the Proceeds of Crime Act 1996 ('the Act') to the alleged proceeds of past criminal activities. In the first case the defendants challenged the validity of certain orders made by the High Court in purported exercise of certain powers conferred by the Act. In both cases declarations have been sought that some or all of the sections of the Act are invalid having regard to the provisions of the Constitution.

Non-constitutional issue

The High Court granted orders pursuant to sections 2, 3, 7 and 9 of the Act prohibiting the defendants from disposing of a sum of £300,00 held in a solicitor's client account appointing a receiver to take possession of the £300,000 and requiring the defendants to deliver an affidavit specifying all the property and the income therefrom in their possession or control during the past 10 years.

An officer of the Criminal Assets Bureau lodged an affidavit giving details of previous convictions and of involvements in various criminal activities.

The proceedings against the defendants were brought by way of plenary summons including applications for interim and interlocutory orders and the appointment of a receiver. The High Court judge emphatically rejected the evidence of the defendants in regard to the alleged legitimate sources of the £300,000. He was satisfied that the orders sought and granted did not cause any injustice.

The defendants made various submissions that the High Court had no jurisdiction to make such orders, that £80,000 of the £300,000 was situate in a UK bank outside the jurisdiction and that the alleged crimes had occurred prior to the Act. The judge held these submissions to be without foundation and pointed out that there was nothing in the Act prohibiting the procedures followed.

Constitutional issue

In these proceedings Garda officers gave evidence as to the problems posed by the significant extension of the practice of 'money laundering' the proceeds of illegal activities such as the import and sale of drugs.

The principal argument made by the appellants was that the provisions of the Act essentially formed part of the criminal law and not of the civil law and that the persons affected were deprived of the most important safeguards which were historically a feature of the criminal law. Specifically the presumption of innocence was reversed, the standard of proof was on the balance of probabilities rather than reasonable doubt, there was no provision for trial by jury in respect of any of the issues and the rule against double jeopardy was ignored.

The submissions by the appellants relied on Irish court decisions relating mainly to fiscal legislation and US court decisions relating to forfeiture of properties. It was not convincing to say that these proceedings were in rem rather than in personam against the alleged wrongdoers. It was also significant that the Act involved a requirement for mens rea. The Act permitted oppressive delays of up to 7/10 years and the procedures were so unfair as to be unconstitutional. No particulars of alleged crimes were provided and the admission of hearsay evidence denied the right to confront and cross examine. The guarantee of private property under the Constitution was violated and the Act was retrospective in effect and purported to apply to property situate outside the State.

In response the court pointed out the Act enjoys a presumption of constitutionality and that in respect of any provision of the Act open to two or more constructions one of which is constitutional it must be presumed that the Oireachtas intended only the constitutional construction. It is also to be presumed that the Oireachtas intended that all procedures under the Act would be conducted in accordance with the principles of constitutional justice but subject to review by the courts.

The main argument that the procedures under ss 2, 3 and 4 of the Act are limited in nature does not stand up to analysis. Following the initial ex parte application an interim order the defendants have ample opportunity to challenge any further order. The general question as to whether statutory proceedings resulting in the forfeiture of property are civil or criminal in nature has been considered by the courts in this country and in the US. In an income tax case [*McLoughlin v Tuite* [1989] IR 82] it was held that the imposition of penalties for failure to deliver returns of income was an offence against the community at large and the sanction was penal in its nature but notwithstanding was not a criminal offence. Even if it were assumed that mens rea is an essential ingredient under ss 3 or 4 of the Act that would not of itself deprive the proceedings of their civil character. In any event such an assumption is a misconception because it may well be that the person against whom the order is made may not have been involved in any criminal activity and may not have been aware that the property constituted the proceeds of crime.

The relevant US decisions concluded that the punitive and deterrent purposes of their legislation were sufficient to uphold against constitutional challenge the application of forfeiture statutes of unlawful activity. These authorities lend considerable weight to the view that in rem proceedings for the forfeiture of property, even where accompanied by parallel proceedings for the prosecution of criminal offences arising out of the same event, are civil in character.

The further submissions by the appellants are not well founded. The procedures under the Act do not predicate unreasonable delays since the person can apply to the court at any time within the 7 year period. The High Court will apply constitutional justice in the hearing of any procedure and will decide on the weight, if any, to be given to hearsay evidence. The onus of proof in civil proceedings is based on the balance of probabilities and does not render the provisions unconstitutional. As regards the privilege of self incrimination the factual position herein cannot be equated with a statutory provisions under criminal law obliging a person to give evidence. The abridgement of property rights in the circumstances herein is considered to be a permissible delimitation of property rights for the purposes of Article 43 of the Constitution. The legislature is authorised to provide for, where certain conditions are met, the making of mandatory rather than discretionary orders. There is no substance in the retrospective or extra territorial arguments. The provisions of the European Convention on Human Rights are not relevant insofar as the European Convention has not yet been made part of the domestic law of the State.

This novel legislation imposing on the court obligations to make 'appropriate' orders and refrain where there 'would be a serious risk of injustice' and to award and determine compensation may be expected to give rise to difficulties in practice if not in principle but the resolution of such problems must await another day.

Held by Keane CJ in dismissing the appeals that:

(i) The High Court had jurisdiction to make the orders sought pursuant to the Proceeds of Crime Act 1996.

(ii) There was nothing in the Act prohibiting the procedures taken by the Garda representative Michael F Murphy.

(iii) The relevant provisions of the Act were civil in character and did not form part of the criminal law.

(iv) The proceedings were in rem rather than in personam.

(v) Mens rea was not an essential ingredient of the provisions.

(vi) The standard of proof was in accordance with civil proceedings there is no substance in the retrospective or territorial arguments.

(vii) The punitive and deterrent purposes of the Act justified a permissible limitation of property rights.

(viii) The Act and the procedures herein did not violate the provisions of the Constitution.

Legislation:
Proceeds of Crime Act 1996 (ss 2, 3, 4, 7, 8, 9),
Criminal Assets Bureau Act 1996, Customs Consolidation Act, 1876,
Customs (Temporary Provisions) Act 1948,
Constitution of Ireland Articles 29(3), 38, 40(1), 43,
Scrap Iron (Control of Exhaust) Act 1938,
Income Tax Act 1918 (s 30(1)),
Income Tax Act 1967 (s 300)
Offences against the State (Amendment) Act 1985,
Companies Act 1963 (s 297)

Cases referred to in judgment
Nestor v Murphy [1979] IR 326
Re Maudslay, Sons & Field (1900) 1 Ch 1002
Caudron v Air Zaire [1985] IR 716
Melling v O'Mathghamhna [1962] IR 1
AG v Southern Industrial Trust (1960) 94 ILTR 161

United States v Ursery 518 US 267
Republic of India v Indian Steamship Company (No 2) [1998] AC 878
Clancy v Ireland [1988] IR 326
McLoughlin v Tuite [1989] IR 82
O'Keefe v Ferris [1993] 3 IR 165
Cox v Ireland [1992] 2 IR 503
King v AG [1981] IR 233
McDonald v Bord na gCon (No 2) [1965] IR 217
East Donegal Co-op v AG [1970] IR 317
The State (Gettins) v Judge Fawsitt [1945] IR 183
O'Cronin v Brennan [1939] IR 274
Proprietary Articles Trade Association v AG of Canada [1931] AC 310
Caledo-Toledo v Pearson Yacht Leasing Company (1974) 416 US 663
McIntosh v Lord Advocate [2001] 2 All ER 638
Phillips v United Kingdom (5 July 2001, unreported), High Court

Supreme Court – 18 October 2001

Keane CJ, In these cases the defendants/respondents and the plaintiff/appellant respectively have sought declarations that some or all of the provisions of the Proceeds of Crime 1996 hereafter the '1996 Act') are invalid having regard to the provisions of the Constitution. In the first case, the defendants/respondents have also challenged the validity of certain orders made by the High Court in purported exercise of certain powers conferred by the 1996 Act on the court. The first part of this judgment is concerned with the non-constitutional issue raised in the first case. The second part is the judgment of the court on the constitutional issue raised in both cases.

The non-constitutional issue

The plaintiff in the first proceedings is a Detective Chief Superintendent in An Garda Síochána. He has instituted the proceedings as a member of the gardaí within the meaning of the 1996 Act and in them he seeks:

> (1) An order pursuant to s 2 and thereafter pursuant to s 3 of the 1996 Act prohibiting the defendants and each of them and such other person as the court might order from disposing or otherwise dealing with the property described in the schedule to the plenary summons, ie the sum of £300,000 standing to the credit of the second named defendant (hereafter 'PB') and/or PC Ltd in the client account of the fourth named defendant (hereafter 'the solicitor').
>
> (2) An order pursuant to s 7 of the 1996 Act appointing a receiver to take possession of the property or such portion of the property as the court might order.
>
> (3) An order pursuant to s 9 of the 1996 Act requiring the first defendant and PB to swear and deliver affidavits specifying all the property of which they are in possession or control and the income and sources of income of each of the defendants during the past ten years.

In an affidavit, sworn on the 28 July 1997, Det Sgt William P O'Brien, a bureau of fleer of the Criminal Assets Bureau appointed under s 8(1) of the Criminal Assets Bureau Act 1996, said that the first named defendant (hereafter 'GM') had been involved in facilitating armed robberies and hijackings since 1975. He said that he was a known 'facilitator' providing guns and transport (sometimes stolen) for such criminal activity and was particularly well known as a receiver of large quantities of stolen property.

Mr O'Brien said that GM had one criminal conviction, involving stolen property, having been convicted on 15 January 1988 by the Dublin Circuit Court for receiving stolen goods valued £107,000 approximately, in respect of which conviction he received a sentence of five years imprisonment.

Mr O'Brien said that, in common with a number of other prominent criminals who had been active in armed robberies, GM became involved in the importation of controlled drugs, mainly cannabis and ecstasy, on his release from prison and, in association with known large scale drug dealers, organised the transport by other persons of drugs so as to ensure that, if the shipments were intercepted by gardaí or customs, he would not be liable to criminal convictions.

Mr O'Brien said that he believed GM was the person behind, or at least partly involved in, the financing of a shipment of 50 kilos of cannabis resin which was seized by gardaí at the M50 motorway, Dublin, while in the possession of one John Doran. He said that the latter had been a close associate of GM since 1975 at least and had been sentenced to 12 years imprisonment in November 1994 in respect of this offence.

Mr O'Brien said that GM was named in a trial in England in early 1997 by one Michael Boyle, who has been tried for attempted murder, as the person who had hired him (Boyle) to murder his intended victim. Mr O'Brien said that GM's wife and one or more of his children reside at a stated address In Palmerston, Dublin, but that GM himself had left Ireland and was staying at a stated address in the Netherlands. The apartment in question was owned by one Johannes Anthonius Bolung who had been charged in The Netherlands with a violation of the Opium Act, handling and receiving stolen goods, and five cases of theft, assault and battery and fraud.

Mr O'Brien said that PB had been a close associate of GM for some time. He had stood trial in April 1995 in England with one Edward Phelan: both were convicted on 12 counts of theft and forgery and sentenced to three years imprisonment. PB absconded during the final week of his trial and was convicted in his absence. Mr O'Brien said that he had been informed by the London Metropolitan Police that extradition proceedings in respect of PB had failed in September 1996 but were likely to be recommenced. As part of the sentence, PB was prohibited from being a director of a company for a period of five years, but he (Mr O'Brien) had been informed by PB and the solicitor that it was intended to appeal the conviction.

Mr O'Brien said that the statements made by 1 am In the affidavit as to the activities of GM were based on garda information in his possession, the source and precise contents of which he did not wish to reveal for operational reasons.

Mr O'Brien said that an extensive investigation had been carried out by bureau officers of the Criminal Assets Bureau. Doing their investigations, the solicitors' offices were searched pursuant to a search warrant issued under s 14 of the Criminal Assets Bureau Act 1996. Mr O'Brien said that in the course of that search a file was seized which was suspected to contain evidence of the whereabouts of the proceeds of the criminal activities of GM. On examination, the file was found to contain instructions in July 1996 from GM and one David Doran to the effect that finds would be deposited in the client account of the solicitor to be at the disposal of PB in connection with a property deal in the United Kingdom to the value of one million pounds. He said that the file also indicated that the third named defendant (hereafter 'the company') was controlled by GM and PB.

Mr O'Brien said that on the 23 July 1997 he called to the offices of the solicitor, who informed him that he was holding approximately £300,000 in his client account for PB. He said that the sum of £300,000 was shortly to be paid out in pursuance of an agreement dated 30 May 1997 in a transaction involving the purchase of United States railroad bonds.

Mr O'Brien said that he subsequently telephoned the solicitor and advised him that he (Mr O'Brien) suspected that the £300,000 was the proceeds of crime and was being 'laundered' using his client account. He requested him not to deal in any way with the finds. The solicitor denied knowing any person by the name of GM or that he was a client of the office. Mr O'Brien said that he urged him to check his client ledgers and any other client files he might have had. Mr O'Brien said that the solicitor in the course of the conversation told him that he was under pressure from his client and asked him (Mr O'Brien) to fax a message to him advising that money laundering was suspected. However, before he had time to send him a fax, he received two faxes from the solicitor advising that:

(a) he was obliged to follow his client's instructions until ordered otherwise, and

(b) seeking copies of the files seized and complaining about references to a criminal conviction in England of PB.

He subsequently sent a fax to the solicitor requesting him not to remove any monies referable to PB, GM or any associate companies.

Mr O'Brien said that he believed that GM and his associates were extremely violent criminals and were likely to attempt to use violence or threats of violence to force the solicitor to make the monies available.

The plaintiff applied to the High Court (Smyth J) on the 28 July 1997 ex-parte for liberty to issue and serve a concurrent plenary summons against GM, for an order pursuant to s 2 of the 1996 Act restraining the defendants or any of them or any person having notice of the making of the order from disposing or otherwise dealing with the sum of £300,000 and appointing Barry Galvin, solicitor, of the Criminal Assets Bureau as the receiver of float sum. Those orders were granted by Smyth J and the plaintiff thereupon brought a notice of motion seeking similar restraining orders against each of the defendants, an order pursuant to s 7 of the 1996 Act appointing a receiver to take possession of the sum of £300,000 and an order requiring GM, PB and the company to swear and deliver an affidavit specifying all property etc of which they were in possession or control.

In a preliminary report exhibited with an affidavit filed by him on the making of that application, Mr Galvin said that, immediately following the making of the ex-parte order by Smyth J, he travelled to the offices of the solicitor in Dun Laoghaire where he met the solicitor. The solicitor told him that that he had paid some of the £300,000 into his client account in the Ulster Bank, Dun Laoghaire and that the balance had been lodged by him into a solicitor's reserve account in a branch of the National Westminster Bank in London. Having telephoned the bank in London, he told Mr Galvin that the amount to credit in that account was £181,356.20 sterling and that the balance standing to credit in the Dun Laoghaire bank was £118,643.80. At Mr Galvin's request, the solicitor signed an authority directing the London bank to give to Det Gda Clíona Richardson a bank draft in the amount of £181,365.20 sterling payable to Mr Galvin. He also received from Mr H a cheque in the amount of £118,643.80 drawn on the Ulster Bank client account. Det Gda Richardson travelled to London on the 28 July 1997 and collected a bank draft in favour of Mr Galvin in the amount of £181,365.20 which she gave to Mr Galvin. Those sums were paid to a receivership account opened by Mr Galvin at the Camden Street branch of the Bank of Ireland.

In a further affidavit dated the 7 October 1997, Mr O'Brien said that in the course of a search of premises which he did not wish to identify he had seized copies of two bank drafts in the amount of £25,000 sterling and £23,000 both payable to GM and purportedly endorsed by him which, he said, together with other monies totalling £169,746.36 were lodged by credit transfer to the client account of the solicitor in his Dun Laoghaire bank on the 30 September 1996. He said that he also searched the dwelling house of PB on the authority of a search warrant, during the course of which a document was seized purporting to be a contract dated the 28 April 1996. He said that, as a result of an examination of a computer also seized during the course of the search, it was ascertained that this contract had been only recently created and that it was proposed to present this document which he described as fabricated before the High Court on affidavit as a false explanation of the source of part of the £300,000. He referred to reports prepared by a member of the staff of the Criminal Assets Bureau who was a qualified system administrator in computer applications and a detective garda in the computer crime investigation unit in support of this averment.

Affidavits were filed by PB and the solicitor. For reasons which will appear shortly, it is unnecessary to deal with their contents in any detail. It is sufficient to say that PB denied that the sun of £300,000 came from GM or represented in any way the proceeds of crime. The solicitor, although accepting that there were references to GM indicating that monies from him had come into the solicitor's client account and that there were also references in his correspondence with the London bank to 'our client GM', denied that GM was at any stage a client of his office.

No appearance was entered in the proceedings by GM. The remaining defendants entered appearances and made submissions on the hearing of the application for the interlocutory order pursuant to s 3(1) of the 1996 Act, which was heard by O'Higgins J over a period of 28 days. As already noted, in addition to a number of non-constitutional issues being raised, the respondents were also given leave to challenge the constitutionality of the 1996 Act. In a reserved judgment delivered on the 4 June 1999, O'Higgins J determined both the non-constitutional and the constitutional issues in favour of the plaintiff end granted an order pursuant to s 3 of the 1996 Act prohibiting the defendants and each of them from disposing or for otherwise dealing with the sum of £300,000 and appointing Mr Galvin receiver over the sum. From that judgment and order, PB, the company and the solicitor have now appealed to this court.

In the course of his judgment, O'Higgins J made a number of findings of fact which can be summarised as follows. He did not accept the evidence of the solicitor that he had never received any monies from GM or that the latter was not his client. As to the source of the monies, having considered the evidence in detail, the learned High Court judge rejected in emphatic language the explanation for its genesis offered by PB and said that the latter had been involved in what he described as:

> a premeditated, calculated, sophisticated and outrageous attempt to deliberately mislead this court.

He said that in the result he was satisfied that the respondents were in possession and control of £300,000 and that this money constituted, directly or indirectly, the proceeds of crime or was acquired in whole or in part with, or in connection with, property that, directly or indirectly, constituted the proceeds of crime.

The specific findings of fact on which the learned High Court judge founded his conclusion that the sum of £300,000 constituted the proceeds of crime and that the plaintiff was entitled to the relief which he was seeking were not contested on the appeal. The second and third named respondents had, however, contested the jurisdiction of the High

Court to make the orders in question on a number of grounds, including the unconstitutionality of the 1996 Act, in the High Court and those grounds were again advanced on the hearing of the appeal in this court.

Before the non-constitutional issues are considered, I should set out the relevant provisions of the 1996 Act. It is described in its long title as:

> An Act to enable the High Court, as respects the proceeds of crime, to make orders for the preservation and, where appropriate, the disposal of the property concerned and to provide for related matters.

Section 2 deals with what are described as 'interim orders'. Subsection (1) provides that:

> Where it is shown to the satisfaction of the [High] Court on application to it ex parte in that behalf by a member or an authorised officer –
>
> (a) that a person is in possession or control of -
>
>   (i) specified property that the property constitutes, directly or indirectly, proceeds of crime, or
>
>   (ii) specified property that was acquired, in whole or in part, with or in connection with property that, directly or indirectly, constitutes proceeds of crime, and
>
> (b) that the value of the property or, as the case may be, the total value of the property referred to in both subparagraphs (i) and (ii), of paragraph (a) is not less than £10,000 the Court may make an order ('an interim order') prohibiting the person or any other specified person or any other person having notice of the order from disposing of or otherwise dealing with the whole or, if appropriate, a specified part of the property or diminishing its value during the period of 21 days from the date of the making of the order.

Subsection (2) provides that an interim order may contain such provisions, conditions and restrictions as the court considers necessary or expedient and shall provide for notice of it to be given to the respondent and any other person who appears to be or is affected by it, unless the court is satisfied that it is not reasonably possible to ascertain his, her or their whereabouts.

Subsection (3) provides that, where an interim order is in force, the court, on the application of the respondent or any other person claiming ownership of any of the property concerned may discharge or, as may be appropriate, vary the interim order. That can be done where it is shown to the satisfaction of the court that the property concerned or a part thereof is not, directly or indirectly the proceeds of crime or that the value of the property is less than £10,000.

Subsection (4) provides that the court shall, on an application at any time by the applicant, discharge an interim order.

Unless an interim order is so discharged, it is to continue in force by virtue of subsection (5) until the expiration of the period of 21 days from the date of its making. It then lapses, unless an application for the making of an interlocutory order is brought during that period: if such an application is brought, the interim order is to lapse upon:

(a) the determination of the application,

(b) the expiration of the ordinary time for bringing an appeal from the determination,

(c) if such an appeal is brought, the determination or abandonment of it or of any further appeal or the expiration of the ordinary time for bringing any further appeal, whichever is the latest.

Section 3 deals with interlocutory orders. Subsection (1) provides that:

Where, on application to it in that behalf by the applicant, it appears to the Court, on evidence tendered by the applicant, consisting of or including evidence admissible by virtue of section 8:

(a) that a person is in possession or control of –

    (i) specified property and that the property constitutes, directly or indirectly, proceeds of crime, or

    (ii) specified property that was acquired, in whole or in part, with or in connection with property that, directly or indirectly, constitutes proceeds of crime, and

(b) that the value of the property or, as the case may be, the total value of the property referred to in both subparagraphs (i) and (ii) of paragraph (a) is not less than £10,000,

the Court shall make an order ('an interlocutory order') prohibiting the respondent or any other specified person or any other person having notice of the order from disposing of or otherwise dealing with the whole or, if appropriate, a specified part of the property or diminishing its value, unless, it is shown to the satisfaction of the Court, on evidence tendered by the respondent or any other person -

(i) that that particular property does not constitute, directly or indirectly, proceeds of crime and was not acquired, in whole or in part, with or in connection with property that, directly or indirectly, constitutes proceeds of crime, or

(ii) that the value of all the property to which the order would relate is less than £10,000.

Provided, however, that the Court shall not make the order if it is satisfied that there would be a serious risk of injustice.

Subsections (3) and (4) contain similar provisions to those contained in s 2(3) and (4), The only difference being that, in the case of an interlocutory order, the court may also discharge or vary the order where it is satisfied that it 'causes any other injustice'.

Section 8 provides inter alia that:

(1) Where a member or an authorised officer states -

(a) in proceedings under s 2, on Affidavit or, if the Court so directs, in oral evidence, or in proceedings under s 3, in oral evidence, that he or she believes either or both of the following, that is to say:

    (i) that the respondent is in possession or control of specified property and that the property constitutes, directly or indirectly, proceeds of crime,

    (ii) that the respondent is in possession of or control of specified property and that the property was acquired, in whole or in part, with or in connection with property that, directly or indirectly, constitutes proceeds of crime,

and that the value of the property or, as the case may be, the total value of the property referred to in both paragraphs (i) and (ii) is not less than £10,000, then, if the Court is satisfied that there are reasonable grounds for the belief aforesaid, the statement shall be evidence of the matter referred in paragraph (id or in paragraph (ii) or in both, as may be appropriate, and of the value of the property.

(2) The standard of proof required to determine any question arising under this Act shall be that applicable to civil proceedings.

Section 4 provides for 'disposal orders'. Subsection (1) empowers the court, where an interlocutory order has been in force for not less than 7 years, to make an order on the application of the applicant directing that the whole, or if appropriate a specified part of the property be transferred to the Minister for Finance or such other person as the court may determine subject to such terms and conditions as may be specified. The order is to be made, unless it is shown to the satisfaction of the court that it did not constitute, directly or indirectly, the proceeds of crime.

Section 7(1) which provides for the appointment of a receiver is as follows:

> Where an interim order or an interlocutory order is in force, the Court may at any time appoint a receiver -
>
> (a) to take possession of any property to which the order relates,
>
> (b) in accordance with the Court's directions, to manage, keep possession or dispose of or otherwise deal with any property in respect of which he or she is appointed,
>
> subject to such exceptions and conditions (if any) as may be specified by the Court, and may require any person having possession or control of property in respect of which the receiver is appointed to give possession of it to the receiver.

The first ground on which the order made in the High Court was challenged was that the court had no jurisdiction to make the interim order appointing Mr Galvin as receiver or the interlocutory order to the same effect. It was submitted that, under the terms of s 7(1), such an order could be made only where an interim order was 'in force'. Since the receiver was appointed by the same order of Smyth J dated the 28 July 1997 as also made a restraining order under s 2, the interim order was not, it was said, 'in force' at the time the receiver was appointed.

I am satisfied that this submission is wholly unsustainable. It was quite clear from the terms of the order that the order restraining the defendants from disposing of or otherwise dealing with the property was made first. At that point, the order was, within the meaning of s 7(1) 'in force' and the High Court had jurisdiction to make the further order, which it did, appointing the receiver.

There is nothing whatever in the section to indicate that the legislature intended that an unspecified interval of time, whether measured in minutes, hours or days, should elapse between the application for an interim order and the appointment of a receiver. I have not the slightest doubt that it was envisaged that the two applications could be made at the same time, which is what happened here.

It was also suggested that the interlocutory order which effectively continued the appointment of Mr Galvin as receiver was also made without jurisdiction since, as the £300,000 had been lodged to the credit of these proceedings, there was nothing further for him to do. At worst, however, the appointment of Mr Galvin under the interlocutory order was otiose, the learned High Court judge was no doubt proceeding on the reasonable basis that, were a further order not made appointing him as receiver, his appointment under the interim order might be regarded as having come to an end when that order was spent.

The second ground of objection was that, at the time the interlocutory order was made, no person was 'in possession or control' of the sum of £300,000. Once the receiver had lodged the money in question in the bank to the credit of these proceedings, it was said, the monies were in the possession or control of the High Court, which is not a juristic person.

If this submission were correct, it would inevitably follow that, in every case where a receiver was appointed following the making of an interim order but before an interlocutory order was made, the interlocutory order could never be made, since at that stage the property would be in the 'possession or control' of the court. A construction leading to so patently absurd and unintended a result should not be adopted unless the language used leaves no alternative: see *Nestor v Murphy* [1979] IR 326. At the stage when the application for an interlocutory order is made, the property can be said to be in the 'possession or control' of the receiver, but since the restraining order can be made prohibiting 'the respondent or any other specified person' from disposing of or dealing with the property account the fact that it is in the receiver's possession or control is of no consequence. I am satisfied that this argument is without foundation.

The third ground of objection was that, at the stage when the order was made under s 2 and s 7, £180,000 approximately of the money was in a bank account in London. It was submitted that there was no jurisdiction to make the order in respect of that sum because:

> (1) No enactment - and this, it was said, applied particularly to a penal enactment such as the present - applies to transactions and property outside the State, unless the enactment expressly so provides, which it did not in this case.

> (2) The rights and liabilities of persons in connection with the property are, under private international law, governed by the lex situs in this case English law, which did not provide for the civil forfeiture of this sum.

> (3) The confiscation of property in another State was contrary to the principles of public international law and was in violation of Articles 29.3 and 8 of the Constitution.

On the facts as already summarised, no issue appears to have arisen for determination in relation to this matter. The solicitor, at the request of the receiver, transferred the money in the bank account in London to the latter. If he had declined so to do, an issue might then have arisen as to whether the receiver's demand could have been enforced by the court. That did not happen.

However, even apart from that consideration, I am satisfied that the submissions made on the topic have no foundation. It is settled law that courts, in the exercise of their equitable jurisdiction, can appoint receivers over property which is not within the jurisdiction. In *In Re Maudslay. Sons & Field* [1900] 1 Ch. 602, Cozens-Hardy J (as he then was) said at p 611:

> It is well settled that the court can appoint receivers over property out of the jurisdiction. This power, I apprehend, is based upon the doctrine that the court acts in personam. The court does not, and cannot, attempt by its order to put its own officer in possession of foreign property, but it treats as guilty of contempt any party to the action in which the order is made who prevents the necessary steps being taken to enable its officer to take possession according to the laws of the foreign country ...

There is no reason to attribute to the legislature in the case of the 1996 Act an intention that the powers of a receiver appointed under the Act were to be any less extensive than those of a receiver appointed by the court in the exercise of its general jurisdiction.

While a number of authorities were cited in the course of argument in support of the principle of international law that courts will not permit within their jurisdiction the exercise of sovereign authority by another jurisdiction, I do not find it necessary to refer to them in any detail since they do not arise for consideration in this case. In the present case, the order of the High Court was intended to secure compliance by a person within the jurisdiction of the court with an order of the court directing the transfer of property in his possession and control to a receiver appointed by the court. That order was in no sense an attempt to exercise sovereign authority in another jurisdiction. Similarly, the rules of private international law providing for the devolution of certain property in accordance with the lex situs have no application whatever to the facts of the present case and require no further consideration.

The fourth ground of objection related to the form of the proceedings. It was submitted that the plenary summons claimed interim and interlocutory relief and the appointment of a receiver only: it did not claim any substantive relief.

It was said that this was an impermissible mode of procedure, having regard to the decision of this court in *Caudron v Air Zaire* [1985] IR 716.

No rules of court have been made prescribing the procedure to be followed in applications under the 1996 Act and, specifically, indicating whether they are to be initiated by way of plenary summons, special summons, notice of motion or some other mode. There was therefore no reason in principle why the proceedings should not have been initiated by way of plenary summons claiming the only relief which was required at that stage, ie orders under s 2, s 3, s 7 and s 9. It would seem at least debatable whether an application for a disposal order under s 4 should have been included at that stage, since, as already noted, that relief could not be granted by the court until the expiration of a period of seven years from the date of the making of the interlocutory order. In the event, however, the learned High Covert judge indicated that, in his view, the plenary summons should be amended so as to include a claim under s 4 and such an application was made and granted following the judgment on the interlocutory application.

I can see no defect in any of these procedures and the decision of this court in *Caudron* is of no relevance. In that case, no substantive relief was claimed or could have been claimed and this court held that, in such circumstances, a plaintiff could not claim a Mareva injunction as a discrete remedy not depending on any specific cause of action relied on in the plenary summons. That is wholly distinguishable from the present case where the plaintiff is claiming express reliefs under specific statutory provisions. I am satisfied that there is no substance in the procedural points on which the respondents rely.

The fifth submission was that the 1996 Act does not apply to the proceeds of alleged crimes committed before it came into force and that, accordingly, if the allegations made in the affidavits grounding the proceedings are correct, they do not justify the making of orders, since they refer to crimes allegedly committed before the 1996 Act came into force.

Section 1(1) of the 1996 Act provides that:

In this Act, save where the context otherwise requires -

'Proceeds of crime' means any property obtained or received at any time (whether before or after the passing of this Act) by or as a result of or in connection with the commission of an offence ...

It was submitted that an enactment of the Oireachtas should not be construed as having retrospective effect in the absence of plain and unambiguous language giving it such effect: see the judgment of this court in *Hamilton v Hamilton* [1982] IR 466 at 484. It was further submitted that it could not have been the intention of the Oireachtas to confiscate the proceeds of crimes committed decades or even centuries ago.

I can find no ambiguity whatever in the definition of 'proceeds of crime' in s 1(1). It expressly extends to property obtained or received before the passing of the Act by or as a result of or in connection with the commission of an offence. Property so obtained or received must, by definition, have been obtained or received after the offence had been committed and, accordingly, the Act in express terms applies to the proceeds of crimes committed before it came into force. A remarkably strained argument was advanced to the effect that the words 'in connection with' could extend to, for example, a ship bought in order to import drugs and that it was only in that context that property obtained before the passing of the Act was to be captured. There is, however, nothing whatever in the section to support so fanciful and artificial a construction. If the legislature had intended the words 'before or after the passing of this act' to have so limited an application, they would have so provided. I am satisfied that the definition in plain and unambiguous language extends to property obtained or received at any time before the passing of the 1996 Act by or as a result of or in connection with the commission of an offence.

The sixth submission was that the applicant in proceedings under the 1996 Act was obliged to identify the crimes in question and when, where and by whom they were alleged to have been committed. It is unnecessary in this case to consider whether, and if so to what extent, the applicant in proceedings under the 1996 Act must satisfy the court that the property whose disposition he seeks to restrain is the proceeds of a specific crime. In this case, the plaintiff gave detailed evidence as to the nature of the criminal activities allegedly committed by GM which were the source of the property sought to be frozen. (This evidence was undoubtedly hearsay, but, as already noted, such evidence is admissible under s 8.) This evidence was accepted by the learned High Court judge and his findings of fact in this context have not been disputed on the hearing of this appeal. Accordingly, no argument on this ground can succeed.

Finally, it was submitted that the learned High Court judge should, at the outset, have ruled on the question as to the onus of proof resting on the plaintiff, ie whether he was obliged to satisfy the court on the balance of probabilities that the sum of £300,000, constituted the proceeds of crime within the meaning of the 1996 Act or simply that there was a fair question to be argued as to whether they were. It was claimed that until such a ruling was made the respondents (to quote their written submissions) 'could not join issue with the applicant on the facts'.

This is clearly wrong. The respondents were not in any way precluded from joining issue with the plaintiff on any of the facts. It was open to them to cross-examine the deponents who had given evidence in support of the application and to adduce evidence themselves. They could then have made whatever submissions they thought appropriate in the light of the evidence on the appropriate onus of proof. Their election not to cross examine and not to adduce oral evidence was a matter for them and they cannot now be heard to complain of the result.

I am satisfied that the learned High Court judge was entirely correct in rejecting, as he did, all the arguments advanced in this case in relation to the non-constitutional issues and I would, accordingly, affirm the order of the High Court.

The constitutional issue

This is the judgment of the court as to the claim made in both proceedings that the 1996 Act was invalid having regard to the provisions of the Constitution.

That was the sole claim made on behalf of the plaintiff in the second of these proceedings. In her judgment (reported in [1998] 3 IR 185), McGuinness J dismissed the plaintiffs claim. In the first proceedings, O'Higgins J in the reserved judgment already referred to also dismissed the plaintiff's claim to the same effect.

The second proceedings were a sequel to proceedings entitled 'The High Court 1996 No 10143P between Michael F Murphy, plaintiff and John Gilligan, Geraldine Gilligan, Tracy Gilligan and Warren Gilligan, defendants' in which an order was made by the High Court pursuant to s 3 of the 1996 Act preventing the plaintiff from disposing or otherwise dealing with the properties specified therein. Those proceedings were grounded on an affidavit by the applicant who is also the plaintiff in the first proceedings, in which he deposed to his belief that the property forming the subject matter of the application was directly or indirectly the proceeds of crime. He said that his belief was supported by the fact that the plaintiff had been involved in crime for a lengthy period and had accumulated very substantial assets in a short period of time without his enjoying any apparent lawful source of income. The applicant also averred that the gardaí believed that the plaintiff had a significant involvement in the importation of narcotics. The plaintiff did not swear an affidavit in those proceedings.

In those proceedings, evidence was given by senior Garda officers as to the problems posed for the law enforcement agencies of the State by the significant extension of the practice of 'money laundering' the proceeds of illegal activities, such as the import and sale of drugs on a substantial scale.

The relevant provisions of the 1996 Act are set out in the judgment of Keane CJ on the non-constitutional issues arising in the first proceedings.

The principal argument advanced on behalf of the appellants in this court was that the provisions of the 1996 Act essentially formed part of the criminal law and not of the civil law and that the persons affected by those provisions were deprived of some of the most important safeguards which were historically a feature of the criminal law. Specifically, the presumption of innocence was reversed, the standard of proof was on the balance of probabilities rather than beyond reasonable doubt, there was no provision for a trial by jury in respect of any of the issues and the rule against double jeopardy was ignored.

The features of the Act which the appellants pointed to as being indicative of its criminal nature can be summarised as follows:

(i) it was of general application;

(ii) it made no provision for compensation or reparation being paid to any of the victims of the alleged crimes;

(iii) its clear policy was the deterrence of crime;

(iv) relief under the Act could only be obtained where the assets were shown to be the proceeds of crime;

(v) the necessity for mens rea, an ingredient associated exclusively with the criminal law, was implicit in the jurisdiction given to the court to grant relief to the persons affected where there was 'a serious risk of injustice';

(vi) the applicant in each case was a senior Garda officer attached to the Criminal Assets Bureau;

(vii) powers exclusively associated with the criminal law, eg the use of search warrants, were used to assist in the plaintiff's case.

In support of the submission that the procedures provided under the Act are essentially criminal in nature rather than civil, the appellants relied on the decision of this court in *Melling v O'Mathghamhna* [1962] IR 1. They submitted that the decision of the former Supreme Court in *Attorney General v Southern Industrial Trust* (1960) 94 ILTR 161, relied on by the respondents, went no further than holding that the penalties imposed in fiscal legislation for contravention of fiscal laws are not necessarily criminal in nature. The 1996 Act was not of a fiscal nature.

The appellants also relied on a number of United States decisions, particularly those of the Supreme Court, which, they said, supported their contention that legislation such as the 1996 Act was criminal in nature. They referred in particular to *Peisch v Ware* 4 Cranch 347; *United States v Halvers* 490 US 435; *Austin v United States* 509 US 602; *Department of Revenue v Kurth Ranch* 511 US 767; *United States v Ursery* 518 US 267; *United States v Bagakaiiam* 524 US 321. They accepted that the decision of the majority in *Ursery* was not in their favour, but submitted that this court should prefer the dissenting judgment of Stevens J in that case.

They further submitted that the constitutional problems which flowed from the absence of the traditional safeguards of the criminal law were not resolved by treating the proceedings as essentially in rem rather than proceedings which effectively punished persons for alleged wrongdoing. They submitted that the decision of the House of Lords in *Republic of India v Indian Steamship Company (No. 2)* [1998] AC 878, that characterising actions as in rem was no longer an appropriate way of resolving questions of substance, should be followed in this jurisdiction.

The appellants further submitted that the decision of the High Court (Barrington J) in *Clancy v Ireland* [1988] IR 326, which had been relied on by the respondents in the High Court, was of no assistance to them, since the points relied on by the appellants in the present case had not been raised or argued in that case. They submitted that the decisions of this court in *McLoughlin v Tuite* [1989] IR 82 and *O'Keeffe v Ferris* [1993] 3 IR 165 relied on in the High Court were also distinguishable. The first concerned a fiscal law and was a case in which there was no mens rea requirement of any kind. The second concerned the statutory remedy available to a liquidator or creditor of an insolvent company which was designed to ensure reparation for losses caused to the company by the defendants' wrongdoing, an entirely different situation from that addressed in the 1996 Act.

The appellants also relied on a number of other features of the 1996 Act as demonstrating that it was invalid having regard to the provisions of the Constitution.

First, it was submitted that the Act permitted of delays which were so oppressive in their nature as to render the Act unconstitutional. Thus, in the present case, a period of over 15 months had elapsed between the making of the order under s 2 and the hearing of the interlocutory application under s 3. They said that this was compounded by the stipulation in s 4(1) that what was effectively the trial of the action (ie the application for a disposal order) could not take place until at least seven years had elapsed from the making of the interlocutory order.

Secondly, it was submitted that the procedures permitted under the Act were so unfair as to be unconstitutional. In the first place, it was said that the maxim audi alteram partem was violated in that there was no provision to ensure that respondents to applications under the Act were told of the case they had to meet. Thus, in the present case the plaintiff was not ordered to deliver a statement of claim, the appellants were not furnished with particulars of the crimes alleged to be involved and no order for discovery had been made.

Secondly, the provision for the admission of hearsay evidence meant that the appellants were deprived of the right to confront and cross examine the witnesses relied on by the plaintiff. Thirdly, there was no 'equality of arms' between the parties to proceedings under the 1996 Act as required by Article 40.1 of the Constitution guaranteeing equality before the law. Thus, the appellants were not entitled to proper pleadings, particulars and discovery and evidence of opinion was permitted in the case of the plaintiff under s 8(1)(b) but not in the case of the respondents. Fourthly, the complete reversal of the onus of proof in favour of the plaintiff was a manifestly unfair procedure, even if the proceedings were properly characterised as civil.

Thirdly, it was submitted that the entire scheme of the 1996 Act and in particular s 9 - under which the respondent could be required to file an affidavit specifying its proper and income - contravened the privilege against self-incrimination. A respondent wishing to challenge an order sought under s 3 might well be obliged to disclose information that could then be used to incriminate him.

Fourthly, it was submitted that the Act was so overboard in its sweep that it constituted an abdication of legislative responsibility. Thus, the expression 'proceeds of crime' was extraordinarily vague and sweeping and the same could be said of the power given to the court to make or refrain from making orders where there was *'a serious risk of injustice'*. Similarly, the vagueness of the Act was in contravention of the requirement laid down in the European Court of Human Rights in the *Sunday Times case* 2 EHRR 245 where the term 'prescribed by law' was explained. It was also contrary to the law as laid down by this court in *King v Attorney General* [1981] IR 233 and *Cox v Ireland* [1992] 2 IR 503.

Fifthly, it was submitted that the Act violated the guarantee of private property under the Constitution, since there was no provision for compensation in the event of any person other than the owner of the properly seeking it or for bona fide purchasers of the proceeds of crime.

Sixthly, it was submitted that the Act impermissibly interfered with the judicial function in a number of respects. The obligation on the court to discharge an interim or interlocutory order on the request of the applicant was a fettering of the court's discretion which was not permitted by the Constitution.

The seventh submission was that s 3(5)(c) of the Act was unconstitutional because it purports to authorise and/or recognise the possibility of an appeal from the Supreme Court to a non-specified court or authority.

The appellants finally submitted that, if contrary to the arguments advanced by them on the non constitutional issues, the court found that the Act applied to property abroad and or was retrospective in its effect, it was invalid having regard to the provisions of Article 29.3 and 8 of the Constitution and because it violated the unenumerated right of a citizen not to have a penalty or other penal burden imposed that was more severe than that applying at the time of the commission of the wrong.

The court begins its consideration of this issue by noting that the 1996 Act enjoys a presumption of constitutionality and that the onus was on the appellants to establish that it was invalid having regard to the provisions of the Constitution.

It also follows that, if in respect of any provision or provisions of the Act two or more constructions are reasonably open; one of which is constitutional and the other is unconstitutional, it must be presumed that the Oireachtas intended only the constitutional construction: see *McDonald v Bord na Con (No 2)* [1965] IR 217. It also follows that, in accordance with the decision of the court in *East Donegal Co-operative v Attorney General* [1970] IR 317, it is to be presumed that the Oireachtas intended that any proceedings, procedures, discretions or adjudications permitted, provided for or prescribed by the Act would be conducted in accordance with the principles of constitutional justice and that any departure from those principles would be restrained or corrected by the courts.

The court addresses first the argument on behalf of the appellants that the procedures permitted under the Act are essentially criminal in nature and that the absence of some of the most important safeguards available under our system of criminal justice to persons charged with criminal offences renders the legislation unconstitutional.

It is almost beyond argument that, if the procedures under s 2, s 3 and s 4 of the 1996 Act constituted in substance, albeit not in form, the trial of persons on criminal charges, they would be invalid having regard to the provisions of the Constitution. The virtual absence of the presumption of innocence, the provision that the standard of proof is to be on the balance of probabilities and the admissibility of hearsay evidence taken together are inconsistent with the requirement in Article 38.1 of the Constitution that:

> no person shall be tried on any criminal charge save in due course of law.

It is also clear that, if these procedures constitute the trial of a person on a criminal charge, which, depending on the value of the property, might not constitute a minor offence, the absence of any provision for a trial by jury of such a charge in the Act would clearly be in violation of Article 38.5 of the Constitution.

The central issue, on this aspect of the case, is, accordingly, whether the procedures prescribed by the Act are in substance criminal in nature. The statutory scheme established under the 1996 Act may be summarised as follows. The applicant, who must be a senior Garda officer, may obtain on an ex parte application to the High Court an order prohibiting a person who is in possession or control of specified property (an expression which would obviously include the owner of the property) from disposing or dealing with the property if it is shown to the satisfaction of the court that it constitutes, directly or indirectly, the proceeds of crime. That order remains in effect for no longer than 21 days unless, before the expiration of that period, an application for a further order is made. This application must be made on notice to the person against whom the ex parte order was made or anyone else claiming to be the owner of the property. Again, the court, if satisfied that the property constitutes, directly or indirectly, the proceeds of crime, may make an order to the same effect as the interim order, unless it is satisfied that there would be 'a serious risk of injustice'. That order then remains in force and, where it has been so in force for at least seven years, the court may make, on the application of the Garda officer, a 'disposal order' transferring the property to the Minister for Finance or such other person as the court may determine. However, in the interval between the making of the interlocutory order and the expiration of that seven year period, the court may discharge the order on the application either of the Garda officer or the person to whom it was directed or who claims an interest in the proper. In the latter case, the order is to be made by the court where it is satisfied that the property was not, directly or indirectly, the proceeds of crime or that it would cause 'any other injustice'.

The effect of the statutory scheme, accordingly, is to 'freeze' property which senior members of the gardaí suspect of representing the proceeds of crime for an indefinite period, subject to the limitations indicated. It is not in dispute - and indeed is a circumstance strongly relied upon on behalf of the appellants - that this unquestionably draconian legislation was enacted by the Oireachtas because professional criminals have developed sophisticated and elaborate forms of what has become known as 'money laundering' in order to conceal from the authorities the proceeds of their criminal activities. In the two cases under appeal, the alleged activities were the importation and sale in this country of substantial quantities of illegal drugs, but the legislation is not, of course, restricted in its effect to that particular form of criminal activity.

The appellants urge that the resultant legislation is a hasty, ill-considered and disproportionate reaction to that particular phenomenon which unjustifiably and dangerously erodes their constitutional rights.

Unless an order is made under s 4 at the expiration of the seven year period for the disposal of the proper, Be owner of the properly does not cease to be its owner by virtue of anything done in exercise of the powers conferred by the Act. He or she is, however, in effect deprived of the beneficial enjoyment of flee property even before such a disposal order is made, the only provision for compensation being where the ex parte or interlocutory order is discharged or lapses or is varied, the compensation then being payable solely to the owner of the properly. The orders which the court is empowered to make, accordingly, under the Act may equate to the forfeiture of the property in question and the appellants contend that such a procedure cannot be deprived of its essentially punitive and criminal nature by being given a statutory vesture appropriate to civil proceedings.

The general question as to whether proceedings authorised by statute which may result in the forfeiture of property are civil or criminal in nature has been considered in a number of authorities to which the court was referred.

In *Attorney General v Southern Industrial Trust Ltd and Anor*, the High Court and the former Supreme Court considered the validity of the provisions of s 207 of the Customs Consolidation Act 1876 ('the 1876 Act') and s 5 of the Customs (Temporary Provisions) Act 1945 ('the 1945 Act') which empowered the court in proceedings brought by way of information by the Attorney General to determine that goods which had been illegally exported from the State - in that case a motor car - should be forfeited and condemned. The car in question was the subject of a hire purchase agreement between the first defendant and the second defendant and it was not in issue in the proceedings (which were not defended by the second defendant) that it had been illegally exported to Northern Ireland by the second defendant. It was also not in dispute that the first defendant had acted in a wholly bona fide manner and had not been privy in any way to the illegal export of the car.

The constitutional validity of the relevant legislation was challenged by the first defendant on two grounds, ie that it constituted a criminal procedure without the safeguard of due process and a trial by jury required under Article 38 and that it violated the private property rights of the first defendant guaranteed under Articles 40 and 43 of the Constitution.

In the High Court, Davitt P rejected both these challenges to the constitutionality of the relevant legislation and his conclusions were upheld on appeal by the Supreme Court. The first defendants had relied, in support of their first ground of challenge, on the earlier decision of the Supreme Court in *The State (Gettins) v Judge Fawsitt* [1945] IR 183.

In that case the prosecutor had exported a quantity of eggs in contravention of an emergency powers order which brought Into operation certain provisions of the Scrap Iron (Control of Export) Act 1938 and rendered him liable to the same penalties, detention and proceedings to which a person was liable under s 186 of the 1876 Act for illegally importing prohibited goods.

That section provided that, in the case of an offence under the Customs Acts, an offender was, for each offence, to forfeit either treble the value of the goods or £100 at the election of the commissioners and might either be detained or proceeded against by summons. Section 11 of the amending Act of 1879 enabled the relevant proceedings to be brought in the superior courts of common law in the name of the Attorney General or by information in the name of an officer of Customs and Excise before one or more justice or justices. The Revenue Commissioners had elected to proceed for a penalty of £100 in the District Court where the proceedings were dismissed. The complainant having appealed, the Circuit Court reversed the dismissal and convicted *Gettins*, who was ordered to pay a penalty of £100 or, in default, to be imprisoned for six months. A conditional order of certiorari having been obtained to quash the conviction and order on the grounds that the proceedings were criminal proceedings and that no appeal lay from the acquittal, a divisional court of the High Court held that the proceedings were not criminal proceedings and discharged the conditional order, following an earlier decision of a divisional court in *O'Croinin v Brennan* [1939] IR 274. On appeal, the Supreme Court by a majority (Sullivan CJ, Murnaghan and Geoghegan JJ, O'Byrne and Black JJ dissenting) held that the proceedings were or criminal proceedings and allowed the appeal.

Delivering the judgment of the majority in that case, Murnaghan J distinguished the case from that of the *Attorney General v Casey* [1930] IR 163. That was also a case in which the Attorney General had proceeded by way of information in the High Court to recover certain penalties from the defendant under the provisions of s 30(1) of the Income Tax Act 1918 on the ground that he had fraudulently concealed part of his income for the year in question. The defendant had sought an order that the action be tried by a judge with a jury, but had been refused and, on the hearing of the appeal in the Supreme Court, it was argued on his behalf inter alia that the proceedings were criminal proceedings.

That argument was rejected by the court, all three members - Kennedy CJ, Fitzgibbon J and Murnaghan J - being of the view that the proceedings were in the form of an action for debt and were accordingly civil. The fact that the statute which imposed the penalty also made the defaulter amenable to the criminal law by indictment or otherwise in respect of the same facts did not, in the view of the court, render the instant proceedings criminal in nature. While Murnaghan J dissented, he did so on the ground that, even accepting that the proceedings were civil in nature, a charge of fraudulent intent under the then law constituted an issue which required resolution by a jury.

Davitt P concluded that the case before him was governed by the decision in *Casey* that it was essentially a civil proceeding which did not seek to make anyone amenable for a criminal offence and that the fact that, in order to lay the ground for an order of forfeiture, the Attorney General had to establish facts which showed that the second named defendant had committed a criminal offence did not render the instant proceedings criminal in nature. While he did not seek expressly to distinguish the decision in *Gettins*, it is to be inferred from his judgment that the learned President would have treated that case as also distinguishable on the ground that in that case the Revenue Commissioners had elected to proceed by way of complaint in the District Court and that this constituted the prosecution of a criminal offence in contrast to proceedings initiated by the Attorney General in the High Court.

On appeal, those conclusions were upheld m the judgment of the court, delivered by Lavery J. Having expressed disquiet at the form of the proceedings, which, in the light of the admissions and agreed statement of facts, indicated that both parties were anxious to obtain something in the nature of an advisory judgment from the court, the learned judge said:

> The first question raised is whether a proceeding of this kind is criminal in character so as to require that the trial should be by a jury.
>
> Article 38 of the Constitution is relied on.
>
> It provides:
>
> Article 38(1). No person shall be tried on any criminal charge save in due course of law.
>
> Article 38(5). Save in the case of the trial of offences under s 2, s 3 or s 4 of this article no person shall be tried on any criminal charge without a jury.
>
> It was not adverted to in argument but the present proceeding is one in rem and not in personam.
>
> No person is on trial here. This circumstance might be sufficient to dispose of the submission, but in the opinion of the court the proceeding is not a criminal charge but is civil in character.
>
> No question of mens rea or of fraud arises. If the exportation is not lawful the forfeiture follows: nor does any question of imprisonment or even of pecuniary penalties directly arise.

Lavery J then went on to say that the matter was in any event determined by authority and to uphold the conclusions of Davitt P in relation to three earlier decisions already referred to. He cited the following passage from the decision of Murnaghan J in *Gettins*:

> The information at the suit of the attorney General is civil because it is a relic of medieval procedure, while the proceedings before the District Justice have all the marks of criminal proceedings for which the punishment is a penalty with imprisonment in default of payment.

Lavery J commented:

> It will be seen that the learned judge emphasises the liability to imprisonment. It is certainly unnecessary in the present case to consider whether such liability always makes a procedure where it is involved a criminal one. It is sufficient to say that no such liability is here involved and that *Gettins*'s case is clearly distinguishable both on this ground and also because the learned judge distinguishes proceedings by information in the High Court by the Attorney General - which is the form of the present proceedings - and accepts that they are civil in character.

The court was not invited to hold that *Southern Industrial Trust* was wrong in law and should not be followed. (It should be pointed out, however, that, in the light of subsequent decisions, it cannot be regarded as correctly stating the law on the second ground of challenge relating to the private property guarantees.) It was, however, urged that the case was distinguishable on the ground that it related to fiscal legislation: it was said that, for somewhat anomalous historical reasons, revenue proceedings against tax defaulters had usually been treated as civil matters. It was also submitted that there could be a forfeiture under s 5 of the 1945 Act, even where the owner had a full defence to a prosecution under the Act, eg where the vehicle had been stolen from him. In contrast, it was submitted that forfeiture under the 1996 Act was invariably predicated on crimes having been committed. It was also submitted that the procedure under the 1945 Act did not provide for the establishment of mens rea: the provisions of the 1996 Act enabling the court to grant relief to the owner of the property where there was a serious risk of injustice clearly indicated that mens rea was an essential ingredient of the forfeiture procedure under the 1996 Act.

It was further submitted that the procedures permitted under the 1996 Act, even if reconcilable with the Constitution when considered solely in the light of the *Southern Industrial Trust* decision, were repugnant to the Constitution in the light of the later decision of the Supreme Court in *Melling v O'Mathahamhna and Another* [1962] IR 1, which must next be considered.

In that case, the plaintiff was charged in the District Court on fifteen charges relating to smuggling of butter into the State in contravention of the Dairy Produce (Price Stabilisation) Act 1935 and s 186 of the 1876 Act. The Revenue Commissioners, under the provisions of s 186, elected to proceed for a penalty of £100 in respect of each of the charges. The prosecution was resisted on the ground that the District Court had no jurisdiction to try the charges because they were not minor in nature and hence could only be tried by a judge and a jury. The matter was adjourned in order to enable proceedings to be brought in the High Court claiming a declaration that the relevant provisions of the 1876 Act and the amending Act of 1879 were inconsistent with the provisions of the Constitution of Saorstát Éireann and the Constitution of Ireland.

The High Court having refused to grant that declaration, an appeal was brought to the Supreme Court.

That court (Maguire CJ, Lavery, Kingsmill Moore, Ó Dálaigh and Maguire JJ) were unanimously of the view that the offences were criminal offences, but a majority, (Maguire

CJ, Lavery and Maguire JJ) were also of the view that they were minor offences which could be tried in a summary manner.

Three judgments were delivered in the course of his judgment, Lavery J said that in his opinion the case was indistinguishable from *Gettins*, but went on to say:

> Apart from authority, it seems to me clear that a proceeding, the course of which permits the detention of the person concerned, the bringing of him in custody to a Garda station, the entry of a charge in all respects in the terms appropriate to the charge of a criminal offence, the searching of the person detained and the examination of papers and other things found upon him, the bringing of him before a District Justice in custody, the admission to bail to stand his trial and the detention in custody if bail be not granted or is not forthcoming, the imposition of a pecuniary penalty with the liability to imprisonment if the penalty is not paid has all the indicia of a criminal charge. The penalty is clearly punitive in character, being £100 or treble the duty paid value of the goods.

In his judgment, Kingsmill Moore J, in a passage which is strongly relied on by the appellants in the present case, referred to some definitions of a 'crime' which had found favour with judges or text book writers. In *Proprietary Articles Trade Association v Attorney General for Canada* [1931] AC 310 at 324, Lord Atkin had said that it could be discovered by reference to one standard alone, ie 'Is the act prohibited with penal consequences?' The then current edition of Cross and Jones had suggested as a definition:

> A crime is a legal wrong the remedy for which is the punishment of the offender at the instance of the State.

Kenny, in the earlier editions of *Outlines of Criminal Law*, had said that:

> Crimes are wrongs whose sanction is punitive and is remissible by the Crown if remissible at all.

The learned judge said that in his view an offence under s 186 of the 1876 Act would fall within these text book definitions and went on to say:

> The offences enumerated in s 186 possess several features which are regarded as indicia of crimes.
>
> (i) They are offences against the community at large and not against an individual. Blackstone defines a crime as a 'violation of the public rights and duties due to the whole community, considered as a community': 4 Bl Comm 5.
>
> (ii) The sanction is punitive, and not merely a matter of fiscal reparation, for the penalty is £100 or three times the duty paid value of the good; and failure to pay, even where the offender has not the means, involves imprisonment.
>
> (iii) They require mens rea for the act must be done 'knowingly' and 'with intend to evade the prohibition or restriction': *Frailey v Charlton* (1920) 1 KB 147. If *O'Croinin v Brennan* purports to decide that mens rea is not a necessary ingredient of an offence under s 186 I would not regard it as correctly decided. Mens rea is not an invariable ingredient of a criminal offence, and even in a civil action of debt for a penalty it may be necessary to show that there was mens rea where the act complained of is an offence 'in the nature of a crime': *Lee v Dangler, Grant & Co* (1892) 2 QB 337; *Badge v Whitehead* (1892) 2 QB 355; but where mens rea is made an element of an offence it is generally an indication of criminality. '

The learned judge went on to subject the decision in *Gettins* case to an exhaustive analysis (with which, it should be noted, Lavery J in his judgment expressly agreed) and concluded that the decision of the Court in that case had been to the effect that proceedings under s 186 of the 1876 Act were criminal and that this was supported by other authorities in both this jurisdiction and in England.

He summed up his view as follows:

> It appears to me that the weight of authority is in favour of the view that prosecutions before a District Justice under s 186 are criminal prosecutions in which a criminal charge is brought against a person accused of an offence, and I accede more readily to this weight of authority because it coincides with my own clear and strong view of the question.

In the course of his judgment, (Ó Dálaigh J (as he then was), having noted that (a) one of the chief characteristics of civil liability, as contrasted with criminal liability, was the obligation to make reparation and not to have to suffer imprisonment if unable to make reparation, and (b) that certain acts, such as assaults, could be the subject of criminal as well as civil proceedings, went on to point to those features of s 186 of the 1876 Act which, in his view, rendered the proceedings permitted thereunder criminal nature.

He said:

> The vocabulary of s 186 of the Act of 1876 is the vocabulary of the criminal law; the preliminary detention in jail unless bail be found (s 197) and the right to enter, search and seize goods in a defendant's house or premises (ss 204 and 205) are, as yet, unfamiliar features of civil litigation. In their initiation, conclusion and consequences proceedings under s 186 have all the features of a criminal prosecution. Note that Parliament in inserting directions in the form of conviction (set out in Schedule C to the Act and directed by s 223 of the Act to be used) speaks unequivocally: I quote:
>
>> 'Where the party has been convicted of an offence punishable by pecuniary penalty and imprisonment in default of payment.'
>
> Finally, the mode of withdrawal of proceedings is the time-honoured formula employed by the Attorney General in criminal charges - nolle prosequi (s 256). Well might Mr Justice Murnaghan say, as he did in *Gettins*'s Case:
>
>> ... the proceedings before the District Justice have all the marks of criminal procedure and are in no way distinguishable from criminal proceedings for which the punishment is a penalty with imprisonment in default of payment.

It is a notable feature of this case that the court's earlier decision in *Southern Industrial Trust* although referred to in the course of the arguments, is not mentioned in any of the judgments. The decisions taken together, however, made it clear beyond doubt that, where proceedings were taken by the Attorney General for the condemnation and forfeiture of illegally exported goods, they were civil in nature, but where the Revenue Commissioners elected to proceed by way of summons in the District Court seeking the imposition of a penalty, they were criminal in nature. The court, at a later part of this judgment, considers how the reasoning by which those conclusions were reached should be applied to the present case. There are, however, three later decisions of the High Court and this court which were also referred to in the course of argument and which must next be considered.

The first these is *Clancy v Ireland*. That arose out of the enactment by the Oireachtas of s 2 of the Offences Against the State (Amendment) Act 1985.

Section 22 of the Offences Against the State Act 1939 provided that where the government had declared a particular organisation to be an unlawful organisation which should be suppressed, its property was to be forfeited to, and vested in, the Minister for Justice. Section 2 of the amending legislation provided that, where in the opinion of the Minister, monies held by a bank would, but for the operation of s 22 of the 1939 Act, be the property of an unlawful organisation, the Minister could require the bank to pay the monies into the High Court on a specified day and in the meantime to refrain from doing any act or making any omission inconsistent with that requirement. The Act contained further provisions entitling a person claiming to be the owner of the money to apply to the High Court for an order directing the payment of the money to him, where he showed to the satisfaction of the court that the monies were not monies to which s 22 of the 1939 Act applied and that he was the owner of the monies.

Such an order having been made in respect of monies held upon a joint account in the names of the plaintiffs in a bank, they issued proceedings claiming that the monies were not held for the benefit of an unlawful organisation and declarations that the relevant provisions of the 1985 Act were invalid having regard to the provisions of the Constitution. The laconic and unsatisfactory report of the case gives no indication as to the nature of the arguments advanced at the hearing in the High Court. It appears from the judgment of Barrington J that the grounds on which the legislation was attacked were that it violated the plaintiff's rights of private property under the Constitution and deprived him of the fair procedures to which he was entitled under a number of decisions of this court, in particular *In Re Haughey* [1971] IR 217.

Barrington J rejected both grounds of challenge. The learned judge said that he was satisfied that the abridgement of property rights provided for under the Act was a permissible delimitation of properly rights for the purposes of Article 43 and was not a breach of fair procedures, citing with approval the decision of the US Supreme Court in *Calero-Toledo v Pearson Yacht Leasing Company* (1974) 416 US 663, an authority to which it will be necessary to refer at a later stage.

McLoughlin v Tuite was a case in which the plaintiff had failed to comply with a notice by an inspector of taxes requiring him to deliver returns of income for certain income tax years. He was sued by the inspector claiming penalties arising under s 500 of the Income Tax Act 1967 arising from his failure to comply with the terms of the notice. Judgment having been entered in favour of the inspector, the plaintiff issued proceedings seeking a declaration that s 500 of the 1967 Act was repugnant to the Constitution in that it imposed a criminal penalty other than in a manner permitted by the Constitution.

Carroll J, in the course of her judgment, considered the decisions in *Casey* and *Melling v O'Mathghamhna* and cited the extracts already quoted in this judgment from the judgments of Lavery J, Kingsmill Moore J and Ó Dálaigh J in the latter case. Applying the indicia specified in the judgment of Kingsmill Moore J, she concluded that two of them were present in the procedures under s 500, ie if an offence was created, it was one against the community at large and the sanction provided was penal in its nature, although there was no provision for imprisonment in default of payment of the penalty.

She was, however, also satisfied that mens rea was not an ingredient in a failure to make a return of income. She also considered that the indicia mentioned in the judgment of Ó Dálaigh J were all absent in the provisions relating to penalties under s 500. The learned judge concluded that the imposition of a penalty where there was a default in making a return was not indicative of a criminal offence and that, accordingly, the provision was not repugnant to the Constitution.

That judgment was upheld on appeal by this court. Having considered the decision of the former court in *Melling v O'Mathghamhna,* Finlay CJ, delivering the judgment of the court, said:

> ... The only feature which could be said to be common between the provisions of s 500 and s 508 (of the Income Tax Act 1967) and the ordinary constituents of a criminal offence is that the payment of a sum of money is provided for which is an involuntary payment and which is

not related to any form of compensation or reparation necessary to the State but is rather a deterrent or sanction. The court is not satisfied that the provision for a penalty in that fashion in a code of taxation law, with the general features which have been shortly outlined in this judgment, clearly establishes the provisions of the section as creating a criminal offence.

The last case in the series of Irish decisions is *O'Keeffe v Ferris*. That case arose out of the provision in s 297 of the Companies Act 1963 empowering the High Court, on the application of the liquidator or any creditor or contributory of a company in winding up, to declare that persons who are knowingly parties to the carrying on of the business in a fraudulent manner are to be personally responsible, without any limitation of liability, for all or any of the debts or other liabilities of the company. It also provided that where the business is so carried on, the persons knowingly party to its being carried on in that manner were to be liable on conviction to imprisonment or fines or bow. The liquidator of an insolvent company having instituted proceedings against one of the directors claiming relief under s 297, the latter then instituted proceedings seeking a declaration that s 297 was unconstitutional or, alternatively, that the manner in which the liquidator sought to invoke it against the plaintiff was invalid as it amounted to a trial of criminal offence without due procedures for a criminal trial.

In the High Court, Murphy J, having referred to the judgments in *Melling* said that some of the indicia of a criminal offence identified in those judgments were not present at all in the impugned subsection and those that were present were ambiguous. In a passage which is of some relevance in the present proceedings, the learned judge pointed out that it would not be correct to treat the procedure under s 297(1) as conforming to the generally accepted concept of compensation or reparation recovered in civil proceedings, since the applicant for the relief did not have to be the particular creditor who had been defrauded by the manner in which the business of a company was carried on. However, in his view, that feature of itself did not mean that the proceedings were criminal in form. He was satisfied that it was the clear intention of the Oireachtas that the remedy afforded the section was a civil remedy and not a criminal one. He accordingly dismissed He plaintiff's claim.

That judgment was upheld in this court. Delivering the judgment of the court, O'Flaherty J referred to a submission on behalf of the plaintiff that the procedure under the section was 'an ersatz civil proceeding which was really criminal in nature', an expression which was also adopted by counsel for the appellants in the present case. In the course of his judgment, O'Flaherty J says:

> It is clear, in the first instance, that the subsection in question does not create a criminal offence. To hold that it did would be to disregard the provisions of both subsection (3) and subsection (4) of s 297. Further, none of the indicia of a criminal offence identified in *Mellings* case are present: there is no prosecutor; there is no offence created; there is no mode of trial of a criminal offence prescribed and there is no criminal sanction imposed. Indeed, the court did not understand counsel for the plaintiff to press this point. Rather, the plaintiff's case was put on the basis that the civil proceedings were really a disguise for what was truly an attempt by the Oireachtas to impose a criminal sanction in a civil context. The court rejects this construction of the section. It holds that the section is clearly within the policy entitlement of the Oireachtas to enact; it is designed to protect creditors and others who may fall victim of people engaged in fraud ... It is true that the proof of fraud will be to the civil standard, but it is also so that the more serious the allegation made in civil proceedings, then the more astute must the judge be to find that the allegation in question has been proved.

The court is satisfied that the decision in *Melling* does not support the submissions advanced on behalf of the appellants in these cases. Even if it is assumed in their favour that the presence of mens rea is an essential ingredient which must be established before an order can be made under s 3 or s 4, that would not of itself deprive the proceedings of their civil character. It is clear from the judgments of Lavery J (with whom Maguire CJ and Maguire J concurred) and from the judgment of Ó Dálaigh J that the ratio of that decision was that the presence of a number of indicia, which are conspicuously absent in the present case, rendered the proceedings criminal in character, viz the provision for the detention of the person concerned, the bringing of him in custody to a Garda station, the searching of the person detained, his admission to bail, the imposition of a pecuniary penalty with liability to imprisonment in default, the reference in the statute to a party having been 'convicted of an offence' and the provision for the withdrawal of proceedings by the entry of a nolle prosequi. The court is satisfied that the emphasis placed by the appellants on the three elements indicated by Kingsmill Moore J as essential ingredients of a criminal offence is misplaced: in another passage in his judgment, cited by Finlay CJ in *McLoughlin v Tuite*, he refers expressly to some of these indicia as pointing clearly to the criminal nature of the proceedings. In contrast, in proceedings under s 3 and s 4 of the 1996 Act, there is no provision for the arrest or detention of any person, for the admission of persons to bail, for the imprisonment of a person in default of payment of a penalty, for a form of criminal trial initiated by summons or indictment, for the recording of a conviction in any form or for the entering of a nolle prosequi at any stage.

The court is in any event satisfied that the submission that the establishment of mens rea by the applicant is essential if an order under s 3 or s.4 is to be made is fundamentally misconceived. Two conditions alone must be met before an order is made under those sections: that a person is in possession or control of a specified property which constitutes the proceeds of crime or was acquired in connection with such property and that its value is not less than £10,000. The orders can be made even though it has not been shown to the satisfaction of the court that there was mens rea on the part of the person in possession or control of the property. This is so, whether mens rea in this context is being used in the sense of 'a general disposition to do something that was morally wrong in the old canonical sense' or in the sense adopted in the authorities at a later stage of 'an intention to commit the particular wrong mentioned in the definition of the relevant offence'. (The distinction between the two forms of mens rea is helpfully discussed in *Criminal Liability* by McCauley and McCutcheon.) The fact that the person in possession or control of the property against whom the order is sought may not himself or herself have been in any way involved in any criminal activity and, specifically, may not have been aware that the property constituted the proceeds of crime would not prevent the court from making the order freezing the property under s 2 or s 3, unless it was satisfied that there would be 'a serious risk of injustice'. If the legislature had intended that no such order should be made unless it had first been established that the person in possession or control of the proper had acquired it with a criminal intent it would have said so. No doubt the court might decline to make the order in a case where the person in possession or control was in a position to establish that he or she had purchased the particular property in good faith for valuable consideration: it might, on the other hand, make the order in circumstances where an innocent recipient of the property had made no payment for it.

It also follows that one of the grounds on which it was sought to distinguish the decision in Southern Industrial Trust - that there was no requirement of mens rea under the statutory provision in question - is not well founded.

Moreover, the court is satisfied that a further ground of distinction urged in respect of that decision, that the order of forfeiture could be made even though the owner of the property was innocent of any crime in respect of it, has not been established. Although the making of the orders under ss 3 and 4 is undoubtedly predicated on the commission of a crime by some person or persons, the same could be said of the provisions under consideration in *Southern Industrial Trust*: although the first defendant was not guilty of any criminal offence, the second defendant had undoubtedly committed the offence of exporting the car without a licence. It is clear from the judgments both in the High Court and the Supreme Court that the order could not have been made had the car not been illegally exported.

The appellants submit that the sequence of cases from *Casey* to *McLoughlin v Tuite* do not support the findings in the High Court that the 1996 Act is constitutional because they were all cases in which revenue offences were under consideration. Black J, in his dissenting judgment in *Gettins*, said: 'I doubt whether the application of logical principles is a sure guide at all in dealing with the traditional doctrine that proceedings in respect of revenue offences are in their nature civil, for I regard that tradition as itself wholly illogical. It is, nonetheless, well recognised.'

The learned judge was there referring to a procedure by way of summons in the District Court which the majority of the court found to be criminal in its nature. It is at this stage beyond argument that the procedures under consideration in *Casey Southern Industrial Trust* and *McLoughlin v Tuite* were all found to be civil in character and - in the case of the two last mentioned decisions - constitutionally valid. The evasion of tax and the smuggling of goods are unquestionably serious criminal offences but it would, in the view of the court, leave the law in a truly illogical and anomalous condition if procedures for the recovery of penalties or the forfeiture of goods in such cases were constitutionally valid while similar procedures in respect of crimes of at least equal gravity, such as the sale of illegal drugs on a substantial scale, were held to be repugnant to the Constitution.

That conclusion receives significant support from the United States authorities to which the court was referred. Since in that jurisdiction trial by jury is a constitutional requirement in a wide range of civil proceedings as well as in indictable crimes, the cases in general dealt with a different issue, ie as to whether the existence of parallel procedures for the forfeiture of property and the prosecution of criminal offences was in violation of the constitutional prohibition of 'double jeopardy'. Since, however, in determining whether the double jeopardy principle had been violated, it was necessary to consider whether the forfeiture proceedings were civil or criminal in their nature, the decisions are of assistance in considering the issue that has arisen in this case. They are conveniently reviewed in the opinion of the United States Supreme Court delivered by Rehnquist CJ in *United States v Ursery* (1996) 135 L Ed 2D549.

In that case, the government had instituted forfeiture proceedings against the respondent's house, alleging that it had been used to facilitate illegal drug transactions. Shortly before *Ursery* settled that claim, he was indicted and later convicted of manufacturing marijuana. The government also filed an in rem complaint against various properties seized from two other persons alleging that each item was subject to forfeiture because it was involved in money laundering.

In his opinion, Rehnquist CJ noted that, since the earliest years of the United States, Congress had authorised the government to seek parallel in rem civil forfeiture actions and criminal prosecutions based on the same underlying events. He cited the following passage from an earlier case of *Various Items of Personal Property v United States* 282 US 577, in which the court said:

> [This] forfeiture proceeding is in rem. It is the property which was proceeded against, and, by resort to legal fiction, held guilty and condemned as though it were conscious instead of inanimate and insentient. In a criminal prosecution it is the wrongdoer in person who is proceeded against, convicted and punished. The forfeiture is no part of the punishment for the criminal offence ...

Rehnquist CJ also referred to the earlier decision of the Supreme Court in *Calero-Toledo v Pearson Yacht Leasing Company*, which was adopted with approval by Barrington J in *Clancy v Ireland*. *Calero-Toledo* was a case in which a statutory forfeiture scheme under which a yacht had been seized and on which marijuana was discovered was challenged on the ground that, since the owner, who was unaware of the wrongful use of the yacht by the lessee, was not notified of the proposed seizure, it violated the due process requirements of the Constitution. It was also contended that the statute was in breach of the private property guarantees under the Constitution.

Delivering the opinion of the court, Brennan J pointed out that, at common law, the value of an inanimate object directly or indirectly causing the accidental death of a King's subject was forfeited to the Crown as a deodand.

This in turn, he said, was traceable to biblical and pre-Judeo/Christian practices.

He also referred to the forfeiture which resulted at common law from conviction for felonies and treason, the basis for them being that a breach of the criminal law was an offence to the King's peace which was felt to justify denial of the right to own property. Having referred to the wide range of forfeiture statutes which had been enacted in the United States, the learned judge commented that contemporary federal and state forfeiture statutes reached virtually any type of property that might be used in the conduct of a criminal enterprise, in a passage clearly relevant to the present case, he added:

> Despite this proliferation of forfeiture enactments, the innocence of the owner of property subject to forfeiture has always uniformly been rejected as a defence. Thus, Mr Justice Story observed in *The Palmyra* 12 Wheat 1 (1827), that a conviction for piracy was not a prerequisite to a proceeding to forfeit a ship allegedly engaged in piratical aggression in violation of a federal statute.

In the result, the opinion of the court in *Calero-Toledo* was that the statute under consideration furthered the punitive and deterrent purposes that had, in previous cases, been found sufficient to uphold, against constitutional challenge, the application of forfeiture statutes to the property of innocents.

While the dissenting opinion of Stevens J in *Ursery* was relied on by the appellants, the court is satisfied that, on examination, even if it were to be regarded as more persuasive than the opinion of the majority in that case, it does not support the submissions of the appellants. The learned judge drew a distinction between the forfeiture of funds which he described as 'the proceeds of unlawful activity' and the seizure of *Ursery*'s house, in respect of which, he said, there was no evidence that it had been purchased with the proceeds of unlawful activity. His opinion undoubtedly takes issue with the opinion of the majority in the same case that proceedings in rem are in general civil rather than criminal in character as being too sweeping and inconsistent with earlier decisions of the court, but the substance of his opinion can be found in this passage:

> There is simply no rational basis for characterising the seizure of this respondent's home as anything other than punishment for his crime. The house was neither proceeds nor contraband and its value had no relation to the government's authority to seize it.

That passage reflects three categories of property identified by Justice Stevens as being subject to forfeiture and his analysis as to why in some circumstances the forfeiture would constitute 'punishment' and in others not.

An examination of the analysis made by Judge Stevens would properly commence with the unusual (in this jurisdiction) title of the consolidated proceedings in which judgment was delivered. The report is entitled *'United States, Petitioner v Guy Jerome Ursery (No 95-345) United States, Petitioner v $405,089.23 in United States currency et al (No 95-346).'*

The facts of the case should now be set out in more detail. The US government had instituted civil forfeiture proceedings under specific legislation against Guy Ursery's house alleging that it had been used to facilitate illegal drug transactions. That claim was settled by Ursery who was then charged and convicted of manufacturing marijuana in violation of certain statutory prohibitions. In the other proceedings (the Arnt and Wren proceedings) the US government instituted proceedings in rem against currency seized from the accused, Messrs Arnt and Wren, on the basis that it was involved in money laundering or represented the proceeds of felonious drug transactions. That litigation was deferred while Messrs Arnt and Wren were successfully prosecuted for their illegal activities. The government then sought to revive the forfeiture proceedings. Issues arose as to whether the criminal proceedings in the *Ursery* case or the forfeiture proceedings in the Arnt and Wren proceedings involved an infringement of the double jeopardy rule. The ultimate decision of the majority of the Supreme Court was that there was no double jeopardy as the forfeiture did not involve the punishment of a wrongdoer.

It was in that context that Justice Stevens disposed shortly and clearly of the issue of punishment insofar as it arose in the case involving Messrs Arnt and Wren. He said in the second paragraph of his judgment:

> In Number 95/346 the government has forfeited $405, 089.23 in currency. Those funds are the proceeds of unlawful activity. They are not property that respondents have any right to retain. The forfeiture of such proceeds, like the confiscation of money stolen from a bank, does not punish respondents because it exacts no price in liberty or lawfully derived property from them. I agree that the forfeiture of such proceeds is not punitive and therefore I concur in the court's disposition of Number 95/356.

Again, Justice Stevens readily accepted that drugs seized by the police in pursuance of the search warrant in Mr Ursery's house were correctly forfeited as the defendant had no right to retain contraband. It was on the third issue namely, the right of the United States to forfeit the respondent's residence because it had been used 'to facilitate the manufacture and distribution of marijuana' that Justice Stevens found himself in disagreement with his colleagues. Judge Stevens was scathing in his comments on the argument that the forfeiture of a valuable house, (which was the undoubted property of the defendant), because it was used for a very limited purpose in conjunction with what appears to have been a minor breach of the drug trafficking legislation, was not punitive.

Furthermore, he was dismissive in that case, as were the House of Lords subsequently in *Republic of India v Indian Steamships Company Limited (No 2)* of the suggestion that there was 'some mystical difference between in rem and in personam proceedings such that only the latter can give rise to double jeopardy concerns'.

Whilst his reasoning in that regard is impressive, his views did not gain the support of any of his colleagues nor do they accord with the legal precedents established in this jurisdiction. *The Attorney General v Southern Industrial Trust* (1960) 90 ILTR 161 is clear authority for the proposition that a motor car used in the course of an illegal activity could be subject to a forfeiture, notwithstanding the fact that the owner did not participate in and had no knowledge of that activity.

Even if this Court were to review the decision in the *Southern Industrial Trust* Case by reversing it or restricting its application, that would not assist the appellants. The issue in the present case does not raise a challenge to a valid constitutional right of property. It concerns the right of the State to take, or the right of a citizen to resist the State in taking, property which is proved on the balance of probabilities to represent the proceeds of crime. In general such a forfeiture is not a punishment and its operation does not require criminal procedures. Application of such legislation must be sensitive to the actual property and other rights of citizens but in principle and subject, no doubt, to special problems which may arise in particular cases, a person in possession of the proceeds of crime can have no constitutional grievance if deprived of their use.

The court is satisfied that the United States authorities lend considerable weight to the view that in rem proceedings for the forfeiture of property, even where accompanied by parallel procedures for the prosecution of criminal offences arising out of the same events, are civil in character and that this principle is deeply rooted in the Anglo-American legal system. The court notes that in *Republic of India v Indian Steamship Company Ltd (No 2)*, Lord Steyn in the course of his speech pointed to the fact that to treat the ship as a defendant in admiralty proceedings because they were in rem had always been a fiction. As already noted, there are observations to the same effect in the dissenting opinion of Stevens J in *Ursery*. It may be, as Holmes pointed out in *The Common Law* that principles of this nature may outgrow their origins in a different historical era and would now find their justification in considerations of public policy or the common good. It is sufficient, however, to say that the secure place of the principles as to civil forfeiture in our law and their congruence with the Constitution is clearly reflected in the decisions in *Southern Industrial Trust* and *McLoughlin v Tuite*.

As to the other modern Irish authorities to which the court was referred, the decision in *Clancy* is not, in the view of the court, of any assistance in determining the issue as to whether proceedings of this character are civil or criminal in nature as the report does not indicate whether that issue was raised in the case: since it is not referred to in the judgment of the learned High Court judge, it seems safer to assume that it was not. The decision of this court in *O'Keeffe v Ferris* usefully illustrates that the principle established in *Southern Industrial Trust* and *McLoughlin v Tuite* is by no means confined to revenue cases.

The court is satisfied that the appellants failed to discharge the onus on them of establishing that the sections referred to in the 1996 Act were invalid having regard to the provisions of the Constitution on this ground.

The next feature of the Act which the appellants relied on as rendering the Act unconstitutional was that it permitted delays which were oppressive in their nature.

The court, in considering this submission, finds it unnecessary to express any view as to whether the surprisingly lengthy period which elapsed between the making of the order under s 2 in the first case and the hearing of the interlocutory application under s 3 was wholly or in part the fault of the appellant in that case, as contended by the respondents. It is sufficient to say that the procedure under the Act is perfectly capable of being operated in such a manner as to ensure that no unreasonable delay elapses between the making of the interim order and the interlocutory order: that indeed is clearly what the Act envisaged, since under s 2(5), the order is to lapse after the expiration of the period of 21 days from the date of its making, unless an application for the making of an interlocutory order is brought during that period. As to the claim that the period of seven years which must elapse before a disposal order is made is unduly oppressive, that rests on the misconception that the application for a disposal order can in some sense be equated to the trial of an action in respect of which the legislation earlier provides for interlocutory orders being made. That is clearly not the nature of the scheme provided for in the Act. A person who is affected by the provisions of an interlocutory order can apply at any time before the expiration of the seven year period for an order discharging or modifying the interlocutory order. The court is satisfied that the submission that the procedure is so oppressive as to be unconstitutional because of this time limitation is not well founded.

As to the submission that the procedures permitted under the Act are so unfair as to be unconstitutional, it is necessary to recall again that it is to be presumed that the Oireachtas intended that procedures provided for under the Act would be conducted in accordance with the principles of constitutional justice and that any departure from those principles will be restrained or corrected by the courts. The appellants complain that the maxim audi alteram partem was violated because, in the first case, the plaintiff was not ordered to deliver a statement of claim, the appellant was not furnished with particulars of the crimes alleged to be involved and no order for discovery was made. These orders were either made in a proper exercise of the jurisdiction of the High Court or they were not. If they were not, the appropriate course for the appellant to have taken was to appeal to this court. It accordingly has to be assumed that the orders were made in accordance with the principles of constitutional justice by the High Court judges concerned. In any event, the court is satisfied that in any case brought under the procedures laid down by the Act, the affidavits grounding the interim and interlocutory application of necessity will indicate to the respondents the nature of the case being made on behalf of the applicant. Nor is the provision for the admission of hearsay evidence of itself unconstitutional: it was a matter for the court hearing the application to decide what weight should be given to such evidence. The court is satisfied that there is no substance in these grounds of challenge to the constitutionality of the legislation.

As to the submission that there was no 'equality of arms' between the parties because evidence of opinion was permitted in the case of the applicant but not in the case of the respondents, the court is satisfied that no such inequality has been demonstrated: the respondents to an application under s 2 or s 3 will normally be the persons in possession or control of the property and should be in a position to give evidence to the court as to its provenance without calling in aid opinion evidence. A similar submission was advanced in respect of the extent to which the onus of proof was reversed in applications under the Act, but the court is satisfied that, having regard to its conclusion that these are civil proceedings this did not, of itself, render the provisions unconstitutional.

In this connection, the court was referred to the recent decision of the Privy Council in *McIntosh v Lord Advocate* [2001] 2 All ER 638. In that case, an issue arose as to whether certain provisions of the Proceeds of Crime (Scotland) Act 1994 were incompatible with Article 6(2) of the European Convention for the Protection of Human Rights and Fundamental Freedoms. Those provisions were in somewhat similar terms to those contained in the Criminal Justice Act 1994 which enable a court to make a confiscation order requiring a person convicted of a drug trafficking offence to pay a certain sum. Those procedures are in contrast to the procedures under the 1996 Act, where e precondition for the conviction of the person against whom the freeing order is to be directed does not exist. The court, however, would adopt with approval the following passage from the speech of Lord Hope of Craithead as to the approach a court should adopt in considering provisions of this nature, whether in the context of the Constitution or of the European Convention of Human Rights. He said (at p 654):

> People engage in this activity [drug trafficking] to make money and it is notorious that they hide what they are doing. Direct proof of the proceeds is often difficult, if not impossible. The nature of the activity and the harm it does to the community provide a sufficient basis for the making of these assumption [ie assumptions that property held by the accused could in certain circumstances be assumed to have been received in connection with drug tracking]. They serve a legitimate aim in the public interest of combating that activity. They do so in a way that is proportionate. They relate to matters that ought to be within the accused's knowledge, and they are rebuttable by him at a hearing before a judge on the balance of probabilities. In my opinion a fair balance is struck between the legitimate aim and the rights of the accused.

(See also the recent decision of the European Court of Human Rights in *Phillips v United Kingdom*) (5 July 2001, unreported). A further argument that the Act necessarily involves the contravention of the privilege against self-incrimination rests on the assumption that a respondent wishing to challenge an order sought under s 3 might be obliged to disclose information that could then be used to incriminate him. Parties to civil proceedings, whatever their nature, may find themselves in a position where they are reluctant to adduce evidence beneficial to them because it might also expose them to the risk of a criminal prosecution. That factual position, however, cannot be equated to a statutory provision obliging a person to give evidence even in circumstances where his or her evidence might be incriminating. Similarly, the fact that a person can be required to file an affidavit specifying his or her property and income cannot, on any view, be equated to a statutory provision requiring a person to adduce evidence which may incriminate him or her. The court is satisfied that these grounds of challenge are also without foundation.

It was also argued that the Act was so over broad in its sweep that it constituted an abdication of legislative responsibility. This was based in the first instance on what was described as the vague and sweeping nature of the expression 'proceeds of crime'. The court notes, however, that in every case before an order can be made the court must be satisfied on the balance of probabilities that on the evidence adduced to it in that particular case the property in respect of which the freezing order is sought was the proceeds of crime. Similarly, while the power of the court to extend relief to persons claiming an interest in the properly where there is 'a serious risk of injustice' is undoubtedly wide in its scope, that can only be in ease of the individuals whose rights may be affected and the court, in applying these provisions, will be obliged to act in accordance with the requirements of constitutional and natural justice.

The court is satisfied that these submissions are also not well founded. It was also submitted that the Act violated the guarantees of private property rights under the Constitution. The court has already noted that in *Clancy* Barrington J adopted as a correct statement of the law in this jurisdiction the opinion of the United States Supreme Court in *Calero-Toledo* and rejected a challenge to the constitutionality of analogous procedures under s 2 of the Offences Against the State (Amendment) Act 1985, concluding that the abridgement of proper rights thus effected was a permissible delimitation of property rights for the purposes of Article 43 of the Constitution. The court is satisfied that the law on this matter was correctly stated by Barrington J in that decision and rejects the challenge to the constitutionality of the 1996 Act advanced on that ground.

It was further submitted that the Act was invalid having regard to the provisions of the Constitution in requiring the High Court to make orders of a specific nature in certain circumstances defined in the Act on the ground that this is an unwarranted interference with the exercise of the judicial function. The court is satisfied that there is no substance in this contention: it is perfectly permissible for the legislature to provide that, where certain conditions are met, the making of an order of a particular nature by a court may be mandatory rather than discretionary: see *The State (O'Rourke) v Kelly* [1983] IR 58.

The Act was also challenged on the grounds that, if, contrary to the arguments advanced in the first case, it did permit the making of retrospective orders and orders which were extraterritorial in their effect, this was in contravention of the Constitution. The court is satisfied that there is no substance in this submission. The Act does not offend in any way the prohibition in Article 15.5 against declaring acts to be infringements of the law which were not so at the date of their commission. The fact that it enables the court to make orders in respect of property constituting the proceeds of crimes committed before the coming into force of the legislation is not in any sense a contravention of that prohibition. Nor is the fact that the legislation may be operated so as to require the compliance of citizens within the jurisdiction with orders of the court directing the transfer of property in their possession or control to a receiver appointed by the court in circumstances where the property is in another jurisdiction constitute in any way a breach of the principles of international law which the State accepts under Article 29 of the Constitution.

It was also submitted that s 3(5)(c) of the Act was unconstitutional as authorising and/or recognising the possibility of an appeal from this court to a non specified court or authority. The court is satisfied that the words 'or if any further appeal' in s 2(5)(c) are, at worst, surplusage and, in accordance with well established principles of statutory construction, can be disregarded where the result would otherwise be unconstitutional or would, as in this case, produce an absurd or anomalous result.

It was finally submitted by the appellants that the provisions of the European Convention on Human Rights ought to be considered as being part of the 'generally recognised principles of international law' and that the Act was in breach of the convention. It was submitted that since Article 29.3 provides that 'Ireland accepts the generally recognised principles of international law as its rule of conduct in its relations with other States' and the convention confers rights on individuals, any legislative measure which was in conflict with the provision of the convention must be considered repugnant to the Constitution having regard in particular to Article 29.3.

This case concerns the application of domestic legislation to persons within the jurisdiction of the State. In these circumstances it is not relevant or necessary to consider the application of the 'principles of international law' in this case and in particular whether the provisions of the European Convention on Human Rights ought to be treated as included in those 'principles', as Article 29.3 of the Constitution makes clear that these general principles, whatever their content, govern relations with other sovereign states at an international level.

Furthermore, Article 29.6 expressly provides that no international agreement shall be part of the domestic law of the State save as may be determined by the Oireachtas. The European Convention has not yet been made part of the domestic law of the State. As Maguire CJ stated in the judgment of the Supreme Court in *In re Ó Laighleis* [1960] IR At 93:

> The Oireachtas has not determined that the Convention of Human Rights and Fundamental Freedoms is to be part of the domestic law of the State, and accordingly this Court cannot give effect to the Convention if it be contrary to domestic law or purports to grant rights or impose obligations additional to those of domestic law.

No argument can prevail against the express command of Section 6 of Article 29 of the Constitution before judges whose declared duty is to uphold the Constitution and the laws. The Court accordingly cannot accept the idea that the primacy of domestic legislation is displaced by the State becoming a party to the Convention for the Protection of Human Rights and Fundamental Freedoms.

The convention itself recognises that it does not of itself have direct effect in the domestic law of the parties to it by providing remedies at international level for breaches of the convention by any of the High Contracting Parties. It is accordingly, unnecessary to express any opinion on whether the legislation is, as alleged, in breach in any way of the convention. The court is, accordingly, satisfied that the appellants have failed to discharge the onus on them of establishing that the sections referred to in the 1996 Act were invalid having regard to the provisions of the Constitution on any of these grounds.

Having regard to the importance and novelty of the legislation it may be as well to emphasise that the decision of this court is based upon the record of the evidence adduced in the High Court and the arguments arising therefrom. Whilst these arguments were extensive they were necessarily confined to matters in which the appellants had an existing interest. Issues which were merely hypothetical were not open for debate or subject to decision and, in the result, the constitutionality of the Act was considered solely in the light of those issues which were the subject of submissions in this court.

It is indeed probable that the special character of the legislation and the broad nature of the obligations imposed upon the Court to make certain orders which 'it may regard as appropriate'; to refrain from others where it is satisfied 'that there would be a serious risk of injustice' and to award and to determine compensation to be payable by the Minister in certain circumstances in respect of loss incrusted by the owner of property, are among the aspects of the legislation which may be expected to give rise to difficulties in practice if not in principle.

However, the resolution of any such problems must await another day.

The court will in both cases dismiss the appeal and affirm the order of the Court.

Cases reported

A

A & B v WJ Davis (Inspector of Taxes) .... Vol II p 60
AB Ltd v Mac Giolla Riogh (Inspector of Taxes) .... Vol II p 419
AB v JD Mulvey (Inspector of Taxes) .... Vol II p 55
Action Aid Ltd v Revenue Commissioners .... Vol V p 392
AE v The Revenue Commissioners .... Vol V p 686
Agricultural Credit Corporation Ltd, The v JB Vale (Inspector of Taxes) .... Vol I p 474
Airspace Investments Ltd v M Moore (Inspector of Taxes) .... Vol V p 3
Alliance & Dublin Consumers' Gas Co, The v Davis (Inspector of Taxes) .... Vol I p 104
Alliance and Dublin Consumers' Gas Co, The v McWilliams (IOT) .... Vol I p 207
Allied Irish Banks plc v James Bolger & Joan Bolger .... Vol V p 1
Associated Properties Ltd v The Revenue Commissioners .... Vol II p 175
Attorney General v Hamilton [1993] 2 IR 250 .... 1998 p 120
Attorney General v Power & Anor .... Vol V p 525
Attorney General, The v Sun Alliance & London Insurance Ltd .... Vol III p 265
Attorney-General, The v Irish Steel Ltd and Vincent Crowley .... Vol II p 108

B

Bairead, MA (Inspector of Taxes) v Martin C Carr .... Vol IV p 505
Bairead, MA (Inspector of Taxes) v Maxwells of Donegal Ltd .... Vol III p 430
Bairead, MA v M McDonald .... Vol IV p 475
Bank of Ireland Finance Ltd v The Revenue Commissioners .... Vol IV p 217
Bedford (Collector-General) v H .... Vol II p 588
Beirne (Inspector of Taxes) v St Vincent De Paul Society
    (Wexford Conference) .... Vol I p 383
Belville Holdings Ltd (in receivership and liquidation) v Cronin
    (Inspector of Taxes) .... Vol III p 340
Birch (Inspector of Taxes) v Denis Delaney .... Vol I p 515
BKJ v The Revenue Commissioners .... Vol III p 104
Boland's Ltd v Davis (Inspector of Taxes) .... Vol I p 86
Boland's Ltd v The Commissioners of Inland Revenue .... Vol I p 34
Bourke (Inspector of Taxes) v Lyster & Sons Ltd .... Vol II p 374
Bourke (Inspector of Taxes) v WG Bradley & Sons .... Vol IV p 117
Breathnach (Inspector of Taxes) v MC .... Vol III p 113
Brosnan (Inspector of Taxes) v Mutual Enterprises Ltd .... Vol V p 138
Brosnan (Inspector of Taxes) v Leeside Nurseries Ltd .... Vol V p 21
Brosnan, TJ (Inspector of Taxes) v Cork Communications Ltd .... Vol IV p 349
Browne, JA (Inspector of Taxes) v Bank of Ireland Finance Ltd .... Vol III p 644
Browne Paul and Others v The Revenue Commissioners & Ors .... Vol IV p 323
Burke & Sons Ltd v Revenue Commissioner, Ireland and Attorney General ... Vol V p 418
Byrne v Conroy .... 1998 p 75
Byrne (Terence) v The Revenue Commissioners .... Vol V p 560

C

Carbery Milk Products Ltd v The Minister for Agriculture & Ors .... Vol IV p 492
Carroll Industries Plc (formerly PJ Carroll & Co Ltd) and
    PJ Carroll & Co Ltd v S O'Culachain (Inspector of Taxes) .... Vol IV p 135
Casey (Inspector of Taxes) v AB Ltd .... Vol II p 500
Casey (Inspector of Taxes) v The Monteagle Estate Co .... Vol II p 429
CD v JM O'Sullivan (Inspector of Taxes) .... Vol II p 140
Cherry Court v The Revenue Commissioners .... Vol V p 180
City of Dublin Steampacket Co, The (In liquidation) v The Revenue
    Commissioners .... Vol I p 318
City of Dublin Steampacket Co, The v Revenue Commissioners .... Vol I p 108
Cloghran Stud Farm v AG Birch (Inspector of Taxes) .... Vol I p 496
Colclough v Colclough .... Vol II p 332
Collins, Daniel & Ors (as executor of the will of Michael Byrne (Deceased))
    and Daniel Collins v J D Mulvey (Inspector of Taxes) .... Vol II p 291
Commission of the European Communities v Ireland Case C-358/97 .... 2000 p 287
Commissioners of Inland Revenue v The Governor and Company of The
    Bank of Ireland .... Vol I p 70
Commissioners of Inland Revenue, The v The Dublin and Kingstown
    Railway Co .... Vol I p 119
Companies Act 1963-1983, The v Castlemahon Poultry
    Products Ltd .... Vol III p 509
Companies Act 1963-1983, The v M F N Construction Co Ltd
    (in liquidation) .... Vol IV p 82
Connolly (Inspector of Taxes) v Denis McNamara .... Vol II p 452
Connolly (Inspector of Taxes) v WW .... Vol II p 657
Connolly, Edward v AG Birch (Inspector of Taxes) .... Vol I p 583
Connolly, Peter v The Collector of Customs and Excise .... Vol IV p 419
Coombe Importers Ltd (In Liq), Re & Re the Companies Acts 1963-1990, Re ... 1998 p 59
Cooper-Flynn, Beverly v RTE, Charlie Bird and James Howard .... 2001 p 97
Corr, F (Inspector of Taxes) v F E Larkin .... Vol II p 164
Crilly, Derek v T & J Farrington Limited and John O'Connor .... 2000 p 65
Criminal Assets Bureau v Gerard Hutch .... 1999 p 65
Criminal Assets Bureau v John Kelly .... 2000 p 225
Criminal Assets Bureau v Patrick A McSweeney .... 2000 p 215
Cronin (Inspector of Taxes) v C .... Vol II p 592
Cronin (Inspector of Taxes) v Cork & County Property Co Ltd .... Vol III p 198
Cronin (Inspector of Taxes) v IMP Midleton Ltd .... Vol III p 452
Cronin (Inspector of Taxes) v Lunham Brothers Ltd .... Vol III p 363
Cronin (Inspector of Taxes) v Strand Dairy Ltd .... Vol III p 441
Cronin (Inspector of Taxes) v Youghal Carpets (Yarns) Ltd .... Vol III p 229
Crowe Engineering Ltd v Phyllis Lynch and Others .... Vol IV p 340
Cummins (Decd), In Re Estates of, O'Dwyer & Charleton v Keegan & Ors .... Vol V p 367
Cunard Steam Ship Co Ltd, The v Herlihy (Inspector of Taxes), and
    The Cunard Steam Ship Co Ltd v The Revenue Commissioners .... Vol I p 330
Curtin (Inspector of Taxes) v M Ltd .... Vol II p 360

Curtis, Gerard and Brendan Geough v The Attorney General and
  The Revenue Commissioners .... Vol III p 419
Cusack, Patrick v Evelyn O'Reilly and The Collector General .... Vol IV p 86

D

Daly, Michael v The Revenue Commissioners & Ors .... Vol V p 213
Davis (Inspector of Taxes) v Hibernian Bank Ltd .... Vol I p 503
Davis, RG (Inspector of Taxes) v The Superioress, Mater Misericordiae
  Hospital, Dublin .... Vol I p 387
Davis, WJ (Inspector of Taxes) v X Ltd .... Vol II p 45
Davoren, Estate of Mary Davoren, Thomas O'Byrne v Michael Davoren
  & Anne Coughlan .... Vol V p 36
De Brun (Inspector of Taxes) v K .... Vol III p 19
Deighan, Michael v Edward N Hearne, Attorney General & Ors .... Vol III p 533
Denny & Sons (Ireland) Ltd T/A Kerry Foods v Minister for Social Welfare .. Vol V p 238
Dilleen, TA (Inspector of Taxes) v Edward J Kearns .... Vol IV p 547
Diners Club Ltd, The v The Revenue and The Minister for Finance .... Vol III p 680
Director of Public Prosecutions v George Redmond .... 2000 p 273
Director of Public Prosecutions v Martin McLoughlin .... Vol III p 467
Director of Public Prosecutions v Michael Cunningham .... Vol V p 691
Director of Public Prosecutions v Robert Downes .... Vol III p 641
Director of Public Prosecutions v Seamus Boyle .... Vol IV p 395
Dolan (Inspector of Taxes) v AB Co Ltd .... Vol II p 515
Dolan, JD (Inspector of Taxes) v "K" National School Teacher .... Vol I p 656
Donovan (Inspector of Taxes) v CG Crofts .... Vol I p 115
Downing, Estate of Teresa (Owner) .... Vol I p 487
Doyle & Ors v An Taoiseach & Ors .... Vol III p 73
Dunnes Stores (Oakville) Ltd v MC Cronin (Inspector of Taxes) .... Vol IV p 68
Dunnes Stores v Gerard Ryan and The Minister for Enterprise, Trade and Employment
  .... 2000 p 261

E

EG v Mac Shamhrain (Inspector of Taxes) .... Vol II p 352
Erin Executor and Trustee Co Ltd (as trustee of Irish Pension Fund Property
  Unit Trust) v the Revenue Commissioners .... Vol V p 76
Evans & Co v Phillips (Inspector of Taxes) .... Vol I p 43
Executors and Trustees of AC Ferguson (Deceased) v Donovan (IOT) .... Vol I p 183
Exported Live Stock (Insurance) Board, The v TJ Carroll (IOT) .... Vol II p 211

F

Fennessy (Inspector of Taxes) v John McConnellogue .... Vol V p 129
Fitzgerald, Martin v Commissioners of Inland Revenue .... Vol I p 91
Flynn, W (Inspector of Taxes) v (1) John Noone Ltd, and
  Flynn, W (Inspector of Taxes) v (2) Blackwood & Co (Sligo) Ltd .... Vol II p 222
Forbes, Cyril v John Tobin And Janet Tobin .... 2001 p 71
Forbes (Inspector of Taxes) v GHD .... Vol II p 491

Forde, Michael Decision by Appeal Commissioners... Vol IV p 348
Frederick Inns Ltd, The Rendezvous Ltd, The Graduate Ltd,
    Motels Ltd (In Liquidation) v The Companies Acts 1963-1983................... Vol IV p 247

G

Gayson, Michael v Allied Irish Banks Plc .... 2000 p 105
G O'C & A O'C, In the Matter of, (Application of Liam Liston
    (Inspector of Taxes)) .... Vol V p 346
GH Ltd v Browne (Inspector of Taxes) .... Vol III p 95
Gilbert Hewson v JB Kealy (Inspector of Taxes) .... Vol II p 15
Gilligan v Criminal Assets Bureau, Galvin, Lanigan & Revenue
    Commissioners .... Vol V p 424
Gilligan, John v Criminal Assets Bureau, Revenue Commissioners
    & Others .... 2001 p 135
Governor & Co of the Bank of Ireland v MJ Meeneghan & Ors......................... Vol V p 44
Great Southern Railways Co, The v The Revenue Commissioners.................... Vol I p 359
Green & Co (Cork) Ltd v The Revenue Commissioners..................................... Vol I p 130
Griffin, Francis v Minister for Social, Community and Family Affairs .... 2001 p 125
Guinness & Mahon Ltd v Browne (Inspector of Taxes)..................................... Vol III p 373
Guinness, Arthur Son & Co Ltd v Commissioners of Inland Revenue
    Arthur Guinness Son & Co Ltd v Morris (Inspector of Taxes) .... Vol I p 1

H

Hammond Lane Metal Co Ltd, The v S O'Culachain (IOT) .... Vol IV p 187
Haughey and Others v Attorney General and Others .... 1998 p 119
Hayes, C (Inspector of Taxes) v RJ Duggan... Vol I p 195
Healy, John v SI Breathnach (Inspector of Taxes) .... Vol III p 496
Hearne, EN (Inspector of Taxes) v O'Cionna & Ors
    t/a JA Kenny & Partners .... Vol IV p 113
Heron, Peter C & Ors v The Minister For Communications .... Vol III p 298
HH v MJ Forbes (Inspector of Taxes).. Vol II p 614
Hibernian Insurance Company Limited v MacUimis (Inspector of Taxes)
    ....Vol V p 495, 2000 p 75
Hibernian Transport Companies Ltd, In re ....Vol V p 194
Hodgins, JT (Inspector of Taxes) v Plunder & Pollak (Ireland) Ltd .... Vol II p 267
Hogan, Michael v Steele And Co Ltd and Electricity Supply Board .... 2000 p 269
Howth Estate Co v WJ Davis (Inspector of Taxes) .... Vol I p 447
HT Ltd, In re (In Liquidation) & Ors.. Vol III p 120
Hughes, HPC (Inspector of Taxes) v Miss Gretta Smyth
    (Sister Mary Bernard) & Ors.. Vol I p 411
Hussey, J (Inspector of Taxes v M J Gleeson & Co Ltd.................................... Vol IV p 533
H Williams (Tallaght) (In Receivership and Liquidation) and
    the Companies Act 1963-1990, In the Matter of...Vol V p 388

I

Irish Agricultural Machinery Ltd v O'Culachain (IOT) .... Vol III p 611
Irish Nationwide Building Society v The Revenue Commissioners................. Vol IV p 296

Irish Provident Assurance Co Ltd (In Liquidation) v Kavanagh (IOT) .... Vol I p 45
Irwin, Liam J v Michael Grimes .... Vol V 209

J

JW v JW .... Vol IV p 437

K

K Co v Hogan (Inspector of Taxes) .... Vol III p 56
Kealy, J B (Inspector of Taxes) v O'Mara (Limerick) Ltd .... Vol I p 642
Kearns (Edward J) v Dilleen (Inspector of Taxes) .... Vol V p 514
Keller, Karl v The Revenue Commissioners & Ors .... Vol IV p 512
Kelly, HF (Inspector of Taxes) v H .... Vol II p 460
Kelly, JF (Inspector of Taxes) v Cobb Straffan Ireland Ltd .... Vol IV p 526
Kennedy (Inspector of Taxes) v The Rattoo Co-operative Dairy
    Society Ltd .... Vol I p 315
Kennedy, Giles J v EG Hearne, the Attorney General & Ors .... Vol III p 590
Kenny, J v Revenue Commissioners, Goodman & Gemon Ltd
    (Notice Parties) .... Vol V p 363
Kerrane, JG (Inspector of Taxes) v N Hanlon (Ireland) Ltd .... Vol III p 633
Kill Inn Motel Ltd (In Liquidation) v The Companies Acts 1963/1983 .... Vol III p 706
King (Evelyn Spain), The v The Special Commissioners .... Vol I p 221
King (Harris Stein), The v The Special Commissioners .... Vol I p 62
Kinghan, Albert v The Minister for Social Welfare .... Vol III p 436
Knockhall Piggeries v JG Kerrane (Inspector of Taxes) .... Vol III p 319

L

Louth, James & Ors v Minister for Social Welfare .... Vol IV p 391
Lynch, Mary v Moira Burke & AIB Banks plc .... Vol V p 271

M

MacAonghusa (Sean) (Inspector of Taxes) v Ringmahon Company
    .... 1999 p 81, 2001 p 117
MacCarthaigh, DA (Inspector of Taxes) v Francis Daly .... Vol III p 253
MacDaibheid (Inspector of Taxes) v SD .... Vol III p 1
MacDermott (Inspector of Taxes) v BC .... Vol III p 43
MacGiolla Mhaith (Inspector of Taxes) v Cronin & Associates Ltd .... Vol III p 211
MacGiolla Riogh (Inspector of Taxes) v G Ltd .... Vol II p 315
MacKeown (Inspector of Taxes) v Patrick J Roe .... Vol I p 214
Madigan, PJ & Or v The Attorney General, Revenue Commissioners & Ors .. Vol III p 127
Manning, David v John R Shackleton & Cork County Council .... Vol IV p 485
Mara (Inspector of Taxes) v GG (Hummingbird) Ltd .... Vol II p 667
Masser, AH Ltd (In receivership) & Ors v Revenue Commissioners .... Vol III p 548
Maye, John v Revenue Commissioners .... Vol III p 332
McAuliffe, Tony v The Minister for Social Welfare .... Vol V p 94
McCabe (Inspector of Taxes) v South City & County Investment Co Ltd
    .... Vol V p 107, 1998 p 183
McCall (Deceased) v Commissioners of Inland Revenue .... Vol I p 28
McCann, Charles Ltd v S O'Culachain (Inspector of Taxes) .... Vol III p 304

McCrystal Oil Co Ltd v The Revenue Commissioners & Ors.......................... Vol IV p 386
McDaid, Charles v His Honour Judge David Sheehy, DPP & Ors.................. Vol IV p 162
McDaid, Charles v His Honour Judge Sheehy & Ors .... Vol V p 696
McElligott p & Sons Ltd v Duigenan (Inspector of Taxes).............................. Vol III p 178
McGarry (Inspector of Taxes) v Limerick Gas Committee .... Vol I p 375
McGarry, L v W S (Inspector of Taxes) ....Vol II p 241
McGarry, W S (Inspector of Taxes) v EF ....Vol II p 261
McGarry, WS (Inspector of Taxes) v JA Spencer ....Vol II p 1
McGrath, Patrick & Ors v JE McDermott (Inspector of Taxes) .... Vol III p 683
McGurrin, L (Inspector of Taxes) v The Champion Publications Ltd.............. Vol IV p 466
McHugh (Inspector of Taxes) v A ....Vol II p 393
McLoughlin, Edward and Thomas Marie Tuite v Revenue
 Commissioners and The Attorney General .... Vol III p 387
McMahon,T & Ors v Rt Hon Lord Mayor Alderman & Burgess of Dublin ..... Vol V p 357
McMahon, J (Inspector of Taxes) v Albert Noel Murphy .... Vol IV p 125
McNally, Daniel v S O Maoldhomhniagh .... Vol IV p 22
McNamee, Estate of Thomas & Or, v The Revenue Commissioners.................Vol V p 577
Millhouse Taverns Ltd and the Companies Act 1963-1999, Re .... 2001 p 77
Milverton Quarries Ltd v The Revenue Commissioners ....Vol II p 382
Minister for Labour, The v PMPA Insurance Co Ltd
 (Under administration)... Vol III p 505
Minister for Social Welfare v John Griffiths .... Vol IV p 378
Molmac Ltd v MacGiolla Riogh (Inspector of Taxes)......................................Vol II p 482
Moloney (Inspector of Taxes) v Allied Irish Banks Ltd as executors
 of the estate of Francis J Doherty (Deceased)... Vol III p 477
Monahan, Patrick (Drogheda) Ltd v O'Connell (Inspector of Taxes).............. Vol III p 661
Mooney, TB v EP O'Coindealbhain and The Revenue Commissioners .... Vol IV p 62
Mooney (Inspector Of Taxes) v McSweeney ....Vol V p 163
Most Honourable Frances Elizabeth Sarah Marchioness
 Conyngham, The v Revenue Commissioners .... Vol I p 231
Moville District Board Of Conservators v D Ua Clothasaigh
 (Inspector of Taxes) ....Vol II p 154
Muckley, Bernard and Anne, v Ireland, AG & Revenue Commissioners .... Vol III p 188
Mulvey, JD (Inspector of Taxes) v Denis J Coffey .... Vol I p 618
Mulvey, JD (Inspector of Taxes) v RM Kieran .... Vol I p 563
Murnaghan Brothers Ltd v S O'Maoldhomhnaigh .... Vol IV p 304
Murphy (Inspector of Taxes) v Asahi Synthetic Fibres (Ireland) Ltd .... Vol III p 246
Murphy, Frances & Mary Murphy v The Attorney General ....Vol V p 613
Murphy, John B v District Justice Brendan Wallace & Ors .... Vol IV p 278
Murphy, S (Inspector of Taxes) v Dataproducts (Dublin) Ltd............................ Vol IV p 12
Murphy, Sean (Inspector of Taxes) v The Borden Co Ltd .... Vol III p 559

N

Navan Carpets Ltd v S O'Culachain (Inspector of Taxes) .... Vol III p 403
Noyek, A & Sons Ltd (In voluntary liquidation) v Edward N Hearne .... Vol III p 523

O

O'Broin, SP (Inspector of Taxes) v (1) Mac Giolla Meidhre, and
  O'Broin, SP (Inspector of Taxes) v (2) Finbar Pigott .... Vol II p 366
O'C, JB v PCD and A Bank .... Vol III p 153
O'Cahill (Inspector of Taxes) v Albert Harding & Ors .... Vol IV p 233
O'Callaghan, Thomas v JP Clifford & Ors .... Vol IV p 478
O'Cleirigh (Inspector of Taxes) v Jacobs International Ltd Inc .... Vol III p 165
O'Coindealbhain (Inspector of Taxes) v Breda O'Carroll .... Vol IV p 221
O'Coindealbhain (Inspector of Taxes) v KN Price .... Vol IV p 1
O'Coindealbhain (Inspector of Taxes) v TB Mooney .... Vol IV p 45
O'Coindealbhain, EP (Inspector of Taxes) v The Honourable
  Mr Justice Sean Gannon .... Vol III p 484
O'Conaill (Inspector of Taxes) v JJ Ltd .... Vol III p 65
O'Conaill (Inspector of Taxes) v R .... Vol II p 304
O'Conaill (Inspector of Taxes) v Z Ltd .... Vol II p 636
O'Connell, Patrick J (Inspector of Taxes) v Fyffes Banana Processing Ltd
  .... 1999 p 71, 2000 p 235
O'Connell, Patrick J (Inspector of Taxes) v Tara Mines Ltd .... 2001 p 79
O'Connell (Patrick J) (Inspector of Taxes) v Thomas Keleghan
  .... 2000 p 113, 2001 p 103
O'Connlain (Inspector of Taxes) v Belvedere Estates Ltd .... Vol III p 271
O'Culachain (Inspector of Taxes) v McMullan Brothers Ltd .... Vol V p 200
O'Culachain, S (Inspector of Taxes) v Hunter Advertising Ltd .... Vol IV p 35
O'Culachain, S v McMullan Brothers .... Vol IV p 284
O'Dwyer (Inspector of Taxes) and the Revenue Commissioners v Irish
  Exporters and Importers Ltd (In Liquidation) .... Vol I p 629
O'Dwyer, JM (Inspector of Taxes) v Cafolla & Co .... Vol II p 82
O'Dwyer, JM (Inspector of Taxes) v The Dublin United Transport
  Co Ltd .... Vol II p 115
O'Grady (Inspector of Taxes) v Laragan Quarries Ltd .... Vol IV p 269
O'Grady (Inspector of Taxes) v Roscommon Race Committee .. Vol IV p 425, Vol V p 317
O'Laoghaire (Inspector of Taxes) v CD Ltd .... Vol III p 51
O'Leary, Edward v The Revenue Commissioners .... Vol IV p 357
O'Loan, HA (Inspector of Taxes) v Messrs M J Noone & Co .... Vol II p 146
O'Reilly, Gerald v W J Casey (Inspector of Taxes) .... Vol I p 601
O'Rourke v Revenue Commissioners .... Vol V p 321
O'Shea (Inspector of Taxes) v Coole Park View Service Station Limited .... 2000 p 247
O'Shea (Inspector of Taxes) v Michael Mulqueen .... Vol V p 134
O'Siochain, Sean (Inspector of Taxes) v Bridget Neenan .... Vol V p 472, 1998 p 111
O'Siochain, S (Inspector of Taxes) v Thomas Morrissey .... Vol IV p 407
O'Srianain (Inspector of Taxes) v Lakeview Ltd .... Vol III p 219
O'Sullivan (Inspector of Taxes) v p Ltd .... Vol II p 464
O'Sullivan JM (Inspector of Taxes) v Julia O'Connor, as
  Administratrix of Evelyn H O'Brien (Deceased) .... Vol II p 61
O'Sullivan v The Revenue Commissioners .... Vol V p 570
O hArgain, L (Inspector of Taxes) v B Ltd .... Vol III p 9
O Laochdha, (Inspector of Taxes) v Johnson & Johnson (Ireland) Ltd .... Vol IV p 361

Orange, James G v The Revenue Commissioners ....Vol V p 70
Orr, Michael (Kilternan) Ltd v The Companies Act 1963-1983,
    and Thornberry Construction (Irl) Ltd v The Companies Act 1963-1983.... Vol III p 530

P

Pairceir (Inspector of Taxes) v EM...Vol II p 596
Pandion Haliaetus Ltd, Ospreycare Ltd & Or v Revenue Commissioners....... Vol III p 670
Parkes (Roberta) v David Parkes .... 1998 p 169
Pharmaceutical Society of Ireland, The v Revenue Commissioners .... Vol I p 542
Phillips (Inspector of Taxes) v Keane.. Vol I p 64
Phillips (Inspector of Taxes) v Limerick County Council...................................... Vol I p 66
Phonographic Performance (Ireland) Ltd v J Somers (IOT)............................. Vol IV p 314
Pine Valley Developments Ltd & Ors v Revenue Commissioners................... Vol IV p 543
Prior-Wandesforde, Captain RH v Revenue Commissioners .... Vol I p 249
Proes v Revenue Commissioners..Vol V p 481
Property Loan & Investment Co Ltd v Revenue Commissioners........................Vol II p 25
Private Motorists Provident Society Ltd & WJ Horgan
    v Minister for Justice...Vol V p 186
Purcell v Attorney General.. Vol IV p 229
Purcell, Joseph v AG Ireland & The Minister for the Environment ....Vol V p 288

Q

Quigley, JJ (Inspector of Taxes) v Maurice Burke .... Vol IV p 332, Vol V p 265

R

Racing Board, The v O'Culachain.. Vol IV p 73
Rahinstown Estates Co v M Hughes, (Inspector of Taxes) .... Vol III p 517
Revenue Commissioners v ORMG... Vol III p 28
Revenue Commissioners v Arida Ltd .... Vol IV p 401, Vol V p 221
Revenue Commissioners v Associated Properties Ltd..Vol II p 412
Revenue Commissioners v Colm O Loinsigh ....Vol V p 98
Revenue Commissioners v Daniel Anthony Moroney & Ors ....Vol V p 589
Revenue Commissioners v Edward Doorley ....Vol V p 539
Revenue Commissioners v Henry Young ....Vol V p 294
Revenue Commissioners v HI.. Vol III p 242
Revenue Commissioners v L & Co..Vol II p 281
Revenue Commissioners v Latchford & Sons Ltd.. Vol I p 240
Revenue Commissioners v Orwell Ltd ....Vol II p 326
Revenue Commissioners v R Hilliard & Sons Ltd ....Vol II p 130
Revenue Commissioners v Sisters of Charity of the Incarnate Word .... 1998 p 65
Revenue Commissioners v Switzer Ltd ....Vol II p 19
Revenue Commissioners v Y Ltd ....Vol II p 195
Right Hon Earl of Iveagh v The Revenue Commissioners................................. Vol I p 259
Robinson, WA T/A James Pim & Son v JD Dolan (IOT)................................. Vol I p 427
Rowan, In the Goods of Bernard Louis (Deceased) Joseph Rowan v
    Vera Agnes Rowan & Ors... Vol III p 572

S

S Ltd v O'Sullivan .... Vol II p 602
S W Ltd v McDermott (Inspector of Taxes) .... Vol II p 661
Saatchi & Saatchi Advertising Ltd v McGarry (Inspector of Taxes)
.... Vol V p 376, 1998 p 99
Simple Imports Limited and Another v Revenue Commissioners and Others ..... 2001 p 57
Smyth EA & Weber Smyth v The Revenue Commissioners .... Vol V p 532
Stamp (Deceased) In the matter of, v Noel Redmond & Ors .... Vol IV p 415
State, The (at the Prosecution of Patrick J Whelan) v Michael Smidic
 (Special Commissioners of Income Tax) .... Vol I p 571
State, The (Calcul International Ltd and Solatrex International Ltd)
 v The Appeal Commissioners and The Revenue Commissioners .... Vol III p 577
State, The (FIC Ltd) v O'Ceallaigh (Inspector of Taxes) .... Vol III p 124
State, The (Melbarian Enterprises Ltd) v The Revenue
 Commissioners .... Vol III p 290
State, The (Multiprint Label Systems Ltd) v The Honourable Justice
 Thomas Neylon .... Vol III p 159
Stephen Court Ltd v JA Browne (Inspector of Taxes) .... Vol V p 680
Sugar Distributors Ltd v The Companies Acts 1963-90 .... Vol V p 225
Sunday Tribune Limited (in Liquidation) .... 1998 p 177
Swaine (Inspector of Taxes) v VE .... Vol II p 472
Swan (Deceased), In re Hibernian Bank Ltd v Frances Munro & Ors .... Vol V p 565

T

Taxback Limited v The Revenue Commissioners .... Vol V p 412
Texaco Ireland Ltd v S Murphy (Inspector of Taxes) .... Vol IV p 91
Tipping, WJ (Inspector of Taxes) v Louis Jeancard .... Vol II p 68
Travers, John v Sean O'Siochain (Inspector of Taxes) .... Vol V p 54
Trustees of The Ward Union Hunt Races, The v Hughes (IOT) .... Vol I p 538

U

Ua Clothasaigh, D (Inspector of Taxes) v Patrick McCartan .... Vol II p 75
United Bars Ltd (In receivership), Walkinstown Inn Ltd
 (In receivership) and Raymond Jackson v Revenue Commissioners .... Vol IV p 107
Urquhart D (Decd), In Re the Estate of, & The Revenue Commissioners
 v AIB Ltd .... Vol V p 600

V

Vale, JB (Inspector Of Taxes) v Martin Mahony & Brothers Ltd .... Vol II p 32
Veterinary Council, The v F Corr (Inspector of Taxes) .... Vol II p 204
Viek Investments Ltd v The Revenue Commissioners .... Vol IV p 367

W

W Ltd v Wilson (Inspector of Taxes) .... Vol II p 627
Warnock & Ors practicing as Stokes Kennedy Crowley & Co
 v The Revenue Commissioners .... Vol III p 356
Waterford Glass (Group Services) Ltd v The Revenue Commissioners .... Vol IV p 187
Wayte (Holdings) Ltd (In Receivership) v EN Hearne (IOT) .... Vol III p 553

Wiley, Michael v The Revenue Commissioners.. Vol IV p 170
Williams Group Tullamore Ltd v Companies Act 1963-1983.......................... Vol III p 423
Wing v O'Connell (Inspector of Taxes).. Vol I p 155
WLD Worldwide Leather Diffusion Ltd v Revenue Commissioners................... Vol V p 61

Cases reported and considered

A

A & B v WJ Davis (Inspector of Taxes) 2 ITC 350, Vol II p 60
AG Moore & Co v Hare 6 TC 572, [1915] SC 91, Vol II p 32, 515
AB Ltd v Mac Giolla Riogh (Inspector of Taxes) 3 ITC 301, Vol II p 419
AB v JD Mulvey (Inspector of Taxes) 2 ITC 345, [1947] IR 121, Vol II p 55
   Cited also at: Vol III p 373
Abbey Films Ltd v Ireland [1981] IR 158, Vol III p 533
Abbot Laboratories Ltd v Carmody 44 TC 569, Vol III p 65
Aberdeen Construction Co Ltd v CIR [1978] 52 TC 281 Vol V p 163
Aberdeen Construction Group v IRC [1987] AC 885, 2000 p 114, 2001 p 105
Absalom v Talbot 26 TC 166, [1944] AC 204, Vol II p 281
Action Aid Ltd v Revenue Commissioners Vol V p 392
Adams, Re [1967] IR 424, Vol III p 572
Addie, Robert & Sons' Collieries v CIR 8 TC 671, [1924] SC 231, Vol I p 91,
   Vol II p 32, 382
Administration des Douanes v Societe Anonyme Gondrant Freres and Societe Anonyme
   Garancini (Case 169/80) [1981] ECR 1931 1998 p 76
AE v The Revenue Commissioners [1984] ILRM 301, Vol V p 686
AG (New South Wales) v Quin [1990] 170 CLR 1, Vol IV p 170
AG for Manitoba v AG for Canada [1925] AC 561, Vol III p 73
AG of Hong Kong v NG Yuen Shiu [1983] 2 AC 629, Vol IV p 170
AG of Jamaica v Williams [1998] AC 357, 2001 p 58
AG v Black IR 6 Ex 308, Vol II pp 154, 204
AG v Carlton Bank [1899] 2 QB 158 Vol V p 539, 2000 p 236
AG v Casey [1930] IR 163, Vol III p 387
AG v De Preville [1900] 1 QB 223 Vol V p 539
AG v Delaney [1876] IR 10 CL 125, Vol I p 542, Vol V p 539
AG v Doorley [1933] IR 750, Vol II p 326
AG v Great Eastern Co 5 AC 473, Vol II p 241
AG v Hamilton [1993] 2 IR 250, 1998 p 120
AG v Hope IR 2 CL 308 Vol V p 539
AG v Irish Steel Ltd and Vincent Crowley 2 ITC 402, Vol II p 108
AG v Jameson [1905] 2 IR 218 Vol V p 532, 577
AG v London County Council No 1 4 TC 265, [1901] AC 26, Vol I pp 447, 487, 515
AG v London County Council No 2 5 TC 242, [1907] AC 131, Vol I p 487
AG v Metropolitan Water Board 13 TC 294, [1928] 1 KB 833, Vol II p 332, Vol III p 229
AG v Pettinger 6 H & N 733, Vol I p 259
AG v Ryan's Car Hire Ltd [1965] IR 642 2000 p 269
AG v Southern Industrial Trust Ltd [1947] ILTR 174, Vol III pp 127, 387, 2001 p 137
AG v Sun Alliance & London Insurance Ltd [1985] ILRM 522, Vol III p 265
AG v Seccombe [1990] 2 KB 688 2000 p 63
AG v Till 5 TC 440, Vol III p 229
Agricultural Credit Corporation Ltd, The v JB Vale (Inspector of Taxes) 2 ITC 46
   [1935] IR 681, Vol I p 474
   Cited also at: Vol III, Vol I p 629, Vol III p 1, 373,

Aikman v Aikman 3 Macq HL 877, Vol I p 259
Ainsworth v Wilding [1896] 1 Ch 673, Vol III p 340
Airspace Investments Ltd v M Moore (Inspector of Taxes) Vol V p 3
Ajayi v RT Briscoe (Nig) Ltd [1964] 1 WLR 1326 Vol V p 589
Alianze Co Ltd v Bell 5 TC 60, 172 [1904] 2 KB 645, [1905] 1 KB 184, [1906] AC 18 Vol II p 515
Allchin v Coulthard 25 TC 430, [1943] AC 607, Vol II p 332
Alliance & Dublin Consumers' Gas Co, The v RG Davis (Inspector of Taxes) 1 ITC 114, [1926] IR 372, Vol I p 104
Cited also at: Vol I pp 474, 629
Alliance and Dublin Consumers' Gas Co v McWilliams 1 ITC 199, [1928] IR 1, 1 LTR 201, Vol I p 427
Cited also at: Vol I p 164, 207
Allied Irish Banks Ltd v Ardmore Studios International [1972] unrep Vol V p 226
Allied Irish Banks plc v James Bolger & Joan Bolger Vol V p 1
Almeida-Sanchez v US [1973] 413 US 266 Vol V p 614
Amalgamated Meat Packers Ltd, In re the [unrep], Vol III p 452
Amalgamated Property Co v TENAS Bank [1982] QB 84, Vol IV p 492
American Thread Co v Joyce 106 LT 171, 29 LTR 266, 6 TC 1 & 163, Vol I pp 28, 583, Vol II p 68
Ammonia Soda Co v Chamberlain [1918] 1 Ch 266, Vol II p 515
Anderson v Laneville 9 Moo PC 325, Vol I p 259
Anderton and Halstead Ltd v Birrell (Inspector of Taxes) [1932] I KB 271, Vol II pp 195, 627, Vol IV p 505
Anderton v Lambe [1981] 43 Ch D, Vol IV p 1
Andrews v Astley [unreported], Vol I p 64
Andrews v Partington [1791] 3 Bro CC 401 Vol V p 37
Anglo Persian Oil Co Ltd v Dale 16 TC 253, [1932] 1 KB 124, Vol I p 642, Vol II p 515
Anheuser Busch v The Controller of Patents Design and Trade Marks [1987] IR 329, Vol IV p 485
Antelope, The, 10 Wheaton 66 Vol V p 45
Appenroot v Central Middlesex Assessment Committee [1937] 2 KB 48, Vol II p 515
Apple and Pear development Council v Commissioners of Customs and Excise Case 102/86 (1988) ECR 1443 2000 p 287
Archbishop of Thyateira v Hubert 168 LT 190, 25 TC 249, Vol II p 68
Archbold Thomson Black and Company v Betty 7TC 158 , 2001 p 118
Archer-Shee v Baker 11 TC 749, 759, [1927] 1 KB 109, [1927] AC 844, Vol II p 393 Vol III p 477
Arthur Guinness Son & Co Ltd v CIR Arthur Guinness Son & Co Ltd v Morris (Inspector of Taxes) 1 ITC 1, [1923] 2 IR 186, Vol I p 1
AS v RB, WS and Registrar General [1984] ILRM 66, Vol IV p 437
Ashbury Railway Carriage and Iron Co v Riche, Vol IV p 247
Ashcroft, Clifton-V-Strauss, Re (1927) 1 Ch 313 Vol V p 295
Ashton Gas Co v Attorney General [1906] AC 10 Vol V p 565
Ashwander v Tennessee Valley Authority 297 US 288 Vol V p 696
Assets Co Ltd v Forbes 34 SLR 486, 3 TC 542
Associated Portland Cement Manufacturers Ltd v Kerr 27 TC 103, [1945] 2 AER 535, [1946] 1 AER 68, Vol II p 515

Associated Portland Cement Manufacturers Ltd v The Prices Commission [1975] 119 So 30, 63, [1975] ICR 34, Vol IV p 135
Associated Properties Ltd v The IRC 3 ITC 25, [1951 IR 140, Vol II p 175
Athenaeum Life Assce Society, In re [1858] Ch 4 Kay & J 304 Vol V p 226
Atherton v British Insulated & Helsby Cables Ltd 10 TC 155, [1925] 1 KB 421, [1926] AC 205, Vol I p 642, Vol II pp 32, 45, 222, 267, 360, 500, 515, 602, Vol III p 95, Vol IV p 425, Vol V p 496
Atkinson, In re, 31 Ch D 577 Vol V p 526
Attorney General of New Zealand v Ortiz [1984] AC 1 Vol V p 45
Attorney General v Power & Anor Vol V p 525
Cited also at: [1906] 2 IR 272, Vol III p 104
Ayerst v C & K (Construction) Ltd [1974] 1 AER 670, Vol IV p 247
Aylmer v Mahaffy 10 TC 594 & 598, [1925] NIR 167, Vol II p 374

B

Bach v Daniels 9 TC 183, [1925] 1 KB 526, Vol 1 p 515, Vol II pp 315, 636
Bagge v Whitehead [not reported], Vol III p 387
Bairead, MA (Inspector of Taxes) v Martin C Carr Vol IV p 505
Bairead, MA (Inspector of Taxes) v Maxwells of Donegal Ltd [1986] ILRM 508, Vol III p 430
Bairead, MA v M McDonald Vol IV p 475
Balgownie Land Trust Ltd v CIR 14 TC 684, Vol III p 1
Balkan-Import-Export GmbH v Hauptzollamt Berlin-Packhof (Case 118/76) [1977] ECR 1177 1998 p 76
Bank of Ireland Finance Ltd v The IRC Vol IV p 217
Bank of Ireland v Caffin [1971] IR 123, Vol IV p 437
Bank of Ireland v Kavanagh [Judgment delivered 19 June 1987], Vol IV p 407
Bank of Ireland v Rockfield Ltd [1979] IR 21 Vol V p 226
Bankline Ltd v CIR 49 TC 307, Vol III p 633
Barclays Bank v Siebe Gorman [1979] 2 Lloyd's Rep 142, Vol III p 548
Barker (Christopher) & Sons v CIR [1919] 2 KB 222, Vol III p 211
Barnardo's Homes v CIR 7 TC 646, [1921] 2 AC 1, Vol III p 477
Baroness Wenlock v River Dee Co [1885] 10 AC, Vol II p 241
Barrington's Hospital v Commissioner of Valuation [1975] IR 299, Vol II p 661
Bartlett v Mayfair Property Co [1898] 2 Ch 28, Vol II p 130
Baxendale v Murphy 9 TC 76 [1924] 2 KB 494, Vol I p 601
Baytrust Holdings Ltd v IRC [1971] 1 WLR 1333, Vol III p 661
Beak v Robson 25 TC 33, [1943] AC 352, Vol II p 515
Bean v Doncaster Amalgamated Collieries 27 TC 296, [1944] 2 AER, Vol II p 515
Beauchamp v FW Woolworth Plc [1989] STC 510 HL Vol V p 138
Beaumont, In Re, deceased [1980] Ch 444, [1979] 3 WLR 818 Vol V p 614
Bebb v Bunny 8 TC 454, 1 K & J 217, Vol II p 332
Bede Steam Shipping Co Ltd, In re [1917] 1 Ch 123 Vol V p 532
Bedford (Collector-General) v H [1968] IR 320, Vol II p 588
Beechor v Major [1865] BLT 54 Vol V p 271
Beirne (Inspector of Taxes) v St Vincent De Paul Society (Wexford Conference) 1 ITC 413 Vol I p 383
Beke v Smith (1836) 2 M & W 191 1998 p 76

Belgian State and Grand Duchy of Luxembourg v Martens (Cases 178, 179 and 180/73) [1974] ECR 383 1998 p 76
Belgium and Luxembourg v Mertens [1974] ECR 1998 p 76
Bell Bros Ltd, Re, ex parte Hodgson (1) 65 TLR 245 Vol V p 532
Bell Bros Pty Ltd v Shire of Serpentine-Jarrahdale [1969] 121 CLR 137 Vol V p 614
Bell v Kennedy LR 1 SC Appeal p 307, I S & D 307, LRIA SC 441, Vol I p 259
Belmont Farm v Minister for Housing 60 LGR 319 Vol V p 357
Belmont Finance Corporation Ltd v Williams Furniture Ltd (No 2) [1980] 1 AER 393, Vol IV p 247
Beloff v Pressdram Ltd [1973] 1 All ER 241 1998 p 177
Belville Holdings Ltd (Receivership and liquidation) v Cronin (Inspector of Taxes) [1985] IR 465, Vol III p 340
Beni Felkai Mining Co Ltd, Re [1934] 1 Ch 406, Vol III p 523
Bennet v Marshall 22 TC 73, [1938] 1 KB 591, Vol II pp 68, 393
Benson (Inspector of Taxes) v Yard Arm Club Ltd 53 TC 67, [1979] STC 266, Vol III p 219, Vol IV p 284
Benyon & Co Ltd v Ogg 7 TC 125, Vol I p 629
Berkeley v Edwards [1988] IR 219 , 2001 p 58
Berry v Farrow [1914] 1 IR 358, Vol II p 332
Berry v Fisher [1903] IR 484, Vol IV p 415
Best v Samuel Fox & Co Ltd [1952] AC 716, Vol IV p 437
Beynon and Co Ltd v Ogg 7 TC 125, Vol I pp 1, 28
Bickerman v Mason per Reps TL 2976, Vol IV p 22
Biddell Brothers v Clemens Horst Company [1911] 1 KB 934, Vol I p 130
Birch (Inspector of Taxes) v Denis Delaney 2 ITC 127, [1936] IR 517, 531, Vol I p 515 Cited also at: Vol I p 583, Vol II pp 315, 429, 472, 596, Vol III pp 1, 9
Birmingham v District Land Co v London & North Investment Railway Co [1888] 40 Ch D 268 Vol V p 589
BKJ v The IRC Vol III p 104
Blake and Others v AG [1982] IR 117, [1981] ILRM 34, Vol III p 127, Vol IV pp 187, 323.
Blakiston v Cooper 5 TC 347, [1907] 1 KB 702, 2 KB 688, [1909] AC 104, Vol I p 155
Bolam v Regent Oil Co Ltd 37 TC 56, Vol II p 515
Boland v An Taoiseach [1974] IR 338 Vol V p 614
Boland's Ltd v Davis (Inspector of Taxes) 1 ITC 91, [1925] ILTR 73, Vol I p 86 Cited also at: Vol III p 363.
Boland's Ltd v The CIR 1 ITC 42, Vol I p 34
Bolson J & Son Ltd v Farrelly 34 TC 161, Vol III p 253
Bomford v Osborne [1942] AC 14, 23 TC 642, Vol II pp 241, 515
Bonner v Basset Mines Ltd 6 TC 146, Vol II p 382
Bord na gCon v Stokes [November 1975], Vol IV p 73
Boulton v Bull [1795], Vol III p 441
Bourke v AG [1972] IR 36, 2000 p 65
Bourke (Inspector of Taxes) v Lyster & Sons Ltd 3 ITC 247, Vol II p 374
Bourke (Inspector of Taxes) v WG Bradley & Sons [1990] IR 379, Vol IV p 117
Bourne and Hollingsworth v the CIR 12 TC 483, Vol II p 429
Bowers v Harding 3 TC 22, Vol II p 366
Bowlby, In re, [1904] 2 Ch 685 Vol V p 526
Bowles v The AG and Others 5 TC 685, [1912] 1 Ch 123 p 135, Vol I p 583

Boyd v Shorrock [not reported], Vol III p 332
BP Australia Ltd v Commissioner of Taxation of the Commonwealth of Australia [1966] AC 224, Vol II p 515
Bradbury v The English Sewing Cotton Co Ltd 8 TC 481, [1923] AC 744, Vol I p 583
Bradbury v United Glass Bottle Manufacturers Ltd 38 TC 369, Vol II p 515
Bradshaw v Blundon 36 TC 397, Vol III p 373
Brady v Donegal County Council [1989] ILRM 282, 2000 p 261
Bray v Best [1989] STC 159, Vol IV p 407
Breathnach v McCann 3 ITR 112, [1984] ILRM 679 Vol V p 200
Breathnach, SI (Inspector of Taxes) v MC [1984] IR 340, Vol III p 113
Cited also at: Vol III p 219
Breen v The Minister for Defence [unreported, SC 20 July 1990], Vol IV p 170
Brennan and Others v AG and Wexford Co Co [1983] ILRM 449 (HC), [1984] ILRM 355 (SC), Vol III p 127
Brennan v AG [1984] ILRM 355, Vol IV pp 229, 323
Brice v The Northern Association Co [1911] 2 KB 577, [1912] 2 KB 41, [1913] AC 610, 6 TC 327, Vol I p 474
Brickwood & Co v Reynolds 3 TC 600, [1898] 1 QB 95, Vol I p 642
Brighton College v Marriott 10 TC 213, [1925] 1 KB 312, [1926] AC 192, Vol I pp 387, 542, Vol II p 211
Bristow (Inspector of Taxes) v Dickinson and Co Ltd 27 TC 157, 62 TLR 37, [1946] KB 321, Vol II pp 140, 374
British Airways v C & E Commissioners [1989] STC 182, Vol IV p 349
British American Tobacco Co v The IRC [1943] AC 335, [1941] 2 KB 270, Vol II p 175
British Broadcasting Corporation v Johns 41 TC 471, Vol IV p 73
British Insulated & Helsby Cables Ltd v Atherton [1926] AC 205 Vol V p 680
British Legion peterhead Branch v CIR 35 TC 509, Vol III p 253
British Mexican Petroleum Co v Jackson 16 TC 570, Vol II p 281
British Railways Board v C & E Commissioners [1977] STC 221, Vol IV p 349
British Sugar Manufacturers Ltd v Harris (Inspector of Taxes) [1938] 2 KB 220, Vol II p 195, Vol IV p 505
British Transport Commission v Gourley [1955] 3 All ER 796,, 2000 p 269
Briton Ferry Steel Co Ltd v Barry 23 TC 414, [1940] 1 KB 463, Vol II p 315
Brocklebank, Re, 23 QBD 461, Vol II p 130
Broken Hill Property Co Ltd v Commissioners of Taxation 41 ALJR 377, Vol III pp 113, 120, 219, Vol IV p 284.
Brosnan (Inspector of Taxes) v Leeside Nurseries Ltd Vol V p 21
Brosnan (Inspector of Taxes) v Mutual Enterprises Ltd Vol V p 138
  Cited also 1999 p 82
Brosnan, TJ (Inspector of Taxes) v Cork Communications Ltd Vol IV p 349
Brown v Donegal County Council [1980] IR 132, 146, Vol III p 19
Browne & Bank of Ireland Finance Ltd [1991] 1 IR 431, 3 ITR 644 Vol V p 139
Browne Paul and Others v The IRC and Others [1991] 2 IR 58, Vol IV p 323
Cited also at: Vol IV p 125
Browne v Burnley Football & Athletic Co Ltd 53 TC 357, [1980] STC 424, Vol IV p 425, Vol V p 317
Browne v Burnley Football and Athletic Co Ltd 53 TC 537

Browne, JA (Inspector of Taxes) v Bank of Ireland Finance Ltd [1987] IR 346 [1991] 1 IR 431, Vol III p 644
Browns Transport Ltd v Kropp (1958) 100 CLR 263, Vol III p 73
BSC Footwear Ltd v Ridgeway 47 TC 495, Vol IV p 135
Buchanan Ltd, Peter v McVey [1954] IR 89 Vol V p 45, 226, 1998 p 76
Buckley v AG [1950] IR 67 Vol V p 696
Bucks v Bowers [1970] Ch D 431, Vol III p 633
Bula Ltd v Tara Mines Ltd [1994] ILRM 111 Vol V p 266
Bullcroft Main Collieries Ltd v O'Grady [1932] 17 TC 93, Vol II p 267, 360
Bullimore v C & E Commissioners MAN/86/145, Vol IV p 349
Burke & Sons Ltd v Revenue Commissioner, Ireland and Attorney General Vol V p 418
Burmah Steamship Co Ltd v CIR [1931] SC 156, [1931] SLT 116, 16 TC 67, Vol I p 427
Burman v Thorn Domestic Appliances (Electrical) Ltd [1982] STC 179, Vol III p 165
Button v West Cork Railway [1883] 23 Ch D, Vol III p 706
Byrne v Grey [1988] IR 31 , 2001 p 58
Byrne (Terence) v The Revenue Commissioners Vol V p 560
Byrne v Conroy 1998 p 75
Byrne v Ireland [1972] IR 241 Vol V p 614

C

C & E Commissioners v Zinn and Others [1988] STC 57, Vol IV p 349
Cadwalader 12 SC LTR 499, 5 TC 101, Vol I p 259
Café Brandy Syndicate v CIR 12 TC 358 1998 p 100
Cafolla v AG [1985] IR 486, Vol IV p 323
Cahill v Harding 4 ITR 233 Vol V p 134
Cahill v Sutton [1980] IR 269, Vol III p 127, 419
Caledo-Toledo v Pearson Yacht Leasing Company (1974) 416 US 663 , 2001 p 138
California Copper Syndicate v Harris 5 TC 159, [1904] 41 SLR 691, 6F 894, Vol I pp 474, 503, 629, Vol III p 644
Campbell v Hall [1774] 1 Cowp 204 ([1558-1774] AER Rep 252 Vol V p 322
Camille and Henry Dreyfus Foundation v CIR (1955) 36 TC 126 1998 p 66
Cannon Industries Ltd v Edwards 42 TC 265, [1966] 1 AER 456, Vol II p 614
Cape Brandy Syndicate v CIR 12 TC 358
Cape Brandy Syndicate v CIR 12 TC 358, [1921] 1 KB 64, Vol I pp 1, 28, Vol III pp 56, 477, Vol IV p 91, Vol V p 376, 472
Capital and National Trust Ltd v Golder 31 TC 265, Vol III p 95, Vol V p 496, 680, 2000 p 76
Carbery Milk Products Ltd v The Minister for Agriculture and Others Vol IV p 492
Carlisle and Silloth Golf Club v Smith 6 TC 198, [1912] 2 KB 177, [1913] 3 KB 75 Vol I pp 387, 515
Carr v CIR [1944] 2 AER 163, Vol III p 211
Carroll Group Distributors Ltd v GAJF Bourke Ltd Vol V p 108, 1998 p 183
Carroll Industries Plc (formerly PJ Carroll & Co Ltd) and PJ Carroll & Co Ltd v S O'Culachain (Inspector of Taxes) [1988] IR 705, Vol IV p 135
Cited also at: Vol IV p 304
Carroll v Mayo County Council [1967] IR 364, Vol II p 636
Carson v Cheyney's Executor 38 TC 240, [1959] AC 412, [1958] 3 AER 573, Vol III p 484, Vol IV p 135

Cary v Cary 2 Sch and Lef 173, Vol I p 601
Casdagli v Casdagli [1919] AC p 177, Vol I p 259
Casey (Inspector of Taxes) v AB Ltd [1965] IR 575, Vol II p 500
Casey (Inspector of Taxes) v The Monteagle Estate Co 3 ITC 313, [1962] IR 106, Vol II p 429
Cassidy v Minister for Industry and Commerce [1978] IR 297, Vol III p 73, Vol V p 288
Cassidy v Minister of Health (1978) IR 207 Vol V p 239
Caudron v Air Zaire [1985] IR 716 , 2001 p 137
Cavan Co-Operative Society, Re [1917] 2 IR 608, Vol III p 319
Cayzer Irvine & Co Ltd v CIR 24 TC 491, Vol II p 472
CCSV v Minister for the Civil Service [1984] 3 AER 935, Vol IV p 170
CD v JM O'Sullivan (Inspector of Taxes) 2 ITC 422, [1949] IR 264, Vol II p 140
Cecil v CIR [1919] 36 TLR 164, Vol III p 211
Cenlon Finance Co Ltd v Ellwood 40 TC 176, [1961] 2 AER 861, [1961] Ch 634, [1962] AC 782, [1974] ITC No 10, Vol II p 627, Vol III p 56, Vol IV p 187
Central London Property Trust Ltd v High Trees House Ltd [1947] KB 130, Vol V p 589
Chambers v Fahy Supreme Court, unrep, 1931 Vol V p 472
Chamney v Lewis [1932] 17 TC 318, Vol II pp 393, 491
Chancery Lane Safe Deposit and Office Co Ltd v CIR 43 TC 83, Vol II p 627
Chantrey Martin & Co v Martin [1952] 2 AER 691, Vol IV p 332, Vol V p 266
Charente Steamship Co v Wilmot 24 TC 97, [1941] 2 KB 386, Vol II p 602
Charge Card Services Ltd, Re, Vol III p 680
Charles Brown & Co v CIR 12 TC 1256, Vol I p 427
Charles McCann v O'Culachain [1985] IR 298, [1986] IR 196, 3 ITR 304 Vol V p 21, 515
Charleston Federal Savings and Loan Assn v Alderson [1945] 324 US 182, Vol III p 127
Charterbridge Corporation v Lloyds Bank [1969] 2 AER, Vol IV p 247
Chaulk v R [1990] 3 Scr 13 Vol V p 213
Cherry Court v The Revenue Commissioners Vol V p 180
Chettiar v Chettiar [1962] 2 WLR 548; [1962] AC 294 1998 p 169
Chevron Oil Co v Huson [1971 404 US 97 Vol V p 614
Chibett Robinson 9 TC 48, 132 LTR 31, Vol I p 155
Chicago, Indianapolis & Louisville Railway Co v Hackett [1931] 228 US 559 Vol V p 614
Chicot County Drainage District v Baxter State Bank [1940] 308 US 371 Vol V p 614
Chinn v Collins [1981] AC 533, [1981] 2 WLR 14, [1981] 1 AER 189, [1980] 54 TC 311, Vol III p 683
Cipriano v City of Houma [1969] 395 US 701 Vol V p 614
CIR v Alexander von Glehn & Co [1920] 2 KB 553, Vol II p 515
CIR v Anderstrom 13 TC 482, [1928] SC 224, Vol II pp 393, 491
CIR v Barclay Curle and Co Ltd 45 TC 221, Vol III pp 113, 120, 219
CIR v Birmingham Theatre Royal Estate Co Ltd 12 TC 580, Vol I p 447, Vol III p 253
CIR v Brender and Cruickshank 46 TC 574, Vol IV p 45
CIR v Buchanan 37 TC 365, [1957] 3 WLR 68, Vol II p 352
CIR v Burrell 9 TC 27, [1924] 2 KB 52, Vol I p 318
CIR v Carron Co 45 TC 18 1999 p 82
CIR v Cock Russel & Co Ltd 29 TC 387, Vol IV p 135
CIR v Cola 38 TC 334, [1959] SLT 122, Vol II p 515
CIR v Dalgety & Co 15 TC 216, Vol III p 403
CIR v Forrest 3 TC 117, 15 AC 334, Vol I p 542

CIR v Forsyth Grant 25 TC 369, [1943] SC 528, Vol II p 636, Vol IV p 1
CIR v Forth Conservancy Board [1930] SC 850, [1931] AC 540, 47 TLR 429, 16 TC 103, Vol I p 656, Vol II p 154, Vol IV p 73
CIR v Fraser 24 TC 498, Vol III p 253
CIR v Gas Lighting Improvement Co Ltd [1922] KB 381, 12 TC 503, Vol I p 447
CIR v George Burrell and William Burrell 9 TC 27, [1924] 2 KB 52, 129 LTR 542, Vol I p 45
CIR v Granite City Steamship Co [1927] Sess Cas 705, 13 TC 1, Vol II p 515, Vol III p 165
CIR v Gribble [1913] 3 KB 212, Vol III p 611
CIR v Hendersons Executors 16 TC 282, Vol III p 477
CIR v Hyndland Investment Co Ltd 14 TC 694, Vol III p 1
CIR v Kingston Railway Co 1 ITC 131, Vol I p 387
CIR v Lambhill Ironworks Ltd 31 TC 393, Vol III p 65
CIR v Land Securities Investment Trust Ltd 45 TC 495 Vol III p 95, Vol V p 139
CIR v Livingston and Others 11 TC 538, Vol III pp 1, 253, 373
CIR v Lysaght 13 TC 511, [1928] AC 234, Vol I p 259
CIR v Mackinlay's Trustees 22 TC 305, [1938] SC 765, Vol II p 627
CIR v Maxse 12 TC 41, Vol III pp 178, 211
CIR v Metrolands 54 TC 679 , 2001 p 105
CIR v Morton [1941] SC 467, 24 TC 259, Vol II p 82
CIR v Newcastle Breweries 12 TC 926, 95 LJ, KB 936, 97 LJ, KB 735, Vol II p 515, Vol III p 165
CIR v Payne 110 LJKB 323, 23 TC 610, Vol II p 82
CIR v Peebleshire Nursing Association 11 TC 335, [1927] SC 215, Vol I p 387
CIR v Pullman Car Co Ltd 35 TC 221, 1999 p 82
CIR v Ramsay [1935] 154 LT 141, 20 TC 79, Vol II p 222, 464, 602
CIR v Ransom (William) & Son Ltd 12 TC 21, Vol III p 178
CIR v Reinhold 34 TC 389, Vol III p 1
CIR v Robins Brothers Ltd 43 TC 266, Vol IV p 425
CIR v Saunders & Pilcher 31 TC 314, Vol III p 304
CIR v Scott Adamson 17 TC 679, [1933] SC 23, Vol II p 482
CIR v Scottish & Newcastle Breweries Ltd 55 TC 252, Vol III pp 113, 120, 219
CIR v Scottish Central Electric Power Co 13 TC 331, [1930] SC 226, 15 TC 761, Vol II p 32, Vol III p 403
CIR v Sneath [1932] 2 KB 362, 17 TC 149, Vol II p 326
CIR v Sneath 17 TC 149, [1932] 2 KB 362, Vol I p 571
CIR v South Behar Railway Co Ltd 12 TC 657, [1925] AC 476, Vol I p 387
CIR v Sparkford Vale Co-operative Society Ltd 133 LT 231, 12 TC 891, Vol I p 315
CIR v The Budderpore Oil Company Ltd 12 TC 467, Vol I p 629
CIR v The Dublin and Kingstown Railway Co [1930] IR 317, 1 ITC 131, Vol I p 359
CIR v The Edinburgh and Bathgate Railway Co 12 TC 895, [1926] Sess Cas 862, Vol I p 359
CIR v The Governor & Co of The Bank of Ireland 1 ITC 74, [1925] 2 IR 90, Vol I p 70
CIR v The Korean Syndicate Ltd [1920] 1 KB 598, 12 TC 181 p 205, Vol I p 447
CIR v The Scottish Automobile & General Insurance Co Ltd [1932] SC 87, 16 TC 381, Vol I p 474, 629
CIR v The Tyre Investment Trust Ltd 132 LT 59, 12 TC 646 pp 655 and 656, Vol I p 447

CIR v The Yorkshire Agricultural Society 13 TC 58, [1928] 1 KB 611, Vol I p 542
CIR v Toll Property Co Ltd 34 TC 13, Vol III p 1
CIR v Trustees of Joseph Reid, Deceased 30 TC 431, [1947] SC 700, [1949] LJR 701, Vol II p 464
CIR v Von Glehn & Co Ltd 12 TC 232, [1920] KB 553, Vol I p 195
CIR, The v The Dublin and Kingstown Railway Co [1930] IR 317, Vol I p 119
City of Dublin Steampacket Co, The (in liquidation) v The Revenue Commissioners 1 ITC 285, [1930] IR 217, Vol I p 318
City of Dublin Steampacket Co, The v IRC 1 ITC 118, [1926] IR 436, Vol I p 108
Cited also at: Vol I p 387
City of London Contract Corporation v Styles [1887] 2 TC 239, Vol II p 515
City of London Real Property Co Ltd v Jones 15 TC 266, [1930] AC 432, Vol I pp 487, 515
Cityview Press Ltd v An Chomhairle Oiliuna [1980] IR 381, Vol III p 127, Vol IV p 162
Clancy v Ireland [1988] IR 326 , 2001 p 138
Clerical, Medical and General Life Assurance Society v Carter 2 TC 437, 22 QBD 444, Vol I p 45
Cleveleys Investment Trust Company v CIR 1975 TC 300 Vol V p 163, 2000 p 114, 2001 p 105
Clifford & O'Sullivan, Re [1921] 2 AC 570, Vol III p 290
Clinch v IRC [1974] IQB 76, Vol III p 356
Clitheroes Estate, In re, 31 Ch D 135 Vol V p 526
Cloghran Stud Farm v AG Birch (Inspector of Taxes) 2 ITC 65, [1936] IR 1, Vol I p 496
Cited also at: Vol I p 515, Vol II p 315
Clover Clayton & Co v Hughes [1910] AC 242 (p 256), Vol I p 427
CM v TM (No 2) [1990] 2 IR 52, [1991] ILRM 268, Vol IV p 437
CM v TM [1987] IR 152, [1988] ILRM 456, Vol IV p 437
Coates v Holker Estates Co [1961] 40 TC 75, Vol II p 657
Codman v Hill [1919], Vol III p 253
Colclough v Colclough [1965] IR 668, Vol II p 332
Cole Bros Ltd v Phillips (Inspector of Taxes) [1981] STC 671, [1982] STC 311, Vol IV pp 68, 284
Cole Bros v Phillips [1980] Ch D 518, 55 TC 188, Vol III p 219
Cole Bros v Phillips [1981] STC 671 Vol V p 200
Coleman's Depositaries Ltd and Life and Health Assurance Association, Re [1907] 2 KB 798, Vol III p 159
Collco Dealings Ltd v IRC 39 TC 509, [1961] 1 AER 762, Vol III p 246
Collins v Adamson 21 TC 400, [1937] 4AE 236, [1938] 1 KB 477, Vol II p 515
Collins v IRC 12 TC 773, [1925] SC 151, Vol I p 240
Collins, Daniel and Michael Byrne, Daniel Collins and Redmond Power as executor of the will of Michael Byrne, deceased, and Daniel Collins v J D Mulvey (Inspector of Taxes) 3 ITC 151, [1956] IR 233, Vol II p 291
Collyer v Hoare & Co Ltd [1931] 1 KB 123, 17 TC 169, [1932] AC 407, Vol I pp 447, 515
Colquohoun v Brooks 2 TC 490, [1889] 14 AC 493, Vol I p 183, Vol II pp 393, 491
Coltness Iron Co v Black 1 TC 287, Vol II p 382
Colville v CIR 8 TC 422, [1923] SC 423, 60 SCLR 248, Vol I p 601
Combe v Combe [1951] 2 KB 215 Vol V p 589
Commercial Structures Ltd v Briggs 30 TC 477, [1948] 2 AER 1041, Vol II pp 195, 627

Commission of the European Communities v Council of the European Communities [1973] ECR 575, Vol IV p 170
Commission of the European Communities v Denmark C47/88, Vol IV p 512
Commission v Federal Republic of Germany Cases 107/84 (1985) ECR 2655 , 2000 p 287
Commission v France and UK (Cases 92and 93/87) [1989] ECR 405 1998 p 76
Commission of the European Communities v Ireland Case C-358/97 2000 p 287
Commission v Netherlands Case 235/85 (1987) ECR 1485 , 2000 p 287
Commissioners of Inland Revenue v Dowdall O'Mahony & Co Ltd 33 TC 259 1998 p 66
Commissioner of Inland Revenue v Granite City Steamship Co Ltd 13 TC 1 Vol V p 496
Commissioners of Inland Revenue v Gull 21 TC 374 1998 p 66
Commissioner of Inland Revenue v Wilsons Executors 18 TC 465 Vol V p 496
Commissioner of Taxes v Nchanga Consolidated Copper Mines [1964] 2 WLR 339, 1 AER 208, Vol II pp 515, 602
Commissioners for Special Purposes of Income Tax v Pemsel 3 TC 53, [1891] AC 531, Vol I pp 221, 387, 542, Vol II p 661
Commissioners of Inland Revenue v Land Securities Investment Trust Ltd 45 TC 495 Vol V p 680
Commissioners of Taxes v Melbourne Trust Ltd [1914] AC 1001, 84 LJPC 21, 30 TLR 685, Vol I p 474
Companies Act 1908 v Ross & Boal Ltd [1924] 1 IR 129, Vol III p 332
Companies Act 1963-1983, The v Castlemahon Poultry Products Ltd [1986] IR 750, [1987] ILRM 222, Vol III p 509
Companies Act 1963-1983, The v MFN Construction Co Ltd (in liquidation) Vol IV p 82
Compton, In re [1945] Ch 123; [1945] 1 AER 198; 114 LJ Ch 99; 172 LT 158; 61 TLR 167; 89 SJ 142, Vol V p 37.
Connolly (Inspector of Taxes) v Denis McNamara 3 ITC 341, Vol II p 452
Connolly (Inspector of Taxes) v WW Vol II p 657
Connolly Peter v The Collector of Customs and Excise Vol IV p 419
Connolly, Edward v AG Birch (Inspector of Taxes) 2 ITC 201, [1939] IR 534, Vol I p 583
Cited also at: Vol II p 472, Vol III p 9
Construction Industry Training Board v Labour Force Ltd [1970] 3 AER 220, Vol III p 505, Vol IV p 391
Cook, Exparte, 29 LJQ B 68, Vol I p 221
Cooke v Beach Station Caravans Ltd [1974] 49 TC 514, [1974] STC 402, Vol IV pp 68, 425, Vol V p 317
Cooke v Walsh [1984] IR 710 Vol V p 696
Cookson v Lee 23 LJ Ch NS p 473, Vol II p 241
Coombe Importers Ltd (In Liq) & Re the Companies Acts 1963-1990, 1998 p 59
Cooper v Stubbs 10 TC 29, [1925] 2 KB 753, Vol I p 629, Vol II pp 204, 614
Cooper, In re, [1911] 2 KB 550, Vol II p 332
Cooper-Flynn, Beverly v RTE, Charlie Bird and James Howard , 2001 p 97
Co-operative Insurance Society v Richardson [1955] CLY 1365, Vol III p 43
Copeman v Coleman 22 TC 594, [1939] 2 KB 484, Vol II p 82
Cormacs Trustees v The Commissioners of Inland Revenue [1924] SC 819 Vol V p 181
Corporation of Birmingham v Barnes 19 TC 195, Vol III pp 165, 253
Corponeto and Others Cases 231/87 and 129/88 (1989) ECR 3233, 2000 p 287
Corr, F (Inspector of Taxes) v F E Larkin 3 ITC 13, [1949] IR 399, Vol II p 164
Costa v ENEL [1964] ECR 585 1998 p 76

Costa Rica Railway Co Ltd v CIR 29 TC 34, Vol II p 429
Cottin v Blane [1975] 2 ANSTR 544, Vol III p 265
Courtauld v Leigh LR 4 Ex at 149 Vol V p 570
Cowan v Seymour 7 TC 372, [1920] 1 KB 500, Vol I pp 155, 618
Cox v Glue 5 CB 533, Vol II p 636
Cox v Hickman 8 HCL 268, Vol III p 467
Cox v Ireland [1992] 2 IR 503 , 2001 p 138
Cox v Murray [1919] 1 IR 358, Vol II p 332
Cox v Rabbits 3 AC 478, Vol I p 601
Craddock v Zevo Finance Co Ltd 27 TC 267, [1944] 1 AER 566, 174 LT 385, Vol II p 419
Craignish, Re, [1892] 3 Ch 192, Vol I p 259
Craven's Mortgage, Re, 8 TC 651, [1907] 2 Ch 448, Vol II p 332
Crilly, Derek v T & J Farrington Limited and John O'Connor 2000 p 65
Criminal Assets Bureau v Gerard Hutch 1999 p 65
Criminal Assets Bureau v John Kelly 2000 p 225
Criminal Assets Bureau v Patrick A McSweeney 2000 p 215
Croft v Sywell Aerodrome 24 TC 126, [1942] 1 AER 110, Vol II p 315
Cronin (Inspector of Taxes) v C [1968] IR 148, Vol II p 592
Cronin (Inspector of Taxes) v Cork & County Property Co Ltd [1986] IR 559, Vol III p 198 Cited also at: Vol III p 271, Vol IV p 135
Cronin (Inspector of Taxes) v IMP Midleton Ltd Vol III p 452
Cronin (Inspector of Taxes) v Lunham Brothers Ltd [1986] ILRM 415, Vol III p 363
Cronin (Inspector of Taxes) v Strand Dairy Ltd Vol III p 441 Cited also at: Vol III p 611, Vol IV p 35, 533, 526, Vol V 21
Cronin (Inspector of Taxes) v Youghal Carpets (Yarns) Ltd [1985] IR 312, [1985] ILRM 666, Vol III p 229
Cronin v Strand Dairy 3 ITR 441 Vol V p 21
Cronk, John & Sons Ltd v Harrison [1936] 120 TC 112, Vol III p 683
Crosby v Wadsworth [1805] 6 East 602, Vol II p 636
Crowe Engineering Ltd v Phyllis Lynch and Others Vol IV p 340
Crowley v Ireland [1980] IR 102 Vol V p 614
Cullen v AG LR 1 HL 190 Vol V p 539
Cullen v Cullen [1962] IR 268 Vol V p 589
Cummins, In the Matter of the Estates of: O'Dwyer & Charleton v Keegan & Ors Vol V p 367
Cunard Steam Ship Co Ltd, The v Herlihy (Inspector of Taxes), and The Cunard Steam Ship Co Ltd v IRC 1 ITC 373, [1931] IR 287, 307, Vol I p 330
Currie v CIR & Durant v CIR [1921] 12 TC 245, Vol III p 211
Curtin (Inspector of Taxes) v M Ltd 3 ITC 227, [1960] IR 59, Vol II p 360
Curtis, Gerard & Brendan Geough v AG &IRC [1986] ILRM 428, Vol III p 419
Cusack Patrick v Evelyn O'Reilly and The Collector General Vol IV p 86
Cyril Lord Carpets Ltd v Schofield 42 TC 637, Vol III p 165

D

D & GR Rankine v CIR 32 TC 520, [1952] SLT 153, Vol II p 429, Vol IV p 135
Dagnall, In re, 12 TC 712, [1896] 2 QB 407, Vol I p 108
Dale v CIR [1953] 34 TC 468, Vol II p 596
Dale v Johnson 32 TC, Vol III p 661
Daly, Michael v The Revenue Commissioners & Ors Vol V p 213

Daphne v Shaw [1926] 11 TC 256, Vol II p 602, Vol III pp 113, 120
Date v Mitcalfe [1928] 1 KB 383, 13 TC 41, [1927] WN 271, Vol I p 221
Davis (Inspector of Taxes) v Hibernian Bank Ltd 2 ITC 111, Vol I p 503
Cited also at: Vol II p 419, Vol III p 373
Davis (Inspector of Taxes) v The Superioress, Mater Misericordiae Hospital Dublin [1933] IR 481, 1 ITR 387 Vol V p 6
Davis v Adair [1895] 1 IR 379, Vol I p 259
Davis v Johnson [1978] 1 AER 841, CA 1132 HL (E), Vol III p 113, 120
Davis v M 2 ITC 320, [1947] IR 145, Vol II p 500, 515
Davis, RG (Inspector of Taxes) v The Superioress, Mater Misericordiae Hospital, Dublin 2 ITC 1, [1933] IR 480, 503, Vol I p 387
Cited also at: Vol III p 178, Vol V p 6
Davis, WJ (Inspector of Taxes) v X Ltd 2 ITC 320, [1946] ILTR 57, [1947] ILTR 157 Vol II p 45
Davoren, Estate of Mary Davoren Vol V p 36
Dawson v Dawson 11 Jur 984, Vol II p 332
De Brun (Inspector of Taxes) v K [1981] IR 117, [1982] ILRM 13, Vol III p 19
Cited also at: Vol III pp 56, 113, 120, 304, 319, 441, 477, 533, 611, 683, Vol IV pp 91, 349, 526, 547, 2001 p 80
De Burca v The Attorney General [1976] IR 38 Vol V p 614
De Nicolls v Saunders LR 5, CP 589, Vol II p 222
Dearle v Hall 15 TC 725, 3 Russell Reports 1, Vol II p 592
Deaton v AG [1963] IR 170, [1962] 98 ILTR 99, Vol III pp 419, 533, Vol IV p 278
Defrenne v Sabena [1976] 2 CMLR 98 Vol V p 614
Deighan, Michael v Edward N Hearne, AG and Others [1986] IR 603, [1990] IR 499, Vol III p 533
Cited also at: Vol III p 590, Vol IV p 505,1999 p 65
Dennehy v Minister for Social Welfare [Unreported HC 26 July 1984], Vol IV p 437
Denny & Sons (Ireland) Ltd T/A Kerry Foods v Minister for Social Welfare Vol V p 238
Denny & Sons Irl Ltd v Minister for Social Welfare [1998] 1 IR 34 , 2001 p 127
Depoix v Chapman 28 TC 462, [1947] 2 AER 649, Vol II p 241
Derry v Inland Revenue [1927] SC 714 Vol V p 614
Derry v The CIR [1927] Sess Cas 714, 13 TC 30, Vol II p 75
Deuchar v Gas Light & Coke Co [1925] AC, Vol II p 241
Deutsche Bank Aktiengesellschaft v Murtagh & Anor [1995] 1 ILRM 381, 2000 p 216
Dewar v IRC 19 TC 561, Vol III p 484
Dickson v Fitch's Garage [1975] STC 480 Vol V p 200
Diggines v Forestal Land, Timber and Railways Co Ltd 15 TC 630, [1931] AC 380, Vol II p 304
Dilleen, TA (Inspector of Taxes) v Edward J Kearns Vol IV p 547
Diners Club Ltd, The v The Revenue and The Minister for Finance [1988] IR 158, Vol III p 680
Dinning v Henderson 3 de G & S 702, Vol II p 332
Diplock v Wintle [1948} Ch 465, Vol IV p 247
Ditcher v Denison 11 Moore PC 325 p 337, Vol II p 108
Diver v McCrea [1908] 42 ILTR 249 Vol V p 271
Diver v McCrea [1908] 42 ILTR 249.

Dixon v Fitch's Garage Ltd 50 TC 509, [1975] STC 480, [1975] 3 AER 455, Vol III p 219,
   Vol IV pp 68, 284, 425
Dixon, Heynes v Dixon, Re, [1900] 2 Ch 561, Vol III p 265
Dolan (Inspector of Taxes) v AB Co Ltd [1969] IR 282, 104 ILTR 101, Vol II p 515
Cited also at: Vol II p 602
Dolan v Corn Exchange [1975] IR 315 Vol V p 322
Dolan v Joyce and Kirwan [1928] IR 559, Vol II p 1
Dolan v Neligan [1967] IR 247, Vol III p 403, Vol V p 322, 614
Dolan, JD (Inspector of Taxes) v "K" National School Teacher 2 ITC 280, [1944] IR 470,
   Vol I p 656
Cited also at: Vol II p 592, Vol III p 484, Vol IV p 221
Donald v Thomson 8 TC 272, [1922] SC 237, Vol II p 636
Donovan (Inspector of Taxes) v CG Crofts 1 ITC 214, [1926] IR 477, Vol I p 115
Cited also at: Vol I p 183, Vol II p 75
Douglas v Douglas CR 12 Eq 643, Vol I p 259
Downing, Estate of Teresa (Owner) 2 ITC 103, [1936] IR 164, Vol I p 487
Downing's Estate, Re, 1 ITC 103, [1936] IR 164, Vol II p 332
Doyle & Others v An Taoiseach & Others [1986] ILRM 522, Vol III p 73
Cited also at: Vol IV p 162
Doyle and Others v Government of Ireland and Others [1981] ECR 735, Vol III p 73
Doyle, In Re Evelyn (SC) 21 Dec 1955 Vol V p 614
DPP v Byrne [1995] 1 ILRM 279, 2000 p 274
DPP v Humphrys [1977] AC 1, [1976] 2 WLR 837, [1976] 2 AER 497, Vol III p 419
DPP v Luft & Anor 2 AER 569, [1976] 3 WLR 32, Vol III p 28
DPP v Lynch [1982] IR 64, [1981] ILRM 389, Vol III p 419
DPP v George Redmond 2000 p 273
DPP v Martin McLoughlin [1986] IR 355, [1986] ILRM 493, Vol III p 467
Cited also at: Vol IV p 378, 2001 p 127
DPP v McCormick CCA 18/04/2000, 2000 p 274
DPP v McDonagh [1996] 2 ILRM 469, 2000 p 65
DPP v Michael Cunningham Vol V p 691
DPP v Ottewell [1970] AC 642, 649, Vol III p 19
DPP v Robert Downes [1987] IR 139, [1987] ILRM 665, Vol III p 641
Cited also at: Vol IV p 395
DPP v Seamus Boyle Vol IV p 395
Draper v AG [1984] IR 277, [1984] ILRM 643, Vol IV p 437
Drexl, In re, No 299/86, Vol IV p 512
Drummond v CIR 32 TC 263, [1951] SC 482, Vol II p 636
Dublin Corporation v Building and Allied Trade Union & Ors [SC] unrep 24 July 1996
   Vol V p 322
Dublin Corporation v Flynn [1980] IR 357, Vol III p 419
Dublin Corporation v M'Adam 20 LR IR 497, Vol II p 211
Duggan & Others v An Taoiseach & Others [unreported 11 April 1988], Vol IV pp 170,
   229
Duke of Westminster v CIR 151 LTR 489, 51 TLR 467, 19 TC 490, [1936] AC 1,
   Vol I pp 601, 618, 629, Vol II pp 222, 515
Duncan v O'Driscoll [1997] ELR 38 , 2001 p 127
Duncan's Executors v Farmer [1909] Sess Cas 1212, 46 SCLR 857, 5 TC 417, Vol I p 618

Dunn Trust (In Voluntary Liquidation) v Williams 31 TC 477, Vol III p 373, 644
Dunne v Hamilton [1982] ILRM 290, Vol III p 356
Dunnes Stores (Oakville) Ltd v MC Cronin (Inspector of Taxes) Vol IV p 68
Dunnes Stores v Gerard Ryan and The Minister for Enterprise, Trade and Employment 2000 p 261
Duple Motor Bodies Ltd v IRC [1961] 1 WLR 739, Vol III p 198
Duple Motor Bodies Ltd v Ostime 39 TC 537, Vol IV p 135
Durbeck's, Re, [1981] ECR 1095, Vol IV p 492
DWS Corporation v Minister of National Revenue [1968] 2 Ex CR 44, 1999 p 82

E

Eadie v CIR 9 TC 1, [1924] 2 KB 198, Vol I p 115, Vol II p 75
Earl Beatty v CIR 35 TC 30, Vol II p 627
Earl Howe v CIR 7 TC 289 Vol V p 108
Earl of Derby v Aylmer 6 TC 665, Vol III p 113, 120
East Cork Foods v O'Dwyer Steel [1978] IR 103 Vol V p 322, 614
East Donegal Co-operative Livestock Marts Ltd v AG [1970] IR 317, 104 ILTR 81, Vol III pp 73, 127, 590, Vol V p 614, 1998 p 120
Eastend Dwellings Co Ltd v Finsbury Borough Council [1953] AC 109 , 2001 p 105
East India Trading Co Inc v Carmel Exporters and Importers Ltd [1952] 1 AER 1053, Vol II p 281, 2001 p 138
East Realty and Investment Co v Schneider Granite Co [1916] 240 US 55, Vol III p 127
Eastmans Ltd v Shaw 43 TLR 549, 14 TC 218, Vol II pp 32, 515, Vol III p 95, Vol V p 680
Ebrahimi v Westbourne Galleries Ltd [1973] AC 379 Vol V p 226
Edinburgh Life Assurance Co v Lord Advocate 5 TC 472, Vol IV p 135
Educational Company v Fitzpatrick No 2 [1961] IR 345 1998 p 120
Edward J Kearns v Dilleen (Inspector of Taxes) Vol V p 514
Edwards (Inspector of Taxes) v Bairstow [1956] AC 14
Edwards (Inspector of Taxes) v Bairstow 36 TC 207, [1956] AC 14, Vol II pp 515, 614, 636, Vol III pp 1, 178, 211, 219, 253, 644, Vol IV p 135, Vol V p 139, 200
EG v Mac Shamhrain (Inspector of Taxes) 3 ITC 217, [1958] IR 288, Vol II p 352
Eglinton Silica Brick Co Ltd v Marrian [1924] Sess Cas 946, 61 SC LR 601, 9 TC 92, Vol II p 115
Egyptian Delta Land and Investment Co Ltd v Todd 14 TC 119, [1929] AC 1, Vol I p 259
Egyptian Hotels Ltd v Mitchell 6 TC 542, CA [1914] 3 KB 118, [1915] AC 1022, Vol I p 359, Vol II p 68
Eisher v Macomber 252 US 207, Vol IV p 135
Ellerker v Union Cold Storage Co Ltd 22 TC 195, Vol III p 304
Elliott v Elliott 9 M & W 23, Vol I p 130
Elmhirst v The CIR 21 TC 381, [1937] 2 KB 551, Vol I p 563
Emery, John & Sons v CIR 20 TC 213, [1935] SC 802, [1937] AC 91, Vol I p 515, 583, Vol II pp 429, 472
Emery's Investment Trusts, In re [1959] 1 Ch 410 1998 p 169
English Crown Spelter Co Ltd v Baker 5 TC 327, 99 LTR 353, Vol I p 642
Ensign Tankers (Leasing) Ltd v Stokes (Inspector of Taxes) [1989] STC 705, [1992] 2 AER 275 Vol V p 6
Erichsen v Last 4 TC 422, 8 QBD 414, Vol I p 330, 387

Erin Executor and Trustee Co Ltd (as trustee of Irish Pension Fund Property Unit Trust) v the Revenue Commissioners Vol V p 76
Essex County Council v Ellman (1989) STC 31T Vol V p 108, 1998 p 183
Estate of Persse, Re, [1888, unreported, Land Judges Court], Vol II p 332
Estate of Peter Kelly, Re, [1908, unreported], Vol II p 332
Euratom Decision 88/376/ EEC, 2000 p 287
European Communities v Hellenic Republic [1989] ECR 2965 1998 p 76
Evans & Co v Phillips (Inspector of Taxes) 1 ITC 38, Vol I p 43
Evans Medical Supplies Ltd v Moriarty 37 TC 540, [1956] 1 WLR 794, Vol II p 602
Evans v Wheatley 38 TC 216, Vol II p 515
Executors and Trustees of AC Ferguson, The (deceased) v Donovan (Inspector of Taxes) 1 ITC 214, [1927] ILTR 49, [1929] IR 489, Vol I p 183
Exham v Beamish [1939] IR 336, Vol II p 154
Exparte Brett [1897] 1 IR 488, Vol I p 28
Exported Live Stock (Insurance) Board, The v TJ Carroll (Inspector of Taxes) 3 ITC 67, [1951] IR 286, Vol II p 211
Cited also at: Vol IV p 73

F

Faccini Dore v Recreb [1995] All ER European Cases 1998 p 76
Falcke v Scottish Imperial Insurance Co 34 Ch D 234, Vol I p 601
Fall v Hitchen 49 TC 433, Vol III p 43, Vol IV p 45
Farmer v The Juridicial Society of Edinburgh [1914] Sess Cas 731, 6 TC 467 [1914], Vol I p 542
Farmer v The Scottish North American Cross Ltd Vol V p 139
Farrell v Alexander [1975] 3 WLR 642, 650-1, [1977] AC 59, Vol III p 19, 229
Federal Commissioners of Taxation v Broken Hill Property Ltd , 2001 p 80
Federal Commissioners of Taxation v Utah Development (1996) 76 ATC 4119 , 2001 p 80
Federal Commissioners of Taxation v ICI Australia Ltd [1972] 127 CLR 529, 3 ATR 321, Vol IV p 68
Federal Commissioner of Taxation v Westraders Pty Ltd [1980] 114 CLR 35, Vol III p 683
Fee v Collendars Trustees [1927] SLT (Sh Ct) 17, Vol II p 32
Feeny v Pollexfen and Co Ltd [1931] IR 589, Vol III p 661
Fennessy (Inspector of Taxes) v John McConnellogue Vol V p 129
Ferguson v Dawson & Partners CA [1976] Vol V p 239, 1998 p 177
Ferguson v Noble [1919] 2 SC LT 49, 7 TC 176, [1919] SC 534, Vol I p 231
Ferguson, Re [1935] IR 21, Vol II p 332
Figgis Deceased, In re [1969] 1 Ch 123, [1968] 2 WLR 1173, [1968] 1 All ER 999, Vol V p 272
Finden v Stephens 2 Ph 142, Vol I p 601
Findlay's Trustees v IRC [1938] 22 ATC 437 Vol V p 577
Finlay v Murtagh [1979] IR 249, Vol IV p 117
Finucane v McMahon [1990] 1 IR 165 Vol V p 272
Firma A Racke v Hauptzollamt Mainz (Case 98/78) [1979] ECR 69 1998 p 76
Firman, Re, [not rep], Vol III p 387
First National Commercial Bank plc v Angland [1996] IR 75, 1999 p 65
Fitzgerald v Persse Ltd [1908] IR 279, Vol II p 130

Fitzgerald, Martin v CIR 1 ITC 100, [1926] IR 182, 585 , Vol I p 91
Cited also at: Vol II pp 32, 45, 222, 267, 360, Vol IV p 425
Fleming v Ranks (Ireland) Ltd [1983] ILRM 541, 2000 p 216
Fleming v Wilkinson 10 TC 416, Vol II p 393, 491
Floor v Davis (Inspector of Taxes) [1978] STC 436, 2000 p 114
Flynn, W (Inspector of Taxes) v (1) John Noone Ltd, and Flynn, W (Inspector of Taxes) v (2) Blackwood & Co (Sligo) Ltd 3 ITC 79, Vol II p 222
Cited also at: Vol II pp 222, 464, 515, Vol III p 683
Foley v Fletcher [1858] 3 H & N 769 Vol V p 108, 1998 p 183
Food Controller v Cork [1923] AC 647, Vol I p 45
Forbes, Cyril v John Tobin And Janet Tobin , 2001 p 71
Forbes (Inspector of Taxes) v GHD 3 ITC 365, [1964] IR 447, Vol II p 491
Forbes v Forbes Kay 341, Vol I p 259
Forde, Michael Decision by Appeal Commissioners Vol IV p 348
Forsyth v Thompson 23 TC 374, Vol I p 164
Foster v Elsley 19 Ch D 419, Vol I p 601
Franconini v Franconini 11 Jur NS 124, Vol I p 427
Franklin v British Railways Board (1994) PIQRI, 2000 p 269
Fraser (Inspector of Taxes) v London Sportscar Centre Ltd [1985] STC 688, [1985] 59 TC 63, Vol III p 611, Vol IV p 304
Frasers (Glasgow) Bank Ltd v CIR 40 TC 698, Vol III p 373
Frederick Inns Ltd, The Rendezvous Ltd, The Graduate Ltd, Motels Ltd (In Liquidation) v The Companies Acts 1963-1983 Vol IV p 247
Freidson v Glynn Thomas [1922] WN 251, Vol I p 64
Fry v Burma Corporation Ltd 15 TC 113, [1930] 1 KB 249, [1930] AC 321, Vol I p 571, 583
Fry v IRC [1959] Ch 86, Vol III p 56
Fry v Salisbury House Estate Ltd [1930] 1 KB 304, 143 LT 77, [1930] AC 432, Vol II p 429, 596, Vol V p 680
Furniss v Dawson [1984] AC 474, [1984] 2 WLR 226, [1984] 1 AER 530, [1984] 55 TC 324, [1984] STC 153, Vol III p 670, 683, Vol IV p 547, Vol V p 6, 108, 163, 515 1998 p 183
Furse, In re (1980) 3 AER 344 Vol V p 481
Furtado v Carndonald Fening Co [1907] SC 36, 20 TC 223, Vol I p 515

G

G O'C & A O'C (Application of Liam Liston (Inspector Taxes)), In the Matter of Vol V p 346
G v An Bord Uchtala [1980] IR 32, [1979] 113 ILTR 25, Vol IV p 437
G v Director of Public Prosecutions [1994] 1 IR 374
G v DPP [1994] 1 IR 374, Vol V p 362
Gaffney v Gaffney [1975] IR 133, Vol IV p 437
Garforth v Tankard Carpets Ltd 53 TC 342, Vol III p 340
Gartside v IRC [1968] 2 WLR 277, Vol III p 104
Garvey v Ireland [1981] IR 75 Vol V p 696
Gascoigne v Gascoigne [1918] 1 KB 223 1998 p 169
Gason v Rich 19 LR (Irl) 391 Vol V p 272
Gatien Motor Co v Continental Oil [1979] IR 406, Vol IV p 269
Gayson, Michael v Allied Irish Banks Plc 2000 p 105

General Medical Council v CIR 13 TC 819, [Reported 139 LTR 225], Vol I p 542
General Nursing Council for Scotland v The CIR 14 TC 645, [1929] SC 664, Vol I p 542
General Reversionary Interest and Investment Co Ltd v Hancock 7 TC 358, [1939] 1 KB 25, Vol II p 515
George Ingelfield Ltd, In re [1933] Ch 1 Vol V p 515
Germyn Street Turkish Baths Ltd [1971] 3 AER 184, Vol III p 423
GH Ltd v Browne (Inspector of Taxes) [1984] ILRM 231, Vol III p 95
Gibbon v Pearse [1905] 1KB 816, Vol IV p 332
Gibbs v Mersey Docks Trustees [Not reported], Vol II p 241
Gilbert Hewson v JB Kealy (Inspector of Taxes) 2 ITC 286, Vol II p 15
Gilbert v CIR [1957] 248 F 2d 399, Vol III p 683
Gillies v CIR 14 TC 329, [1929] SC 131, Vol I p 411
Gilligan v Criminal Assets Bureau, Galvin, Lanigan & Revenue Commissioners Vol V p 424
Gilligan, John v Criminal Assets Bureau, Revenue Commissioners & Others, 2001 p 135
Gisbourne v Gisbourne [1877] 2 AC 300, Vol IV p 340
Glamorgan Quarter Sessions v Wilson 5 TC 537, [1910] 1 KB 725, Vol II p 332
Glanely v Wightman 17 TC 634, [1933] AC 613, Vol II p 315
Glasgow Corporation v Inland Revenue [1959] SLT 230 Vol V p 614
Glenboig Union Fireclay Co Ltd v CIR 12 TC 427, [1922] Sess (HL) 112, Vol I p 1, 427, Vol II p 515
Gliksten 14 TC 364, Vol I p 164
Global Plant Ltd v Secretary of State for Health and Social Security [1971] 3 AER 385, [1971] 2 WLR 269, [1972] 1 QB 139, Vol III p 43, Vol IV p 45
Glover v BLN Ltd (No 2) [1973] IR 432, 2000 p 269
Gold Coast Selection Trust v Humphrey 30 TC 209, [1948] AC 459, [1946] 2 AER 742, [1948] 2 AER 379, Vol II p 419
Golden Horse Shoe Ltd v Thurgood [1934] 1 KB 548, Vol II p 515
Golder v Great Boulder Proprietary Gold Mines Ltd 33 TC 75, [1952] 1 AER 360, Vol II p 500
Golding (Inspector of Taxes) v Kaufman [1985] STC 152, Vol IV p 547, Vol V p 515
Goldstein v CIR [1966] 364 F 2nd 734, Vol III p 683
Goodman International and Anor v Hamilton [1992] IR 54 1998 p 120
Gordon and Blair Ltd v Cronin 40 TC 358, Vol III p 363
Gordon v Dunleavy [1928] IR 595, Vol II p 291
Goslings and Sharpe v Blake 2 TC 450, 23 QBD 324, Vol II p 332
Gould v Curtis 6 TC 293, [1913] 2 KB 84, Vol II p 661
Governor & Co of the Bank of Ireland v MJ Meeneghan & Ors Vol V p 44
Governors of Rotunda Hospital v Coman 7 TC 517, [1921] 1 AC 1, 36 TLR 646, Vol I p 387, 515
Government of India, Ministry of Finance (Revenue Division) v Taylor [1955] AC 491 1998 p 76
Gowers and Others v Walker and Others 15 TC 165, [1930] 1 Ch p 262, Vol II p 108
Graham v District Justice Carroll (unreported, HC 9 December 1987), Vol IV p 278
Graham v Greene [1925] 9 TC 309, Vol II p 614, Vol III p 363
Graham v Minister for Industry and Commerce [1933] IR 156, Vol III p 43, Vol IV p 45, Vol V p 239
Grainger v Gough 3 TC 462, [1896] AC 325, Vol I p 330

Granite Supply Association Ltd Kitton 5 TC 168, 43 SCLR 65, [1905] 8F 5, Vol I p 91, Vol II pp 32, 45, 382, 515
Granville Building Co Ltd v Oxby 35 TC 245, Vol III p 1
Gray & Co Ltd v Murphy 23 TC 225, Vol I p 164
Gray and Gillet v Tiley 26 TC 80, Vol III p 1
Gray v Formosa [1963] p 259, Vol IV p 437
Gray v Holmes 30 TC 467, [1949] TR 71, Vol II p 452
Great Northern Railway Co v Sunburst Oil & Refining Co [1932] 287 US 358 Vol V p 614
Great Southern Railways Co, The v The IRC 1 ITC 298, [1930] IR 299, Vol I p 359
Green & Co (Cork) Ltd v The IRC 1 ITC 142, [1927] IR 240, Vol I p 130
Green & Others v Minister for Agriculture [1990] ILRM 364, Vol IV p 323
Green v Favourite Cinemas Ltd 15 TC 390, Vol II p 464
Green v IRC ITC 142, [1927] IR 240, Vol I p 240
Green v J Gliksten & Sons Ltd [1928] 2 KB 193, [1929] AC 381, 14 TC 364, Vol I p 427
Green, JW & Co Ltd v the IRC [1927] IR 240, [1927] ILTR 145, Vol IV p 304
Greene v Louisville and Interurban Railway Co [1917] 244 US 499, Vol III p 127
Greenhalgh v Arderne Cinemas Ltd & Others [1950] 2 AER 1120, Vol III p 423
Greenore Trading Co Ltd [unreported] 28 March 1980, Vol III p 423
Gresham Life Assurance Society Ltd v Bishop 4 TC 464, [1903] 2 KB 171, Vol III p 484
Gresham Life Assurance Society v AG [1916] 1 Ch 228, Vol I p 34
Gresham Life Assurance Society v Styles 3 TC 185, [1892] AC 309, Vol I pp 1, 515, Vol IV p 135
Griffin, Francis v Minister for Social, Community and Family Affairs , 2001 p 125
Griffin v Illinois [1956] 351 US 12 Vol V p 614
Griffiths (Inspector of Taxes) v Harrison (Waterford) Ltd, JP [1962] 1 AER 909, Vol V p 6
Griffiths v Mockler 35 TC 135; [1953] 2 AER 805, Vol II p 366
Griffiths v The Queen (1997) ICLR 293, 2000 p 274
Grimes v Wallace [1994] unrep, 4 March 1994 Vol V p 210
Grocock v Grocock [1920] 1 KB 1, Vol I p 629
Groome v Fodhla Printing Co [1943] IR 380, Vol II p 360
Grove v Young Men's Christian Association 88 LT 696, 4 TC 613, Vol I p 387
Guardians of Parish of Brighton [1891] 2 QN 157, Vol II p 175
Guardians of the Banbury Union v Robinson 4 QB 919 Vol V p 560
Guildford Corporation v Brown [1915] 1 KB 256, Vol III p 441, 611
Guinness & Mahon Ltd v Browne (Inspector of Taxes) Vol III p 373
Cited also at: Vol III p 644
Gulbenkian Settlement Trusts, In re [1970] AC 508; [1968] 3 WLR 1127; [1968] 3 AER 785; Vol V p 37

H

H & G Kinemas Ltd v Cooke 18 TC 116, Vol III p 178
H Williams (Tallaght) (in Receivership and Liquidation), In the Matter of Vol V p 388
Hall v IRC 12 TC 382, [1921] LJ 1229, Vol I p 240
Hallett's Estate, Re, [1879] 13 Ch D 696, Vol IV p 247
Hallstrooms Pty Ltd v Federal Commissioners of Taxation [1946] 72 CLR 634, Vol II p 515
Hamerton v Overy 35 TC 73, Vol II p 366
Hamilton v CIR 16 TC 28, Vol III p 229
Hamilton v Hamilton [1982] IR 466, [1982] ILRM 290, Vol III p 73, Vol IV p 162

Hamilton v Linaker [1923] IR 104, Vol II p 332
Hammond Lane Metal Co Ltd, The v S O'Culachain (Inspector of Taxes) [1990] IR 560, Vol IV p 187
Cited also at: Vol V p 6
Hampton (IOT) v Fortes Auto-Grill Ltd [1980] STC 80, 53 TC 691, Vol IV pp 68, 284
Hanbury, In re 38 TC 588 Vol V p 108, 1998 p 183
Hancock v General Reversionary and Investment Co 7 TC 358, [1919] 1 KB 25, Vol II p 32
Hanlon v North City Milling Co [1903] 2 IR 163 Vol V p 532
Harbutts Plasticine Ltd v Wayne Tank and Pump Company Limited [1971] All ER 225, 2000 p 269
Harling v Celynen Collieries Workmen's Institute 23 TC 558, [1940] 2 KB 465, Vol II p 482
Harrision, JP (Watford) Ltd v Griffith 40 TC 281, Vol III p 373
Hartland v Diggines 10 TC 247, [1926] AC 289, Vol II p 452
Harvey v Caulcott 33 TC 159, Vol II p 472, Vol III p 1, 9, 373
Harvey v Minister for Social Welfare [1990] ILRM 185 Vol V p 696
Haughey, Re [1971] IR 217, Vol III p 590, Vol V p 614, 1998 p 120
Haughey and Others v Attorney General and Others 1998 p 119
Hay v O'Grady 1 IR 210 Vol V p 272
Hayes, C (Inspector of Taxes) v RJ Duggan 1 ITC 269, [1929] IR 406, Vol I p 195
Cited also at: Vol II p 291
Healy, John v SI Breathnach (Inspector of Taxes) [1986] IR 105, Vol III p 496
Cited also at: Vol V p 98
Heaney v Ireland [1994] 2 ILRM 420 Vol V p 213
Hearne, EN (Inspector of Taxes) v O'Cionna and Others T/A JA Kenny & Partners Vol IV p 113
Heather v p E Consulting Group Ltd 48 TC 293, Vol IV p 135
Helby v Matthews [1895] AC 471 Vol V p 515
Helby v Rafferty [1979] 1 WLR 13 Vol V p 614
Hedley Byrne & Co Ltd v Heller & Partners Ltd, 2000 p 105
Henderson v Folkestone Waterworks Co [1885] 1 TLR 329 Vol V p 614
Henley and Co 1 TC 209, 9 Ch D 469, Vol I p 45
Henriksen v Grafton Hotels Ltd 24 TC 453, [1942] 1 KB 82, [1942] 2 KB 184, Vol II p 515
Herbert v McQuade 4 TC 489, [1902] 2 KB 631, Vol I pp 155, 427, 618, Vol II p 261
Heron Peter C and Others v The Minister For Communications [1985] IR 623, Vol III p 298
Heydon's case 3 Rep 75 Vol V p 539
HH v MJ Forbes (Inspector of Taxes) Vol II p 614
Cited also at: Vol III p 178
Hibernian Insurance Company Limited v MacUimis (Inspector of Taxes) Vol V p 495, 2000 p 75
Hibernian Transport Companies Ltd, In re Vol V p 194
High Wycombe Squash Club Ltd v C & E Commissioners [1976] VAT TR 156, Vol IV p 349
Highland Railway Co v Balderston 26 SC LR 657, 2 TC 485, Vol II p 32
Hill v East and West India Dock Co 9 AC 448, Vol II p 130
Hill v Gregory 6 TC 39, [1912] 2 KB 70, Vol I p 515

Hill v Mathews 10 TC 25, Vol II p 115
Hinchcliffe (Inspector of Taxes) v Crabtree 47 TC 419, Vol IV p 125
Hinches, Dashwood v Hinches, Re, [1921] 1 Ch 475, 19 TC 521, Vol I p 515
Hinton v Madden and Ireland Ltd 38 TC 391, [1959] 3 AER 356, 1 WLR 875, Vol II p 602, Vol III pp 113, 120
Hitchcock v Post Office [1980] ICR 100, Vol IV p 45
Hochstrasser v Mayes 38 TC 673, [1958] 3 WLR 215, [1959] Ch 22, [1960] AC 376, Vol II p 452, Vol IV p 407
Hodgins, JT (Inspector of Taxes) v Plunder & Pollak (Ireland) Ltd 3 ITC 135, [1957] IR 58, Vol II p 267
Cited also at: Vol II pp 382 500, 515, 602, Vol III p 65
Hoechst Finance Ltd v Gumbrell [1983] STC 150, Vol III p 95, Vol V p 496, 680, 2000 p 76
Hoeper v Tax Commission of Wisconsin [1931] 284 US 206 Vol V p 615
Hogan, Michael v Steele And Co Ltd and Electricity Supply Board 2000 p 269
Holland v Hodgson [1872] LR 7 CP 328, Vol III p 332
Holroyd v Wyatt 1 de G & S 125, Vol II p 332
Holt v IRC [1953] 1 WLR 1488 Vol V p 295, 577, 2001 p 105
Hood Barrs v CIR 27 TC 385, [1945] 1 AER 500 (on appeal [1946] 2 AER 768), Vol II p 82
Hope-Edwards v Blackburne [1901] 1 Ch 419, Vol I p 487
Horsfall, exparte [1827] 108 ER 820, Vol IV p 332
Houghland v RR Low (Luxury Coaches) Ltd [1962], Vol III p 253
Howard v Commissioner for Public Works [1993] ILRM 665, 2000 p 65
Howe (Earl) v CIR 7 TC 289 1998 p 184
Howe, Ex parte Brett, Re, [1871] 6 Ch App 838, 841, Vol III p 265
Howth Estate Co v WJ Davis (Inspector of Taxes) 2 ITC 74, [1936] ILTR 79, Vol I p 447
Cited also at: Vol II p 429
HT Ltd, Re (in Liquidation) and Others [1984] ILRM 583, Vol III p 120
Cited also at: Vol III p 523
Hudson Bay Co Ltd v Stevens 101 LT 96, 25 TLR 709, 5 TC 424, Vol I pp 1, 474
Hudson v Wrightson 26 TC 55, Vol III p 9
Hughes v Metropolitan Railway Co [1877] 2 AC 439 Vol V p 589
Hughes v Utting and Co Ltd 23 TC 174, [1940] AC 463, Vol II p 472
Hughes, HPC (Inspector of Taxes) v Miss Gretta Smyth (Sister Mary Bernard) and Others 1 ITC 418, [1933] IR 253, Vol I p 411
Cited also at: Vol II p 82
Humble v Humble 12 Beav 43, Vol II p 332
Humphrey v Peare 6 TC 201, [1913] 2 IR 462, Vol I p 1, 155
Huntington v Attrill [1893] AC 150 Vol V p 45
Huntley v Gaskell [1906] AC 56, Vol I p 259
Hussey, J (Inspector of Taxes v M J Gleeson & Co Ltd Vol IV p 533, Vol V p 22
Hutton v The West Cork Railway Co [1883] 23 Ch D 654, Vol III p 706, Vol IV p 247
Hyam v CIR [1929] SC 384, 14 TC 479, [1929] SC LT 361, Vol II p 32

I

Iarnrod Eireann v Ireland unrep, 28 April 1995 Vol V p 213
Imperial Chemical Industries of Australia & New Zealand Ltd v Federal Commissioner of Taxation [1970] 120 CLR 396, 1 ATR 450, Vol IV p 68

Imperial Tobacco Co Ltd v Kelly 25 TC 292, [1943] 1 AE 431, [1943] 2 AE 119, Vol II p 281
Income Tax Commissioners of Bihar and Orissa Singh [1942] 1 AER 362, Vol II p 500
Incorporated Law Society of Ireland v Carroll & Ors [1995] 3 IR 145, 2000 p 216
Industrie en Handelsonderreming Vreugdenhil BV v Commission (Case 282/90) [1992] ECR 1937 1998 p 76
Indyka v Indyka [1966] 3 AER 583 (CA), [1967] 2 AER 689, [1969] 1 AC 33, Vol IV p 437
Ingram v IRC [1986] Ch 585, [1986] 2 WLR 598, Vol III p 683
Ingram, JG & Son Ltd v Callaghan 45 TC 151, Vol III p 363
Inland Revenue Commissioners v Duke of Westminster [1979] 3 AER 775 Vol V p 6
Inland Revenue Commissioners v Plummer [1935] AER 295 Vol V p 6
Inspector of Taxes v Kiernan [1981] IR 117, 3 ITR 19 Vol V p 22, 108, 515, 1998 p 183, 1999 p 72
Inspector of Taxes v Kiernan 3 ITR 19 000 p 236
International Fishing Vessels Ltd v The Minister for the Marine [1989] IR 149, Vol IV p 485
Inverclyde, Re [1924] SC 18, Vol II p 326
Inwards v Baker [1965] 2 QB 29 Vol V p 589
Ioannides v Republic of Cyprus 6 Nov 1978 Vol V p 615
IRC v Barclay Curle & Co [1969] 45 TC 221, Vol IV pp 68, 425
IRC v Blott [1921] 2 AD 171, Vol IV p 135
IRC v Broadway Cottages Trust [1955] CJ 20; [1954] 3 WLR 438; [1954] 3 AER 120; 98 SJ 588; 47 R & IT 574; 35 TC 577, Vol V p 37
IRC v Burmah Oil Co Ltd [1981] 54 TC 200, [1982] STC 30, Vol III p 683
IRC v City of Glasgow Police Athletic Association 34 TC 76, [1953] AC 380, Vol II p 393
IRC v Clay [1914] 3 KB 466 Vol V p 577
IRC v Cock Russell 29 TC 387, 28 ATC 393, [1949] 2 AER 889, Vol II p 419
IRC v Crossman & Ors [1937] AC 26 Vol V p 577
IRC v Doorley [1933] IR 750, Vol II p 25, 195, Vol III p 683, Vol IV p 22, 91
IRC v Duke of Westminster [1936] AC 1, [1935] 104 LJ (KB) 383, 153 LT 223, 51 TLR 467, 19 TC 490, Vol II p 464, Vol III p 683, Vol V p 163
IRC v Europa Oil (NZ) Ltd [1971] AC 760, [1971] 2 WLR 55, Vol III p 683
IRC v Falkirk Temperance Cafe 11 TC 353, [1927] SC 261, Vol I p 387
IRC v Fraser 24 TC 498, Vol III p 178
IRC v Frere [1965] AC 402, Vol III p 403
IRC v Lysaght 13 TC 511, [1928] AC 234, Vol II p 32
IRC v Metrolands Property Finance Ltd [1981] STC 195 Vol V p 347
IRC v N 101 ILTR 197, Vol III p 319
IRC v National Federation of Self Employed and Small Businesses Ltd [1982] AC 617, Vol IV p 229
IRC v Newcastle Breweries Ltd 12 TC 927, 42 TLR 609, Vol I p 207
IRC v Paterson 9 TC 163, Vol III p 484
IRC v Plummer [1980] AC 896, [1979] 3 WLR 689, [1979] 3 AER 775, [1979] 54 TC 1, [1979] STC 793, Vol III p 683, Vol V p 108, 1998 p 183
IRC v Ramsey (1935) 20 TC 70 Vol V p 108, 1998 p 184
IRC v Reid's Trustees [1949] AC 361, Vol III p 56
IRC v Rossminster and Others [1980] AC 952 , 2001 p 58

IRC v Scottish & Newcastle Breweries Ltd [1981] STC 50, [1982] STC 296, Vol IV pp 68, 284, 425
IRC v Sneath 17 TC 149, 48 TLR 241, [1932] 2 KB 362, Vol II p 374
IRC v Strong 15 SLR 704, Vol I p 155, 427
IRC v The Duke of Westminster [1936] AC p 19 & 24, Vol II p 175
IRC v Thompson [1937] 1 KB 290, Vol III p 553
IRC v Wesleyan and General Assurance Society [1946] 2 AER 749, [1946] 62 TLR 741 (CA), [1948] 1 AER 555, [1948] 64 TLR 173, 30 TC 11 (HL), Vol II p 464, Vol III p 683
IRC v Wolfson [1949] WN 190, Vol II p 175
Irish Agricultural Machinery Ltd v O'Culachain (Inspector of Taxes) [1987] IR 458, [1990] IR 535, Vol III p 611, Vol V p 22
Cited also at: Vol IV pp 35, 125, 361, 533, Vol V p 22
Irish Creamery Milk Suppliers Association and Others v The Government of Ireland and Others [not reported], Vol III p 73
Irish Nationwide Building Society v The IRC Vol IV p 296
Irish Permanent Building Society v Registrar of Building Societies, Irish Life Building Society and Others [1981] ILRM 242, Vol III p 28
Irish Provident Assurance Co Ltd (In Liquidation) v Kavanagh (Inspector of Taxes) 1 ITC 52, [1930] IR 231, Vol I p 45
Cited also at: Vol I p 318
Irish Bank Ltd, Re [1999] 1 ILRM 321, 2000 p 65
Irish Shell and BP Ltd v Costello [1981] ILRM 66, Vol IV p 269, Vol V p 108, 515, 1998 p 184
Irwin v Michael Grimes Vol V p 209

J

James, Ex parte [1874] 8 Ch App 609 Vol V p 615
Jarrold v Good 40 TC 681
Jarrold v John Good & Sons Ltd 40 TC 681, Vol III p 219, Vol IV p 68, Vol V p 200
JB O'C v PCD and A Bank 3 ITR 153 Vol V p 347
Jeffrey v Rolls-Royce Ltd 40 TC 443, [1960] 2 AER 640, Vol II p 602
Jenkins Productions Ltd v CIR 29 TC 142, EPT Leaflet No 21 [1944] 1 AER 610, Vol II p 130
Jennings v Kinder 38 TC 673, [1959] Ch 22, [1958] 3 WLR 215, Vol II p 452
Jennings v Middlesborough Corporation 34 TC 447, Vol III p 253
Johnson v New Jersey [1966] 384 US 719 Vol V p 615
Jones v CIR 7 TC 310 Vol V p 108, 1998 p 184
Jones v Cwmmorthin Slate Co 1 TC 267, Vol II p 382
Jones v Flint 19 Ad & E 753, Vol II p 636
Jones v Leeming [1930] AC 415, Vol II p 204
Jones v Nuttall 10 TC 349, Vol III p 319
Jones v The Mersey Docks 11 HL Ca 480, Vol II p 211
Jones v The South West Lancashire Coal Owners' Association Ltd [1927] AC 827, Vol II p 211
Jones v Wright 13 TC 221, 44 TLR 128, 139 LTR 43, Vol I p 601
Jones, In re [1933] Ch 842 Vol V p 565
Jones, In re, 26 Ch D 736 Vol V p 526
Jones, Samuel & Co (Devondale) Ltd v CIR 32 TC 513, [1952] SLT 144, Vol II p 267, Vol III p 65

Jordan and Harrison v MacDonald and Evans [1952] ITLR 101, Vol IV p 45
Joyce, Re [1946] IR 277, Vol III p 572
Julius v The Bishop of Oxford 5 AC 214 p 222, Vol I p 104
JW v JW Vol IV p 437

K

K Co v Hogan (Inspector of Taxes) [1985] ILRM 200, Vol III p 56
Cited also at: Vol IV p 547
Kahn v Shevin [1974] 416 US 351 Vol V p 615
Kealy, JB (Inspector of Taxes) v O'Mara (Limerick) Ltd 2 ITC 265, [1942] IR 616,
   Vol I p 642
Cited also at: Vol II pp 25, 45, 222, 500, 602
Keenan Brothers Ltd [1985] ILRM 641, Vol III p 548, Vol V p 108, 1998 p 184
Keir v Gillespie 7 TC 473, 478, Vol III p 319
Keller, Karl v The IRC and Others Vol IV p 512
Kelly, HF (Inspector of Taxes) v H 3 ITC 351, [1964] IR 488, Vol II p 460
Kelly, JF (Inspector of Taxes) v Cobb Straffan Ireland Ltd Vol IV p 526, Vol V p 22
Kellystown Co v Hogan [1985] ILRM 200 Vol V p 515
Kelsall Parsons & Co, v CIR 21 TC 608, [1938] SC 238, Vol II p 515
Kemp (as Hawkins' Executor) v Evans 20 TC 14, Vol II p 393
Kennard Davis v CIR 8 TC 341, Vol II p 326, Vol III pp 229, 403
Kennedy (Inspector of Taxes) v The Rattoo Co-operative Dairy Society Ltd 1 ITC 282,
   Vol I p 315
Cited also at: Vol III p 533
Kennedy, Giles J v EG Hearne, AG and Others [1987] IR 120, [1988] IR 481, [1988]
   ILRM 53, 531, Vol III p 590
   Cited also 1998 p 120
Kenny J v Revenue Commissioners, Goodman & Gemon Ltd (Notice Parties) Vol V p 363
Kenny v AG 11 LR IR 253 Vol V p 539
Kenny v Harrison & Anor [1902] 2 KB 168, Vol III p 661
Kensington Income Tax Commissioners v Aramayo 6 TC 279 & 613, [1916] 1 AC 215, Vol
   II p 291
Kent v Sussex Sawmills Ltd (1947) IR 177 Vol V p 108, 1998 p 184
Kerrane, JG (Inspector of Taxes) v N Hanlon (Ireland) Ltd [1987] IR 259, Vol III p 633
Kidston v Aspinall [1963] 41 TC 371, Vol II p 627, Vol IV p 187
Kiely v Minister for Social Welfare (No 2) [1977] IR 267 1998 p 120
Kill Inn Motel Ltd (In Liquidation) v The Companies Acts 1963/1983 Vol III p 706
Kilmarnock Equitable Co-operative Society Ltd, Re, 42 TC 675, Vol III p 65, 304
Kilroy v Parker [1966] IR 309 Vol V p 37
King (Harris Stein), The v The Special Commissioners 1 ITC 71, Vol I p 62
King v AG [1981] IR 233, Vol III p 127, 2001 p 138
King v Foxwell 3 Ch D 518, Vol I p 259
King, The v British Columbia Fir and Cedar Timber Co Ltd [1932] AC 441, Vol I p 164
King, The v Earl Cadogan [1915] 3 KB 485, Vol II p 464
King, The v The Commissioners for Special Purposes of Income Tax (ex parte King (Evelyn
   Spain), The v The Special Commissioners 1 ITC 227, [1934] IR 27, Vol I p 221
Kinghan, Albert v The Minister for Social Welfare Vol III p 436
Kinsela v Russell Kinsela Property in Liquidation [1986] 4 NSWLR 722, Vol IV p 247
Kiriri Cotton Co Ltd v Dewani [1960] AC 192 Vol V p 615

Kirke's Trustees v CIR (Supra) 11 TC 323, [1927] SC HL 56, 136 LT 582, Vol II p 115
Kirkness v John Hudson & Co Ltd 36 TC 28, Vol III p 477
Knetsch v US [1960] 364 US 361, Vol III p 683
Knight v Calder Grove Estates 35 TC 447, Vol II p 382
Knight's, Re, 5 Coke Rep 54B, Vol II p 222
Knockhall Piggeries v JG Kerrane (Inspector of Taxes) 1985] ILRM 655, Vol III p 319
Knowlton v Moore [1900] 178 US 41, 77 Vol V p 615
Knox v Guidea 11th ILR 482, Vol I p 583

L

L v W S McGarry,(Inspector of Taxes), Vol II p 241
Lady Beresford v Driver [1851] 2 OLJ (Ch) 476, Vol IV p 332
Lands Allotment, Re, [1894] 1 Ch 616\1986 4 NSWLR 722, Vol IV p 247
Larkins v National Union of Mineworkers [1985] IR 671 Vol V p 45
Larner v London County Council [1949] 2 KB 683 Vol V p 615
Lauderdale Peerage, Re, 10 AC 692, Vol I p 259
Law Shipping Co Ltd v CIR 12 TC 621, [1924] SC 74, Vol II p 267
Lawlor v Flood High Court, unrep, 2 July 1999, 2000 p 65
Lawrie, Wm p v CIR 34 TC 20, [1952] SLT 413, Vol II p 360, Vol IV p 425
Laycock v Freeman Hardy and Willis Ltd 22 TC 288, [1939] 2 KB 1, Vol II p 315
Le Mesurier v Le Mesurier [1985] AC 517, Vol IV p 437
Le Soleil Ltd v Minister of National Revenue 73 DTC 5093, Vol IV p 466
Leach v Pogson 40 TC 585, Vol III p 253
Lean and Dickson v Ball 10 TC 345, 655, Vol III p 319
Lee v Dangar Grant & Co [not reported], Vol III p 387
Leeder v Counsel [1942] 1 KB 264, Vol II p 204
Leeds Permanent Benefit Building Society v Mallandaine 3 TC 577, [1897] 2 QB 402,
Leeds Permanent Building Society v Proctor [1982] STC 821, [1982] 3 AER 925, Vol IV pp 68, 284
Lehnhausen v Lake Shore Auto Parts Co [1973] 410 US 356 Vol V p 615
Leicestershire County Council v Faraday [1941] 2 KB 205, Vol IV p 332, Vol V p 266
Leigh v Dickson 15 QBD 85, Vol I p 601
Leigh v IRC 11 TC 590, [1928] 1 KB 73, Vol III p 484
Leigh v Taylor [not reported], Vol III p 332
Leitch v Emmott 14 TC 633, [1929] 2 KB 236, Vol I p 563, Vol IV p 1
Levene v IRC 13 TC 486, [1928] AC 217, Vol I pp 259, 375, 387
Lewis Merthyr Consolidated Collieries Ltd [1929] 1 Ch 498, Vol IV p 107, Vol V p 388
Lewis, Exparte, 21 QBD 191, Vol I p 221
Lincoln Wagon and Engine Co Ltd v CIR 12 TC 494, Vol II p 429
Linkletter v Walker [1965] 381 US 618 Vol V p 615
Liquidator of Irvine and Fullerton Property Investment Society v Cuthbertson 43 SC LR 17, Vol II p 25
Lismore RDC v O'Malley 36 ILTR 54, 56, Vol II p 241
Lister & Co v Stubbs (1890) 45 Ch D 1, 2000 p 216
Liverpool & London & Globe Insurance Co v Bennett [1911] 2 KB 577, [1913] AC 610, 6 TC 327, Vol I p 447, Vol III pp 633, 644
Lloyd v Sulley 21 SC LR 482, 2 TC 37, Vol I p 259
Lomax v Newton 24 TC 558, 216 LT 419, [1953] 1 WLR 1123, [1953] 2 AER 801, Vol II pp 366, 460

London and Northern Estates Co v Harris 21 TC 197, [1937] 3 AER 252, 106 LJKB 823, Vol II p 429
London County Council v AG 4 TC 265, [1901] AC 26, Vol II pp 222, 332, 393
London County Freehold and Leasehold Properties Ltd v Sweet 24 TC 412, [1942] 2 AER 212, 58 TLR 281, Vol II p 429, Vol V p 496
London Investment & Mortgage Co v Worthington 38 TC 86, Vol III p 165
London Library v Carter 2 TC 594, Vol II p 661
London School Board v Northcraft [1889] 2 Hudsons BC 4 Ed 147, Vol IV p 332
Lord Advocate v Jaffrey [1921] 1 AC 146, Vol IV p 437
Lord Chetwode v IRC [1977] 1 WLR 248, Vol III p 403
Lord Cromwell v Andrews Cro Eliz 15, Vol II p 222
Lord Glanely v Wightman 17 TC 634, [1933] AC 618, Vol I p 496
Lord Inverclyde's Trustees v Inland Revenue [1924] SC 14, Vol II p 195
Lord Inverclyde's Trustees v Millar 9 TC 14, [1924] SC 14, Vol II p 25, Vol III p 246
Lord Massey v CIR [1918] 2 KB 584 Vol V p 108, 1998 p 184
Lord Mostyn v London 3 TC 294, [1895] 1 QB 170, Vol I p 515
Lord Sudeley's, Re, [unrep], Vol III p 477
Lord Vestey's Executors and Vestey v IRC [1951] Ch 209, [1950] 2 AER 891 (HL), [1949] 1 AER 1108, [1949] 31 TC 1 (CA), Vol III p 683
Lothian Chemicals v IRC 11 TC 508, Vol IV p 135
Lothian Chemical Company Ltd v Rogers (1926) 11 TC 508, 2000 p 76
Louisville Gas and Electric Co v Coleman [1928] 277 US 32, Vol III p 127
Louth, James & Others v Minister for Social Welfare Vol IV p 391
Loveridge, Drayton v Loveridge, Re, [1902] 2 CH 865, Vol I p 427
Lowe and Others v IRC [1983] STC 816, Vol IV p 135
Lowndes v de Courcy (SC) 7 April 1960 Vol V p 589
Lucas and Chesterfield Gas & Water Board, Re, [1909] 1 KB 16, Vol III p 298
Luipaard's Vlei Estate and Gold Mining Co Ltd v IRC 15 TC 573, [1930] 1 KB 593, Vol I pp 487, 583, Vol II p 332, Vol III p 229
Luke v IRC [1963] AC 557, Vol IV p 162
Lumsden v IRC [1914] AC 877 Vol V p 539
Lupton v Cadogan Gardens Developments 47 TC 1, [1971] 3 AER 460, Vol III p 253
Lupton v RA and AB Ltd [1968] 2 AER 1042, Vol III p 253
Lupton v SA and AB 47 TC 598 Vol V p 61
Lurcott v Wakely and Wheeler [1911] 1KB 905, Vol II p 267
Lynch, Mary v Moira Burke & AIB Banks plc Vol V p 271
Lynham v Butler (No 2) [1933] IR 74, [1932] 67 ILTR 75, [1932] LJ IR 72, Vol III p 533
Lyons, J & Co Ltd v AG [1944] Ch D 281, 1 AER 477, [1944] Cr 287, Vol III p 219, Vol IV p 68, Vol V p 200
Lysaght v CIR 13 TC 511, [1928] AC 234, Vol I pp 249, 387

M

M v An Bord Uchtala [1975] IR 140, [1977] IR 287, Vol V p 615, 696
MacAonghusa (Sean) (Inspector of Taxes) v Ringmahon Company 1999 p 81, 2001 p 117
MacAuley v The Minister for Post and Telegraphs [1966] IR 345, Vol III p 533
MacCarthaigh, DA (Inspector of Taxes) v Francis Daly [1985] IR 73, [1986] ILRM 24, 116, Vol III p 253
MacDaibheid (Inspector of Taxes) v SD Vol III p 1
MacDermott (Inspector of Taxes) v BC Vol III p 43

Macduff, Re, 13 TC 846, [1896] Second Chancery p 466 and 467, Vol I p 542
MacGiolla Mhaith (Inspector of Taxes) v Cronin & Associates Ltd Vol III p 211
MacGiolla Riogh (Inspector of Taxes) v G Ltd 3 ITC 181, [1957] IR 90, Vol II p 315
MacKeown (Inspector of Taxes) v Patrick J Roe 1 ITC 206, [1928] IR 195, Vol I p 214
Cited also at: Vol I p 618
MacLaine & Co v Eccott [1926] AC 424, 10 TC 481, Vol I pp 330, 571
Maclaine v Gatty [1921] 1 AC 376 Vol V p 615
MacLennan, In re [1939] 1 Ch 750 Vol V p 565
Macsaga Investments Co Ltd v Lupton 44 TC 659, Vol III p 253
Madeleine Vionnet et Cie v Wills [1940] 1 KB 72, Vol II p 281
Madigan PJ & p Madigan v AG, The Revenue Commissioners and Others [1986] ILRM 136, Vol III p 127
Cited also at: Vol IV p 323
Maher and Nugent's Contract, In re (1910) IR 167 Vol V p 560
Maher v The Attorney General [1973] IR 140 Vol V p 615
Mahon v Butler [1997] 3 IR 169, 2000 p 216
Mahoney's, Re, [1910] 2 IR 741, Vol I p 221
Maire v Wood and Others [1958] SLT 326, Vol III p 467
Malcolm v Lockhart 7 TC 99, [1919] AC 463, Vol I p 496, Vol II p 315
Mallalieu v Drurnmond (Inspector of Taxes) [1983] STC 665, 1999 p 82
Mallandin Investments Ltd v Shadbolt 23 TC 367, Vol I p 164
Mallett v Stavely Coal & Iron Co Ltd [1928] 2 KB 405, 13 TC 772, Vol II p 222, 515
Malone & Others v Manton 131 LTR 144, Vol II p 222
Malone v Harrison [1979] 1 WLR 1353 Vol V p 615
Mann Crossman & Paulin Ltd v Compton [1947] 1 AER 742, 28 TC 410, Vol II p 515
Manning, David v John R Shackleton & Cork County Council Vol IV p 485
Mara (Inspector of Taxes) v GG (Hummingbird) Ltd [1982] ILRM 421, Vol II p 667
Cited also at: Vol III pp 9, 43, 178, 211, 219, 253, 373, 441, 496, 644, Vol IV pp 117, 125, 233, 269, 284, 349, Vol V p 6, 22, 98, 139, 201, 239, 1999 p 82, 2000 p 247, 2001 p 80
Marbury v Madison [1803] 5 US 49 Vol V p 615
Marchioness of Ormonde v Brown 17 TC 333, Vol II p 491
Margerison v Tyre Soles Ltd 25 TC 59 (not reported elsewhere), Vol II p 515
Margrett v Lowestoft Water and Gas Co 19 TC 481, Vol II p 267
Mark Fishing Co v United Fishermen and Allied Workers Union 24 DLR (3rd ed) p 585, Vol III p 467, 2001 p 127
Market Investigations Ltd v Minister for Social Security [1968] 2 AER 732, [1969] 2 QB 173, Vol III p 43, Vol IV p 45, Vol V p 239
Marleasing SA v La Commercial Internacional de Alimentacionsia [1990] 1 ECR 4135 1998 p 76
Marron v Cootehill (No 2) Rural District Council [1915] AC 792 Vol V p 539
Marsden & Sons Ltd v CIR [not reported] 12 TC 217, Vol I p 642
Marshall (IOT) v Kerr [1983] STC 360 Vol V p 347
Marshall v Crutwell [1875] LR 20 Eq 328, 44 LJ Ch 504, 39 JP 775 Vol V p 272
Martin v Lowry [1926] 1 KB 550, [1927] AC 312, 41 TLR 574, 11 TC 297, Vol I pp 155, 629
Mason v New South Wales [1959] 102 CLR 108 Vol V p 615
Masser, AH Ltd (Receivership) & Others v The Revenue Commissioners Vol III p 548
Massey v Crown Life Insurance [1978] 2 AER 576 Vol V p 239

Mathews v Cork County Council 5 TC 545, [1910] 2 IR 521, Vol I p 45
Matthews v Chicory Marketing Board (1938) 60 CLR 263, Vol III p 73
Maxwell v McLure 6 Jur NS 407, 8 WR 370, Vol I p 259
Maudslay, Sons & Field, Re (1900) 1 Ch 1002 , 2001 p 137
Maye, John v The IRC [1986] ILRM 377, Vol III p 332
Mayfair Property Co, Re, [1898] 2 CH 28, Vol II p 326
Mayo Perrott v Mayo Perrott [1958] IR 336, [1958] 93 ILTR 195, Vol IV p 437
McAuliffe, Tony v The Minister for Social Welfare Vol V p 94 (1995) ILRM 189 Vol V
 p 239
McC v KED [1985] IR 697, [1987] ILRM 189, Vol IV p 437
*McCabe (Inspector of Taxes) v South City & County Investment Co Ltd
 Vol V p 107, 1998 p 183*
McCall (deceased) v CIR 1 ITC 31, Vol I p 28
McCall v Bradish-Ellames [1950] IJR 16, 84 LTR 78, Vol IV p 367
*McCann, Charles Ltd v S O'Culachain (Inspector of Taxes) [1985] IR 298, [1986] IR 196,
 Vol III p 304, 2000 p 236*
Cited also at: Vol III pp 441, 611, Vol IV p 35, 361, 466, 526, 533 p 547, Vol V p 21
McCausland, Samuel v Ministry of Commerce [1956] NILR 36, Vol III pp 304, 441, 611,
 Vol IV p 35, 533, Vol V p 22
McConnells Trustees CIR [1927] SLT 14 Vol V p 295, 532
McCrystal Oil Co Ltd v The IRC and Others Vol IV p 386
*McDaid, Charles v His Honour Judge David Sheehy, the Director of Public Prosecutions &
 Ors [1991] IR 1, Vol IV p 162, Vol V p 696*
McDonald v Bord Na gCon [1964] IR 350, [1965] IR 217, Vol III pp 387, 577, 590,
 Vol V p 288, 615, 696, 1998 p 120
McDonald v Bord na gCon (No 2) [1965] IR 217 , 2001 p 138
McDonald v Shand 39 TLR 444, 8 TC 420, Vol I p 214
McDougall v Smith [1918] 7 TC 134, Vol II p 596
McElligott p & Sons Ltd v Duigenan (Inspector of Taxes) [1985] ILRM 210, Vol III p 178
McEnery, In re [1941] IR 323 Vol V p 37
McEvoy v Belfast Banking Co [1935] Ac 24, [1834] NI 67; [1933] 68 ILTR 3, [1934] All
 ER 800, [1934] 103 LJPC 137, 151 LT 501, 40 Com Cas 1, Vol V p 272, 1998 p 169
*McGarry (Inspector of Taxes) v Limerick Gas Committee 1 ITC 405, [1932] IR 125,
 Vol I p 375*
Cited also at: Vol II pp 500, 515, 1999 p 82
McGarry, W S (Inspector of Taxes) v EF 3 ITC 103, [1954] IR 64, Vol II p 261
McGarry, WS (Inspector of Taxes) v JA Spencer 2 ITC 297, [1946] IR 11, Vol II p 1
McGee v The Attorney General [1974] IR 284 Vol V p 615
McGlinchey v Wren [1982] IR 154, [1983] ILRM 169, Vol III p 533, 2000 p 236
*McGrath Patrick & Ors v JE McDermott (Inspector of Taxes) [1988] IR 258, [1988] ILRM
 181, 647, Vol III p 683, Vol V p 6, 108, 163, 295, 472, 515, 1998 p 184*
Cited also at: Vol III p 271, Vol IV pp 91, 547, Vol V pp 6, 108, 163, 295, 472, 515
 1999 p 63, 72, 82
McGurrin, L (Inspector of Taxes) v The Champion Publications Ltd Vol IV p 466
McHugh (Inspector of Taxes) v A 3 ITC 257, [1958] IR 142, [1959] ILTR 125, Vol II p 393
McIntosh v Lord Advocate [2001] 2 All ER 638 , 2001 p 138
McIntyre v CIR 12 TC 1006, Vol III p 211
McKenna v Eaton Turner 20 TC 566, [1937] AC 162, Vol II p 68

McKenna v Herlihy [1920] 7 TC 620, Vol II p 636
McKinlay v H T Jenkins & Son Ltd 10 TC 372, Vol II p 281
McKinley v Minister for Defence [1992] 2 IR 333, Vol IV p 437
McLaren v Needham 39 TC 37, Vol II p 515
McLaughlin v Mrs Blanche Bailey 7 TC 508, [1920] IR 310 & 316, Vol I p 496,
    Vol II p 315
McLellan Rawson and Co Ltd v Newall 36 TC 117, Vol III p 1
*McLoughlin, Edward and Thomas Marie Tuite v The Revenue Commissioners and AG
    [1986] IR 235, [1986] ILRM 304, [1990] IR 83 , Vol III p 387, 2000 p 274*
Cited also at: Vol III p 533, 641, Vol IV p 395, 2001 p 138
McMahon v The Attorney General [1972] IR 69 Vol V p 615
McMahon, J (Inspector of Taxes) v Albert Noel Murphy Vol IV p 125
McMahon, T & Ors v Rt Hon Lord Mayor Alderman & Burgess of Dublin Vol V p 357
McMillan v Guest [1941] 1 KB 258, [1942] AC 561, 24 TC 190, Vol II p 68
McNally, Daniel v S O Maoldhomhniagh Vol IV p 22, Vol V p 515
Cited also at: Vol IV p 547
McNamee & Ors v The Revenue Commissioners, In the Matter of the Estate of Vol V p 577
McPhail v Doulton [1971] AC 424; [1970] 2 WLR 1110; [1970] 2 AER 228; 114 SJ 375
    Vol V p 37
McRae v CIR [1960] 34 Tax Court of US Reports 20, Vol III p 683
McSweeney v Mooney [1997] 3 IR 424 , 2001 p 105
McTaggart v Strump 10 TC 17, [1925] SC 599, Vol II p 464
Meenaghan v Dublin County Council [1984] ILRM 616, Vol IV p 485
Melling v O'Mathghamhna and Anor [1962] IR 1, Vol III p 387, Vol IV p 395,
    2001 p 137
Mersey Docks and Harbour Board v Lucas 2 TC 25, [1903] 8 AC 891, Vol I pp 387, 601,
    656, Vol II pp 154, 211, 592, Vol III p 484, Vol V p 539
Mersey Docks v Cameron 11 HL Ca 443, Vol II p 211
Mesco Properties Ltd, Re, [1979] 1 WLR 558, Vol III p 523
Michelham, Re, [1921] 1 Ch 705, Vol II p 332
Middlesex Justices 2 QBD 510, Vol I p 221
Mikrommatis v Republic of Cyprus [1961] 2 RSCC 125 Vol V p 615
Miley v Rooney 4 TC 344, [1918] 1 IR 455, Vol I p 542
Millheim v Barewa Oil & Mining Co NL [1971] WAR 65 Vol V p 226
Millhouse Taverns Ltd and the Companies Act 1963-1999, Re , 2001 p 77
Milnes v J Beam Group Ltd 50 TC 675, Vol III p 340
Milverton Quarries Ltd v The IRC 3 ITC 279, [1960] IR 224, Vol II p 382
Minister for Agriculture v Norgo Ltd [1980] IR 155 Vol V p 691
Minister for Fisheries v Sealy [1939] IR 21 Vol V p 221
Minister for Industry and Commerce v Hale and Others [1967] IR 50, Vol III p 43
Minister for Justice v Siucre Eireann [1992] IR 215 Vol V p 226
*Minister for Labour, The v PMPA Insurance Co Ltd (under administration) [1990] IR 284,
    Vol III p 505*
Cited also at: Vol IV p 391
Minister for Social Welfare, The v John Griffiths Vol IV p 378
Cited also at: 2001 p 127
Minister of Finance v Smith [1927] AC 193, Vol I p 195

Minister of National Revenue v Anaconda American Brass Ltd [1956] 1 AER 20, [1956] AC 85 Vol II p 515, Vol III p 198, Vol IV p 135
Mitchell v B W Noble Ltd 43 TLR 102, [1927] 1 KB 719, 137 LTR 33, 11 TC 372, Vol I p 375, Vol II p 500, 515
Mitchell v CIR 25 TC 380, [1943] SC 541, Vol II p 636
Mitchell v Egyptian Hotels Ltd [1915] AC 1022; 6 TC 542, Vol I p 183
Mitchell v Ross 40 TC 11, Vol III p 43
Mogul of Ireland v Tipperary (NR) CC [1976] IR 260 Vol V p 272
Mohanlal Hargovino of Jubbulpore v Commissioners of Income Tax [1949] AC 521, 28 ATC 287, Vol II p 515
Molmac Ltd v MacGiolla Riogh (Inspector of Taxes) 3 ITC 376, [1965] IR 201, 101 ILTR 114, Vol II p 482
Moloney (Inspector of Taxes) v Allied Irish Banks Ltd as executors of the estate of Francis J Doherty deceased [1986] IR 67, Vol III p 477
Monahan Patrick (Drogheda) Ltd v O'Connell (Inspector of Taxes) Vol III p 661
Montreal Coke and Manufacturing Co v Minister for National Revenue [1944] 1 All ER 743 , 2001 p 118
Mooney (Inspector Of Taxes) v McSweeney Vol V p 163, 2000 p 114
Mooney v O'Coindealbhain (No 2) [1992] 2 IR 23 Vol V p 326
Mooney, TB v EP O'Coindealbhain & The Revenue Commissioners Vol IV p 62 Cited also at: Vol V p 326
Moore & Co v Hare [1915] Sess Cas 91, 52 SC LR 59, 6 TC 572, Vol II p 45, 500
Moorhouse v Lord 10 HC Cas 272, Vol I p 259
Morant v Wheal Grenville Mining Co 3 TC 298, Vol II p 382
Morgan v Tate and Lyle 35 TC 367, [1953] Ch 601, [1955] AC 21, Vol II p 500, 515, 1999 p 82
Morgan, In re, 24 Ch D 114 Vol V p 526
Morice v The Bishop of Durham 10 TC 86 p 539, [1925] 10 Vesey 522, Vol I p 542
Morrow v Carty [1957] NI 174 Vol V p 589
Morse v Stedeford 18 TC 457, Vol II p 515
Moses v Macferlan [1760] 2 Burr 1005, Vol IV p 247, Vol V p 615
Most Honourable Frances Elizabeth Sarah Marchioness Conyngham, The v IRC 1 ITC 259, [1928] ILTR 57, 136, Vol I p 231
Moville District Board Of Conservators v D Ua Clothasaigh (Inspector of Taxes) 3 ITC 1, [1950] IR 301, Vol II p 154
Mowleim, Re, 43 LJ CH 354, Vol I p 427
Moynihan v Greensmyth [1977] IR 55 Vol V p 615
Muckley, Bernard and Anne Muckley v Ireland, The Attorney General and The IRC [1985] IR 472, [1986] ILRM 364, Vol III p 188
Mullingar RDC v Rowles 6 TC 85, [1913] 2 IR 44, Vol I pp 1, 427
Mulloy v Minister for Education [1975] IR 88, Vol III p 127
Multipar Syndicate Ltd v Davitt (Inspector of Taxes) [1945] 1 AER 298, Vol IV p 505
Mulvey, JD (Inspector of Taxes) v Denis J Coffey 2 ITC 239, [1942] IR 277, Vol I p 618
Mulvey, JD (Inspector of Taxes) v RM Kieran 2 ITC 179, [1938] IR 87, Vol I p 563
Munby v Furlong 50 TC 491, Vol III pp 113, 120
Municipal Mutual Insurance Ltd v Hills Vol XVI TC p 448, Vol II p 211
Murnaghan Brothers Ltd v S O'Maoldhomhnaigh [1991] 1 IR 455, Vol IV p 304
Murphy v Roche [1987] IR 106, 2000 p 261

Murph's Restaurants, In re [1979] ILRM 141 Vol V p 226
Murphy & Ors v AG [1982] IR 241, Vol III pp 127, 188, Vol V p 424
Murphy (Inspector of Taxes) v Asahi Synthetic Fibres (Ireland) Ltd [1985] IR 509, [1986] IR 777, Vol III p 246
Murphy v Dublin Corporation [1972] IR 215, [1972] 107 ILTR 65, Vol III p 533
Murphy v Minster for Industry and Commerce [1987] IR 295, Vol IV p 378
Murphy v Roche [1987] IR 106 Vol V p 696
Murphy, Frances & Mary Murphy v The Attorney General Vol V p 613
Murphy, John B v District Justice Brendan Wallace and Others Vol IV p 278
Murphy, S (Inspector of Taxes) v Dataproducts (Dublin) Ltd [1988] IR 10, Vol IV p 12
Murphy, Sean (Inspector of Taxes) v The Borden Co Ltd, Vol III p 559
Murray v Ireland & AG [1985] IR 532, [1985] ILRM 542, Vol IV p 437
Murtagh Properties Ltd v Cleary [1972] IR 330, Vol III p 127, Vol IV p 323, Vol V p 615
Musker v English Electric Co Ltd 41 TC 556, (Ch D) 106 SJ 511, Vol II p 602

N

N McS v Inspector of Taxes Vol V p 294
Narich Property Ltd v Commissioner of Payroll Tax [1984] ICR 286, Vol IV p 45
Nashville, Chattanooga & St Louis Railway v Browning [1940] 310 US 362 Vol V p 615
Nathan, Re, 12 QBD 461, Vol I p 221
National Bank of Scotland v The Lord Advocate 30 SL Rep 579 Vol V p 560
National Bank of Wales, Re, [1897] 1 Ch 298, Vol II p 175
National Bank v Baker 17 TC 381, [1932] 1 KB 668, Vol I pp 474, 503
National Irish Banks Ltd v Radio Telefís Éireann SC, 20 March 1998 1998 p 120
National Provident Institution v Brown 8 TC 57, [1921] 2 AC 222, Vol I p 515
National Provincial Bank of England v Jackson 33 Ch D 1 Vol V p 560
Naval Colliery Co Ltd v CIR 12 TC 1017, Vol III p 95
Navan Carpets Ltd v S O'Culachain (Inspector of Taxes) [1988] IR 164, Vol III p 403 Vol V p 326
Neale v City of Birmingham Tramways Company [1910] 2 Ch 464, Vol II p 175
Nesbitt v Mitchell 11 TC 211, Vol II p 115, 2001 p 137
Nestor v Murphy [1979] IR 326, Vol IV p 162
Nevile Reid & Co Ltd v CIR 12 TC 545, Vol I p 130, Vol III p 611
New York Life Assurance Co v Styles 2 TC 460 [1914] 14 AC 381 (p 389), Vol I p 387
Newcastle City Council v Royal Newcastle Hospital [1959] AC 248, Vol II p 636
Newman Manufacturing Co v Marrable [1931] 2 KB 297 Vol V p 539
Nicoll v Austin 19 TC 531, Vol II p 452
Nixon v Commissioner of Valuation [1980] IR 340, Vol III p 319
Noble, BW Ltd v IRC 12 TC 923, Vol II p 175
Nolder v Walters 15 TC 380, Vol II p 366
Nord Getreide v Haupdzolla MT Hamburg-Jones [1985] ECR 3127 1998 p 76
Norris v AG [1984] IR 36, Vol IV p 437, 1998 p 120
Northend v White & Leonard [1975] 1 WLR 1037, Vol III p 633
Northern Association Co v Russell 26 SLR 330, 2 TC 551, Vol I p 474
Northern Bank Finance Co Ltd v Quinn & Anor [1979] ILRM 221 Vol V p 226
Northern Insurance Co v Russell 2 TC 571, Vol III p 373
Norton v Shelby County [1886] 118 US 425 Vol V p 615

Cases reported and considered

Noyek, A & Sons Ltd (in Voluntary liquidation) v Edward N Hearne [1988] IR 772,
  Vol III p 523
Nugent-Head v Jacob 30 TC 83, [1947] 1 KB 17, Vol II p 75

O

O hArgain, L (Inspector of Taxes) v B Ltd [1979] ILRM 56, Vol III p 9
O Laochdha, (Inspector of Taxes) v Johnson & Johnson (Ireland) Ltd [1991] 2 IR 287,
  Vol IV p 361
O'B v S [1984] ILRM 86, Vol IV pp 415, 437
O'Brien v Bord na Mona [1983] IR 255, [1983] ILRM 314, Vol III pp 533, 590,
  Vol IV p 512
O'Brien v Commissioner for Tipperary (South Riding) Board of Health [1938] IR 761,
  Vol III p 43
O'Brien v Keogh [1972] IR 144, Vol III p 127, Vol V p 615
O'Brien v Manufacturing Engineering Co Ltd [1973] IR 334, 108 ILTR 105, Vol III p 127,
  Vol V p 615
O'Broin, SP (Inspector of Taxes) v (1) Mac Giolla Meidhre, and O'Broin, SP (Inspector of
  Taxes) v (2) Finbar Pigott 3 ITC 235, [1959] IR 98, Vol II p 366
O'Byrne v Minister for Finance [1959] IR 1, 94 ILTR 11, Vol III p 127, Vol V p 615
O'C, JB v PCD and A Bank [1985] IR 265, Vol III p 153
O'Cahill (Inspector of Taxes) v Albert Harding and Others Vol IV p 233
O'Callaghan, Thomas v JP Clifford and Others Vol IV p 478
O'Cleirigh (Inspector of Taxes) v Jacobs International Ltd Incorporated [1985] ILRM 651,
  Vol III p 165
O'Coindealbhain (Inspector of Taxes) v Breda O'Carroll [1989] IR 229, Vol IV p 221, Vol
  V p 472, 1998 p 111
O'Coindealbhain (Inspector of Taxes) v KN Price [1988] IR 14, Vol IV p 1
O'Coindealbhain (Inspector of Taxes) v TB Mooney [1990] IR 422, Vol IV p 45,
  Cited also at: Vol V p 239, 323, 326
O'Coindealbhain, EP (Inspector of Taxes) v The Honourable Mr Justice Sean Gannon
  [1986] IR 154, Vol III p 484
O'Conaill (Inspector of Taxes) v JJ Ltd Vol III p 65
O'Conaill (Inspector of Taxes) v R 3 ITC 167, [1956] IR 97, Vol II p 304
O'Conaill (Inspector of Taxes) v Z Ltd Vol II p 636
O'Connell, Patrick J (Inspector of Taxes) v Fyffes Banana Processing Ltd
  1999 p 71, 2000 p 235
O'Connell, Patrick J (Inspector of Taxes) v Tara Mines Ltd , 2001 p 79
O'Connell (Patrick J) (Inspector of Taxes) v Thomas Keleghan 2000 p 113, 2001 p 103
O'Connlain (Inspector of Taxes) v Belvedere Estates Ltd [1985] IR 22, Vol III p 271
O'Croinin and Quinn v Brennan [1939] IR 274, Vol III p 387, 2001 p 13
O'Culachain, S (Inspector of Taxes) v Hunter Advertising Ltd Vol IV p 35
  Cited also at: Vol IV p 466, 533, Vol V p 22 376
O'Culachain (Inspector of Taxes) v McMullan Brothers Ltd Vol IV, p 284, 1998 p 100
  Cited also at: Vol IV p 425, Vol V p 200, 317, 482, 2001 p 80
O'Dwyer (Inspector of Taxes) & IRC v Irish Exporters and Importers Ltd (In Liquidation)
  2 ITC 251, [1943] IR 176, Vol I p 629
  Cited also at: Vol II p 82
O'Doherty v AG [1941] IR 569, 2000 p 216

O'Dwyer, JM (Inspector of Taxes) v The Dublin United Transport Co Ltd 2 ITC 437, [1949] IR 295, Vol II p 115
O'Farrell & Another, Re, [1960] IR 239, [1958] 95 ILTR 167, Vol III p 533
O'Flaherty v Browne [1907] 2 IR 416 Vol V p 272
O'G, T v AG [1985] ILRM 61, Vol IV p 437
O'Grady (Inspector of Taxes) v Laragan Quarries Ltd [1991] 1 IR 237, Vol IV p 269
O'Grady (Inspector of Taxes) v Roscommon Race Committee Vol IV p 425, Vol V p 317
O'Grady v Bullcroft Main Collieries 17 TC 93, Vol III p 65, Vol IV p 425
O'Kane, J & R & Co v CIR 12 TC 303, HL 126 LT707, 56 ILTR 57, Vol I p 1
O'Keeffe v An Bord Pleanala [1992] ILRM 69, Vol IV pp 170, 512
O'Keefe v Ferris [1993] 3 IR 165 , 2001 p 138
O'Laoghaire (Inspector of Taxes) v CD Ltd Vol III p 51
O'Leary, Edward v The IRC Vol IV p 357
O'Loan, HA (Inspector of Taxes) v Messrs M J Noone & Co 2 ITC 430, [1949] IR 171, Vol II p 146
Cited also at: Vol III p 178
O'Mahony v Horgan & Others [1996] 1 ILRM 161, 2000 p 216
O'R v O'R [1985] IR 367, Vol III p 533
O'Reilly, Gerald v W J Casey (Inspector of Taxes) 2 ITC 220, [1942] IR 378, Vol I p 601
O'Rourke v Revenue Commissioners Vol V p 321
O'Shea (Inspector of Taxes) v Michael Mulqueen Vol V p 134
O'Shea (Inspector of Taxes) v Coole Park View Service Station Limited 2000 p 247
O'Siochain, Sean (Inspector of Taxes) v Bridget Neenan Vol V p 472, 1998 p 111
O'Siochain, Sean (Inspector of Taxes) v Thomas Morrissey Vol IV p 407
O'Srianain (Inspector of Taxes) v Lakeview Ltd Vol III p 219
Cited also at: Vol IV pp 68, 284, Vol V p 317
O'Sullivan (Inspector of Taxes) v p Ltd 3 ITC 355, Vol II p 464
Cited also at: Vol III p 683, Vol V p 295
O'Sullivan JM (Inspector of Taxes) v Julia O'Connor, as Administratrix of Evelyn H O'Brien, Deceased 2 ITC 352, [1947] IR 416, Vol II p 61
O'Sullivan v The Revenue Commissioners Vol V p 570
Oakey Abattoir Pty Ltd v Federal Commissioner of Taxation 84 ATC 4718, Vol III p 683
Oakthorpe Holdings Ltd, In Re [1989] ILRM 62 Vol V p 388
Odeon Associated Theatres Ltd v Jones 48 TC 257, [1971] 1 WLR 422, [1972] 2 AER 407, ITR Vol III p 198, Vol IV pp 135, 304
Odhams Press Ltd v Cook 56 TLR 704, [1938] 2 AER 312, 4 AER 545, 23 TC 233, Vol I p 642
Ogilvie v Kitton [1908] Sess Cas 1003, 5 TC 338, Vol I p 183
Old Battersea and District Building Society v The CIR [1898] 2 QBD 294, Vol IV p 296
Old Bushmills Distillery Company Ltd, Exparte Brydon, Exparte Bank of Ireland [1896] 1 IR 301, Vol I p 28
Olive & Partington Ltd v Rose 14 TC 701, Vol II p 115
Oppenheim v Tobacco Securities Trust Co Ltd [1951] AC 297; [1951] 1 AER 31; [1951] 1 TLR 118 Vol V p 37
Orange, James G v The Revenue Commissioners Vol V p 70
Oriental Inland Steam Co, Re, [1874] Ch App 557, Vol IV p 247
Ormond Investment Co Ltd v Betts 13 TC 400, [1927] 2 KB 326, [1928] AC 143, 138 LT 600, Vol I p 447, Vol II p 429, 482, 1998 p 66

Orr, Michael (Kilternan) Ltd v The Companies Act 1963-1983, and Thornberry
   Construction (Irl) Ltd v The Companies Act 1963-1983 [1986] IR 273, Vol III p 530
Osler v Hall & Co [1923] 1 KB 720, 17 TC 68, Vol II p 55
Ostime v Australian Mutual Provident Society 39 TC 492, [1959] 3 AER 245, Vol III p 246
Oughtred v IRC [1959] 3 WLR 906, Vol IV pp 187, 367
Ounsworth v Vickers Ltd 6 TC 671, [1915] 3 KB 267, Vol I pp 91, 642, Vol II p 32, 45,
   515, Vol IV p 425
Overseers of the Savoy v Art Union of London 12 TC 798, [1894] 2 QB 62, Vol I p 542
Owen v Sassoon 32 TC 101, Vol III p 633
Owens v Greene and Freeley v Greene [1932] IR 225, [1932] 67 ILTR 161 Vol V p 272
Oxford Benefit Building & Investment Society [1896] 35 Ch 502 Vol V p 186, 195

P

Paddington Burial Board v CIR 13 QBD 9, Vol II p 211
Page Boy Couriers Ltd, Re ILRM 510 , 2001 p 77
Page v The International Agency & Industrial Trust Ltd [1893] 62 LJ Ch 610 Vol V p 186,
   195
Pairceir (Inspector of Taxes) v EM Vol II p 596
Palmer v Johnson 13 QBD 351 Vol V p 539
Palser v Grinling Property Holding Co Ltd [1948] AC 291 Vol V p 686
Panama, New Zealand and Australian Royal Mail Co, Re, 5 Ch App 318, Vol III p 661
*Pandion Haliaetus Ltd, Ospreycare Ltd, Osprey Systems Design Ltd v The IRC [1987] IR
   309, [1988] ILRM 419, Vol III p 670*
Paperlink v AG [1984] ILRM 373, Vol IV p 323
Parchim [1918] AC 157, Vol I p 130
Parke v Daily News [1962] 2 AER 929, Vol III p 706, Vol IV p 247
Parke v Walker & Ors (1961) SLT 251 , 2001 p 127
Parker & Cooper Ltd v Reading & Anor [1926] 1 Ch 975 Vol V p 226
Parker v Chapman 13 TC 677, Vol III p 484
Parker v Great Western Railroad Co [1856], Vol III p 441
Parker v Walker and Others [1961] SCT 252, Vol III p 467
Parkes (Roberta) v David Parkes 1998 p 169
Parsons v AG [1943] Ch 12 Vol V p 600
Parsons v Kavanagh [1990] ILRM 560, Vol IV p 323
Partington v AG [1869] LR 4 HL 100, Vol I p 601, Vol II p 332, Vol III p 683,
   Vol V p 163, 539
Partington, Ex parte, 6 QB 649, Vol II p 130
Partridge v Mullandaine 2 TC 179, [1886] 18 QBD 276, Vol I pp 155, 195, Vol III p 484
Paterson, John (Motors) Ltd v CIR 52 TC 39, Vol III p 559
Patrick v Broadstone Mills [1954] 1 AER 163, [1954] 1 WLR 158, 35 TC 44, Vol II p 515,
   Vol IV p 135
Patterson v Marine Midland Ltd [1981] STC 540 Vol V p 139
Pattinson Deceased, In re, Graham v Pattinson [1885] 1 TLR 216 Vol V p 272
Pattison v Marine Midland Ltd [1984] 2 WLR 11 Vol V p 139
Pearse v Woodall-Duckham Ltd [1978] STC 372, Vol IV p 135
Pearson v IRC [1980] 2 WLR 871, Vol III p 104
Peel v London North Western Rly [1907] 1 Ch D p 5, Vol II p 241
Penrose v Penrose [1933] Ch 793 Vol V p 600

Pepper v Hart [1993] 1 All ER 42, 2000 p 65
People (AG) v Bell [1969] IR 24 Vol V p 221
Perkins Executor v IRC 13 TC 851, Vol III p 484
Perrin v Dickson 14 TC 608, [1929] 2 KB 85, [1930] 1 KB 107, Vol II p 464,
   Vol V p 10, 1998 p 184
Perry v Astor [1943] 1 KB 260, 19 TC 255, [1935] AC, Vol II p 82
Peter Dodson 77 Cr App Reps 1983, Vol III p 153
Peter Merchant Ltd v Stedeford 30 TC 496, Vol II p 515
Petrotim Securities Ltd v Ayres [1964] 1 AER 269, 41 TC 389, Vol III p 253, 340, 373
*Pharmaceutical Society of Ireland, The v The Revenue Commissioners 2 ITC 157
   [1938] IR 202, Vol I p 542*
Philips v Bourne 27 TC 498, [1947] 1 KB 533, Vol III p 19, 319
*Phillips (Inspector of Taxes) v Keane 1 ITC 69, [1925] 2 IR 48, Vol I p 64
Cited also at: Vol II p 460*
*Phillips (Inspector of Taxes) v Limerick County Council 1 ITC 96, [1925] 2 IR 139,
   Vol I p 66*
Phillips v United Kingdom (5 July 2001, unreported), High Court , 2001 p 138
Phillips v Whieldon Sanitary Potteries Ltd 65 TLR 712, 33 TC 213, Vol II pp 267, 360
*Phonographic Performance (Ireland) Ltd v J Somers (Inspector of Taxes) [1992] ILRM
   657, Vol IV p 314*
Pickford v Quirke 13 TC 251, Vol III p 253
Pickles v Foulsham 9 TC 261, [1923] 2 KB 413, [1925] AC 458, Vol I p 259, Vol II p 68
Pigs and Marketing Board v Donnelly (Dublin) Ltd [1939] IR 413, Vol III p 127,
   Vol IV p 162
Pilcher v Logan [1914] 15 SR NSW 24, Vol III p 484
Pine Valley Developments Ltd, Daniel Healy and Others v The IRC Vol IV p 543
Platt v AG of New South Wales 3 AC 336, Vol I p 259
PMPA Garages Ltd, In re [1992] IR 332 Vol V p 323
Pooley, Re, 40 Ch D 1, Vol I p 601
Pollypeck International Plc v Nadir (No 2) [1992] 4 All ER 769, 2000 p 216
Potts' Exeuctors v IRC [1951] AC 443, [1951] 1AER 76, [1951] 1 TLR 152, [1950] 32 TC
   211, Vol III p 683
Power Lane Manufacturing Co v Putnan [1931] 2 KB 309 Vol V p 540
Poynting v Faulkner 5 TC 145, 93 LT 367, Vol I p 155
Prestcold (Central) Ltd v Minister of Labour [1969] 1 AER 69, Vol III p 611
Preston, Re, [1985] 2 WLR 836, Vol III p 356
Pretore di Cento v A person or persons unknown (Case 110/76) [1977] ECR 851 1998 p 76
Pretoria-Pietersburg Railway Co Ltd v Elwood 95 LT 468, 98 LT 741, 6 TC 508, Vol I
   p 427
Prince v Mapp (Inspector of Taxes) [1970] 1 WLR 260 1999 p 82
Prior-Wandesforde, Captain RH v The IRC 1 ITC 248, Vol I p 249, Vol V p 481
*Private Motorists Provident Society Ltd (in liquidation) and WJ Horgan v
   Minister for Justice Vol V p 186*
Private Motorists Provident Society Ltd (in liquidation), In the Matter of, 23 June 1995,
   1995 ITR 159 Vol V p 195
Proes v The Revenue Commissioners Vol V p 481
Property Loan & Investment Co Ltd v The IRC 2 ITC 312, [1946] IR 159, Vol II p 25

Proprietary Articles Trade Association v AG of Canada [1931] AC 310, Vol IV p 395, 2001 p 138
Pryce v Monmouthshire Canal Co 4 AC 197 Vol V p 540
Punjab Co-Operative Bank Ltd Amritsar v Income Tax Commissioner Lahore [1940] AC 1055, Vol III p 373
Punton v Ministry of Pensions and National Insurance [1963] 1 AER 275, Vol II p 491
Purcell, Joseph v AG Ireland & The Minister for the Environment
Purcell, Joseph v Attorney General & Ors Vol IV p 229, Vol V p 288
Pyrah v Annis 37 TC 163, [1956] 2 AE 858, [1957] 1 AER 186, Vol II p 515
Pryce v Monmouthshire Canal Company 4 All Cas 197, 2000 p 236

Q

Queen v The Pharmaceutical Society of Ireland [1896] 2 IR 384 and 385, Vol I p 542
Queen, The v Bishop of Oxford 4 QBD 245 p 261, Vol II p 108
Queensland Stations Property Ltd v Federal Commr of Taxation (1945) 70 CLR 539 Vol V p 239
Quigley, JJ (Inspector of Taxes) v Maurice Burke [1991] 2 IR 169, Vol IV p 332 Vol V p 265
Quinn v Leathen [1901] AC 495, Vol II p 500
Quinn's Supermarket v AG [1972] IR 1, Vol III p 127, Vol IV pp 323, 437, Vol V p 615

R

R (County Councils North Riding and South Riding County Tipperary) v Considine [1917] 2 IR 1, Vol I p 221
R v Buttle 39 LJ MC 115, Vol II p 175
R v Chief Metropolitan Magistrate ex parte Secretary of State for the Home Department [1989] 1 AER 151 1998 p 76
R v Commissioners for Special Purposes of Income Tax 2 TC 332, 21 QBD 313, Vol I p 221
R v Commissioners for Special Purposes of Income Tax 7 TC 646, [1920] 1 KB 26, Vol I p 221
R v Commissioners of Income Tax for the City of London 91 LTR 94, Vol I p 221
R v Cotham [1898] 1 QB 802, Vol III p 290
R v Crawshaw Bell C C 303, 8 Cox 375, Vol I p 195
R v Criminal Injuries Compensation Board, ex parte Lain [1967] 2 QB 864, [1967] 3 WLR 348, [1967] 2 AER 770, Vol III p 290
R v General Income Tax Commissioners for Offlow 27 TLR 353, Vol I p 221
R v Gregory 5 B and AD 555, Vol I p 195
R v Inland Revenue Commissioners ex p Unilever Plc (1996) STC 681 Vol V p 418
R v National Insurance Commissioner; ex parte Hudson [1972] AC 944 Vol V p 615
R v Peters [1886] 16 QBD 636, Vol III p 19
R v R [1984] IR 296, [1985] ILRM 631, Vol III p 533, 590, 2000 p 216
R v The Governor of Pentonville Prison ex parte Khubchandani (1980) 71 Crim App R 241 1998 p 76
R v Waller [1910] 1 KB 364 Vol V p 691
R v Woodhouse [1906] 2 KB 501, Vol III p 290
R & V Haegeman v Commission (Case 96/71) [1972] ECR 1005 1998 p 76
Rabbitt v Grant [1940] IR 323, Vol II p 32
Racing Board v Inspector of Taxes, Vol IV p 73

Radio Pictures Ltd v CIR 22 TC 106, Vol II p 281
Rahill v Brady [1971] IR 69, Vol III p 19
Rahinstown Estates Co v M Hughes, (Inspector of Taxes) [1987] ILRM 599, Vol III p 517
Ramsay, WT Ltd v Inland Revenue Commissioners [1981] 1 AER 165 Vol V p 6
Ramsay, WT Ltd v IRC [1982] AC 300, [1981] 2 WLR 449, [1981] 1 AER 865, [1981] 54 TC 101, [1981] STC 174, Vol III p 104, 683, Vol IV p 547, Vol V p 108, 295, 164 1998 p 184
Ramsey, WT Ltd v CIR 54 TC 101 Vol V p 515, 2000 p 114, 2001 p 105
Ramsey v Liverpool Royal Infirmary [1930] AC 588, Vol III p 572
Ranelaugh (Earl) v Hayes [1683] 1 Vern 189, Vol III p 265
Ransom v Higgs [1973] 2 AER 657, [1974] 1 WLR 1594, [1974] 3 AER 949, [1974] 50 TC 1, Vol II p 614, Vol III pp 572, 683
Reade v Brearley [not reported] 17 TC 687, Vol I p 656
Readymix (Eire) Ltd v Dublin County Council and the Minister for Local Government [SC] unrep, 30 July 1974 Vol V p 357
Readymix Concrete v Commissioner of Taxation (Australia) [unreported], Vol III p 441
Readymix Concrete v Minister for Pensions [1968] 1 AER 433, Vol IV p 45, Vol V p 239
Reed v Cattermole 21 TC 35, [1937] 1 KB 613, Vol II p 452
Reed v Seymour 11 TC 625, [1906] 2 KB 594, [1926] 1 KB 588, 42 TLR 514, 135 LTR 259, Vol I p 155, 618
Rees Roturbo Development Syndicate Ltd v Ducker (CIR) 13 TC 366, Vol I p 474, 629
Reg v Bow Road Justices, ex parte Adedigba [1968] 2 QB 572, Vol III p 19
Reg v Commissioners of Woods and Forests 15 QB 767, Vol I p 221
Reg v Galsworthy [1892] 1 QB 348, Vol II p 241
Reg v IRC, ex parte Fed of Self-Employed [1982] AC 617, Vol IV p 170
Reg v Labourchere 12 QBD 328, Vol I p 427
Reg v Lords of the Treasury 16 QB 357, Vol I p 221
Regent Oil Co Ltd v Strick [1966] AC 295 Vol V p 139
Regina and Jones [1978] 1 WLR 195, Vol III p 153
Regina v Inspector of Taxes ex parte Clarke [1974] 1 QB 220, Vol III p 159
Reid, re [1921] 64 DLR 598, 50 OLR 595 Vol V p 272
Reid's Trustees v Dawson (1915) SC (HL) 47 Vol V p 540
Reids Trustees v CIR [1929] 14 TC 512, Vol III p 477
Reilly v McEntee [1984] ILRM 572 Vol V p 366
Religious Tract and Book Society of Scotland v Forbes 33 SLR 289, 3 TC 415, Vol I p 387
Rellim Ltd v Vise 32 TC 254, Vol III p 1
Republic of Cyprus v Demetriades [1977] 12 JSC 2102 Vol V p 615
Republic of India v Indian Steamship Company (No 2) [1998] AC 878 , 2001 p 138
Revenue Commissioners, The v ORMG [1984] ILRM 406, Vol III p 28
Revenue Commissioners, The v Arida Ltd Vol V p 221
Revenue Commissioners, The v Associated Properties Ltd 3 ITC 293, Vol II p 412
Revenue Commissioners, The v Colm O Loinsigh Vol V p 98
Revenue Commissioners, The v Daniel Anthony Moroney & Ors Vol V p 589
Revenue Commissioners, The v Doorley [1933] IR 750, Vol V p 539, 1998 p110, 184, 2000 p 236, 247
Cited also at: Vol II p 25, 195, 326, Vol III p 683, Vol IV p 22, 91, Vol V p 108, 376
Revenue Commissioners, The v Henry Young Vol V p 294

Revenue Commissioners, The v HI Vol III p 242
Cited also at: Vol V p 393
Revenue Commissioners, The v L & Co 3 ITC 205, Vol II p 281
Revenue Commissioners, The v Latchford & Sons Ltd 1 ITC 238, Vol I p 240
Revenue Commissioners, The v Orwell Ltd 3 ITC 193, Vol II p 326
Revenue Commissioners, The v R Hilliard & Sons Ltd 2 ITC 410, Vol II p 130
Revenue Commissioners, The v Sisters of Charity of the Incarnate Word 1998 p 65
Revenue Commissioners, The v Switzer Ltd 2 ITC 290, [1945] IR 378, Vol II p 19
  Vol II p 130
Revenue Commissioners, The v Y Ltd 3 ITC 49, Vol II p 195
Rex (Waterford County Council) v Local Government Board [1902] 2 IR 349, Vol III p 590
Rex v BC Fir and Cedar Lumber Co Ltd 17 TC 564, 147 LT 1, Vol I p 427
Rex v Dibdin [1910] p 57, Vol II p 130
Rex v General Commissioners of Income Tax for the City of London (ex parte Gibbs and Others) [1940] 2 KB 242, [1942] AC 402, 24 TC 221, Vol II p 55
Rex v James Whitney 1 Moody 3, Vol III p 19
Rex v Sarah Chapple [1804] Russell & Ryan 77, Vol III p 19
Rex v Special Commissioners of Income Tax 20 TC 381, (ex parte Elmhirst [1936] 1 KB 487), Vol I p 571
Reynolds v Times Newspapers & Others [1998] 3 All ER 961, 2001 p 98
Rhodesia Railways Ltd v Collector of Income Tax, Bechuanaland Portectorate [1933] AC 368, Vol II p 32, 267
Rhymney Iron Co Ltd v Fowler [1896] 2 QB 79, Vol I p 164
Richardson, Re, 50 LJ Ch 488, Vol I p 130
Richmond's Trustees v Richmond [1935] SC 585 Vol V p 565
Ricketts v Colquhoun 10 TC 118, KBD [1924] 2 KB 347, CA [1925] 1 KB 725, HL [1926] AC 1, Vol I p 64, Vol II pP 366, 460
Ridge Securities Ltd v CIR 44 TC 373, Vol III p 253, 373
Right Hon Earl of Iveagh, The v IRC 1 ITC 316, [1930] IR 386, 431, Vol I p 259
Cited also at: Vol I p 375, 387
River Estates Ltd v Director General of Inland Revenue [1984] STC 60, Vol III p 178
River Estates, Re, [1984] STC 60, Vol III p 178
Roache v Newsgroup Newspapers Ltd & Others [1998] EMLR 161, 2001 p 98
Roberts v Williamson 26 TC 201, [1944] 60 TLR 561, Vol II p 241
Robertson v MacDonagh [1880] 6 LR IR 433, Vol III p 484
Robinson v Corry 18 TC 411, [1934] 1 KB 240, Vol II p 452
Robinson v Scott Bader Co Ltd 54 TC 757, Vol IV p 73
Robinson, WA, t/a James Pim & Son v JD Dolan (Inspector of Taxes) 2 ITC 25, [1935] IR 509, Vol I p 427
Cited also at: Vol III p 165
Roche v Minister for Industry & Commerce [1978] IR 149 Vol V p 696
Roche v p Kelly & Co Ltd [1969] IR 100, Vol IV p 45, Vol V p 239
Rodgers v ITGWU and Others [1978] ILRM 51, Vol IV p 323
Rogers v Inland Revenue 16 SC LR 682, 1 TC 225, Vol I p 259
Rolled Steel Ltd v British Steel Corporation [1986] 1 Ch 246, Vol IV p 247
Rolls v Miller [1884] 27 Ch D 71 Vol V p 686
Rolls-Royce Ltd v Jeffrey 40 TC 443, [1962] 1 AER 801, Vol II p 602
Rompelman v Minister Van Financien, case 268/83 Vol V p 76

Rondel v Worsley [1969] 1 AC 191, Vol III p 484
Roper v Ward [1981] ILRM 408, Vol IV p 247
Rorke v CIR [1960] 1 WLR 1132, 39 TC 194, Vol II p 515
Rosyth Building and Estates Co Ltd v p Rogers (Surveyor of Taxes) [1921] Sess Cas 372, 58 SLR 363, 8 TC 11, Vol I p 447, 515
Routledge & Co Ltd [1904] 2 Ch 474, Vol II p 130
Rowan, In the Goods of Bernard Louis, Deceased, Joseph Rowan v Vera Agnes Rowan and Others [1988] ILRM 65, Vol III p 572
Rowan's Trustees v Rowan [1940] SC 30 Vol V p 565
Rownson, Drew & Clydesdale Ltd v CIR 16 TC 595, Vol I pp 164, 427
Rowntree & Co v Curtis 8 TC 678, [1925] 1 KB 328, Vol II p 32
Royal Bank of Canada v IRC [1972] 1 Ch 665, Vol III p 356
Royal Bank of Ireland & O'Shea [1943] 77 ILTR Vol V p 1
Royal College of Surgeons of England v CIR 4 TC 344, [1899] 1 QB 871, Vol I p 542
Royal Crown Derby Porcelain Co Ltd v Russell [1949] 2 KB 417, Vol III p 19, 533
Royal Insurance Co Ltd v Stephen 14 TC 22, 44 TLR 630, Vol I p 503, Vol III p 373
Royal Insurance Co Ltd v Stephen 44 TLR 630, 14 TC 22, Vol I p 474, Vol II p 419
Royal Liver Friendly Society [1870] LR 5 Exch 78, Vol IV p 296
Royster Guano Co v Virginia [1920] 253 US 412, Vol III p 127
Russell v Aberdeen Town and County Bank 2 TC 321, 13 AC 418, Vol II p 515
Russell v Russell [1985] 315, Vol IV p 437
Russell v Scott [1936] 55 CLR 440, [1936] 36 SR NSW 454, 53 NSWWN 178 Vol V p 272
Russell v Scott [1948] AC 422, Vol III p 56
Russell v Wakefield Waterworks Co [1875] LR 20 Eq 474, Vol IV p 247
Russian Petroleum Co Ltd [1907] 2 Ch 540, Vol II p 130
Rustproof Metal Window CoLtd v CIR 29 TC 243, 177 LT 657, Vol II p 602
Ryall v Hoare 8 TC 521, [1923] KB 447, Vol I p 155, 474
Ryan v Asia Mill 32 TC 275, Vol II p 515
Ryan v Oceanic Steam Navigation Co Ltd [1914] 3 KB 731, Vol I p 330
Ryan v The Attorney General [1965] IR 294 Vol V p 615
Ryans Car Hire v Attorney General [1965] IR 642 Vol V p 272
Ryle Brehon Airlines v Ming (1995) 3 WLR 64 Vol V p 412

S

S Ltd v O'Sullivan Vol II p 602
S v S [1983] IR 68, Vol IV p 437
S W Ltd v McDermott (Inspector of Taxes) Vol II p 661
SA Roquette Freres v French State (Case 145/79) [1980] ECR 3333 1998 p 77
Saatchi & Saatchi Advertising Ltd v Kevin McGarry (Inspector of Taxes) Vol V p 376 1998 p 99
Salisbury House Estate Ltd v Fry [1930] 1 KB 304, [1930] AC 432, 15 TC 266, Vol I pp 447, 487, 515, Vol II p 315, Vol III p 95, Vol IV p 1
Salvesen's Trustee's v CIR [1930] SLT 387 Vol V p 532, 577
San Paulo (Brazilian) Railway Co v Carter 73 LT 538, 3 TC 407, Vol I p 183
Sargeant (Inspector of Taxes) v Eayers 48 TC 573, 2000 p 76
Sargood Bros v The Commonwealth [1910] 11 CLR 258 Vol V p 615
Saunders (GL) (in liquidation), in Re [1986] 1 WLR 215 Vol V p 387
Saunders v Dixon 40 TC 329, Vol II p 515

Saunders, GL Ltd (in liquidation), Re, [1986] 1 WLR 215, [1985] 130 SJ 166, [1985] 83 LS Gaz 779, Vol IV p 107
Saxone Lilley and Skinner Holdings Ltd v CIR 44 TC 122, Vol III p 65
Scales v George Thompson & Co Ltd 13 TC 83, Vol III p 178
Schofield v Hall 49 TC 538, [1975] STC 353, Vol III pp 113, 120, 219, Vol IV pp 68, 284, 425
Scoble v Secretary of State for India 4 TC 618 Vol V p 108, 1998 p 184
Scottish Co-operative Wholesale Society v Meyer [1958] 3 AER 66, Vol III p 423
Scottish Golf Club [1913] 3 KB 75, Vol I p 515
Scottish Investment Trust Co v Forbes 3 TC 231, Vol I p 474, Vol II p 419, Vol III p 373
Scottish Provident Institution v Farmer [1912] Sess Case 452, 6 TC 34 p 38, Vol I p 1
Scottish Widows Fund Life Assurance Society Ltd v Farmer 5 TC 502, Vol III p 484
Seaham Harbour Dock Co v Crook 16 TC 333, Vol III p 165
Sebel Products Ltd v Commissioners of Customs and Excise [1949] Ch 409 Vol V p 615
Sebright, Re, [1944] 1 Ch 287, Vol II p 332
Secretan v Hart 45 TC 701, Vol IV p 135
Secretary of State for India v Scoble 4 TC 618, [1903] AC 299, Vol II p 464
Sergeant (Inspector of Taxes) v Eayrs 48 TC 573 Vol V p 496
Severn Fishery Board v O'May [1919] 2 KB 484, 7 TC 194, Vol II p 154, 204, Vol IV p 73
Shadford v H Fairweather and Co Ltd 43 TC 291, Vol III p 1
Sharkey v Wernher 36 TC 275, [1954] 2 AER 753, [1955] 3 AER 493, Vol II p 315, Vol III p 253, 340
Shaw v Lawless 5 CI & F 129, Vol I p 601
Shell-Mex v Manchester Garages [1971] 1 WLR 612, Vol IV p 269
Shepherd v Harrison LR 5 HL 116, Vol I p 130
Sherdley v Sherdley [1987] STC 217, Vol III p 683
Sherry [not rep], Re, Vol III p 387
Shilton v Wilmhurst [1991] STC 88 , 2001 p 105
Sillar, Re, [1956] IR 344, Vol III p 572
Simmons v Heath Laundry Company [1910] 1 KB 543 1998 p 177
Simple Imports Limited and Another v Revenue Commissioners and Others , 2001 p 57
Simpson v Tate 9 TC 314, Vol II p 366
Simpson v The Grange Trust Ltd 19 TC 231, [1934] 2 KB 317, and in the House of Lords 50 TLR 389, Vol I p 447
Simpson v The Grange Trust Ltd 19 TC 231, 51 TLR 320, [1934] 2 KB 317, Vol II p 429
Sinclair v Brougham [1914] AC 415, Vol IV p 247
Sinclair v Cadbury Brothers 18 TC 157, Vol III p 65
Singer v Williams [1918] 2 KB 432, [1921] 1 AC 41, 7 TC 419, Vol I p 583, Vol II pp 82, 491
Small v Easson 12 TC 351, [1920] SC 758, Vol II p 500
Smart v Lincolnshire Sugar Co Ltd 20 TC 643, Vol III p 165
Smidth and Co v Greenwood 8 TC 193, [1920] 3 KB 275, [1921] 3 KB 583, [1922] 1 AC 417, Vol I p 330
Smith v Incorporated Council of Law Reporting for England and Wales 6 TC 477, [1914] 3 KB 674, Vol II p 32, 393, 515
Smith v Lion Brewery Co Ltd 5 TC 568, [1911] AC 155, Vol I p 515, 642
Smith v The Law Guarantee and Trust Society Ltd [1904] Ch 569, Vol I p 45
Smith, John & Son v Moore 12 TC 266, [1921] 2 AC 13, Vol II p 515

Smyth EA & Weber Smyth v The Revenue Commissioners [1931] IR 643, Vol V p 532
Smyth v Revenue Commissioners [1931] IR 643, Vol V p 577
Smyth v Stretton 20 TLR 443, 5 TC 41, Vol I p 155
Society of the Writers to the Signet v CIR 2 TC 257, [1886] 14 Sess Cas 34, Vol I p 542
Solamon v Solamon & Co Ltd [1897] AC 22, Vol IV p 247
Solicitors Act 1954, Re, [1960] IR 239, Vol III p 577
Solomon v Commissioners of Customs and Excise 2 QB 116, Vol III p 246
Somerville v Somerville 5 Ves 750, 758, Vol I p 259
Sother Smith v Clancy 24 TC 1 Vol V p 108, 1998 p 184
South Australia v The Commonwealth [1941] 65 CLR 373 Vol V p 615
South Behar Railway Co v IRC 12 TC 657, [1925] AC 485, Vol I p 108, 318
Southampton & Itchen Bridge Co v Southampton Local Board [Not reported], Vol II p 241
Southern Railway of Peru v Owen 36 TC 602, [1957] AC 334, Vol II p 515
Southern v Aldwych Property Trust Ltd 23 TC 707, [1940] 2 KB 266, 56 TLR 808, Vol II pp 95, 429, Vol V p 680
Southern v Borax Consolidated Ltd 23 TC 597 [1940] 4 AER 412, [1941] 1 KB 111, Vol II pp 45, 267, 500, 515
Southwell v Savill Bros 4 TC 430, [1901] 2 KB 349, Vol II pp 32, 45, 515, 2000 p 76
Spaight v Dundon [1961] IR 201, Vol IV p 437
Spanish Prospecting Co Ltd [1911] 1 Ch 92, Vol I p 1
Spencer v McGarry 2 ITC 297, [1946] IR 11, Vol II p 241
Spencer v Metropolitan Board of Works LR 22 Ch Div 149 Vol V p 570
Spurway v Spurway [1894] 1 IR 385, Sel and 28 ILTR 2, Vol I p 259
Spyer v Phillipson [1931] 2 Ch 183, Vol III p 332
St Andrew's Hospital (Northampton) v Shearsmith 2 TC 219, 19 QBD 624, Vol I p 387
St John's School Mount Ford & Knibbs v Ward 49 TC 523 Vol V p 201
St Johns School v Ward 49 TC 524, Vol III p 219
St Lucia Usines and Estates Co Ltd v Colonial Treasurer of St Lucia 131 LT 267, [1924] AC 508, Vol I p 214
Stainers Executors v Purchase 32 TC 408, Vol IV p 135
Stamp deceased, In the matter of John Patrick Stamp v Noel Redmond & Ors Vol IV p 415
Standing v Bowring [1885] 31 Ch D 282, 55 LJ Ch 218, 54 LT 191, 34 WR 204, 2 TLR 202 Vol V p 272
Stanley v Gramaphone and Typewriter Ltd 5 TC 358, [1908] 2 KB 89-95, Vol I p 28
State (at the prosecution of Brookfield Securities Ltd) v The Collector Customs and Excise [Unreported], Vol IV p 419
State (Carmody), The v De Burca (HC) 1970, unrep Vol V p 691
State (Creedon) v Criminal Injuries Compensation Tribunal [1988] IR 51, Vol IV p 485
State (Daly) v Minister for Agriculture [1987] IR 1965, Vol IV p 485
State (DPP) v Walsh [1981] IR 412, Vol IV p 437
State (Elm Developments Ltd) v An Bord Pleanala [1981] ILRM 108, Vol IV p 505
State (Gettins) v Judge Fawsitt [1945] IR 183 , 2001 p 138
State (Healy) v Donoghue [1976] IR 325, Vol IV p 478, Vol V p 615
State (Hully) v Hynes 100 ILTR 145 1998 p 77
State (Keegan and Lysaght) v Stardust Victims Compensation Tribunal [1986] IR 642, Vol IV p 170, Vol IV p 512
State (Keegan) v Stardust Victims Compensation Tribunal [1986] IR 658, 2000 p 261

State (Keller) v Galway County Council and Another [1958] IR 142, Vol III p 290
State (McFadden) v The Governor of Mountjoy Prison [1981] ILRM 113 1998 p 77
State (Multiprint Label System Ltd) v President of Circuit Court [1984] ILRM 545, Vol IV
    p 505
State (Nicolaou) v An Bord Uchtala [1966] IR 567, [1966] 102 ILTR 1, Vol III p 127,
    Vol IV p 437, Vol V p 615
State (O'Duffy) v Bennet & Ors [1935] IR 70 Vol V p 691
State (O'Rourke) v Kelly [1983] IR 58, Vol IV p 278
State (Quinn) v Ryan [1965] IR 70 1998 p 120
State (Ryan) v IRC [1934] IR 13, Vol I p 563, Vol II p 326
State (Walsh) v An Bord Pleanala [1981] ILRM 535, Vol IV p 505
State Board of Tax Commissioners v Jackson [1931] 283 US 527, Vol III p 127
State v Sealy [1939] IR 21, Vol IV p 401
State, (Sheerin) v Kennedy [1966] IR 379, Vol V p 615, 1998 p 120
*State, The (at the prosecution of Patrick J Whelan) v Michael Smidic (Special
    Commissioners of Income Tax) 2 ITC 188, [1938] IR 626, Vol I p 571*
    Cited also at: Vol II p 374
*State, The (Calcul International Ltd and Solatrex International Ltd) v The Appeal
    Commissioners and The Revenue Commissioners Vol III p 577*
State, The (FIC Ltd) v O'Ceallaigh (Inspector of Taxes) Vol III p 124
*State, The (Melbarian Enterprises Ltd) v The Revenue Commissioners [1985] IR 706,
    Vol III p 290*
*State, The (Multiprint Label Systems Ltd) v The Honourable Justice Thomas Neylon [1984]
    ILRM 545, Vol III p 159*
State, The State (Sheerin) v Kennedy [1966] IR 379 Vol V p 615
Stedeford v Beloe 16 TC 505, [1931] 2 KB 610, [1932] AC 388, Vol I p 618, Vol II p 393
Steer, Re, 3 H & N 599, Vol I p 259
Stephen Court Limited v JA Browne (Inspector of Taxes) (1984) ILRM 231 Vol V p 496
Stephen Court Ltd v JA Browne (Inspector of Taxes) Vol V p 680
    Cited also at 2000 p 76
Stevens (Inspector of Taxes) v Tirard [1940] 23 TC 321, Vol IV p 221
Stevenson, Jordon & Harrison Ltd v Macdonald [1952] 1 TLR 101 1998 p 177
Stockport Schools [1898] 2 Ch 687, Vol IV p 296
Stonegate Securities Ltd v Gregory [1980] IR 241 , 2001 p 77
Strong and Company of Romsey Ltd v Woodfield (Surveyor of Taxes) 5 TC 215 ,
    1999 p 82, 2001 p 118
Stovall v Denno [1967] 388 US 293 Vol V p 615
Strick v Regent Oil Co 43 TC 1, [1964] AC 295, [1966] 1 AER 585, Vol II p 515,
    Vol IV p 135
Stubart Investments Ltd v The Queen [1984] CTC 294, 84 DTC 6305, Vol III p 683
Styles v The New York Life Insurance Co LR 14 AC 381, Vol II p 211
Sugar Distributors Ltd v The Companies Acts 1963-90 Vol V p 225
Sulley v AG 29 LJ Ex 464, 2 TC 149, Vol I pp 183, 330
Sulley v Royal College of Surgeons Edinburgh 29 SC LR 620, [1892] 3 TC 173,
    Vol I p 542
Sunday Tribune Limited (in Liquidation), Re, 1998 p 177
Sun Insurance Officer v Clark 6 TC 59, [1912] AC 443, Vol II pp 211, 515, Vol IV p 135

Sun Life Assurance Society v Davidson 37 TC 330, Vol III p 95, Vol V p 496, 680, 2000 p 76
Sun Newspapers v Federal Commissioner of Taxation [1938] 61 CLR 337, Vol II p 515
Sunday Tribune Ltd (in liquidation), In the matter of the [1984] IR 505 Vol V p 239
Superwood Holdings v Sun Alliance Insce Group [1995] unrep Vol V p 226
Sutherland v CIR 12 TC 63, 55 SC LR 674, EPD Leaflet No 9, Vol I p 1, Vol III p 253
Swaine (Inspector of Taxes) v VE 3 ITC 387, [1964] IR 423, 100 ILTR 21, Vol II p 472
Cited also at: Vol III p 1, 9
Swan Brewery Co Ltd (No 2) ACLR 168 Vol V p 226
Swan, Deceased; Hibernian Bank Ltd v Frances Stewart Munro & Ors Vol V p 565
Swedish Central Railway Co Ltd v Thompson 9 TC 342, [1925] AC 495, Vol II p 68
Swire, Re, 30 Ch D 239, Vol III p 340
Switzer v Commissioners of Valuation [1902] 2 IR 275, Vol II p 241
Symons v Weeks [1983] STC 195, Vol IV p 135

T

T v T [1983] IR 29, [1982] ILRM 217, Vol IV p 437
Tasker, W & Sons Ltd [1905] 1 Ch 283, Vol II p 130
Taxback Limited v The Revenue Commissioners Vol V p 412
Taylor Clarke International Ltd v Lewis (Inspector of Taxes) 1997 STC 499 Vol V p 164, 2001 p 105
Tebrau (Johore) Rubber Syndicate Ltd v Farmer [1910] SC 906, 47 SLR 816, 5 TC 658, Vol I pp 1, 474
Tempany v Hynes [1976] IR 101, Vol IV p 304, 367
Temperley v Visibell Ltd 49 TC 129, Vol IV p 1
Tennant v Smith 3 TC 158, [1892] AC 150, Vol II p 452, Vol V p 540
Texaco (Ireland) Ltd v Murphy (No 2) [1992] 1 IR 399 Vol V p 326
Texaco (Ireland) Ltd v Murphy (No.3) [1992] 2 IR 300, 4 ITR 91 Vol V p 323
Texaco Ireland Ltd v S Murphy (Inspector of Taxes) [1989] IR 496, [1991] 2 IR 449, Vol IV p 91,
Cited also at: Vol V p 376
Thomas Merthyr Colliery Co Ltd v Davis [1933] 1 KB 349, Vol I p 164
Thomas v Richard Evans & Co Ltd 11 TC 790, Vol I p 164
Thomas, In re [1982] 4 AER 814 Vol V p 45
Thomas, Weatherall v Thomas, In re [1900] 1 Ch 319, Vol II p 32
Thompson Magnesium Elektron Ltd [1944] 1 AER 126, 26 TC 1, Vol II p 515
Thomson v Goold & Co [1910] AC 409 1998 p 77
Thomson Hill Ltd v Comptroller of Income Tax [1984] STC 251, Vol IV p 135
Thomson v Bensted 7 TC 137, [1919] Sess Cas 8, Vol I p 259
Thomson v St Catherines College, Cambridge [1919] AC 468 Vol V p 615
Thorley, Re, [1891] 2 Ch 613, Vol I p 601
Tilley v Wales [1943] AC 386, Vol IV p 407
Tillmans and SS Knutsford [1908] 2 KB 385, Vol IV p 296
Tilson, In re [1951] IR 1 Vol V p 615
Timpson's Executors v Yerberry 20 TC 155, Vol II p 592
Tinker v Tinker [1970] p 136 1998 p 169
Tipping, WJ (Inspector of Taxes) v Louis Jeancard 2 ITC 360, [1948] IR 233, Vol II p 68
Todd v Egyptian Delta Land & Investment Co Ltd 14 TC 119, [1929] AC 1, Vol II p 68
Tomadini v Administrazione delle Finanze dello Steto [1979] EC Vol II 1814, Vol IV p 492

Tool Metal Manufacturing Co Ltd v Tungsten Electric Co Ltd [1955] 1 WLR 761 Vol V p 589
Tormey v Ireland & AG [1985] IR 289, [1985] ILRM 375, Vol III p 577, Vol IV p 437
Trans- Prairie Ltd v Minister of National Revenue 70 DTC 6351, 1999 p 82, 2001 p 118
Travers v Holley [1953] p 246, [1953] 3 WLR 507, [1953] 2 AER 794, Vol IV p 437
Travers, John v Sean O'Siochain (Inspector of Taxes) Vol V p 54
Trevor v Whitworth [1887] 12 Appeal Cases 414, Vol IV p 247
Trinidad Petroleum Development Co v IRC 21 TC 1, [1937] 1 KB 408, Vol II p 332, Vol III p 229
Trustees of Psalms and Hymns v Whitwell 7 TLR 164, 3 TC 7, Vol I p 387
Trustees of the Tollemach Settled Estates v Coughtrie 30 TC 454, [1961] AC 880, Vol II p 491
Trustees of The Ward Union Hunt Races, The v Hughes (Inspector of Taxes) 2 ITC 152, Vol I p 538
Tryka Ltd v Newall 41 TC 146, Vol III p 363
Tuck & Sons v Priester [1887] 19 QBD 629, 638, Vol III p 19
Tucker (Inspector of Taxes) v Granada Motorway Services Ltd (1979) STC 393 Vol V p 496
Turner v Cuxson 2 TC 422, 22 QBD 150, Vol I p 155
Turner v Last 42 TC 517, Vol III p 1
Turton v Cooper 5 TC 138, 92 LTR 863, [1907] 2 KB 694, Vol I p 155, 618
Tyler, In Re [1907] 1 KB 865 Vol V p 615
Tzu Tsai Cheng v The Governor of Pentonville Prison [1973] AC 931 1998 p 77

U

Ua Clothasaigh, D (Inspector of Taxes) v Patrick McCartan 2 ITC 367, [1948] IR 219, Vol II p 75,
Cited also at: Vol V p 615
Udny V Udny LR 1 SC Appeals 441, Vol I p 259, Vol V p 481
Ulster Investment Bank Ltd v Euro Estates & Drumkill Ltd [1982] ILRM 57 Vol V p 226
Union Cold Storage Co v Jones 8 TC 725, 129 LTR 512, Vol I p 642, Vol II p 500
United Bars Ltd (Receivership), Walkinstown Inn Ltd (Receivership) and Raymond Jackson v The IRC [1991] IR 396
Cited also at: Vol V p 388
United Collieries Ltd v The Commissioners of the Inland Revenue 12 TC 1248, Vol II p 382
United States of America v Inkley [1989] 1 QB 255 Vol V p 45
United States v Peltier [1975] 422 US 531 Vol V p 615
United States of American Trucking Association (1940) 310 US 543/544, 2000 p 65
United Steel Companies Ltd v Cullington (No 1) 23 TC 71, 162 LT 23, Vol II p 515
United States v Ursery 518 US 267 , 2001 p 138
University of London Press Ltd v University Tutorial Press Ltd [1916] 2 Ch 601, [1916] WN 321, Vol III p 496
Unwin v Hanson [1891] 2 QB 115, Vol III p 19
Urquhart, D & Revenue Commissioners v AIB Ltd [1979] IR 197 Vol V p 366
Urquhart, D (Decd) & Revenue Commissioners v AIB Ltd, In the Matter of the Estate of Vol V p 600
Cited also at: [1979] IR 197, Vol V p 366

Usher's Wiltshire Brewerey Ltd v Bruce [1915] AC 433, 6 TC 399, [1919] 1 KB 25, Vol I pp 91, 642, Vol II p 222, 267, 500, 515, Vol III p 198, Vol IV p 135

V

Vacuum Oil Co Proprietaries v Comrs of Taxation (25 February 1964), Vol II p 515
Vale, JB (Inspector Of Taxes) v Martin Mahony & Brothers Ltd 2 ITC 331, [1947] IR 30, Vol II p 32
Cited also at: Vol II p 267, 360, 515
Vallambrosa Rubber Co Ltd v Farmer 5 TC 529, [1910] SC 519, Vol I pp 91, 642, Vol II p 32, 382, 515, Vol IV p 425
Vestey v IRC (1962) 2 WLR 221 1998 p 184
Von Colson v Landnordhein-Westfalen Case 14/83 [1984] ECR 1891 1998 p 77
Van Den Berghs Ltd v Clark [1935] AC 431, 19 TC 390, Vol I p 642, Vol II pp 32, 222, 515
Van Hool McArdle Ltd (in liquidation), Re, IRC v Donnelly [1983] ILRM 329, Vol III p 523
Vestey v IRC (1962) 2 WLR 221 Vol V p 108
Veterinary Council, The v F Corr (Inspector of Taxes) 3 ITC 59, [1935] IR 12, Vol II p 204
VIEK Investments Ltd v The IRC [1991] 2 IR 520, Vol IV p 367
Cited also at: Vol III p 9, Vol IV pp 323, 437
Vodafone Cellular Ltd v Shaw (Inspector of Taxes) [1997] STC 734,1999 p 82

W

W Ltd v Wilson (Inspector of Taxes) Vol II p 627
Cited also at: Vol IV p 187
W v W [1993] 2 IR 476 Vol V p 482
Wagner Miret v Fondo de Grantia Salaril case [1993] ECR I 6911 1998 p 77
Waldie & Sons Ltd v Commissioners of IR [1919] Sess Cas 697, 12 TC 113 p 118, Vol I p 447
Wales v Graham 24 TC 75, Vol II p 366
Wales v Tilley [1943] AC 386, Vol IV p 407
Walker v Boyd [1932] LJ 402, Vol II p 32
Walker v Giles [1848] 6 CB 662, Vol IV p 296
Wandesforde's 1 ITC 248, [unreported 23 May 1928], Vol I p 259
Warnock and Others practising as Stokes Kennedy Crowley & Co v The IRC [1985] IR 663, [1986] ILRM 37, Vol III p 356
Warrender v Warrender [1835] 2 C & F 488, Vol IV p 437
Waterford Glass (Group Services) Ltd v The Revenue Commissioners [1990]1 IR 334, Vol IV p 187
Cited also at: Vol IV p 367, Vol V 181
Watkins v US (1956) 354 US 178 1998 p 120
Watson v Everitt v Blunden 18 TC 402, Vol I p 601
Watson v Hornby 24 TC 506, [1942] 2 AER 506, Vol II p 315
Watson v Rowles 95 LJKB 959, 42 TLR 379, 11 TC 171, Vol II p 68
Wayte (Holdings) Ltd (Receivership) v EN Hearne (Inspector of Taxes) [1986] IR 448, Vol III p 553
Webb v Ireland [1988] IR 353, Vol IV p 170, 492
Wedick v Osmond and Co [1935] IR 838 p 845, Vol I p 542
Welbeck Securities v Powlson [1986] STC, [1987] STC 468, Vol IV p 547, Vol V p 515
Wellaway v Courtier [1918] 1 KB 200, Vol II p 636

Wemyss v Wemyss Trustee [1921] SC p 40-41, Vol I p 259
Werle & Co v Colquhoun 2 TC 402, 20 QBD 753, Vol I p 28, 387
Westcott v Woolcombes Ltd [1987] STC 600
West Mercia Safetyware Ltd (In Liquidation) v Dodd and anor [1988] Butterworths Company Law Cases 250, Vol IV p 247
West v Phillips 38 TC 203, Vol III p 1, 373
Westcott v Woolcombes Ltd [1987] STC 600, 2000 p 114
Westcombe v Hadnock Quarries Ltd 16 TC 137, Vol III p 165
Westminister Bank Ltd v Osler 17 TC 381, 146 LTR 441, 148 LTR 41, Vol I p 474, 503, Vol II p 419, Vol III p 373
Westminster Bank Ltd v Riches 28 TC 159, Vol II p 332
Westminster v CIR 19 TC 490, [1936] AC 1, Vol I p 515
Weston v Hearn 25 TC 425, [1943] 2 AER 421, Vol II p 452
Westwinds Holdings Co Ltd [unreported] 21 May 1974, Vol III p 423
Whelan, Norah and Others v Patrick Madigan [High Court, 18 July 1978], Vol III p 332
Whicker v Hume 7 HLC p 160, Vol I p 259
Whimster & Co v CIR 12 TC 813, Vol IV p 135, Vol II p 419, Vol III p 198
White, In re, [1892] 2 Ch 217, Vol I p 601
Whiteley Ltd, William v The King [1909] 101 LT 741 Vol V p 615
Wiley, Michael v The IRC [1989] IR 351, Vol IV p 170
Wilks v Heeley [1832] 1 Cr & M 249, Vol III p 265
William's Executors v CIR 26 TC 23, Vol I p 164
Williams Group Tullamore Ltd v Companies Act 1963-1983 Vol III p 423
Williams v Corbet 8 Sim 349, Vol I p 601
Williams v Grundys Trustees 18 TC 271, [1934] 1 KB 524, Vol II p 627
Williams v Singer 7 TC 387, [1921] 1 AC 65, Vol III p 477
Wilson (Inspector of Taxes) v Dunnes Stores (Cork) Ltd Vol III p 403
Wilson Box (Foreign Rights) Ltd v Brice 20 TC 736, Vol III p 1
Wilson v John Lane [unreported], Vol III p 441
Wilson v West Sussex Co Council [1963] 2 QB 764 Vol V p 357
Wimpey International Ltd v Warland, Associated Restaurants Ltd v Warland [1987] Simons Tax Intelligence since reported [1988] STC 149, [1989] STC 273, Vol IV p 284, Vol V p 201
Winans v AG [1904] AC 287, Vol I p 259
Wing v O'Connell (Inspector of Taxes) 1 ITC 170, [1927] IR 84, Vol I p 155
Cited also at: Vol I pP 427, 618, Vol II p 261, Vol III p 165
Winget Ltd: Burn v The Company, Re [1924] 1 Ch p 550, Vol II p 108
Winsconsin v Pelican Insurance Co [1887] 127 US 265 Vol V p 45
Wisdom v Chamberlain [1969] 1 AER 332, 45 TC 92, Vol III p 253, Vol V p 6
WLD Worldwide Leather Diffusion Ltd v The Revenue Commissioners Vol V p 61
Wolmershausen v Gullick [not reported], Vol III p 265
Woolwich Building Society v IRC [1993] AC 70 Vol V p 323

X

Xenos v Wickham LR 2 HL 296 Vol V p 560
XX Ltd v O hArgain, Judgment of Kenny J, 20/6/75, Vol III p 1

Y

Yarmouth v France [1880] 19 QBD 646, [1887] 19 QBD 647, Vol II p 602, Vol III pp 113, 120, 219, Vol IV pp 68, 425, Vol V p 201, 317
Yates (Inspector of Taxes) v Starkey (1951) Ch 465 Vol V p 472
Yates v Starkey 32 TC 38, [1951 Ch 465, Vol IV p 221
Yeates and Others v the Minister for Posts and Telegraphs and Others [1978] ILRM 22,
Young v IRC 12 TC 827, [1926] SC 30, Vol I p 240
Young v Racecourse Betting Control Board 38 TC 426, Vol IV p 73
Young v Robertson 4 Macq HL 314 Vol V p 540
Young v Sealey [1949] Ch 278, [1949] 1 All ER 92, [1949] LJR 529, [1948] 93 SJ 58 Vol V p 272
Young's Estate, Re [1918] 1 IR 30, Vol II p 332
Yuill v Wilson STC 1980, Vol III p 340

Statutes considered

Adaptation of Enactments Act 1922
....1998 p 120
Adoption Act 1952
....Vol V p 696
   s 4.. Vol IV p 415
   s 26(2)... Vol IV p 415
Acquisition of Land (Assessment of Compensation) Act 1919
....Vol IV p 485
   s 2...Vol III p 298
Capital Acquisition Tax Act 1976
   s 2...Vol III p 104
   s 15-18 ....Vol V p 295, 680
   s 21...Vol V p 200
   s 39... 2000 p 62
      (4)..Vol V p 295
   s 52(2)..Vol V p 295
   s 56.. Vol IV p 340
   s 58(3)...Vol V p 221
   s 146...Vol V p 138
   Sch 2 Pt 1 para 9 ....Vol V p 686
Central Bank Act 1971
   s 2...Vol III p 559, 664
   ss 7 to 31 ....Vol III p 559, 664
   s 58...Vol III p 559, 664
Capital Gains Tax Act 1975
   s 3... Vol IV p 515, 547
   s 8... Vol IV p 515, 547
      (2)... Vol IV p 543
      (5)... Vol IV p 217
   s 11(1), (2) .... 2000 p 114
   s 12..Vol III p 683, Vol V p 163
   s 19..Vol III p 559, 664
   s 28... Vol IV p 1
   s 33... Vol II p 683
   s 46...Vol V p 163, 2001 p 104
   s 47... Vol IV p 515, 547
   s 49(1) .... Vol IV p 125
   Sch 2 para 2 ....2000 p 114, 2001 p 104
   Sch 4 paras 6, 7, 11(4) .... Vol IV p 217
   Sch 4 para 8(2)(*b*) .... Vol IV p 125
   Sch 4 para 11(1), (6) .... Vol IV p 543
Common Law Procedure (Ireland) Act 1854
....Vol V p 70

Companies (Consolidation) Act 1908
- s 69 .... Vol V p 532
- s 82(2) .... Vol V p 532
- s 107 .... Vol II p 108
- s 209 .... Vol II p 108

Companies Act 1963
- s 8 .... Vol IV p 247
- s 89 .... Vol V p 226
- s 98 .... Vol III p 548, Vol IV p 91, Vol V p 388
- s 147 .... Vol IV p 247
- s 150 .... Vol IV p 247
- s 201(3) .... Vol IV p 82
- s 202 .... Vol IV p 82
- s 205 .... Vol III p 423
- s 214 .... 2001 p 77
- s 225 .... Vol V p 186
- s 230 .... Vol V p 186
- s 231(e) .... 2001 p 77
- s 235 .... Vol V p 186
- s 244 .... Vol III p 120
- s 281 .... Vol III p 523
- s 285 .... Vol III p 120, 509, 548
- .... Vol IV p 82, Vol V p 388
- s 297 .... 2001 p 137

Companies Act 1990
- s 8 .... Vol V p 226
- s 14 .... Vol V p 226
- s 19 .... 2000 p 261
- s 21 .... 2000 p 261
- s 134 .... Vol V p 388
- s 227 .... Vol V p 226

Constitution of Ireland 1937
- .... Vol V p 70
- Article 6 .... 1998 p 120
- Article 15 .... 1998 p 120
- Article 18 .... 1998 p 120
- Article 28 .... 1998 p 120
- Article 29.3 .... 2001 p 137
- Article 30 .... 1998 p 120
- Article 34 .... Vol V p 70, 1999 p 65
- Article 34(1) .... Vol III p 590
- Article 34.3.4 .... Vol III p 419
- Article 37 .... 1999 p 65
- Article 38 .... 2001 p 137
- Article 38.1 .... Vol III p 387, 419
- Article 38.2 .... Vol III p 419
- Article 38.5 .... Vol III p 419

Constitution of Ireland 1937 (contd)

Article 40 .... Vol V p 70, 614, 1998 p 120, 1999 p 65
Article 40.1 .... Vol III p 188, Vol IV p 437, Vol V p 481, 2001 p 137
Article 40.3 .... Vol III p 188, 590
.... Vol IV p 437
Article 41 .... Vol III p 188, Vol IV p 437
.... Vol V p 614
Article 43 .... Vol V p 70, 2001 p 137
Article 50 .... Vol V p 481, 1998 p 120

Conveyancing Act 1881
   s 14 .... Vol V p 589

Conveyancing Act 1891
   s 7 .... Vol V p 181

Copyright Act 1963
   s 1 .... Vol IV p 314
   s 17 .... Vol IV p 314

Corporation Tax Act 1976
   .... Vol III p 611
   s 1 .... Vol III p 53
      (1) .... Vol V p 107, 1998 p 183
   s 2 .... Vol IV p 415
   s 4 .... Vol III p 670
   s 6 .... Vol III p 553, Vol V p 107, 1998 p 183
   s 8 .... Vol I p 330
      (1) .... Vol IV p 12
      (2) .... Vol IV p 12
   s 9 (1) .... Vol V p 107, 1998 p 183
   s 10 .... Vol V p 107, 1998 p 183
   s 11 .... Vol III p 553
      (i) .... Vol V p 107, 1998 p 183
      (iii) .... Vol V p 107, 1998 p 183
   s 13 .... Vol V p 107, 1998 p 183
   s 15 .... Vol I p 447, Vol II p 429, Vol V p 680
      (1) .... 2000 p 76
      (6) .... 2000 p 76
   s 16(1) .... Vol III p 363
      (2) .... Vol III p 340
   s 21 .... Vol IV p 91, Vol V p 200
   s 25 .... Vol I p 86, Vol III p 340
   s 27(1) .... Vol III p 363
   s 28 .... Vol III p 430
   s 37 .... Vol IV p 475
   s 52 .... Vol IV p 401
   s 54 .... Vol III p 304, 2001 p 80
   s 58 .... Vol IV p 633, 2001 p 80
      (3) .... Vol III p 229, Vol V p 221
   s 59 .... Vol IV p 633

Corporation Tax Act 1976 (contd)
>s 78 .... Vol III p 304
>s 83 .... Vol III p 246
>s 84 .... Vol III p 246
>>(1) .... Vol III p 517
>s 87(8) .... Vol III p 246
>s 100 .... Vol III p 517
>s 101 .... Vol III p 517
>s 107 .... 2000 p 76
>s 131 .... Vol III p 373
>s 140 .... Vol III p 533
>s 142 .... Vol III p 553
>s 143 .... Vol III p 120
>s 145 .... 1999 p 72, 2000 p 236
>s 146 .... Vol III p 559, 644, Vol V p 138, 2000 p 76
>s 147 .... Vol III p 553
>s 151 .... Vol III p 246
>s 155 .... Vol IV p 12, Vol III p 246
>.. Vol V p 226
>s 156 .... Vol V p 226
>>(1)(*b*) .... Vol III p 246
>s 162 .... Vol III p 211
>s 182 .... Vol III p 363
>s 184 .... Vol III p 363
>s 307 .... Vol III p 253
>Sch 1 para 10 .... Vol IV p 91
>Sch 3 s 164 .... Vol III p 56

Courts of Justice Act 1936
>s 38 .... Vol V p 322
>s 65 .... Vol V p 195

Courts (Supplemental Provisions) Act 1961
>.. Vol III p 641, Vol IV p 395
>s 52 .... Vol V p 221

Courts Acts 1924-1981
>.. Vol III p 641

Courts Act 1981
>s 22 .... Vol III p 403
>>(1) .... Vol V p 322

Court Officers Act 1926
>... Vol V p 186, 195

Courts of Justice Act 1924
>s 38(3) .... Vol IV p 437
>s 94 .... Vol III p 387

Courts of Justice Act 1936
>s 38 .... Vol V p 322
>s 65 .... Vol V p 186, 195

228

Courts of Justice Act 1936 (contd)
    s 76 .... Vol IV p 278

Courts of Justice Act 1961
    .... Vol V p 221

Criminal Assets Bureau Act 1996
    s 8 .... 1999 p 65, 2001 p 137

Criminal Justice Act 1988 (UK)
    s 71 .... Vol V p 45
    s 77(8) .... Vol V p 45

Criminal Justice Act 1993
    s 2 .... 2000 p 274

Customs Consolidation Act 1876
    .... 2001 p 137
    s 186 .... Vol IV p 395
    s 204 .... Vol IV p 386
    s 205 .... 2001 p 58

Customs and Inland Revenue Regulation Act 1890
    s 30 .... Vol IV p 386

Customs Act 1956
    .... Vol V p 348

Customs (Temporary Provisions) Act 1948
    .... 2001 p 137

Customs and Excise (Miscellaneous Provisions) Act 1988
    s 5(1) .... 2001 p 58

Debtors (Ireland) Act 1840
    s 26 .... Vol V p 322

Domicile and Recognition of Foreign Divorces Act 1986
    .... Vol IV p 437

Double Taxation Relief (Taxes on Income and Capital Gains) [UK] Order 1976 (SI 319/1976)
    .... Vol V p 129
    Article 15 .... Vol V p 54
    Article 18(2) .... Vol V p 54

Enforcement of Court Orders Act 1926
    s 2 .... Vol IV p 86
    s 13 .... Vol IV p 86

Ethics in Public Office Act 1995
    .... 1998 p 120

Excise Management Act 1827
    s 86 .... Vol IV p 278
    s 90 .... Vol IV p 278

Excise Collection and Management Act 1841(4 & 5 Vict c 20)
    s 24 .... Vol III p 265

Executive Power (Consequential Provisions) Act 1937
.... 1998 p 120
Extradition Act 1965
   s 50 .... 1998 p 76
Farm Tax Act 1985
.... Vol III p 229
   s 3 .... Vol V p 288
   s 9 .... Vol V p 288
Finance Act 1894
   s 1 .... Vol V p 600
   s 2(1)(a) .... Vol V p 600
   s 5(3) .... Vol V p 526
   s 7(5) .... Vol V p 294, 532, 577
   s 10 .... Vol V p 577
   s 22(2)(a) .... Vol V p 600
Finance (1909-1910) Act 1910
   s 59(2) .... Vol V p 589
   s 74(5) .... Vol IV p 187
Finance Act 1910 Pt V
   ss 73-75 .... Vol V p 570
Finance Act 1915
   s 21(2) .... 2000 p 76
   s 41(1) .... 2000 p 76
Finance Act (No 2) 1915
   s 45(5) .... Vol I p 1
   Sch IV Pt I
     rule 1 .... Vol I p 240
   Sch IV Pt III .... Vol I p 34
Finance Act 1918
   s 33 .... 2000 p 76
   s 35 .... Vol I p 28
Finance Act 1920
   s 16 .... Vol II p 596
   s 17 .... Vol V p 539
   s 52 .... Vol III p 56
     (2) .... Vol I p 70, 108
       (I) .... Vol I p 359
         (a) .... Vol I p 108, 119
         (b) .... Vol I p 330
   s 53 .... Vol I p 629, Vol II p 382
.... Vol III p 56
     (2)(b) .... Vol II p 412
     (h) .... Vol II p 195
   s 54(1) .... Vol II p 130
   Pt V .... Vol I p 627

Finance Act 1921
    s 21 .... Vol IV p 386
    s 30(1)(*c*) .... Vol I p 383
    s 53 .... Vol I p 315, Vol II p 195
    Sch 2 Pt II
        rule 1 .... Vol I p 130

Finance Act 1922
    s 18 .... Vol II pp 393, 452
    s 20 .... Vol II p 82
        (1) .... Vol II p 352
        (1)(*c*) .... Vol I p 411

Finance Act 1923
    s 17 .... Vol V p 539

Finance Act 1924
    s 10 .... Vol I p 656

Finance Act 1925
    s 11 .... Vol V p 565
    s 12 .... Vol I pp 249, 259

Finance Act 1926
    s 24(*a*) .... Vol IV p 395
    s 25(1) .... Vol IV p 395
    Sch 1 Pt II .... Vol II p 491
        s 1(3) .... Vol II p 304
        s 2(2) .... Vol II p 304

Finance Act 1929
    s 5 .... Vol I p 571
    s 8(1) .... Vol I p 146
    s 9 .... Vol II p 515
        (2) .... Vol I p 146
    s 10 .... Vol I p 563, Vol II p 304
    .... Vol III p 568
    s 11 .... Vol I pp 563, Vol II p 393
    .... Vol II pp 304, 464, 491
    s 12 .... Vol II pp 55, 115
    s 14 .... Vol II p 482
    s 17 .... Vol I p 618
    s 18 .... Vol II p 304
    s 33(1)(*d*) .... Vol II p 25
    Sch 1 Pt II .... Vol I p 393, Vol II p 61
    Sch 2 para (3) .... Vol II p 304

Finance Act 1932
    s 3(4) .... Vol V p 565
    s 4 .... Vol I p 393
    s 46 .... Vol V p 539

Finance Act 1935
- s 6 .... VOL I p 583
- (1) .... Vol II p 472
- s 21 .... Vol V p 696
- (8) .... Vol IV p 162

Finance Act 1937
- s 2 .... Vol II p 82
- (1) .... Vol II p 352

Finance Act 1939
- s 3 .... Vol V p 565
- s 7 .... Vol II p 315

Finance Act 1940
- s 3 .... Vol V p 393
- s 18 .... Vol IV p 386

Finance Act 1941
- s 32 .... Vol V p 589
- s 36(4) .... Vol II p 175
- s 39 .... Vol II p 19

Finance Act 1944
- s 14 .... Vol II p 175

Finance Act 1946
- s 24 .... Vol II p 195

Finance Act (No 2) 1947
- s 13(1) .... 1998 p 169
- (4) .... 1998 p 169
- (5) .... 1998 p 169
- s 23 .... Vol V p 570

Finance Act 1956
- Pt V .... Vol II p 602

Finance Act 1958
- s 23 .... Vol IV p 323
- s 24 .... Vol IV p 323
- s 25 .... Vol IV p 323
- s 26 .... Vol IV p 323

Finance Act (No 2) 1959
- .... Vol IV p 82
- s 13(1) .... Vol II p 588

Finance Act 1962
- s 22 .... Vol IV p 162

Finance Act 1963
- s 34(4)(*d*)(i) .... Vol III p 419
- (iii) .... Vol III p 419

Finance Act 1964
- s 26 .... Vol III p 56

Finance Act 1965
- s 23 .... 2000 p 114

Finance Act 1967
- s 12 .... Vol V p 393
- s 138-143 .... Vol V p 393
- s 153 .... Vol V p 393
- s 241 .... Vol V p 317
- s 439 .... Vol V p 393

Finance Act 1968
- s 7 .... Vol III p 590
- s 8 .... Vol III p 590, 1998 p 59
- s 11 .... 1998 p 59
- s 14 .... Vol IV p 91
- s 43(1) .... Vol IV p 170

Finance Act 1969
- s 2 .... Vol III p 496, Vol V p 98
- s 3 .... Vol V p 393
- s 65(1) .... Vol III p 533

Finance Act 1970
- s 17 .... Vol IV p 269, 304
- s 20 .... Vol III p 484
- s 24 .... Vol IV p 187
- s 26 .... Vol IV p 68

Finance Act 1971
- s 22 .... Vol IV p 22
- s 25 .... Vol IV p 22
- s 26 .... Vol V p 200

Finance Act 1972
- ss 14-25 .... Vol IV p 340
- Sch 1 .... Vol IV p 340

Finance Act 1973
- s 34 .... Vol III p 670

Finance Act 1974
- s 8 .... Vol V p 393
- s 13 .... Vol IV p 1
- (1) .... Vol III p 319
- s 15 .... Vol IV p 1
- s 17 .... Vol IV p 1
- s 21 .... Vol IV p 1
- s 22 .... Vol V p 680
- s 31 .... Vol III p 246
- s 59 .... Vol III p 356

Finance Act 1975
- s 12 .... Vol IV p 1
- s 25 .... Vol V p 348

233

Finance Act 1975 (contd)

    s 31 .... Vol I p 130, Vol III pp 51, 178
        (1) .... Vol IV p 304
        (2) .... Vol IV p 135

Finance Act 1976

    s 21 .... Vol IV p 269
    s 26 .... Vol III p 51
    s 30 .... Vol IV pp 62, 91
        (4) .... Vol V p 322
    s 41 .... 2000 p 59
    s 46 .... Vol IV p 162, Vol V p 696

Finance Act 1977

    s 43 .... Vol III p 611
    Pt V Sch 1 .... Vol III p 611

Finance Act 1978

    .... Vol V p 322
    s 46 .... Vol IV p 91
    ss 138-142 .... Vol V p 614

Finance Act 1980

    s 1 .... Vol V p 393
    s 2 .... Vol V p 393
    s 8 .... Vol V p 129
    s 18 .... Vol V p 129
    s 21 .... Vol III p 188
    s 38-51 .... Vol V p 226
    s 39 .... Vol III p 611, Vol IV p 35
    .... Vol IV pp 361, 526
        (1), (2) and (5) .... 1999 p 72, 2000 p 236
    s 41(2) .... Vol III p 304, Vol IV p 35
    .... Vol IV p 466
        (4) .... Vol IV p 466
        (8) .... Vol V p 376, 1998 p 99
    s 42 .... Vol IV p 361, Vol V p 221
    s 57 .... Vol IV p 478
    s 79 .... Vol III p 73
    Pt I Ch VI .... Vol III p 441, Vol V p 21

Finance Act 1982

    Sch 2 .... Vol IV p 35
    s 4. .... Vol IV p 323
    s 26 .... Vol IV p 35
    s 69(1) .... Vol IV p 395

Finance Act 1983

    s 3 .... Vol IV p 437
    s 9 .... Vol III p 533
    s 18 .... Vol III p 153, Vol V p 348
    s 19 .... Vol I p 195, Vol II p 291, Vol V p 424

Finance Act 1983 (contd)
- s 56 .... Vol III p 120
- s 94 .... Vol III p 387, Vol IV p 395
  - (2) .... Vol IV p 478
  - (4) .... Vol IV p 478
  - (9) .... Vol IV p 478
- s 95 .... Vol III p 127

Finance Act 1983 (No 15)
- s 9 .... Vol III p 533

Finance Act 1984
- s 12 .... 2000 p 58

Finance Act 1986
- s 46 .... Vol III p 253
- s 48(2) .... Vol V p 210
- s 96(1) .... Vol IV p 187

Finance Act 1987
- s 14 .... Vol V p 213
- s 15 .... Vol V p 213
- s 17-19 .... Vol V p 213
- s 53 .... Vol IV p 278

Finance Act 1988
- s 1 .... Vol V p 424
- s 7 .... Vol V p 424
- s 16 .... Vol V p 210
- s 54 .... 2000 p 216
- s 72 .... 2000 p 105
- s 73 .... Vol V p 70

Finance Act 1989
- s 86 .... Vol V p 6
- s 92 .... 2000 p 55

Finance Act 1990
- s 14 .... Vol V p 213
- s 26 .... Vol V p 213
- s 41(1) .... Vol V p 376, 1998 p 99
  - (5) .... 1999 p 72, 2000 p 236

Finance Act 1992
- s 15 .... Vol V p 472
- s 242 .... Vol IV p 419

Finance Act 1995
- s 10 .... Vol V p 472
- s 105 .... 2000 p 59

Finance Act (Miscellaneous Provisions) 1956
- .... 2001 p 80
- s 13(3) .... Vol III p 452

Finance Act (Miscellaneous Provisions) 1968
- s 17 .... Vol II p 667
- s 18 .... Vol III p 271
  - (2) .... Vol III p 198

Finance Act (Miscellaneous Provisions) 1968 (No 7)
- s 17 .... Vol III p 9

Finance (Excise Duties) (Vehicles) Act 1952
.... Vol IV p 170

Finance (Taxation of Profits of Certain Mines) Act 1974
.... Vol IV p 91, 2001 p 80

Fraudulent Conveyances Act 1635
.... Vol III p 706

Garda Síochána Pension Order 1981
.... 1998 p 113

Holidays (Employees) Act 1973
.... Vol III p 505

Health Act 1970
- s 52 .... 2000 p 65
- s 53 .... 2000 p 65
- s 55 .... 2000 p 65

Imposition of Duties Act 1957
.... Vol IV p 162

Industrial Development Act 1969
- s 33 .... Vol IV p 22

Interpretation Act 1937
- s 11 .... Vol III pp 559, 644

Income Tax Act 1843
.... 1998 p 183

Income Tax Act 1918
- Sch B .... Vol II p 636
  - rule 8 .... Vol II p 1, Vol II p 241
- Sch D .... Vol I p 330, 474, 496, 515
  .... Vol II p 32, 45, 140, 164
  .... 360, 374, 419
- Sch D Case I .... Vol I p 427, 629
  .... Vol II p 211, 291, 315, 500,
  - rule 3 & 6 602
- Sch D Cases I & II .... Vol I p 86
  - rule 1(1) .... Vol I p 642
  - rule 2 .... Vol II p 382
  - rule 3 .... Vol I p 375, 642, Vol II p 515
    - (*a*) .... Vol II p 222
    - (*d*) and (g) .... Vol II p 267
  - rule 4 .... Vol II p 115

Income Tax Act 1918 (contd)
- rule 7 .... Vol I p 43 rule 11
- .... Vol II p 55
- Sch D Cases II & VI .... Vol I p 195
- Sch D Case III .... Vol I pp 45, 393, 491
- .... Vol II pp 15, 393, 464, 568, 592
  - rule 2 (s 17) .... Vol II p 304
  - rule 4 .... Vol III p 19
  - rule 5 .... Vol II p 222
- Sch D Case IV
  - rule 2(*a*) .... Vol I p 259
- Sch D Case V
  - rule 3 .... Vol I p 249
- Sch D Case VI .... Vol II p 204, 261
- Sch E .... Vol I p 155, 601
- .... Vol II p 68, 452
  - rule 1 .... Vol I p 214, 618
  - rule 5 .... Vol I p 214
  - rule 7 .... Vol II p 261
  - rule 9 .... Vol I p 64, Vol II pp 366, 460
- Case VI .... Vol II p 154
  - rule 16 .... Vol I pp 115, 563, Vol II p 75
  - rule 21 .... Vol I p 487
- s 5 .... Vol I p 231
- s 16 .... Vol V p 565
- s 25 .... Vol I p 221
- s 29 .... Vol V p 565
- s 31 .... 2001 p 137
- s 33 (1) .... Vol I p 447, Vol II p 429
- s 100(2) .... Vol I p 642
- s 133 .... Vol I p 571
- s 137 .... Vol I p 571
- s 149 .... Vol I p 1, 571, 656
  - (1)(*e*) .... Vol II p 60
- s 186 .... Vol II p 1, 241
- s 187 .... Vol II pp 1, 241
- s 202 .... Vol I p 221
- s 209 .... Vol I p 642, Vol II p 515
- Sch 1 .... Vol III p 56

Income Tax Act 1967
- .... Vol II pp 366, 460, Vol III p 1
- Sch E .... Vol III p 467
- s 1 .... Vol III p 559, 644
- .... Vol IV p 73
- s 4 .... Vol V p 108, 1998 p 183
- s 7(*a*) .... Vol III p 533
- s 11 .... Vol III p 9
  - (1) .... Vol V p 496

237

Income Tax Act 1967 (contd)

s 12	Vol III p 9
s 17	Vol II p 641
s 25	Vol II p 393
s 52	Vol V p 108, 1998 p 183
s 53	Vol I pp 1, 28, 45, 115, 119, 207, 231, 231
	Vol I pp 318, 427, 474, 629
	Vol II pp 60, 164, 204, 304, 393, 491, 592, 614
	Vol III pp 165, 484, 568, Vol IV pp 45, 73, 135, 1998 p 183
	Vol V p 108
s 53(1)	Vol III pp 559, 644
s 54	Vol V p 21
s 57	Vol I p 130
s 58	Vol I p 146
	Vol I p 91
s 61	Vol I pp 104, 375, 503, 642
	Vol II pp 32, 45, 267, 281, 360
	Vol II pp 382, 500, 515, 602
	Vol IV p 187, 425, Vol V p 496
	2000 p 55, 2000 p 56, 2001 p 118
s 61(*a*)	Vol IV p 22
(*e*)	Vol V p 138
(*f*)	Vol V p 138
s 62(2)	Vol IV p 304
s 76	Vol I pp 249, 259, Vol II p 304, Vol V p 481
s 80	Vol IV p 187
s 81	Vol IV p 187
(5)(*d*)	Vol III p 95, Vol V p 680
(6)(a)(i)	Vol V p 680
s 83	Vol IV p 187
s 91	Vol IV p 187
s 105	Vol III p 477, 553
s 109	1998 p 113
s 110	Vol I pp 214, 601, 656, Vol II pp 261, 452
	Vol III p 43, 505, Vol IV p 45
	Vol IV p 221, 391, 407, 2000 p 114, 2001 p 104
s 111	Vol IV p 221
s 114	Vol I p 618, Vol IV pp 233, 407
	Vol V p 134
s 115	Vol IV p 221
(1)(*a*)	Vol V p 134
s 117	Vol II p 452, Vol IV p 323
s 118	Vol IV p 323
s 119	Vol IV p 323
s 120	Vol IV p 323
s 126	Vol III p 590, Vol V p 322
s 127	Vol II p 641
s 128	Vol II p 641

Income Tax Act 1967 (contd)

s 129	Vol III p 590
s 131	Vol III p 590
s 133(1)	Vol II p 588
s 138	Vol V p 129, 614
s 146	Vol V p 496
s 161(1)	Vol III p 670
s 162	Vol III p 290, 298
s 169	Vol V p 348
(4)	Vol III p 387
s 172	Vol IV p 478
(4)	Vol V p 348
s 174(1)	Vol IV p 332
(*a*)	Vol V p 265
s 176	Vol IV p 221
s 178(1)	Vol III p 387
s 184	1999 p 65
(2)	Vol III p 533
s 186	Vol I p 34, Vol II p 627
	Vol IV p 187
s 192	Vol IV p 188, Vol V p 129, 614
s 193	Vol I p 115
s 194	Vol I p 563, Vol II p 75
	Vol V p 424
s 195	Vol V p 424, 614
(1)	Vol V p 129
s 196	Vol V p 614
s 197	Vol V p 614
s 198	Vol V p 614
s 200	Vol I p 183
s 207	Vol III p 553
s 212	Vol III p 553
s 220(5)	Vol II p 661
s 224	1998 p 113
s 238	Vol III p 387
s 239	Vol V p 108, 1998 p 183
s 240	Vol III p 387
s 241	Vol III p 113, 219
	Vol IV p 68, 425, Vol V p 6
(1)	Vol V p 200
(5)	Vol III p 253
s 244	Vol IV p 91
s 245	Vol IV p 91
s 252	Vol III p 253
s 254	Vol III p 65
s 255	Vol III p 65, 661, 2000 p 56
(1)(d)	Vol V p 357
s 282	Vol III p 253

Income Tax Act 1967 (contd)

s 296 .... Vol III p 253, 387
s 300 .... 2001 p 137
s 307 .... Vol III p 332
s 333 .... Vol I p 542, 1998 p 66
s 334 .... Vol I p 383, 1998 p 66
s 348 .... Vol I p 538
s 349 .... Vol III p 28
s 361 .... Vol III p 246
s 416 .... Vol I p 221, 571, 618, 629
.... Vol II p 55, Vol III pp 332, 577
.... Vol IV pp 62, 73, 91, 125, 187
s 416 .... 1999 p 65
   (6) .... Vol III p 533, Vol V p 210
s 428 .... Vol III p 159, 198, 611, 1998 p 111
.... Vol IV p 401, 505
.... Vol V p 54, 76, 163, 221, 481, 496,
.... 1999 p 72, 2000 p 76,114,, 236,, 247, 2001 p 104
s 428(*b*) .... Vol III p 340
   (9) .... Vol IV p 91, Vol V p 322
s 429 .... Vol II p 374, Vol III p 219
.... Vol IV pp 125, 401, 407, 505
s 430 .... Vol I p 487, Vol II p 332
.... Vol III pp 159, 198, 496, 559, 611, 644
.... Vol IV pp 62, 125, 401, 425, 505
.... Vol V p 54, 138, 221, 481
s 438 .... Vol I p 411
s 439 .... Vol III p 242
s 440 .... Vol II p 82
s 443 .... Vol II p 352
.... Vol IV p 221
s 448 .... Vol II p 82
s 478 .... Vol V p 424
s 485 .... Vol III p 533, 590, 1999 p 65
s 488 .... Vol III p 577
s 496 .... Vol III p 559, 644
s 498 .... Vol V p 322
s 500 .... Vol III p 387, 641
.... Vol IV p 395, 478
s 501 .... Vol III p 577, Vol IV p 478
s 502 .... Vol IV p 478
s 503 .... Vol IV p 395
s 506 .... Vol IV p 478
s 507 .... Vol IV p 478
s 508 .... Vol III p 387
s 527 .... Vol IV p 73
s 542(2) .... Vol V p 348

Income Tax Act 1967 (contd)
    s 550 .... Vol V p 322
        (1) .... Vol IV p 91
        (2A)(*c*) .... Vol IV p 62
    Pt XXVI .... Vol III p 577
    Sch 2 para 3 .... Vol I p 64
Income Tax Act 1970 (UK)
    s 130(*f*) .... Vol V p 138
Inland Revenue Regulations Act 1890
    s 21 .... Vol V p 691
Labour Exchange Act 1909
    .... Vol III p 253, Vol IV p 45
Limited Partnerships Act 1907
    .... Vol III p 253
Local Government (Planning and Development) Act 1963
    s 5 .... Vol V p 357
    s 528(6) .... Vol V p 357
Local Government (Planning and Development) Act 1976
    .... Vol IV p 543
Local Government (Planning and Development) Act 1982
    .... Vol IV p 543
Local Government (Tolls Road) Act 1979 .... 2000 p 287
Minerals Development Act 1940
    s 14 .... Vol V p 696
Offences against the State (Amendment) Act 1985
    .... 2001 p 137
Partnership Act 1890
    .... Vol III p 253
Petty Sessions (Ireland) Act 1851
    s 22 .... Vol IV p 278
    s 42 .... Vol IV p 278
Poor Law Act 1834 (4 & 5 Wm 4 c 76)
    s 86 .... Vol V p 560
Poor Relief (Ireland) Act 1838 (1 & 2 Vict c 56)
    s 96 .... Vol V p 560
Preferential Payments in Bankruptcy (Ireland) Act 1889
    .... 1998 p 59
Proceeds of Crime Act 1996
    ss 2, 3, 4, 7, 8, 9 .... 2001 p 137
Prosecution of Offences Act 1974
    .... Vol III p 641
    s 3 .... Vol IV p 395, Vol V p 691

Racing Board and Racecourses Act 1945
    s 4 .... Vol IV p 73
    ss 14-16 .... Vol IV p 73
    s 27(1) .... Vol IV p 73
Revenue Act 1898 (61 & 62 Vict c 46)
    s 13 .... Vol V p 560
Revenue Act 1911
    s 15 .... Vol V p 570
Road Traffic Act 1988 (UK)
    s 157 .... 2000 p 65
Roads Act 1993 .... 2000 p 287
Sale of goods Act 1893
    .... Vol V p 21
Scrap Iron (Control of Exhaust) Act 1938 .... 2001 p 137
Sea Fisheries Protection Act 1933
    s 9 .... Vol IV p 401
Settled Land Act 1882
    .... Vol V p 526, 600
Social Welfare Act 1952
    s 27(2) .... Vol V p 472
Social Welfare Act 1976
    s 18(1) .... Vol V p 472
Social Welfare (Consolidation) Act 1981
    .... Vol IV p 113
    s 2 .... Vol V p 472
        (4) .... Vol IV p 378
    s 5(1) .... Vol IV p 378
    s 9 .... Vol III p 509
        (1),(2) .... Vol IV p 378
    s 10 .... Vol III p 509, 1998 p 59
        (1),(3) .... Vol IV p 378
    s 92 .... Vol IV p 221, Vol V p 472, 1998 p 111
    s 94 .... Vol IV p 221, 1998 p 111
    s 95 .... Vol V p 472, 1998 p 111
    s 111 .... Vol V p 239
    s 114 .... Vol IV p 391
    s 298 .... Vol V p 239
    s 299 .... Vol III p 436, Vol V p 239
Social Welfare Act 1982
    s 2 .... Vol V p 472
Social Welfare (Consolidation) Act 1993
    .... Vol V p 95
    s 16
        (1) .... 1998 p 59

Social Welfare (Consolidation) Act 1993 (contd)
> s 16 (2) ....1998 p 59
> s 271..2001 p 126
> s 301 ....1998 p 59

Social Welfare (No 2) 1993
> Part III ....2001 p 126

Stamp Duties (Ireland) Act 1842
> s 38...Vol V p 539

Stamp Duties Act 1854
> s 1...Vol V p 570

Stamp Act 1870
> s 17...Vol V p 1
> ss 96-99..Vol V p 570

Stamp Duties Management Act 1891 (54 & 55 Vict c 38)
> s 10 ....Vol V p 560

Stamp Act 1891
> s 1... Vol IV p 187
> s 3... Vol IV p 187
> s 12...Vol V p 570
> s 13... Vol IV p 367, Vol V p 181
> s 14...Vol V p 363
>   (4)...Vol V p 1
> s 23...Vol V p 570
> s 54... Vol IV p 187, 367
> ss 59-61..Vol V p 570
> ss 175-78..Vol V p 570

Succession Act 1965
> ....Vol III p 559
> 9(2)...Vol V p 600
> 10 ....Vol V p 367
> 67(1)...Vol V p 367
> 111 ....Vol V p 600
>   (1)...Vol V p 367
> 115 ....Vol V p 367, 600
> 120 ....Vol V p 367
> Pt VIII ....Vol V p 271

Succession Duty Act 1853
> s 18...Vol V p 539

Taxes Consolidation Act 1997
> s 81(2) .... 1999 p 82
> s 86(i) ....2001 p 118
> s 112 ....2000 p 57
> s 271 ....2000 p 57
> s 552 ....2000 p 55
> s 573 ....2000 p 55

Taxes Consolidation Act 1997 (contd)
    s 669 .... 2000 p 57
    s 849 .... 2000 p 216
    s 933 .... 1999 p 65
    s 955(2)(a) .... 1999 p 65
    s 966 .... 2000 p 216
        (5)(a) .... 1999 p 65
    s 997 .... 2000 p 61
    s 998 .... 2000 p 216
    s 1002
        (8) .... 2000 p 216
    s 1017 .... 2000 p 58
    s 1052 .... 2000 p 274
    s 1078 .... 2000 p 274
    s 1082 .... 2000 p 274
    s 1097 .... 1999 p 65

Taxes Management Act 1880
    s 59 .... Vol I p 1

Tribunal of Inquiry (Evidence) Act 1921
    .... 1998 p 120

Tribunal of Inquiry (Evidence) (Amendment) Act 1979
    .... 1998 p 120

Unemployment Assistance Act 1933
    .... Vol III p 253, Vol IV p 45

Unfair Dismissals Act 1977
    .... Vol V p 239

Value Added Tax Act 1972 (No 22)
    .... 2001 p 72
    Sch 1 .... 2000 p 58
        (12) .... Vol III p 680
    Sch 2 .... 2000 p 58
    Sch 4 .... Vol IV p 117
    Sch 6 .... Vol IV p 349, 2000 p 58
    s 1(1) .... Vol III p 611
    s 2 .... Vol IV p 117, 314
    s 3   (1)(*f*) .... Vol V p 76
        (5) (b)(iii) .... 2000 p 247
    s 4 .... 2000 p 58
        (4) .... Vol V p 76
    s 5 .... Vol IV p 117, 314
    s 8 .... Vol V p 61
    s 9 .... Vol V p 61
    s 10 .... Vol III p 332, Vol V p 418
        (9) .... Vol V p 76

Value Added Tax Act 1972 (contd)
 s 10 (10) .... Vol V p 76
 s 11 .... Vol IV p 117, Vol V p 418
 s 12 .... Vol V p 76, 412
 s 16 .... Vol V p 412
 s 19 .... Vol V p 412
 s 20(1) .... Vol V p 412
 s 25 .... Vol III p 332
 .... Vol V p 76, 2000 p 247
 s 26 .... Vol IV p 478
 s 27 .... Vol IV p 386, 478
 s 32 .... Vol V p 76
 s 43 .... Vol V p 418

Value Added Tax Act (Amendment) Act 1978 (No 34)
 s 3 .... Vol IV p 314

Value Added Tax Act (UK) 1983
 s 39(3) .... Vol V p 45

Waiver of Certain Tax, Interest & Penalties Act 1993
 s 2 .... Vol V p 210
  (2) .... 1999 p 65
 s 3 .... Vol V p 210
  (6) .... 1999 p 65

Wills Act 1837
 .... Vol V p 271

Regulations and Statutory Instruments

Agricultural Levies (Export Control) Regulations 1983 (UK)
 .... 1998 p 76
EC Council Directive No 77/388/EEC
 .... Vol V p 76
EC Council Directive No 81/77/EEC
 .... 1998 p 76
EC Council Directive No 83/182/EEC of 28 March 1983
 .... Vol IV p 512
EEC Regulations
 804/68 and 2682/72 .... Vol IV p 492
EEC Council Regulations
 729/1970, 974/1971 and 667/85 .... 1998 p 76
European Communities (Companies) Regulations 1973
 SI 163/1973 .... Vol V p 226
European Communities (Exemption from Import Charges of
 Certain Vehicles etc Temporarily Imported) Regulations 1983
 SI 422/1983 .... Vol IV p 512
Farm Tax (Adjusted Acreage) Regulations
 SI 321/1986 .... Vol V p 288

Farm Tax Regulations 1986
    SI 237/1986 .... Vol V p 288
Finance Act 1966
    SI 152/1970 .... Vol III p 73
    SI 160/1979 .... Vol III p 73
Hydrocarbon Oil (Rebated Oil) Regulations 1961 Article 8,
    FA 1959 SI 28/1960 .... Vol IV p 113
Imposition of Duties Order 1975
    SI 221/1975 .... Vol IV p 162, Vol V p 696
Imposition of Duties (No 236) (Excise Duties on Motor Vehicles etc) 1979
    SI 57/1979 para 12... Vol IV pp 170, 512
    SI 353/1984 .... Vol IV p 512
Income Tax (Employments) Regulations 1960
    .... Vol III p 590, Vol V p 322
    rule 2 .... Vol IV p 113
    SI No 28/1960... Vol II p 588, Vol III p 590
Social Welfare (Collection of Employment Contributions by the
Collector General) Regulations 1979
    SI 77/1979 .... Vol III p 467, 509
Social Welfare (Collection of Employment Contributions) Regulations 1989
    SI 302/1989. .... Vol IV p 378
Superior Court Rules
    SI 15/1986
    Order 84
        r 20(4) .... Vol V p 363
        r 25(5) .... Vol V p 363
    Order 99
        r 1 .... 2001 p 97
Supreme Court & High Court (Fees) Order 1984
    SI 19/1984 as amended by SI 36/1985 .... Vol III p 530
Treaty of Rome
    Article 38 .... 1998 p 76
    Article 39 .... 1998 p 76
    Article 177 .... Vol III p 73
    Article 235 .... 1998 p 76
VAT Regulations 1979
    SI 63/1979 .... Vol V p 76
VAT (Refund of Tax)(No 13) Order 1980
    SI 263/1980 .... Vol IV p 170
VAT (Exported goods) Regulations 1992
    (SI 438/1992) .... Vol V p 412
VAT Registration Regulation 1993
    SI 30/1993 .... Vol V p 61

Destination Table (Taxes Consolidation Act 1997)

This table may be used to trace the present location of older legislation as re-enacted in the Taxes Consolidation Act, 1997.

Former Enactment   *Destination in TCA 1997*

Finance Act 1928 (1928 No 11)
   s 34 (2) .... s 872(1)

Income Tax Act 1967 (1967 No 7)
   Pt I
   s 1 .... Definitions of "assurance company", ... ss 2(1), 3(1)
                     "commencement of this Act",
                     "municipal rate", "National Debt
                     Commissioners" and "repealed
                     enactments" in ITA 1967 s 1(1)
                     unnecessary (obsolete)
       (2) .... Unnecessary (construction)
       (3) .... Unnecessary (interpretation)
       (4) .... Unnecessary (interpretation)
       (5) .... Rep by CTA 1976 s 164 and Sch 3 Pt II
       (6) .... Unnecessary (obsolete)
   2 .... s 3(2), (3)
   3 .... s 1(2)
   4 .... s 12
   5 .... s 14(2)
   6 .... s 14(1)
   7 .... Rep by FA 1972 s 46(1) and Sch 4 Pt I
   8 .... s 1087
   Pt II
   ss 9-42......... Rep by FA 1969 s 65(1) and Sch 5 Pt I
   43 .... Rep by FA 1996 s 132(2) and Sch 5 Pt II
   44 .... Rep by FA 1969 s 65(1) and Sch 5 Pt I
   45 .... Rep by FA 1969 s 65(1) and Sch 5 Pt I
   46 .... Rep by FA 1997s 146(2) and Sch 9 Pt II
   Pt III
   s 47 .... s 17(1)
   48 .... s 33
   49 (1), (2) .... s 34
   49 (3) .... Rep by DR&IA 1967 s 4 and Sch 6
   50 .... s 35
   51 .... ss 17(2), 32
   Pt IV
   s 52 .... s 18(1), (3)
   53 .... s 18(2), (3)
   54 (1) .... s 654
      (2)(a) .... s 655(3)
      (2)(b),(3), . Rep by FA 1969 s 65(1) and Sch 5 Pt I
      (4)
   55 .... s 54
   56 (1)-(3) .... s 56
      (4)-(6) .... Rep by FA 1969 s 65(1) and Sch 5 Pt I
   57 .... s 81(1)
   58 (1) .... s 65(1)
      (2)-(4) .... s 66
      (5), (6) .... s 67

Former Enactment   *Destination in TCA 1997*

Income Tax Act 1967 (1967 No 7) (contd)

```
s 58A......... (s 58A inserted by FA 1995 s 19)................... s 68
  59 ............................................................ s 69
  60 ............................................................ s 65(2)-(4)
  61 ............................................................ s 81(2)
  62 (1)(a), (b) ................................................. s 89(2)
     (b)(proviso).................................................. s 656(2)
     (2)........................................................... s 89(1)(a), (c)
  63 ............................................................ s 84
  64 .........Rep by CTA 1976 s 164 and Sch 3 Pt I
  65 ..........Unnecessary (spent)
  66 ..........Rep by FA 1969 s 65(1) and Sch 5 Pt I
  67 (1)-(3A) .................................................... s 85
     (4)........Rep by FA 1969 s 31
  68 (1)......................................................... s 108
     (2)........Rep by FA 1997 ................................... ss 146(2) and Sch 9 Pt II
  69 (1), (2) ... Definition of "capital allowance".............. s 1007(1), (2)
                 rep by FA 1975 s 33 and Sch 1 Pt II
  69 (3)......................................................... ss 880(3), 1007(3)
  70 (1)-(3A) .................................................... s 880(2)-(6)
     (3B) ........................................................ s 900(3)
     (4).......................................................... s 1052(4)(a), (c), (e)
     (5).......................................................... s 880(1)
  71 (1)......................................................... s 1008(1)
     (2)(a), (b) ................................................. s 1008(2)
         (c) .....Unnecessary (spent)
     (3)-(5)...................................................... s 1008(3)-(5)
  72 ............................................................ s 1010
  73 ............................................................ s 1012
  74 ............................................................ s 1011
  75 ............................................................ s 70(1)
  76 (1)......................................................... s 71(1)
     (2)(a)....................................................... s 71(2)
         (b) .....Rep by CTA 1976 s 164 and Sch 3 Pt I
     (3).......................................................... s 71(3)
     (4)........Rep by FA 1994 s 157(1)
     (5), (6) .................................................... s 71(5), (6)
     (7), (8) ....Rep by CTA 1976 s 164 and Sch 3 Pt I
  77 (1)......................................................... s 70(2)
     (2).......................................................... s 70(3)
     (3), (4) ....Ceased by FA 1990 s 17(2)
     (5).......................................................... s 70(4)
  78 ..........Rep by FA 1969 s 65(1) and Sch 5 Pt I
  79 ............................................................ s 74
  80 (1)......................................................... ss 96(1), 888(1)
     (2).......................................................... s 96(2)
     (3)........Unnecessary (obsolete)
     (4), (5) .................................................... s 96(3), (4)
  81 (1)......................................................... ss 75(1), 96(1)
     (2).......................................................... s 75(2)
```

Former Enactment　　　　　　　　　　　　　　　　　　　　　　*Destination in TCA 1997*
Income Tax Act 1967 (1967 No 7) (contd)

```
s  81 (3)(a) .................................................... s 75(3)
         (b), (c).. Ceased by FA 1990 s 18(2)
         (4)-(8) ................................................. s 97
         (9), (10)... Unnecessary (spent)
    82   ........ Rep by FA 1997 s 146(2) and Sch 9 Pt II
    83   ............................................................ s 98
    84   ............................................................ s 99
    85   ............................................................ s 100
    86   ............................................................ s 75(4)
    87   ........ Rep by FA 1969 s 65(1) and Sch 5 Pt I
    88 (1) ...................................................... s 918(4)
       (2), (3).... Rep by FA 1969 s 65(1) and Sch 5 Pt I
    89   ............................................................ s 384
    89A ........ Rep by FA 1996 s 132(2) and Sch 5 Pt II.
                 (s 89A inserted by F(MP)A 1968 s 7)
    90   ............................................................ s 101
    91   ............................................................ s 102
    92   ............................................................ s 103
    93 (1), (2) ................................................. s 104
       (3) ....................................................... s 1087(2)
    94   ............................................................ s 888
    95   ........ Rep by FA 1969 s 65(1) and Sch 5 Pt I
    96-103...... Unnecessary (obsolete)
    104  ........ Rep by FA 1969 s 65(1) and Sch 5 Pt I
    105. ........................................................... s 52
    106  ........ Rep by FA 1997 s 146(2) and Sch 9 Pt II
    107. ........................................................... s 107
    108  ........ Rep by CTA 1976 s 164 and Sch 3 Pt I
Pt V
s  109. ........................................................... s 19(1)
   110. ........................................................... s 112
   111  ........ Deleted by FA 1990 s 19(b) with saver for
                 enactments which refer to s 111
   112. ........................................................... s 113
   113. ........................................................... s 948
   114(1)-(5) .................................................. s 123(1)-(5)
       (6) ....... Unnecessary (spent)
       (7) ....................................................... s 123(6)
   115(1) ...................................................... s 201(2)
       (1A)(a)................................................... s 201(3)
           (b).... Unnecessary (operative date)
       (2)-(4) ................................................. s 201(4)-(6)
       (5)-(7) ................................................. s 201(1)
       (8) ....................................................... s 201(7)
   116. ........................................................... s 117
   117. ........................................................... s 118
   118(1), (2) ................................................ s 119(1), (2)
       (3) ....... Deleted by FA 1969 s 32(a)
       (4) ....................................................... s 119(3), (4)
       (5) ....... Deleted by FA 1969 s 32(a)
```

Former Enactment   *Destination in TCA 1997*
Income Tax Act 1967 (1967 No 7) (contd)

s 119(1), (2) .... s 116(1)

    (3), (4) .... s 116(3), (4)

120(1) .... s 897(6)

    (2) .... s 897(7)

    (3) .... Unnecessary (duplication)

121 .... Rep by FA 1973 s 42

    (1), (3) .... s 116(1)

122(2) .... s 116(2)

123 .... s 120

124 .... s 983

125 .... s 984(1), (2)

126 .... s 985

127(1)(a)-(f), ... s 986(1)(a)-(j), (g), (h)

      (ff) ..... Deleted by FA 1974 s 11 and Sch 1 Pt II

    (2) .... s 986(2)

    (3)(a)(i) .... s 986(3)(a)

      (ii) ... Deleted by FA 1974 s 11 and Sch 1 Pt II

    (b) .... s 986(3)(b)

    (c) ...... Deleted by FA 1974 s 11 and Sch 1 Pt II

    (4)-(5A) .... s 986(4)-(6)

    (6) .... Unnecessary (spent)

    (7) .... s 986(7)

127A .... (s 127A inserted by FA 1992 s 233) .... s 903

128(1),(1A),(2) .... s 987(1)-(3)

    (3) .... Deleted by FA 1982 s 60(2)

    (4) .... s 987(4)

129 .... s 991(1)

130 .... Ceased by FA 1974 s 71(a)

131 .... s 993(1)-(4)

132 .... s 994

133 .... s 997

Pt VI

s 134-136 ...... Rep by FA 1974 s 86 and Sch 2 Pt I

137 .... s 458

138 .... s 461

138A(1)-(6) .. (s 138A inserted by FA 1980 s 3 .... s 462
          and substituted by FA 1985 s 4)

    (7) .... Rep by FA 1996 s 132(2) and Sch 5 Pt II

138B .... (s 138B inserted by FA 1980 s 3) .... s 472

139   Ceased by FA 1982 s 2(3) and Sch 1

140 .... Ceased by FA 1982 s 2(3) and Sch 1

141(1)-(6) .... s 465

    (7) .... Rep by FA 1996 s 132(2) and Sch 5 Pt II

142 .... s 466

142A .... (s 142A inserted by FA 1982 s 5(1)) .... s 473

143 .... Ceased by FA 1992 s 4(a)

144 .... Rep by FA 1979 s 32(1)

145(1)-(3) .... s 470(1)-(3)

    (3A) ...... Rep by FA 1996 s 132(2) and Sch 5 Pt II

    (4) .... s 470(4)

    (5) .... Rep by FA 1996 s 132(2) and Sch 5 Pt II

146 .... s 459(1)

Destination Table (Taxes Consolidation Act 1997)

Former Enactment   *Destination in TCA 1997*
Income Tax Act 1967 (1967 No 7) (contd)

s 147 .... Rep by FA 1969 s 65(1) and Sch 5 Pt I	
148 .... Rep by FA 1969 s 65(1) and Sch 5 Pt I	
149.	s 459(2)
150 .... Rep by FA 1969 s 65(1) and Sch 5 Pt I	
151 .... Ceased by FA 1992 s 4(a)	
152 .... Ceased by FA 1992 s 4(a)	
153.	s 1032
154.	s 1016, Sch 32, para 21(1)

Pt VII

s 155.	s 849
156.	s 850
157.	s 853
158.	s 854
159.	s 855
160.	s 856(1), (2)
161.	s 852(1), (2)
162.	s 851
163.	s 857(1)-(3)
164.	s 860
165.	s 861(1)
166(1) .... Unnecessary (continuity)	
(2)	s 862

Pt VIII

s 167 .... Rep by F(MP)A 1968 s 6(1)	
168 .... Rep by F(MP)A 1968 s 6(1)	
169(1)(a) ..... Rep by FA 1969 s 65(1) and Sch 5 Pt I	
(b)-(4)	s 877
170.	s 878
171 .... Rep by F(MP)A 1968 s 6(1)	
172(1), (2), (4), (6)	s 879(1)-(4)
(3) .... Rep by F(MP)A 1968 s 6(1)	
(5)	s 1052(4)(a), (c), (e)
173(1)-(7), (9)	s 889(10)
173(8) .... Deleted by FA 1982 s 60(2)(b)(ii)	
174.	s 900(1), (2), (4)
175.	s 891
176.	s 890
177 .... Rep by FA 1997 s 146(2) and Sch 9 Pt II	
178.	s 897(1)-(5)
179 .... Rep by F(MP)A 1968 s 6(1)	
180 .... Rep by FA 1969 s 65(1) and Sch 5 Pt I	
181.	s 918(1)-(3)
182.	s 920
183(1)(a)	s 921(2)
(b)..... Rep by FA 1969 s 65(1) and Sch 5 Pt I	
(2)-(5)(a)	s 921(3)-(6)
183(5)(b)..... Rep by FA 1969 s 65(1) and Sch 5 Pt I	
(6) .... Rep by FA 1969 s 65(1) and Sch 5 Pt I	
(7)	s 921(1)
184.	s 922
185.	s 923

Former Enactment   *Destination in TCA 1997*
Income Tax Act 1967 (1967 No 7) (contd)

s 186 .... s 924
    187(1) .... s 928(1)
        (2) .... Rep by FA 1996 s 132(2) and Sch 5 Pt II
        (3) .... s 964(2)
    188(1) .... s 863
        (2) .... Rep by FA 1974 s 86 and Sch 2 Pt I
    189 .... s 867
    190 .... s 929
    191(1)-(5) .... s 930
        (6) .... Deleted by FA 1995 s 15(c)
Pt IX
s 192 .... s 1015
    193 .... s 1016
    194 .... s 1017
    195 .... s 1018
    195A(1)-(6) ... (s 195A inserted by FA 1983 s 6) .... s 1020
        (7) .... Unnecessary (commencement)
    195B .... (s 195B inserted by FA 1993 s 10(1)) .... s 1019
    195C .... (s 195C inserted by FA 1993 s 10(1)) .... s 1021
    196 .... s 1022
    197 .... s 1023
    198 .... s 1024
    199 .... Rep by FA 1994 s 157(1)
    200 .... s 1034
    201 .... s 1035
    202 .... s 1036
    203 .... s 1037
    204 .... s 1038
    205 .... s 1039
    206 .... Rep by FA 1994 s 157(1)
    207 .... s 1044
    208 .... s 1045
    209 .... s 1046(1), (2)
    210(1), (2) .... s 1047
        (3) .... Rep by FA 1969 s 65(1) and Sch 5 Pt I
    211(1)-(3) .... s 1048
        (4) .... Deleted by FA 1973 s 6
    212 .... s 1049
    213 .... s 1050
Pt X
ss 214-217 ...... Rep by CTA 1976 s 164 and Sch 3 Pt I
Pt XI
    218 .... Definition of "capital allowance" .... s 698
              rep by FA 1975 s 33 and Sch 1 Pt II
    219(1) .... s 699(1)
        (2) .... Rep by CTA 1976 s 164 and Sch 3 Pt I
        (3) .... Unnecessary (transitional)
        (4)(a) ..... Unnecessary (spent)
          (b), (c) .... s 699(2)
    220(1)-(5), (7) . Rep by FA 1978 s 52(1) and Sch 3 Pt I
        (6) .... Rep by CTA 1976 s 164 and Sch 3 Pt I
    221 .... Rep by CTA 197 s 164 and Sch 3 Pt I 6

Former Enactment   *Destination in TCA 1997*
Income Tax Act 1967 (1967 No 7) (contd)

Pt XII

s 222	Rep by FA 1972 s 46(2) and Sch 4 Pt II
223	Rep by FA 1972 s 46(1) and Sch 4 Pt I
224(1), (2), (4)	s 126(1), (2)
(3), (5), (6) ...	Rep by FA 1979 s 6
225	s 790
226	Rep by FA 1972 s 46(2) and Sch 4 Pt II with saver in FA 1972 Sch 1 Pt III para 4 (substituted by FA 1997 s 146(1) and Sch 9 para 5(3)) for enactments which refer to ITA 1967 Pt XII Ch II
227	Rep by FA 1972 s 46(2) and Sch 4 Pt II with saver in FA 1972 Sch 1 Pt III para 4 (substituted by FA 1997 s 146(1) and Sch 9 para 5(3)) for enactments which refer to ITA 1967 Pt XII Ch II
228	Rep by FA 1972 s 46(2) and Sch 4 Pt II with saver in FA 1972 Sch 1 Pt III para 4 (substituted by FA 1997 s 146(1) and Sch 9 para 5(3)) for enactments which refer to ITA 1967 Pt XII Ch II
229	Rep by FA 1972 s 46(2) and Sch 4 Pt II with saver in FA 1972 Sch 1 Pt III para 4 (substituted by FA 1997 s 146(1) and Sch 9 para 5(3)) for enactments which refer to ITA 1967 Pt XII Ch II
230	Rep by FA 1972 s 46(2) and Sch 4 Pt II with saver in FA 1972 Sch 1 Pt III para 4 (substituted by FA 1997 s 146(1) and Sch 9 para 5(3)) for enactments which refer to ITA 1967 Pt XII Ch II
231	Rep by s 46(2) and Sch 4 Pt II FA 1972 with saver in FA 1972 Sch 1 Pt III para 4 (substituted by FA 1997 s 146(1) and Sch 9 para 5(3)) for enactments which refer to ITA 1967 Pt XII Ch II
232	Rep by FA 1972 s 46(2) and Sch 4 Pt II with saver in FA 1972 Sch 1 Pt III para 4 (substituted by FA 1997 s 146(1) and Sch 9 para 5(3)) for enactments which refer to ITA 1967 Pt XII Ch II
233	Rep by FA 1972 s 46(2) and Sch 4 Pt II with saver in FA 1972 Sch 1 Pt III para (substituted by FA 1997 s 146(1) and Sch 9 para 5(3)) for enactments which refer to ITA 1967 Pt XII Ch II
234	Rep by FA 1972 s 46(2) and Sch 4 Pt II with saver in FA 1972 Sch 1 Pt III para 4 (substituted by FA 1997 s 146(1) and Sch 9 para 5(3)) for enactments which refer to ITA 1967 Pt XII Ch II
235(1)-(5)	s 784(1)-(5)
(6)	s 783(4)
(7)(a)-(c)	s 783(3)
(d)....	Rep by FA 1996 s 132(2) and Sch 5 Pt II
(8)	s 783(2)
(9)	s 783(1)(a), (c)
(10)	s 784(6)

Former Enactment   *Destination in TCA 1997*

Income Tax Act 1967 (1967 No 7) (contd)

s 235A(1)-(6) ... (s 235A inserted by FA 1974 s 66) . . . . s 785
    (7). . . . . . . Unnecessary (transitional)
  236(1). . . . . s 787(6)
    (1A)-(2B) . . . . s 787(8)-(12)
    (2C) . . . . . . Unnecessary (transitional)
    (3)-(7). . . . . s 787(1)-(5)
    (8). . . . . s 787(13)
    (9). . . . . s 787(14)
    (10). . . . . . . Rep by FA 1974 s 86 and Sch 1 Pt I
    (11). . . . . s 787(7)
  237 . . . . Rep by CTA 1976 s 164 and Sch 3 Pt I
  238(1), (2) . . . . s 787(15), (16)
    (3), (4) . . . . s 783(5), (6)
  239 . . . . s 788
  240 . . . . s 789
  241(1)(a) . . . . s 284(1)
      (b) . . . . s 284(2)(a), (3)
      (c) . . . . s 300(1)
   proviso. . . . . s 284(2)(b)
    (1A) . . . . . . Unnecessary (obsolete)
    (2). . . . . s 299(1)
    (3). . . . . s 304(4)
    (4). . . . . s 304(2)
    (5). . . . . s 298(1)
    (6). . . . . s 284(4)
    (6A) . . . . s 284(5)
    (7)-(9). . . . . Rep by FA 1996 s 132(2) and Sch 5 Pt II
    (9A)(a) . . . . s 316(1)(a)
      (b) . . . . s 316(2)
    (10). . . . . ss 284(6), 301(1)
    (11)(a). . . . . s 284(7)
      (b) . . . . s 406
  241A(1), (2) . . . (s 241A inserted by FA 1994 s 24(a)). . . . . s 291
    (3). . . . . s 301(1)
  242 . . . . Rep by FA 1996 s 132(2) and Sch 5 Pt II
  243 . . . . Rep by FA 1996 s 132(2) and Sch 5 Pt II

Pt XIV

s 244(1). . . . . s 763(2)
    (2),(2A). . . . . s 764
    (3)-(7). . . . . s 765
    (8), (9) . . . . s 763(5), (6)
  245 . . . . s 670
  246 . . . . Unnecessary (obsolete)
  247 . . . . Unnecessary (obsolete)
  248 . . . . Unnecessary (obsolete)
  249 . . . . Rep by FA 1996 s 132(2) and Sch 5 Pt II
  250 . . . . Unnecessary (obsolete)

Former Enactment *Destination in TCA 1997*
Income Tax Act 1967 (1967 No 7) (contd)

Pt XV

s 251(1) .... ss 283(2), 300(1)
    (2) .... s 316(3)
    (3) .... Unnecessary (operative date)
    (4) (a),(b), Unnecessary (spent)
    (bb)(i),(bbb),
    (c)
    (bb)(ii), (d)... s 283(3)
    (5) .... s 304(3)(b)
    (6) .... s 283(1)
    (7) .... s 283(6)
252... ss 298(1), 299(1), 304(4)
253... ss 301(2), 304(6)(b)
254(1)(a), (b)... s 271(2), (4)
    (c) .... ss 271(1), 320(1)
    (d), (e) .... ss 278(1), (2), (6), 305
    (2) .... Unnecessary (spent)
    (2A).. s 271(4)
    (2B)...... Unnecessary (spent)
    (3) .... s 271(6)
    (3A)...... Deleted by FA 1994 s 22(1)
    (4)(a) .... s 316(3)
    (b) .... s 317(2)
    (5) .... s 304(4)
    (6) .... s 304(2), (3)(a)
    (7) .... s 271(5)
255(1)-(5) .... s 268(1)-(3), (5)-(8)
    (6) .... s 320(2)
256... s 270
257... s 268(4)
258 .... Unnecessary (operative date)
259 .... Rep by FA 1996 s 132(2) and Sch 5 Pt II
260... s 316(1)(a)
261... s 316(2)
262 .... Rep by FA 1996 s 132(2) and Sch 5 Pt II
263(1) .... Unnecessary (interpretation)
    (2), (3) .... s 282
    (4) .... ss 270, 268(4)
264... s 272
265... s 274(1), (3), (4), (5), (8)
266... s 277
267... s 278(1), (3), (4), (5), (6)
268... s 269
269... s 281
270... s 280
271......... Definitions of "initial allowance" .... s 288(4)(a)
    "wear and tear allowance" unnecessary
272(1)-(3) .... s 288(1)-(3)
    (4) .... s 288(4)(b)

Former Enactment   *Destination in TCA 1997*
Income Tax Act 1967 (1967 No 7) (contd)

s 272(5)(a), (b) .... s 288(5)
      (c) ..... Unnecessary (spent)
    (6) .... s 288(6)
273(1) .... s 290
    (2) .... Rep by FA 1996 s 132(2) and Sch 5 Pt II
274 .... s 292
275 .... s 293
276 .... s 294
277 .... s 289
278 .... s 295
279 .... s 296
280 .... s 297
281 .... s 298(2)
282 .... s 300
283(1) .... s 301(1)
    (2) .... Rep by FA 1969 s 65(1) and Sch 5 Pt I
284 .... s 754
285 .... s 755
286 .... s 756
287 .... Unnecessary (obsolete)
288 .... s 757
289 .... Unnecessary (obsolete)
290(1)-(3) .... s 758
    (4) .... Unnecessary (obsolete)
291 .... s 759
292 .... s 761
293 .... s 760
294(1)-(5) .... s 303(1)-(5)
    (6) .... s 302(1)
    (7) .... s 303(6)
    (8) .... s 302(2)
    (9) .... s 303(7)
    (10) .... s 302(1)
    (11), (12) .... s 303(8), (9)
295 .... s 304(2), (4), (5), (6)(a)
296(1) .... s 305(1)
    (2) .... Unnecessary (obsolete)
    (3)-(5) .... s 305(2)-(4)
297 .... s 306
298 .... s 311
299(1)-(3) .... s 312(2)-(4)
     (4)(a), ... s 312(5)
      (b),(i),
      (b)(ii)
       (b)(iii) .... s 762(2)(a)
    (5) .... s 312(6)
    (6) .... s 312(1)
300 .... s 313
301 .... s 314
302 .... s 315

Former Enactment	Destination in TCA 1997

Income Tax Act 1967 (1967 No 7) (contd)

s 303(1)	ss 316(1), 762(2)(b)
(2)	s 316(2)
(3)	s 317(2)
304(1)	ss 318, 320(1)
(2)-(6)	s 320(2)-(6)
305	s 769
306 .... Rep by FA 1996 s 132(2) and Sch 5 Pt II	
(1)	s 381(1)
(1A)...... Rep by FA 1997 s 146(2) and Sch 9 Pt II	
(1AA) .... Ceased by FA 1990 s 27(2)(a)	
(1AAA)-(6)	s 381(2)-(7)
307(1)	s 381(1)
(1A)...... Repealed by FA 1997 s 146(2) and Sch 9 Pt II	
(1AA) .... Ceased by FA 1990 s 27(2)	
(1AAA)-(6)	381(2)-(7)
308 .... Unnecessary (spent)	
309(1), (2)	s 382(1), (2)
(3) .... Rep by FA 1969 s 65(1) and Sch 5 Pt I	
310	s 383
311	s 385
312	s 386
313(1), (2)	s 387
(3) .... Unnecessary (spent)	
314(1)	s 388
(2) .... Rep by FA 1975 s 33 and Sch 1 Pt II	
315	s 389
316	s 390(1), (3)
317(1) ...... Definition of "capital allowances"	s 391(1)
deleted by FA 1975 s 33 and Sch 1 Pt II	
(2)(a) from ... Rep by FA 1997 s 146(2) and Sch 9 Pt II	
"In paragraph (a)"to end	
(b)-(d)	s 391(2)
318	s 392
319	s 393
320	s 394
321	s 395
322	s 391(3)
323-328 ...... Rep by CTA 1976 s 164 and Sch 3 Pt I	
329-332 ...... Ceased by FA 1983 s 7	
333	s 207(1), (2)
334(1) (a), (c)	s 208(2)
(b)..... Rep by FA 1969 s 65(1) and Sch 5 Pt I	
(2) .... Rep by FA 1969 s 65(1) and Sch 5 Pt I	
(2A)	s 208(3)
(3)	s 208(1)
335	s 211(1)-(4)
336	s 213(1), (2)
337 .... Ceased by FA 1993 s 43(1)	
338	s 206

Former Enactment   *Destination in TCA 1997*
Income Tax Act 1967 (1967 No 7) (contd)

```
339 (1) ....... Rep by F(MP)A 1968 s 3(5) and Sch Pt IV
    (2)........................................... ss 207(3), 211(5), 213(3)
    (3)....... Rep by F(MP)A 1968 s 3(5) and Sch Pt IV
    (4)........................................... ss 207(4), 211(6), 213(4)
340(1)............................................ s 204(2)
    (2)(a)-(c)....................................... s 204(1)
    (d), (ff),  .. Rep by FA 1983 s 120 and Sch 4
    (g)
    (e), (f) .... Rep by FA 1997 s 146(2) and Sch 9 Pt II
    (3)....... Rep by FA 1983 s 120 and Sch 4
341 ......... Rep by DR&IA 1967 s 4 and Sch 6
342 ......... Rep by DR&IA 1967 s 4 and Sch 6
343 ......... Rep by FA 1997 s 62(2)
344 ......... Rep by FA 1996 s 132(2) and Sch 5 Pt II
345 ........................................... s 199
346 ......... Rep by FA 1996 s 132(2) and Sch 5 Pt II
347 ......... Rep by CTA 1976 s 164 and Sch 3 Pt I
348 ........................................... s 215
349 ........................................... s 235
350 ........................................... s 216
351-352 ...... Rep by FA 1969 s 65(1) and Sch 5 Pt I
353 ........................................... s 193 Sch 32, para 2
354 ........................................... s 194
```
Pt XXII
```
s 355 ......... Rep by FA 1977 s 54(1)(a) and Sch 2 Pt I
356 ......... Rep by FA 1977 s 54(1)(b) and Sch 2 Pt II
357 ......... Rep by FA 1977 s 54(1)(a) and Sch 2 Pt I
358(1)........ Unnecessary (saver for FA 1950 s 12)
    (2), (3) .................................... s 833
359 ........................................... s 834
360 ......... Rep by FA 1996 s 132(2) and Sch 5 Pt II
361(1)-(7)....................................... s 826(1)-(7)
    (8)......................................... s 826(9)
362 ......... Rep by FA 1987 s 23 with saver
363 ......... Rep by CTA 1976 s 166 and Sch 4 Pt II
364 ......... Rep by CTA 1976 s 166 and Sch 4 Pt II
365 ......... Rep by FA 1977 s 146(2) and Sch 9 Pt II
366 ......... Rep by FA 1977 s 146(2) and Sch 9 Pt II
```
Pt XXIII
```
s 367 ........................................... s 748
368 ........................................... s 749
369(1)........................................... s 750
369(2)........ Rep by FA 1977 s 54(1)(a) and Sch 2 Pt I
370 ........................................... s 751
```
Pt XXIV
```
s 371 ........................................... s 752
372 ........................................... s 753
```
Pt XXV
```
s 373 ......... Rep by CTA 1976 s 164 and Sch 3 Pt I
374 - 414 ..... Rep by CTA 1976 s 164 and Sch 3 Pt I
415 ........................................... s 932
    (1)-(7)(f)..................................... s 933(1)-(7)(f)
    (7)(g) ..... Unnecessary (obsolete)
    (8)......................................... s 933(8)
```

Former Enactment   *Destination in TCA 1997*

Income Tax Act 1967 (1967 No 7) (contd)

s 415(8A)	Deleted by FA 1983 s 9(a)(i)(IV)	
(9)		s 933(9)
(10)		s 942(9)
(11)	Rep by FA 1974 s 86 and Sch 2 Pt I	
416		s 933(1)-(7)(f)
417	Ceased by FA 1976 s 30(8)	
418	Ceased by FA 1971 s 17(3)	
419	Rep by FA 1997 s 146(2) and Sch 9 Pt II	
420	Deleted by FA 1983 s 9(b)	
421		s 934
422		s 935
423		s 936
424		s 937
425		s 938
426		s 939
427		s 940
428		s 941
429		s 942(1)-(8), (10)
430		s 943
431		s 944
432 (1)		ss 864(1), 949(1)
(2)-(4)		s 949(2)-(4)

Pt XXVII

s 433		s 237
434 (1)-(5A)		s 238(1)-(6)
(6)	Unnecessary (obsolete)	
(7)	Unnecessary (spent)	
(8)		s 238(7)
435	Rep by CTA 1976 s 164 and Sch 3 Pt I	
436-437	Rep by FA 1969 s 65(1) and Sch 5 Pt I	

Pt XXVIII

s 438		s 791(2)-(4)
439		s 792(1)-(4)
440	Ceased by FA 1995 s 12(3)	
441		s 793
442		s 791(1)
443(1)		s 795
443(2), (3)		s 794(2), (3)
(4)	Ceased by FA 1995 s 12(3)	
(5)		s 794(4)
444		s 796(1), (2)(a), (b), (c)
445		s 794(5)
446		s 797
447	Definition of "child" rep by FA 1996 s 132(2) and Sch 5 Pt II, definition of "minor" unnecessary (duplication)	s 794(1)s 794(1)
448(1), (3), (4)		s 798(1)-(3)
(2)	Rep by FA 1996 s 132(2) and Sch 5 Pt II	
449		s 812 (1), (2), (4)

Pt XXIX

s 450		s 799

Former Enactment *Destination in TCA 1997*
Income Tax Act 1967 (1967 No 7) (contd)

s 451 . . . . s 800
   452 . . . . s 801(1)-(8)
   453 . . . . s 802
   454 . . . . s 803
   455 . . . . s 804

Pt XXX

s 456 . . . . Rep by CTA 1976 s 164 and Sch 3 Pt I
   457 . . . . Rep by CTA 1976 s 164 and Sch 3 Pt I
   458 . . . . s 1091

Pt XXXI

s 459 . . . . s 60
   460 . . . . s 61
   461 . . . . s 62
   462 . . . . s 63
   462A . . . . (s 462A inserted by FA 1994 s 15) . . . . s 64
   463 . . . . s 42
   464 . . . . s 43
   465 . . . . s 45(1)
   466 . . . . s 36
   467-468(2) . . . . Rep by FA 1997 s 146(2) and Sch 9 Pt II
   468(3) . . . . s 47
   469 . . . . Rep by FA 1997 s 146(2) and Sch 9 Pt II
   470 . . . . s 50
   471 . . . . Rep by FA 1997 s 146(2) and Sch 9 Pt II
   472(1) . . . . Sch 32, para 1(1)
      (2) . . . . Rep by FA 1997 s 146(2) and Sch 9 Pt II
   473 . . . . Rep by FA 1997 s 146(2) and Sch 9 Pt II
   474 . . . . s 49, Sch 32 para 1(2)
   475 . . . . s 51
   476 . . . . Rep by FA 1996 s 132(2) and Sch 5 Pt II
   477 (1) . . . . s 960
      (2), (3) . . . . Rep by FA 1996 s 132(2) and Sch 5 Pt II
   478 . . . . s 961
   479 . . . . Rep by FA 1996 s 132(2) and Sch 5 Pt II
   480 . . . . Rep by FA 1996 s 132(2) and Sch 5 Pt II
   481 . . . . Rep by FA 1969 s 65(1) and Sch 5 Pt I
   482(1), (2) . . . . s 971
      (3) . . . . Rep by FA 1996 s 132(2) and Sch 5 Pt II
   483 . . . . Rep by IT(A)A 1967 s 1
   484(1)-(4) . . . . s 972(1)-(4)
      (5) . . . . Unnecessary (obsolete)
      (6), (7) . . . . s 972(5), (6)
   485(1), (2) . . . . s 962(1), (2)
      (3), (4) . . . . Rep by FA 1974 s 86 and Sch 2 Pt I
      (5) . . . . s 962(3)
   485(6) . . . . Unnecessary (spent)
   486(1), (2), (4) . . . . s 963
      (3) . . . . Rep by FA 1997 s 146(2) and Sch 9 Pt II
   487 . . . . s 964(1)
   488 . . . . s 966
   489 . . . . s 965
   490 . . . . Rep by FA 1967 s 25 and Sch 3 Pt I

Destination Table (Taxes Consolidation Act 1997)

Former Enactment   *Destination in TCA 1997*
Income Tax Act 1967 (1967 No 7) (contd)

s 491	s 998
492	s 968
493	s 969
494 (1)	s 970
(2) .... Rep by FA 1996 s 132(2) and Sch 5 Pt II	
495 .... Rep by FA 1996 s 132(2) and Sch 5 Pt II	
496 .... Rep by FA 1997 s 146(2) and Sch 9 Pt II	
497	s 460
498	s 865
499 .... Unnecessary (operative date)	
500(1)-(3)	s 1052(1)-(3)
(4)	s 1052(4)(a)-(e)
501	s 1053(1)-(4)
502	s 1053(5)-(7)
503	s 1054(2)-(4)
504	s 1060
505	s 1055
506	s 1069(2)
507	s 1068
508	s 1061
509	ss 1054(1), 1069(1)(a)
510	s 1062
511	s 1063
512	s 1065
513	s 1059
514	s 1070
515	s 1057
516	s 1056
517	s 1064
518	s 1066
519	s 874
520	s 1058
521	s 1067
522-524 ...... Rep by FA 1974 s 86 and Sch 2 Pt I	
525	s 127(1)-(5)
526-527 ...... Rep by FA 1974 s 86 and Sch 2 Pt I	
528	s 926
529 .... Ceased by FA 1971 s 17(3)	
530-531 ...... Rep by CTA 1976 s 164 and Sch 3 Pt I	
532 .... Rep by FA 1974 s 86 and Sch 2 Pt I	
533	s 866
534	s 1090
535	s 1088
536	s 868
537	s 870
538	s 875
539	s 901
540 .... Rep by FA 1996 s 132(2) and Sch 5 Pt II	
541	s 873

Former Enactment   *Destination in TCA 1997*
Income Tax Act 1967 (1967 No 7) (contd)

```
s  542(1). . . . . . . . Rep by F(MP)A 1968 s 3(5) and Sch Pt IV
      (2). . . . . . . . . . . . . . . . . . . . . . . . . . . . . . . . . . . . . . . . . . . . . . s 869(1)
      (3). . . . . . . . Deleted by FA 1975 s 29
      (4)-(7). . . . . . . . . . . . . . . . . . . . . . . . . . . . . . . . . . . . . . . . s 869(2)-(5)
   543 . . . . . . . . . . Rep by FA 1996 s 132(2) and Sch 5 Pt II
   544 (1) . . . . . . . . . . . . . . . . . . . . . . . . . . . . . . . . . . . . . . . . . . . s 837
      (2). . . . . . . . Rep by FA 1969 s 65(1) and Sch 5
   545 (1) . . . . . . . . . . . . . . . . . . . . . . . . . . . . . . . . . . . . . . . . . . . s 1096
      (2). . . . . . . . Rep by FA 1969 s 65(1) and Sch 5 Pt I
   546 . . . . . . . . . . Ceased by FA 1990 s 27(2)(a)
   547 . . . . . . . . . . . . . . . . . . . . . . . . . . . . . . . . . . . . . . . . . . . . . . s 483(1)-(3)
   548 . . . . . . . . . . Rep by FA 1969 s 65(1) and Sch 5 Pt I
   549 . . . . . . . . . . . . . . . . . . . . . . . . . . . . . . . . . . . . . . . . . . . . . . s 1004
   550 (1) . . . . . . . . . . . . . . . . . . . . . . . . . . . . . . . . . . . . . . . . . . . s 1080(1)
      (2). . . . . . . . Ceased by FA 1990 s 24
      (2A) . . . . . . Rep by FA 1997 s 146(2) and Sch 9 Pt II
      (3)-(5). . . . . . . . . . . . . . . . . . . . . . . . . . . . . . . . . . . . . . . . . s 1080(2)-(4)
   551(1), (2)(a) . . . . . . . . . . . . . . . . . . . . . . . . . . . . . . . . . . . . . s 1081
      (2)(b) . . . . . Rep by FA 1974 s 86 and Sch 2 Pt I
   552 . . . . . . . . . . Unnecessary (commencement)
   553 . . . . . . . . . . . . . . . . . . . . . . . . . . . . . . . . . . . . . . . . . . . . . . s 111
Pt XXXVIII
s  554 . . . . . . . . . . Unnecessary (commencement and repeals)
   555 . . . . . . . . . . Unnecessary (obsolete)
   556 . . . . . . . . . . Unnecessary (savings in relation to ITA 1967)
   557 . . . . . . . . . . Rep by FA 1996 s 132(2) and Sch 5 Pt II
   558 . . . . . . . . . . Rep by FA 1996 s 132(2) and Sch 5 Pt II
   559 . . . . . . . . . . Unnecessary (continuity and construction)
   560 . . . . . . . . . . Unnecessary (continuity)
   561 . . . . . . . . . . Unnecessary (short title)
Sch 1 . . . . . . . . . . . . . . . . . . . . . . . . . . . . . . . . . . . . . . . . . . . . . . . Sch 2
Pt I       . . . . . . . . . . . . . . . . . . . . . . . . . . . . . . . . . . . . . . . . . . . . . Pt 2
Pt II      . . . . . . . . . Rep by FA 1997 s 146(2) and Sch 9 Pt II.
Pts III-V. . . . . . . . . . . . . . . . . . . . . . . . . . . . . . . . . . . . . . . . . . . Pts 3-5
Pt VI      . . . . . . . . . . . . . . . . . . . . . . . . . . . . . . . . . . . . . . . . . . . . Pt 1
Sch 2
   Rule 1(1), (2). . . . . . . . . . . . . . . . . . . . . . . . . . . . . . . . . . . . . . . s 925
      (3) . . . . . . . Rep by FA 1996 s 132(2) and Sch 5 Pt II
      2. . . . . . . . . . . . . . . . . . . . . . . . . . . . . . . . . . . . . . . . . . . . . . s 19(2)
      3. . . . . . . . . . . . . . . . . . . . . . . . . . . . . . . . . . . . . . . . . . . . . . s 114
      4. . . . . . . . . . . . . . . . . . . . . . . . . . . . . . . . . . . . . . . . . . . . . . s 115
      5-7. . . . . . . Rep by FA 1976 s 81 and Sch 5 Pt I
Sch 3
para1-11 . . . . . . . . . . . . . . . . . . . . . . . . . . . . . . . . . . . . . . . . . . . Sch 3
      12, 13 . . . . . . . . . . . . . . . . . . . . . . . . . . . . . . . . . . . . . . . . . . s 201(1)(a)
      14 . . . . . . . . . . . . . . . . . . . . . . . . . . . . . . . . . . . . . . . . . . . . Sch 3
Sch 4
para1(1) . . . . . . . . . . . . . . . . . . . . . . . . . . . . . . . . . . . . . . . . . . . s 459(3)
      (2), (3) . . . . Rep by F(MP)A 1968 s 3(5) and Sch Pt IV
   2(1),(3),(4),(5) . . . . . . . . . . . . . . . . . . . . . . . . . . . . . . . . . . . . . s 459(4)
      (2). . . . . . . . Rep by F(MP)A 1968 s 3(5) and Sch Pt IV
      3 . . . . . . . . . Rep by F(MP)A 1968 s 3(5) and Sch Pt IV
Sch 5 . . . . . . . . . . Deleted by FA 1996 s 13(b)
```

Former Enactment   *Destination in TCA 1997*

Income Tax Act 1967 (1967 No 7) (contd)

Sch 6
- Pt I .... Rep by FA 1977 s 54 and Sch 2 Pt I
- II .... Rep by FA 1977 s 54 and Sch 2 Pt I
- III, para 1 .... s 73
  - para 2-5 ... Rep by FA 1977 s 54 and Sch 2 Pt I
- Sch 7 .... Rep by FA 1977 s 54 and Sch 2 Pt I
- Sch 8 .... Sch 25
- Sch 9 .... Unnecessary (obsolete)
- Sch 10 .... Sch 24
  - para 1-4 .... para 1-4(1)
  - 5, 6 .... para 5, 6
  - 7 .... Rep by CTA 1976 s 166(2) and Sch 4 Pt II
  - 8-14 .... para 7-13
- Sch 11 .... Sch 21
- Sch 12 .... Sch 22
- Sch 13 .... Rep by FA 1996 s 132(2) and Sch 5 Pt II
- Sch 14 .... Rep by FA 1967 s 25 and Sch 3
- Sch 15 .... Sch 29
- Sch 16 .... Rep by CTA 1976 s 164 and Sch 3 Pt I
- Sch 17 .... Sch 27
- Sch 18 .... Sch 28
  - para I .... Rep by FA 1969 s 65(1) and Sch 5 Pt I
  - II-IX .... paras 1-8
- Sch 19 .... Unnecessary (repeals)

Income Tax (Amendment) Act 1967 (1967 No 7)

- Preamble ..... Unnecessary (obsolete)
- s 1 .... Unnecessary (cesser of ITA 1967 ss 480(2), (3), 483)
- 2 .... Unnecessary (short title)

Finance Act 1967 (1967 No 17)

- s 1 .... Unnecessary (spent)
- 2 .... Insertion of ITA 1967 s 139(5)
- 3 .... Amendment of ITA 1967 s 141(1) .... s 465
- 4 .... Amendment of ITA 1967 s 142(1) .... s 466
- 5 .... Substitution of ITA 1967 s 251(4) .... ss 283(2), 300(1)
- 6 (1) ...... Substitution of ITA 1967 s 254(1) .... s 271(2), (4)
- (2) .... Insertion of ITA 1967 s 262(4) .... s 316(2)
- 7 .... Amendment of ITA 1967 s 335 .... s 211(1)-(4)
- 8 .... Amendment of ITA 1967 s 344
- 9 (1) ...... Amendment of ITA 1967 ss 383, 386(2) .... s 963
- (2)(a) .... Amendment of ITA 1967 s 386 .... s 963
- (b) ..... Amendment of ITA 1967 s 387 .... s 964(1)
- (c) ..... Amendment of ITA 1967 s 389
- 10 .... Substitution of ITA 1967 s 523
- 11 (1),(2),(2A) .... s 285(1), (2), (3)
- (3) .... s 299(2)
- (4) .... s 285(8)
- 12 (1) .... s 469(1)
- proviso to definition of "dependant" .... s 469(4)
- (2)(a), (c) .... s 469(2)
- (b) ..... Deleted by FA 1972 s 9
- (3) .... s 469(3)

Former Enactment   *Destination in TCA 1997*

Finance Act 1967 (1967 No 17) (contd)

s 12 (4) .... s 469(5)
     (5) .... s 469(6)
     (6) .... Amendment of ITA 1967s 153(1)(d) .... s 1032
     (7) .... Amendment of ITA 1967 s 193 .... s 1016

Pt V

s 25 .... Unnecessary (application of schedule)
   26 .... Unnecessary (care and management)
   27(2), (6) ..... Unnecessary (construction and commencement)
   Sch 3, Pt I .... Repeal of ITA 1967 s 490 and Sch 14

Finance (Miscellaneous Provisions) Act 1968 (1968 No 7)

s 1 (1) .... Substitution of ITA 1967 s 156(1) .... s 850
    (2) .... Unnecessary (obsolete)
   2 .... Insertion of ITA 1967 s 181(3) .... s 918(1)-(3)
   3 (1) .... Amendment of ITA 1967 .... ss 860, 933(1)-(7)(f),
                ss 164(2), 416(5),   935, 942(1)-(8), (10)
                418(6), 422(3), 429(3)
    (2)-(5) .... Unnecessary (application of schedules)
    (6) .... Amendment of SR&O No 48 of 1928
              and SIs Nos 152 of 195, 28 of 1960
              and 231 of 1961
   4 (1) .... Substitution of ITA 1967 s 186(2) .... s 920
    (2) .... Unnecessary (spent)
    (3) .... Amendment of ITA 1967 s 211 .... s 1048
    (4) .... Substitution of ITA 1967 s 526(6)
    (5)(a) ..... Amendment of ITA 1967 s 498 .... s 865
       (b) ..... Unnecessary (spent)
   5 (1) .... s 876
    (2) .... Amendment of ITA 1967 Sch 15 .... Sch 29
   6 (1) .... Repeal of ITA 1967 ss 167, 168,
              171, 172(3), 179
    (2) .... Amendment of ITA 1967 s 169(1) .... s 877
    (3) .... Amendment of ITA 1967 s 169(4) .... s 877
    (4) .... Amendment of ITA 1967 s 170(1) .... s 878
    (5) .... Amendment of ITA 1967 s 176(1) .... s 890
    (6) .... Amendment of ITA 1967 s 177
    (7) .... Amendment of ITA 1967s 211(3) .... s 1048
   7 (1) .... Insertion of ITA 1967 s 81(4)(f), s 89A .... s 97
    (2) .... Unnecessary (spent).
   8 .... Amendment of ITA 1967 Sch 15 .... Sch 29
   9 (1), (2) .... s 200(1)
    (3) .... Unnecessary (commencement)
   13 .... Rep by CTA 1976 s 164 and Sch 3 Pt II
   14 .... Unnecessary (obsolete)
   15 .... Rep by CTA 1976 s 164 and Sch 3 Pt II

Pt IV

16 (1),(2),(4) .. Definition of "control" unnecessary (obsolete) .... s 639
    (3) .... Ceased by FA 1996 s 131(9)(b)
   17 .... s 640
   18 .... s 641
   19 .... s 642
   20 (1)(a) ..... Unnecessary (operative date)
      (b)-(17) .... s 643
   21 .... s 644
   22 .... s 645

Destination Table (Taxes Consolidation Act 1997)

Former Enactment   *Destination in TCA 1997*

Finance (Miscellaneous Provisions) Act 1968 (1968 No 7)

s 23 (1)-(3),(5) .... s 646
     (4) .... Rep by FA 1974 s 86 and Sch 2 Pt I
  24 (1) .... Unnecessary (commencement)
     (2) .... Unnecessary (obsolete)

Pt V

  27 .... s 999
  29 (2) .... Unnecessary (construction)
Sch Pt I .... Amendment of ITA 1967 ss 1(1), 13(1), ... ss 2(1), 3(1),
               37(1)(f)(ii), 38, 41(3), 50(3)(4), 54(4),   35, 84, 1012,
               60(3), 73(3), 76(5)(6), 81(6), 82(2)(a),   71(5)-(6),73, 97,
               90(2)(3), 113(1)(2), 120(1)(c)(2),   101, 948, 897(6),
               156(2)(3)(4), 164(2), 190(1), 191(4)(5),   850, 860, 929, 930,
               194(2)(c), 195(3)(a), 203(1)-(3), 204,   1017, 1018, 1037, 1038,
               214(2), 228(3), 238(1)(2), 240(1), 241(1),   787(15)-(16),789,284(1),
               245(14), 259, 296(3)(4), 301(1), 307(5)(6),   670, 305(2)-(4), 314,
               315(1)(2), 367(3), 371(7)(c), 379(1),   381(2)-(7), 389, 748, 752,
               382(2), 397, 413(1), 414, 416(1)-(9), 417,   933(1)-(7)(f),934,
               418(1)(2)(3)(6), 421(2), 422(1)(2), 424,   935, 937, 938, 939,940,
               425(1), 426(1), 427(a), 428(1)(9),   941,942(1)-(8)(10), 943,
               429(1)(2), 430(1), 431(1)(2), 432(1)-(4),   944,864(1),949(1)-(4),
               437(1)(2), 441(2), 446(2), 462(3)(4),   793, 797, 1053(1)-(4),
               501(1)(c), 506, 529, 537(2), 542(6), 549(5),   1069(2), 870, 869(2)-(5),
               553(2), Sch 6 Pt III para 1(2), 3(2)(3),   1004,111,Sch 21,Sch 22,
               4(1)(2), Sch 10 para 13(1), Sch 11 para 3(4),   Sch 24 paras 7-13
               Sch 12 para 2(1)(2), 3(2),(5), Sch 16 paras
               1-3, 10
Sch Pt II ...... Amendment of ITA 1967 ss 49(1), 152(6), ... ss 34,
               181(1)(a), 460(a), 484(3), 530(1),   918(1)-(3), 61, 972(1)-(4),
               531(1)-(3), Sch 1 Pt I para 3, 4,   Sch 2 Pt 2,
               Sch1 Pt II para 1, 3, Sch 1 Pt III para 1, 2,   Sch 2 Pts 3-5
               Sch 1 Pt IV para 3, 9, Sch 2 para 6(1)(2),   Sch 2 Pt 1,
               Sch 6 Pt II para (3), Sch 16 para 4, 5, 7, 8,
               11, Sch 16 para 10
Sch Pt III...... Amendment of ITA 1967 ss 36(2), 152(4)(b), ... ss 857(1)-(3); 207(3),
               163(2), 339(2), 530(5), 536(1), Sch 1 Pt I   211(5),213(3);1054(2)-
               para 4, 5, Sch 4 para 1(1), 2(3), Sch 17 Pt I,   (4); 868; Sch 2 Pt 2; 459(4); Sch
                                                                27, 459(3),
Sch Pt IV....... Repeal of ITA 1967 ss 22(2), 153(3),
               339(1)(3), 542(1), Sch 4 para 1(2)(3), 2(2), 3
               Amendment of ITA 1967 ss 29(1), 30, 35, ... ss 800, 868, 111
               36(1), 214(1)(2), 329(1), 332(1), 451(5),   Sch 2 Pt 2, Sch 2 Pt 1
               496(1), 530(4), 536(2), 544(2),
               553(1)(2), Sch 1 Pt I para 5, Sch 1 Pt IV
               par1(1), Sch 4 para 2(1), Sch 6 Pt II para (1)

Finance Act 1968 (1968 No 33)

s 1 .... Unnecessary (spent)
   2 .... s 768
   3 .... s 480
   4 .... Rep by FA 1996 s 132(2) and Sch 5 Pt II
   5 .... Rep by FA 1969 s 65(1) and Sch 5
   6 (1)-(5) .... s 886
     (6) .... Amendment of ITA 1967 s 508(1)..................... s 1061
   7 (1), (2) .... s 989(2), (3)
     (3) .... Rep by FA 1974 s 71
     (4), (5) .... s 989(4), (5)
     (6) .... Unnecessary (duplication)
     (7) .... Unnecessary (duplication)

Former Enactment   *Destination in TCA 1997*

Finance Act 1968 (1968 No 33) (contd)

s 7 (8)........Definition of "income tax month" .... s 989(1)
              unnecessary (duplication)
  8 (1),(2) (4) .... s 990
    (3).........Rep by FA 1974 s 71
  9 (a)... s 991(2)(a)
    proviso ..Rep by FA 1974 s 71
    (b).. s 991(2)(b)
  10 .... s 992
  11 .... s 1000
  12 ....Amendment of ITA 1967 s 138(1) .... s 461
  13 ....Rep by FA 1983 s 17(1)
  14 ....Amendment of ITA 1967 s 244 .... s 126(1), (2)
  15 ....Insertion of ITA 1967 s 416(8A) .... s 933(1)-(7)(f)
  16 ....Amendment of ITA 1967 s 421(3) .... s 944
  17 ....Amendment of ITA 1967 s 523(1)(b)
  27-30 ....Rep by CTA 1976 s 164 and Sch 3 Pt II

Pt VIII

s 34 ....Rep by CTA 1976 s 164 and Sch 3 Pt III
  35 ....Rep by CTA 1976 s 166 and Sch 4 Pt II
  36 ....Rep by CTA 1976 s 164 and Sch 3 Pt III
  37 (1)... ss 203(1), 109(1)
  37 (2)... s 203(2)
  37 (3)-(7).. s 109(2)-(6)
  37 (8).........Unnecessary (duplication)
  37 (9).........Unnecessary (operative date)
  38 ....Substitution of ITA 1967 s 251(4) .... s 283(3)
  39 ....Amendment of ITA 1967 s 254(2) .... s 271
  41 ....Rep by Trustee Savings Banks Act 1989
  47 ....Unnecessary (care and management).
  48 (2), (5) ....Unnecessary (construction and commencement)

Finance (No 2) Act 1968 (1968 No 37)

s 1 ....Unnecessary (interpretation)
  8 .... s 46
  10 ....Unnecessary (care and management)
  11 (4) ....Unnecessary (construction)

Finance Act 1969 (1969 No 21)

s 1 ....Unnecessary (spent)
  2 .... s 195(1)-(11)
  3 (1),(2),(4) .... s 467
    (3).........Rep by FA 1996 s 132(2) and Sch 5 Pt II
    (5).........Amendment of ITA 1967 s 153(1)(d) .... s 1032
    (6).........Rep by FA 1980 s 19 and Sch 1 Pt III
    (7).........Amendment of ITA 1967 s 497........................ s 460
    (8).........Rep by FA 1980 s 19 and Sch 1 Pt III
  4 ....Rep by FA 1996 s 132(2) and Sch 5 Pt II
  5 ....Rep by FA 1996 s 132(2) and Sch 5 Pt II
  6 ....Unnecessary (obsolete)
  7 ....Amendment of FA 1967 s 12(2) .... s 469(2)
  8 ....Amendment of ITA 1967 s 125(a) .... s 984(1), (2)
  9 ....Amendment of ITA 1967 s 138........................ s 461
  10 ....Amendment of ITA 1967 s 141........................ s 465
  11 ....Amendment of ITA 1967 s 142(1) .... s 466
  12 ....Substitution of ITA 1967 s 157(c)..................... s 853
  13 ....Insertion of ITA 1967 s 193(2A) .... s 1016
  14 ....Insertion of ITA 1967 s 246(1A)

Destination Table (Taxes Consolidation Act 1997)

Former Enactment   *Destination in TCA 1997*

Finance Act 1969 (1969 No 21) (contd)

s 15	Amendment of ITA 1967 s 374(2)	
16	Amendment of ITA 1967 s 402	
17	Insertion of ITA 1967 s 523(5)	
18 (1)	Definition of "farming" rep by FA 1996 s 132(2) and Sch 5 Pt II	s 232(1)
(2)(a)	Rep by FA 1974 s 14	
(b)		s 231
(c)		s 232(2)
19		s 53
20	Rep by CTA 1976 s 164 and Sch 3 Pt I	
21	Amendment of ITA 1967 Sch 6 Pt III para 1	s 73
22	Substitution of ITA 1967 s 81	ss 75, 96, 97
23	Substitution of ITA 1967 s 82	
24	Substitution of ITA 1967 s 89	s 384
25		s 1041
26 (1)-(4)		s 106
(5)	Unnecessary (duplication)	
(6)	Unnecessary (operative date)	
27	Amendment of ITA 1967 s 80	ss 96, 882
28	Substitution of ITA 1967 s 90	s 101
29	Substitution of ITA 1967 s 93	s 103
30	Amendment of ITA 1967 s 65	
31	Amendment of ITA 1967 s 67	s 85
32	Amendment of ITA 1967 s 118	s 119
33 (1)	Unnecessary (application of schedule)	
51-54	Rep by CTA 1976 s 164 and Sch 3 Pt II	
63 (1)		s 48(2)
(2)		s 48(1)(a)
64 (1), (2)	Amendment of ITA 1967 s 255	s 790
(3), (4)		s 274(6), (7)
(5)	Unnecessary (operative date)	
65	Unnecessary (repeals)	
66	Unnecessary (care and management)	
67 (2), (7)	Unnecessary (construction and commencement)	
Sch 4, Pt I	Amendment of ITA 1967 ss 53(1), 83, 84(1), 86, 89A, 92(1), 94, 162(3)(a), 183(1), 184(1), 214(3), 267(5)(a), 307(1), 316(2), 334(1), 335, 336, 433, 434, Sch 18 and F(MP)A 1967 s 18(2)(g)	ss 18(2)(3), 75(4), 98, 99, 103, 888, 851, 921, 922, 278(1)(3)-(6), 381(1),390 (1)(3), 208(2), 211(1)-(4), 213(1),(2),237,238(1)-(6), Sch 28, 641
Sch 5, Pt I	Repeal of ITA 1967 ss 2(2)(d), 9-42, 44, 45, 54(3)(4), 56(4)(5)(6), 66, 75(2)(ii), 78, 87, 88(2)(3), 95, 104, 106(2), 147, 148, 150, 169(1)(a), 180, 183(1)(b), (5)(b)(6), 210(3), 243(3), 244(6)(b), 245(8)(a), 267(5)(6), 283(2), 309(3), 334(1)(b)(2), 351, 352, 385(2), 436, 437, 477(2)(a), (b), 480(6), 481, 524(3)(a), 545(2),548, Sch 18 para 1 and FA 1968 s 5	
	Amendment of ITA 1967 ss 1(1), 2(1)(c), 4, 52(1)(b), 53(1), 54(2), 60(1), 61(c), 86, 107(1), 169(2), 183(1), 186(1), 219(1), 235(7)(c),251(1),322, 333(1)(a),388, 416(1), 480(1), 485, 533, 544(1), Sch 15	ss 2(1), 3(1); 3(2)(3); 12; 18(1)(3); 18(2)(3); 655(3); 65(2)-(4); 81(2); 75(4); 107;877;921(2);924; 699(1);784(1)-(5); 283(2), 300(1);391(3); 208(2); 933(1)-(7)(f); 866; 837 962(1)(2); Sch 29
Sch 5, Pt III	Repeal of ITA 1967 s 404(7), (8)	

Former Enactment   *Destination in TCA 1997*
Finance Act 1970 (1970 No 14)

s 1 ....Unnecessary (spent).
    2 (1), (2) ....Ceased by FA 1971 s 2
      (3)........Insertion of ITA 1967 s 153(1)(dd) ....s 1032
      (4)........Amendment of ITA 1967 s 193(6) ....s 1015
    2 (5)........Amendment of ITA 1967 s 497.........................s 460
    3 (1)........Amendment of ITA 1967 s 6 ....s 14(1)
      (2)........Unnecessary (operative date)
    4 ....Amendment of FA 1967 s 11(1) and
              FA 1969 s 4(1)......................................s 285(1)-(3)
    5 ....Insertion of ITA 1967 s 127(1)(ff)
    6 ....Amendment of ITA 1967 s 134
    7 ....Amendment of ITA 1967 s 135(1)
    8 ....Amendment of ITA 1967 s 136
    9 ....Amendment of ITA 1967 s 138(3) ....s 461
    10 ....Amendment of ITA 1967 s 141(1A)(a)..................s 465
    11 ....Amendment of ITA 1967 s 142(1) ....s 466
    12 ....Amendment of ITA 1967 s 221(2)(h)(i)
    13 ....Amendment of ITA 1967 s 236(1) and Sch 5............s 787(6)
    14 (1),(2),(3) ....s 287
      (4)..s 301(1)
      (5).......Amendment of ITA 1967 s 241(7)
    15 ....Amendment of ITA 1967 s 331(3)
    16 ....Amendment of ITA 1967 s 332(8)
    17(1).......Definitions of "construction ....ss 530(1), 531(11)(c)
              contract", construction
              paymentscard" and "construction
              tax deduction card" deleted by FA
              1992 s 28(a)(ii)

(2),(2A),(3) ....s 531(1), (3), (4),
(4),(5), (6),   (5), (6), (8), (9), (10)
(6A), (6B)
(7)(a), (b)..s 531(11)(a), (b)
(c) ....Deleted by FA 1992 s 28(e)(iii)
(8), (9), (10)..s 531(12), (13), (14),
(10A),(10B) ....(15), (16), (7), (2)
(11)(12)
(13) ....s 530(2)
(14),(15),(16), ..s 531(17), (18)
(17),(19),(20)
17A ....(s 17A inserted by FA 1992 s 233)....................904
18 ....s 197
19(1), (2), (2A) ....s 279
    (3) ....Unnecessary (construction)
    (4) ....Unnecessary (operative date)
    (5) ....Unnecessary (operative date)
20(1) ....s 91(3)
   (2) ....s 91(1)
   (3)(a)-(d) ....s 91(2)
    (e).......Unnecessary (operative date)
   (4) ....s 91(4)
   (5)(a) ......Rep by FA 1975 s 33 and Sch 1 Pt II
    (b), (c)(d)...s 91(5)
21 ....s 95
22 ....s 92

Former Enactment   *Destination in TCA 1997*
Finance Act 1970 (1970 No 14) (contd)

s 23 (1), (2), (3).. s 90(1)-(3)
       (4) s 89(1)(b)
          (5) .... s 90(4)
          (6) .... Unnecessary (operative date)
    24 (1), (2)(a)... s 87
       (2)(b)..... Rep by CTA 1976 s 164 and Sch 3 Pt II
    24 (3) .... Unnecessary (operative date)
    25 .... s 93
    26 (1)-(4) .... s 94
       (5) .... Unnecessary (operative date)
   Pt VI
s 57 (1) .... Unnecessary (duplication)
       (2)-(4) .... s 829
       (5) .... Unnecessary (obsolete)
    58 .... Amendment of FA 1968 s 35(3)(b)
    59 (1),(2),(3)... ss 38, 48(1)(b)
       (5) .... Amendment of ITA 1967 s 474(1)
       (6) .... s 48(2)
    61 .... Unnecessary (care and management)
    62 (2), (7).... Unnecessary (construction and commencement)

Finance (No 2) Act 1970 (1970 No 25)

s   1 .... Ceased by FA 1972 s 10
    7 .... Unnecessary (care and management)
    8 (2), (5).... Unnecessary (construction and commencement)

Finance Act 1971 (1971 No 23)
   Pt I
s   1 .... Unnecessary (obsolete)
    2 .... Unnecessary (cesser of FA 1970 s 2)
    3 .... Amendment of ITA 1967 s 58
               (amendment ceased by FA 1990 s 14(2))
    4 (1)-(4),(6).. s 72
       (5) .... Unnecessary (operative date)
    5 .... s 86
    6 .... Amendment of ITA 1967 s 134
    7 .... Amendment of ITA 1967 s 135
    8 .... Amendment of ITA 1967 s 136
    9 .... Insertion of ITA 1967 s 139(6)
   10 .... Amendment of ITA 1967 s 142(1)..................... s 466
   11 (1), (2) .... s 468
       (3) .... Deleted by FA 1980 s 5
       (4) .... Rep by FA 1996 s 132(2) and Sch 5 Pt II
       (5) .... Amendment of ITA 1967 s 153(1)(d) .... s 1032
       (6) .... Deleted by FA 1980 s 5
       (7) .... Amendment of ITA 1967 s 497 .... s 460
       (8) .... Deleted by FA 1980 s 5
   12 .... Amendment of ITA 1967 s 244 .... ss 763-765
   13 .... Amendment of ITA 1967 s 251(4)(c).................. ss 283(2), 300(1)
   14 .... Amendment of ITA 1967 s 254(2)
   15 .... Amendment of ITA 1967 s 336 .... s 213(1), (2)
   16 (1)(a), (b).. Amendment of ITA 1967 s 443
       (c)..... Amendment of ITA 1967 s 444
       (2), (3) .... s 796(2)(d), (e), (f)
   17 (1), (2)(a).. Amendment of ITA 1967 s 550 .... s 1080(1)
       (2)(b)..... Unnecessary (operative date)
       (3) .... Unnecessary (cesser of ITA 1967 ss 418, 529)

Former Enactment *Destination in TCA 1997*
Finance Act 1971 (1971 No 23) (contd)

s 18 .... Amendment of ITA 1967 s 419
   19 .... Amendment of ITA 1967 ss 428, 429, ... ss 941, 942(1)-(8)(10)
   20 (1)-(4), (6) .... s 1082
      (5)........ Unnecessary (operative date)
   21 (1)(a) ..... Insertion of FA 1970 s 17(2)(aa)
     (b),(c),(d).. Unnecessary (obsolete)
     (2)........ Insertion FA 1970 s 17(6A), (6B), (6C) .... s 531(5)(6)(8)(9)(10)
     (3)........ Unnecessary (obsolete)
   22 .... Unnecessary (spent)
   23 .... Unnecessary (obsolete)
   24 .... Unnecessary (obsolete)
   25 .... Unnecessary (obsolete)
   26 (1),(2),(2A).. s 285(1), (2), (3)
     (3).. s 299(2)
     (4).. s 285(8)
     (5)........ Amendment of FA 1970 s 14(1) .... s 287

Pt VI
s 54 .... Unnecessary (care and management)
   55 (2), (6) .... Unnecessary (construction and commencement)

Finance Act 1972 (1972 No 19)

Pt I
s 1 (1)........ Rep by FA 1974 s 86 and Sch 2 Pt I
    (2)........ Amendment of ITA 1967 s 522
   2 .... Amendment of ITA 1967 ss 127(1), 128(1) .... ss 986(1)(a)-(j), 987(1)-(3)
   3 .... Amendment of ITA 1967 s 135
   4 .... Amendment of ITA 1967 s 138......................... s 461
   5 .... Amendment of ITA 1967 s 141......................... s 465
   6 .... Amendment of ITA 1967 s 142(1) .... s 466
   7 .... Amendment of ITA 1967 s 485(5) .... s 962(1), (2)
   8 .... Amendment of ITA 1967 s 486......................... s 963
   9 .... Amendment of FA 1967 s 12(2) .... s 469(2)
   10 .... Unnecessary (cesser of F(No 2)A 1970 s 1)
   11 .... Rep by FA 1997 s 146(2) and Sch 5 Pt II
   12 .... Unnecessary (repeals)
   13 (1), (2), ... Definitions of "ordinary share...................... s 770
     (4)   capital", "proprietary director" and
           "proprietary employee" rep by FA
           1975 s 86 and Sch 2 Pt III, definition
           of "Revenue Commissioners"
           unnecessary
     (3)........ Rep by FA 1974 s 86 and Sch 2 Pt II
   14 .... s 771
   15 (1)... s 772(1)
     (2)(a)-(e),(g)... s 772(2)
     (2)(f)...... Rep by FA 1974 s 64
     (3).. s 772(3)
     (4)........ The matter from "In applying this.................... s 772(4)
           subsection" to end rep by FA 1996
           s 132(2) and Sch 5 Pt II
     (5)-(7).. s 772(5)-(7)
   15 (8)........ Unnecessary (operative date)
   16 (1), (2), (3) .... s 774(1), (3), (5)
     (4)... s 774(6), Sch 32 para 26
     (5).. s 774(7)
     (6)........ Rep by FA 1996 s 132(2) and Sch 5 Pt II

Former Enactment *Destination in TCA 1997*
Finance Act 1972 (1972 No 19) (contd)

```
s  16 (7) ................................................. s 774(2)
    16A ......... (s 16A inserted by FA 1997 s 41 ) .......... s 775
    17 (1), (2) ............................................. s 776
        (3) ....... Rep by FA 1996 s 132(2) and Sch 5 Pt II
        (4) ....... Unnecessary (operative date)
    18 (1)(a), (2)-(5) ...................................... s 772
        (b) ..... Rep by FA 1996 s 132(2) and Sch 5 Pt II
        (6) ....... Insertion of ITA 1967 s 2(2)(cc) .......... s 3(2), (3)
        (7) ....... Unnecessary (operative date)
    19 ...................................................... s 778
    20 ...................................................... s 779
    21 (1)-(4), .. s 780
    (5)(a), (6), (7)
        (5)(b) ..... Unnecessary (operative date)
    22 (1)-(4) .............................................. s 781
        (5) ....... Unnecessary (operative date)
    23 ...................................................... s 782
    24 ......... Rep by FA 1996 s 132(2) and Sch 5 Pt II
    25 ......... Rep by FA 1996 s 132(2) and Sch 5 Pt II
Pt V
s  42 (1) ....... Amendment of ITA 1967 s 251(4)
       (2) ....... Amendment of ITA 1967 s 246(1)
    43 ...................................................... s 212
    46 ......... Unnecessary (repeals)
    47 ......... Unnecessary (care and management)
    48 (2), (5) .... Unnecessary (construction and commencement)
Sch 1, Pt I .............................................. Sch 23, Pt I,
    para 1, 2 ............................................... para 1, 2
    3(1)-(3) ................................................ para 3
        (4) ...... Unnecessary (operative date)
    4, 5 .................................................... para 4, 5
Sch 1, Pt II ..... Unnecessary (obsolete)
Sch 1, Pt III
    para 1 ........ Amendment of ITA 1967 s 63 ............... s 84
        2 ........ Amendment of ITA 1967 s 115(1) ........... s 201(2)
        3 ........ Amendment of ITA 1967 Sch 15 ............. Sch 29
        4 ........ Saver for enactments which contain reference
                   to ITA 1967 Pt XII Ch II (substituted by FA
                   1997 s 146(1) and Sch 9 para 5(3))
Sch 1, Pt IV ..... Rep by FA 1996 s 132(2) and Sch 5 Pt II
Sch 1, Pt V ...... Rep by FA 1996 s 132(2) and Sch 5 Pt II
Sch 1, Pt VI
    paras 1-4 ...... Sch 23, Pt 2, paras 6-9
        5 ........ Insertion of ITA 1967 s 2(2)(dd) ......... s 3(2), (3)
Sch 3 ......... Amendment of ITA 1967 ss 1(1), 8(1), (2) ..... ss 2(1), 3(1), s 1087
Sch 4 ......... Repeal of ITA 1967 ss 7, 63(a), (b), (c) and
                proviso, 152(5), 222, 223, Pt XII Ch II
```

Finance Act 1973 (1973 No 19)

```
s   1 (1) ....... Amendment of ITA 1967 s 129 .............. s 991(1)
       (2) ....... Unnecessary (operative date)
    2 ......... Amendment of ITA 1967 s 138(3) ............. s 461
    3 ......... Amendment of ITA 1967 s 141 ................ s 465
    4 ......... Amendment of ITA 1967 s 142(1) ............. s 466
    5 ...................................................... Sch 32, para 21(2)
    6 ......... Unnecessary (deletion of ITA 1967 s 211(4) )
```

Former Enactment   *Destination in TCA 1997*

Finance Act 1973 (1973 No 19) (contd)

s 7	Amendment of ITA 1967 s 229(1)(i)	
8	Amendment of ITA 1967 s 246	
9 (1)	Amendment of ITA 1967 s 251(4)(d)	s 283(3)
(2)		s 283(7)
proviso	Unnecessary (operative date)	
10	Amendment of ITA 1967 s 254(2)	s 316(3)
11	Amendment of ITA 1967 s 272	s 288
12	Amendment of ITA 1967 s 336	s 213(1), (2)
13	Amendment of ITA 1967 s 357(3)	
14	Insertion of ITA 1967 s 387(4)	
15	Insertion of ITA 1967 s 439(1)(ii)(a)	s 792(1)-(4)
16	Amendment of FA 1971 s 22(2)	
17	Amendment of FA 1971 s 26(1)	s 285(1), (2), (3)
18	Amendment of FA 1972 s 21	s 780
19 (1), (2)		s 192
(3)	Unnecessary (operative date)	
20		s 209
21		s 767
22		s 993(5)
23	Deleted by FA 1992 s 4	
24	Rep by FA 1982 s 20(7)	
25		ss 373(2)(a), 374
26		ss 373(2)(a), 375
27		ss 373(2)(a), 377
28		ss 373(2)(a), 378
29		ss 373(2)(a), 379
30 (1), (5), (6)		s 373(1), (2)(a), (3)
(2), (3), (4)		s 380
31	Unnecessary (spent)	
32	Rep by FA 1977 s 54 and Sch 2 Pt I	
33 (1)(a),(b),(c)		s 13(1)
(d)	Unnecessary (duplication)	
(2), (3),	s 13(2)-(6)	
(4), (5), (7)		
(6)	Unnecessary (commencement)	
34 (1), (2)		s 234(1), (2)(a)
(2A)-(7)		s 234(3)-(8)
35		s 1089(1)
39	Rep by CTA 1976 s 164 and Sch 3 Pt III	
40 (1)-(5)		s 275
(6)	Unnecessary (obsolete)	
(7)	Unnecessary (construction and operative date)	
41	Insertion of ITA 1967 s 117(7), (8)	s 118
42	Unnecessary (cesser of ITA 1967 s 121)	
43	Amendment of ITA 1967 s 128	s 987
44	Insertion of ITA 1967 s 335(2), (3), (4)	s 211(1)-(4)
45	Amendment of ITA 1967 s 413(2)	
46	Amendment of ITA 1967 s 503(2)	s 1054(2)-(4)
92 (1)		ss 39(1), 48(1)(c)
(2)(a)		s 39(2)
(b)		s 48(2)
(4)	Amendment of ITA 1967 s 474(1)	s 49, Sch 32 para 1(2)
97	Unnecessary (care and management)	
98(2), (6)	Unnecessary (construction and commencement)	
Sch 1	Deleted by FA 1992 s 4(b)	

Former Enactment   *Destination in TCA 1997*

Finance Act 1973 (1973 No 19) (contd)

Sch 2	....	Rep by FA 1977 s 54 and Sch 2 Pt I
Sch 3		
paras 1, 3-5,7,8	....	Sch 1
2	....	Amendment of ITA 1967 Sch 15 ...... Sch 29
6	....	Unnecessary (obsolete)
Sch 4	....	Rep by FA 1977 s 54 and Sch 2 Pt I
Sch 5	....	Deleted by FA 1996 s 13(b)
Pt I		
para 1-5	....	Sch 9, para 1 to 5
6(a),(c)- (e)	....	Sch 9, para 6(a)-(d)
(b)	......	Unnecessary (duplication)
7, 9	....	Sch 9 para 7, 8
8, 10	......	Rep by CTA 1976 s 164 and Sch 3
Pt II	....	Unnecessary (duplication)

Finance (Taxation of Profits of Certain Mines) Act 1974 (1974 No 17)

s 1 (1)	......	Definition of "tax" unnecessary .... s 672(1)
		(duplication)
(2),(6),(7)	....	s 672(2), (3), (4)
(3)-(5)	....	Unnecessary (construction)
2 (1)	....	s 673(1)
proviso	...	Deleted by FA 1990 s 93(a)
(2)	....	Unnecessary (spent)
(3)	....	Unnecessary (obsolete)
(4)	....	s 673(3)
3 (1)	....	Unnecessary (spent)
(2)-(5)	....	s 674(1)(a), (2), (3), (4)
4	....	s 675
5	....	s 676
6	....	s 677
7 (1), (3), (4)	....	s 678
(2)	....	Unnecessary (spent)
7A	....	(s 7A inserted by FA 1990 s 39(d)) .... s 679(1)(a),(2)-(5)
8	....	s 680
8A(1)-(9)	....	(s 8A inserted by FA 1996 s 34) .... s 681
8A (10)	......	Unnecessary (obsolete)
9	....	Rep by CTA 1976 s 164 and Sch 3 Pt II
10	....	s 682(1)-(3)
11	....	s 683
12	....	Rep by CTA 1976 s 164 and Sch 3 Pt II
13-15	....	Rep by CTA 1976 s 164 and Sch 3 Pt I
16-17	....	Rep by CTA 1976 s 164 and Sch 3 Pt II
18	....	Unnecessary (short title, construction and commencement)

Finance Act 1974 (1974 No 27)

Pt I		
s 1	....	Amendment of ITA 1967 s 1(1)
2	....	Amendment of ITA 1967 s 4
3	....	Unnecessary (obsolete)
4	....	s 59
5 (1)	....	s 237(1)(b), (2)
proviso	...	Rep by CTA 1976 s 164 and Sch 3 Pt 1
(2), (3)	....	s 16
6	....	Unnecessary (obsolete)
7	....	Amendment of ITA 1967 s 142(1)

Former Enactment   *Destination in TCA 1997*

Finance Act 1974 (1974 No 27) (contd)

s 8 (1)		s 464
(2)	Rep by FA 1996 s 132(2) and Sch 5 Pt II	
9	Substitution of ITA 1967 s 152(1)	
10	Unnecessary (cesser of charge to sur-tax)	
11	Unnecessary (supplementary)	
12	Unnecessary (commencement)	
13 (1)		s 654
(2), (3)	Rep by FA 1983 s 120 and Sch 4	
14	Unnecessary (repeal of FA 1969 s 18(2)(a))	
15		s 655(1), (2)
16 (1)		s 657(1)
(2)		s 657(2)
(3)	Deleted by FA 1976s 14(1)(c)	
(4)		s 657(3)
(5)		s 657(1)
17-19	Rep by FA 1983 s 120 and Sch 4	
20	Ceased by FA 1983 s 24	
20A	Unnecessary (spent)	
20B(1)	(s 20B inserted by FA 1981 s 10)	s 657(4)
(2)		s 657(5)
proviso	Unnecessary (obsolete)	
(3)		s 657(6)
(4)		s 657(7)
(5)		s 657(8)
(6)		s 657(9)
(7)		s 657(10)
(8)		s 657(11)
(9)		s 657(12)
21	Ceased by FA 1980 s 24	

Finance Act 1974 (1974 No 27)

s22(1)	Section 658 is applied on a modified basis by Sch 32 para 23 to reflect the application of FA 1974 s 22 in relation to certain old expenditure	s 658(1)
(2)		s 658(2)(a)
proviso		s 658(2)(b)
(2A)		s 658(3)
(2B)		s 658(4)
(2C)	Deleted by FA 1994 s 23	
(3)		s 658(5)
(4)	Deleted by FA 1982 s 16	
(5)		s 658(6)
(6)		s 658(7)
(7)		s 658(8)
(8)		s 658(9)
proviso		s 658(10)
(9)		s 658(11)
(10)		s 658(12)
(11)		s 658(13)
23	Rep by CTA 1976 s 164 and Sch 3 Pt I	
24	Unnecessary (obsolete)	

Destination Table (Taxes Consolidation Act 1997)

Former Enactment   *Destination in TCA 1997*
Finance Act 1974 (1974 No 27) (contd)

s 25	s 660
26 .... Amendment of ITA 1967 s 307	s 381(1)
27 (1)-(6) .... Definitions of "basis year" unnecessary (obsolete) and "market gardening" unnecessary (duplication)	s 662
(7) .... Rep by CTA 1976 s 164 and Sch 3 Pt II	
28 .... Rep by FA 1983 s 120 and Sch 4	
29 .... Substitution of ITA 1967 s 496	
30 .... Rep by FA 1996 s 132(2) and Sch 5 Pt II	
31 (1), (2), (4)	s 246(1), (2), (4)
(3)(a) ..... Rep by FA 1996 s 132(2) and Sch 5 Pt II	
(3)(b)-(g)	s 246(3)
32	s 245
33	s 247(1)-(3)
34	s 248(1)-(3)
35(1)-(3)	s 249
35(4), (5)	ss 247(4), (5), 248(4), (5)
36	s 253
37	s 254
38 .... Rep by FA 1997 s 146(2) and Sch 9 Pt II	
39	s 255
40 .... Rep by FA 1996 s 132 (2) and Sch 5 Pt II	
41 (1)-(6)	s 813
(7) .... Unnecessary (obsolete)	
42 (1) .... Amendment of ITA 1967 s 61(l)	s 82(2)
(2) .... Unnecessary (commencement)	
43 .... Insertion of ITA 1967 s 75(3), (4)	s 70(1)
44 .... Rep by FA 1997 s 146(2) and Sch 9 Pt II	
45 .... Amendment of ITA 1967 s 77(3)	
46	s 71(4)
47 .... Substitution of ITA 1967 s 219(1)	s 699(1)
48 .... Amendment of ITA 1967 s 221(2)	
49 .... Amendment of ITA 1967 ss 231(4)(a), 232(2), 233(2)(a)	
50 .... Rep by FA 1996 s 132(2) and Sch 5 Pt II	
51 (1) .... Amendment of ITA 1967 s 535(1)(b)	s 1088
(2) .... Unnecessary (operative date)	
52 .... Rep by FA 1997 s 146(2) and Sch 9 Pt II	
54 .... Rep by FA 1997 s 146(2) and Sch 9 Pt II	
55	s 814
56 (1), (2), (3)(b), (c), (4)	s 816
(3)(a) ..... Rep by CTA 1976 s 164 and Sch 3 Pt II	
57 preamble, (1)-(7) and (8)(a)-(c),(e),(f)	s 806
(d) ..... Unnecessary (obsolete)	
(9) .... Unnecessary (operative date)	
58	s 807
59(1)-(5)	s 808
(6) .... Amendment of ITA 1967 Sch 15	Sch 29
60	s 809
61	s 810
62(1), (2)	s 105
(3) .... Unnecessary (obsolete)	

Former Enactment   *Destination in TCA 1997*
Finance Act 1974 (1974 No 27) (contd)

s 63	Amendment of F(MP)A 1968 s 20	s 643
64(1)	Unnecessary (cesser of FA 1972 s 115(2)(f) and ITA 1967 Sch 3 proviso para 4)	
(2)	Substitution of FA 1972 Sch 1 Pt III para 4	
65	Amendment of ITA 1967 s 235	ss 783-784
66	Insertion of ITA 1967 s 235A	s 785
67	Amendment of ITA 1967 s 236 and Sch 5	s 787
69	Amendment of ITA 1967 s 429	s 942(1)-(8), (10)
70	Amendment of ITA 1967 s 489(1)	s 965
71	Unnecessary (cesser of ITA 1967 s 130, FA 1969 ss 7(3), 8(3) and 9(a)(proviso)	
72		s 988
73 (1)-(4)		s 898
(5)	Amendment of ITA 1967 Sch 15	Sch 29
74		s 671
Pt IV		
s 86	Unnecessary (application of schedule)	
87	Unnecessary (care and management)	
88(2), (5)	Unnecessary (construction and commencement)	
Sch 1, Pt I	Amendment of ITA 1967 ss 137-141, 143, 146, 149, 153, 193, FA 1969 s 3, FA 1971 s 11	ss 193, 458, 459(1)-(2), 460, 461, 462, 465, 467, 468, 472, 1032, 1032
Sch 1, Pt II	Amendment of ITA 1967 ss 115(1)(b), 127, 133(1), 195, 233(2), 406(5), 434(1), 435(1), 451(5), 488, 497, 525(1), 528, 530, 543, Sch 1 Pt I para 1(c), Sch 1 Pt II para 1(b), Sch 16 para 8, 9, FA 1967 s 12(2), FA 1968 ss 3, 34(6)	ss 201(2), 986, 997 1018, 238(1)-(6), 800, 966, 460, 127(1)-(5), 926, Sch 2, 469(2), 480
Sch 2, Pt I	Repeal of ITA 1967 ss 134, 135, 136, 144(3), 188(2), 198, 236(10), s 387(4)(c), 396(4), 410(4), 416(11), 485(3)(4), 522, 523, 524, 526, 527, 532, 551(2)(b), Sch 10 para 5(1)(b) and proviso, F(MP)A 1968 ss 3(6)(a)(b) (c)(i)(c)(vi), 23(4), FA 1972 s 1(1)	
	Amendment of ITA 1967 ss 2(2)(c), 3, 70(1)(c), 116(1), 117(1), 145(1), 162(2), 172(1)(c), 187(1), 191(2), (3), 192(1), 194(1)(a), 196, 231(2)(3), 288(2), 291, 293, 329(1)(b), 332(1)(b), 344(4), 345, 356, 361, 365, 336(b), 387(3)(a), 419, 420, 441(1), 446(1), 465, 486(1), 489(1), 491(1), 492(1), 493, 501(1)(c), 502(2), 505, 511, 521, 539(1), 547(3), 549(1), 550, 552(2), 554(4), 555, 556(1), 559(1), Sch 6 Pt II para 1, 10 Pt III para (3)(1), Sch para 1(1), 5(1)(a), Sch 15, IT(A)A 1967 preamble para 2, FA 1968 ss 6(2)(a), 37(6), 48(2), F(No 2)A 1968 ss 8, 11(4), FA 1969 ss 63(1), 67(2), FA 1970 ss 19(5), 62(2), FA 1971 s 20(2), FA 1972 s 48(2), FA 1973 ss 33(1)(d), (6), 98(2)	ss 1(2), 3(2)(3), 45(1), 48(2), 117, 118, 199, 470(1)-(3),483(1)-(3), 757, 759, 760, 793, 797, 826(1)-(7)(9), 851, 879(1)-(4), 880(2)-(6), 886, 901, 928(1), 930, 963,965, 968, 969, 998, 1000,1004, 1015, 1017, 1022, 1053(1)-(4),1054(2)-(4), 1055, 1063, 1067, 1080(1), 1082, Sch 24 paras 1(1), 6, Sch 29
Sch 2, Pt II	Repeal of definitions of "ordinary share capital", "proprietary director", "proprietary employee" in FA 1972 s 13(1), (3)	
Sch 3	Repealed by FA 1983 s 120 and Sch 4	

Destination Table (Taxes Consolidation Act 1997)

Former Enactment			*Destination in TCA 1997*
Finance Act 1975 (1975 No 6)			

s 1 .... Amendment of ITA 1967 s 142(1)..................... s 466
  2 .... Amendment of ITA 1967 s 143(3)(b)
  3 .... Amendment of ITA 1967 s 251(4)(d) .... ss 283(2), 300(1)
  4 .... Insertion of ITA 1967 s 254(2A) .... s 271(4)
  5 .... Amendment of ITA 1967 s 264 .... s 272
  6 .... Amendment of FA 1971 s 22(2)
  7 .... Amendment of FA 1971 s 26(1)....................... s 285(1)-(3)
  8 .... Amendment of FA 1973 s 8
  9 .... Amendment of FA 1973 s 19......................... s 192
 10 .... Amendment of FA 1974 s 3
 11 (1) ...... Substitution of FA 1974 s 6(1)
s 11 (2) ...... Unnecessary (application of schedule)
 12 .... Substitution of FA 1974 s 13(1)..................... s 654
 13 .... Amendment of FA 1974 s 15(3)...................... s 655(1), (2)
 14 (1) ...... Amendment of FA 1974 s 16........................ s 657(1)
    (2) ...... Unnecessary (operative date)
 15 .... Amendment of FA 1974 s 17(4)
 16 .... Amendment of FA 1974 s 20(1)
 17 .... Amendment of FA 1974 s 21(1)
 18 .... Amendment of FA 1974 s 22......................... s 658
 19 .... Amendment of ITA 1967 s 80........................ ss 96, 888(1)
 20 .... Amendment of ITA 1967 s 83 .... s 98
 21 (1)-(7) .... s 947
    (8) ...... Rep by CTA 1976 s 164 and Sch 3 Pt II
 22 .... Unnecessary (application of schedule)
 25 .... Amendment of ITA 1967 s 542 .... s 869
 26 .... Amendment of FA 1968 s 9(b)....................... s 991(2)(b)
 27 .... Amendment of FA 1973 s 35......................... s 1089(1)
 28 .... Unnecessary (obsolete)
 29 .... s 319
 30 .... Rep by CTA 1976 s 164 and Sch 3 Pt I.
 31 .... Rep by FA 1996 s 132(2) and Sch 5 Pt II
 31A .... Rep by FA 1996 s 132(2) and Sch 5 Pt II
 32 .... Amendment of FA 1974 s 41(7)
 33 (1) .... s 2(1)
    (2) ...... Unnecessary (application of schedule)
 34 (1)....... Amendment of ITA 1967 s 255(1) .... s 268(1)-(3),(5)-(8)
    (2)(a)(i) .... s 271(4)(b)
         (ii)... s 272(3)(b)
         (iii) .... ss 272(4)(b), 274(1)(b)(ii)
      (b)..... Unnecessary (spent)
    (3) ...... Unnecessary (operative date)
 35 .... Unnecessary (application of schedule)
 56 .... Unnecessary (care and management)
 57(2), (5) .... Unnecessary (construction and commencement)
Sch 1
Pt I   .... Amendment of ITA 1967 ss 138, 139, 140,.............. ss 460,461,
                141, FA 1969 s 3 FA 1971 s 11, FA 1974 s 8   464-466,
                                                                     467, 1032
Pt II .... Amendment of ITA 1967 ss 69(1), 218, ... ss 1007(1)-(2), 698,)
                317(1), 236(3), 314, FA 1970 s 20(5)(a),   391(1), 787(6), 662
                FA 1971 s 22, FA 1973 39(1)(b), (7),
                FA 1974 s 27(1)
Pt III .... Amendment of ITA 1967 s 288(2), ... ss 757, 59
                F(TPCM)A 1974 ss 1, 7(4), 11(2)
Sch 2
Pt I   .... Unnecessary (obsolete)
Pt II .... Amendment of ITA 1967 Sch 15 .... Sch 29

Former Enactment *Destination in TCA 1997*

Finance Act 1975 (1975 No 6) (contd)

Pt III .... Amendment of ITA 1967 ss 81(3), 91(1)(b), 92(2)
Sch 3 .... Rep by FA 1996 s 132(2) and Sch 5 Pt II
Sch 5 .... Rep by FA 1996 s 132(2) and Sch 5 Pt II

Finance (No 2) Act 1975 (1975 No 19)

s 1 .... Unnecessary (obsolete)
   3 .... Unnecessary (care and management)
   4 .... Unnecessary (short title, construction and commencement)

Capital Gains Tax Act 1975 (1975 No 20)

s 1 .... Unnecessary (short title)
   2 (1)(3)(4) .... s 5
      (2). .... Rep by FA 1996 s 132(2) and Sch 5 Pt II
      (5). .... s 3(4)
      (6). ...... Unnecessary (construction)
      (7). ...... Unnecessary (construction)
      (8). ...... Unnecessary (construction)
   3 (1)-(3) .... s 28
      (4). .... Deleted by FA 1992 s 60(1)(b)
   4(1)-(4)(6)-(8) .... s 29(1)-(7)
      (2) proviso . Rep by FA 1977 s 54 and Sch 2 Pt I
      (5). .... s 30
   5 (1). .... s 31
      (2). .... s 979
      (3). .... s 1042
   6 .... Rep by CGT(A)A 1978 s 17 and Sch 2
   7(1). .... s 532(1)
      (2). .... ss 545(1), 546(1)
   8 (1). .... s 534
      (2). .... s 535(2)
      (3). .... s 567(2)
      (4), (5), (6) .... s 537
      (7). .... s 535(1)
   9 .... s 547
   10 (1). .... s 542(1)
      (2). .... s 539
      (3). .... s 542(2)
   11 .... s 545(2), (3)
   12 (1). .... s 546(2)
      (2). .... s 546(3)
      (3), (4), (5) .... s 538
      (6). .... s 546(4)
      (7). .... s 546(5)
   13 .... s 1028
   14 .... s 573
   15 (1), (9), (11) .... s 574
      (2). .... s 575
      (3), (8) .... s 576
      (4)-(5A)(6)(12). .... s 577
      (7). .... s 578
      (10). .... s 567(1)

Former Enactment   *Destination in TCA 1997*

Capital Gains Tax Act 1975 (1975 No 20) (contd)

Former Enactment	Destination in TCA 1997
s 16	s 601(1), (2), (4), (5)
17	s 602
18	s 603
19 (1)	s 607(1)(a), (b), (c), (d), (f)
(2)	s 607(2)
20	s 593
20A .... (s 20A inserted by FA 1993 s 24)	s 594
20B .... (s 20B inserted by FA 1994 s 58)	s 595
21	s 608(2)-(4)
22	s 609
23	s 610, Sch 15, Pt I
24	s 613
25	s 604
26(1)-(6)	s 598
(7) .... Rep by CGT(A)A 1978 s 17 and Sch 2	
27(1)(a)-(c),	s 599
(2)-(4)	
(d) .... Rep by FA 1996 s 132(2) and Sch 5 Pt II	
28	s 597
29(1)-(3), (5)	s 536
(4) .... Rep by CGT(A)A 1978 s 17 and Sch 2	
30	s 612
31 (1)-(4), (6)	s 731(1)-(5)(a)
(5)	Sch 32, para 25
32	s 732
33 (1)-(6)	s 549
(7) .... Ceased by FA 1996 s 131(9)(a)	
(8) .... Rep by FA 1996 s 132(2) and Sch 5 Pt II	
34	s 550
35 (1)-(3), (5)	s 589
35 (4) .... Deleted by CTA 1976 s 140(2) and Sch 2 Pt II, para 3(2)	
36	s 590(1)-(9)
37	s 579
38	s 828(1)-(3)
39	s 611
40	s 569
41	s 570
42	s 572
43	s 1005
44 (1)	s 981
(2)	s 563(1)
45	s 543
46 (1)-(6)	s 541(1)-(6)
(7)(a)-(d)	s 541(7)(a), (b), (c), (g)
47(1)-(6)(8)-(11)	s 540
(7) .... Rep by CGT(A)A 1978 s 17 and Sch 2	
48	s 533
49 (1)-(6)	s 548(1)-(6)
(7) .... Rep by FA 1997 s 146(2) and Sch 5 Pt II	

Former Enactment	Destination in TCA 1997
Capital Gains Tax Act 1975 (1975 No 20) (contd)	

s 50	(1)........Amendment of PCTA 1927 s 1	
	(2)........Amendment of IRRA 1890 s 39	
s 51	(1).........For leases only, otherwise unnecessary (application of schedules)	s 566
	(2)...	s 544(8)
Sch 1, Pt I		
para 1	....	s 544(1)-(6)
Sch 1, Pt I		
para 2	....	s 551
	3(1)-(5)...	s 552
	(6)..	s 828(4)
	(7)..	s 565
	4..	s 554
	5(1), (2), (4)..	s 555
	(3)..	s 544(1)
	6..	s 557
	7..	s 559
	8..	s 560(1), (2)
	9..	s 560(3), (4), (5)
	10...	s 561
	11...	s 562
	12...	s 564
	13.......Rep by CGT(A)A 1978 s 17 and Sch 2	
	14(1)-(5)..	s 581
	(6)......Rep by CGT(A)A 1978 s 17 and Sch 2	
	15...	s 596
Sch 1, Pt II......Rep by CGT(A)A 1978 s 17 and Sch 2		
Sch 2		
para 1	....	s 583
	2(1)-(7)(9)..	s 584
	(8).......Rep by CGT(A)A 1978 s 17 and Sch 2	
	2A........(para 2A inserted by FA 1990 s 87).....................	s 733
	3..	s 585
	4..	s 586(1), (2)
	5..	s 587(1)-(3)
	5A.......(para 5A inserted by FA 1997 s 70)....................	s 588
	6..	s 600(1)-(5)
Sch 3	....	Sch 14
para 1	....	para 2
	2..	para 3
	3..	para 4(1)-(6)
	4..	para 5
	5..	para 6
	6..	para 7
	7..	para 8
	8..	para 9
	9..	para 10
	10...	para 1

Destination Table (Taxes Consolidation Act 1997)

Former Enactment	*Destination in TCA 1997*

Capital Gains Tax Act 1975 (1975 No 20) (contd)

Sch 4
   para 1(1).. s 849(1), (2)
        (2) .... s 931(1)
        (3) .... ss 851, 976(1)

Sch 4
   para 2(1).. ss 931(2), 976(2)
        (2) .... ss 29(8), (9), 567(3), (4), 849(3)-(6), 861(1), 863, 864, 865, 869, 870, 875, 931(3), 949, 976(3), 999, 1043, 1051, 1083, Sch 1

       3(1)(3)-(5) .... s 913(1), (3)-(5), (7)
        (2) .... ss 874, 913(2), 1077(1)
        (6) .... s 1077(2)
   para 4.. s 914
       5... s 915
       6... s 916
       7... s 917
       8(1) .... s 945
       (2)(a)-(i),(k)
        (2)(j) .... Rep by CGT(A)A 1978 s 17 and Sch 2
       9... s 946
       10(1) .... s 913(8)
        (2) .... s 1029
       11(1)-(10A).. s 980
        (11) .... Unnecessary (operative date)
       12... s 568
       13... s 544(7)
       14... s 911
       15... s 982
       16... s 871
       17... s 977
       18... s 978
       19... s 913(6)

Corporation Tax Act 1976 (1976 No 7)

Pt I
s 1 (1), (2), (3)... s 21
      (4) .... Unnecessary (cesser of corporation profits tax)
      (5) .... s 4(1)
   2... s 129
   3... s 24
   4... s 864(2)
   5... s 152(1), (2)

Pt II
   6 (1), (2), (3)... s 26(1), (2), (3)
      (4) .... Rep by FA 1997s 146(2) and Sch 9 Pt II
      (5) .... s 849
      (6) .... Amendment of PCTA 1927 s 1
      (7) .... Amendment of IRRA 1890 s 39
   7... s 919(6)

Former Enactment   *Destination in TCA 1997*

Corporation Tax Act 1976 (1976 No 7) (contd)

s 8 (1), (2), (3)	s 25
(4)	ss 1040, 1046(3)
9	s 27
10	s 243(1), (2), (4)-(9)
10A(1)(a), ...(s 10A inserted by FA 1992 s 46(1)(a))	s 454(1)
(b)(ii)	
(b)(i) .....Unnecessary (obsolete)	
(2), (3)	s 454(2), (3)
11 (1), (2)(b),	s 76
(3)-(8)	
(2)(a) .....Unnecessary (obsolete)	
12 (1) to(7)	s 77
(8)........Rep by FA 1996 s 132(2) and Sch 5 Pt II	
12A.........(s 12A inserted by FA 1994 s 95(a))	s 79
13 (1)	s 78(1)
(1A)......Matter from "and section. 132(2) shall have effect" to the end. Unnecessary (obsolete)	s 78(2)
(1B)	s 78(3)(a), (b)
(1C), (2)	s 78(4), (5)
13 (3)(a), (c)	s 78(6)
(b) .....Rep by CGT(A)A 1978 s 17 and Sch 2	
(4), (5)	s 78(7), (8)
14(1), (2)	s 307
(3)-(8)	s 308
14A.........(s 14A inserted by FA 1994 s 56(b))	s 402
15	s 83
16 (1)-(8)(10)	s 396
(9)........Ceased by FA 1983 s 51	
16A.........(s 16A inserted by FA 1992 s 46(1)(c))	s 455
17 (1).......Definitions of "farming" and "market gardening" unnecessary (duplication)	s 663(1)
(2)-(4)	s 663(2)-(4)
(5)........Matter from "In this. subsection" to "section 157" unnecessary (obsolete)	s 663(5)
18 (1)-(3)	s 397
(4).......Ceased by FA 1983 s 51	
19	s 399
20	s 400
21 (1).......Unnecessary (application of income tax provisions for purposes of corporation tax)	
(2).......Unnecessary (non-application of income tax provisions)	
(3).......Unnecessary (obsolete).	
(4)	s 309
22 (1)	s 827
(2)	s 826(8)
23 (1)	ss 826(1)-(7), (9), 827
(2)-(4)-(5)	Sch 24, para 4(2)
24	s 156

Former Enactment   *Destination in TCA 1997*
Corporation Tax Act 1976 (1976 No 7) (contd)

s 25 (1)-(7)	s 157
(8) Ceased by FA 1983 s 51	
26 (1)-(3), (3) proviso para (a), (4)-(6)	s 158
(3) proviso Ceased by FA 1983 s 51 para (b)	
27 (1)-(7)	s 401
(8) Unnecessary (obsolete)	
Pt III	
s 28 Ceased by FA 1988 s 33(2)	
28A(1) (s 28A inserted by FA 1996 s 44)	s 22(1)(a)
(2)-(8)	s 22(2)-(8)
(9) Unnecessary (obsolete)	
28A(10)	s 457
29	s 844
30 (1) Unnecessary (interpretation)	
(2)-(4)	s 700
(5)(a) Amendment of ITA 1967 s 219	s 699(1)
(b) Unnecessary (obsolete)	
31 (1)-(3) Ceased by FA 1986 s 34(a)	
(4) Unnecessary (obsolete)	
(5)	s 702(2)
(6) Ceased by FA 1986 s 34(a)	
(7) Unnecessary (obsolete)	
(8)	s 702(1)
(9) Rep by FA 1992 s 43(4)	
(10) Unnecessary (spent)	
32 (1), (2)	s 1009(2), (3)
(3)(a)-(d)	s 1009(4)
(c)(proviso) Unnecessary (spent)	
(4)	s 1009(5)
(5)	s 1009(1)
33 (1)-(1B)(2)	s 707
(3)	s 728
33A(1)-(5), (s 33A inserted by FA 1992 s 44) (7), (8)	s 708
(6) Unnecessary (spent)	
33B (s 33B inserted by FA 1993 s 11(c))	s 712
34	s 709
35	s 710(1)-(5)
35A (s 35A inserted by FA 1993 s 11(d))	s 711
36	s 713(1)-(6)
36A(1)-(6)(8) (s 36A inserted by FA 1993 s 11(f))	s 723
(7)	s 706(4)
36B (s 36B inserted by FA 1993 s 11(f))	s 724
36C (s 36C inserted by FA 1993 s 11(f))	s 725
37 Deleted by FA 1982 s 42	
38	s 714
39	s 715
40	s 716
41	s 717(1), (3)-(6)
42(1)-(5), (8)	s 718
(6), (7) Rep by FA 1977 s 54 and Sch 2 Pt I	
43	s 726

Former Enactment   *Destination in TCA 1997*
Corporation Tax Act 1976 (1976 No 7) (contd)

s 44 .... s 727
   45 .... s 729(1)-(6)
   46 .... s 730
   46A......... (s 46A inserted by FA 1992 s 44(d))................. s 719
                Definitions of "collective investment
                undertaking", "market value", "trading
                company" and "units" deleted by
                FA 1993 s 11(j)(i)
   46B(1) .... (s 46B inserted by FA 1992 s 44(d)).................. s 720(1)
   (proviso)... s 720(2)
   paras (iii)-(v)
   (proviso) ..... Unnecessary (spent)
   para (i), (ii)
     (2)-(4).. s 720(3)-(5)
   47 .... Deleted by FA 1992 s 44(e)
   48 .... s 721
   49 .... s 722
   50 (1)......... Unnecessary (declaratory)
     (2)-(4)... s 706(1)-(3)
   51(1)-(3)(a) .... s 845
     (4)-(6)
     (3)(b), (c) .. Rep by FA 1996 s 132(2) and Sch 5 Pt II
   52 (1)-(4)(6) .... s 846
   52 (5)........ Rep by FA 1996 s 132(2) and Sch 5 Pt II
Pt IV
s 53-63 .... Unnecessary (spent)
   64 .... s 145(1), (2)(a), (3)-(10)
   65 .... s 146
   66 .... Ceased by CTA 1976 s 66A(3)
   66A(1)(2)(a)... (s 66A inserted by FA 1992 s 35(a))................ s 145(11)(a)(b)
                Definitions of "the adjusted average
                relieved distribution", "the average
                relieved distribution" and "the relieved
                distribution". Unnecessary (spent)
     (2)(b) ..... Unnecessary (redundant)
     (3)........ Unnecessary (cesser of CTA 1976 ss 66 and 67)
     (proviso)... Rep by FA 1997 s 146(2) and Sch 9 Pt II
     (4)........ Rep by FA 1997 s 146(2) and Sch 9 Pt II
   67 .... Ceased by CTA 1976 s 66A(3)
   68 .... Rep by FA 1996 s 132(2) and Sch 5 Pt II
   69-75 .... Unnecessary (spent)
   76(1),(2)(a)(ii),... s 144
   (2)(b),(3)-(8)
     (2)(a)(i).... Unnecessary (obsolete)
   76A(1) .... Unnecessary (obsolete) (s 76A inserted by FA 1992 s 35(b))
     (2)........ Unnecessary (cesser of CTA 1976 s 76(2)(a)(i))
     (proviso)... Rep by FA 1997 s 146(2) and Sch 9 Pt II
     (3)........ Rep by FA 1997 s 146(2) and Sch 9 Pt II
   77 .... Unnecessary (spent)
Pt VI
s 78 .... Unnecessary (spent)
Pt VII
s 79 .... Ceased by FA 1988 s 33(2)
   80 .... Rep by FA 1997 s 61(2)

Former Enactment   *Destination in TCA 1997*

Corporation Tax Act 1976 (1976 No 7) (contd)

Pt VIII

s 81	s 142
82	s 143

Pt IX

s 83 (1)	Unnecessary (declaratory)	
(2), (3)		s 20
83 (4)		s 153(1)
(5)		s 152(3)
84		s 130
84A(1)	Section 84A as inserted by FA 1984 s 41 was substituted by FA 1989 s 21(1) but FA 1989 s 21(2) saved provisions of s 84A as it existed before the substitution in respect of certain types of loans. Section 134 of the Bill reflects those provisions while s 133 of the Bill reflects provisions of s 84A as substituted by FA 1989 s 21(1) and as subsequently amended	s 134(3)
(2)		s 134(5)
(3)		ss 134(1)(a), 133(7)
(3A)(a)		s 133(8)(b)
(proviso)	Unnecessary (spent)	
(b)		s 133(8)(c)
(c)		s 133(8)(d)
(d)		s 133(8)(e)
(e)		s 133(8)(a)
(3B)(a)	(s 84A(3B) was substituted by FA 1992 s 40(b) as respects certain loans advanced after 20.12.91; accordingly the original s 84A(3B) (inserted by FA 1991 s 28(a)) still applies for loans advanced before that date)	s 133(9)(a)
(proviso)		133(9)(b)
(3B)(b)		ss 133(9)(c),
(proviso)		s 133(11)
(a)	These three references relate to s 84A(3B) as substituted by FA 1992 s 40(b)	s 133(10)(a)
(b)		s 133(10)(b))
(b)(proviso)		s 133(11))
(4)		s 134(1)(b)
(4A)(a)		s 133(13)(b)
(b)	(s 84A(4A)(b) proviso (para (a) is spent)	s 133(13)(c)
(4A)(c)		s 133(13)(a)
(5)		s 134(1)(a), (c)
(6)		s 134(1)(a)
(7)-(8)	Unnecessary (spent)	
(9)		s 134(4)
(10)		s 134(6)
(9)		s 133(1)(d)
(10)		s 133(4)
85		s 131

Former Enactment   *Destination in TCA 1997*

Corporation Tax Act 1976 (1976 No 7) (contd)

s 86	s 132
87	s 135
88	s 136
89	s 137
90	Ceased by FA 1983 s 51
91	Ceased by FA 1983 s 51
s 92	Unnecessary (spent)
93	s 140

Pt X

s 94	s 430
95	s 431
96	s 436
97	s 437
98 (1)-(7), (9)	s 438
(8)	Unnecessary (spent)
99 (1), (2), (4)	s 439
(3)	Unnecessary (spent)
100	Section 100(4) definition of "distributable income" para (b). Unnecessary (spent) ... s 434
101	s 440
102	s 432
103	s 433
104	s 435

Pt XI

s 105	s 410
106	Rep by FA 1992 s 50
107	s 411
108	s 412
109	s 413
110	s 414
111	s 415
112	s 416
113	s 417
114	s 418
115	s 419
116	s 420
116A(1)(a), (b),(ii),(2)-(4) (b), (5)	(s 116A inserted by FA 1988 s 34) ... s 456
(b)(i), (4)(a)	Unnecessary (spent)
117(1)-(3)(a), (b), (d), (4)	s 421
(3)(c)	Unnecessary (spent)
118	s 422
119	s 423
120	Definition of "connected person" in ... s 424. s 120(5) unnecessary (obsolete)
121	s 425
122(1)-(5)	s 426
(6)	Unnecessary (obsolete)

Destination Table (Taxes Consolidation Act 1997)

Former Enactment   *Destination in TCA 1997*
Corporation Tax Act 1976 (1976 No 7) (contd)

s 123	s 427
124	s 428
125	s 429
Pt XII	
126	s 614
127	s 615
128	s 553
129(1)-(6)(b)	s 616
129(6)(c)(7)	s 590(11)
130	s 617
131	s 618
132	s 619
133	s 620
134	s 626
135	s 623
136	s 624
137	s 625
138	s 621
139(1)-(6) .... The matter from "and section 157" to end in s 139(6) unnecessary (obsolete)	s 622
Pt XIII	
s 140(1) .... Unnecessary (application of schedule)	
(2) .... Unnecessary (application of schedule)	
(3) .... Unnecessary (construction)	
Pt XIV	
s 141(1)-(1B)(3)	s 882(2)-(5)
(2)	s 1073
142(1)	s 883
(proviso).. Unnecessary (obsolete)	
(2)	s 1074
143(1)-(6), (7)(a),(b),(d)	s 884
(7)(c), (8)	s 1071
(9)-(11)	s 1072
(12)(a)	s 930
(b)	s 861(2)
(c)	ss 861(2), 884
144	s 919(1)-(5)
145(1), (2)	s 973
145(3)	s 1080
(4)	s 1082
(5)	s 974
146(1)	s 864, Pt 40 Ch I, s 949
(2)	s 856(3)
147(1), (2)	ss 207(3), (4), 211(5), (6), 213(3), (4), 483(1)-(3), 860, 861(1), 862, 863, 865, 868, 869, 870, 873, 874, 875, 886,

Former Enactment	Destination in TCA 1997
Corporation Tax Act 1976 (1976 No 7) (contd)	
s 142(1), (2) (contd)	898, 901, 928(1), 929, 947, 998, 1004, 1049, 1055, 1056, 1057, 1058, 1066, 1067, 1068, 1069, 1070, 1081(1)
(3), (4)	ss 1059, 1060, 1061, 1062, 1063, 1065, 1076(2)
147(5)	s 857(4)
148	s 1064
149	s 1075
150	s 647
s 151(1)-(13)	s 239
(14) . . . . Amendment of ITA 1967 s 434	s 238(1)-(6)
152	s 240
153 . . . . Rep by FA 1996 s 132(2) and Sch 5 Pt II	
154	ss 882(1), 1076(1)
Pt XV	
s 155(1), (2)	s 1(2)
(3), (4)	s 2(2), (3)
(5)	ss 2(1), 4(1)
(6)-(8) . . . . . Unnecessary (construction)	
(9)-(13)	s 4(2)-(6)
156	s 9
157 . . . . Ceased by FA 1996 s 131	
158	s 11
159	s 590(10)
160	s 1033
161	s 927
162(1)-(6)	s 441
(7) . . . . Unnecessary (obsolete)	
163	s 830
164 . . . . Unnecessary (application of schedule)	
165 . . . . Unnecessary (non-application of FA 1924 s 38 for corporation tax)	
166 . . . . Unnecessary (application of schedule)	
167 . . . . Ceased by FA 1983 s 51(2)	
168 . . . . Ceased by FA 1983 s 51(2)	
169 . . . . Unnecessary (obsolete)	
170 . . . . (s 170(3A)(a) (proviso) is spent)	s 141
171	s 2(4)
172 . . . . Unnecessary (relates to introduction of corporation tax)	
Pt XVI	
s 173 . . . . Unnecessary (relates to commencement of corporation tax)	
174 . . . . Unnecessary (relates to winding up of corporation profits tax)	
174(3)(proviso)	Sch 32, para 18(2)
175	Sch 32, para 19
176 . . . . Unnecessary (spent)	
177	Sch 32, para 8
178	s 139
179 . . . . Unnecessary (spent)	
180 . . . . Unnecessary (commencement)	
181 . . . . Unnecessary (spent)	
182(1)-(3), (3)(proviso)	
para (a),(bb),	

Destination Table (Taxes Consolidation Act 1997)

Former Enactment	*Destination in TCA 1997*
Corporation Tax Act 1976 (1976 No 7) (contd)	
s 182(4)	Sch 32, para 16(1)-(4)
(3)(proviso)... Unnecessary (obsolete)	
para (b),(c)	
183	Sch 32, para 17
184(1)	Sch 32, para 18(1)
(2)	Sch 32, para 18(3)
184(3)	Sch 32, para 18(4)(a), (b)
(proviso)	Sch 32, para 18(4)(c)
para (iiA)	
(proviso) . Unnecessary (obsolete)	
para (i)-(iii)	
(4)	Sch 32, para 18(5)
185 .... Unnecessary (spent)	
186 .... Unnecessary (application of schedule)	
187 .... Unnecessary (obsolete)	
188 .... Unnecessary (short title and construction)	
Sch 1	
para 1 .... Definition of "tax" in para 1(3) unnecessary (duplication)	s 321(1)-(7)
2	s 321(8)
3	s 321(9)
4 .... Unnecessary (obsolete)	
5 .... Unnecessary (obsolete)	
6 .... Substitution of ITA 1967 s 241	s 284
7 .... Substitution of ITA 1967 s 242	
8 .... Substitution of ITA 1967 s 243	
9 .... Substitution of ITA 1967 s 244	s 763(2)
10 ...... Substitution of ITA 1967 s 245	s 670
11 ...... Substitution of ITA 1967 s 246	
12 ...... Substitution of ITA 1967 s 247	
13 ...... Substitution of ITA 1967 s 248	
14 ...... Substitution of ITA 1967 s 249	
15 ...... Substitution of ITA 1967 s 251	ss 283(2), 300(1), 316(3)
16 ...... Substitution of ITA 1967 s 252	ss 298(1), 299(1), 304(4)
17 ...... Substitution of ITA 1967 s 254	ss 271(1), (2), (4), 278(1), (2), (6), 305, 320(1)
18 ...... Substitution of ITA 1967 s 256	s 270
19 ...... Substitution of ITA 1967 s 258	
20 ...... Substitution of ITA 1967 s 259	
21 ...... Substitution of ITA 1967 s 260	s 316(1)(a)
22 ...... Substitution of ITA 1967 s 262	
23 ...... Substitution of ITA 1967 s 264	s 272
24 ...... Substitution of ITA 1967 s 265	s 274(1), (3), (4), (5), (8)
25 ...... Substitution of ITA 1967 s 266	s 277
26 ...... Substitution of ITA 1967 s 267	s 278(1), (3), (4), (5), (6)
27 ...... Substitution of ITA 1967 s 270	s 280
28 ...... Substitution of ITA 1967 s 271	s 288(4)(a)
29 ...... Substitution of ITA 1967 s 272	s 288
30 ...... Substitution of ITA 1967 s 274	s 292
31 ...... Substitution of ITA 1967 s 275	s 293
32 ...... Substitution of ITA 1967 s 279	s 296
33 ...... Substitution of ITA 1967 s 280	s 297
34 ...... Substitution of ITA 1967 s 282	s 300
Sch 1	
para 35 ...... Substitution of ITA 1967 s 284	s 754
36 ...... Substitution of ITA 1967 s 285	s 755
37 ...... Substitution of ITA 1967 s 286	s 756
38 ...... Substitution of ITA 1967 s 288	s 757
39 ...... Substitution of ITA 1967 s 290	s 758

Former Enactment *Destination in TCA 1997*
Corporation Tax Act 1976 (1976 No 7) (contd)

Sch 1 (contd)
para 40 .... Substitution of ITA 1967 s 291 .... s 759
    41 .... Substitution of ITA 1967 s 292 .... s 761
    42 .... Substitution of ITA 1967 s 293 .... s 760
    43 .... Substitution of ITA 1967 s 294 .... ss 302, 303
    44 .... Substitution of ITA 1967 s 295 .... s 304(2),(4)-(6)(a)
    45 .... Substitution of ITA 1967 s 297 .... s 306
    46 .... Substitution of ITA 1967 s 299 .... ss 312, 762
    47 .... Substitution of ITA 1967 s 301 .... s 314
    48 .... Substitution of ITA 1967 s 302 .... s 315
    49 .... Substitution of ITA 1967 s 303 .... ss 316(1)(2), 317(2),
                                                                                    762(2)(b)
    50 .... Substitution of ITA 1967 s 304 .... ss 318, 320(1), (2), (6)
    51 .... Substitution of ITA 1967 s 305 .... s 769
    52 .... Substitution of ITA 1967 s 306 .... s 381
    53 .... Substitution of FA 1967 s 11 .... s 285(1), (2), (3), (8), 299(2)
    54 .... Substitution of FA 1968 s 4
    55 .... Substitution of FA 1969 s 4
    56 .... Substitution of FA 1970 s 14 .... ss 287, 301(1)
    57 .... Substitution of FA 1971 s 22
    58 .... Substitution of FA 1971 s 23
    59 .... Substitution of FA 1971 s 24
    60 .... Substitution of FA 1971 s 26 .... ss 285(1), (2), (3), (8),
                                                                                    288, 299(2)
    61 .... Substitution of FA 1973 s 9(2) .... s 283(7)
    62 .... Substitution of FA 1973 s 25 .... ss 373(2)(a), 374
    63 .... Substitution of F(TPCM)A 1974 s 1 .... s 672
    64 .... Substitution of F(TPCM)A 1974 s 2 .... s 673
    65 .... Substitution of F(TPCM)A 1974 s 3
    66 .... Substitution of F(TPCM)A 1974 s 4 .... s 675
    67 .... Substitution of F(TPCM)A 1974 s 5 .... s 676
    68 .... Substitution of F(TPCM)A 1974 s 6 .... s 677
    69 .... Substitution of F(TPCM)A 1974 s 7 .... s 678
    70 .... Substitution of FA 1974 s 22 .... s 658
    71 .... Substitution of FA 1974 s 25 .... s 660
    72 .... Substitution of FA 1975 s 34 .... s 248(1)-(3)

Sch 2, Pt I
para 1 .... Amendment of ITA 1967 s 1 .... ss 2(1), 3(1)
    2 .... Amendment of ITA 1967 s 8 .... s 1087
    3 .... Amendment of ITA 1967 s 83 .... s 98
    4 .... Amendment of ITA 1967 s 169 .... s 877
    5 .... Amendment of ITA 1967 s 181(1) .... s 918(1)-(3)
    6 .... Amendment of ITA 1967 s 183(1) .... s 921
    7 .... Amendment of ITA 1967 s 184(2)(a) .... s 922
    8 .... Amendment of ITA 1967 s 186(1) .... s 924
    9 .... Amendment of ITA 1967 s 239(6)
    10 .... Amendment of ITA 1967 s 329
    11 .... Amendment of ITA 1967 s 331
    12 .... Amendment of ITA 1967 s 332

Sch 2, Pt I
para 13 .... Amendment of ITA 1967 s 333(1)(b) .... s 207(1), (2)
    14 .... Amendment of ITA 1967 s 335(1) .... s 211(1)-(4)
    15 .... Amendment of ITA 1967 s 336 .... s 213(1), (2)
    16 .... Amendment of ITA 1967 s 337(2)
    17 .... Amendment of ITA 1967 s 367(7)
    18 .... Amendment of ITA 1967 s 369(1) .... s 750
    19 .... Amendment of ITA 1967 s 370 .... s 751
    20 .... Amendment of ITA 1967 s 371 .... s 752

Former Enactment *Destination in TCA 1997*
Corporation Tax Act 1976 (1976 No 7) (contd)

Sch 2 Pt I (contd)
  para 21   Amendment of ITA 1967 s 372   s 753
       (1) . . . . . . Amendment of ITA 1967 s 449(1). . . . . s 812 (1), (2), (4)
       (2). . . . . s 812(3)
     23 . . . . Amendment of ITA 1967 s 450(2)(d) . . . . s 799
     24. . . . . s 801(9)
     25 . . . . Amendment of ITA 1967 s 458(1). s 1091
     26. . . . . s 51
     27. . . . . s 483(4)
     28 . . . . Amendment of ITA 1967 Sch 12. . . . . Sch 22
     29 . . . . Unnecessary (obsolete)
     30. . . . . s 109
     31. . . . . Sch 32, para 26
     32 . . . . Amendment of FA 1973 s 24
     33. . . . . s 375
     34. . . . . s 23
     35. . . . . s 234(2)(b)
     36(1), (3) . . . . Sch 1, para 1, 2, 5
       (2) . . . . . Unnecessary (obsolete)
     37 . . . . Amendment of F(TPCM)A 1974 s 8(1). . . . . s 680
     38. . . . . s 682(4)
     39 . . . . Substitution of F(TPCM)A 1974 s 11 . . . . s 682(1)-(3)
     40 . . . . Amendment of F(TPCM)A 1974 s 18(2)
     41 . . . . Amendment of FA 1974 s 4(b). . . . . s 59
     42 . . . . Amendment of FA 1974 s 31(3)(f). s 246(1), (2), (4
     43 . . . . Amendment of FA 1974 s 33(1). . . . . s 247(1)-(3)
     44 . . . . Amendment of FA 1974 s 38(2)
     45. . . . . s 813
     46 . . . . Amendment of FA 1974 s 54
     47(1) . . . . s 814
       (2) . . . . . Amendment of FA 1974 s 55. . . . . s 814
     48. . . . . s 671
     49 . . . . Unnecessary (obsolete)
     50 . . . . Unnecessary (spent)

Sch 2, Pt II
  para 1 . . . . Amendment of CGTA 1975 s 2(1). . . . . s 5
     2 . . . . Amendment of CGTA 1975 s 33(7)(b)
     3 . . . . Amendment of CGTA 1975 s 35 . . . . s 589
     4 . . . . Amendment of CGTA 1975 s 36(1), (8) . . . . s 590(1)-(9)
     5 . . . . Amendment of CGTA 1975 s 36(4)(d) . . . . s 590(1)-(9)
     6. . . . . ss 563(2), 975(2)
     7. . . . . s 548(7)
     8 . . . . Amendment of CGTA 1975 Sch 1 par 2(1). . . . . s 551
     9 . . . . Amendment of CGTA 1975 Sch 1. . . . . s 552
             par 3(3)(a)(ii), (iii)

Sch 3, Pt II
  para10 . . . . Amendment of CGTA 1975 Sch 1 para 22(1)(a)
     11. . . . . Sch 14, para 4(7)
     12. . . . . s 975(1)
     13 . . . . Unnecessary (spent)
Sch 3, Pt I . . . . . . Repeal of ITA 1967 ss 64, 76(7), (8), 108, Pt X,
              ss 219(2), 220(6), 221, 237, Pt XIX Ch III, s 347,
              Pt XXV, s 435, Pt XXX Ch I, Pt XXXVI Ch II,
              Sch 16, FA 1969 s 20, FA 1973 ss 11, 24(2),

Former Enactment *Destination in TCA 1997*
Corporation Tax Act 1976 (1976 No 7) (contd)

Sch 3, Pt I (contd) F(TPCM)A 1974 ss 13, 14, 15, 16, FA 1974 ss 4
proviso, 23, 54(4), FA 1975 ss 5, 18, 30
Amendment of ITA 1967 ss 1(1), 75(2), ss 2(1), 3(1); 70(1);
76(2), 316(2), 371(7)(c), 432(3)(a), 543, 71(2); 390(1), (3); 752
FA 1972 s 16(4), FA 1973 ss 24(8), 26, 949(2)-(4); s 774(6), Sch 32
FA 1974 s 5(1) para 26; 373(2)(a), 375;
s 237(1)(b), (2)

Sch 3, Pt II Repeal of ITA 1967 s 1(5), FA 1967 s 21,
F(MP)A 1968 ss 13, 15, FA 1968 Pt IV,
s 48(4), FA 1969 Pt VI, FA 1970 s 24(2)(b),
FA 1971 ss 46, 49, 50, FA 1972 s 43
(insofar as it relates to corporation tax),
FA 1973 s 37, F(TPCM)A 1974 ss 12, 17,
FA 1974 ss 27(7), 53, 56(3)(a),
FA 1975 s 21(8)
Amendment of ITA 1967 ss 555(1)(e),556, ... ss 48, 95, 373, 13(1),
559(1), FA 1969 s 63 , FA 1970 s 21, 234(1)(2)(a), 1089(1),
FA 1973 ss 30, 33, 34(2), 35, 98(2), Sch 1, 682(1)-(3), 813,
Sch 3 para 7, F(TPCM)A 1974 s 10, 671, 75(1), 96(1), 97,
FA 1974 ss 41(2), 74, FA 1975 s 28, Sch 2 102, 103, Sch 29

Sch 3, Pt III .....Repeal of FA 1968 ss 34, 36, FA 1973 s 39,
FA 1974 s 68

Sch 4, Pt I.......Amendment of ITA 1967 ss 355, 361(1), ... s 826(1)-(7), Sch 24, 829
Sch 10, FA 1970 s 57

Sch 4, Pt II......Repeal of ITA 1967 ss 363, 364, Sch 10
para 3(1), 7, FA 1968 s 35Sch 24 paras 7-13
Amendment of ITA 1967 Sch 10 para 8(3)(c) .... Sch 24 paras 7-13

Sch 5 ....Unnecessary (spent)

Finance Act 1976 (1976 No 16)
Pt I
s 1 ....Amendment of ITA 1967 s 128(4) .... s 987(4)
    2 ....Amendment of ITA 1967 s 142(1) .... s 466
    3 ....Amendment of ITA 1967 s 174......................... s 900(1), (2), (4)
    4 ....Insertion of ITA 1967 s 197(1A)....................... s 1023
    5 ....Amendment of ITA 1967 s 316(2) .... s 390(1), (3)
    6 (1)........Amendment of ITA 1967 s 477.......................... s 960
      (2)........Amendment of FA 1971 s 20(2) .... s 1082
    7 ....Amendment of ITA 1967 s 497........................ s 460
    8 ....Amendment of ITA 1967 s 525(1) .... s 127(1)-(5)
    9 ....Amendment of F(No 2)A 1975 s 1
    10 ....Unnecessary (obsolete)
    11 (1)-(3).. s 881
       (4)........Amendment of ITA 1967 Sch 15 .... Sch 29
       (5)........Amendment of ITA 1967 s 169(1) .... s 877
    12 ....Rep by FA 1996 s 132(2) and Sch 5 Pt II
    13 .... s 805
    14 ....Substitution of FA 1968 s 11
    15 ....Rep by FA 1996 s 132(2) and Sch 5 Pt II
    16 ....Rep by FA 1996 s 132(2) and Sch 5 Pt II
    17(1)-(3)(a)(4)(b).. s 996
       (3)(b), ...Unnecessary (obsolete)
       (4)(a)
    18 ....Amendment of FA 1974 s 21
    19 ....Rep by FA 1983 s 120 and Sch 4
    20 ....Amendment of FA 1970 s 17 .... ss 530, 531
    21 ....Substitution of FA 1970 s 17......................... ss 530, 531
    22 .... s 57
    23 ....Rep by FA 1978 s 5
    24 ....Amendment of FA 1973 ss 31, 37

Destination Table (Taxes Consolidation Act 1997)

Former Enactment   *Destination in TCA 1997*

Finance Act 1976 (1976 No 16) (contd)

s 25	Rep by FA 1997 s 146(2) and Sch 9 Pt II	
26	Amendment of FA 1975 s 31(1), insertion of FA 1975 s 31A and Sch 5	
27	Insertion of CTA 1976 s 54(4)	
28	Unnecessary (obsolete)	
29		s 1089(2)
30	Rep by FA 1997 s 146(2) and Sch 9 Pt II	
31		s 373(2)(b)
32		s 376
33	Rep by FA 1978 s 52(1) and Sch 4 Pt I	
34		s 905

Pt VI

s 81 (1), (3)(a)	Unnecessary (application of schedule)	
82	Unnecessary (care and management)	
83 (2), (6)	Unnecessary (construction and commencement)	
Sch 1, Pt I	Amendment of ITA 1967 ss 138, 141(1A)	ss 458, 465
Sch 5, Pt I	Repeal of ITA 1967 s 125(a) and Sch 2 Rules 5, 6, 7	
	Amendment of ITA 1967 ss 157(c), 557	s 853

Finance Act 1977 (1977 No 18)

s 1	Amendment of ITA 1967 s 142	s 466
2 (1)	Amendment of ITA 1967 s 236	s 787
(2)	Unnecessary (application of schedule)	
3	Amendment of FA 1974 s 59(3)	s 808
4	Amendment of ITA 1967 s 477(1), (2) and FA 1976 s 6(2)(b)	ss 960, 1082
5 (1)	Unnecessary (obsolete)	
(2)	Unnecessary (application of schedule)	
6 (1), (2)	Unnecessary (obsolete)	
(3)	Unnecessary (application of schedule)	
7	Rep by FA 1980 s 2	
8	Substitution of FA 1974 s 54	
9	Amendment of FA 1974 s 15(3)	s 655(1), (2)
10	Amendment of FA 1974 s 16(1)	s 657(1)
11	Substitution of FA 1974 s 19	
12 (a)	Amendment of FA 1974 s 21	
(b)	Insertion of FA 1974 s 21	
13	Unnecessary (obsolete)	
14		Sch 32, para 23(2)
15	Ceased by FA 1982 s 26(1)	
16 (1), (2)	Amendment of CTA 1976 ss 13, 37	s 78
(3)	Ceased by FA 1982 s 31(2)	
17	Amendment of FA 1982 s 28	
18	Ceased by FA 1982 s 26(1)	
19 (1), (2)	Unnecessary (spent)	
(3)	Rep by FA 1982 s 26(2) and Sch 2	
20-32	Unnecessary (obsolete)	
33	Amendment of CGTA 1975 s 3(3)	s 28
34	Amendment of CGTA 1975 s 31, Sch 32 para 25	s 731(1)-(5)(a),
35	Substitution of CGTA 1975 s 32	s 732
36		s 6
37	Unnecessary (spent)	
38	Amendment of FA 1973 s 8(1)	

Former Enactment *Destination in TCA 1997*
Finance Act 1977 (1977 No 18) (contd)

s 39 (1)-(5)..... Definition of "the former Agreements" .... s 832
  unnecessary (obsolete)
  (2)........ Unnecessary (spent)
  (4)(b) ..... Rep by FA 1996 s 132(2) and Sch 5 Pt II
  proviso
  40 .... Unnecessary (spent)
  41 (1)........ Amendment of CTA 1976 s 171....................... s 2(4)
  (2)........ Unnecessary (operative date)
  42 .... Unnecessary (application of schedule)
  43 .... Unnecessary (application of schedule)
  53 .... s 825
  54 (1)........ Unnecessary (application of schedule)
  55 .... Unnecessary (care and management)
  56 (2), (7) .... Unnecessary (construction and commencement)
  Sch 1, Pt I....... Amendment of ITA 1967 Sch 5
  Sch 1, Pt II...... Amendment of ITA 1967 ss 1(1), 153(1),................ ss 2(1), 3(1); 1032;
    497, 525(1), CTA 1976 ss 66(3)(b), 82(6)   460; 127(1)-(5); 143
  Sch 1, Pt III ..... Amendment of ITA 1967 s 138(1), (2).................. s 461
  Sch 1, Pt IV ..... Amendment of CTA 1976 ss 58(10), 109(1), ... s 413; 109(2)-(6);
    176(6)(a), Sch 5 para 1(6), FA 1968   774(6); Sch 32 para 26;
    s 37(4), FA 1972 s16(4), FA 1973 ss 24(9),   373(2)(a), 375; 814
    26, FA 1974 s 55(4)
  Sch 1, Pt V...... Amendment of FA 1975 ss 31, 31A, Sch 3,
    Sch 5, and FA 1976 s 12
  Sch 2, Pt I....... Repeal of ITA 1967 ss 355, 357, 369(2),
    Sch 6 Pts I, II, and III, paras 2, 3, 4, 5,
    Sch 7, FA 1973 ss 32, 38, and Sch 2, 4,
    CGTA 1975 s 4(2) proviso, CTA 1976
    s 42(6), (7), SI No 143 of 1975
    Amendment of FA 1968s 35(2)
  Pt II .... Repeal of s 356

Finance Act 1978 (1978 No 21)

s 1 .... Amendment of ITA 1967 s 142........................ s 466
  2 .... Substitution of ITA 1967 s 143(3)
  3 .... Amendment of ITA 1967 s 193........................ s 1016
  4 (1)........ Amendment of ITA 1967 s 236........................ s 787
  (2)........ Unnecessary (application of schedule)
  5 .... Unnecessary (cesser of FA 1976 s 23)
  6 .... Unnecessary (obsolete)
  7 .... Substitution of FA 1973 s 19......................... s 192
  8 .... s 250
  9 .... Rep by FA 1996 s 132(2) and Sch 5 Pt II
  10 (1)-(6)..... Unnecessary (obsolete)
  (7)........ Amendment of ITA 1967 s 193(2) .... s 1016
  11 (1)........ Substitution of ITA 1967 s 211(2) .... s 1048
  (2)........ Substitution of ITA 1967 s 504(2) .... s 1060
  12 (1)........ Amendment of FA 1974 s 13 .... s 654
  (2)........ Insertion of FA 1974 Sch 3
  13 .... Amendment of FA 1974 s 15 .... s 655(1), (2)
  14 .... Amendment of FA 1974 Pt I Ch II
  15 (1), (2) .... s 661
  (3)........ Unnecessary (duplication)
  16 (1)........ Amendment of ITA 1967 s 477 .... s 960
  (2)........ Unnecessary (obsolete)
  17 .... Unnecessary (spent)
  18 .... Unnecessary (obsolete)
  19 .... Substitution of ITA 1967 s 30
  20 .... Amendment of FA 1977 Pt I Ch IV
  21 .... Amendment of CTA 1976 s 28
  22 .... Amendment of FA 1971 s 26(1) .... s 285(1), (2), (3)

Former Enactment   *Destination in TCA 1997*

Finance Act 1978 (1978 No 21) (contd)

s 23	Amendment of FA 1973 s 8(1)	
24	Amendment of FA 1977 s 40(1)	
25 (1)		s 273(1)
(2)		s 273(2)
(2A)		s 273(3)
(3)		s 273(8)
26		s 310
27 (1)	Amendment of FA 1975 s 31A	
(2)	Amendment of FA 1976 s 12	
28 (1)	Unnecessary (obsolete)	
(2)	Unnecessary (obsolete)	
(3)	Amendment of CTA 1976 s 45	s 729(1)-(6)
(4)	Amendment of CTA 1976 s 64(3)(c)(ii)	s 145(1), (2)(a), (3)-(10)
(5)	Amendment of CTA 1976 s 79(6)	
(6)	Amendment of CTA 1976 s 178(1)	
(7)	Unnecessary (spent)	
46	Amendment of ITA 1967 ss 129, 550, FA 1970 s 17(6A), FA 1971 s 20(2), CTA 1976 ss 145, 152	ss 991(1); 1080(1); 531(5)(6)(8)(9); 1082; 973, 974, 1080, 1082; 240
47		s 1092
s 52 (1)	Unnecessary (application of schedule)	
53	Unnecessary (care and management)	
54 (2), (8)	Unnecessary (construction and commencement)	
Sch 1		
Pt I	Amendment of ITA 1967 Sch 5	
Pt II	Amendment of ITA 1967 s 138	ss 461, s 464 and FA 1974 s 8
Pt III	Rep by FA 1996 s 132(2) and Sch 5 Pt II	
Pt IV	Insertion of FA 1974 Sch 3	
Sch 2	Unnecessary (obsolete)	
Sch 4	Repeal of ITA 1967 s 220 (in so far as it is unrep) and FA 1976 s 33	

Capital Gains Tax (Amendment) Act 1978 (1978 No 33)

s 1 (1)		s 1(2)
(2)	Unnecessary (interpretation)	
(3)-(5)	Unnecessary (construction)	
2	Substitution of CGTA 1975 s 3(3)	s 28
3 (1)-(7)		s 556(1)-(7)
4	Ceased by FA 1982 s 30(2)	
5		s 605
6 (1)	Substitution of CGTA 1975 s 14(1)	s 573
(2)	Unnecessary (operative date)	
7 (1)	Substitution of CGTA 1975 s 15(4)(b)	s 577
(2)	Unnecessary (operative date)	
8	Substitution of CGTA 1975 s 27	s 599
9	Insertion of CGTA 1975 s 28(2A)	s 597
10	Substitution of CGTA 1975 s 39(1)	s 611
11	Amendment of CTA 1976 ss 13, 37	s 78
12	Amendment of CTA 1976 s 90	
13	Amendment of CTA 1976 s 127(1)	s 615
14	Amendment of CTA 1976 s 132(2)	s 619
15	Amendment of CGTA 1975 Sch 4	ss 29(8)(9), 544(7), 567 (3)(4), 568, 849(1)(2), 849 (3)-(6), 851, 861(1), 863-865, 869-871, 874, 875, 911, 913-917, 931, 945, 946, 949, 976, 977, 978, 980, 982, 999,

Former Enactment   *Destination in TCA 1997*

Capital Gains Tax (Amendment) Act 1978 (1978 No 33) (contd)

s 15 (contd) .... Sch 1, 1029, 1043, 1051,
                                                                                                                   1077(1), 1077(2), 1083

    16 .... Unnecessary (application of schedule)
    17 .... Unnecessary (application of schedule)
    18 .... Unnecessary (short title, construction and commencement)

Sch 1

    para 1 .... s 556(8), (9)
        2 .... Unnecessary (obsolete)
        3 .... The matter from "and .... s 582
                section 4" to the end is unnecessary (obsolete)
        4 .... s 580
        5 .... Substitution of CGTA 1975 Sch 2 para 2(3) .... s 584
        6 .... Unnecessary (obsolete)
        7 .... s 546(6)
        8 .... s 601(3)
        9 .... Substitution of CGTA 1975 s 32(3) .... s 732
      10 .... s 558

Sch 2 .... Repeal of CGTA 1975 ss 6, 26(7), 29(4),
               47(7), Sch 1 Pt I para 13, 14(6) and PtII,
               Sch 2 para 2(8), Sch 4 para 8(2)(j), CTA
               1976 s 13(3)(b)
               Amendment of CGTA 1975   ss 545(2)(3), 601(1)(2)(4)(5)
               ss 11(1), (2),16(4), 51(2),   544(8), 544(7)
               Sch 4 para 13, FA 1977 s 16(3)

Finance Act 1979 (1979 No 11)

s 1 .... Substitution of ITA 1967 s 142(1A) .... s 466
     2 (1) .... Amendment of FA 1977 s 5
       (2) .... Unnecessary (application of schedule)
     3 (1), (2) .... Unnecessary (obsolete)
       (3) .... Unnecessary (application of schedule)
     4 .... Insertion of ITA 1967 s 138A .... s 462
     5 .... Rep by FA 1996 s 132(2) and Sch 5 Pt II
     6 .... Unnecessary (cesser of ITA 1967 s 224(3),
               (5), (6), otherwise obsolete)
     7 .... Unnecessary (spent)
     8 (1 .... ss 125(1), 471(1)
       (2)(a) .... s 471(2)
         (b) ..... Rep by FA 1996 s 132(2) and Sch 5 Pt II
       (3) .... s 471(3)
       (4) .... s 125(3)
       (4A) .... s 125(4)
       (5) .... Unnecessary (operative date)
       (6) .... s 125(2)
     9 .... Amendment of ITA 1967 s 496(2)(b), FA .... s 250
               1974 ss 38(1), 44, 52(b), FA 1978 s 8(2)
   10 .... Rep by FA 1982 s 8(8)
   11 .... Rep by FA 1980 s 16
   12 .... Amendment of ITA 1967 s 488(5) .... s 966
   13 .... Amendment of FA 1974 ss 15, 19 .... s 655(1), (2)
   14 .... Unnecessary (spent)
   15 .... Amendment of FA 1974 s 20
   16 .... Amendment of FA 1974 s 21(1)
   17 .... Amendment of ITA 1967 s 307 .... s 381(1)
   18 .... Amendment of ITA 1967 s 308

Former Enactment   *Destination in TCA 1997*

Finance Act 1979 (1979 No 11) (contd)

s 19	Substitution of ITA 1967 s 318(1)	s 392
20	Substitution of ITA 1967 s 319(1)	s 393
21	Amendment of CTA 1976 ss 10(6), 169, FA 1978 s 18(5) proviso	s 243(1), (2), (4)-(9)
22	Insertion of FA 1977 s 25A	
23	Amendment of FA 1975 s 31A and FA 1976 s 12	
24	Amendment of FA 1971 s 22	
25	Amendment of FA 1978 s 25(1)	s 273(1)
26	Unnecessary (obsolete)	
27	Substitution of FA 1976 s 25	
28 (1)-(3)		s 786
(4)	Amendment of ITA 1967 s 239(8)	s 788
(5)	Amendment of CTA 1976 s 50(4)(a)	s 706(1)-(3)
29	Amendment of ITA 1967 s 517 and CTA 1976 s 148	s 1064
30	Insertion of ITA 1967 s 70(3A), (3B)	ss 880(2)-(6), 900(3)
31		s 902
32 (1)	Unnecessary (repeal of ITA 1967 s 144)	
(2)	Unnecessary (declaratory)	
(3)	Unnecessary (obsolete)	
33	Insertion of ITA 1967 s 439(1A)	s 791(2)-(4)
34	Amendment of ITA 1967 Sch 12	Sch 22
35	Insertion of CGTA 1975 s 25(9A)	s 604
36	Amendment of CGTA 1975 s 27(1) s 599	
37 (1)	Unnecessary (CGTA 1975 cesser of s 31(4))	
(2)	Amendment of CGTA 1975 s 31(5)	
58	Unnecessary (care and management)	
59 (2), (6)	Unnecessary (construction and commencement)	
Sch 1		
Pt 1	Amendment of ITA 1967 ss 1(1), 153(1)(dd), 497, 525(1)	ss 2(1), 3(1), 1032, 460, 127(1)-(5)
Pt II	Amendment of ITA 1967 s 138, FA 1974 s 8	ss 461, 464
Sch 2	Unnecessary (obsolete)	

Finance Act 1980 (1980 No 14)

Pt I

s 1		s 187
2(1)-(4),(6),(7)		s 188
(5)	Unnecessary (cesser of FA 1977 s 7)	
s 3	Substitution of ITA 1967 ss 138, 138A Insertion of ITA 1967 138B	ss 461, 462, 472
4 (1), (2)	Unnecessary (obsolete)	
(3)	Unnecessary (application of schedule)	
5	Amendment of FA 1971 s 11	s 468
6	Amendment of ITA 1967 ss 143, 152(1)	
7	Rep by FA 1997 s 146(2) and Sch 9 Pt II	
8	Unnecessary (obsolete)	
9	Amendment of ITA 1967 s 3	s 1(2)
10	Amendment of ITA 1967 s 115 and Sch 3	s 201, Sch 3
11	Amendment of ITA 1967 s 336	s 213(1), (2)
12	Amendment of ITA 1967 s 340(2)	s 204(1)
13	Substitution of ITA 1967 s 344(1), (2)	
14	Amendment of ITA 1967 s 447 and FA 1971 s 20(2)	ss 794(1), 1082
15	Amendment of FA 1979 s 7(1) and Sch 2	
16	Unnecessary (FA 1979 cesser of s 11)	

| Former Enactment | Destination in TCA 1997 |

Finance Act 1980 (1980 No 14) (contd)

s 17	Amendment of ITA 1967 ss 58, 72, 77, 241, 244, 245, 296	ss 65(1); 1010; 70(2); 284, 300(1); 763-735; 670; 305(1)
18	Substitution of ITA 1967 Pt IX Ch I	
19	Unnecessary (application of schedule)	
20	Unnecessary (obsolete)	
21	Unnecessary (obsolete)	
22	Amendment of FA 1974 ss 15, 19	s 655(1), (2)
23	Unnecessary (obsolete)	
24	Unnecessary (FA 1974 cesser of ss 20, 21)	
25	Rep by FA 1983 s 120 and Sch 4	
26	Ceased by FA 1988 s 52(3)	
27	Substitution of FA 1974 s 22(2)	s 658(2)(a)
28	Rep by FA 1996 s 132(2) and Sch 5 Pt II	
37	Amendment of FA 1977 Pt I Ch I	
38		s 442(1)
39		s 443
39A(1)-(7)(10)	Definition of "EEC Treaty" unnecessary (obsolete)	s 445
(2) proviso	Deleted by FA 1988 s 35	
(8), (9)	Deleted by FA 1989 s 23	
39B(1)-(7)(a), (b),(8)-(10)		s 446(1)-(12)
(7)(c)	Rep by FA 1988 s 36(1)	
39C		s 449
39D		s 450
40		s 442(2)
41 (1)		s 448(1)
(2)		s 448(2)(a)
(3)-(5)(8)(9)		s 448(3)-(7)
(6), (7)	Unnecessary (obsolete)	
42 (1)-(4)	Unnecessary (obsolete)	
(5)	Substitution of CTA 1976 s 58(10)	
(6)	Amendment of CTA 1976 s 64	s 145(1), (2)(a), (3)-(10)
43	Unnecessary (obsolete)	
44		s 453
45 (1)-(3), (5)-(8)		s 147, Sch 32 para 4
(1A) 1st proviso para (a)	Unnecessary (obsolete)	
(4)	Unnecessary (obsolete)	
46		s 148
47 (1)	Amendment of CTA 1976 s 182	Sch 32, para 16(1)-(4)
(2)		Sch 32, para 5(2)
48 (1)	Amendment of CTA 1976 s 184	Sch 32, para 18
(2)		Sch 32, para 6(2)
49		s 149
50		s 444
51		ss 151, 447
52	Amendment of FA 1977 s 40(1)	
53 (1)	Amendment of FA 1975 s 31A	
(2)	Amendment of FA 1976 s 12	
(3)-(6)	Unnecessary (obsolete)	
54	Amendment of ITA 1967 ss 416(5), 421	ss 933(1)-(7)(f), 934
55	Substitution of ITA 1967 s 4	s 12
56	Amendment of FA 1973 s 24	

Former Enactment   *Destination in TCA 1997*

Finance Act 1980 (1980 No 14) (contd)

s 57	Amendment of ITA 1967 ss 448(5), 500	ss 798(1)-(3), 1052
58	Amendment of ITA 1967 s 265(4)	s 274(1), (3), (4), (5), (8)
59	Substitution of ITA 1967 s 516	s 1056
60	Substitution of FA 1976 s 34(2)	s 905
61	Amendment of CGTA 1975 ss 2(3), 13(4), 25(9A)(b), Sch 4 para 10(2)	ss 5, 1028, 604, 1029
62	Amendment of CGTA 1975 ss 7(1), 46	ss 532(1), 541
Pt VI		
89	Substitution of FA 1978 s 47(1)	s 1092
95	Unnecessary (care and management)	
96 (2), (7)	Unnecessary (construction and commencement)	
Sch 1		
Pt I	Amendment of ITA 1967 s 141(1A), FA 1969 s 3	ss 465, 467
Pt II	Substitution of ITA 1967 Sch 3	s 201(1)(a), Sch 3
Pt III	Amendment of ITA 1967 ss 82(3), 139, 145(2), 183(7), 307(2)(a)(i), Sch 15, FA 1967 s 12, FA 1969 s 3(1)(a), FA 1974 ss 8(1), 28(6), FA 1976 s 11(3) Repeal of FA 1969 ss 3(6), (8), FA 1978 s 3, FA 1979 s 7(2)(b)	ss 470(1)-(3), 921(1) 381(2)-(7), Sch 29, 469(1), 467, 464, 881

Finance Act 1981 (1981 No 16)

1	Amendment of FA 1980 ss 1, 2	ss 187, 188
2 (1), (2)	Unnecessary (obsolete)	
(3)	Unnecessary (application of Schedule)	
3	Amendment of FA 1980 s 8	
4	Amendment of ITA 1967 s 128	s 987(1)-(3)
5	Amendment of ITA 1967 s 198(1)	s 1024
6	Rep by FA 1997 s 146(2) and Sch 9 Pt II	
7	Amendment of FA 1970 s 17(2)	s 531(1), (3), (4)
8 (a)	Amendment of FA 1979 s 7	
(b)	Amendment of FA 1979 Sch 2	
9	Amendment of ITA 1967 ss 81(3),111(1)(b), 553(2), FA 1970 s 23(2), F(TPCM)A 1974 s 11(1), (2)	ss 75(3); 111, 90(1)-(3), 683
10	Insertion of FA 1974 s 20B	s 683
11	Insertion of ITA 1967 s 334(2A)	s 208(3)
12	Amendment of ITA 1967 s 477(2)	
13	Rep by FA 1996 s 132(2) and Sch 5 Pt II	
15 (1)	Amendment of CTA 1976 s 6(4)	
(2), (3)	Unnecessary (obsolete)	
16	Substitution of CTA 1976 s 143(1), (2)	s 884
17 (a)	Insertion of FA 1980 s 39(1A)-(1D)	s 443
(b)	Insertion of FA 1980 s 39A	s 445
18	Rep by FA 1997 s 146(2) and Sch 9 Pt II	
19	Amendment of FA 1973 s 34(3)	s 234(3)-(8)
20 (1)	Amendment of FA 1975 s 31A	
(2)	Amendment of FA 1976 s 12	
(3), (5), (6)	Unnecessary (obsolete). There is no s 20(4)	
21	Unnecessary (obsolete)	
22	Insertion of CTA 1976 s 152(4)	s 240
23 (1)(a)		ss 325(1), 326(1), 327(1), 329(1), (2)
(b)		s 329(7)
(c)		s 329(9)(a)
(1)(d)	Unnecessary (obsolete)	

Former Enactment	Destination in TCA 1997

Finance Act 1981 (1981 No 16) (contd)

s 23 (2)	ss 325(2), 326(4), 327(2)
proviso	ss 325(3), 326(5), 327(3)
(3)(a)	ss 325(4), 326(6), 327(4)
(b), (c)	s 329(8)
(4)	s 329(6)
(5)	ss 325(5), 326(7), 327(5)
(6)(a)	ss 325(6)(a), 326(8), 327(7)
(b)	s 325(6)(b)
(7)(a)	ss 325(7)(a), 326(9), 327(7)
(b)	s 325(7)(b)
(8)	s 329(3)
(9)(a)	s 329(4)(a)
(b)	s 329(5)
(10)	s 329(11)
(11)	s 329(12)
23 .... Sch 32, para 14 .. Sch 32, para 14 of the Bill saves the provisions of s 23 FA 1981 (in so far as that section applied to areas other than the Custom House Docks Area)	
24 (1)	s 326(1)
(2)(a)	s 326(1)
(b)	s 326(1)
(c) ..... Unnecessary (obsolete)	
(d) ..... Unnecessary (obsolete)	
s 24 (2) (e)	s 326(8), (9)
(f)	s 326(9)
(g)	s 329(4)(b)
(3)	s 326(10)
24 .... Sch 32, para 14. . Sch 32, para 14 of the Bill saves the provision of FA 1981 s 24 (in so far as that section applied to areas other than the Custom House Docks Area)	
25	Sch 32, para 9
26	Sch 32, para 10
27 .... Amendment of ITA 1967 s 254(1)	s 271
28 .... Substitution of F(MP)A 1968 s 17(1)	s 640
29 (1) .... Unnecessary (declaratory)	
(2)(a) ..... Substitution of F(MP)A 1968 s 18	s 641
(b) ..... Unnecessary (obsolete)	
(3) .... Substitution of F(MP)A 1968 ss 20, 21, 22	ss 643-645
(4) .... Amendment of ITA 1967 Sch 15	Sch 29
52	s 1093
53 .... Unnecessary (care and management)	
54 (2), (7) .... Unnecessary (construction and commencement)	
Sch 1 .... Amendment of ITA 1967 ss 138A, 138B(1), 141(1A), FA 1969 s 3(1), FA 1971 s 11(2)	ss 462, 472, 465, 467, 468

Finance Act 1982 (1982 No 14)

s 1 .... Amendment of FA 1980 ss 1(2), 2(6)	ss 187, 188
2 (1), (2) .... Unnecessary (obsolete)	
(3) .... Unnecessary (application of schedule)	
3 .... Amendment of FA 1980 s 8	
4 (1) .... Unnecessary (commencement)	

Former Enactment   *Destination in TCA 1997*

Finance Act 1982 (1982 No 14) (contd)

s 4 (2)-(6), (9)		s 121
(7)	Amendment of ITA 1967 s 178(1)	s 897(1)-(5)
(8)	Amendment of ITA 1967 Sch 15	Sch 29
5 (1)	Insertion of ITA 1967 s 142A	s 473
(2)	Amendment of ITA 1967 s 198(1)(a)	s 1024, Sch 29 and Sch 15
6	Rep by FA 1996 s 132(2) and Sch 5 Pt II	
7	Insertion of ITA 1967 s 152(1A)	
8 (1)-(5), (7), (9)		s 122
(6)	Amendment of ITA 1967 s 178(1)	s 897(1)-(5)
(8)	Unnecessary (cesser of FA 1979 s 10)	
9 (1), (2)		s 205
(3)	Unnecessary (commencement)	
10	Amendment of ITA 1967 s 485(5)	s 962(3)
11	Amendment of ITA 1967 s 486	s 963
12	Amendment of FA 1979 s 7(1) and Sch 2	
13	Rep by FA 1996 s 132(2) and Sch 5 Pt II	
14	Amendment of ITA 1967 s 477(2)	s 960
15	Amendment of FA 1974 s 21A(1)	
16	Amendment of FA 1974 s 22	s 658(1)
18		s 225
19 (1)-(2A),		s 482(1)-(4),
(3)-(4A)(5)		(5), (6), (7)
(6)		s 482(10)
20 (1)-(6), (8)		s 840
(7)	Unnecessary (cesser of FA 1973 s 24)	
21	Rep by FA 1997 s 146(2) and Sch 9 Pt II	
22	Rep by FA 1997 s 146(2) and Sch 9 Pt II	
23	Unnecessary (obsolete)	
24 (1)	Amendment of FA 1975 s 31A	
(2)	Amendment of FA 1976 s 12	
25	Unnecessary (obsolete)	
26 (1)(a)	Unnecessary (cesser of FA 1977 ss 15, 17(1)(a), 18)	
(b)	Unnecessary (obsolete)	
(2)	Unnecessary (application of schedule)	
27 (1)	Amendment of CTA 1976 s 6(4)	
(2)	Unnecessary (obsolete)	
(3)	Unnecessary (obsolete)	
(4)	Amendment of ITA 1967 s 550	s 1080(1)
28	Unnecessary (spent)	
29	Unnecessary (interpretation)	
30 (1)	Amendment of CGTA 1975 s 3	s 28
(2)	Unnecessary (cesser of CGT(A)A 1978 s 4)	
(3)	Unnecessary (obsolete)	
31 (1)	Amendment of CTA 1976 s 13	s 78
(2)	Unnecessary (cesser of FA 1977 s 16(3))	
32	Amendment of CGTA 1975 ss 13(4), 16 and CGT(A)A 1978 Sch 1	ss 546(6), 556(8)(9), 558, 580, 582, 584, 601, 732, 1028,
33	Insertion of CGTA 1975 s 5(3)	s 1042
34 (1)	Substitution of CGTA 1975 Sch 4 para 11(5)	s 980
(2), (3)	Unnecessary (obsolete)	
35	Amendment of CTA 1976 s 90(4)	
36 (1)		s 648
(2)-(3A)	Deleted by FA 1992 s 60(2)	
(4)-(6)		s 649
(7)	Deleted by FA 1992 s 68(b)	
37		s 650

Former Enactment *Destination in TCA 1997*
Finance Act 1982 (1982 No 14) (contd)

```
s 38  ................................................... s 651
  39  ................................................... s 652
  40 (1), (2) ........................................... s 653
     (3). . . . . . . .Insertion of CTA 1976 s 25(8)
        (a) ............................................. s 607(1)(e)
        (b) . . . . .Ceased by FA 1992 s 24(2)
  42 (a). . . . . . . .Substitution of CTA 1976 s 36(3)(a). . . . . . . . . . . . . . . . . . s 713(1)-(6)
     (b). . . . . . . .Deletion of CTA 1976 s 37
  43  . . . . . . . . . .Unnecessary (spent)
  44  . . . . . . . . . .Unnecessary (spent)
  45  . . . . . . . . . .Unnecessary (spent)
  46  . . . . . . . . . .Unnecessary (spent)
  47  . . . . . . . . . .Unnecessary (spent)
  48  . . . . . . . . . .Unnecessary (spent)
  49  . . . . . . . . . .Unnecessary (spent)
  50  . . . . . . . . . .Definition of "ordinary share . . . . . . . . . . . . . . . . . . . . . . . . s 509
                 capital" unnecessary (duplication)
  51 (1)-(7). . . . . . . . . . . . . . . . . . . . . . . . . . . . . . . . . . . . . . . . . . . . . . . . . . . s 510
     (8). . . . . . . .Amendment of ITA 1967 Sch 15 . . . . . . . . . . . . . . . . . . . . . . Sch 29
  52 ..................................................... s 511
  53 ..................................................... s 512
  54 ..................................................... s 513
  55 ..................................................... s 514
  56 ..................................................... s 515
  57 ..................................................... s 516
  58 ..................................................... s 517
  58A. . . . . . . . . .(s 58A inserted by FA 1997 s 50) . . . . . . . . . . . . . . . . . . . . . . s 518
  59 ..................................................... s 1082
  60  . . . . . . . . . .Amendment of ITA 1967 ss 128, 173(6),  . . . . . . . . . . . . . . . ss 987(1)-(3), 889(10)
                 426(3), 500, FA 1968 s 6(5), CTA 1976        939, 1052, 886, s 145(1),
                 s 64(9), FA 1976 s 34(4), FA 1979 s 31(5),   (2)(a), (3)-(10), 905, 902,
                 FA 1980 s 45(8)                              s 147, Sch 32 para 4
  61  . . . . . . . . . .Amendment of ITA 1967 s 371. . . . . . . . . . . . . . . . . . . . . . . . s 752
  62  . . . . . . . . . .Insertion of CGTA 1975 s 9(3), (4). . . . . . . . . . . . . . . . . . . . . s 547
  63 ..................................................... ss 586(3), 587(4)
  104 . . . . . . . . . .Unnecessary (care and management)
  105(2), (7) . . . .Unnecessary (construction and commencement)
  Sch 1  . . . . . . . . . .Amendment of ITA 1967 ss 138, 138A, . . . . . . . . . . . . . . . . . ss 461, 462, 464-468
                 141(1A), 142(1), FA 1969 s 3(1), FA 1971
                 s 11(2), FA 1974 s 8(1).
                 Cesser of ITA 1967 ss 139, 140
  Sch 2, Pt I
     para 1  . . . . . . . .Unnecessary (cesser of FA 1977 s 19(3))
          2, 3  . . . . . .Unnecessary (spent)
  Sch 2, Pt II
     para 1  . . . . . . . .Amendment of FA 1980 s 41(2) . . . . . . . . . . . . . . . . . . . . . . . s 448(2)(a)
          2  . . . . . . . .Unnecessary (spent)
          3  . . . . . . . .Amendment of FA 1980 ss 47(2), 48(2) . . . . . . . . . . . . . . . . Sch 32, paras 5(2), 6(2)
          4  . . . . . . . .Unnecessary (spent)
  Sch 3 . . . . . . . . . . . . . . . . . . . . . . . . . . . . . . . . . . . . . . . . . . . . . . . . . . . . . Sch 11
```

Finance Act 1983 (1983 No 15)

```
  Pt I
  s 1   . . . . . . . . . .Amendment of FA 1980 s 1(2) . . . . . . . . . . . . . . . . . . . . . . . s 187
    2   . . . . . . . . . .Amendment of FA 1980 s 8
    3   . . . . . . . . . . . . . . . . . . . . . . . . . . . . . . . . . . . . . . . . . . . . . . . . . . . . s 1025
```

Former Enactment   *Destination in TCA 1997*

Finance Act 1983 (1983 No 15) (contd)

s 4		s 1026(1), (2)
5	Amendment of FA 1982 s 6	
6	Insertion of ITA 1967 s 195A	s 1020
7	Unnecessary (cesser of ITA 1967 Pt XX)	
8	Amendment of ITA 1967 s 344	
9	Amendment of ITA 1967 ss 416, 421, 428, 429, 430, deletion of s 420	ss 933(1)-(7)(f), 934, 941, 942(1)-(8), (10), 943
10	Amendment of ITA 1967 s 496(2A)	
11	Substitution of FA 1974 s 15	s 655(1), (2)
12	Amendment of FA 1974 s 20A	
13	Amendment of FA 1982 s 13(1)	
14	Substitution of ITA 1967 s 307(1A)	
15	Amendment of FA 1974 s 22	s 658
16	Unnecessary (spent)	
17 Preamble	Unnecessary (declaratory).	
(1)	Unnecessary (cesser of FA 1968 s 13)	
(2)	Amendment of ITA 1967 s 175	s 891
18		s 908
19 (1), (2)		s 58
(3)	Unnecessary (duplication)	
(4)	Unnecessary (operative date)	
19A	(s 19A inserted by DCITPA 1996 s 12)	s 859
20		s 909
21 (1), (2)		s 892
(3)	Amendment of ITA 1967 Sch 15	Sch 29
22 (1), (2)		s 885
(3)	Amendment of ITA 1967 Sch 15	Sch 29
23		s 1086
24	Amendment of FA 1982 s 58(1)	s 517
25	Substitution of FA 1982 ss 21(3), 23(3)	
26 (1)	Amendment of FA 1975 s 31A	
(2)	Amendment of FA 1976 s 12	
(3), (4)	Unnecessary (obsolete)	
27	Unnecessary (spent)	
28 (1)	Unnecessary (cesser of FA 1978 s 28(1))	
(2)	Unnecessary (obsolete)	
(3)	Unnecessary (obsolete)	
29	Unnecessary (spent)	
30	Unnecessary (spent)	
31	Amendment of FA 1982 ss 43, 44, 45, 46	
32		s 220
33	Amendment of CTA 1976 s 56(1)	
34	Amendment of FA 1978 Sch 2	
35	Insertion of CTA 1976 s 98(9)	s 438
36	Substitution of CTA 1976 s 143(7)	s 1071
37	Substitution of CTA 1976 s 146(1)	s 864, Pt 40 Ch I, s 949
38		s 159
39		s 160
40		s 161
41		s 162
42 (1)		s 163
(2)	Unnecessary (obsolete)	
43		s 164
44		s 165
45		s 166

Former Enactment   *Destination in TCA 1997*

Finance Act 1983 (1983 No 15) (contd)

s 46	(1)-(8)	s 167
	(9) Unnecessary (spent)	
47	(1)-(3)	s 168
	(4) Amendment of ITA 1967 s 361(1)	s 826(1)-(7)
47A	(s 47A inserted by FA 1995 s 37)	s 169
48	(1),(2)(a), (3)(4)	s 170
	(2)(b) Unnecessary (spent)	
49	Unnecessary (spent)	
50	(1)-(10), (11)(a)-(d)	s 171
	(12), (13)	
	(11)(e) Rep by FA 1997 s 146(2) and Sch 9 Pt II	
51	Unnecessary (cesser of CTA 1976 ss 16(9), 18(4), 25(8), 26(3) proviso para (b), 90, 91, 167, 168)	
52	Unnecessary (spent)	
53		s 172
54	Rep by FA 1988 s 70(2)	
55	Amendment of CGTA 1975 Sch 4 para 8	s 945
56	(1) Unnecessary (operative date)	
	(2)-(10)	s 571
Pt V		
s 94		s 1078
Pt VII		
s 120	Unnecessary (application of schedule)	
121	Unnecessary (care and management).	
122(2), (6)	Unnecessary (construction and commencement)	
Sch 4	Repeal of ITA 1967 s 340(2)(d)(ff)(g), (3), FA 1974 ss 13(2)(3), 17, 18, 19, 21A, 28, Sch 3, FA 1976 s 19, FA 1980 s 25 Amendment of FA 1974 ss 13(1), 20B(3)(b), FA 1978 s 15(2)	ss 654, 657(6), 661

Finance Act 1984 (1984 No 9)

s 1	Amendment of FA 1980 ss 1(2), 2(6)	ss 187, 188
2	Unnecessary (obsolete)	
3	(1), (2) Unnecessary (obsolete)	
	(3) Unnecessary (application of schedule)	
4	Amendment of FA 1982 s 6(2)	
5	Amendment of ITA 1967 s 142A(2)(a)(i)	s 473
6	Amendment of ITA 1967 s 432(1)	ss 864(1), 949(1)
7	Unnecessary (cesser of FA 1968 s 41(9))	
8	Amendment of FA 1969 s 3(1)	s 467
9	Substitution of ITA 1967 s 349	s 235
10	Amendment of FA 1983 s 16	
11(1)(3)(4)		s 488(1)-(3)
(2)	Unnecessary (obsolete)	
12 (1)		s 489(1)
1st proviso	Deleted by FA 1991 s 15(1)(a)	
2nd proviso		s 489(2)
(2), (7)		s 488(1)
(3)		s 489(3), (6)
1st proviso		s 489(4)
2nd proviso		s 489(5)

Former Enactment   *Destination in TCA 1997*
Finance Act 1984 (1984 No 9) (contd)

Former	Destination
s 12 (4)	s 489(7)
(5)	s 489(8)
(6)	s 489(9)
(6A)	s 489(10)
(8)	s 489(11)
(9) Rep by FA 1996 s 132(2) and Sch 5 Pt II	
(10)	s 489(12)
(10A)	s 489(13)
(11)	s 489(15)
proviso . Deleted by FA 1996 s 17(c)(ii)	
13 (1)-(2C)	s 490
(2) proviso. Deleted by s 25(c)(i) FA 1993	
(3) Amendment of ITA 1967 s 198(1)	s 1024
13A (s 13A inserted by FA 1989 s 9)	s 491
13B (s 13B inserted by FA 1996 s 20)	s 492
14	s 493
14A (s 14A inserted by FA 1995 s 17(1)(d))	s 494
15 (1)-(12)	s 495
(13) Deleted by FA 1991 s 15(d)	
16 (1)-(3)	s 496
(2)(a)(iii) .. Deleted by FA 1991 s 15(e)(i)	
(4)	s 488(4)
16A (s 16A inserted by FA 1995 s17(1)(g))	s 497
17	s 498
18	s 499
19	s 500
20	s 501
21	s 502
22	s 503
23	s 504
24 (1)-(8)	s 505
(9) Amendment of ITA 1967 Sch 15	Sch 29
25	s 506
26 (1)-(4)	s 507
(1A) Deleted by FA 1991 s 15(1)(f)	
27	s 508
28 (1)	ss 45(2), 48(3)
(2)	ss 45(3), 48(4)
(3)	ss 45(4), 48(5)
29 (1) Definition of "tax" unnecessary (duplication)	s 815(1)
(2)	s 815(2)
(2A)	s 815(3)
(3)(a)	s 815(4)
(b) Unnecessary (obsolete)	
(4), (5)	s 815(5), (6)
29 (6) Amendment of ITA 1967 Sch 15	Sch 29
(7) Unnecessary (operative date)	
30 Amendment of FA 1976 s 30	
31 Amendment of FA 1982 ss 56(1), (2), 58(1) and Sch 3	ss 515, 517, Sch 11
32	s 484
33 Rep by FA 1996 s 132(2) and Sch 5 Pt II	

Former Enactment   *Destination in TCA 1997*

Finance Act 1984 (1984 No 9) (contd)

s 34	Unnecessary (spent)	
35	Amendment of ITA 1967 ss 251(4)(d), 254(2A)(a), 264(1) proviso para (ii), (3) proviso para (ii), 265(1) proviso para (ii)	ss 271(4), 272, 274(1)(3)-(5),(8)
36		s 268(1)(a)(ii), (9)(a)
37	Amendment of FA 1981 s 23 Sch 32, para 14	ss 325, 326, 327, 329
38	Amendment of FA 1981 s 25	Sch 32, para 9
39	Amendment of FA 1981 s 26(1)	Sch 32, para 10
40 (1)-(10)(a)		s 403
(10)(b)	Unnecessary (obsolete)	
(11)	Unnecessary (obsolete)	
41	Insertion of CTA 1976 s 84A	ss 134, 134(1)(4)
42 (1), (2), (3)		s 138
(4), (5)	Unnecessary (obsolete)	
43	Amendment of FA 1978 Sch 2 Pt I	
44	Amendment of FA 1982 ss 43, 44, 45, 46	
45 (a)	Amendment of FA 1980 s 38	s 442(1)
(b)	Amendment of FA 1980s 39	s 443
46	Amendment of FA 1983s 51(2)	
47	Amendment of FA 1983s 52	
48-65	Rep by FA 1996 s 132(2) and Sch 5 Pt II	
66 (a)		s 607
(b)	Ceased by FA 1988 s 70(2)(b)	
67	Insertion of CGTA 1975 s 25(10A)	s 604

Pt VI

s 115	Unnecessary (care and management)	
116(2), (7)	Unnecessary (construction and commencement)	

Sch 1

Pt I	Amendment of ITA 1967 ss 1(1), 153(1)(dd),497, 525(1)	ss 2(1), 3(1), 1032, 460 127(1)-(5)
Pt II	Amendment of ITA 1967 ss 138, 138A	ss 461, 462
Sch 2		Sch 10

Finance Act 1985 (1985 No 10)

s 1	Amendment of FA 1980 ss 1(2), 2(6),	ss 187, 188
2	Amendment of FA 1984 s 2	
3 (1), (2)	Unnecessary (obsolete)	
(3)	Unnecessary (application of schedule)	
4	Substitution of ITA 1967 s 138A	s 462
5	Amendment of FA 1982 s 6	
6 (1)	Substitution of ITA 1967 s 125	s 984(1), (2)
(2)		s 984(3)
7	Amendment of ITA 1967 s 142A(2)	s 473
8	Amendment of ITA 1967 s 344	
9	Amendment of FA 1968 ss 7(5), 8	ss 989(4), (5), 990
10 (1)(a)		s 664(1)(a)
(b)	Unnecessary (obsolete)	
(2)-(6)		s 664(2)-(6)
11	Amendment of FA 1983 s 16	
12	Amendment of ITA 1967 s 550(4)	s 1080(2)-(4)
13	Amendment of FA 1984 ss 11(1), 12(4), 15(7)(b), 26, 27(8)	ss 488(1)-(3), 489(7) 495, 507, 508
14 (1)	Substitution of FA 1969 s 18(2)(b)	
(2)	Unnecessary (operative date)	
15	Substitution of FA 1973 s 21	s 767
16	Unnecessary (spent)	

Former Enactment   *Destination in TCA 1997*

Finance Act 1985 (1985 No 10) (contd)

s 17 (1)	Amendment of FA 1975 s 31A	
(2)	Amendment of FA 1976 s 12	
(3)	Unnecessary (application)	
18	Amendment of FA 1984 ss 49, 51	
19	Unnecessary (spent)	
20	Amendment of ITA 1967 ss 251(4)(d), 254(2A)(a), 264(1) proviso para (ii), 264(3) proviso para (ii), 265(1) proviso para (iii)	ss 283(3), 271(4) 272, 274(1)(3)-(5)(8)
21	Sch 32, para 11. . Sch 32 para 14 of the Bill saves the provisions of FA 1985 s 21 (in so far as that section applied to areas other than the Custom House Docks Area)	
(1)(a)		s 327(1)(a)
(b)	Unnecessary (construction)	
(2)(a)(i)		s 327(1)
(ii)		s 327(3)(a)(ii)
(iii)	Unnecessary (spent)	
(iv)		s 327(1)
(v)	Unnecessary (obsolete)	
(vi)		s 327(1)
(vii)		s 329(9)(b)
(viii)		s 327(4)
(ix)		s 327(6), (7)
(x)		s 327(7)
(xi)		s 329(4)(b)
(xii)		s 329(12)
(b)	Unnecessary (obsolete)	
(3)		s 327(8)
(4)		s 327(9)
(5)		s 329(10)
22 (1)		ss 326(1), 329(1)
(2)		s 326(2)
(3)		s 326(3)
(4)	Unnecessary (spent)	
(5)		s 329(10)
22	Sch 32, para 11. . Sch 32, para 14 of the Bill saves the provisions of FA 1985 s 22 (in so far as that section applied to areas other than the Custom House Docks Areas)	
23 (1)	Substitution of CTA 1976 s 6(4)	
(2)	Unnecessary (spent)	
24		s 218
25	Amendment of FA 1983 s 52	

Pt V

s 60	Amendment of ITA 1967 s 143(5)	

Pt VI

s 69		s 44
70	Unnecessary (care and management)	
71 (2), (7)	Unnecessary (construction and commencement)	

Former Enactment *Destination in TCA 1997*
Finance Act 1985 (1985 No 10) (contd)
    Sch 1 . . . . Amendment of ITA 1967 ss 138, 141(1A), ... ss 461, 465, 467, 468
                                                                                                                            FA 1969 s 3(1), FA 1971 s 11(2)

Finance Act 1986 (1986 No 13)
  s 1 . . . . Amendment of FA 1980 s 2(6) . . . . s 188
      2 . . . . Amendment of FA 1984 s 2
      3 (1), (2) . . . . Unnecessary (obsolete)
        (3). . . . . Unnecessary (application of schedule)
      4 . . . . Substitution of ITA 1967 s 141 . . . . s 465
      5 . . . . Amendment of FA 1967 s 12(1) . . . . s 469(1)
      6 . . . . Amendment of FA 1982 s 6
      7 . . . . Insertion of FA 1979 s 8(6) . . . . s 125(2)
      8 . . . . Rep by FA 1997 s 146(2) and Sch 9 Pt II
      9 (1)(a), ... s 128(1)
        (b)(i), (iii)
          (b)(ii). . . Unnecessary (obsolete)
        (2)-(11)(a). . . . . s 128(2)-(11)
        (11)(b) . . . . Amendment of ITA 1967 Sch 15 . . . . Sch 29
    10 (1), ... Rep by FA 1992 s 12 for share options . . . . Sch 32, para 7
      (2)(a)(b), (6)   granted on or after 29.1.92. Section 10
                              still applies to share options granted
                          before that date
      (2)(c), (3)-(5) . . Unnecessary (obsolete)
    11 . . . . Substitution of FA 1982 s 52(7), (8) . . . . s 511
    12 (1)-(8). . . . . Definitions of "full-time director". . . . . s 479
                      and "full-time employee"
                      deleted by FA 1996 s 12 and
                      definition of "ordinary share capital"
                      unnecessary (duplication)
        (9). . . . . Deleted by FA 1996 s 132(2) and Sch 5 Pt II
    13 . . . . Amendment of FA 1984 s 12(11) . . . . s 489(15)
    14 . . . . Ceased by FA 1992 s 13
    15 (1). . . . . Amendment of FA 1975 s 31A
      (2). . . . . Amendment of FA 1976 s 12
      (3). . . . . Unnecessary (application)
    16 . . . . Unnecessary (obsolete)
    17-30 . . . . Rep by FA 1997 s 146(2) and Sch 9 Pt II
    31 . . . . Definition of "operative. . . . . s 256
                      date" unnecessary (spent)
    32 . . . . s 257
    33 (1)-(9), ... s 258
    (a)-(d), (10)
        (9)(e) . . . . . Rep by FA 1997 s 146(2) and Sch 9 Pt II
    33A(1),(2), ... (s 33A inserted by FA 1996 s 42) . . . . s 260
    (2) proviso
    para (b),(3),(4)
    (2) proviso   Unnecessary (obsolete)
    para (a)
    34 (a). . . . . Unnecessary (cesser of CTA 1976 s 31(1), (2), (3), (6))
      (b). . . . . Amendment of CTA 1976 s 31(4), (9)
    35 (1)(a)-(cc). . . . . s 261
      (d), (e) . . . . Deleted by FA 1992 s 22(1)(b)(ii)
      (2)-(4). . . . . Unnecessary (obsolete)
      (5). . . . . Unnecessary (cesser of ITA 1967 s 344)
    36 . . . . s 262

Destination Table (Taxes Consolidation Act 1997)

Former Enactment	Destination in TCA 1997

Finance Act 1986 (1986 No 13) (contd)

s 37(1)		s 263
(1) proviso		
para (ii),(2)		
(1) proviso	Unnecessary (obsolete)	
para (i) (3), (4)		
37A	(s 37A inserted by FA 1992 s 22(1)(c))	s 264
37B	(s 37B inserted by FA 1992 s 22(1)(c))	s 265
38		s 266
39		s 267
40 (1)	Amendment of ITA 1967 Sch 15	Sch 29
(2)	Amendment of FA 1983 s 94(2)	s 1078
41 (1), (2)	Definition of "designated area" unnecessary (obsolete)	s 322(1)
(3)		s 322(4)
42	Sch 32, para 11 of the Bill saves the provisions of FA 1986 s 42 (in so far as that section applied to areas other than the Custom House Docks Area)	Sch 32, para 11
(1)	Definitions of "multi-storey car-park", "qualifying period" and "the relevant local authority" unnecessary (obsolete)	s 323(1)
(2)		s 323(2)(a), (3)(a)
1st proviso		s 323(2)(b)
2nd proviso		s 323(4)
(3)	Deleted by FA 1991 s 22(2)	
(4)	Unnecessary (obsolete)	
(4)proviso		s 323(3)(b)
(5), (6), (8), (9)	Unnecessary (obsolete)	
(7)		s 323(5)
43	Deleted by FA 1994 s 35(1)(b)	
44	Sch 32, para 12 of the Bill saves the provisions of FA 1986 s 44 (in so far as that section applied to areas other than the Custom House Docks Area)	Sch 32, para 12
(1)(a)(b)	Definition of "qualifying period" and "the relevant local authority" unnecessary (obsolete)	s 328(1)
(b) proviso	Deleted by FA 1995 s 32(1)(c)	
44 (1)(c)(f)(g)	Unnecessary (obsolete)	
(d)		s 329(9)(b)
(e)		s 328(3)
(2)		s 328(2)
(3)		s 329(12)
(4)	Rep by FA 1996 s 132(2) and Sch 5 Pt II	
(5)	Amendment of ITA 1967 s 198(1)	s 1024
45	Sch 32, para 13 of the Bill saves the provisions of FA 1986 s 45 (in so far as that section applied to areas other than the Custom House Docks Area)	Sch 32, para 13
(1)(a)(c)		s 324(1)
(b)	Unnecessary (obsolete)	
(2)		s 324(2)
1st proviso para (a)	Unnecessary (obsolete)	
1st proviso para (b)		s 324(3)
2nd proviso	Unnecessary (obsolete)	

Former Enactment   *Destination in TCA 1997*
Finance Act 1986 (1986 No 13) (contd)

s 46 (1)-(3) .... s 1013(1)-(3)
    (4) .... Rep by FA 1997 s 146(2) and Sch 9 Pt II
    (5) .... Unnecessary (obsolete)
    (6) .... s 1013(4)(b)
47 .... Amendment of FA 1985 s 16(1)(b)(i)
48 (1)-(4) ..... Definitions of "specified date" (obsolete) and .... s 1084(1)-(4)
              "tax" (duplication) unnecessary
49 .... Amendment of FA 1976 s 30(1)
50 (1) .... s 373(2)(c)
    (2) .... Amendment of FA 1976 s 32 .... s 376
51 .... Amendment of FA 1981 s 25(1) .... Sch 32, para 9
52 (1) .... s 317(3)
    (2) .... Insertion of ITA 1967 s 264(3A) .... s 272
53 .... Amendment of FA 1984 s 40 .... s 403
54 .... Insertion of CTA 1976 s 84A(10) .... s 133(4)
55 (1) .... Amendment of CTA 1976 ss 25(5), 26(4) .... ss 157, 158
    (2) .... Unnecessary (operative date)
56 (1) .... Amendment of CTA 1976 s 70
    (2) .... Amendment of CTA 1976 s 39A
57 (1) .... Substitution of CTA 1976 s 155(10) .... s 4(2)-(6)
    (2) .... Unnecessary (operative date)
58 .... Unnecessary (spent)
59 (a) .... Insertion of CTA 1976 s 33(1A), (1B) .... s 707
    (b) .... Insertion of CTA 1976 s 39(4A) .... s 715
    (c) .... Insertion of CTA 1976 s 40(1A) .... s 716
    (d) .... Amendment of CTA 1976 s 50 .... s 706(1)-(3)
60 .... Amendment of CGTA 1975 s 3(3) .... s 28
61 .... Unnecessary (spent)

Pt VI

112(1), (2) .... s 7
    (3) .... Unnecessary (operative date)
113(1)-(3) ..... Definition of "tax" in s 113(1) unnecessary (duplication) ... s 887
    (4) .... Unnecessary (cesser)
    (5) .... s 928(2), (3)
    (6) .... s 967
114(1) .... Amendment of ITA 1967 s 429 .... s 942(1)-(8), (10)
    (2) .... Amendment FA 1976 s 30
    (3) .... Amendment of FA 1983 s 107
    (4) .... Unnecessary (operative date)
115 .... s 1001
116(1) .... Substitution of ITA 1967 s 161 .... s 852(1), (2)
    (2) .... s 852(3)
117 .... Unnecessary (care and management)
118(2), ... Unnecessary (construction and commencement)
    (7), (8)
Sch 1 .... Amendment of ITA 1967 ss 138, 138A(2), ... ss 461, 462
              138B(1), FA 1974 s 8(1)   472, 464
Sch 2 .... Rep by FA 1992 s 12
Sch 3 .... Unnecessary (obsolete)
Sch 4
    Pt I, II .... Sch 5
    Pts III, IV, ... Unnecessary (obsolete)
    V, VI, VII

Income Tax (Amendment) Act 1986 (1986 No 34)

s 1 .... Substitution of ITA 1967 s 110 .... s 112
   2 .... Unnecessary (short title and construction)

Former Enactment   *Destination in TCA 1997*
Finance Act 1987 (1987 No 10)

Pt I
s 1 .... Amendment of FA 1982 s 6
    2 (1) .... Unnecessary (duplication)
       (2) .... s 664(1)(a)
       proviso .... s 664(1)(b)(i)
    3 .... Amendment of FA 1986 s 16
    4 .... Rep by FA 1994 s 157(1)
    5 .... Amendment of FA 1986 s 14
    6 .... Rep by FA 1997 s 146(2) and Sch 9 Pt II
    7 (1)-(4) .... s 259
       (5) .... Unnecessary (construction)
    8 .... Amendment of FA 1984s 12 .... ss 488, 489
    9 .... Insertion of FA 1984 s 13(2A), (2B), (2C) .... s 490
   10 .... Insertion of FA 1984 s 15(3A), (13) .... s 495
   11 .... Amendment of FA 1984 s 16 .... ss 488(4), 496
   12 .... Insertion of FA 1984 s 26(1A) and .... Sch 10
              substitution of Sch 2 para 1
   13 .... s 520
   14 .... s 521
   14A .... (s 14A inserted by FA 1988 s 8(c)) .... s 522
   15 .... s 523
   16 .... s 524
   17 .... s 525
   18 .... s 526
   19 .... s 527
   20 .... s 528
   21 .... s 529
   22 (1) ...... Amendment of FA 1975 s 31A
      (2) .... Amendment of FA 1976 s 12 .... s 77
      (3) .... Unnecessary (application)
   23 (1) ...... Unnecessary (repeal of ITA 1967 s 362)
      (2) .... s 835
   24 .... s 286
   25 (1) .... s 317(1)
      (2) .... s 317(4)
   26 .... Amendment of FA 1984 s 40(10)(a) .... s 403
   27 (1)(a) .... Unnecessary (obsolete)
      (1)(b) .... s 322(2)
      (2) .... s 322(3)
   28 (1) ...... Par (iv) of definition of "qualifying ship" .... s 407(1)
              deleted by FA 1990 s 42(1)
      (2) .... s 407(3)
      (3) .... Insertion of FA 1980 s 39(1CC1) .... s 443
      (4) .... s 407(4)
      (5)(a) .... s 407(6)
        (b) .... ss 133(1)(d), 134(1)(d)
   29 .... Insertion of FA 1980 s 39(1CC2) .... s 443
   30 .... Insertion of FA 1980 s 39B .... s 446(1)-(12)
   31 .... Insertion of FA 1980 s 39(1CC3) .... s 443
   32 .... Unnecessary (spent)
   33 .... Amendment of CTA 1976 s 79
   34 .... s 220

Former Enactment   *Destination in TCA 1997*
Finance Act 1987 (1987 No 10) (contd)

   s 35 (1)-(20) .... s 481, Sch 32 para 22
        (21) .... Unnecessary (obsolete)
        (22) .... Rep by FA 1997 s 146(2) and Sch 9 Pt II
   Pt VI
     52 .... Amendment of ITA 1967 s 162(3) .... s 851
     54 .... Unnecessary (care and management)
     55(2), (7) ..... Unnecessary (construction and commencement)

Finance Act 1988 (1988 No 12)

   Pt I
   s 1 .... Amendment of FA 1980 ss 1(2), 2(6) .... ss 187, 188
      2 .... Amendment of FA 1986 s 2
      3 (1), (2) .... Unnecessary (obsolete)
        (3) .... Unnecessary (application of schedule)
      4 .... Amendment of FA 1982 s 6
      5 (1) .... Unnecessary (spent)
        (2) .... Unnecessary (construction)
      6 .... Amendment of FA 1986 Sch 2
      7 .... Amendment of FA 1984 s 16(2)(a)
      8 .... Amendment of FA 1987 Pt I Ch III
      9 (1) .... Definition of "relevant chargeable period" .... ss 950(1), 955(5)(a)
          obsolete except for purposes of s 955(5)
        (2), (3) .... s 950(2), (3)
        (4) .... Deleted by FA 1991 s 45(b)
     10 (1)-(12) .... (s 10(12) also provided for the amendment .... s 951
          of ITA 1967 Sch 15)
     11 .... s 952
     12 .... s 953
     13 .... s 954
     14 (1), (2) .... s 955(1), (2)(a)
        (2) proviso .... s 955(2)(b)
        para (a)-(e)
        para (f) .... Unnecessary (obsolete)
        (3), (4) .... s 955(3), (4)
        (5) .... s 955(5)(b)(i)
     15 .... s 956
     16 .... s 1084(1), (5)
     17 .... s 957
     18 (1)-(3), ... s 958(2)-(5)
   (3)1st proviso
   (3) 2nd proviso
        paras (a),(b) .... s 958(6)(a), (b)
        para (c) .... Unnecessary (spent)
        (3A)-(6) .... s 958(7)-(10)
        (7) .... s 958(1)
     19 (1) .... Rep by FA 1997 s 146(2) and Sch 9 Pt II
        (2) .... Amendment of ITA 1967 s 550 .... s 1080(1)
     20 (1) to(4) ... Ceased by FA 1990 s 27(2)(b)
        (5) .... (The cesser of FA 1988 s 20 by FA 1990 s 27 .... s 959(7)
          does not effect the provision of s 20(5))
     21 (1) .... s 959(1)
        (2) .... s 1069(1)(b)
        (3), (4), (5) .... s 959(2), (3), (4)

Destination Table (Taxes Consolidation Act 1997)

Former Enactment	Destination in TCA 1997

Finance Act 1988 (1988 No 12) (contd)

s 21	(6)	Rep by FA 1997 s 146(2) and Sch 9 Pt II	
	(7), (8)		s 959(5), (6)
22		Rep by FA 1997 s 146(2) and Sch 9 Pt II	
23	(1)	Amendment of FA 1975 s 31A	
	(2)	Amendment of FA 1976 s 12	
	(3)	Unnecessary (application)	
24	(1)		s 373(2)(d)
	(2)	Unnecessary (obsolete)	
25		Amendment of FA 1986 s 44(1)(a)	s 328(1)
26		Unnecessary (spent)	
27		Amendment of FA 1981 s 23	ss 325(1), 326(1), 327(1), 329(1)(2)
28		Amendment of FA 1985 s 21	ss 326, 327, 329, Sch 32, para 11
29		Amendment of FA 1985 s 22	Sch 32, para 11
30	(1)		ss 774(4)(a), 608(1)(a), 717(2)(a)
	(2)(a)		s 774(4)(b)
	(b)		s 608(1)(b)
	(c)		s 717(2)(b)
31	(1)	Unnecessary (obsolete)	
	(2)	Unnecessary (application of schedule)	
32	(1)	Amendment of FA 1980 s 45	s 147, Sch 32 para 4
	(2)	Unnecessary (obsolete)	
	(3)	Unnecessary (application of schedule)	
33	(1)	Substitution of CTA 1976 s 1(1)	s 21
	(2)	Unnecessary (cesser of CTA 1976 ss 28, 79)	
	(3)	Unnecessary (application of schedule)	
34		Insertion of CTA 1976 s 116A	s 456
35		Amendment of FA 1980 s 39A(2)	s 445
36	(1)	Rep FA 1980 s 39B(7)(c)	
	(2)	Unnecessary (obsolete)	
	(3)	Amendment of FA 1980 s 39B(6)	s 446(1)-(12)
	(4)		s 451
37			s 452
38		Insertion of FA 1974 s 31(3)(cc)	s 246(3)
39			s 217
40	(1)	Amendment of FA 1987 s 28(1)	s 407(1)
	(2)	Unnecessary (obsolete)	
	(3)	Amendment of FA 1987 s 28(4)(c)	s 407(4)
41			s 222
42			Sch 32, para 3
43		Amendment of ITA 1967 s 251	ss 283(2)(3)(6), 300(1), 304(3)(b), 316(3)
44		Insertion of ITA 1967 s 254(7)	ss 271(1)(2)(4)-(6), 278(1), (2), (6), 304(2)(3)(a)(4), 305, 316(3), 317(2), 320(1)
45		Amendment of ITA 1967 s 265	s 274(1), (3)-(5), (8)
46		Substitution of FA 1967 s 11(2)	s 285(1), (2), (3)
47		Substitution of FA 1971 s 26(2)	s 285(1), (2), (3)
48		Substitution of FA 1978 s 25(2)	s 273(2)
49		Amendment of FA 1981 s 25(1)	Sch 32, para 9
50		Amendment of ITA 1967 ss 254(2A)(a), 264(1) proviso para (ii), 264(3) proviso para (ii), 265(1) proviso para (iii)	s 271(4), 272, 274(1)(3)-(5)(8)

Former Enactment	Destination in TCA 1997
Finance Act 1988 (1988 No 12) (contd)	
s 51 (1)(a)	ss 271(3)(a), 273(5)(a), 283(4)(a), 285(5)(a)
(b) .....Unnecessary (obsolete)	
(c)	ss 273(5)(b), 285(5)(b)
(cc)	ss 271(3)(b), 273(5)(c), 285(5)(c)
proviso	ss 271(3)(b), 273(5)(c), 283(4)(b), 285(5)(c)
(d)	ss 274(2), 285(5)(d)
(2)(a),(c),(d)	s 283(3)(a)
(b) .....Unnecessary (obsolete)	
(3)	s 285(4)
(4)(a)	s 271(4)(a)
(b)	s 273(4)
(5)	s 274(2)
(6)	ss 271(1), 273(1), 283(1), 285(1)
52 (1)........Amendment of FA 1974 s 22	s 658(1)
(2)........Amendment of FA 1977 s 14(1)	Sch 32, para 23(2)
(3)........Cesser of FA 1980 s 26 (unnecessary)	
70 (1)(a) .....Insertion of ITA 1967 s 467A	
(b) .....Amendment of ITA 1967 s 474(1)	s 49, Sch 32 para 1(2)
(2)(a)	s 607(1)(d)
(b) .....Unnecessary (cesser of FA 1983 s 54 and FA 1984 s 66(6) (in so far as it relates to Bord Telecom Eireann))	
71 (1), (2)(a)	s 1006
(2)(b) .....Unnecessary (obsolete)	
72 (1)-(6).....Unnecessary (obsolete)	
(7)........Amendment of FA 1983 s 23(4)	s 1086
73 (1)-(16), (18)	s 1002
(17)........Deleted by FA 1992 s 241(e)	
74 (1), (2)	s 8
(3)........Unnecessary (commencement)	
76 ....Unnecessary (care and management)	
77 (2), (7), (8) .Unnecessary (construction and commencement)	
Sch 1 ....Amendment of ITA 1967 ss 138, 138A(2), 138B(1)	ss 461, 462, 472
Sch 2 ....Unnecessary (obsolete)	
Sch 3 ....Unnecessary (obsolete)	
Finance Act 1989 (1989 No 10)	
s 1 ....Amendment of FA 1980 ss 1, 2	ss 187, 188
2 ....Amendment of FA 1984 s 2	
3 ....Amendment of FA 1982 s 6	
4 (1)-(6)	Sch 32, para 20
(7)........Rep by FA 1996 s 132(2) and Sch 5 Pt II	
4 (8)........Amendment of ITA 1967 s 198(1)	s 1024
5 ....Insertion of FA 1969 s 2(5A)-(5D)	s 195(1)-(11)
6 ....Amendment of FA 1982 s 8(1)(a)	s 122
7 ....Rep by FA 1997 s 146(2) and Sch 9 Pt II	
8 ....Ceased by FA 1992 s 4	
9 ....Amendment of FA 1984 ss 12(1), 16(2)(2A), 17, insertion of s 13A	s 489(1)(2), 493, 496, 498,
10	s 995

Former Enactment   *Destination in TCA 1997*
Finance Act 1989 (1989 No 10) (contd)

s 11 (1)	Amendment of FA 1975 s 31A	
(2)	Amendment of FA 1976 s 12	
(3)	Unnecessary (spent)	
(4)	Unnecessary (application)	
12 (1)		s 373(2)(e)
(2)	Amendment of FA 1976 s 32	s 376
13	Substitution of ITA 1967 s 251(7)	
14	Substitution of ITA 1967 s 254(7)	s 271(5)
15	Amendment of FA 1974 s 22(2)	s 658(2)(a)
16	Insertion of FA 1978 s 25(3)	s 273(8)
17	Amendment of FA 1981 s 26	Sch 32, para 10
18 (1)		s 734(1)(a), (c)
(2)-(9), (11),(11A),(12)		s 734(2)-(12)
(10)	Deleted by FA 1993 s 20(b)	
19 (1), (2), (3)		s 893
(4)	Amendment of ITA 1967 Sch 15	Sch 29
20	Substitution of CTA 1976 s 36(2)	s 713(1)-(6)
21 (1)	Substitution of CTA 1976s 84A	s 134(3)
(2)(a)		ss 133(3), 134(2)
(2)(b)	Unnecessary (spent)	
22	Amendment of FA 1980 ss 38, 39(1CC)	ss 442(1), 443
23	Deletion of FA 1980 s 39A(8), (9)	
24	Amendment of FA 1980 s 45	s 147, Sch 32 para 4
25 (1)-(3)		s 154(1)-(3)
(4)		s 154(6)
26	Substitution of FA 1984 s 42(1)	s 138
27 (1)	Amendment of CTA 1976 s 100(3)(h)	s 434
(2)	Amendment of FA 1980 s 41(1)	s 448(1)
(3)	Unnecessary (operative date)	
28	Amendment of FA 1987 s 35	s 481, Sch 32, para 22
29	Amendment of CGTA 1975 Sch 4 para 11	s 980
30	Amendment of FA 1986 s 61(1)	
31 (1)	Amendment of FA 1988 s 70(2)	s 607(1)(d)
(2)	Unnecessary (operative date)	
32	Amendment of CGTA 1975 s 19	s 607(1)(a)-(d)(f), (2)
33		s 610, Sch 15, Pt I

Pt VI

86		s 811
87	Insertion of CGTA 1975 s 33(5A)	s 549
88 (1)-(7)		s 817
(8)	Unnecessary (operative date)	
89 (1)	Amendment of ITA 1967 s 433(1)	s 237
(2)		s 242

Pt VII

95 (1)(a)	Insertion of ITA 1967 s 467B	
(b)	Amendment of ITA 1967 s 474(1)	s 49, Sch 32 para 1(2)
(2)	Amendment of CGTA 1975 s 19(d)	s 607
98 (1)	Amendment of FA 1973 s 92(1)	ss 39(1), 48(1)(c)
(2)	Amendment of FA 1984 s 66(a)	s 607
99	Unnecessary (care and management)	
100(2), (7), (8)	Unnecessary (construction and commencement)	

Former Enactment   *Destination in TCA 1997*
Finance Act 1989 (1989 No 10) (contd)

Sch 1 .... Sch 1 para 1(7)(e) rep by FA 1997 s 146(2) .... Sch 18 para 1
para 1(1)-(6),   and Sch 9 Pt II
(7)(a)-(d), (8)

para 2 .... para 2
para 3 .... Amendment of ITA 1967 Sch 15, ... Sch 29
                FA 1983 s 94(2)

Judicial Separation and Family Law Reform Act 1989 (1989 No 6)

s 26 .... s 1027(a)

Finance Act 1990 (1990 No 10)

s 1 .... Amendment of FA 1980 ss 1, 2 .... ss 187, 188
   2 .... Amendment of FA 1984 s 2
   3 .... Amendment of FA 1982 s 6
   4 .... Amendment of FA 1969 s 3(1) .... s 467
   5 (1), (2) .... s 189
     (3) .... Unnecessary (commencement)
   6 .... Amendment of FA 1989 s 8
   7 .... s 190
   8 .... Amendment of FA 1976 s 13(2) .... s 805
   9 .... Amendment of FA 1980 s 28(3)
   10 .... Amendment of FA 1984 ss 11(1), 12, 16 .... s 488(1)-(3), 489(1), 496
   11 .... s 251
   12 .... Amendment of ITA 1967 Sch 3 .... s 201(1)(a), Sch 3
   13 (1), (3), (4) .... s 214
      (2) .... Unnecessary (commencement)
   14 (1) .... Amendment of ITA 1967 s 58 .... ss 65(1), 66, 67
      (2) .... Unnecessary (cesser of FA 1971 s 3)
   15 .... Substitution of ITA 1967 s 60 .... s 65(2)-(4)
   16 .... Unnecessary (spent)
   17 (1)(a) .... Amendment of ITA 1967 Pt IV Ch IV
      (b) ..... Amendment of ITA 1967 Sch 6 .... s 73
      (2) .... Unnecessary (cesser of ITA 1967 s 77(3)(4))
   18 (1) .... Amendment of ITA 1967 ss 81(3), 89 .... ss 75(3), 384
      (2) .... Unnecessary (cesser of ITA 1967 s 81(3)(b)(c))
   19 (a) .... Substitution of ITA 1967 s 110 .... s 112
      (b) .... Unnecessary (deletion of ITA 1967 s 111
                with saver for any enactment which refers to
                ITA 1967 s 111)
   20 (1) .... Amendment of ITA 1967 Sch 18 .... Sch 28
      (2) .... Amendment of FA 1974 s 20B .... s 657(4)(5)
      (3) .... Unnecessary (cesser of FA 1980 s 17 Table
                Pt I para (a), (b) and FA 1981s 9(a), (b))
      (4) .... Unnecessary (spent)
   21 .... Unnecessary (spent)
   22 (1) .... Amendment of ITA 1967 ss 262(2), 297(2) .... s 306
      (2) .... Amendment of FA 1974 s 22(2A)(c) .... s 658(3)
   23 (1) .... Amendment of ITA 1967 s 70 .... ss 880(1)-(6), 900(3),
                                                                        1052(4)(a)(c)(e)
      (2) .... Amendment of ITA 1967 s 172 .... ss 879(1)-(4),
                                                                        1052(4)(a)(c)(e)
      (3) .... Amendment of FA 1988 ss 9, 10 .... ss 950, 951, 955(5)(a).
      (4) .... Unnecessary (spent)
      (5) .... Unnecessary (commencement)
   24 (a) .... Amendment of ITA 1967 s 477(1) .... s 960
      (b) .... Unnecessary (cesser of ITA 1967 s 550(2)
                and FA 1982 s 27(4))
      (c) .... Amendment of CTA 1976 s 6(4)
      (d) .... Amendment of FA 1988 s 18 .... s 958

Former Enactment *Destination in TCA 1997*
Finance Act 1990 (1990 No 10) (contd)

s 25 (1) .... Amendment of FA 1986 s 48 .... s 1084(1)-(4)
    (2) .... Unnecessary (operative date)
    (3) .... Unnecessary (spent)
  26 (1) .... Unnecessary (invalid)
    (2) .... Unnecessary (spent)
    (3) .... Unnecessary (spent)
  27 (1) .... Amendment of ITA 1967 s 236(11) .... s 787(7)
    (2) .... Unnecessary (cesser of ITA 1967
               ss 307(1AA), 546 and FA 1988 s 20)
  28 .... Substitution of ITA 1967 s 421(2) .... s 934
  29 (1)(2)(5)(6) .... s 1014
    (3) .... Amendment of CGTA 1975 s 2(1) .... s 5
    (4) .... Amendment of CTA 1976 s 1(5) .... s 4(1)
    (7) .... Unnecessary (operative date)
  30 (1) .... Amendment of FA 1986 ss 42(1), 44(1)(a), ... Sch 32 paras 11, 12, 13
               45(1)(a)
    (2) .... Amendment of FA 1989 s 4(1)(a) .... Sch 32 para 20
  31 .... Amendment of FA 1987 s 27(1)(a)(ii)
  32 .... Amendment of FA 1986 s 45(2) .... Sch 32 para 13
  33 (1) .... ss 324(4)(b), 333(4)(b),
                                                     345(8)(b), 354(5)(b),
                                                     370(8)(b)

    (2)(a) .... Definition of "qualifying premises" .... ss 324(4)(a),
            unnecessary (duplication),   333(4)(a), 345(8)(a), 354(5)(a),
                                                     370(8)(a)

  33 (2)(b) ..... Unnecessary (obsolete)
  34 (1)(a) .... ss 155(1), 489(14)(a)
    (b)(i) ... Unnecessary (obsolete)
   (1)(b)(ii) .... ss 155(2)(c), 489(14)(b)
    (2) .... ss 155(2)(a), 489(14)(c)(d)
    (3) .... s 155(3)
    (4) .... s 489(14)(e)
    (5), (6) .... s 155(4), (5)
  35 (1), (2) .... s 735
    (3) .... Unnecessary (operative date)
  36 .... Unnecessary (obsolete)
  37 .... Unnecessary (obsolete)
  38 .... Amendment of FA 1989 s 25(3)(a) .... s 154(1)-(3)
  39 (a)-(c) .... Amendment of F(TPCM)A 1974 ss 2(1), ... ss 673(1), 674(1)(a)(2)-(4),
               3(2), 4(1)   675
    (d) .... Insertion of F(TPCM)A 1974 s 7A .... s 678
  40 .... Amendment of FA 1980 s 38 .... s 442(1)
  41 (1) .... Amendment of FA 1980 s 39 .... s 443
    (2) .... Unnecessary (spent)
    (3) .... Unnecessary (obsolete)
    (4)(a) .... s 133(1)(e)
      (b) ..... Unnecessary (duplication)
    (5) .... s 403(9)(a)
    (6) .... s 442(1)
  42 (1) .... Amendment of FA 1987 s 28(1) .... s 407(1)
    (2) .... Unnecessary (obsolete)
  43 .... Substitution of CTA 1976 s 10(4) .... s 243(1), (2), (4)-(9)
  44 (1) .... Insertion of CTA 1976 s 116(10) .... s 420
    (2) .... Unnecessary (spent)
  45 .... Unnecessary (spent)

Former Enactment   *Destination in TCA 1997*
Finance Act 1990 (1990 No 10) (contd)

s 46	Amendment of CTA 1976 s 84A	ss 133, 134
47	Amendment of CTA 1976 s 101	s 440
48	Amendment of CTA 1976 s 162	s 441
49	Amendment of CTA 1976 s 151	ss 238(1)-(6), 239
50	Insertion of CTA 1976 s 152(4)	s 240
51 (1), (2)		s 241
(3)	Substitution of ITA 1967 s 434(5A)	s 238
(4)	Unnecessary (operative date)	
52	Amendment of FA 1980 s 41(1)	s 448(1)
53	Amendment of CTA 1976 s 58(10)	
54	Substitution of CTA 1976 s 143(1)	s 884
55	Amendment of FA 1983 s 50	s 171
56	Substitution of FA 1983 s 24	s 517
57		s 703
58	Amendment of CTA 1976 s 129(2)	s 616
59		s 704
60		s 705
61	Amendment of ITA 1967 s 337	
62		s 740
63		s 741
64		s 742
65		s 743
66		s 744
67		s 745
68		s 746
69 (1)-(7)		s 747
(8)	Unnecessary (obsolete)	
70	Amendment of ITA 1967 s 241(1)	s 284(1)(2)(a)(b),(3), 300(1)
71	Amendment of FA 1967 s 11	s 285(1), (2), (3)
72	Amendment of FA 1971 s 26	ss 285(1)(2)(3)(8), 287, 299(2)
73	Amendment of ITA 1967 s 251	ss 283(2), 300(1), 316(3)
74	Amendment of ITA 1967 s 254	ss 271(1)(4)(6), 278(1)(2)(6), 305, 320
75	Insertion of FA 1970 s 19(2A)	s 279
76	Amendment of FA 1978 s 25	s 273(1)(2)(3)(8)
77	Amendment of FA 1974 s 22	s 658
78	Amendment of ITA 1967 s 265(1)	s 274(1)(3)-(5)(8)
79	Amendment of ITA 1967 s 276	s 294
80	Substitution of FA 1988 s 51(2), (3), (4)	ss 283(3)(a), 285(4), 271(4)(a), 273(4)
81 (1)(a)		ss 271(3)(c), 273(7)(a)(i), 283(5), 285(7)(a)(i)
(b)		s 273(7)(a)(ii)
(c)		s 285(7)(a)(ii)
(1) proviso		ss 273(7)(b), 285(7)(b)
(2)(a), (b)		s 283(3)(b)
(c)	Unnecessary (obsolete)	
(3)		s 285(6)
(4)		s 271(4)(a)
(5)		s 273(6)
82	Amendment of CGTA 1975 s 3(3)	s 28
83	Amendment of CGTA 1975 s 36	s 590(1)-(9)
84	Amendment of CGTA 1975 s 26	s 598
85	Amendment of CGTA 1975 s 27(3)	s 599

Former Enactment   *Destination in TCA 1997*
Finance Act 1990 (1990 No 10) (contd)

s 86	.... Amendment of CGTA 1975 Sch 1 para 15(3)	s 596
87	.... Insertion of CGTA 1975 Sch 2 para 2A................	s 733

Pt VII

s 131	.... Insertion of FA 1970 s 17(14)-(17)	s 531(17), (18)
136	.... Insertion of FA 1982 Sch 3 para 4A...................	Sch 11
137	.... Insertion of FA 1986 Sch 2 para 15	
138(1)	....	ss 45(3),(4)(a), 48(4)(a),(5)(a)
(2)	.... Amendment of FA 1984 s 28......................	ss 45(2)-(4), 48(3)-(5)
139	.... Unnecessary (care and management)	
140(2), (8)	.... Unnecessary (construction and commencement)	
Sch 1	.... Unnecessary (obsolete)	
Sch 2	.... Unnecessary (obsolete)	
Sch 3	....	Sch 16
Sch 4	....	Sch 17
Sch 5	....	Sch 19
Sch 6	....	Sch 20

Finance Act 1991 (1991 No 13)

Pt I

s 1	.... Amendment of FA 1980 ss 1, 2	ss 187, 188
2 (1), (2)	....	s 15
(3)	.... Unnecessary (application of schedule)	
3 (1), (2)	.... Unnecessary (obsolete)	
(3)	.... Unnecessary (application of schedule)	
4 (1), (2)	....	s 463
(3)	.... Rep by FA 1996 s 132(2) and Sch 5 Pt II	
(4)	.... Unnecessary (commencement)	
5	.... Amendment of FA 1989 s 8	
6	.... Amendment of ITA 1967 s 110	s 112
7	.... Insertion of ITA 1967 s 138B(3).....................	s 472
8	.... Substitution of ITA 1967 s 142A(2)(b)	s 473
9	.... Amendment of FA 1982 s 6	
10 (1)	.... Unnecessary (interpretation)	
(2)	....	s 664(1)(a), (b)(ii)
11	.... Amendment of FA 1986 s 31(1).....................	s 256.
12	....	s 773
13	....	s 210
14	.... Amendment of FA 1984 ss 12, 13	ss 488(1), 489, 490, 1024
15 (1)	.... Amendment of FA 1984 ss 12, 13, 13A, 15, ... 16, 26	ss 488(1)(4), 489, 490, 491, 495, 496, 507, 1024,
(2)	.... Amendment of FA 1984 Sch 2 para 1	Sch 10
16	.... Unnecessary (obsolete)	
17 (1)	.... Amendment of FA 1984 s 13	s 490
(2)	.... Amendment of FA 1984 s 15(2).....................	s 495
(3)(a)	..... Unnecessary (obsolete)	
(b)	..... Ceased by FA 1994 s 17	
(4)	.... Unnecessary (interpretation)	
18 (1)	.... Amendment of FA 1975 s 31A	
(2)	.... Amendment of FA 1976 s 12	
(3)	.... Amendment of FA 1980 s 28	
(4)	.... Unnecessary (application)	
19 (1)	.... Amendment of FA 1989 s 18(1).....................	s 734
(2)	....	s 734(1)(b)
(3)	.... Unnecessary (obsolete)	
20 (1), (3)	....	s 230
(2)	....	s 610, Sch 15, Pt I

Former Enactment	Destination in TCA 1997
Finance Act 1991 (1991 No 13) (contd)	

s 21	(1)	Amendment of FA 1986 s 45	Sch 32, para 13
	(2)	Unnecessary (operative date)	
22	(1)		s 271(4)(a)
	(2)(a)	Unnecessary (cesser of FA 1986 s 42(3))	
	(b)	Unnecessary (operative date)	
23		Amendment of FA 1970 s 19	s 279
24			s 408
25		Amendment of FA 1974 s 22	s 658
26			s 276
27		Amendment of FA 1984 s 29	s 815(1)(2)
28		Amendment of CTA 1976 s 84A	ss 133(7)(13), 134(1)(4)-(6)
29		Insertion of CTA 1976 s 87(4)(e)	s 135
30	(1)	Amendment of CTA 1976 s 35	s 710(1)-(5)
	(2)		s 710(6)
31			s 110
32	(1)	Amendment of FA 1980 s 39(3)(a)	s 443
	(2)	Unnecessary (operative date)	
33		Amendment of FA 1980 s 39A	s 445
34		Amendment of FA 1980 s 39B(2)	s 446(1)-(12)
35		Amendment of FA 1990 s 41(6)	s 442(1)
36			s 831
37		Unnecessary (obsolete)	
38		Substitution of FA 1988 s 30(1)	ss 774(4)(a), 608(1)(a), 717(2)(a)
39		Amendment of FA 1990 s 45(2)(a)	
40		Amendment of FA 1988 s 41(1)(a)	s 222
41			s 220
42		Amendment of CGTA 1975 s 26	s 598
43	(1), (2)		s 606
	(3)	Unnecessary (operative date)	
44		Amendment of FA 1989 s 33(2)	s 610, Sch 15, Pt I
45		Amendment of FA 1988 s 9	ss 950(1)-(3), 955(5)(a).
46		Amendment of FA 1988 s 10	s 951
47		Amendment of FA 1988 s 12	s 953
48		Insertion of FA 1988 s 13(7)	s 954
49		Amendment of FA 1988 s 14(5)	s 955(5)(b)(i)
50		Amendment of FA 1988 s 15(1)	s 956
51		Amendment of FA 1988 s 17(1)	s 957
52		Amendment of FA 1988 s 18	s 958(2)-(5)
53		Amendment of FA 1988 s 21	s 959(1)
54-55		Rep by FA 1997 s 156(1)(a)	
56	(1)(a)(i)		s 325(1)
	(ii)	Unnecessary (spent)	
	(iii)	Rep by FA 1997 s 156(1)(b)	
	(iv)	Unnecessary (spent)	
	(b)		s 325(1)
	(bb)	Unnecessary (obsolete)	
	(c)	Unnecessary (obsolete)	
	(2)		s 325(2)
	proviso	Rep by FA 1997 s 156(1)(b)	
57	(1)(a)	Rep by FA 1997 s 156(1)(c)	
	(b)(i)		s 327(1)
	(ii),(iii)	Unnecessary (obsolete)	
	(2)	Rep by s 156(1)(c)	
	(3)(a)(i)		s 327(1)
	(ii)	Unnecessary (obsolete)	
	(aa)		s 327(1)
	(b)	Unnecessary (obsolete)	

Former Enactment   *Destination in TCA 1997*

Finance Act 1991 (1991 No 13) (contd)

```
s  57  (3)(bb) . . . .  Unnecessary (obsolete)
           (c) . . . . .  Unnecessary (obsolete)
       58  (1)(a) . . . . .  Rep by FA 1997 s 156(1)(d)
           (b)(i) . . . . . . . . . . . . . . . . . . . . . . . . . . . . . . . . . . . . . . . . . . . . . .  s 326(1)
           (ii)(iii) . . . .  Unnecessary (obsolete)
           (2) . . . . . . . .  Rep by FA 1997 s 156(1)(d)
           (3)(a) . . . . . . . . . . . . . . . . . . . . . . . . . . . . . . . . . . . . . . . . . . . . . .  s 326(1)
           (b) . . . . .  Unnecessary (obsolete)
           (c) . . . . .  Unnecessary (obsolete)
       59  . . . . . . . . .  Definitions of "the Act of 1975", . . . . . . . . . . . . . . . . . . . . . .  s 173
                      "the Act of 1976" unnecessary
                      (duplication) and "relevant day"
                      unnecessary (operative date)
       60  . . . . . . . . . . . . . . . . . . . . . . . . . . . . . . . . . . . . . . . . . . . . . . . . . . . . . . .  s 174
       60A . . . . . . . . . (s 60A inserted by FA 1997 s 39(b)) . . . . . . . . . . . . . . . . . . . .  s 175
       61  . . . . . . . . . . . . . . . . . . . . . . . . . . . . . . . . . . . . . . . . . . . . . . . . . . . . . . .  s 176
       62  . . . . . . . . . . . . . . . . . . . . . . . . . . . . . . . . . . . . . . . . . . . . . . . . . . . . . . .  s 177
       63  . . . . . . . . . . . . . . . . . . . . . . . . . . . . . . . . . . . . . . . . . . . . . . . . . . . . . . .  s 178
       64  . . . . . . . . . . . . . . . . . . . . . . . . . . . . . . . . . . . . . . . . . . . . . . . . . . . . . . .  s 179
       65  . . . . . . . . . . . . . . . . . . . . . . . . . . . . . . . . . . . . . . . . . . . . . . . . . . . . . . .  s 180
       66  . . . . . . . . . . . . . . . . . . . . . . . . . . . . . . . . . . . . . . . . . . . . . . . . . . . . . . .  s 181
       67  . . . . . . . . . . . . . . . . . . . . . . . . . . . . . . . . . . . . . . . . . . . . . . . . . . . . . . .  s 182
       68  (1)-(3) . . . . . . . . . . . . . . . . . . . . . . . . . . . . . . . . . . . . . . . . . . . . . . . .  s 183
           (4) . . . . . . .  Amendment of ITA 1967 Sch 15 . . . . . . . . . . . . . . . . . . . . . . . .  Sch 29
       69  . . . . . . . . .  Insertion of FA 1983 ss 45(9), 47(1)(c) . . . . . . . . . . . . . . . .  ss 166, 168I
       70  . . . . . . . . . . . . . . . . . . . . . . . . . . . . . . . . . . . . . . . . . . . . . . . . . . . . . . .  s 184
       71  . . . . . . . . . . . . . . . . . . . . . . . . . . . . . . . . . . . . . . . . . . . . . . . . . . . . . . .  s 185
       72  . . . . . . . . . . . . . . . . . . . . . . . . . . . . . . . . . . . . . . . . . . . . . . . . . . . . . . .  s 186
Pt VII
s  126  . . . . . . . . .  Amendment of ITA 1967 s 141(4) . . . . . . . . . . . . . . . . . . . . . .  s 465
       128  . . . . . . . . .  Amendment of FA 1970 s 17(5)(a) . . . . . . . . . . . . . . . . . . . . .  s 531(5)(6)(8)(9),
       130(1) . . . . . . .  Amendment of FA 1988 s 73(1) . . . . . . . . . . . . . . . . . . . . . . .  s 1002
           (2) . . . . . . .  Unnecessary (operative date)
       131  . . . . . . . . .  Unnecessary (care and management)
       132(2), (8) . . . .  Unnecessary (construction and commencement)
       Sch 1, Pt I . . . . . .  Amendment of ITA 1967 s 1(1), FA 1974 . . . . . . . . . . . . . . .  ss 2(1), 3(1)
                      s 3(1), and cesser of FA 1974 s 3
       Sch 1, Pt II . . . . .  Amendment of ITA 1967 ss 138, 138A(2). . . . . . . . . . . . . . .  ss 461, 462
       Sch 2 . . . . . . . . . . . . . . . . . . . . . . . . . . . . . . . . . . . . . . . . . . . . . . . . . . . . . . .  Sch 6
```

Oireachtas (Allowance to Members)
 and Ministerial and Parliamentary Offices
(Amendment) Act 1992 (1992 No 3)

```
s  4   . . . . . . . . . . . . . . . . . . . . . . . . . . . . . . . . . . . . . . . . . . . . . . . . . . . . . . .  s 836
```

Finance Act 1992 (1992 No 9)

```
s  1   . . . . . . . . .  Amendment of FA 1980 ss 1, 2 . . . . . . . . . . . . . . . . . . . . . . . .  ss 187, 188
       2  (1)(a) . . . . .  Amendment of FA 1991 s 2
           (b) . . . . .  Unnecessary (obsolete)
           (2)(a) . . . . .  Amendment of ITA 1967 s 198 . . . . . . . . . . . . . . . . . . . . . .  s 1024
           (b) . . . . .  Unnecessary (spent)
       3   . . . . . . . . .  Amendment of FA 1982 s 6
       4   . . . . . . . . .  Unnecessary (cesser of ITA 1967 ss 143, 151,
                      152, FA 1973 s 23 and Sch 1, FA 1989 s 8)
       5   . . . . . . . . .  Amendment of ITA 1967 s 432(1) . . . . . . . . . . . . . . . . . . . .  ss 864(1), 949(1)
       6   . . . . . . . . .  Amendment of FA 1972 ss 15(3), 21(2), 22 . . . . . . . . . . . .  ss 772(3), 780, 781
```

Former Enactment   *Destination in TCA 1997*
Finance Act 1992 (1992 No 9) (contd)

s	7	(1)......Insertion of FA 1979 s 8(4A)	s 125(3)
		(2)......Unnecessary (operative date)	
	8	......Amendment of FA 1982 s 4	ss 121, 897(1)-(5), Sch 29
	9	......Amendment of FA 1982 s 8(1)	s 122
	10	......Amendment of FA 1987 s 13(1)	s 520
	11	......Amendment of FA 1987 s 14	s 521
	12	......Cesser of FA 1986 s 10 and Sch 2, but only as respects share options granted on or after 29 January 1992	Sch 32, para 7(1)
	13	......Unnecessary (cesser of FA 1986 s 14)	
	14	(1)-(3)	s 252
		(4)......Insertion of FA 1974 s 34(3)	s 248(1)-(3)
	15	(1)	s 126(3)(a)
		(2)	s 126(3)(b)
		proviso	s 126(4)
		(3)	s 126(6)
		(4)	s 126(7)
	16	......Amendment of FA 1977 s 36(a)	s 6
s	17	(1)......Amendment of FA 1982 s 56 and Sch 3 para 1(4)	s 515, Sch 11
		(2)......Unnecessary (spent)	
	18	(1)......Substitution of ITA 1967 s 525	s 127(1)-(5)
		(2)......Substitution of ITA 1967 s 115(1)(b)	s 201(2)
		(3)	s 127(6)
	19	(1)......Insertion of FA 1973 s 34(2A)	s 234(3)-(8)
		(2)......Amendment of CTA 1976 s 170	s 141
	20	......Amendment of FA 1980 s 28(3)	
	21	(1)	s 373(2)(f)
		(2)......Amendment of FA 1976 s 32	s 376
	22	(1)......Amendment of FA 1986 ss 31, 35, insertion of ss 37A, 37B	ss 256, 261, 264, 265
		(2)......Unnecessary (operative date)	
	23	(1)......Amendment of FA 1986 s 46(2)	s 1013(1)-(3)
		(2)(a)......Unnecessary (operative date)	
		(b)	s 1013(5)(a)
	23	(3)	s 1013(5)(b)
	24	(1)(a)......Insertion of ITA 1967 s 467C	
		(b)......Amendment of ITA 1967 s 474(1)	s 49, Sch 32 para 1(2)
		(2)(a)......Amendment of CGTA 1975 s 19(d)	s 607
		(b)......Unnecessary (cesser of FA 1982 s 41 in so far as it relates to Bord Gais Eireann)	
	25		s 405
	26	(1)-(3), (5) . Rep by FA 1996 s 132(2) and Sch 5 Pt II	
		(4)......Insertion of ITA 1967 s 241(6A)	s 284(5)
	27	(1)......Amendment of ITA 1967 s 255(1)(bb)	s 268(1)-(3), (5)-(8)
		(2)......Unnecessary (operative date)	
	28	......Amendment of FA 1970 s 17	ss 530(1)(2), 531
	29	......Amendment of FA 1986 ss 41(2), 42, 44(1)(a), 45(1)(a)	ss 322(1), s 323(1), 324(1), 328(1), Sch 32, para 11
	30	......Amendment of FA 1987 s 27(1)(a)(ii)	
	31	......Amendment of FA 1989 s 4(1)	Sch 32, para 20
	32	......Amendment of FA 1988 s 18(3)(b)	s 958(2)-(5)
	33	(1)......Amendment of FA 1988 s 21	ss 959, 1069(1)(b)
		(2)......Unnecessary (operative date)	
	34	......Amendment of FA 1991 ss 56(1)(a), 57, 58	s 325(1)
	35	......Insertion of CTA 1976 ss 66A, 76A	s 145(11)(a), (b)
	36		s 736

Former Enactment   *Destination in TCA 1997*
Finance Act 1992 (1992 No 9) (contd)

  s 37 (1) .... s 154(3)(a), (4)
       (2) .... s 154(5)
     38 (1) .... Substitution of CTA 1976 s 83(4) .... s 153(1)
       (2) .... s 153(2)
     39 .... Definition of "the definition of scientific research"..... s 763(1)(3)(4)
             unnecessary (obsolete)
     40 .... Amendment of CTA 1976 s 84A...................... ss 133, 134
     41 .... Substitution of FA 1989 s 21(2)...................... ss 133(3), 134(2)
      (1) .... Amendment of ITA 1967 ss 464,..................... ss 45(1), 49, 50,
             470, 474(2)   Sch 32 para 1(2)
     42 (2) .... s 398(1)
      (3)(a)..... Unnecessary (spent)
        (b)... s 398(2)
      proviso... Unnecessary (spent)
      (4) .... Unnecessary (obsolete)
     43 (1)-(3) .... Unnecessary (spent)
     43 (4) .... Unnecessary (repeal of CTA 1976 s 31(9))
     44 (a), (b).... Amendment of CTA 1976 s 33 .... ss 707, 728
      (c), (d).... Insertion of CTA 1976 ss 33A, 46A, 46B .... ss 708, 719, 720
      (e) .... Unnecessary (deletion of CTA 1976 s 47)
      (f) .... Amendment of CTA 1976 s 50(1)
     45 .... s 487
     46 (1)(a)..... Insertion of CTA 1976 s 10A........................ s 454
       (b)..... Amendment of CTA 1976 s 16(1) .... s 396
       (c)..... Insertion of CTA 1976 s 16A........................ s 455
      (2) .... Amendment of CTA 1976 s 116A..................... s 456
     47 .... Amendment of FA 1980 s 39....................... s 443
     48 .... Unnecessary (spent)
     49 (1) .... Insertion of CTA 1976 s 25(5A) .... s 157
      (2) .... Insertion of CTA 1976 s 26(4A) .... s 158
     50 (1) .... Amendment of CTA 1976 s 105 .... s 410
      (2) .... Unnecessary (repeal of CTA 1976 s 106)
      (3) .... Unnecessary (operative date)
     51 (1) .... Amendment of FA 1983 s 44....................... s 165
      (2) .... Unnecessary (operative date)
     52 .... Amendment of FA 1980 s 39A .... s 445
     53 .... Amendment of FA 1980 s 39B...................... s 446(1)-(12)
     54 .... Substitution of FA 1980 s 41(1)..................... s 448(1)
     55 (1), (2) .... s 1085(1), (2)
      (3) .... Unnecessary (operative date)
     56 .... s 88
     57 .... Amendment of FA 1988 s 39....................... s 217
     58 .... Amendment of FA 1987 s 35(1)..................... s 481, Sch 32, para 22
     59 .... Amendment of CGTA 1975 ss 13(4), ... s 655(1)(2), 601(3)
             16(1)(2), CGT(A)A 1978 Sch 1 para 8
     60 (1) .... Substitution of CGTA 1975 s 3(3)................... ss 283(2), 300(1)
      (2) .... Unnecessary (deletion of FA 1982 s 36(2),
             (3), (3A))
     61 .... s 600(6)
     62 (1) .... Insertion of CGTA 1975 s 9(5) .... s 272
      (2) .... Unnecessary (operative date)
     63 .... Amendment of CGTA 1975 s 47
     64 .... s 630
     65 .... s 631
     66 .... s 632
     67 .... s 633
     68 .... Amendment of FA 1982 s 36....................... s 648

Former Enactment **Finance Act 1992 (1992 No 9) (contd)** *Destination in TCA 1997*

Former		Destination
s 69		s 634
70		s 635
71		s 636
72		s 637
73	Amendment of CTA 1976 s 132(2).	s 619
74		s 638
75		s 684
76		s 685
77		s 686
78		s 687
79		s 688
80 (1), (2)		s 689
(3)	Unnecessary (operative date)	
81 (1)-(5), (7)		s 690
(6)	Unnecessary (obsolete)	
82		s 691
83		s 692
84		s 693
85		s 694
86		s 695
87		s 696
88		s 697
226	Definition of "relevant chargeable period" unnecessary (obsolete). ITA 1967 s 226(7) also provided for the amendment of Sch 15	s 894
227	Amendment of ITA 1967 ss 94, 173, 176	ss 888, s 889(10), 890
228		s 899
229	Amendment of FA 1989 s 19	s 893
230(1)-(6)	Definition of relevant chargeable period" unnecessary (obsolete).	s 895
(7)	Unnecessary (operative date)	
230A	(s 230A inserted by FA 1995 s 41)	s 896
231	Substitution of FA 1986 s 6	
232	Substitution of FA 1976 s 34	s 905
233	Insertion of ITA 1967 s 127A	s 903
234	Amendment of ITA 1967 s 128(1)	s 987(1)-(3)
235	Insertion of FA 1970 s 17A	s 904
236		s 906
237		s 912
238	Amendment of FA 1979 s 31	s 902
239	Amendment of FA 1983 s 20	s 909
240	Amendment of FA 1983 s 23	s 1086
241	Amendment of FA 1988 s 73	s 1002
242		s 1094
243(a)(i), (b)	Amendment of FA 1983 s 94	s 1078
(ii)	Rep by FA 1996 s 132(2) and Sch 5 Pt II	
244	Amendment of FA 1988 s 9(1)	ss 950(1)-(3), 955(5)(a).
245	Insertion of FA 1986 s 48(3)	s 1084(1)-(4)
246	Insertion of CGTA 1975 Sch 4 para 3(4A)	s 913(1), (3)-(5), (7)
247	Amendment of CTA 1976 s 143	ss 861(2), 884, 930, 973, 974, 1071, 1072, 1080, 1082

Former Enactment   *Destination in TCA 1997*

Finance Act 1992 (1992 No 9) (contd)

s 248	Amendment of ITA 1967 ss 128(1A), 173(6), 426(3), 500(1)(2), FA 1979 s 31(5), FA 1980 s 45(8), FA 1983 s 112(1)(a)(3)	s 987(1)-(3), 889(10), 939, 1052(1)-(3), 902, 147, Sch 32 para 4
253	Unnecessary (care and management)	
254(2), (8), (9)	Unnecessary (construction and commencement)	
Sch 1	Substitution of Table to FA 1982 s 4(4)	s 121
Sch 2		Sch 13

Finance (No 2) Act 1992 (1992 No 28)

s 1	Insertion of FA 1980 s 41(9)	s 448(3)-(7)
2	Amendment of FA 1980 s 45(3)	s 147, Sch 32 para 4
3	Amendment of FA 1986 ss 31(1),	s 256, 256, 265 37A(1), 37B(1)
29	Unnecessary (care and management)	
30 (2)	Unnecessary (construction and commencement)	

Finance Act 1993 (1993 No 13)

Pt I

s 1	Amendment of FA 1980 ss 1, 2	ss 187, 188
2 (1)	Amendment of FA 1991 s 2	s 15
(2)	Unnecessary (application of schedule)	
3 (1), (2)	Unnecessary (obsolete)	
(3)	Unnecessary (application of schedule)	
4	Amendment of FA 1982 s 6	
5	Rep by FA 1997 s 146(2) and Sch 9 Pt II	
6	Substitution of FA 1990 s 11	
7 (1)	Insertion of ITA 1967 s 115(1A)	s 201(3)
(2)		s 124
8 (a)	Amendment of ITA 1967 s 115	s 201(2)
(b)	Amendment of ITA 1967 Sch 3	s 201(1)(a), Sch 3
9	Unnecessary (spent)	
10	Insertion of ITA 1967 ss 195B, 195C,	ss 1019, 1021
11	Amendment of CTA 1976 ss 33, 36, 38, 43, 46A, 50, substitution of s 46, insertion of ss 33B, 35A, 36A, 36B, 36C	s 706(1)-(3), 707, 711, 712, 713(1)-(6), 714, 719, 726, 724, 725
12 (1)	Unnecessary (spent)	
(2)(a)	Unnecessary (spent)	
(b)		Sch 32, para 24
13		s 737
14 (1)-(3)		s 838(1)-(3)
(4)(a)-(c), (d)-(f)		s 838(4)
(c)proviso	Unnecessary (operative date)	
(5)		s 838(5)
(6)(a), (c)		s 838(6)
(b)	Unnecessary (operative date)	
(7)		s 838(7)
15 (1)	Amendment of FA 1986 ss 31(1),35(1),37A	s 256, 261, 264
(2)	Unnecessary (spent)	
16		s 839
17		s 738
18		s 739
19	Amendment of CGTA 1975 s 31(4)	
20	Amendment of FA 1989 s 18	s 734
21	Amendment of FA 1984 s 29(2A)(b)	s 980
22	Amendment of CTA 1976 s 16(5)	s 396
23	Amendment of CTA 1976 s 33A(1)	s 708
24	Insertion of CGTA 1975 s 20A	s 594

Former Enactment　　　　　　　　　　　　　　　　　　　　*Destination in TCA 1997*
Finance Act 1993 (1993 No 13) (contd)

s 25	Amendment of FA 1984 ss 11, 12, 13, 13A, 493, 495, 496, 503 503, 1024,	s 488(1)(2)(3), 489, 490, 14, 15, 16, 22, 23
26	Amendment of FA 1986 s 12(2)	s 479
27 (1)-(3)	Definitions of "full-time working officer or employee" and "personal company" deleted by FA 1995 s 74	s 591(1)-(4)
(4)(a)(b)(i), (iv)		s 591(5)
(4)(ii)(iii)	Deleted by FA 1995 s 74	
(5)		s 591(6)
proviso	Unnecessary (spent)	
(6)-(13)		s 591(7)-(14)
(14)	Unnecessary (obsolete)	
(15)	Unnecessary (operative date)	
28	Rep by FA 1996 s 132(2) and Sch 5 Pt II	
29 (1)		s 482(1)(a)
(2)		s 482(9)
30 (1)	Amendment of FA 1986 ss 42, 44(1), 45	s 328(1), Sch 32 paras 11, 13
(2)	Unnecessary (operative date)	
31	Amendment of FA 1989 s 4(1)	Sch 32, para 20
32	Amendment of FA 1991 ss 56(1)(a), 57, 58	s 325(1), 326(1), 327(1),
33 (1)	Substitution of FA 1988 s 51(1)(a)	ss 271(3)(a), 273(5)(a), 283(4)(a)(5)(a)
(2)	Unnecessary (operative date)	
34 (1)	Substitution of ITA 1967 ss 254(4)(b),	s 317(2), 317(2), 769 303(3), 305(2)(b)
(2)	Substitution of FA 1974 s 22(11)	s 658(1)
(3)	Substitution of FA 1986 s 52(1)(a)(i)	s 317(3)
(4)	Unnecessary (operative date)	
35 (1)(a), (2)-(6)		s 701
(b)	Unnecessary (obsolete)	
36	Amendment of FA 1974 s 56	s 816
37		s 223
38	Rep by FA 1997 s 146(2) and Sch 9 Pt II	
39 (1)	Amendment of CTA 1976 s 6(4)	s 26(1), (2), (3)
(2)	Unnecessary (operative date)	
40	Amendment of FA 1988 s 18	s 958
41	Amendment of FA 1993 s 50(6)	
42 (1)	Amendment of CTA 1976 s 1(5)	s 4(1)
(2)	Unnecessary (operative date)	
43	Unnecessary (cesser of ITA 1967 s 337)	
44 (1)	Amendment of FA 1980 s 39	s 443
(2)	Unnecessary (operative date)	
45 (1)	Amendment of CTA 1976 s 84A	s 134(3)
(2)	Unnecessary (operative date)	
46 (1), (2)		s 150
(3), (4)	Unnecessary (spent)	
(5)	Amendment of FA 1980 s 45(7)	s 147, Sch 32 para 4
(6)	Unnecessary (operative date)	
47 (1), (2)		s 80
(3)	Insertion of FA 1980 s 39(1CC10)	s 443
(4)	Unnecessary (commencement)	
48	Amendment of FA 1987 s 35	s 481, Sch 32 para 22
49	Rep by FA 1997 s 146(2) and Sch 9 Pt II	
50	Amendment of CTA 1976 s 10A	s 454(1)
51		s 486
140	Amendment of FA 1992 s 242	s 1094
142	Unnecessary (care and management)	

Former Enactment   *Destination in TCA 1997*

Finance Act 1993 (1993 No 13) (contd)

s 143(2), (8)	Unnecessary (construction and commencement)	
Sch 1	Amendment of ITA 1967 ss 1(1),138, 38A(2)	ss 2(1), 3(1), 461, 462

Waiver of Certain Tax, Interest and Penalties Act 1993 (1993 No 24)

s 10	Amendment of ITA 1967 s 512(1)	s 1065
11	Substitution of ITA 1967 s 516	s 1056
12	Amendment of ITA 1967 Sch 15	Sch 29
13		s 907

Finance Act 1994 (1994 No 13)

Pt I

s 1	Amendment of FA 1980 ss 1, 2	ss 187,188
2	Amendment of FA 1991 s 2 and	ss 2(1), 3(1), 15, 461, 462 FA 1993 Sch 1
3 (1), (2)	Unnecessary (obsolete)	
(3)	Unnecessary (application of schedule)	
4	Insertion of ITA 1967 s 138B(2A)	s 472
5	Amendment of FA 1982 s 6	
6	Rep by FA 1997 s 146(2) and Sch 9 Pt II	
7	Insertion of ITA 1967 s 145(3A)	s 470(1)-(3)
8	Amendment of FA 1967 s 12(2)	s 469(1)
9	Amendment of FA 1982 s 8(1)	s 122
10	Unnecessary (spent)	
11	Amendment of FA 1992 Sch 2	Sch 13
12 (1)	Amendment of FA 1986 ss 35(1), 37A(1)	s 261, 264
(2)	Amendment of FA 1993 s 14(1)(c)	s 838(1)-(3)
13	Amendment of FA 1988 s 18(3)(b)	s 958
14 (1)	Unnecessary (interpretation)	
(2)-(5)		s 195(12)-(15)
15	Insertion of ITA 1967 s 462A	
16 (1)	Amendment of FA 1984 ss 11(1), 14(7A)(a), 16(2)(a)	s 488(1)-(3), 493
(2)	Unnecessary (operative date)	
17	Unnecessary (cesser of FA 1991 s 17(3)(b))	
18 (1)	Substitution of FA 1982 s 19(2)	s 482(1), (2), (3), (4)
(2)		s 482(8)
19 (1)-(6)		s 236
(7)	Unnecessary (commencement)	
20 (1)	Amendment of FA 1987 s 35	s 481, Sch 32 para 22
(2)	Unnecessary (operative date)	
21 (1)		s 373(2)(g)
(2)	Amendment of FA 1976 s 32	s 376
22 (1)	Amendment of ITA 1967 ss 254, 256, 264, 265	s 271, 278(1)(2)(6), 304(4), 305, 316(3), 317(2)
(2)	Unnecessary (operative date)	
23 (1)	Amendment of FA 1974 s 22	s 658
(2)	Unnecessary (operative date)	
24	Insertion of ITA 1967 s 241A, amendment of ss 272(1), 304(1)	ss 288(1)-(3), 291, 301(1), 314
25 (1)	Amendment of FA 1989 s 18	s 734
(2)	Unnecessary (commencement)	
26	Amendment of FA 1984 s 29(2A)	s 815(3)
27	Amendment of CTA 1976 ss 83, 88	ss 20, s 152(3), 153(1)
28	Amendment of FA 1973 s 34(1)	s 234(1), (2)(a)
29 (1)	Insertion of FA 1986 s 46(6)	s 1013(4)(b)
(2)(a)	Unnecessary (operative date)	
(b)		s 1013(4)(c)
30 (1)-(5), (7)		s 404
(6)	Unnecessary (obsolete)	

Former Enactment *Destination in TCA 1997*
Finance Act 1994 (1994 No 13) (contd)

s 31 ....Amendment of FA 1993 s 49(1)(a)
  32 (1)-(4)... s 227
    (5).. s 610, Sch 15 Pt I
  33 ....Amendment of CTA 1976 s 36A(2) .... s 723
  34 ....Amendment of FA 1993 ss 13, 14, 16. .... ss 256, 261, 264, 737, 838
  35 (1)........Amendment of FA 1986 ss 42, 44, 45, ... s 323, 324, 328(1)-(3),
          deletion of s 43   329(9)(b)(12), 1024,
                                                            Sch 32 paras 11,12,13
    (2)........Unnecessary (operative date)
  36 ....Amendment of FA 1987 s 27(1) .... s 322(2)
  37 (1)........Amendment of FA 1991 ss 55, 56, 57, 58. .... s 325(1)(2), 326(1), 327(1)
    (2)........Unnecessary (operative date)
  38 (1), (3), (4) .... s 339
    (2)........Unnecessary (obsolete)
  39 .... s 340
  40 .... s 341
  41 .... s 342
  41A.........(s 41A inserted by FA 1995 s 35(1)(e)) .... s 343
  41B.........(s 41B inserted by FA 1995 s 35(1)(f)).................... s 344
  42 (1)-(7)... s 345(1)-(7)
    (8)........Amendment of FA 1990 s 33 .... ss 324(4)(b), 333(4)(b),
                                                            345(8)(b), 354(5)(b),
                                                            370(8)(b)
  43 .... s 346
  44 .... s 347
  45 .... s 348
  46 (1)-(4), (7) .Proviso to definition of "qualifying premises" .... s 349
          deleted by FA 1995 s 35(1)
    (5)........Rep by FA 1996 s 132(2) and Sch 5 Pt II
    (6)........Amendment of ITA 1967 s 198(1)(a) .... s 1024
  47 .... s 350
  48 (1), (2) ....Amendment of FA 1980 s 39(1A) .... s 443
    (2)........Amendment of FA 1990 s 41 .... s 443
  49 ....Amendment of FA 1988 s 37 .... s 452
  50 (1)........Amendment of CTA 1976 s 84A .... s 134(3)
    (2)... s 133(12)(a)-(d)
    (3)........Unnecessary (operative date)
    proviso(i) .... s 133(12)(e)
    proviso(ii). ..Unnecessary (operative date)
  51 ....Amendment of FA 1992 s 56(2) .... s 88
  52 (1)... s 221(1)
    (2)... s 221(2)(a)(b)
  53 ....Amendment of FA 1980 s 39B(6) .... s 446(1)-(12)
  54 ....Insertion of s 39C, amendment of...................... s 448(1)
          FA 1980 s 41(1)
  55 ....Insertion of FA 1983 s 44(8)........................... s 165
  56 ....Insertion of CTA 1976 ss 12A, 14A .... s 79
  57 ....Amendment of FA 1993 ss 17, 18. .... ss 738, 739
  58 ....Insertion of CGTA 1975 s 20B .... s 595
  59 ....Substitution of FA 1989 s 25(1) .... s 154(1)-(3)
  60 ....Amendment of CTA 1976 s 35(1A) .... s 710(1)-(5)
  61 ....Amendment of FA 1984 s 40 .... s 403
  62 ....Amendment of FA 1987 s 28(1) .... s 407(1)
  63 (1)........Amendment of CGTA 1975 Sch 4 .... 29(8)(9), 544(7), 567(3)(4),
                                                            568, 849(1)(2), 849(3)-(6),
                                                            851, 861(1), 863-865,

Former Enactment   *Destination in TCA 1997*

Finance Act 1994 (1994 No 13) (contd)

s 63 (1)		869-871, 874, 875, 911, 913-917, 931, 945, 946, 949, 976, 977, 978, 980, 982, 999, Sch 1, 1029, 1043, 1051, 1077(1), 1077(2), 1083
(2)	Unnecessary (operative date)	
64 (1), (2)	Amendment of CGTA 1975	s 31731(1)-(5)(a), Sch 32 para 25
(3)		s 731(7)
65	Amendment of FA 1993 s 27	s 591(1)-(4)
66 (1)-(8)		s 592
(8A)	Rep by FA 1997 s 146(2) and Sch 9 Pt II	
(9)	Unnecessary (operative date)	

Pt VII

s 149	s 818
150	s 819
151	s 820
152	s 821
153	s 822
154	s 823
155 ...... Amendment of ITA 1967 s 153	s 1032
156	s 824
157(1) ..... Unnecessary (repeal of ITA 1967 ss 76(4), 199, 206, FA 1987 s 4)	
(2) .... Unnecessary (spent)	
158 .... Unnecessary (commencement)	
161(1)	ss 40(1), 48(1)(d)
(2)(a)	s 40(2)
(2)(b)	s 48(1)(d)
(3) ..... Amendment of ITA 1967 s 474(1)	s 49, Sch 32 para 1(2)
(5) ..... Amendment of FA 1984 s 66	s 607
162(1) ..... Substitution of ITA 1967 s 486(1), (2)	s 963
(2) .... Unnecessary (operative date)	
(2) .... Unnecessary (spent)	
(3) .... Unnecessary (operative date)	
164	s 196
165 .... Unnecessary (care and management)	
166(2), (8) .... Unnecessary (construction and commencement)	
Sch 1 .... Amendment of ITA 1967 ss 138, 138A(2),	ss 461, 462
Sch 2	Sch 4

Finance Act 1995 (1995 No 8)

Pt I

s 1	Amendment of FA 1980 ss 1, 2	ss 187, 188
2	Amendment of FA 1991 s 2	
3 (1), (2)	Unnecessary (obsolete)	s 15
(3)	Unnecessary (application of schedule)	
4	Amendment of FA 1982 s 6	
5	Amendment of ITA 1967 s 142A	s 473
6 (1)-(5)		s 474
(6)	Rep by FA 1996 s 132(2) and Sch 5 Pt II	
(7)	Amendment of ITA 1967 s 198(1)(a)	s 1024
7 (1)-(8)		s 477
(9)(a)	Amendment of ITA 1967 s 198(1)(a)	s 1024
(b)	Amendment of ITA 1967 Sch 15	Sch 29

Former Enactment *Destination in TCA 1997*
Finance Act 1995 (1995 No 8) (contd)

s 7 (10)....... Rep by FA 1996 s 132(2) and Sch 5 Pt II
  8 (1)(a)(c) .... s 848(1)
    (b) ...... Unnecessary (obsolete)
    (2)-(5)(a).. s 848(2)-(5)
    (5)(b) .... s 848(1)(a)
    (6), (7) .... s 848(6), (7)
  9 .... Amendment of FA 1982 s 8(1) .... s 122
  10 (1)....... Substitution of FA 1992 s 15(2) .... s 126(3)(b)
    (2)....... Amendment of FA 1994 s 10
  11 (1)....... Amendment of FA 1986 s 31(1) .... s 256
    (2)....... Amendment of FA 1993 s 14(3) .... s 838(1)-(3)
  12 (1)....... Amendment of ITA 1967 ss 443, 444, ... ss 794(1)-(5), 795
              445, 447
    (2)....... Unnecessary (operative date)
    (3)....... Unnecessary (cesser of ITA 1967 ss 440, 443(4))
  13 (1)(a) ..... Insertion of ITA 1967 s 439(1A)....................... s 792(1)-(4)
    (b) ..... Unnecessary (operative date)
    (2)....... Amendment of ITA 1967 s 439....................... s 792(1)-(4)
  13 (3).. Sch 32, para 27
  14 (1)....... Insertion of ITA 1967 s 94(e) .... s 888
    (2)....... Amendment of FA 1992 ss 226(1), 228(1) .... ss 894, 899
    (3)....... Unnecessary (operative date)
  15 .... Amendment of ITA 1967 s 191..................... s 930
  16 .... Amendment of FA 1982 s 56 and Sch 3 .... s 515, Sch 11
  17 (1)....... Amendment of FA 1984 ss 11(1), 12, 13, 15,............. ss 488, 489, 490, 494, 495,
              16, 22, 23, insertion of ss 14A, 16A,   496, 498, 503, 504
    (2)....... Unnecessary (operative dates)
  18 (1)....... Amendment of FA 1970 s 17 .... ss 530(1), 531(11)
    (2)....... Unnecessary (operative date)
  19 .... Insertion of ITA 1967 s 58A .... s 68
  20 .... Amendment of FA 1982 s 19 .... s 482
  21 .... Rep by FA 1996 s 132(2) and Sch 5 Pt II
  22 .... Rep by FA 1996 s 132(2) and Sch 5 Pt II
  23 (1)... s 373(2)(g)
    (2)....... Amendment of FA 1976 s 32 .... s 376
  24 (1)....... Amendment of ITA 1967 s 265(1)(c) .... s 274(1), (3), (4), (5), (8)
    (2)....... Unnecessary (operative date and cesser of
              FA 1994 s 22(1)(d)(i))
  25 (1)....... Amendment of ITA 1967 s 272....................... s 288(1)-(3)
    (2)....... Unnecessary (operative date)
  26 .... Amendment of FA 1988s 51(1)...................... ss 271(3)(a), 273(5)(a),
                                                           283(4)(a), 285(5)(a)
  27 .... Substitution of FA 1990 s 81(1) .... ss 273(7)(b), 285(7)(b)
  28 .... Amendment of FA 1994 s 49(1) .... s 452
  29 .... s 847
  30 (1)....... Amendment of FA 1986 s 48(2) .... s 1084(1)-(4)
    (2)....... Unnecessary (operative date)
  31 .... Amendment of FA 1988 s 18 .... s 958
  32 (1)....... Amendment of FA 1986 ss 41, 42, 44................. s 322(1), 323,
                                                           Sch 32 paras 11, 12
    (2)....... Unnecessary (operative date)
  33 .... Amendment of FA 1987 s 27(1)(b)................... s 322(2)-(3)
  34 (1)....... Amendment of FA 1991 ss 54(3), 55, 56, ... s 325(1)(2)
              57(2), 58(2)
    (2)....... Unnecessary (operative date)

Destination Table (Taxes Consolidation Act 1997)

Former Enactment	Destination in TCA 1997

Finance Act 1995 (1995 No 8) (contd)

s 35 (1)	Amendment of FA 1994 ss 38(1), 39, 40, 41, 42(1), 43(1), 46(1), insertion of ss 41A, 41B	s 339, 340, 341, 342, 343, 344, 345(1)-(7), 346, 349
(2)	Unnecessary (operative date)	
36 (1)	Amendment of FA 1987 s 35	s 481, Sch 32 para 22
(2)	Unnecessary (operative date)	
37	Insertion of FA 1983 s 47A	s 169
38	Amendment of FA 1989 s 18(1)	s 734(1)(a), (c)
39	Amendment of FA 1994 s 27	ss 20, s 152(3), 153(1)
40		s 198
41	Insertion of FA 1992 s 230A	s 896
42	Amendment of FA 1992 ss 75(1), 77(1)	ss 684, 686
43		s 224
44 (1), (2)		s 220
(3)		s 610, Sch 15 Pt I
45 (1)	Unnecessary (obsolete)	
(2)	Unnecessary (application of schedule)	
46 (1)		s 351
(2)	Unnecessary (obsolete)	
47		s 352
48		s 353
49 (1)-(4)		s 354(1)-(4)
(5)	Amendment of FA 1990 s 33	ss 324(4)(b), 333(4)(b), 345(8)(b), 354(5)(b), 370(8)(b)
49A	(s 49A inserted by FA 1996 s 30)	s 355
50		s 356
51		s 357
52		s 358
53		s 359
54 (1)	Substitution of CTA 1976 s 1(1)	s 21
(2)	Unnecessary (application of schedule)	
55 (1)	Amendment of CTA 1976 s 162(4)	s 441
(2)	Unnecessary (operative date)	
proviso	Unnecessary (obsolete)	
56	Amendment of FA 1992 s 45(1)(a)	s 487
57 (1)		s 221(1)
(2)		s 221(2)(c)(d)
58	Amendment of CTA 1976 s 141	ss 882(2)-(5), 1073
59 (1)-(4)		s 766
(5)	Unnecessary (obsolete)	
60	Amendment of CTA 1976 s 23	ss 826(1)-(7), (9), 827, Sch 24, para 4(2)
61	Amendment of FA 1980 s 41(1)(b)	s 448(1)
62	Insertion of FA 1980 s 39D	s 446(1)-(12)
63	Amendment of FA 1980 s 39C	s 449
64	Insertion of CTA 1976 s 43(2A)	s 726
65	Substitution of FA 1980 s 39B(6)(c)(iiia)	s 446(1)-(12)
66 (1), (2)		s 1085(3), (4)
(3)	Unnecessary (operative date)	
67	Amendment of FA 1993 s 51	s 486
68	Insertion of CGTA 1975 s 20A(4)	s 594
69	Amendment of CTA 1976 s 46B(1)	s 720(1)(2)
70 (1)	Amendment of CGTA 1975 Sch 4 para 4(1)	s 914
(2)	Unnecessary (operative date)	

Former Enactment   *Destination in TCA 1997*

Finance Act 1995 (1995 No 8) (contd)

s 71 (1) . . . . Amendment of CGTA 1975 s 26 . . . . s 598
    (2) . . . . Unnecessary (operative date)
  72 (1) . . . . Amendment of CGTA 1975 s 27(4)(a) . . . . s 599
    (2) . . . . Unnecessary (operative date)
  73 (1) . . . . Insertion of FA 1982 s 39(4), (5) . . . . s 652
    (2) . . . . Unnecessary (operative date)
  74 (1) . . . . Amendment of FA 1993 s 27 . . . . s 591
    (2) . . . . Unnecessary (operative date)
  75 . . . . Amendment of FA 1995 s 66 . . . . s 1085(3), (4)
  76 . . . . Amendment of CGTA 1975 Sch 4 para 11 . . . . s 980

Pt VII

s 167 . . . . Amendment of FA 1986 ss 31(1), 37(1) . . . . ss 256, 263
  168 . . . . Amendment of ITA 1967 s 175(4) . . . . s 891
  169 . . . . Amendment of FA 1994 s 152(1) . . . . s 821
  170 . . . . Amendment of FA 1994 s 154(2) . . . . s 823
  172 . . . . s 1079
  173(1) . . . . Amendment of ITA 1967 ss 416, 421, 422, ... ss 864(1), 933(1)-(7)(f),
                            423, 424, 427, 428, 429, 432   934, 935,936, 937, 940,
                                                                                    941, 942(1)-(8), (10),
                                                                                    949(1)-(4)
    (2) . . . . Substitution of FA 1969 s 2(5B) . . . . s 195(1)-(11)
    (3) . . . . Unnecessary (application).
  173 (4) . . . . Unnecessary (operative date)
  174 . . . . Amendment of FA 1986 s 115
  175 . . . . s 910
  176 . . . . s 1003
  177(1)-(6) . . . . s 1095
    (7) . . . . Unnecessary (operative date)
  178 . . . . Unnecessary (care and management)
  179(2), (8), (9) . Unnecessary (construction and commencement)
Sch 1 . . . . Amendment of ITA 1967 ss 138, 138A(2) . . . . s 461, s 462
Sch 2 . . . . Unnecessary (obsolete)
Sch 3 . . . . Sch 8
Sch 4 . . . . Unnecessary (obsolete)

Family Law Act 1995 (1995 No 26)

s 49 . . . . Amendment of FA 1983 s 4 . . . . s 1026(1), (2)

Finance Act 1996 (1996 No 9)

Pt I

s 1 . . . . Amendment of FA 1980 ss 1, 2 . . . . ss 187, 188
  2 . . . . Amendment of FA 1991 s 2 . . . . s 15
  3 (1), (2) . . . . Unnecessary (obsolete)
    (3) . . . . Unnecessary (application of schedule)
  4 . . . . Unnecessary (obsolete)
  5 . . . . s 478
  6 . . . . Amendment of FA 1982 s 4 . . . . s 121
  7 (1) . . . . Substitution of ITA 1967 s 145(1) . . . . s 470(1)-(3)
    (2) . . . . Unnecessary (operative date)
  8 (1) . . . . Amendment of FA 1992 Sch 2
    (2) . . . . Unnecessary (operative date)
  9 . . . . s 191
  10 . . . . s 664(1)(a), (b)(iii)
  11 (1) . . . . s 656(1)
    (2) . . . . Amendment of ITA 1967 s 62(1)(b) . . . . s 89(2)
  12 . . . . Amendment of FA 1986 s 12 . . . . s 479
  13 (a) . . . . Substitution of ITA 1967 s 236(1A) . . . . s 787(8)-(12)
    (b) . . . . Unnecessary (deletion of ITA 1967 Sch 5)

Former Enactment   *Destination in TCA 1997*
Finance Act 1996 (1996 No 9) (contd)

s 14	.... Amendment of FA 1969 s 2(2)(a)	s 195(1)-(11)
15 (1)-(5), (8)	....	s 475
(6)	.... Rep by FA 1997 s 146(2) and Sch 9 Pt II	
(7)	.... Amendment of ITA 1967 s 198(1)(a)	s 1023
16	.... Amendment of FA 1984 s 11(1).......................	s 488(1), (2), (3)
17	.... Amendment of FA 1984 s 12.......................	ss 488(1), 489
18	.... Amendment of FA 1984 s 13.......................	s 490
19	.... Amendment of FA 1984 s 13A	s 491
20	.... Insertion of FA 1984 s 13B	s 492
21	.... Unnecessary (obsolete)	
22	.... Insertion of FA 1984 s 15(3C).......................	s 495
23	.... Amendment of FA 1984 s 16.......................	s 496
24	.... Amendment of FA 1984 s 16A	s 497
25 (1), (2)	....	s 233
(3)	.... Amendment of CTA 1976 s 93(1)	s 140
(4)	.... Unnecessary (operative date)	
26 (1)	.... Amendment of FA 1984 s 41B(1)	
26 (2)	.... Unnecessary (operative date)	
27	.... Amendment of FA 1991 s 22........................	s 271(4)(a)
28	.... Amendment of ITA 1967 ss 264, 265	s 272, s 274(1),(3)-(5),(8)
29	.... Amendment of ITA 1967 s 255(1)....................	s 268(1)-(3), (5)-(8)
30	.... Insertion of FA 1995 s 49A	s 355
31 (1)	.... Substitution of FA 1987 s 35	s 481, Sch 32, para 22
(2)(a),(3),(4)	....	Sch 32, para 22(1)-(4)
(b)	..... Unnecessary (obsolete)	
(1)	.... Amendment of FA 1973 s 34(1).....................	s 234(1), (2)(a)
(2)	.... Amendment of CTA 1976 s 170	s 141
(3)	.... Unnecessary (operative date)	
33 (1)	.... Substitution of FA 1974 s 31(3)(cc)	
(2)	.... Unnecessary (operative date)	
34	.... Insertion of F(TPCM)A 1974 s 8A	s 681
35 (1)	.... Amendment of FA 1989 s 18(1).......................	s 734
(2)	.... Unnecessary (operative date)	
36 (1)	.... Insertion of FA 1993 s 13(8)(bb)	s 737
(2)	.... Unnecessary (operative date)	
37 (1)	.... Amendment of FA 1993 s 14	s 838
(2)	.... Unnecessary (operative date)	
38 (1)	.... Amendment of FA 1993 s 17.......................	s 738
(2)	.... Unnecessary (operative date)	
39 (1)	....	ss 41, 228, 610
(2)	....	s 228
(3)	....	s 41
(4)	.... Amendment of ITA 1967 s 474(1)....................	s 49, Sch 32 para 1(2)
(5)	.... Amendment of CGTA 1975 s 19(1)...................	s 607(1)(a), (b), (c), (d), (f)
(6)	....	s 610, Sch 15 PtI
39 (7)	.... Unnecessary (repeal of Securitisation (Proceeds of Certain Mortgages) Act, 1995 s 14)	
(8)	.... Unnecessary (operative date)	
40 (1), (2)	....	s 226
(3)	.... Unnecessary (operative date)	
41	.... Amendment of FA 1970 s 17.......................	ss 530(1), 531(11)
42	.... Insertion of FA 1986 s 33A	s 260
43 (1)	.... Amendment of FA 1988 s 51(1)(a)	ss 271(3)(a), 273(5)(a), 283(4)(a), 285(5)(a)
(2)	.... Unnecessary (operative date)	
44	.... Insertion of CTA 1976 s 28A........................	s 22
45 (1)	.... Amendment of CTA 1976 s 12A.....................	s 79
(2)	.... Unnecessary (operative date)	

Former Enactment   *Destination in TCA 1997*
Finance Act 1996 (1996 No 9) (contd)

s 46	Amendment of CTA 1976 s 33A(1)	s 708
47 (1)	Insertion of CTA 1976 s 35A(1A)	s 711
(2)	Unnecessary (operative date)	
48 (1)	Amendment of CTA 1976 s 36(2)	s 713(1)-(6)
(2)	Unnecessary (operative date)	
49 (1)	Amendment of CTA 1976 s 36A(6)	s 723
(2)	Unnecessary (operative date)	
50 (1)	Insertion of CTA 1976 s 46B(4)	s 720(3)-(5)
(2)	Unnecessary (operative date)	
51	Amendment of CTA 1976 s 135	s 623
52 (1)	Amendment of CTA 1976 s 162(4)	s 441
(2)	Unnecessary (operative date)	
proviso	Unnecessary (obsolete)	
53	Amendment of FA 1980 s 39A(6)(c)	s 445
54 (1)	Amendment of FA 1987 s 28	ss 133(1)(d), 134(1)(d), 407(1)(3)(4)(6), 443
(2), (5)		s 407(5)
(3)(a), (4)		s 407(1)
(b)		s 407(2)
55 (1)	Amendment of FA 1991 s 31	s 110
(2)	Unnecessary (operative date)	
56	Amendment of FA 1992 s 56	s 88
57 (1)	Amendment of FA 1995 s 59	s 766
(2)	Unnecessary (operative date)	
58 (1)	Amendment of FA 1983 ss 44(5), 47(1)	ss 165, 168
(2)	Unnecessary (operative date)	
59	Amendment of CGTA 1975 Sch 4 para 11	s 980
60 (1)	Amendment of CGTA 1975 s 26(6)(a)	s 598
(2)	Unnecessary (operative date)	
61 (1)	Insertion of CGTA 1975 s 46(7)	s 541(7)(a)-(c), (g)
(2)	Unnecessary (operative date)	
62 (1)	Insertion of FA 1993 s 27(2A)	s 591(1)-(4)
(2)	Unnecessary (operative date)	
63 (1)	Amendment of FA 1994 s 66	s 592
(2)	Unnecessary (operative date)	
64		s 610, Sch 15
65		s 360
66		s 361
67		s 362
68		s 363
69 (1)-(3), (5)		s 364
(4)	Amendment of ITA 1967 s 198(1)(a)	s 1024
70		s 365

Pt VI

s 130		s 872(2)
131(1)-(8)		s 10
(9)(a)	Unnecessary (obsolete)	
(b)	Unnecessary (cesser of F(MP)A 1968 s 16(3), CGTA 1975 s 33(7), CTA 1976 s 157)	
132(1), (2)	Unnecessary (application of schedules)	
(3)	Unnecessary (construction)	
133	Definition of "farming" and "tax" unnecessary (duplication)	s 665
134		s 666
135		s 667
136		s 668

Destination Table (Taxes Consolidation Act 1997)

Former Enactment   Destination in TCA 1997
Finance Act 1996 (1996 No 9) (contd)

s 137... s 669
Pt VII
s 139 .... Amendment of FA 1995 s 176(2)..................... s 1003
  142 .... Unnecessary (care and management)
  143(2), ... Unnecessary (construction and commencement)
    (7), (8)
Sch 1 .... Amendment of ITA 1967 ss 138, 138A(2), ... ss 461, 462, 465, 467, 468
              141(1), FA 1969 s 3(1), FA 1971 s 11(2)

Sch 5
  Pt I .... Amendment of ITA 1967 ss 2, 79, 145, 146,............. ss 3(2)(3), 74, 237, 238(1)(6),
              149, 153, 195A, 235(7), 239, 241, 297, 299,   306, 312, 386, 390(1)(3),
              312(2), 316, 433(1), 434(1), 468(2), 471(2),   459(1)(2), 460, 762(2)(a),
              497   470(1)-(4), 783(3), 788,
                                                                   1020, 1032, Sch 32, para 1(1)

              Substitution of ITA 1967 ss 137, 321.................. s 458, 395
              Amendment of FA 1967 s 11, FA 1968 s 6,.............. ss 207(3)(4), 211(5)(6),
              FA 1969 s 19 , FA 1971 s 26, FA 1972   213(3)(4), 234, 26(1)-(3),
              Sch 1, FA 1973 s 34, F(TPCM)A 1974 s 1,   273, 273(1)-(3)(8),
              FA 1974 s 62, CTA 1976 ss 6, 50, 102(1),   285(1)-(3)(8), 286, 287,
              147(2), FA 1978 s 25, FA 1980 s 2, FA   299(2), 432, 463, 479,
              1983 ss 3, 94(2), FA 1985 s 10, FA 1986   483(1)-(3), 53, 664(1)(a),
              s 12, FA 1987 s 24, FA 1991 s 4 , FA   672(1), 692, 706(1)-(3),
              1992 s 83, FA 1995 s 177   863, 865, 868, 869, 870,
                                                                   849, 860, 861(1), 862,
                                                                   873, 874, 875, 877, 886,
                                                                   898, 901, 928(1), 929,
                                                                   947, 998, 1004, 1025, 1049,
                                                                   105, 1055, 1056, 1057, 1058,
                                                                   1066, 1067, 1068, 1069,
                                                                   1070, 1078, 1081(1), 1095,
                                                                   Sch 23 Pt I paras 1-5

  Pt II .... Repeal of ITA 1967 ss 43, 89A, 138A(7),
              141(7), 145(3A)(5), 241(7)(8)(9), 242, 243,
              244(4)(e), 247(3), 249, 259, 262, 273(2), 306,
              344, 346, 360, 448(2), 476, 477(2), (3), 479,
              480, 482(3), 494(2), 495, 540, 543, 557, 558,
              Sch 2 rule 1(3), Sch 13, FA 1967 s 12(5)(c),
              FA 1968 s 4, FA 1969 ss 3(3), 4, 5, FA 1971
              s 11(4), FA 1972 ss 16(6), 17(3), 18(1)(b), 24,
              25, Sch 1 Pt II para 1(2), Sch 1 Pts IV, V, FA
              1974 ss 4(c), 8(2), 30, 40, 50, FA 1975 ss 31,
              31A, Sch, 3, Sch 5, CGTA 1975 ss 2(2), 27(1)(d),
              33(8), CTA 1976 ss 12(8), 51(3)(b)(c), 52(5), 68,
              153, FA 1976 ss 12, 15, 16, FA 1977 s 39(4)(b)
              proviso, FA 1978 s 9, Sch 1 Pt III, FA 1979 ss 5,
              8(2)(b), FA 1980 s 28, FA 1981 s 13, FA 1982
              ss 6, 13, FA 1983 s 94(1)(ee), FA 1984 ss 12(9),
              33, Pt I Ch VIII, IX, FA 1986 ss 12(9), 44(4), FA
              1989 s 4(7), FA 1991 s 4(3), FA 1992 ss 26(1)(2)
              (3)(5), 243(a)(ii), FA 1993 s 28, FA 1994 s 46(5),
              FA 1995 ss 6(6), 7(10), 21, 22
              Amendment of ITA 1967 ss 58(5), 186(3), ... ss 59, 67, 76, 114, 207(3)(4),
              187(1), 235(7), 244(5)(b)(6), 245(7), 300(1),   211(5)(6), 213(3)(4), 232(1),
              309, 441, 442, 447, 478, 484(3), 496(1)(c),   246(3), 313, 382(1)(2),
              Sch 2 rule 3, FA 1969 s 18(1), FA 1972   483(1)-(3), 599, 662, 670,
              s 15(4), FA 1974 ss 4(b)(e), 27(2), 31(3), FA   715, 726, 765, 772(4),
              1975 Sch 2 Pt I para 2, CGTA 1975 s 27(3),   783(3), 791(1), 793, 794(1),
              CTA 1976 ss 11(6), 39(2)(b), 43(5)(a),   860, 861(1), 862, 863,
              147(2)   865, 868, 869, 870, 873,
                                                                     874, 875, 886, 898, 901,
                                                                     924, 928(1), 929, 947, 961,

Former Enactment   *Destination in TCA 1997*

Finance Act 1996 (1996 No 9) (contd)

Pt II (contd)   964(2), 972(1)-(4), 998,
1004, 1049, 1055, 1056,
1057, 1058, 1066, 1067,
1068, 1069, 1070, 1081(1)

Disclosure of Certain Information for Taxation and Other Purposes Act 1996 (1996 No 25)

s 5	Insertion of ITA 1967 s 184(3)	s 922
6	Substitution of CTA 1976 s 144(4)	s 919(1)-(5)
10	Insertion of FA 1983 s 18(4A)	s 908
11	Substitution of FA 1983 s 19(2)	s 58
12	Insertion of FA 1983 s 19A	s 859

Criminal Assets Bureau Act 1996 (1996 No 31)

s 23	Substitution of FA 1983 s 19A(3)(a)	s 859
24 (1)	Substitution of ITA 1967 s 184(3)	s 922
(2)	Substitution of CTA 1976 s 144(4)(b)	s 919(1)-(5)

Family Law (Divorce) Act 1996 (1997 No 33)

s 31		s 1027(b)
32	Amendment of FA 1983 s 4	s 1026(1), (2)
35		s 1031

Finance Act 1997 (1997 No 22)

Pt I

s 1	Amendment of FA 1980 ss 1, 2	ss 187, 188
2	Amendment of FA 1991 s 2	s 15
3 (1), (2)	Unnecessary (duplication)	
3 (3)	Unnecessary (application of schedule)	
4 (1)	Amendment of FA 1992 s 15(2)	s 126(3)(b)(4)
(2)		s 126(8)
5 (a)	Insertion of FA 1983 s 4(3)	s 1026(1), (2)
(b)	Unnecessary (repeal of Family Law Act 1995 s 49 and Family Law (Divorce) Act 1996 s 32	
6 (1)	Insertion of ITA 1967 s 127(5A)	s 986(4)-(6)
(2)	Unnecessary (operative date)	
7	Amendment of FA 1996 s 15	s 475
8 (1)-(7), (10),(11)		s 476
(8)	Amendment of ITA 1967 s 137	s 458
(9)	Amendment of ITA 1967 s 198(1)(a)	s 1024
9	Amendment of FA 1984 ss 11, 14A, 16, 16A	ss 488(1)-(4), 494, 496, 497
10	Amendment of FA 1992 s 14	ss 248(1)-(3), 252
11 (1)	Amendment of ITA 1967 s 353	s 193 Sch 32, para 2
(2)	Unnecessary (operative date)	
(3)	Unnecessary (spent)	
(4)	Amendment of ITA 1967 s 178(1)	s 897(1)-(5)
12	Amendment of ITA 1967 s 115(1A)	s 201(3)
13 (1)	Amendment of FA 1970 s 17	ss 530(1), 531(11)
(2)	Amendment of ITA 1967 Sch 15	Sch 29
14		s 202
15	Insertion of FA 1971 s 4(6)	s 72
16		s 485
17 (1)	Amendment of FA 1982 s 19	s 482
(2)	Amendment of FA 1993 s 29(1)	s 482(1)(a)
(3)	Unnecessary (operative date)	
18	Amendment of FA 1996 s 134	s 666
19	Amendment of FA 1996 s 135(1)(b)	s 667
20 (1)-(13)		s 659
(14)	Amendment of FA 1975 s 29	s 319

Destination Table (Taxes Consolidation Act 1997)

Former Enactment	*Destination in TCA 1997*

Finance Act 1997 (1997 No 22) (contd)

s 21 (1)		s 373(2)(i)
(2)	Amendment of FA 1976 s 32	s 1009
22	Amendment of ITA 1967 s 241	ss 284, 298(1), 299(1), 301(1), 304(2)(4), 316(1)(a)(2), 406
23 (1)	Amendment of ITA 1967 ss 265, 266,	ss 274(1) (3)-(5)(8), 277
(2)	Unnecessary (operative date)	
24		s 409
25 (1)-(5), (7)		s 843
(6)	Unnecessary (operative date)	
26	Amendment of FA 1994 ss 38, 39, 42	ss 339, 340, 324(4)(b), 333(4)(b), 345(8)(b), 354(5)(b), 370(8)(b)
27	Amendment of FA 1986 s 45(2), FA 1994 s 42(3), FA 1995 s 49(3)	ss 324(2), 346, 354(1)-(4)
28	Insertion of FA 1980 s 39B(10)	s 446(1)-(12)
29 (1)		s 82(2)
(2)		s 243(3)(b)
(3)		s 390(2)(b)
(4)		s 82(3)
(5)		ss 82(4), 243(3)(c), 390(2)(c)
(6)		ss 82(1), 243(3)(a), 390(2)(a)
30 (1)	Amendment of FA 1987 s 35	s 481, Sch 32 para 22
(2)		Sch 32, para 22(6)-(8)
31 (1)	Amendment of FA 1993 s 14	s 838(1)-(4)
(2)	Unnecessary (operative date)	
32	Amendment of FA 1989 s 18(1)	s 734(1)(a), (c)
33		s 55
34	Amendment of FA 1990 s 138(1)	ss 45(3)(4)(a), 48(4)(a),(5)(a)
35	Substitution of FA 1993 s 17(4)(a)	s 738
36	Amendment of FA 1974 s 31	s 246(1)-(4)
37 (1)		ss 4(1), 136(2),139(1), 143(2)(7), 145(2)(a), (11)(a), 729(5)
(2)	Unnecessary (application of schedule)	
38	Amendment of FA 1992 s 37(1)	s 154(3)(a)(4)(5)
39 (1)(a)	Amendment of FA 1991 s 59	s 173
(b)	Insertion of FA 1991 s 60A	s 175
(2)	Unnecessary (operative date)	
40 (1)	Amendment of FA 1996 s 40(2)	s 226
(2)	Unnecessary (operative date)	
41 (1)(a)	Amendment of FA 1972 s 16	s 774(1)-(3)(5)-(7), Sch 32 para 26
(b)	Insertion of FA 1972 s 16A	s 775
(2)	Amendment of CTA 1976 Sch 2 Pt I para 31	Sch 32 para 26
(3)	Unnecessary (commencement)	
42		s 627
43		s 628
44		s 629
45 (1)	Amendment of ITA 1967 s 464	s 43
(2)	Unnecessary (operative date)	
46 (1)	Amendment of ITA 1967 s 470(1)(b)	s 50
(2)	Unnecessary (operative date)	
47 (1)	Amendment of ITA 1967 s 474(2)	s 49, Sch 32 para 1(2)
(2)	Unnecessary (operative date)	

Former Enactment *Destination in TCA 1997*
Finance Act 1997 (1997 No 22) (contd)

s 48 (1), (2) .... s 842
    (3)........ Unnecessary (operative date)
  49 (1), (2) .... s 220
    (3)... s 610, Sch 15 Pt I
    (4)... Sch 32, para 3
  50 (a)........ Amendment of FA 1982 s 52 .... s 511
    (b)........ Insertion of FA 1982 s 58A................ s 518
    (c)........ Amendment of FA 1982 Sch 3 .... Sch 11
  51 .... s 519
  52 .... s 366
  53 .... s 367
  54 .... s 368
  55 .... s 369
  56 .... s 370(1)-(7)
    (8)........ Amendment of FA 1990 s 33 .... ss 324(4)(a)(b), 333(4)(a)(b), 345(8)(b), 354(5)(b), 370(8)(b)
  57 (1)-(3), (5) .... s 371
    (4)........ Amendment of ITA 1967 s 137............. s 458
  58 .... s 372
  59 (1)........ Substitution of CTA 1976 s 1(1)............ s 21
    (2)........ Unnecessary (application of schedule)
  60 (1)........ Amendment of CTA 1976 s 28A .... s 22(1)(a), (2)-(8)
    (2)........ s 22(1)(b)
    (3)........ Unnecessary (operative date)
  61 (1), (3), (4) .... s 841
    (2)........ Unnecessary (repeal of CTA 1976 s 80)
  62(1), (3)-(5) .... s 229
    (2)........ Unnecessary (repeal of ITA 1967 s 343)
  63 .... s 219
  64 .... Amendment of FA 1992 s 56 .... s 88
  65 .... Amendment of FA 1993 s 51 .... s 454(1)
  66 (1)........ Amendment of FA 1988 s 36(4)(a).......... s 451
    (2)........ Unnecessary (operative date)
  67 (1)........ Insertion of CTA 1976 s 35(1B)............ s 710(1)-(5)
    (2)........ Unnecessary (operative date)
  68 (1)........ Amendment of CTA 1976 s 36............. s 713(1)-(6)
    (2)........ Unnecessary (operative date)
  69 (1)........ Substitution of CTA 1976 s 46A(3)(a) .... s 719
    (2)........ Unnecessary (operative date)
  70 (1)........ Insertion of CGTA 1975 Sch 2 para 5A ... s 588
    (2)........ Unnecessary (operative date)
  71 (1)-(3) .... s 1031
    (4)........ Unnecessary (repeal of s 35 Family Law (Divorce) Act, 1996)
    (5)........ Unnecessary (operative date)
  72 (1)-(3).. s 1030
    (4)........ Unnecessary (repeal of Family Law Act 1995 s 52)
    (5)........ Unnecessary (operative date)
  73 (1)........ Insertion of CGTA 1975 s 15(5A) .... s 577
    (2)........ Unnecessary (operative date)
  74 (1)........ Amendment of CGTA 1975 s 20A .... s 594
    (2)........ Unnecessary (operative date)
  75 (1)........ Amendment of FA 1993 s 27 .... s 591(1)-(5)
    (2)........ Unnecessary (operative date)

Destination Table (Taxes Consolidation Act 1997)

Former Enactment   *Destination in TCA 1997*
Finance Act 1997 (1997 No 22) (contd)

s 76	Amendment of FA 1994 s 66	s 592
77 (1)	Insertion of FA 1982 s 39(3A)	s 652
(2)	Unnecessary (operative date)	
78 (1)	Amendment of CGTA 1975 s 46(7)	s 541(7)(a), (b), (c), (g)
(2)		s 541(8)

Pt VII

s 144		s 37
145		s 244
146(1), (2)	Unnecessary (application of schedule)	
(3)	Unnecessary (interpretation)	
147		s 330
148		s 331
149		s 332
150(1)-(3)		s 333(1)-(3)
(4)	Amendment of FA 1990 s 33	ss 324(4)(b), 333(4)(b), 345(8)(b), 354(5)(b), 370(8)(b)
150(5)		s 333(5)
151		s 334
152		s 335
153		s 336
154		s 337
155		s 338
156(1)	Repeal of FA 1991 ss 54, 55, 56(1)(a)(iii), (2) proviso, 57(1)(a), (2), 58(1)(a), (2)	
(2)	Amendment of ITA 1967 s 137	s 458
(3)	Amendment of CTA 1976 s 33A(1)	s 708
(4)	Amendment of FA 1991 s 56(1)(c)	
157	Amendment of ITA 1967 s 162(3)	s 851
158	Substitution of FA 1983 s 23(2), (3)	s 1086
159		s 858
160(1)	Amendment of FA 1992 s 242(1)	s 1094
165	Unnecessary (care and management)	
166(2), (8), (9)	Unnecessary (construction and commencement)	
Sch 1	Amendment of ITA 1967 ss 138, 138A(2) and FA 1974 s 8(1)	ss 461, 462, 464
Sch 2		
para 1		ss 4(1), 136(2), 139(1), 143(2), (7), 145(2)(a), (11)(a), 729(5)
2		s 729(7)
3 (1)	Unnecessary (operative date)	
(2)	Unnecessary (cesser of FA 1978 s 28(7), FA 1983 s 28(3), FA 1988 Sch 2 Pt I para 4, FA 1990 Sch 1 para 3, FA 1995 Sch 2 para 3)	
(3)		s 145(2)(b)
Sch 3		Sch 12
Sch 4		s 659 Table
Sch 5		Sch 26

Former Enactment	Destination in TCA 1997
Finance Act 1997 (1997 No 22) (contd)	
Sch 6, Pt I	
para 1	ss 26(4), 78(3)(c)
2(1)	Sch 32, para 16(5), 18(6)(a)
(2)	Sch 32, para 18(6)(b)
(3)	Sch 32, para 16(3)(b), 18(4)(b)
Pt II	
para 1(1)	s 448(2)(b)
(2)......Amendment of FA 1980 s 41(2)	s 448(2)(a)
(1)......Amendment of FA 1980 ss 47(2), 48(2)	Sch 32 paras 5(2), 6(2)
2(2)	Sch 32 para 5(3), 6(3)
Sch 9	
Pt I ....Amendment of ITA 1967 ss 1(1), 58(1), 61, 76(1)(c), 77(5), 81(5)(b), 89(2), 137, 138B, 142(1)(b), 183, 197, 198, 225, 239(4), 241(1)(b)(i), 241A, 256, 284(3), 304, 309(2), 310(3), 318(1), 319(1), 349, 429(4), 441(1), 446(1), 450(2), 466(3)(b), 474(1), 484, 492(1)(d), 525(5)(a), Sch 6 Pt III Par 1(2), FA 1967 s 12(1), F(MP)A 1968 s 9, FA 1970 ss 14(2), 19(2A), 59(1), FA 1972 ss 15, 18(5), Sch 1 Pt III para 4, FA 1973 ss 25(1), 34(3), F(TPCM)A 1974 ss 7(4), CGTA 1975 ss 2(1), 25(9A)(a), 38(1), CTA 1976 ss 76, 84A, 93(7), 101(6), 103(3), 124(6), 145(3), 160, 162(5), 170(7), FA 1980 ss 39(1CC), 45(1)(a), FA 1982 ss 8, 58(3), FA 1984 ss 12(7)(b), 13A(1A), 13B(1), 14(1)(a), 15(3C)(b), FA 1986 s 33A(3), FA 1988 s 12, FA 1992 ss 45(1)(a), 84(11), FA 1993 s 14, 35(1)(a), FA 1994 ss 14(3)(b)(i), 45(2), 66(7)(a), FA 1995 s 48(5), FA 1996 s 68(2) s 194, 225 Substitution of ITA 1967 s 354, FA 1982 s 18	ss 3(1), 5, 38, 48(1)(b), 49, 65(1),70(4), 71(1), 73, 81(2), 97, 122, 127(1)-(5), 134(3), 140, 141, 144, 147 195(12)-(15), 2(1), 200(1), 234(3)-(8), 235, 245, 260, 270, 279, 284, 287, 291, 301(1), 316, 318, 320(1), 348, 353, 36, 363, 373(2)(a), 374, 382(1)(2), 383, 384, 392, 393, 406, 428, 433,440, 441, 443, 458, 466, 469(1), 472, 487, 488(1), 491, 492, 493, 495, 517, 592, 604,678, 681, 693, 701, 754, 772,772, 788, 790, 793, 797, 799, 808, 828(1)-(3), 838, 921, 942(1)-(8)(10), 953, 968, 972, 973, 1023, 1024, 1033, Sch 32 paras 1(2), para 4
Pt II ....Repeal of ITA 1967 ss 46, 68(2), 82, 106, 177, 307(1A), 340(2)(e)(f), 365, 366, 419, 467, 467A, 467B, 467C, 468(1)(2), 469, 471, 472(2), 473, 484(5), 486(3), 496, 550(2A), Sch 1 Pt II, Sch 18 para VIII(1), FA 1972 s11, FA 1974 ss 38, 44, 52, 54, CGTA 1975 s 49(7), CTA 1976 ss 6(4), 66A(3) proviso, 66A(4), 76A(2) proviso, (3), FA 1976 ss 25, 30, FA 1980 s 7, FA 1981 ss 6, 18, FA 1982 ss 21, 22, FA 1986 s 8, Pt I Ch III, ss 33(9)(e), 46(4), FA 1987 ss 6, 35(22), FA 1988 ss 19(1), 21(6), 22, FA 1993 s 7, Sch 1 para 1(7)(e), FA 1994 ss 5, 38, 49, FA 1995 s 6, 66(8A), FA 1996 s 15(6).	
Amendment of ITA 1967 ss 1(1), 307(1), 317(2), FA 1974 s 16(5), CGTA 1975 s 32(4)(b), CTA 1976 ss 76(6), 152(3), FA 1983 s 50(11), FA 1986 s 33(9)(d), FA 1989 Sch 1 para 1(7)(d)	ss 2(1), 3(1), 381(1), 144, 171, 240, 258, 657(1), 732, Sch 18 para 1
Sch 10	Sch 7

Index

A

Abandonment

of an option within the meaning of CGTA 1975 s 47(3) *TA Dilleen (Inspector of Taxes) v Edward J Kearns* Vol IV p 547

Absent

landowner returns to take on active farming *EP O'Coindealbhain (Inspector of Taxes) v KN Price* Vol IV p 1

Absolute interest

discretionary trust, when absolute interest passes *BKJ v The Revenue Commissioners* Vol III p 104

Accountants

working papers, whether the inspector of taxes is entitled to call for production of a taxpayer's nominal ledger, whether the nominal ledger formed part of the accountant's working papers *JJ Quigley (Inspector of Taxes) v Maurice Burke* Vol IV p 332, Vol V p 265

Accounting

method of accounting for tax purposes, whether replacement cost basis is acceptable or whether historical cost accounting is the only method of commercial accountancy, *Carroll Industries Plc (formerly PJ Carroll & Co Ltd) and PJ Carroll & Co Ltd v S O'Culacháin (Inspector of Taxes)* Vol IV p 135

Accounting period

accounts made up half-yearly, whether Revenue required to determine accounting period *The Revenue Commissioners v R Hilliard & Sons Ltd* Vol II p 130

Acquisition of Land (Assessment of Compensation) Act 1919

section 2 *Peter C Heron & Others v The Minister for Communications* Vol III p 298

Additional assessments

whether the inspector of taxes had made a "discovery" on finding that inadmissible deductions had been allowed in the computation of the company's tax liability for certain years and whether he was entitled to raise additional assessments for those years *W Ltd v Wilson (Inspector of Taxes)* Vol 11 p 627, *Hammond Lane Metal Co Ltd v S O'Culacháin (Inspector of Taxes)* Vol III p 187

Administration

procedures of Revenue Commissioners, whether unfair and unconstitutional, enforcement order issue to city sheriff after payment of tax, defamation of plaintiff *Giles J Kennedy v E G Hearne, The Attorney General & Others* Vol III p 590

Admissibility

of evidence of illegality *Daniel Collins and Michael Byrne, Daniel Collins and Redmond Power as Executor of the Will of Michael Byrne, deceased and Daniel Collins v J D Mulvey (Inspector of Taxes)* Vol II p 291

Admissibility (contd)

of legislative history of statutory provisions *Derek Crilly v T & J Farrington Limited and John O'Connor* 2000 p 65

Adopted children

whether "issue" included adopted children *In the matter of John Stamp deceased Patrick Stamp v Noel Redmond & Ors* Vol IV p 415

Adoption Act 1952

ss 4, 26(2), adoption heavily qualified, whether permissible to adopt paying provisions of ITA 1967 into corporation tax code while ignoring charging provisions *Wayte (Holdings) Ltd (In Receivership) Alex Burns v E N Hearne* Vol III p 553

Advance payment

received on foot of obligation with bank, whether income from trade *JG Kerrane (Inspector of Taxes) v N Hanlon (Ireland) Ltd* Vol III p 633

Advertising

agency, whether a profession for the purposes of corporation tax surcharge *Mac Giolla Mhaith (Inspector of Taxes) v Cronin & Associates Ltd* Vol III p 211

company producing materials for use in advertising, whether manufacture *S O'Culachain (Inspector of Taxes) v Hunter Advertising Ltd* Vol IV p 35

newspaper publisher, newspapers are "goods" for the purpose of manufacturing relief, whether advertising income is from a separate trade and qualifies for such relief *L McGurrin (Inspector of Taxes) v The Champion Publications Ltd* Vol IV p 466

Agreement

whether an agreement between the taxpayer and the inspector of taxes in relation to an assessment under appeal is binding and conclusive *The Hammond Lane Metal Co Ltd v S O'Culachain (Inspector of Taxes)* Vol IV p 187

construction of documents and transactions *B McCabe (Inspector of Taxes) v South City & County Investment Co Ltd* Vol V p 107, 1998 p 183

Agricultural Society

definition of *The Trustees of The Ward Union Hunt Races v Hughes (Inspector of Taxes)* Vol I p 538

Allowable loss

capital gains tax used for avoidance of tax, whether allowable *Patrick McGrath & Others v JE McDermott (Inspector of Taxes)* Vol III p 683

Allowances

UK resident working in Ireland, wife working in UK, whether he is entitled to married allowance and rate bands *S Fennessy (Inspector of Taxes) v John Mc Connellogue* Vol V p 129

Amnesty

whether customer given negligent advice by bank in relation to availing of amnesty *Michael Gayson v Allied Irish Banks Plc* 2000 p 105

Amnesty (contd)

1993, whether applies *Liam J Irwin (Collector General) v Michael Grimes* Vol V p 209, *Crimianl Assets Bureau v Gerard Hutch* 1999 p 65

Annuity

payable tax free from a trust, the trust is accountable to the Revenue Commissioners for the tax, where such tax is refunded by the Revenue Commissioners to the annuitant is the annuitant accountable to the trust for the tax so refunded *In re Swan, Deceased; The Hibernian Bank Ltd v Munro & Ors* Vol V p 565

paid between group companies, whether capital or revenue *B Mc Cabe (Inspector of Taxes) v South City & County Investment Co Ltd* Vol V p 107

Annual charge

on rental income left to beneficiary provided he continued to manage the property whether remuneration under Schedule E *Gerald O'Reilly v WJ Casey (Inspector of Taxes)* Vol 1 p 601

Annual profits or gains

veterinary body corporate performing Statutory functions, surplus of receipts over expenditure whether liable to tax *The Veterinary Council v F Corr (Inspector of Taxes)* Vol II p 204

Appeals

against a decision of the High Court to refuse on a judicial review application to quash three convictions with six months imprisonment for each offence imposed in the District Court on the appellant for failure to make income tax returns *Thomas O'Callaghan v JP Clifford & Others* Vol IV p 478

new grounds, appellants right to introduce *Boland's Ltd v The Commissioners of Inland Revenue* Vol 1 p 34

to Circuit Court, whether Circuit Court Judge has authority to award costs in tax appeal hearings *The Revenue Commissioners v Arida Ltd* Vol IV p 401, Vol V p 221

to High Court by way of case stated from decision of Circuit Judge, failure to notify the respondent the fact that a case has been stated *A & B v WJ Davis (Inspector of Taxes)* Vol II p 60

summonses served in respect of tax liabilities the subject matter of earlier appeals whether Circuit Court judge has discretion to accept late filing of notice and fee, whether dissatisfaction expressed at the Circuit Court appeal hearings, whether dissatisfaction must be expressed immediately after determination by the Circuit Court, whether notice to county registrar must be lodged within 21 days together with the £20 fee, whether payment of tax denies access to the courts, whether requirements are directory or mandatory, whether tax must be paid before the case stated is determined, whether time lapse after expression of dissatisfaction is fatal *Michael A Bairead v Martin C Carr* Vol IV p 505

time for notice of appeal meaning of "immediately" *The State (Multiprint Label Systems Ltd) v The Hon Justice Thomas Neylon* Vol III p 159

Appeal Commissioners

determinations of 2000 p 55

grounds for setting aside findings of fact by Appeal Commissioners *Mara v GC (Hummingbird) Ltd* Vol II p 687

nature of powers and functions limited or unlimited, determination of tax liability by High Court and Appeal Commissioners whether mutually exclusive *The State (Calcul International Ltd and Solatrex International Ltd) v The Appeal Commissioners and The Revenue Commissioners* Vol III p 577

Appellant

company's accounts, based on current cost accounting convention (ie replacement cost) *Carroll Industries Plc (formerly PJ Carroll & Co Ltd) and PJ Carroll & Co Ltd v S O'Culachain (Inspector of Taxes)* Vol IV p 135

right of, to introduce new grounds of appeal *Boland's Ltd v The Commissioners of Inland Revenue* Vol 1 p 34

Arbitration

compulsory acquisition of land, whether property arbitrator obliged to give breakdown of his award, whether breakdown required for capital gains tax purposes, whether failure by applicant to request an apportionment of the award rules out any further relief, whether applicant can appeal without the breakdown for the award, whether failure to advance further arguments of unfairness amounted to acceptance of the normal practice, *Manning, J v Shackleton, J & Cork Co Council* Vol IV p 485

Artistic exemption

exemption of earnings from original and creative works of artistic or cultural merit, whether journalism qualifies *John Healy v SI Breathnach (Inspector of Taxes)* Vol III p 496

legal text books, refusal by inspector of taxes to grant exemption from income tax under FA 1969 s 2, exemption granted if the books are original and creative works which are generally recognised as having cultural or artistic merit. *Michael Forde Decision* Vol IV p 348

Assessment

basis of assessment under Case III *O'Conaill (Inspector of Taxes) v R* Vol II p 304

basis of, commencement and cessation within a year, whether assessment for the previous year can be reviewed *AB v JD Mulvey (Inspector of Taxes)* Vol II p 55

builder's profits *The State (at the prosecution of Patrick J Whelan) v Michael Smidic (Special Commissioners of Income Tax) and Edward Connolly v AG Birch (Inspector of Taxes)* Vol I p 583

confirmed, allowability of expenses *The King (Harris Stein) v The Special Commissioners* Vol I p 62

joint, whether husband is liable on wife's income, *Gilligan v Criminal Assets Bureau, Galvin, Lanigan & Revenue Commissioners* Vol V p 424

made in the absence of returns, *Criminal Assets Bureau v Gerard Hutch* 1999 p 65

of remuneration paid in year after for work done in earlier year *Bedford (Collector-General) v H* Vol II p 588

whether can be reopened *Boland's Ltd v The Commissioners of Inland Revenue* Vol I p 34

Assigned

personal pension and other assets assigned to company pension continued to be paid to pensioner, whether pensioner liable to tax on pension *Cronin (Inspector of Taxes) v C* Vol II p 592

Associated company

whether a company, resident and trading in Northern Ireland was an associated company of a company resident and trading in the State for the purposes of CTA 1976 s 28 (ie reduced rate of corporation tax for small companies) *MA Bairead (Inspector of Taxes) v Maxwells of Donegal Ltd* Vol III p 430

Auctioneer's commission

whether revenue or capital management expense *Stephen Court Ltd v JA Browne (Inspector of Taxes)* Vol V p 680

Avoidance

dealing in and developing land *O'Connlain (Inspector of Taxes) v Belvedere Estates Ltd* Vol III p 271

sports club, whether set up for tax avoidance or bona fide purposes *Revenue v ORMG* Vol III p 28

whether tax avoidance valid *McGrath v McDermott* Vol III p 683

B

Basis of assessment

commencement and cessation within a year, whether assessment for the previous year can be reviewed *AB v JD Mulvey (Inspector of Taxes)* Vol II p 55

under Case III *O'Conaill (Inspector of Taxes) v R* Vol II p 304

Bank

confidentiality between banks and customers *JB O'C v PCD and A Bank* Vol III p 153

government stocks purchased to comply with Central Bank requirements, whether carrying on trade of dealing in securities, whether liable as profits under Schedule D or exempt capital gains on Government stocks *JA Browne (Inspector of Taxes) v Bank of Ireland Finance Ltd* Vol III p 644

whether personal liability of members is unlimited) *CIR v The Governor and Company of The Bank of Ireland* Vol I p 70

whether Inspector of Taxes entitled to a Court Order *In the Matter of GO'C & AO'C (Application of Liam Liston)* Vol V p 346

Banana ripening

whether qualified for manufacturing relief *PJ O'Connell (Inspector of Taxes) v Fyffes Banana Processing Ltd* 2000 p 235

Bank account

application by Revenue for court order for bank to furnish details of accounts to taxpayers *In re G O'C & A O'C (Application of Liam Liston (Inspector of Taxes))* Vol V p 346

Bad debts
recovered by executor but allowed during lifetime of deceased, whether executor carrying on a trade, whether such bad debts recovered are taxable *CD v J MO' Sullivan* Vol II p 140

Barrister's fees
due prior to his appointment to the bench, fees refused but could be paid to a family company if solicitors so wished *EP O'Coindealbhain (Inspector of Taxes) v The Honourable Mr Justice Sean Gannon* Vol III p 484

Beneficial owner
personal pension and other assets assigned to company pension continued to be paid to pensioner, whether pensioner liable to tax on pension *Cronin (Inspector of Taxes) v C* Vol II p 592

whether director controlled a company and whether managing director was the beneficial owner of, or able to control more than 5% of its ordinary shares *Associated properties Ltd v The Revenue Commissioners* Vol II p 175

Benefit in kind
cars, whether charge to benefit in kind on sales representatives is constitutional *Paul Browne & Others v The Revenue Commissioners & Others* Vol IV p 323

rent paid for employee *Connolly (Inspector of Taxes) v Denis McNamara* Vol II p 452

Bloodstock
animal bought in course of trade, sent to stud after successful racing career and subsequently sold to a syndicate whether amount realised on syndication a trading receipt *Mac Giolla Riogh (Inspector of Taxes) v G Ltd* Vol II p 315

Board of Conservators
surplus revenue, whether annual profits or gains *Moville District Board of Conservators v D Ua Clothasaigh (Inspector of Taxes)* Vol II p 75

Books
barrister's books, whether plant *Breathnach (Inspector of Taxes) v MC* Vol III p 113

Bookmaker
bookmaker convicted and fined in the District Court of offences under the Betting Acts penal warrant for imprisonment, whether constitutional, *John B Murphy v District Justice Brendan Wallace & Others* Vol IV p 278

levies on course betting, whether taxable a income or profits of a trade *The Racing Board v S O'Culachain* Vol IV p 73

profits of a bookmaker from transactions in Irish Hospital Sweepstakes tickets, whether receipts assessable to tax under Schedule D *HH v MJ Forbes (Inspector of Taxes)* Vol II p 164

betting duty, whether necessary for Revenue Commissioners to comply with Regulations Act 1890 before proceedings can commence for failure to pay duty on bets *DPP v Michael Cunningham* Vol V p 691

Breach
customs regulations, seizure by the Revenue Commissioners of an oil tanker *McCrystal Oil Co Ltd v The Revenue Commissioners & Others* Vol IV p 386

Builder's profits

assessment of *The State (at the prosecution of Patrick J Whelan) v Michael Smidic (Special Commissioners of Income Tax)* Vol I p 571 and *Edward Connolly v AG Birch (Inspector of Taxes)* Vol I p 583

capitalised value of ground rents and fines, whether liable to tax *Birch (Inspector of Taxes) v Denis Delaney* Vol I p 515 and *Edward Connolly v AG Birch (Inspector of Taxes)* and *Swaine (Inspector of Taxes) v VE* Vol I p 583

Building societies

company lending money to non-members to purchase property, whether trading as a building society *Property Loan & Investment Co Ltd v The Revenue Commissioners* Vol II p 25

instruments relating to the internal affairs of a society were exempt from stamp duty, whether this exemption extended to a transfer of a premises to a society to conduct its business *Irish Nationwide Building Society v Revenue Commissioners* Vol IV p 296

Business

carried on abroad *The Executors and Trustees of A C Ferguson (deceased) v Donovan (Inspector of Taxes)* Vol I p 183

Brewery

trade or business, whether liability in respect of transactions under DORA requisition orders *Arthur Guinness Son & Co Ltd v Commissioners of Inland Revenue* Vol I p 1

C

Cable television system

whether liable to value added tax on sales to customers *TJ Brosnan (Inspector of Taxes) v Cork Communications Ltd* Vol IV p 349

Cattledealer

whether the taxpayer was a "dealer in cattle" within the meaning of ITA 1918 Sch D Case III rule 4 and ITA 1967 s 78. *De Brun (Inspector of Taxes) v K* Vol III p 19

Capital acquisitions tax

whether succession under Act is automatic or must be claimed *In the Matter of the Estates of Cummins (Decd); O'Dwyer & Ors v Keegan & Ors* Vol V p 367

COMPETENT TO DISPOSE

whether surviving spouse competent to dispose of statutory share in estate *In Re the Estate of Urquhart, D (Decd) & Revenue Commissioners v AIB Ltd* Vol V p 600

FAVOURITE NEPHEW RELIEF

gift of farm to niece - whether niece worked substantially full time on the farm *AE v The Revenue Commissioners* Vol V p 686

valuation of shares in private non-trading company *Revenue Commissioners v Henry Young* Vol V p 294

Capital allowances

barrister's books, whether plant *Breathnach (Inspector of Taxes) v MC* Vol III p 113

expenditure on installation of suspended ceiling in supermarket, whether plant qualifying for capital allowances *Dunnes Stores (Oakville) Ltd v MC Cronin (Inspector of Taxes)* Vol IV p 68

in designated area, whether plant used exclusively in designated area, whether allowance extends to plant used under a hire contract *Daniel McNally v S O Maoldhomhniagh* Vol IV p 22

holiday cottages, whether qualifying for capital allowances *McMahon, T & Ors v Rt Hon Lord Mayor Alderman & Burgess of Dublin* Vol V p 357

industrial building structure for dock undertaking, whether bonded transit sheds used as clearing house and not for storage qualify *Patrick Monahan (Drogheda) Ltd v O'Connell (Inspector of Taxes)* Vol III p 661

poultry house, whether plant and machinery *O'Srianain (Inspector of Taxes) v Lakeview Ltd* Vol III p 219

racecourse stand, *O'Grady (Inspector of Taxes) v Roscommon Race Committee* Vol V p 317

share of, on leasing transaction, involving a purported limited partnership, against his personal income tax liability. *DA MacCarthaigh (Inspector of Taxes) v Francis Daly* Vol III p 253

whether a building which housed offices, a showroom, a canteen, computer department and utilities qualified for industrial building allowance under ITA 1967 s 255 *O'Conaill (Inspector of Taxes) v JJ Ltd* Vol III p 65

whether capital allowances apportioned in accordance with ITA 1967 s 220(5), should be confined to the allowances outlined in Part XVI of that Act *SW Ltd v McDermott (Inspector of Taxes)* Vol II p 661

whether mining operation qualifies for ESR or capital allowances *Patrick J O'Connell (Inspector of Taxes) v Tara Mines Ltd* 2001 p 79

Capitalised

builder's profits capitalised value of ground rents and fines, whether liable to tax *Birch (Inspector of Taxes) v Denis Delaney* Vol I p 515 and *Edward Connolly v A G Birch (Inspector of Taxes)* Vol I p 583 and *Swaine (Inspector of Taxes) v VE* Vol II p 472

Capital expenditure

whether annual interest on loan to redeem preference shares is a deductible expense *Seán MacAonghusa (Inspector of Taxes) v Ringmahon Company* 2001 p 117

Capital gains tax

ACCOUNTABLE PERSON

disposal of property by mortgagee as nominee for mortgagor, accountable person for capital gains tax purposes, repayment of 15% deducted by purchaser in the absence of tax clearance certificate *Bank of Ireland Finance Ltd v The Revenue Commissioners* Vol IV p 217

ALLOWABLE LOSS

capital gains tax used for avoidance of tax, whether allowable *Patrick McGrath & Others v JE McDermott (Inspector of Taxes)* Vol III p 683

Capital gains tax (contd)

valuation of lands as at 6 April 1974 *J McMahon (Inspector of Taxes) v Albert Noel Murphy* Vol IV p 125

CAPITAL GAINS TAX

on sale of lands *EP O'Coindealbhain (Inspector of Taxes) v KN Price* Vol IV p 1

sale of whiskey in a bond by a publican, whether liable to capital gains tax *McCall (deceased) v Commissioners of Inland Revenue* Vol I p 28

CAPITAL LOSS

loss on realisation of *investments The Alliance & Dublin Consumers' Gas Co v Davis (Inspector of Taxes)* Vol I p 207

CLEARANCE CERTIFICATE

on sale of bonds, whether applicant ordinarily resident in the state is entitled to a clearance certificate *The State (FIC Ltd) v O'Ceallaigh* Vol III p 124

whether absence of a clearance certificate prohibited the Revenue Commissioners from repaying tax deducted by purchaser *Bank of Ireland Finance Ltd v The Revenue Commissioners* Vol IV p 217

COMPULSORY ACQUISITION

of land, whether property arbitrator obliged to give breakdown of his award, whether breakdown required for capital gains tax purposes, whether failure by applicant to request an apportionment of the award rules out any further relief, whether applicant can appeal without the breakdown for the award, whether failure to advance further arguments of unfairness amounted to acceptance of the normal practice, *David Manning v John R Shackleton & Cork County Council* Vol IV p 485

COMPULSORY PURCHASE

compensation determined without regard to tax arising on disposal *Peter C Heron & Others v The Minister For Communications* Vol III p 298

of land, whether property arbitrator obliged to give breakdown of his award, whether breakdown required for capital gains tax purposes, whether failure by applicant to request an apportionment of the award rules out any further relief, whether applicant can appeal without the breakdown for the award, whether failure to advance further arguments of unfairness amounted to acceptance of the normal practice *David Manning v John R Shackleton & Cork County Council* Vol IV p 485

DEBT

whether loan notes are a simple debt or a debt on a security *Patrick J O'Connell (Inspector of Taxes) v Thomas Keleghan* 2000 p113

whether a loan with conversion rights constitutes a debt within the meaning of CGTA 1975 s 46(1) *Mooney (Inspector of Taxes) v McSweeney* Vol V p 163

VALUATION OF LAND

agricultural land, appeal against market value at 6 April 1974 as determined by Circuit Court, whether agricultural value the sole determining factor, whether development potential attached on 6 April 1974, whether subsequent planning permission for milk processing plant relevant *J McMahon (Inspector of Taxes) v Albert Noel Murphy* Vol IV p 125

Capital gains tax (contd)

whether CGT chargeable on redemption of loan notes for cash *Patrick J O'Connell (Inspector of Taxes) v Thomas Keleghan* 2001 p 103

Capital or revenue

annuity paid between group companies *B Mc Cabe (Inspector of Taxes) v South City & County Investment Co Ltd* Vol V p 107

auctioneer's commission *Stephen Court Ltd v Browne (Inspector of Taxes)* Vol V p 680

compensation for loss of profits *The Alliance and Dublin Consumers' Gas Co v McWilliams (Inspector of Taxes)* Vol I p 104

dividends from sales of capital assets, whether liable to corporation profits tax *K Co v Hogan (Inspector of Taxes)* Vol III p 56

exchange losson foreign currency loans, whether capital or revenue *TG Brosnan (Inspector of Taxes) v Mutual Enterprises Ltd* Vol V p 138

interest on loan following redemption of share capital, whether allowable against trading income *Sean MacAonghusa v Ringmahon Co* 1999 p 81

lump sum paid on the execution of a lease *W Flynn (Inspector of Taxes) v John Noone Ltd* and *W Flynn (Inspector of Taxes) v Blackwood & Co (Sligo) Ltd* Vol II p 222

management expenses, whether allowable *Hibernian Insurance Co Ltd v MacUimis (Inspector of Taxes)* 2000 p 75

payment in advance on the signing of a lease, whether capital *O'Sullivan (Inspector of Taxes) v p Ltd* Vol II p 464

racecourse stand, whether deductible repairs or non deductible capital expenditure or expenditure qualifying as plant *Michael O'Grady (Inspector of Taxes) v Roscommon Race Committee* Vol IV p 425

removing top-soil from surface of quarry *Milverton Quarries Ltd v The Revenue Commissioners* Vol II p 382

solicitor's fees - payable by investment company *Stephen Court Ltd v Browne (Inspector of Taxes)* Vol V p 680

training grants, whether capital or revenue receipt *O'Cleirigh (Inspector of Taxes) v Jacobs International Ltd Incorporated* Vol III p 165

whether capital expenditure *Airspace Investments Ltd v M Moore (Inspector of Taxes)* Vol V p 3

whether expenditure incurred by petrol marketing company under exclusivity agreements with retailers is revenue or capital *Dolan (Inspector of Taxes) v AB Co Ltd* Vol II p 515

Cars

whether charge to benefit in kind on sales representatives is constitutional *Paul Browne & Others v The Revenue Commissioners & Others* Vol IV p 323

Carry forward

of losses *Molmac Ltd v MacGiolla Riogh (Inspector of Taxes)* Vol II p 482

Case stated

request for, by taxpayer *The King (Harris Stein) v The Special Commissioners* Vol I p 62

Case stated (contd)

time for notice of appeal meaning of "immediately" *The State (Multiprint Label Systems v Thomas Neylon* Vol III p 159

Ceilings

expenditure on installation of suspended ceiling in supermarket, whether plant qualifying for capital *allowances Dunnes Stores (Oakville) Ltd v M C Cronin (Inspector of Taxes)* Vol IV p 68

Certiorari

whether applicant was entitled to order of certiorari where decision is confirmed and enacted *C Mc Daid v His Honour Judge Sheehy & Ors* Vol V p 696

Cessation of business

assessment of builders profits *The State (at the prosecution of Patrick J Whelan) v Michael Smidic (Special Commissioners of Income Tax) and The State (at the prosecution of Patrick J Whelan) v Michael Smidic (Special Commissioners of Income Tax)* Vol I p 571

basis of assessment, commencement and cessation within a year, whether assessment for the previous year can be reviewed *AB v JD Mulvey (Inspector of Taxes)* Vol II p 55

deduction of corporation profits tax and excess corporation profits tax in computing profits for income tax purposes *JM O'Dwyer (Inspector of Taxes) v The Dublin United Transport Co Ltd* Vol II p 115

losses forward *Cronin (Inspector of Taxes) v Lunham Brothers Ltd* Vol III p 363

phasing down of business, whether constituted trading, whether collection of debts constituted trading *The City of Dublin Steampacket Co v Revenue Commissioners* Vol I p 108

Change of ownership

losses forward *M Cronin (Inspector of Taxes) v Lunham Brothers Ltd* Vol III p 363

Chargeable person

joint assessment, whether husband is liable for both incomes *Gilligan v Criminal Assets Bureau, Galvin, Lanigan & Revenue Commissioners* Vol V p 424

Charges

on book debts by deed of mortgage, whether fixed or floating charge *AH Masser Ltd (in receivership) & Others v The Revenue Commissioners* Vol III p 548

Charge card

scheme, the meaning of paid, *The Diners Club Ltd v The Revenue and The Minister for Finance* Vol III p 680

Charity

income from securities and from school, whether for charitable purposes *The Pharmaceutical Society of Ireland v The Revenue Commissioners* Vol I p 542

nun, whether assessable on income from employment which she gives to her order *JD Dolan (Inspector of Taxes) v "K" National School Teacher* Vol I p 656

trade carried on by beneficiary of charity, whether exempt *Beirne (Inspector of Taxes) v St Vincent De Paul Society (Wexford Conference)* Vol I p 383

Charity (contd)

whether a charity "established" in Ireland *Revenue Commissioners v Sister of Charity of the Incarnate Word* 1998 p 65

Charitable bequest

whether it had to be expended in Ireland *The Revenue Commissioners v The Most Reverend Edward Doorley* Vol V p 539

Children

children's pension, whether income of parent for income tax purposes *O'Coindealbhain (Inspector of Taxes) v Breda O'Carroll* Vol IV p 221

father taking his elder children and his mother-in-law into partnership, subsequent assignment of mother-in-law's interest to his younger children whether income of children to be deemed to be income of father *JM O'Dwyer (Inspector of Taxes) v Cafolla & Co* Vol II p 82

increase in widows contributory pension in respect of dependent children, whether taxable on parent *Sean O'Siochain (Inspector of Taxes) v Bridget Neenan* Vol V p 472

settlement of income, deed of appointment by parent in favour of child *E G v Mac Shamhrain, (Inspector of Taxes)* Vol II p 352

whether "issue" included adopted children *In the matter of John Stamp deceased Patrick Stamp v Noel Redmond & Others* Vol IV p 415

Circuit Court

appeal hearings, whether Circuit Court Judge has authority to award costs in tax appeal hearings *The Revenue Commissioners v Arida Ltd* Vol IV p 401, Vol V p 221

summonses served in respect of tax liabilities the subject matter of earlier appeals whether Circuit Court judge has discretion to accept late filing of notice and fee, whether dissatisfaction expressed at the Circuit Court appeal hearings, whether dissatisfaction must be expressed immediately after determination by the Circuit Court, whether notice to county registrar must be lodged within 21 days together with the £20 fee, whether payment of tax denies access to the courts, whether requirements are directory or mandatory, whether tax must be paid before the case stated is determined, whether time lapse after expression of dissatisfaction is fatal *Michael A Bairead v Martin C Carr* Vol IV p 505

whether a Circuit Court Judge hearing an appeal pursuant to ITA 1967 s 429 has jurisdiction to award costs *The Revenue Commissioners v Arida Ltd* Vol IV p 401, Vol V p 221

Club

to promote athletics or amateur games or sports, whether bona fide or tax avoidance *Revenue v ORMG* Vol III p 28

Coal mining

trading as fuel merchants, whether new trade of coal mining was set up or commenced *H A O'Loan (Inspector of Taxes) v Messrs MJ Noone & Co* Vol II p 146

College/Schools
whether operated for charitable purposes *The Pharmaceutical Society of Ireland v The Revenue Commissioners* Vol I p 542

Collector
of vintage motor cars *Karl Keller v The Revenue Commissioners & Others Commencement* Vol IV p 512

Commencement
and cessation within a year, whether assessment for the previous year can be reviewed *AB v JD Mulvey (Inspector of Taxes)* Vol II p 55

fuel merchants, whether new trade of coal mining was set up or commenced *H A O'Loan (Inspector of Taxes) v Messrs M J Noone & Co* Vol II p 146

Company
definition of, within the meaning of FA 1920 s 52(3) *CIR v The Governor and Company of The Bank of Ireland* Vol I p 70

in receivership preferential claim *The Attorney-General, Informant v Irish Steel Ltd and Vincent Crowley, Defendants* Vol II p 108

meetings, whether they took place, whether resolution was passed, whether share issue invalid *In re Sugar Distributors Ltd* Vol V p 225

non-resident *The Cunard Steam Ship Co Ltd v Herlihy (Inspector of Taxes), and The Cunard Steam Ship Co Ltd v Revenue Commissioners* Vol I p 330

Company secretary
role of *Wayte (Holdings) Ltd (In Receivership) Alex Burns v Edward N Hearne* Vol III p 553

Compensation
ex gratia payments, by British government for malicious damage to property or personal injury sustained, whether trading receipt *WA Robinson T/A James Pim & Son v J D Dolan (Inspector of Taxes)* Vol I p 427

for compulsory purchase, determined without regard to tax arising on disposal *Peter C Heron & Others v The Minister For Communications* Vol III p 298

for loss of profits, whether income or capital receipt *The Alliance and Dublin Consumers' Gas Co v McWilliams (Inspector of Taxes)* Vol I p 207 and *F Corr (Inspector of Taxes) v F E Larkin* Vol II p 164

Compulsory sale
to Minister for Finance, in return for sterling equivalents, of dollar balances consisting of income from securities, etc, in the USA whether moneys so received assessable *J M O'Sullivan (Inspector of Taxes) v Julia O'Connor, as Administratrix of Evelyn H O'Brien, Deceased* Vol II p 61

Confidentiality
between banks and customers *JB O'C v PCD and A Bank* Vol III p 153

Inspector of Taxes entitled to Court Order *In the Matter of GO'C & AO'C (Application of Liam Liston (Inspector of Taxes))* Vol V 346

Confirmation of assessment
allowance of expenses where assessment has been confirmed *The King (Harris Stein) v The Special Commissioners* Vol I p 62

Conflict

in terms of deed *AH Masser Ltd (in receivership) & Others v The Revenue Commissioners* Vol III p 548

Constitutional rights

constitution validity of taxing statute applicable to married persons *Bernard Muckley & Anne Muckley v Ireland, AG and Revenue Commissioners* Vol III p 188

to have recourse to High Court denied *Michael Deighan v Edward N Hearn & Others* Vol III p 533

whether charge to benefit in kind on sales representatives is constitutional *Paul Browne & Others v The Revenue Commissioners & Others* Vol IV p 323

whether common law rule of dependant domicile of a wife whether constitutional *JW v JW* Vol IV p 437

whether constitutional right to earn a livelihood infringed - whether legislation requires amendment *James G Orange v The Revenue Commissioners* Vol V p 70

whether undertaking by the State under Article 41.3 to guard the institution of marriage infringed, whether imposition of higher taxes or married couples repugnant to the Constitution *Francis & Mary Murphy v The Attorney General* Vol V p 613

whether Imposition of Duties Act 1957 s 1 is constitutional *C Mc Daid v His Honour Judge Sheehy & Ors* Vol V p 696

whether method of granting credit for Professional services withholding tax is constitutional *Michael Daly v The Revenue Commissioners* Vol V p 213

whether rights to privacy and fair procedures infringed. *Charles J Haughey and Others v Moriarty and Others* 1998 p 119

Construction contracts

whether lorry owners carrying sand and gravel were engaged as subcontractors under a construction contract, whether the lorry owners became the proprietors of the quarry materials *O'Grady v Laragan Quarries Ltd* Vol IV p 269

Contract

availability of remedy of specific performance where VAT not paid pursuant to contract *Cyril Forbes v John Tobin And Janet Tobin* 2001 p 71

Contract of service or contract for services

branch manager of local Employment Office of Dept of Social Welfare *O'Coindealbhain (Inspector of Taxes) v TB Mooney* Vol IV p 45

demonstrator of food products at supermarket *H Denny & Sons (Irl) Ltd v Minister for Social Welfare* Vol V p 238

members of fishing vessel *Minister for Social Welfare v John Griffiths* Vol IV p 378

temporary employee engaged through an employment agency *The Minister for Labour v PMPA Insurance Co Ltd (under administration)* Vol III p 505

wholesale distributor of newspapers *Tony McAuliffe v Minister for Social Welfare* Vol V p 94

winding up, preferential payments, tests applicable *In the Matter of Sunday Tribune* 1998 p 177

Contract for sale

of legal estate, whether a contract for sale of property *Waterford Glass (Group Services) Ltd v The Revenue Commissioners* Vol IV p 187

stamp duties, amount chargeable, contracts and consideration structured to minimise stamp duty *VIEK Investments Ltd v The Revenue Commissioners* Vol IV p 367

Control

by trustees *The Executors and Trustees of AC Ferguson (deceased) v Donovan (Inspector of Taxes)* Vol I p 183

interest paid by a company to a person having controlling interest in the company *The Revenue Commissioners v Associated properties Ltd* Vol II p 412

whether director controlled a company and whether managing director was the beneficial owner of, or able to control more than 5% of its ordinary shares *Associated properties Ltd v The Revenue Commissioners* Vol II p 175

Conveyance for sale

what constitutes a conveyance for sale under Stamp Act of 1891 *Waterford Glass (Group Services) Ltd v The Revenue Commissioners* Vol IV p 187

Co-operative

surplus of from dealing with members, whether trading profits, whether exempt *Kennedy (Inspector of Taxes) v The Rattoo Co-operative Dairy Society Ltd* Vol I p 315

Copyright

whether corporate body exploiting copyrights supplying service within meaning of VATA - Copyright Act 1963 *Phonographic Performance (Ireland) Ltd v J Somers (Inspector of Taxes)* Vol IV p 314

Corporation profits tax

accounting period, whether Revenue Commissioners are required to determine *The Revenue Commissioners v R Hilliard & Sons Ltd* Vol II p 130

company lending money to non-members to purchase property, whether trading as a building society *Property Loan & Investment Co Ltd v The Revenue Commissioners* Vol II p 25

foreign company trading in Ireland provision for devaluation of foreign currency not allowed as deduction from profits *The Revenue Commissioners v L & Co* Vol II p 281

liability to *Commissioners of Inland Revenue v The Governor & Company of The Bank of Ireland* Vol I p 70

paid by a company to a person having controlling interest in that company *The Revenue Commissioners v Associated Properties Ltd* Vol II p 412

surplus of co-op from dealing with members, whether trading profits, whether exempt *Kennedy (Inspector of Taxes) v Rattoo Co-operative Dairy Society Ltd* Vol 1 p 315

whether collection of rents and dividends and distribution of dividends constituted trading *The Commissioners of Inland Revenue v The Dublin and Kingstown Railway Co* Vol I p 119 and *The Great Southern Railways Co v The Revenue Commissioners* Vol I p 359

Corporation profits tax (contd)

whether excess corporation profits tax is exigible for accounting periods in respect of which no corporation profits tax (other than excess corporation profits tax) is payable *The Revenue Commissioners v Orwell Ltd* Vol II p 326

whether phasing down of business constituted trading *The City of Dublin Steampacket Co v Revenue Commissioners* Vol I p 108

Corporation tax

application of income tax provisions to corporation tax *Wayte (Holdings) Ltd (In receivership) Alex Burns v Edward N Hearne* Vol III p 553

deduction of management expenses of investment company *Hibernian Insurance Company Limited v MacUimis (Inspector of Taxes)* 2000 p 75

manufacturing relief for film production, whether relief applies to short advertising films produced for television, whether relief applies for accounting periods prior to FA 1990 *Saatchi & Saatchi Advertising Limited v Kevin McGarry (Inspector of Taxes)* 1998 p 99

manufacturing relief production of materials for use in advertising, whether manufacture *S O'Culachain (Inspector of Taxes) v Hunter Advertising Ltd* Vol IV p 35

surcharge, whether an advertising agency provides professional services for the purposes of corporation tax surcharge *Mac Giolla Mhaith (Inspector of Taxes) v Cronin & Associates Ltd* Vol III p 211

whether annual interest on loan to redeem preference shares is a deductible expense *Seán MacAonghusa (Inspector of Taxes) v Ringmahon Company* 2001 p 117

whether operation is manufacturing or mining *Patrick J O'Connell (Inspector of Taxes) v Tara Mines Ltd* 2001 p 79

Costs

whether a Circuit Court Judge hearing an appeal pursuant to ITA 1967 s 429 has jurisdiction to award costs *Revenue v Arida Ltd* Vol IV p 401, Vol V p 221

Cost accounting

method of accounting for tax purposes, whether replacement cost basis is acceptable or whether historical cost accounting is the only method of commercial accountancy *Carroll Industries Plc (formerly PJ Carroll & Co Ltd) and PJ Carroll & Co Ltd v S O'Culachain (Inspector of Taxes)* Vol IV p 135

Court fees

amount on which court fees are chargeable in liquidation *In re Private Motorists Provident Society Ltd (In Liqdtn) & W J Horgan v Minister for Justice* Vol V p 186, *In re Hibernian Transport Companies Ltd* Vol V p 194

Court order

whether Irish bank account is subject to UK court order restraining taxpayer from accessing funds *Governor & Co of the Bank of Ireland v Michael John Meeneghan & Ors* Vol V p 44

Covenants

to covenantees in Third World countries, whether covenantors entitled to relief under ITA 1967 s 439(1) and whether covenantees entitled to exemption limits under FA 1980 s 1 *Action Aid Ltd v Revenue Commissioners* Vol V p 392

Covenants (contd)

whether an individual was entitled to repayment of tax deducted from payments made under an indenture of covenant pursuant to ITA 1967 s 439(1)(iv) *The Revenue Commissioners v HI* Vol III p 242

Crime

non-payment of excise duty payable on bets entered into by the defendant a registered bookmaker, whether recovery of an excise penalty a criminal matter *The Director of Public Prosecutions v Seamus Boyle* Vol IV p 395

proceeds liable to tax, *Criminal Assets Bureau v Gerard Hutch* 1999 p 65

Criminal Assets Bureau

and assessments for income tax *The Criminal Assets Bureau v John Kelly* 2000 p 225

whether Mareva Injunction proceedings can be brought by plenary summons *The Criminal Assets Bureau v Patrick A McSweeney* 2000 p215

Crime and criminal earnings

Proceeds of Crime Act 1996 *John Gilligan v Criminal Assets Bureau, Revenue Commissioners & Others* 2001 p 135

Currency

compulsory sale of, to Minister for Finance, in return for sterling equivalents, of dollar balances consisting of income from securities, etc, in the USA whether moneys so received assessable *J M O'Sullivan (Inspector of Taxes) v Julia O'Connor, as Administratrix of Evelyn H O'Brien, Deceased* Vol II p 61

Customs duties

locus standi evasion of customs duties on specified goods *Gerard Curtis and Brendan Geough v The Attorney General and The Revenue Commissioners* Vol III p 419

seizure of oil tanker and contents for breach of regulations *McCrystal Oil Co Ltd v The Revenue Commissioners & Others* Vol IV p 386

Customs and Excise duties

milk products, whether a whey or skimmed milk product, whether export refunds on consignments from EC countries to non EC countries, whether re-classification renders products liable for repayment of export refunds, whether Revenue Commissioners responsible for classification whether Revenue Commissioners and state chemist negligent and in breach of duty whether Minister entitled to counterclaim against plaintiff *Carbery Milk Products Ltd v The Minister for Agriculture & Others* Vol IV p 492

whether unconstitutional for applicant to be convicted and fined for keeping hydrocarbon oil in his motor vehicle on which custom and excise duty had not been paid, whether delegation of powers under Imposition of Duties Act 1957 is permissible *Charles McDaid v Hon Judge David Sheehy, DPP & Ors* Vol IV p 162, Vol V p 696

Customs Law

validity of warrants grounding searches and seizures by Customs Officers *Simple Imports Limited and Another v Revenue Commissioners and Others* 2001, p 57

D

Dáil Debates

Evidence, admissibility of legislative history of statutory provision *Derek Crilly v T & J Farrington Limited and John O'Connor* 2000 p 65

Damages

for detinue and conversion arising from seizure by Revenue Commissioners of oil tanker *McCrystal Oil Co Ltd v The Revenue Commissioners & Others* Vol IV p 386

whether undertaking by individual to refund his employer all advances made during absence from work resulting from accident includes such amount as represents income tax, PRSI and pension contributions deducted from gross wages paid *Michael Hogan v Steele And Co Ltd and Electricity Supply Board* 2000 p 269

Dealing in or developing land

building contractors, whether lands the subject matter of a contract for sale entered into during an accounting period constitute trading stock for the year ending in that accounting period, whether inclusion of the lands in the accounts in accordance with good accounting procedure was evidence of the commercial reality of the transaction, whether absence of possession, conveyance of legal estate and planning permission relevant to taxpayer's claim for relief *Murnaghan Brothers Ltd v S O'Maoldhomhnaigh* Vol IV p 304

interest in land acquired and disposed of within one accounting period *M Cronin (Inspector of Taxes) v Cork & County Property Co Ltd* Vol III p 198

property company, whether ordinary principles of commercial accounting apply or whether artificial method of valuation pursuant to F(MP)A 1968 s 18(2) prevails *M Cronin (Inspector of Taxes) v Cork & County Property Co Ltd* Vol III p 198

property company, farm land, letting to partners on conacre, area zoned for development, land transferred to new company, whether land trading stock of company *L O hArgain (Inspector of Taxes) v B Ltd* Vol III p 9

whether the surplus from the sale of property was profit of a trade of dealing in or developing land, or the profit of a business which was deemed by F(MP)A 1968 s 17, to be such a trade *Mara (Inspector of Taxes) v GG (Hummingbird) Ltd* Vol II p 667

Debts

determining restriction in prevention of charging, assigning or otherwise disposing of book debts and other debts *AH Masser Ltd (in receivership) & Others v The Revenue Commissioners* Vol III p 548

on securities, loan notes, liability to capital gains tax *PJ O'Connell (Inspector of Taxes) v T Keleghan* 2000 p 113

whether a loan with conversion rights constitutes a debt within the meaning of CGTA 1975 s 46(1) *Mooney (Inspector of Taxes) v McSweeney* Vol V p 163

Debenture stock

whether loan notes constitute debenture stock *Patrick J O'Connell (Inspector of Taxes) v Thomas Keleghan* 2001 p 103

Deductions

SCHEDULE D CASE I AND II

compensation paid to tenants of adjoining premises for interference with light and air, whether allowable Case I deduction *WJ Davis (Inspector of Taxes) v X Ltd* Vol II p 45

cost of replacement of weighbridge house *JT Hodgins (Inspector of Taxes) v Plunder & Pollak (Ireland) Ltd* Vol II p 267

deduction from excess profits duty for replacement of capital items *Boland's Ltd v The Commissioners of Inland Revenue* Vol I p 34

deduction of corporation profits tax and excess corporation profits tax in computing profits for income tax purposes *J M O'Dwyer (Inspector of Taxes) v The Dublin United Transport Co Ltd* Vol II p 115

deduction of management expenses of investment company Hibernian Insurance Company Limited v MacUimis (Inspector of Taxes) 2000 p 75

expenditure on mill *sanitation JB Vale (Inspector of Taxes) v Martin Mahony & Brothers Ltd* Vol II p 32

expenditure on temporary *premises Martin Fitzgerald v Commissioners of Inland Revenue* Vol I p 91

expenses of promoting Bill in Parliament *McGarry (Inspector of Taxes) v Limerick Gas Committee* Vol I p 375

foreign company trading in Ireland provision for devaluation of foreign currency not allowed as deduction from profits. *The Revenue Commissioners v L & Co* Vol II p 281

formation expenses, whether allowable against trading profits *JB Kealy (Inspector of Taxes) v O'Mara (Limerick) Ltd* Vol I p 642

inadmissible, whether the inspector of taxes had made a "discovery" on finding that inadmissible deductions had been allowed in the computation of the company's tax liability for certain years and whether he was entitled to raise additional assessments for those years *W Ltd v Wilson (Inspector of Taxes)* Vol II p 627

incidental expenses, whether a deduction should be allowed under ITA 1967 Schedule 2 para 3, in respect of incidental expenses *MacDaibheid (Inspector of Taxes) v SD* Vol III p 1

legal fees in defending action in High Court for balance alleged to be due to a building contractor in respect of the construction of cinema, whether allowable Case I deduction *Casey (Inspector of Taxes) v AB Ltd* Vol II p 500

on rebuilding of business premises, whether portion thereof deductible in computing profits *Curtin (Inspector of Taxes) v M Ltd* Vol II p 360

removing top-soil from surface of quarry *Milverton Quarries Ltd v The Revenue Commissioners* Vol II p 382

whether expenditure incurred by petrol marketing company under exclusivity agreements with retailers is revenue or capital *Dolan (Inspector of Taxes) v AB Co Ltd* Vol II p 515

whether expenses of management or by management *Hiberian Insurance Co Ltd v MasUimis (Inspector of Taxes)* Vol V p 495, 2000 p 75

woodlands, whether purchasing and planting of trees is allowable deduction from farming profits *Connolly (Inspector of Taxes) v WW* Vol II p 657

Deductions (contd)

SCHEDULE D CASE III

interest *Phillips (Inspector of Taxes) v Limerick County Council* Vol I p 66

SCHEDULE D CASE V

whether letting fees and legal expenses incurred by the company in respect of first lettings of property qualified as deductions under ITA 1967 s 81(5)(*d*) *GH Ltd v Browne (Inspector of Taxes)* Vol III p 95

SCHEDULE E

travelling expenses *Phillips (Inspector of Taxes) v Keane* Vol I p 64, *SP O'Broin (Inspector of Taxes) v Mac Giolla Meidhre/Finbar Pigott* Vol II p 366 and *HF Kelly (Inspector of Taxes) v H* Vol II p 460

MANAGEMENT EXPENSES

by investment company *Howth Estate Co v WJ Davis (Inspector of Taxes)* Vol I p 447

losses in holding company, whether notional management fees deductible Corporation tax *Belville Holdings Ltd (in receivership and liquidation) v Cronin (Inspector of Taxes)* Vol III p 340

Delegation of powers

by Government to Customs and Excise department whether unconstitutional *Charles McDaid v His Honour Judge David Sheehy, the Director of Public Prosecutions & Others* Vol IV p 162, Vol V p 696

Deposit

company engaged in manufacture and erection of prefabricated buildings deposit of 15 per cent of total cost paid on execution of contract, whether payment on account of trading stock or security for contracts *O'Laoghaire (Inspector of Taxes) v CD Ltd* Vol III p 51

whether expenses of management or by management *Hibernian Insurance Co Ltd v MacUimis (Inspector of Taxes)* Vol V p 495, 2000 p 75

company engaged in manufacture and export of ambulances, deposit received on foot of obligation with bank, whether income from trade *JG Kerrane (Inspector of Taxes) v N Hanlon (Ireland) Ltd* Vol III p 633

Designated areas

capital allowances, whether plant used exclusively in designated area, whether allowance extends to plant used under a hire contract *Daniel McNally v S O Maoldhomhniaigh* Vol IV p 22

Determination of an appeal

assessment of builders profits *The State (at the prosecution of Patrick J Whelan) v Michael Smidic (Special Commissioners of Income Tax)* Vol I p 571

statutory provision requiring person to express dissatisfaction with the determination of a point of law "immediately after the determination" *The State (Multiprint Label Systems Ltd) v The Honourable Justice Thomas Neylon* Vol III p 159

Development of land

trading property company, farm land, letting to partners on conacre, area zoned for development, land transferred to new company, whether land trading stock of company *L O hArgain (Inspector of Taxes) v B Ltd* Vol III p 9

whether the surplus from the sale of property was profit of a trade of dealing in or developing land, or the profit of a business which was deemed by F(MP)A 1968 s 17, to be such a trade *Mara (Inspector of Taxes) v GG (Hummingbird) Ltd* Vol II p 667

Development land

valuation agricultural land, appeal against market value at 6 April 1974 as determined by Circuit Court, whether agricultural value the sole determining factor, whether development potential attached on 6 April 1974, whether subsequent planning permission for milk processing plant relevant *J McMahon (Inspector of Taxes) v Albert Noel Murphy* Vol IV p 125

Director

resident abroad, of a company incorporated in the State but managed and controlled abroad. whether Schedule E employment *WJ Tipping (Inspector of Taxes) v Louis Jeancard* Vol II p 68

Disabled persons

redundancy payments to disabled employees, whether exempt from income tax, whether distinction to be made between disabled employees whose jobs continued and disabled employees whose jobs ceased p *O Cahill (Inspector of Taxes) v Albert Harding & Others* Vol IV p 233

to what extent must disabled persons be disabled to import goods eg motor vehicle free of excise duty *Michael Wiley v The Revenue Commissioners* Vol IV p 170

Discontinuance

of trade *Boland's Ltd v Davis (Inspector of Taxes)* Vol I p 86

Discovery

right to reopen assessment of Inspectors of Taxes *Hammond Lane Metal Co Ltd v S O'Culacháin (Inspector of Taxes)* Vol IV 197 *W Ltd v Wilson (Inspector of Taxes)* Vol II p 627

Discretionary trust

discretionary powers of trustees, meaning of dependents *Crowe Engineering Ltd v Phyllis Lynch and Others* Vol IV p 340

interpretation of residuary bequest, whether bequest failed for uncertainty, whether bequest infringed rule against perpetual trusts *In the Matter of the Estate of Mary Davoren, Deceased; Thomas O'Byrne v Michael Davoren and Anne Coughlan* Vol V p 36

when absolute interest passes *BKJ v The Revenue Commissioners* Vol III p 104

Disposal

of assets at an undervalue by a company *Kill Inn Motel Ltd (In Liquidation) v The Companies Acts 1963/1983* Vol III p 706

of property by mortgagee as nominee for mortgagor, accountable person for capital gains tax purposes, repayment of 15% deducted by purchaser in the absence of tax clearance certificate *Bank of Ireland Finance Ltd v The Revenue Commissioners* Vol IV p 217

Disposal (contd)
paper for paper transaction, capital gains tax implications *PJ O'Connell v T Keleghan* 999-2000 p 143

Disposition of income
deed of appointment by parent in favour of child *EG v Mac Shamhrain, (Inspector of Taxes)* Vol II p 352

deed of trust in favour of charitable objects with provision for re-vestment of income in settlor in certain contingencies, whether income of settlor or trustees *HPC Hughes (Inspector of Taxes) v Miss Gretta Smyth (Sister Mary Bernard) & Others* Vol I p 411

in favour of children *JM O'Dwyer (Inspector of Taxes) v Cafolla & Co* Vol II p 82

Distance trades
Boland's Ltd v Davis (Inspector of Taxes) Vol I p 86

Distributions
interest paid by Irish subsidiary to Japanese parent company on loan from parent company whether tax should be deducted at source under Double Tax Treaty or hether the payment should be treated as distribution under Schedule F *Murphy (Inspector of Taxes) v Asahi Synthetic Fibres (Ireland) Ltd* Vol III p 246

Dividends
from sales of capital assets whether liable to corporation profits tax *K Co v Hogan (Inspector of Taxes)* Vol III p 56

payment of, whether payment through inter-company account was sufficient evidence of actual payment, whether payment of cheque required, whether making of accounting entry a mere record of underlying transaction, whether a dividend declared on 11 December 1980 was received by related company not later than 12 December 1980, whether making of journal entries after 23 December 1980 material evidence *Sean Murphy (Inspector of Taxes) v The Borden Co Ltd* Vol III p 559

whether dividends paid represented profit earning capacity of a company, *E A Smyth v The Revenue Commissioners* Vol V p 532

Doctrines of res judicata and equitable estoppel
Boland's Ltd v The Commissioners of Inland Revenue Vol I p 34

Domicile
Captain R H Prior-Wandesforde v The Revenue Commissioners Vol I p 249, *The Right Hon Earl of Iveagh v The Revenue Commissioners* Vol I p 259, *In the Goods of Bernard Louis Rowan, Deceased Joseph Rowan v Vera Agnes Rowan & Others* Vol III p 572, *Proes v The Revenue Commissioners* Vol V p 481

common law rule that wife takes domicile of dependence of her husband, whether constitutional *JW v JW* Vol IV p 437

DORA requisition orders
liability in respect of transactions under *Arthur Guinness Son & Co Ltd v Commissioners of Inland Revenue* Vol I p 1

Double taxation relief
wife's remuneration taxed in Northern Ireland - whether appellant entitled to double taxation relief in Ireland *John Travers v Sean O'Siochain (Inspector of Taxes)* Vol V p 54

E

Earned income

income from the leasing of premises, whether leasing constitutes trading whether earned income *Pairceir (Inspector of Taxes) v EM* Vol II p 596

Ejusdem generis rule

as applied in interpretation of statutes *M Cronin (Inspector of Taxes) v Lunham Brothers Ltd* Vol III p 370

Emoluments

of office, grant to a President of a college on retirement *JD Mulvey (Inspector of Taxes) v Denis J Coffey* Vol I p 618

of employment, rent paid for employee *Connolly (Inspector of Taxes) v Denis McNamara* Vol II p 452

professional services rendered without prior agreement as regards remuneration payment on termination of services whether chargeable as income *WS McGarry (Inspector of Taxes) v E F* Vol II p 261

Employee

branch manager of local Employment Office of Dept of Social Welfare *O'Coindealbhain (Inspector of Taxes) v TB Mooney* Vol IV p 45

demonstrator of food products at supermarket, whether an employee or self-employed *H Denny & Sons (Irl) Ltd v Minister for Social Welfare* Vol V p 238

whether a member of the crew of a fishing vessel can be an "employee", whether there can be an "employee" without there being a corresponding employer, whether Social Welfare (Consolidation) Act 1981 applies to self employed persons, whether scheme of Act and regulations is limited to employer/employee circumstances whether Minister has unlimited power to make regulations enabling any person to be treated as an employee *The Minister for Social Welfare v John Griffiths* Vol IV p 378

whether director became employee of company *Patrick J O'Connell (Inspector of Taxes) v Thomas Keleghan* 2001 p 103

whether share fishermen employed on contract of service or engaged in a joint venture with boat owner *Francis Griffin v Minister for Social, Community and Family Affairs* 2001 p 125

wholesale distributors of newspapers *Tony McAuliffe v Minister for Social Welfare* Vol V p 94

Employments

appeal as to whether a contract of services or a contract for services - wholesale distributor of newspapers, *Tony McAuliffe v The Minister for Social Welfare* Vol V p 94

branch manager of local Employment Office of Dept of Social Welfare whether the taxpayer was engaged under a contract of service or a contract for services *O'Coindealbhain (Inspector of Taxes) v TB Mooney* Vol IV p 45

contract of service or contract for services, temporary employee engaged through an employment agency *The Minister for Labour v PMPA Insurance Co Ltd (under administration)* Vol III p 505

demonstrator of food products at supermarket, whether an employee or self-employed *H Denny & Sons (Irl) Ltd v Minister for Social Welfare* Vol V p 238

director resident abroad, of a company incorporated in the State but managed and controlled abroad. whether Schedule E employment *W J Tipping (Inspector of Taxes) v Louis Jeancard* Vol II p 68

whether contract for services between skipper of fishing vessel and crew members, *Director of Public Prosecutions v Martin McLoughlin* Vol III p 467

whether dockers working under a pooling arrangement can receive unemployment benefit when they are not occupied unloading ships, whether dockers had a contract of employment with their Association, separate contracts on each occasion of their employment, whether level of earnings material to question of employment *James Louth & Others v Minister for Social Welfare* Vol IV p 391

whether the taxpayer was engaged under a contract of service or a contract for services *McDermott (Inspector of Taxes) v BC* Vol III p 43

Employer's obligations

to deduct PAYE and PRSI from employee's emoluments *EN Hearne (Inspector of Taxes) v O'Cionna & Others T/A J A Kenny & Partners* Vol IV p 113

Enforcement of Revenue Debts

Governor & Co of Bank of Ireland v Michael John Meeneghan and Others Vol V p 44 *In the Matter of the Extradition Acts John Oliver Byrne v Noel Conroy* 1998 p 75

Errors

inadmissible deductions, whether the inspector of taxes had made a "discovery" on finding that inadmissible deductions had been allowed in the computation of the company's tax liability for certain years and whether he was entitled to raise additional assessments for those years *W Ltd v Wilson (Inspector of Taxes)* Vol II p 627

Estate company

expenses of management, company whose business consists mainly in the making of investments *Casey (Inspector of Taxes) v The Monteagle Estate* Co Vol II p 429

Estate duty

whether conveyancing form determines liability *The Attorney General v Power & Anor* Vol V p 525

charitable bequest, whether it had to be expended in Ireland *The Revenue Commissioners v The Most Reverend Edward Doorley* Vol V p 539

Estate duty (contd)

whether due when consideration is stated in receipt clause of deed but payment is not pursued by the disponer *Revenue v Daniel Anthony Moroney & Ors* Vol V p 589

whether surviving spouse competent to dispose of statutory share in estate *In Re the Estate of Urquhart, D (Decd) & Revenue Commissioners v AIB Ltd* Vol V p 600

Estoppel

whether stamped conveyance invalid *Parkes (Roberta) v David Parkes* 1998 p 169

Evasion

locus standi evasion of customs duties on specified goods *Gerard Curtis and Brendan Geough v The Attorney General and The Revenue Commissioners* Vol III p 419

Evasion (contd)

and bank advice relating to availing of tax amnesty *Michael Gaysan v Allied Irish Banks Plc* 2000 p 105

Evidence

secondary evidence that beneficial interest in securities had been transferred not admissible *Gilbert Hewson v JB Kealy (Inspector of Taxes)* Vol II p 15

Ex gratia payments

by British government for malicious damage to property or personal injury sustained, whether trading receipt *WA Robinson T/A James Pim & Son v JD Dolan (Inspector of Taxes)* Vol I p 427

Excess corporation profits tax

whether excess corporation profits tax is exigible for accounting periods in respect of which no corporation profits tax (other than excess corporation profits tax) is payable *The Revenue Commissioners v Orwell Ltd* Vol II p 326

Excess profits duty

accounting period, whether Revenue Commissioners are required to determine *The Revenue Commissioners v R Hilliard & Sons Ltd* Vol II p 130

brewery, whether liability in respect of transactions under DORA requisition orders *Arthur Guinness Son & Co Ltd v Commissioners of Inland Revenue* Vol I p 1

deductions from, expenditure on temporary premises *Martin Fitzgerald v Commissioners of Inland Revenue* Vol I p 91

notional loss in trade from decrease in value of stock not allowed *The Revenue Commissioners v Latchford & Sons Ltd* Vol I p 240

profits, whether ascertained by actual or standard percentage *Boland's Ltd v The Commissioners of Inland Revenue* Vol I p 34

stock relief, definition of trading stock in hand *Green & Co (Cork) Ltd v The Revenue Commissioners* Vol I p 130

whiskey in bond sold by publican *McCall (deceased) v Commissioners of Inland Revenue* Vol I p 28

Exchange loss

on foreign currency loans, whether capital or revenue *TG Brosnan (Inspector of Taxes) v Mutual Enterprises Ltd* Vol V p 138

Excise duty

bookmaker convicted and fined in the District Court of offences under the Betting Acts penal warrant for imprisonment, whether constitutional *John B Murphy v District Justice Brendan Wallace & Others* Vol IV p 278

imposed on proprietors of slaughter houses and exporters of live animals, whether ultra vires and void *Doyle & Others v An Taoiseach & Others* Vol III p 73

non-payment of excise duty payable on bets entered into by the defendant a registered bookmaker, whether recovery of an excise penalty a criminal matter *The Director of Public Prosecutions v Seamus Boyle* Vol IV p 395

publican's licence, whether new licence obtainable, whether application within six year period, meaning of year immediately preceding *Peter Connolly v The Collector of Customs and Excise* Vol IV p 419

Excise duty (contd)

to what extent must disabled persons be disabled to import goods eg motor vehicle free of excise duty *Michael Wiley v The Revenue Commissioners* Vol IV p 170

whether creditor to resort to securities received from principal before proceeding against surety *The Attorney General v Sun Alliance and London Insurance Ltd* Vol III p 265

whether Imposition of Duties Act 1957 s 1 is constitutional *C Mc Daid v His Honour Judge Sheehy & Ors* Vol V p 696

whether zero rated for VAT purposes, *DH Burke & Sons Ltd v The Revenue Commissioners, Ireland and The Attorney General* Vol V p 418

Exclusivity agreements

whether expenditure incurred by petrol marketing company under exclusivity agreements with retailers is revenue or capital *Dolan (Inspector of Taxes) v AB Co Ltd* Vol II p 515

Executor

carrying on trade, recovery by executor of debts allowed as bad debts in lifetime of deceased, whether a trading receipt *CD v JM O'Sullivan (Inspector of Taxes)* Vol II p 140

Exemptions

AGRICULTURAL SOCIETY

definition of *The Trustees of The Ward Union Hunt Races v Hughes (Inspector of Taxes)* Vol I p 538

ARTISTIC

exemption of earnings from original and creative works of artistic or cultural merit, whether journalism qualifies *John Healy v SI Breathnach (Inspector of Taxes)* Vol III p 496

legal text books, refusal by inspector of taxes to grant exemption from income tax under FA 1969 s 2, Exemption granted if the books are original and creative works which are generally recognised as having cultural or artistic merit *Michael Forde Decision* Vol IV p 348

BUILDING SOCIETIES

instruments relating to the internal affairs of a society were exempt from stamp duty, whether this exemption extended to a transfer of a premises to a society to conduct its business *Irish Nationwide Building Society v Revenue Commissioners* Vol IV p 296

CHARITIES

trade carried on by beneficiary of charity, whether exempt *Beirne (Inspector of Taxes) v St Vincent De Paul Society (Wexford Conference)* Vol I p 383

INDUSTRIAL AND PROVIDENT SOCIETIES

surplus of co-op from dealing with members, whether trading profits, whether exempt *Kennedy (Inspector of Taxes) v The Rattoo Co-operative Dairy Society Ltd* Vol I p 315

ORIGINAL AND CREATIVE

writing, school textbooks - whether within the meaning of FA 1969 s 2 *The Revenue Commissioners v Colm O'Loinsigh* Vol V p 98

Expenditure

loan interest payable after redemption of share capital whether allowable trading expense, *Sean MacAonghusa v Ringmahon* 1999 p 81

on installation of suspended ceiling in supermarket whether plant qualifying for capital allowances *Dunnes Stores (Oakville) Ltd v MC Cronin (Inspector of Taxes)* Vol IV p 68

on mill sanitation *JB Vale (Inspector Of Taxes) v Martin Mahony & Brothers Ltd* Vol II p 32

on racecourse stand, whether deductible as repairs *Michael O'Grady (Inspector of Taxes) v Roscommon Race Committee* Vol IV p 425

on rebuilding of business premises whether portion thereof deductible in computing profits *Curtin (Inspector of Taxes) v M Ltd* Vol II p 360

on temporary premises *Martin Fitzgerald v Commissioners of Inland Revenue* Vol I p 91

Expenses

allowance of, where assessment has been confirmed *The King (Harris Stein) v The Special Commissioners* Vol 1 p 62

compensation paid to tenants of adjoining premises for interference with light and air, whether allowable Case I deduction *WJ Davis (Inspector of Taxes) v X Ltd* Vol II p 45

deduction of expenses of management by investment company *Howth Estate Co v W J Davis (Inspector of Taxes)* Vol I p 447

formation expenses, whether allowable against trading profits *JB Kealy (Inspector of Taxes) v O'Mara (Limerick) Ltd* Vol I p 642

from Schedule E *SP O'Broin (Inspector of Taxes) v Mac Giolla Meidhre/Finbar Pigott* Vol II p 366 and *HF Kelly (Inspector of Taxes) v H* Vol II p 460

incidental expenses, whether a deduction should be allowed under ITA 1967 Sch 2 para 3 *MacDaibheid (Inspector of Taxes) v SD* Vol III p 1

of management, investment appraisal expenditure whether allowable as management expense *Hibernian Insurance Co Ltd v MacUimis (Inspector of Taxes)* 2000 p 75

of management, company whose business consists mainly in the making of investments *Casey (Inspector of Taxes) v The Monteagle Estate Co* Vol II p 429

of management, whether tax deductible, meaning of *Hibernian Insurance Company Limited v MacUimis (Inspector of Taxes)* Vol V p 495, 2000 p 75

of management, whether auctioneer's/solicitors fees are revenue or capital - *Stephen Court Ltd v JA Browne (Inspector of Taxes)* Vol V p 680

of promoting bill in Parliament *McGarry (Inspector of Taxes) v Limerick Gas Committee* Vol I p 375

of removing top soil from surface of quarry whether capital or revenue expenditure *Milverton Quarries Ltd v The Revenue Commissioners* Vol II p 382

Export sales relief

ambulances manufactured in the State and exported *JG Kerrane (Inspector of Taxes) v N Hanlon (Ireland) Ltd* Vol III p 633

sale of meat into intervention, exporter need not be owner at time of export *Cronin (Inspector of Taxes) v IMP Midleton Ltd* Vol III p 452

whether mining operation qualifies for ESR or capital allowances *Patrick J O'Connell (Inspector of Taxes) v Tara Mines Ltd* 2001 p 79

Exported Live Stock (Insurance) Board

statutory body, whether carrying on a trade *The Exported Live Stock (Insurance) Board v T J Carroll (Inspector of Taxes)* Vol II p 211

Export refunds

milk products, whether a whey or skimmed milk product, whether export refunds on consignments from EC countries to non EC countries, whether re-classification renders products liable for repayment of export refunds, whether Revenue Commissioners responsible for classification whether Revenue Commissioners and state chemist negligent and in breach of duty whether Minister entitled to counterclaim against plaintiff *Carbery Milk Products Ltd v The Minister for Agriculture & Others* Vol IV p 492

Extension

of period for making distribution of dividends *Rahinstown Estates Co v M Hughes (Inspector of Taxes)* Vol III p 517

Extradition Order

appeal on grounds of a revenue offence, whether EEC levies constitute a tax *John Oliver Byrne v Noel Conroy* 1998 p 75

F

Fair Procedures

constitutional right to fair procedures *Charles J Haughey & Others v Moriarty & Others* 1998 p 119

Farm tax

whether implementation of Farm Tax Act constituted unfair procedures, effect of repeal of that Act, consequences of absence of amending legislation *Purcell v Attorney General* Vol IV p 229, Vol V p 288

Farming

BLOODSTOCK

animal bought in course of trade, sent to stud after successful racing career and subsequently sold to a syndicate whether amount realised on syndication a trading receipt *Mac Giolla Riogh (Inspector of Taxes) v G Ltd* Vol II p 315

CATTLEDEALER

whether the taxpayer was a "dealer in cattle" within the meaning of ITA 1918 Sch D Case III rule 4 and ITA 1967 s 78 *De Brun (Inspector of Taxes) v K* Vol III p 19

MARKET GARDENING

valuation of land occupied for market gardening *L v WS McGarry (Inspector of Taxes)* Vol II p 241

OCCUPATION OF LANDS

whether the appellant company was in occupation of lands, forming part of a military establishment, for the purposes of ITA 1918 Sch B or ITA 1967 *O Conaill (Inspector of Taxes) v Z Ltd* Vol II p 636

Farming (contd)

PIG REARING

whether the activity of intensive pig rearing constituted farming for the purposes of FA 1974 s 13(1) *Knockhall Piggeries v JG Kerrane (Inspector of Taxes)* Vol III p 319

WOODLANDS

whether purchasing and planting of trees is allowable deduction from farming profits *Connolly (Inspector of Taxes) v WW* Vol II p 657

Fees

due to a barrister prior to his appointment to the bench, fees refused but could be paid to a family company if solicitors so wished *EP O'Coindealbhain (Inspector of Taxes) v The Honourable Mr Justice Sean Gannon* Vol III p 484

High Court fees on funds realised by liquidator in course of liquidation, whether applicable to secured creditors or to proceeds of sale of property subject to a fixed charge *Michael Orr (Kilternan) Ltd v The Companies Acts 1963-1983, and Thornberry Construction (Irl) Ltd v The Companies Acts 1963-1983* Vol III p 530

Film production

whether accounting periods prior to FA 1990 qualify for relief *Saatchi & Saatchi Advertising Ltd v Kevin McGarry (Inspector of Taxes)* Vol V p 376

Finality

of Special Commissioners' decision *The King (Evelyn Spain) v The Special Commissioners* Vol I p 221

Finance company

dealing in stocks and shares, whether investments should be valued at cost or market value *AB Ltd v Mac Giolla Riogh (Inspector of Taxes)* Vol II p 419

Fixtures

installation of fixtures subject to low rate of value added tax, whether or not television aerials attached to roof of a house are fixtures *John Maye v The Revenue Commissioners* Vol III p 332

Foreign company

director resident abroad, of a company incorporated in the State but managed and controlled abroad. whether Schedule E employment *WJ Tipping (Inspector of Taxes) v Louis Jeancard* Vol II p 68

foreign company trading in Ireland provision for devaluation of foreign currency not allowed as deduction from profits. *The Revenue Commissioners v L & Co* Vol II p 281

Foreign currency loans

whether exchange loss is capital or revenue *TG Brosnan (Inspector of Taxes) v Mutual Enterprises Ltd* Vol V p 138

Foreign pension

pension received by Irish resident from British company, whether income from foreign possession *McHugh (Inspector of Taxes) v A* Vol II p 393 and *Forbes (Inspector of Taxes) v GHD* Vol II p 491

Foreign property

claim for relief under ITA 1918 Case V rule 3, question of residence and domicile *Captain R H Prior-Wandesforde v the Revenue* Commissioners Vol I p 249 and *The Right Hon The Earl of Iveagh v The Revenue Commissioners* Vol I p 259

Foreign Revenue Debt

UK vat, *Governor & Co of the Bank of Ireland v Meenaghan & Ors* Vol V p 44

Foreign tax

whether recoverable in Ireland *Governor & Co of the Bank of Ireland v Michael John Meeneghan & Ors* Vol V p 44

Foreign trades

basis of assessment under Case III *O'Conaill (Inspector of Taxes) v R* Vol II p 304

Formation expenses

whether allowable against trading profits *JB Kealy (Inspector of Taxes) v O'Mara (Limerick) Ltd* Vol I p 642

Forward purchase contracts

fall in market value of goods before delivery, *The Revenue Commissioners v Latchford & Sons Ltd* Vol I p 240

Fraudulent Conveyances Act 1634 (10 Charles 1)

Kill Inn Motel Ltd (In Liquidation) v The Companies Acts 1963/1983 Vol III p 706

Fuel merchants

whether new trade of coal mining was set up or commenced *HA O'Loan (Inspector of Taxes) v Messrs MJ Noone & Co* Vol II p 146

Functions of courts

and legislature *McGrath & Or v JE McDermott (Inspector of Taxes)* Vol III p 683

Funds in court

whether general rules applicable Schedules A, B, C, D and E apply to the court when paying interest on debts out of funds in court and whether tax deductible from income accrued to funds in court for years prior to 1922/23 *Colclough v Colclough* Vol II p 332

G

Gifts

made by a company *Kill Inn Motel Ltd (In Liquidation) v The Companies Acts 1963/1983* Vol III p 706

whether "marriage gratuity" received on resignation was a retirement payment under ITA 1967 s 114 or was a perquisite of her office under ITA 1967 s 110 *Sean O'Siochain (Inspector of Taxes v Thomas Morrissey Eleanor Morrissey* Vol IV p 407

whether present from employer taxable as gift, or emolument under Schedule E *Wing v O'Connell (Inspector of Taxes)* Vol I p 155

whether gift arises when consideration is stated in receipt clause of deed but payment is not pursued by the disponer *The Revenue Commissioners v Daniel Anthony Moroney & Ors* Vol V p 589

Goods

distinguished from services *Dunnes Stores (Oakville) Ltd v MC Cronin (Inspector of Taxes)* Vol IV p 68

Government stocks

purchased to comply with Central Bank requirements, whether carrying on trade of dealing in securities, whether liable as profits under Schedule D or exempt capital gains on Government stocks *JA Browne (Inspector of Taxes) v Bank of Ireland Finance Ltd* Vol III p 644

Ground rents

whether fines and capitalised value of ground rents are assessable to tax *Birch (Inspector of Taxes) v Denis Delaney* Vol I p 515

Group relief

whether the expression "total income means income before or after the deduction of group relief *Cronin (Inspector of Taxes) v Youghal Carpets (Yarns) Ltd* Vol III p 229

Group companies

recovery of outstanding taxes from a group of companies, whether Revenue Commissioners may appropriate payments between separate companies within the group, whether insolvency of a company is relevant to gratuitous alienation of assets *Frederick Inns Ltd, The Rendezvous Ltd, The Graduate Ltd, Motels Ltd (In Liquidation) v The Companies Acts 1963-1986* Vol IV p 247

H

Hauliers

whether lorry owners carrying sand and gravel were engaged as subcontractors under a construction contract, whether the lorry owners became the proprietors of the quarry materials *O'Grady v Laragan Quarries Ltd* Vol IV p 269

High Court

powers of determination of tax liability by High Court and Appeal Commissioners whether mutually exclusive, nature of powers and functions of Appeal Commissioners limited or unlimited *The State (Calcul International Ltd and Solatrex International Ltd) v The Appeal Commissioners and The Revenue Commissioners* Vol III p 530

High Court fees

on funds realised by liquidator in course of liquidation, whether applicable to secured creditors or to proceeds of sale of property subject to a fixed charge *Michael Orr (Kilternan) Ltd v The Companies Acts 1963-1983, and Thornberry Construction (Irl) Ltd v The Companies Acts 1963-1983* Vol III p 530

Historical cost accounting

method of accounting for tax purposes, whether replacement cost basis is acceptable or whether historical cost accounting is the only method of commercial accountancy *Carroll Industries Plc (formerly PJ Carroll & Co Ltd) and PJ Carroll & Co Ltd v S O'Culachain (Inspector of Taxes)* Vol IV p 135

Holiday cottages

whether qualifying for capital allowances *McMahon, T & Ors v Rt Hon Lord Mayor Alderman & Burgess of Dublin* Vol V p 357

Holidays (Employees) Act 1973

The Minister for Labour v PMPA Insurance Co Ltd (under administration) Vol III p 505

Hospital

whether carrying on a trade *RG Davis (Inspector of Taxes) v The Superioress Mater Misericordiae Hospital, Dublin* Vol I p 387

Husband

and wife, living apart *Donovan (Inspector Of Taxes) v CG Crofts* Vol I p 115

and wife, living together *Ua Clothasaigh (Inspector of Taxes) v McCartan* Vol II p 75

tax paid by a married couple in excess of the amounts payable by a husband and wife if taxed as separate persons, *Francis & Mary Murphy v AG* Vol V p 613

wife's income from securities assessed on husband in first year of wife's income from securities *JD Mulvey (Inspector of Taxes) v RM Kieran* Vol I p 563

I

Illegal trades

not assessable to tax *C Hayes (Inspector of Taxes) v RJ Duggan* Vol I p 195

Immediately

statutory provision requiring person to express dissatisfaction with the determination of a point of law "immediately after the determination" *The State (Multiprint Label Systems Ltd) v The Honourable Justice Thomas Neylon* Vol III p 159

Importation

of used motor vehicles from a Member State *Karl Keller v The Revenue Commissioners & Others* Vol IV p 512

Imprisonment

bookmaker convicted and fined in the District Court of offences under the Betting Acts penal warrant for imprisonment, whether constitutional *John B Murphy v District Justice Brendan Wallace & Others* Vol IV p 278

return of income, failure to make, appeal against a decision of the High Court to refuse on a judicial review application to quash three convictions with six months imprisonment for each offence imposed in the District Court on the appellant for failure to make income tax returns *Thomas O'Callaghan v JP Clifford & Others* Vol IV p 478

Incidental expenses

whether a deduction should be allowed under ITA 1967 Sch 2 para 3, in respect of incidental expenses *MacDaibheid (Inspector of Taxes) v SD* Vol III p 1

Income

accumulated for minor, benefit taken by way of capital *The King (Evelyn Spain) v The Special Commissioners* Vol I p 221

Income (contd)

father taking his elder children and his mother-in-law into partnership, subsequent assignment of mother-in-law's interest to his younger children whether income of children to be deemed to be income of father *JM O'Dwyer (Inspector of Taxes) v Cafolla & Co* Vol II p 82

from the leasing of premises, whether earned income *Pairceir (Inspector of Taxes) v EM* Vol II p 596

not "immediately derived" from a trade of business *JG Kerrane (Inspector of Taxes) v N Hanlon (Ireland) Ltd* Vol III p 633

on estate in course of administration *Moloney (Inspector of Taxes) v Allied Irish Banks Ltd as executors of the estate of Francis J Doherty deceased* Vol III p 477

payment for maintenance of residence not part of total income *The Most Honourable Frances Elizabeth Sarah Marchioness Conyngham v The Revenue Commissioners* Vol I p 231

personal pension and other assets assigned to company pension continued to be paid to pensioner, whether pensioner liable to tax on pension *Cronin (Inspector of Taxes) v C* Vol II p 592

professional services rendered without prior agreement as regards remuneration payment on termination of services whether chargeable as income *WS McGarry (Inspector of Taxes) v EF* Vol II p 261

received on foot of an obligation with bank *JG Kerrane (Inspector of Taxes) v N Hanlon (Ireland) Ltd* Vol III p 633

trust in favour of charitable objects with provision for re-vestment of income in settlor in certain contingencies, whether income of settlor or trustees *HPC Hughes (Inspector of Taxes) v Miss Gretta Smyth (Sister Mary Bernard) & Others* Vol I p 411

whether children's pension is treated as income of the parent or income of the children for income tax purposes *EP O'Coindealbhain (Inspector of Taxes) v Breda O'Carroll* Vol IV p 221

whether increase in widows contributory pension for children is taxable income of parent *Sean O'Siochain (Inspector of Taxes) v Bridget Neenan* Vol V p 472

Income tax

Acts *Michael Deighan v Edward N Hearne & Others* Vol III p 533

appeal to High Court by way of case stated from decision of Circuit Judge, failure to notify the respondent the fact that a case has been stated *A & B v WJ Davis (Inspector of Taxes)* Vol II p 60

application of provisions to corporation tax *Wayte (Holdings) Ltd (In Receivership) Alex Burns v Edward N Hearne* Vol III p 553

assessable profits, not received in the year of assessment *MacKeown (Inspector of Taxes) v Patrick J Roe* Vol I p 214

difference between contracts of and for service *Patrick J O'Connell (Inspector of Taxes) v Thomas Keleghan* 2001 p 103

domicile and ordinary residence *Captain R H Prior-Wandesforde v the Revenue Commissioners* Vol I p 249 and *The Right Hon The Earl of Iveagh v The Revenue Commissioners* Vol I p 259

exemption for agricultural societies *The Trustees of The Ward Union Hunt Races v Hughes (Inspector of Taxes)* Vol I p 538

Income tax (contd)

husband and wife living apart, wife's income assessed on husband *Donovan (Inspector of Taxes) v CG Crofts* Vol I p 115

husband and wife living together *D Ua Clothasaigh (Inspector of Taxes) v Patrick McCartan* Vol II p 75

residence of company *The Cunard Steam Ship Co Ltd v Herlihy (Inspector of Taxes), and The Cunard Steam Ship Co Ltd v Revenue Commissioners* Vol I p 330

school/colleges whether operated for charitable purposes *The Pharmaceutical Society of Ireland v The Revenue Commissioners* Vol I p 542

trust in favour of charitable objects with provision for re-vestment of income in settlor in certain contingencies, whether income of settlor or trustees *HPC Hughes (Inspector of Taxes) v Miss Smyth (Sister Mary Bernard) & Others* Vol I p 411

veterinary, body corporate performing statutory functions, whether profits liable to tax *The Veterinary Council v F Corr (Inspector of Taxes)* Vol II p 204

wife's income from securities assessed on husband in first year of wife's income from securities *JD Mulvey (Inspector of Taxes) v RM Kieran* Vol I p 563

RETURNS

of income, what constitutes a proper return of income for the assessment of income tax *MA Bairead v M McDonald* Vol IV p 475

SCHEDULE A

income tax paid, whether further balance due *Estate Of Teresa Downing (Owner)* Vol I p 487

SCHEDULE B

profits from stallion fees, whether liable to tax under Schedule B or Schedule D income tax paid, whether further balance due *Cloghran Stud Farm v AG Birch (Inspector of Taxes)* Vol I p 496

occupation of lands, whether the appellant company was in occupation of lands, forming part of a military establishment, for the purposes of ITA 1918 Schedule B or ITA 1967 *O Conaill (Inspector of Taxes) v Z Ltd* Vol II p 636

valuation of land occupied for market gardening *L v WS McGarry (Inspector of Taxes)* Vol II p 241

SCHEDULE D

assessment of builders profits *The State (at the prosecution of Patrick J Whelan) v Michael Smidic (Special Commissioners of Income Tax)* Vol I p 571 and *Edward Connolly v AG Birch (Inspector of Taxes)* Vol I p 583

change in nature of trade or new trade, trading as fuel merchants, whether new trade of coal mining was set up or commenced *HA O'Loan (Inspector of Taxes) v Messrs MJ Noone & Co* Vol II p 146

cost of replacement of weighbridge house, whether allowable deduction *JT Hodgins (Inspector of Taxes) v Plunder & Pollak (Ireland) Ltd* Vol II p 267

ex gratia payments, by British government for malicious damage to property or personal injury sustained, whether trading receipt *WA Robinson T/A James Pim & Son v JD Dolan (Inspector of Taxes)* Vol I p 427

management expenses, deduction of, by investment company *Howth Estate Co v WJ Davis (Inspector of Taxes)* Vol I p 447

Income tax (contd)
> nurseries and market gardens, assessment of income by reference to annual profits estimated according to the rules of Schedule D *WS McGarry (Inspector of Taxes) v JA Spencer* Vol II p 1
>
> obsolescence of assets *Evans & Co v Phillips (Inspector of Taxes)* Vol I p 43
>
> payment in advance on the signing of a lease, whether capital *O'Sullivan (Inspector of Taxes) v p Ltd* Vol II p 464
>
> personal pension assigned to company but continued to be paid to pensioner, whether pensioner liable to tax *Cronin (Inspector of Taxes) v C* Vol II p 592
>
> profits from stallion fees, whether liable to tax under Schedule B or Schedule D income tax paid, whether further balance due *Cloghran Stud Farm v AG Birch (Inspector of Taxes)* Vol I p 496
>
> profits of a bookmaker from transactions in Irish Hospital Sweepstakes tickets, whether receipts assessable to tax under Schedule D *HH v MJ Forbes (Inspector of Taxes)* Vol II p 614
>
> trade or business, brewery, whether liability in respect of transactions under DORA requisition orders *Arthur Guinness Son & Co Ltd v Commissioners of Inland Revenue* Vol I p 1
>
> SCHEDULE D, CASE I & II
>
> an obsolescence of assets *Evans & Co v Phillips (Inspector of Taxes)* Vol I p 43
>
> assessment of wife's first years income on husband *JD Mulvey (Inspector of Taxes) v RM Kieran* Vol I p 563
>
> SCHEDULE D, CASE I & II
>
> bad debts recovered *Bourke (Inspector of Taxes) v Lyster & Sons Ltd* Vol II p 374
>
> basis of assessment *JD Mulvey (Inspector of Taxes) v RM Kieran* Vol I p 563
>
> basis of assessment, commencement and cessation within a year, whether assessment for the previous year can be reviewed *AB v JD Mulvey (Inspector of Taxes)* Vol II p 55
>
> bloodstock, animal bought in course of trade, sent to stud after successful racing career and subsequently sold to a syndicate whether amount realised on syndication a trading receipt *Mac Giolla Riogh (Inspector of Taxes) v G Ltd* Vol II p 315
>
> builder's profits, capitalised value of ground rents and fines, whether liable to tax *Birch (Inspector of Taxes) v Denis Delaney* Vol I p 515 and *Edward Connolly v AG Birch (Inspector of Taxes)* Vol I p 583 and *Swaine (Inspector of Taxes) v VE* Vol II p 472
>
> compensation for loss of profits, whether income or capital receipt *The Alliance and Dublin Consumers' Gas Co v McWilliams (Inspector of Taxes)* Vol I p 207
>
> compensation for loss of profits, whether trading receipt *F Corr (Inspector of Taxes) v FE Larkin* Vol II p 164
>
> compensation paid to tenants of adjoining premises for interference with light and air, whether allowable Case I deduction *WJ Davis (Inspector of Taxes) v X Ltd* Vol II p 45
>
> compulsory sale to Minister for Finance, in return for sterling equivalents, of dollar balances consisting of income from securities etc, in the USA whether moneys so received assessable *JM O'Sullivan (Inspector of Taxes) v Julia O'Connor, as Administratrix of Evelyn H O'Brien, Deceased* Vol II p 61

Income tax (contd)

deduction for expenses of promoting bill in Parliament *McGarry (Inspector of Taxes) v Limerick Gas Committee* Vol I p 375

deduction for interest paid *Phillips (Inspector of Taxes) v Limerick County Council* Vol I p 66

deduction of corporation profits tax and excess corporation profits tax in computing profits for income tax purposes *JM O'Dwyer (Inspector of Taxes) v The Dublin United Transport Co Ltd* Vol II p 115

deduction of loss on realisation of investments *The Alliance & Dublin Consumers' Gas Co v Davis (Inspector of Taxes)* Vol I p 104

deduction, legal fees in defending action in High Court for balance alleged to be due to a building contractor in respect of the construction of cinema, whether allowable Case I deduction *Casey (Inspector of Taxes) v AB Ltd* Vol II p 500

discontinuance of trade, set off of losses *Boland's Ltd v Davis (Inspector of Taxes)* Vol I p 86

ex gratia payments, by British government for malicious damage to property or personal injury sustained, whether trading receipt *WA Robinson T/A James Pim & Son v JD Dolan (Inspector of Taxes)* Vol I p 427

execution of document under seal of the Isle of Man, Secondary evidence that beneficial interest in securities had been transferred not admissible *Gilbert Hewson v JB Kealy (Inspector of Taxes)* Vol II p 15

formation expenses, whether allowable against trading profits *JB Kealy (Inspector of Taxes) v O'Mara (Limerick) Ltd* Vol I p 642

hospital and private nursing home whether carrying on a trade *RG Davis (Inspector of Taxes) v The Superioress, Mater Misericordiae Hospital, Dublin* Vol I p 387

SCHEDULE D, CASE I & II

illegal trades, not assessable to tax *C Hayes (Inspector of Taxes) v RJ Duggan* Vol I p 195 and *Daniel Collins and Michael Byrne Daniel Collins and Redmond Power as Executor of the Will of Michael Byrne, deceased and Daniel Collins v JD Mulvey (Inspector of Taxes)* Vol II p 291

income from the leasing of premises, whether leasing constitutes trading whether earned income *Pairceir (Inspector of Taxes) v EM* Vol I p 596

Industrial and Provident Societies, trading with both members and non-members, investments and property purchased out of trading profits, whether the dividends and rents form part of the profits of the trade *The Revenue Commissioners v Y Ltd* Vol II p 195

losses forward *Molmac Ltd v MacGiolla Riogh (Inspector of Taxes)* Vol II p 482

lump sum paid on execution of lease, whether capital payment or rent paid in advance, whether liable under Case I and II or Case III *W Flynn (Inspector of Taxes) v John Noone Ltd, and W Flynn (Inspector of Taxes) v Blackwood & Co (Sligo) Ltd* Vol II p 222

on rebuilding of business premises, whether portion thereof deductible in computing profits *Curtin (Inspector of Taxes) v M Ltd* Vol II p 360

profit on realisation of investments, whether trading profit *Agricultural Credit Corporation Ltd v JB Vale (Inspector of Taxes)* Vol I p 474 and *Davis (Inspector of Taxes) v Hibernian Bank Ltd* Vol I p 503

removing top-soil from surface of quarry *Milverton Quarries Ltd v The Revenue Commissioners* Vol II p 382

Income tax (contd)

    statutory body, whether carrying on a trade *The Exported Live Stock (Insurance) Board v TJ Carroll (Inspector of Taxes)* Vol II p 211

    trade carried on by beneficiary of charity, whether exempt, *Beirne (Inspector of Taxes) v St Vincent De Paul Society (Wexford Conference)* Vol I p 383

    whether expenditure incurred by petrol marketing company under exclusivity agreements with retailers is revenue or capital *Dolan (Inspector of Taxes) v AB Co Ltd* Vol II p 515

    SCHEDULE D, CASE III

    foreign trades, basis of assessment under Case III *O'Conaill (Inspector of Taxes) v R* Vol II p 304

    interest received *Irish Provident Assurance Co Ltd (In Liquidation) v Kavanagh (Inspector of Taxes)* Vol I p 45

    ITA 1918 rule 7 *Evans & Co v Phillips (Inspector of Taxes)* Vol I p 43

    liability to, business carried on abroad *The Executors and Trustees of AC Ferguson (deceased) v Donovan (Inspector of Taxes)* Vol I p 183

    lump sum paid on execution of lease, whether capital payment or rent paid in advance, whether liable under Case I & II or Case III *W Flynn (Inspector of Taxes) v John Noone Ltd, and W Flynn (Inspector of Taxes) v Blackwood & Co (Sligo) Ltd* Vol II p 222

    pension received by Irish resident from British company, whether income from foreign possession *McHugh (Inspector of Taxes) v A* Vol I p 393 and *Forbes (Inspector of Taxes) v GHD* Vol II p 491

    settlement of income, deed of appointment by parent in favour of child *EG v Mac Shamhrain, (Inspector of Taxes)* Vol II p 352

    SCHEDULE D, CASE IV

    illegal trades, not assessable to tax under Case IV *C Hayes (Inspector of Taxes) v RJ Duggan* Vol I p 195

    lump sum paid on execution of lease, whether capital payment or rent paid in advance, whether liable under Case I & II or Case III *W Flynn (Inspector of Taxes) v John Noone Ltd; W Flynn (Inspector of Taxes) v Blackwood & Co (Sligo) Ltd* Vol II p 222

    professional services rendered without prior agreement as regards remuneration payment on termination of services whether chargeable as income *W S McGarry (Inspector of Taxes) v EF* Vol II p 261

    SCHEDULE D, CASE V

    domicile and ordinary residence *Captain RH Prior-Wandesforde v the Revenue Commissioners* Vol I p 249 and *The Right Hon The Earl of Iveagh v The Revenue Commissioners* Vol I p 259

    SCHEDULE E

    benefit in kind, rent paid for employee *Connolly (Inspector of Taxes) v Denis McNamara* Vol II p 452

    branch manager of local Employment Office of Dept of Social Welfare whether the taxpayer was engaged under a contract of service or a contract for services *O'Coindealbhain (Inspector of Taxes) v TB Mooney* Vol IV p 45

Income tax (contd)

calculation of PAYE due in respect of remuneration paid in year following that in which work was done, method of assessment *Bedford (Collector-General) v H* Vol II p 588

deductions *Phillips (Inspector of Taxes) v Keane* Vol I p 64

deductions *SP O'Broin (Inspector of Taxes) v Mac Giolla Meidhre/Finbar Pigott* Vol II p 366 and *HF Kelly (Inspector of Taxes) v H* Vol II p 460

director resident abroad, of a company incorporated in the State but managed and controlled abroad. whether Schedule E employment *WJ Tipping (Inspector of Taxes) v Louis Jeancard* Vol II p 68

interest due on overpayment of PAYE *O'Rourke v Revenue Commissioners* Vol V p 321

nun, whether assessable on earnings which are given to her order *JD Dolan (Inspector of Taxes) v "K" National School Teacher* Vol I p 656

present from employer, whether taxable as gift or emolument *Wing v O'Connell (Inspector of Taxes)* Vol I p 155

remuneration charging section provision in will charging rental income from estate with annual amount payable to beneficiary provided he continued to manage the property *Gerald O'Reilly v WJ Casey (Inspector of Taxes)* Vol I p 601

remuneration of office, grant to a President of a college on retirement *JD Mulvey (Inspector of Taxes) v Denis J Coffey* Vol I p 618

whether contract for services between skipper of fishing vessel and crew members *Director of Public Prosecutions v Martin McLoughlin* Vol III p 467

whether the taxpayer was engaged under a contract of service or a contract for services *McDermott (Inspector of Taxes) v BC* Vol III p 43

SCHEDULE F

interest paid by Irish subsidiary to Japanese parent company on loan from parent company whether tax should be deducted at source under Double Tax Treaty or whether the payment should be treated as distribution under Schedule F *Murphy (Inspector of Taxes) v Asahi Synthetic Fibres (Ireland) Ltd* Vol III p 246

Income tax and corporation profits tax

company in receivership preferential claim *The Attorney-General v Irish Steel Ltd and Vincent Crowley* Vol II p 108

Inducement payments

whether liable to income tax *PJ O'Connell (Inspector of Taxes) v T Keleghan* 2000 p 113

profit/trading receipts *O'Dwyer (Inspector of Taxes) and the Revenue Commissioners v Irish Exporters and Importers Ltd (In Liquidation)* Vol I p 629

Industrial and Provident Societies

surplus of co-op from dealing with members, whether trading profits, whether exempt *Kennedy (Inspector of Taxes) v The Rattoo Co-op Dairy Society Ltd* Vol I p 315

trading with both members and non-members, investments and property purchased out of trading profits, whether the dividends and rents form part of the profits of the trade *The Revenue Commissioners v Y Ltd* Vol II p 195

Industrial building

structure for dock undertaking, whether bonded transit sheds used as clearing house and not for storage qualify *Patrick Monahan (Drogheda) Ltd v O'Connell (Inspector of Taxes)* Vol III p 661

whether a building which housed offices, a showroom, a canteen, computer department and utilities qualified for industrial building allowance under ITA 1967 s 255 *O'Conaill (Inspector of Taxes) v JJ Ltd* Vol III p 65

Information

available to Revenue Commissioners, accountants working papers, whether the inspector of taxes is entitled to call for production of a taxpayer's nominal ledger, whether the nominal ledger formed part of the accountant's working papers *JJ Quigley (Inspector of Taxes) v Maurice Burke* Vol IV p 332, Vol V p 265

transfer of assets to offshore tax havens, whether accountants could be requested to furnish relevant particulars in respect of all their clients *Warnock & Others practising as Stokes Kennedy Crowley & Co v The Revenue Commissioners* Vol III p 356

Inspector

under Companies Act 1990, whether conduct of company warrants appointment *Dunnes Stores v Gerard Ryan and The Minister for Enterprise, Trade and Employment* 2000 p 261

Inspector of taxes

empowered to require of an individual by notice a return of income *Thomas O'Callaghan v JP Clifford & Others* Vol IV p 478

entitlement to recompute standard percentage basis of profits for excess profits duty *Boland's Ltd v The Commissioners of Inland Revenue* Vol I p 34

Interest

deduction for interest paid from interest received *Phillips (Inspector of Taxes) v Limerick County Council* Vol I 66

earned by non-resident company manufacturing through a branch in the State, tax free profits from branch paid into foreign bank account, whether interest earned on foreign bank account is taxable in Ireland *Murphy (Inspector of Taxes) v Dataproducts (Dublin) Ltd* Vol IV p 12

earned on deposit interest after date of liquidation *A Noyek & Sons Ltd (in voluntary liquidation), Alex Burns v Edward N Hearne* Vol III p 523

in possession, whether conveyancing form determines liability to estate duty *The Attorney General v Power & Anor* Vol V p 525

on loan after redemption of share capital, whether allowable as trade expense *Sean MacAonghusa v Ringmahon* 1999 p 81

on overpaid income tax, whether appeal of assessments under wrong Schedule rules out interest on overpayments of tax, whether appeal to nil assessments to tax rules out interest on overpayments on tax *O'Coindealbhain (Inspector of Taxes) v TB Mooney* Vol IV p 45

on overpaid PAYE, whether due or not, *O'Rourke v Revenue Commissioners* Vol V p 321

on repayment of tax *Navan Carpets Ltd v O'Culachain (Inspector of Taxes)* Vol III p 403

Interest (contd)

paid by a company to a person having controlling interest in that company *The Revenue Commissioners v Associated Properties Ltd* Vol II p 412

paid by Irish subsidiary to Japanese parent company on loan from parent company whether tax should be deducted at source under Double Tax Treaty or treated as distribution under Schedule F *Murphy (Inspector of Taxes) v Asahi Synthetic Fibres (Ireland) Ltd* Vol III p 246

repayment of interest on tax paid in mistake of law, common law right to restitution, rate of interest according to Courts of Justice Acts *O'Rourke v Revenue Commissioners* Vol V p 321

stamp duties, new interest and penalty provisions introduced by FA 1991 s 100 came into effect on 1 November 1991 and previous provision for interest and penalties under Stamp Act 1891 s 15 were repealed on 29 May 1991, the date of the passing of FA 1991, whether interest and penalties applied between 29 May 1991 and 1 November 1991 *Edward O'Leary v The Revenue Commissioners* Vol IV p 357 *Terence Byrne v The Revenue Commissioners* Vol V p 560

whether annual interest on loan to redeem preference shares is a deductible expense *Seán MacAonghusa (Inspector of Taxes) v Ringmahon Company* 2001 p 117

Interest and income from securities and possessions

execution of document under seal of the Isle of Man, secondary evidence that beneficial interest in securities had been transferred, not admissible *Gilbert Hewson v JB Kealy (Inspector of Taxes)* Vol II p 15

Interpretation of documents

Court entitled to look at reality of what has been done *Waterford Glass (Group Services) Ltd v The Revenue Commissioners* Vol IV p 194, *B McCabe (Inspector of Taxes) v South City & County Investment Co Ltd* Vol V p 119, 1998 p 183

Interpretation of statutes

of excise duties payable under SI 422/1983 and EC Directive *Karl Keller v The Revenue Commissioners & Others* Vol IV p 512

of statutes, absurdity *K Company v Hogan* Vol III p 56

of statutes, ambiguity *McNally v Maoldhomnaigh* Vol IV p 22

of statutes, ejusdem generis rule *M Cronin v Lunham Brothers Ltd* Vol III p 370

of statutes, exemption *The Revenue Commissioners v Doorley* Vol V p 539

of statutes, mandatory *The Revenue Commissioners v Henry Young* Vol V p 294

of statutes, relief *Texaco Ireland Ltd v Murphy* Vol IV p 91 *O'Coindealbhain v Gannon* Vol III p 484, *McCann v O'Culachain* Vol III p 304 *O'Culachain v McMullan Bros* Vol IV p 284, Vol V p 200, *O'Sullivan v The Revenue Commissioners* Vol V p 570

of statutes, rules of construction *De Brun (Inspector of Taxes) v Kiernan* Vol III p 19, *McGrath v McDermott* Vol III p 683

of taxing act *EP O'Coindealbhain (Inspector of Taxes) v The Honourable Mr Justice Sean Gannon* Vol III p 484

Investments

finance company, dealing in stocks and shares, whether investments should be valued at cost or market value *AB Ltd v Mac Giolla Riogh (Inspector of Taxes)* Vol II p 419

Investments (contd)

profits on realisation of whether trading profits *The Agricultural Credit Corporation Ltd v JB Vale (Inspector of Taxes)* Vol I p 474 and *The Alliance & Dublin Consumers' Gas Co v Davis (Inspector of Taxes)* Vol I p 104 and *Davis (Inspector of Taxes) v Hibernian Bank Ltd* Vol I p 503

Investment company

deduction of expenses of management *Howth Estate Co v WJ Davis (Inspector of Taxes)* Vol I p 447, *Hibernian Insurance Company Limited v MacUimis (Inspector of Taxes)* 2000 p75 and *Casey (Inspector of Taxes) v The Monteagle Estate Co* Vol II p 429

Issue

whether "issue" included adopted children *In the matter of John Stamp deceased Patrick Stamp v Noel Redmond & Others* Vol IV p 415

J

Joint ownership

whether survivor entitled, whether resulting trust *M Lynch v M Burke & AIB plc* Vol V p 271

Joint assessment

whether husband is liable for wife's income *Gilligan v Criminal Assets Bureau, Galvin, Lanigan & Revenue Commissioners* Vol V p 424

Journalism

exemption of earnings from original and creative works of artistic or cultural merit, whether journalism qualifies *John Healy v SI Breathnach (Inspector of Taxes)* Vol III p 496

Judicial function

exercise of by Inspector of Taxes *Michael Deighan v Edward N Hearne & Others* Vol III p 533

exercise of by Appeal Commissioners *The State (Calcul International and Solatrex International Ltd) v The Appeal Commissioners and The Revenue Commissioners* Vol III p 577

Judicial review

application for, re stamp duty *Kenny J v Revenue Commissioners, Goodman & Gemon Ltd (Notice Parties)* Vol V p 363

application re VAT *DH Burke & Sons Ltd v The Revenue Commissioners and Others* Vol V 418, *Taxback Ltd v The Revenue Commissioners* Vol V 412

Jurisdiction

of High Court relating to Social Welfare appeals *Albert Kinghan v The Minister for Social Welfare* Vol III p 436

L

Land

dealing in and developing *O'Connlain (Inspector of Taxes) v Belvedere Estates Ltd* Vol III p 271

Land (contd)

whether the surplus from the sale of property was profit of a trade of dealing in or developing land, or the profit of a business which was deemed by F(MP)A 1968 s 17, to be such a trade *Mara (Inspector of Taxes) v GG (Hummingbird) Ltd* Vol II p 667

Land Purchase Acts

arrears of jointure tax paid under Schedule A, whether further balance due *Estate Of Teresa Downing (Owner)* Vol I p 487

Lease

lump sum paid on execution of lease, whether capital payment or rent paid in advance *W Flynn (Inspector of Taxes) v John Noone Ltd, and W Flynn (Inspector of Taxes) v Blackwood & Co (Sligo) Ltd* Vol II p 222

payment in advance on the signing of a lease, whether capital *O'Sullivan (Inspector of Taxes) v p Ltd* Vol II p 464

Leasing

income from the leasing of premises, whether leasing constitutes trading, whether earned income *Pairceir (Inspector of Taxes) v EM* Vol II p 596

Legal costs

whether a Circuit Court Judge hearing an appeal pursuant to ITA 1967 s 429 has jurisdiction to award costs *The Revenue Commissioners v Arida Ltd* Vol IV p 401, Vol V p 221

Legal fees

in defending action in High Court for balance alleged to be due to a building contractor in respect of the construction of cinema, whether allowable Case I deduction *Casey (Inspector of Taxes) v AB Ltd* Vol II p 500

whether letting fees and legal expenses incurred by the company in respect of first lettings of property qualified as deductions under ITA 1967 s 81(5)(*d*) *GH Ltd v Browne (Inspector of Taxes)* Vol III p 95

Letting expenses

whether letting fees and legal expenses incurred by the company in respect of first lettings of property qualified as deductions under ITA 1967 s 81(5)(*d*) *GH Ltd v Browne (Inspector of Taxes)* Vol III p 95

Lessors

trade carried on *The Great Southern Railways Co v The Revenue Commissioners* Vol I p 359

Liability

of liquidator to employer's contribution of PRSI in respect of "reckonable earnings" of employees, when payable preferential status *The Companies Act 1963-1983 v Castlemahon Poultry Products Ltd* Vol III p 509

of personal representatives *Moloney (Inspector of Taxes) v Allied Irish Banks Ltd as executors of the estate of Francis J Doherty deceased* Vol III p 477

of receiver, to corporation tax *Wayte (Holdings) Ltd (In receivership) Alex Burns v Edward N Hearne* Vol III p 553

Liability (contd)

personal, of members of bank, whether unlimited *CIR v The Governor & Company of The Bank of Ireland* Vol I p 70

Limited

partnership, share of capital allowances on leasing transaction, involving a purported limited partnership, against his personal income tax liability *DA MacCarthaigh (Inspector of Taxes) v Francis Daly* Vol III p 253

Liquidation

court fees, amount on which court fees are chargeable in a liquidation *In re Private Motorists Provident Society ltd (In Liqdtn) & W J Horgan v Minister for Justice* Vol V p 186, *In re Hibernian Transport Companies Limited* Vol V p 194

deferral of revenue debts pending completion of contracts by company *The Companies Act 1963-1983 and MFN Construction Co Ltd (in liquidation) on the application of Patrick Tuffy (liquidator)* Vol IV p 82

whether a sum which arose to the company on the liquidation of a wholly owned subsidiary was part of its trading profits *Guinness & Mahon Ltd v Browne (Inspector of Taxes)* Vol III p 373

whether deposit interest earned on monies held by the official liquidator liable to tax *In Re HT Ltd (in Liquidation) & Others* Vol III p 120

whether assessments of PRSI entitled to super preferential priority *Re Coombe Importers Ltd (In Liq) and Re the Companies Acts 1963-1990* 1998 p 59

Liquidator

liability of, to employer's contribution of PRSI in respect of "reckonable earnings" of employees, when payable preferential status *The Companies Act 1963-1983 v Castlemahon Poultry Products Ltd* Vol III p 509; *Re Coombe Importers Ltd (In Liq) and Re the Companies Acts 1963-1990* 1998 p 59

Loan interest

payable follwoing redemption of share capital whether allowable *Sean Mac Aonghusa v Ringmahon* 1990-2000 p 81

Loan notes

whether capital gains tax deferred pending redemption of, *PJ O'connell v T Keleghan* 2000 p 113

whether loan notes are debenture stock or shares *Patrick J O'Connell (Inspector of Taxes) v Thomas Keleghan* 2001 p 103

Losses

carry forward of losses *Molmac Ltd v MacGiolla Riogh (Inspector of Taxes)* Vol II p 482 and *M Cronin (Inspector of Taxes) v Lunham Brothers Ltd* Vol III p 363

discontinuance of trade, set off of losses *Boland's Ltd v Davis (Inspector of Taxes)* Vol I p 86

in trade, notional, from fall in market value of goods before delivery *The Revenue Commissioners v Latchford & Sons Ltd* Vol I p 240

Lump sum

paid on execution of lease, whether capital payment or rent paid in advance *W Flynn (Inspector of Taxes) v John Noone Ltd, and W Flynn (Inspector of Taxes) v Blackwood & Co (Sligo) Ltd* Vol II p 222

redundancy payments to disabled employees, whether exempt from income tax, whether distinction to be made between disabled employees whose jobs continued and disabled employees whose jobs ceased p *O Cahill (Inspector of Taxes) v Albert Harding & Others* Vol IV p 233

whether paid on account of retirement or due to ill health *B D O'Shea (Inspector of Taxes) v Michael Mulqueen* Vol V p 134

M

Market gardening

valuation of land occupied for market gardening *L v WS McGarry (Inspector of Taxes)* Vol II p 241

Market value

of shares in a private trading company, *E A Smyth v The Revenue Commissioners* Vol V p 532, *In the estate of Thomas McNamee & Others v The Revenue Commissioners* Vol V p 577

Management

expenses, deduction of, by investment company *Howth Estate Co v W J Davis (Inspector of Taxes)* Vol I p 447 and *Casey (Inspector of Taxes) v The Monteagle Estate Co* Vol II p 429, *Hibernian Insurance Company Limited v MacUimis (Inspector of Taxes)* Vol V p 495, 2000 p 75, *Stephen Court Ltd v JA Browne (Inspector of Taxes)* Vol V p 680

losses in holding company, whether notional management fees deductible Corporation tax *Belville Holdings Ltd (in receivership and liquidation) v Cronin (Inspector of Taxes)* Vol III p 340,

Mandamus

finality of Special Commissioners' decision *The King (Evelyn Spain) v The Special Commissioners* Vol I p 221

order for mandamus - clearance certificate *The State (Melbarian enterprises Ltd) v The Revenue Commissioners* Vol III p 291

Manufacturing relief

assembly of agricultural machinery whether manufacturing *Irish Agricultural Machinery Ltd v S O'Culachain (Inspector of Taxes)* Vol III p 661

film production, whether relief given for accounting periods prior to FA 1990 *Saatchi & Saatchi Advertising Ltd v Kevin McGarry (Inspector of Taxes)* Vol V p 376, 1998 p 99

newspaper publisher, newspapers are "goods" for the purpose of manufacturing relief, whether advertising income is from a separate trade and qualifies for such relief *L McGurrin (Inspector of Taxes) v The Champion Publications Ltd* Vol IV p 466

process of ripening bananas whether constituted manufacturing *Charles McCann Ltd v S O'Culachain (Inspector of Taxes)* Vol III p 304, *PJ O'Connell v Fyffes Banana Processing Ltd* 2000 p 235

Manufacturing relief (contd)

processing of and sale of milk produced by the company, whether constituted the manufacture of goods for the purposes of the reduction in corporation tax provided for in FA 1980 Pt I Ch VI *Cronin (Inspector of Taxes) v Strand Dairy Ltd* Vol III p 441

production of day old chicks, whether day old chicks are goods within the meaning of FA 1980, whether process constitutes manufacturing, whether use of extensive plant machinery and skilled workers constitute a process of manufacturing *JF Kelly (Inspector of Taxes) v Cobb Straffan Ireland Ltd* Vol IV p 526, *TG Brosnan (Inspector of Taxes) v Leeside Nurseries Ltd* Vol V p 21

production of films for use in advertising, whether manufacture *S O'Culachain (Inspector of Taxes) v Hunter Advertising Ltd* Vol IV p 35

whether production of J Cloths and nappy liners from bales of fabric is a manufacturing process *D O Laochdha (Inspector of Taxes) v Johnson & Johnson (Ireland) Ltd* Vol IV p 361

whether proper construction of words of s 41 brought advertisements within definition of goods *L McGurrin (Inspector of Taxes) v The Champion Publications Ltd* Vol IV p 466

whether sophisticated system of growth of plants within glasshouses constitute a manufacturing process *TG Brosnan (Inspector of Taxes) v Leeside Nurseries Ltd* Vol V p 21

wholesaler of beers and stouts, also conditions bottled stout, whether conditioning of bottled Guinness constitutes manufacturing process, whether plant and equipment sufficiently sophisticated *J Hussey (Inspector of Taxes) v MJ Gleeson & Co Ltd* Vol IV p 533

Mareva injunction

whether action to freeze person's assets can be brought by plenary summons *The Criminal Assets Bureau v Patrick A McSweeney* 2000 p 215

Marriage gratuity

whether "marriage gratuity" received on resignation was a retirement payment under ITA 1967 s 114 or was a perquisite of her office under ITA 1967 s 110 *Sean O'Siochain (Inspector of Taxes) v Thomas Morrissey* Vol IV p 407

Married persons

aggregation of incomes of married persons unconstitutional *Francis Murphy & Partner v Attorney General* Vol V p 613

aggregation of earned income of married persons unconstitutional *Bernard Muckley and Anne Muckley v Ireland, The Attorney General and The Revenue Commissioners* Vol III p 188

joint assessment whether husband is liable for tax on both incomes *Gilligan v Criminal Assets Bureau, Galvin, Lanigan & Revenue Commissioners* Vol V p 424

living apart *Donovan (Inspector of Taxes) v CG Crofts* Vol I p 115

living together *D Ua Clothasaigh (Inspector of Taxes) v Patrick McCartan* Vol II p 75

wife's income from securities assessed on husband in first year of wife's income from securities *JD Mulvey (Inspector of Taxes) v RM Kieran* Vol I p 563

Married persons (contd)

UK resident working in Ireland, wife working in UK, whether he is entitled to married allowance and rate bands *S Fennessy (Inspector of Taxes) v John Mc Connellogue* Vol V p 129

Meetings

of companies, whether they took place, whether resolution was passed, whether share issue invalid *In re Sugar Distributors Ltd* Vol V p 225

Mill

expenditure on mill sanitation *JB Vale (Inspector of Taxes) v Martin Mahony & Brothers Ltd* Vol II p 32

Mining

whether operation is mining or manufacturing *Patrick J O'Connell (Inspector of Taxes) v Tara Mines Ltd* 2001 p 79

Mistake

whether monies paid in mistake of law recoverable, whether a common law right to repayment *O'Rourke v Revenue Commissioners* Vol V p 321

N

Newspaper publisher

newspapers are "goods" for the purpose of manufacturing relief, whether advertising income is from a separate trade and qualifies for such relief *L McGurrin (Inspector of Taxes) v The Champion Publications Ltd* Vol IV p 466

Non-resident company

manufacturing through a branch in the State, tax free profits from branch paid into foreign bank account, whether interest earned on foreign bank account is taxable in Ireland *S Murphy (Inspector of Taxes) v Dataproducts (Dublin) Ltd* Vol IV p 12

Non-residents - EU

whether entitled to VAT refunds through refunding agencies *Taxback Limited v The Revenue Commissioners* Vol V p 412

Nuns

whether assessable on income from employment which is given to the order *JD Dolan (Inspector of Taxes) v "K" National School Teacher* Vol I p 656

Nurseries and market gardens

assessment of income by reference to annual profits estimated according to the rules of Schedule D *WS McGarry (Inspector of Taxes) v JA Spencer* Vol II p 1

Nursing home

profits derived from hospital and associated private nursing home, whether trade carried on *RG Davis (Inspector of Taxes) v The Superioress Mater Misericordiae Hospital, Dublin* Vol I p 387

O

Obsolescence of assets

Evans & Co v Phillips (Inspector of Taxes) Vol I p 43

Occupation of lands

whether the appellant company was in occupation of lands, forming part of a military establishment, for the purposes of ITA 1918 Sch B or ITA 1967 *O Conaill (Inspector of Taxes) v Z Ltd* Vol II p 636

Option

deed of release, whether release constitutes a sale for stamp duty purposes *In re Cherrycourt v The Revenue Commissioners* Vol V p 180

Original

document not produced, secondary evidence that beneficial interest in securities had been transferred not admissible *Hewson v JB Kealy (Inspector of Taxes)* Vol II p 15

P

Paid

the meaning of, whether charge/credit cards mean paid for *The Diners Club Ltd v The Revenue and The Minister for Finance* Vol III p 680

Partnership

as distinguished form employment *Francis Griffin v Minister for Social, Community and Family Affairs* 2001 p 125

father taking his children into partnership, whether income of children is deemed to be income of father *JM O'Dwyer (Inspector of Taxes) v Cafolla & Co* Vol II p 82

share of capital allowances on leasing transaction, involving a purported limited partnership, against his personal income tax liability *DA MacCarthaigh (Inspector of Taxes) v Francis Daly* Vol III p 253

sole trader admitted partner at beginning of year, during the year the business is sold to limited company, whether sole traders previous year's assessment can be revised *AB v JD Mulvey (Inspector of Taxes)* Vol II p 55

whether capital investment necessary for partnership *Francis Griffin v Minister for Social, Community and Family Affairs* 2001 p 125

Patent rights

whether income from patent rights disregarded for income tax purposes, where payable to non residents, whether tax avoidance scheme *Pandion Haliaetus Ltd & Ors v The Revenue Commissioners* Vol III p 670

PAYE

due in respect of remuneration paid in year following that in which work was done, assessment *Bedford (Collector-General) v H* Vol II p 588

employer's obligations to deduct PAYE and PRSI from employee's emoluments *EN Hearne (Inspector of Taxes) v O'Cionna & Ors T/A JA Kenny & Ptnrs* Vol IV p 113

PAYE regulations

whether procedures unfair and unconstitutional, enforcement order issue to city sheriff after payment of tax, defamation of plaintiff *Giles J Kennedy v E G Hearne, the Attorney General & Others* Vol III p 590

Payment

of dividends, whether payment through inter-company account was sufficient evidence of actual payment, whether payment of cheque required, whether making of accounting entry a mere record of underlying transaction, whether a dividend declared on 11 December 1980 was received by related company not later than 12 December 1980, whether making of journal entries after 23 December 1980 material evidence *Sean Murphy (Inspector of Taxes) v The Borden Co Ltd* Vol II p 559

payment of excise duty deferred *The Attorney General v Sun Alliance and London Insurance Ltd* Vol III p 265

Penalties

non-payment of excise duty payable on bets entered into by the defendant a registered bookmaker, whether recovery of an excise penalty a criminal matter, *The Director of Public Prosecutions v Seamus Boyle* Vol IV p 395

prosecution for payment of a Revenue penalty, whether criminal or civil proceedings *Director of Public Prosecutions v Robert Downes* Vol III p 641

whether penalties for failure to make returns are unconstitutional *Edward McLoughlin and Thomas Marie Tuite v The Revenue Commissioners and The Attorney General* Vol III p 387

whether too linient *The Director of Public Prosecutions v George Redmond* 2000 p 273

Pension

personal pension and other assets assigned to company pension continued to be paid to pensioner, whether pensioner liable to tax on pension *Cronin (Inspector of Taxes) v C* Vol II p 64

social welfare (Consolidation Act 1951 s 299), whether entitled to old age contributory pension, meaning of entry into insurance, definition of contribution year, whether issue open to appeal *Albert Kinghan v The Minister for Social Welfare* Vol III p 436

Personal representatives

liability of personal representatives *Moloney (Inspector of Taxes) v Allied Irish Banks Ltd as executors of the estate of Francis J Doherty deceased* Vol III p 477

Personal rights

of citizen violated *Michael Deighan v Edward N Hearne & Others* Vol III p 533

of citizens *Bernard Muckley and Anne Muckley v Ireland, The Attorney General and The Revenue Commissioners* Vol III p 188

Petrol canopies

whether forecourt canopies at petrol filling stations constitute plant for tax purposes *S O'Culachain v McMullan Brothers* Vol IV p 284, Vol V p 200

Petrol marketing company

whether expenditure incurred under exclusivity agreements with retailers is revenue or capital *Dolan (Inspector of Taxes) v AB Co Ltd* Vol II p 515

Petroleum exploration

whether constitutes scientific research, whether such scientific research qualifies for tax relief by way of an allowance under ITA 1967 s 244 *Texaco Ireland Ltd v S Murphy (Inspector of Taxes)* Vol IV p 91

Pig rearing

whether the activity of intensive pig rearing constituted farming for the purposes of FA 1974 s 13(1) *Knockhall Piggeries v Kerrane (Inspector of Taxes)* Vol III p 319

Plant

barrister's books, whether plant *Breathnach (Inspector of Taxes) v MC* Vol III p 113

expenditure on installation of suspended ceiling in supermarket whether plant qualifying for capital allowances *Dunnes Stores (Oakville) Ltd v MC Cronin (Inspector of Taxes)* Vol IV p 68

poultry house, whether plant and machinery qualifying for capital allowances *O'Srianain (Inspector of Taxes) v Lakeview Ltd* Vol III p 219

racecourse stand, whether deductible repairs or non deductible capital expenditure or expenditure qualifying as plant *Michael O'Grady (Inspector of Taxes) v Roscommon Race Committee* Vol IV p 425, Vol V p 317

whether forecourt canopies at petrol filling stations constitute plant for tax purposes *S O'Culachain v McMullan Brothers* Vol IV p 284, Vol V p 200

Poultry house

whether plant and machinery qualifying for capital allowances *O'Srianain (Inspector of Taxes) v Lakeview Ltd* Vol III p 219

Power of revocation

settlement of income, deed of appointment by parent in favour of child *EG v Mac Shamhrain (Inspector of Taxes)* Vol II p 352

Precedent

whether High Court decisions are binding on Appeals Officers *Francis Griffin v Minister for Social, Community and Family Affairs* 2001 p 125

Preferential claim

in receivership, income and corporation profits tax *The Attorney-General v Irish Steel Ltd and Vincent Crowley* Vol III p 265 and *In Re HT Ltd (in Liquidation) & Others* Vol III p 120

in receivership and liquidation *In the Matter of H Williams (Tallaght) (In Receivership & Liquidation) and the Companies Act 1963-1990* Vol V p 388

preferential creditors priority in receivership *United Bars Ltd (In Receivership), Walkinstown Inn Ltd (In Receivership) and Raymond Jackson v The Revenue Commissioners* Vol IV p 107

status under Companies Act 1963 s 285 *The Companies Act 1963-1983 v Castlemahon Poultry Products Ltd* Vol III p 509

whether assessemnts of PRSI entitled to super preferential priorty *Re Coombe Importers Ltd (In Liq) and Re the Companies Acts 1963-1990* 1998 p 59

Preference shareholders

whether entitled to participate in capital distribution whether entitled to a portion of issue of new ordinary shares *Williams Group Tullamore Ltd v Companies Act 1963 to 1983* Vol III p 423

Premium

on lease payable by instalments, whether allowable under ITA 1967 s 91 *The Hammond Lane Metal Co Ltd v S O'Culachain (Inspector of Taxes)* Vol IV p 187

Printing

and processing in UK, whether manufacturing *S O'Culachain (Inspector of Taxes) v Hunter Advertising Ltd* Vol IV p 35

Privacy

right to privacy *Charles J Haughey v Moriarty and Others* 1998 p 119

Proceeds of Crime Act 1996

constitutional and non-constitutional issues regarding provisions relating to proceeds derived from criminal activity *John Gilligan v Criminal Assets Bureau, Revenue Commissioners & Others* 2001 p 135

jurisdiction of High Court to impose orders under the legislation *John Gilligan v Criminal Assets Bureau, Revenue Commissioners & Others* 2001 p 135

Processes

in form of loannotes, capital gains tax implications *PJ O'Connell v T Keleghan* 2000 p 113

Professional services withholding tax

whether method of granting credit for same is constitutional *Michael Daly v The Revenue Commissioners* Vol V p 213

Profits

FROM ILLEGAL TRADE

Daniel Collins and Michael Byrne, Daniel Collins and Redmond Power as Executor of the will of Michael Byrne, deceased and Daniel Collins v JD Mulvey (Inspector of Taxes) Vol II p 291

FROM STALLION FEES

whether liable to tax under Schedule B or Schedule D income tax paid, whether further balance due *Cloghran Stud Farm v AG Birch (Inspector of Taxes)* Vol I p 496

NOT RECEIVED IN THE YEAR OF ASSESSMENT

MacKeown (Inspector of Taxes) v Patrick J Roe Vol I p 214

OF A TRADE

bad debts recovered, *Bourke (Inspector of Taxes) v Lyster & Sons Ltd* Vol II p 374

compensation for loss of profits, whether income or capital receipt *The Alliance and Dublin Consumers' Gas Co v McWilliams (Inspector of Taxes)* Vol I p 207

derived from hospital and associated private nursing home, whether trade carried on *RG Davis (Inspector of Taxes) v The Superioress, Mater Misericordiae Hospital, Dublin* Vol I p 387

Profits (contd)

profit/trading receipts *O'Dwyer (Inspector of Taxes) and the Revenue Commissioners v Irish Exporters and Importers Ltd (In Liquidation)* Vol I p 629

ON REALISATION OF INVESTMENTS

whether trading profits, *The Agricultural Credit Corporation Ltd v JB Vale (Inspector of Taxes)* Vol I p 474 and *The Alliance & Dublin Consumers' Gas Co v Davis (Inspector of Taxes)* Vol I p 104 and *Davis (Inspector of Taxes) v Hibernian Bank Ltd* Vol I p 503

ON SWEEPSTAKES

C Hayes (Inspector of Taxes) v R J Duggan Vol I p 195

Prosecution

for payment of a Revenue penalty *DPP v Robert Downes* Vol III p 641

PRSI

employer's contribution in respect of "reckonable earnings" of employees, when payable, liability of liquidator preferential status *The Companies Act 1963-1983 v Castlemahon Poultry Products Ltd* Vol III p 509

employer's obligations to deduct PAYE and PRSI from employee's emoluments *EN Hearne (Inspector of Taxes) v O'Cionna & Ors T/A JA Kenny & Ptnrs* Vol IV p 113

whether share fishermen liable to PRSI as self-employed *Francis Griffin v Minister for Social, Community and Family Affairs* 2001 p 125

Publican's licence

excise duty, whether new licence obtainable, whether application within six year period, meaning of year immediately preceding *Peter Connolly v The Collector of Customs and Excise* Vol IV p 419

purchase of, in a bond, by a publican whether trading transaction *McCall (deceased) v Commissioners of Inland Revenue* Vol I p 28

Publishers

newspaper publisher, newspapers are "goods" for the purpose of manufacturing relief, whether advertising income is from a separate trade and qualifies for such relief *L McGurrin (Inspector of Taxes) v Champion Publications Ltd* Vol IV p 466

Q

Quarry

removing top-soil from surface of quarry *Milverton Quarries Ltd v The Revenue Commissioners* Vol II p 382

R

Racing and Racecourses Act 1945

sections 4, 15, 27 *The Racing Board v S O'Culachain* Vol IV p 73

Racecourse stand

whether deductible repairs or non deductible capital expenditure or expenditure qualifying as plant *Michael O'Grady (Inspector of Taxes) v Roscommon Race Committee* Vol IV p 425, Vol V p 317

Racing bodies

whether exemption for Agricultural Societies apply *to The Trustees of The Ward Union Hunt Races v Hughes (Inspector of Taxes)* Vol I p 538

Railways

lines leased to another company at an annual rent *The Commissioners of Inland Revenue and The Dublin and Kingstown Railway Co* Vol I p 119

lessors of railway line, whether a railway undertaking *The Great Southern Railways Co v The Revenue Commissioners* Vol I p 359

Realisation

of assets, meaning of, *In re Private Motorists Provident Society ltd (In Liqdtn) & W J Horgan v Minister for Justice* Vol V p 186, *In re Hibernian Transport Companies Limited* Vol V p 194

Receiver

company in receivership preferential claim *The Attorney-General v Irish Steel Ltd and Vincent Crowley* Vol II p 108

liability to corporation tax *Wayte (Holdings) Ltd (In Receivership) Alex Burns v Edward N Hearne* Vol III p 553

Receivership

preferential creditors priority in receivership *United Bars Ltd (In Receivership), Walkinstown Inn Ltd (In Receivership) and Raymond Jackson v The Revenue Commissioners* Vol IV p 107

Recovery of tax

from a group of companies, whether Revenue Commissioners may appropriate payments between separate companies within the group, whether insolvency of a company is relevant to gratuitous alienation of assets *Frederick Inns Ltd, The Rendezvous Ltd, The Graduate Ltd, Motels Ltd (In Liquidation) v The Companies Acts 1963-1986* Vol IV p 247

Redundancy payments

whether lump sum payments to disabled employees exempt from income tax *O Cahill (Inspector of Taxes) v Albert Harding & Others* Vol IV p 233, *BD O'Shea (Inspector of Taxes) v Michael Mulqueen* Vol V p 134

Refunding agencies - VAT

whether VAT refunds obtainable through refunding agencies *Taxback Limited v The Revenue Commissioners* Vol V p 412

Regulations

betting duty, whether necessary for Revenue Commissioners to comply with Regulations Act 1890 before proceedings can commence for failure to pay duty on bets *DPP v MichaelCunningham* Vol V p 691

Release

deed of, whether release of an option is a sale *In re Cherrycourt v The Revenue Commissioners* Vol V p 180

Religious orders

whether entitled to repayment of tax deducted from payments made under an indenture of covenant pursuant to ITA 1967 s 439(1)(iv) *The Revenue Commissioners v HI* Vol III p 242

Remuneration

calculation of PAYE due in respect of remuneration paid in year following that in which work was done, method of assessment *Bedford (Collector-General) v H* Vol II p 588

charging section provision in will charging rental income from estate with annual amount payable to beneficiary provided he continued to manage the property *Gerald O'Reilly v WJ Casey (Inspector of Taxes)* Vol I p 601

of office, grant to a President of a college on retirement *JD Mulvey (Inspector of Taxes) v Denis J Coffey* Vol I p 618

professional services rendered without prior agreement as regards remuneration payment on termination of services whether chargeable as income *W S McGarry (Inspector of Taxes) v EF* Vol II p 261

Rent

lump sum paid on execution of lease, whether capital payment or rent paid in advance *W Flynn (Inspector of Taxes) v John Noone Ltd, and W Flynn (Inspector of Taxes) v Blackwood & Co (Sligo) Ltd* Vol II p 222

paid by employing company for house occupied voluntarily by employee *Connolly (Inspector of Taxes) v Denis McNamara* Vol II p 452

payment in advance on the signing of a lease, whether capital *O'Sullivan (Inspector of Taxes) v p Ltd* Vol II p 464

Repairs

allowability of *Martin Fitzgerald v Commissioners of Inland Revenue* Vol I p 91

expenditure on roof, whether deductible repairs or non deductible capital expenditure *Michael O'Grady (Inspector of Taxes) v Roscommon Race Committee* Vol IV p 425

new bar and extension to old bar, whether non-deductible capital improvements *Michael O'Grady (Inspector of Taxes) v Roscommon Race Committee* Vol IV p 425

racecourse stand, whether deductible repairs or non deductible capital expenditure or expenditure qualifying as plant *Michael O'Grady (Inspector of Taxes) v Roscommon Race Committee* Vol IV p 425, Vol V p 317

re-design or lower terracing, whether an improvement *Michael O'Grady (Inspector of Taxes) v Roscommon Race Committee* Vol IV p 425

work done to walls whether deductible repairs or non deductible capital expenditure *Michael O'Grady (Inspector of Taxes) v Roscommon Race Committee* Vol IV p 425

Repayments

provision for interest on repayments of tax *Navan Carpets Ltd v S O'Culachain (Inspector of Taxes)* Vol III p 403

stamp duty inadvertently paid, whether repayment due, *Terence Byrne v The Revenue Commissioners* Vol V p 560

Repayments (contd)

whether Revenue can withhold VAT repayments *Taxback Limited v The Revenue Commissioners* Vol V p 412

Repealed legislation

effect of repeal of Farm Tax Act, consequences of absence of amending legislation *Purcell v Attorney General* Vol IV p 229, Vol V p 288

Replacement cost accounting

method of accounting for tax purposes, whether replacement cost basis is acceptable or whether historical cost accounting is the only method of commercial accountancy *Carroll Industries Plc (formerly PJ Carroll & Co Ltd) and PJ Carroll & Co Ltd v S O'Culachain (Inspector of Taxes)* Vol IV p 135

Residence

of company *The Cunard Steam Ship Co Ltd v Herlihy (Inspector of Taxes), and The Cunard Steam Ship Co Ltd v Revenue Commissioners* Vol I p 330

ordinary residence and domicile, Income tax, Sch D, Case V *Captain RH Prior-Wandesforde v the Revenue Commissioners* Vol I p 249 and *The Right Hon The Earl of Iveagh v The Revenue Commissioners* Vol I p 259

UK resident working in Ireland, wife working in UK, whether he is entitled to married allowance and rate bands *S Fennessy (Inspector of Taxes) v John Mc Connellogue* Vol V p 129

whether individual is resident *LJ Irwin (Collector General) v M Grimes* Vol V p 209

whether long term residence determines domicile *Proes v The Revenue Commissioners* Vol V 481

Residential property tax

residential property tax, whether unconstitutional *PJ Madigan & p Madigan v The Attorney General, The Revenue Commissioners & Others* Vol III p 127

Restoration

of destroyed premises under covenant to repair *Martin Fitzgerald v Commissioners of Inland Revenue* Vol I p 91

Retailers Scheme for VAT

interpretation of scheme, *DH Burke & Sons Ltd v The Revenue Commissioners, Ireland and the AG* Vol V p 418

Retirement payments

whether "marriage gratuity" received on resignation was a retirement payment under ITA 1967 s 114 or was a perquisite of her office under ITA 1967 s 110 *Sean O'Siochain (Inspector of Taxes) v Thomas Morrissey* Vol IV p 407

whether lump sum was paid on account of retirement or due to ill health *B D O'Shea (Inspector of Taxes) v Michael Mulqueen* Vol V p 134

Return

of income, what constitutes a proper return of income for the assessment of income tax *MA Bairead v M McDonald* Vol IV p 475; *In the Matter of G O'C & A O'C (Application of Liam Liston (Inspector of Taxes))* Vol V p 346

Return (contd)

of income, failure to make, appeal against a decision of the High Court to refuse on a judicial review application to quash three convictions with six months imprisonment for each offence imposed in the District Court on the appellant for failure to make income tax returns *Thomas O'Callaghan v JP Clifford & Others* Vol IV p 478

whether wife obliged to prepare and deliver a separate return of income *Gilligan v Criminal Assets Bureau & Others* Vol V p 424

Roll over relief

proceeds of sale reinvested in acquisition of further lands, whether rollover relief on transfer of a trade applies *EP O'Coindealbhain (Inspector of Taxes) v KN Price* Vol IV p 1

S

Sanitation

expenditure on mill sanitation, whether allowable deduction from trade profits *JB Vale (Inspector of Taxes) v Martin Mahony & Brothers Ltd* Vol II p 32

Sale

of meat into intervention within the EEC *Cronin (Inspector of Taxes) v IMP Middleton Ltd* Vol III p 452

meaning of sale for stamp duty purposes, whether release of an option is a sale *In re Cherrycourt v The Revenue Commissioners* Vol V p 180

Schedule E

gifts, whether present from employer taxable as gift, or emolument under Schedule E *Wing v O'Connell (Inspector of Taxes)* Vol I p 155

School/colleges

whether operated for charitable purposes *The Pharmaceutical Society of Ireland v The Revenue Commissioners* Vol I p 542

Scientific research

whether petroleum exploration constitutes scientific research, whether such scientific research qualifies for tax relief by way of an allowance under ITA 1967 s 244 *Texaco Ireland Ltd v S Murphy (Inspector of Taxes)* Vol IV p 91

Search warrants

Requirement for Customs Officer to have reasonable grounds for suspicion that goods were on premises *Simple Imports Limited and Another v Revenue Commissioners and Others* 2001, p 57

Validity thereof *Simple Imports Limited and Another v Revenue Commissioners and Others* 2001, p 57

Secondary evidence

not admissible *Gilbert Hewson v J B Kealy (Inspector of Taxes)* Vol II p 15

Seizure

interpleader summons arose out of the seizure by the applicant in his role as Revenue sheriff of goods and chattels claimed to be the property of the claimant in the action *Patrick Cusack v Evelyn O'Reilly & The Honourable Mr Justice Frank Roe & Others* Vol IV p 86

of oil tanker by the Revenue Commissioners *McCrystal Oil Co Ltd v The Revenue Commissioners & Others* Vol IV p 386

Series of transactions

through a chain of companies including the abandonment by the respondent and his wife of their respective options *TA Dilleen (Inspector of Taxes) v Edward J Kearns* Vol IV p 547

with associated companies *O'Connlain (Inspector of Taxes) v Belvedere Estates Ltd* Vol III p 271

Services

supply of, for value added tax purposes, by a solicitor to a non resident, not established in the state but resident in EU, where services deemed to be supplied *JJ Bourke (Inspector of Taxes) v WG Bradley & Sons* Vol IV p 117

whether a contract of services or a contract for services *Henry Denny & Sons (Ir) Ltd v Minister for Social Welfare* Vol V p 238, *O'Coindeabhain v Mooney* Vol III p 45

Settlement of legal action

compensation paid to tenants of adjoining premises for interference with light and air, whether allowable Case I deduction *Davis (Inspector of Taxes) v X Ltd* Vol II p 45

Settlement of income

deed of appointment by parent in favour of child *EG v Mac Shamhrain (Inspector of Taxes)* Vol II p 352

Shares

finance company, dealing in stocks and shares, whether investments should be valued at cost or market value *AB Ltd v Mac Giolla Riogh (Inspector of Taxes)* Vol II p 419

whether loan notes are treated as shares *Patrick J O'Connell (Inspector of Taxes) v Thomas Keleghan* 2001 p 103

Shareholders

whether preference shareholders are entitled to participate in capital distribution whether entitled to a portion of issue of new ordinary shares whether opposition of minority shareholders *Williams Group Tullamore Ltd v Companies Act 1963 to 1983* Vol III p 423

Slaughter houses

excise duty imposed on proprietors of slaughter houses and exporters of live animals, whether ultra vires and void *Doyle & Others v An Taoiseach & Others* Vol III p 73

Single source

foreign trades, basis of assessment under Case III *O'Conaill (Inspector of Taxes) v R* Vol II p 304

Social welfare

employee, whether a member of the crew of a fishing vessel can be an "employee", whether there can be an "employee" without there being a corresponding employer, whether Social Welfare (Consolidation) Act 1981 applies to self employed persons, whether scheme of Act and regulations is limited to employer/employee circumstances whether Minister has unlimited power to make regulations enabling any person to be treated as an employee. *The Minister for Social Welfare v John Griffiths* Vol IV p 378

employer's contribution of PRSI in respect of "reckonable earnings" of employees, when payable, liability of liquidator preferential status *The Companies Act 1963-1983 v Castlemahon Poultry Products Ltd* Vol III p 509

meaning of entry into insurance, definition of contribution year, whether entitled to old age contributory pension, whether issue open to appeal *Albert Kinghan v The Minister for Social Welfare* Vol III p 436

whether dockers working under a pooling arrangement can receive unemployment benefit when they are not occupied unloading ships, whether dockers had a contract of employment with their Association, separate contracts on each occasion of their employment, whether level of earnings material to question of employment *James Louth & Others v Minister for Social Welfare* Vol IV p 391

whether a wholesale distributor of newspapers a self employed person *Tony McAuliffe v Minister for Social Welfare* Vol V p 94

widows contributory pension, whether increase for dependent children liable to tax on parent, *Sean O'Siochain (Inspector of Taxes) v Bridget Neenan* Vol V p 472. 1998 p 111

Solicitors fees

whether allowable as management expense, *Stephen Court Ltd v JA Browne (Inspector of Taxes)* Vol V p 680

Special Commissioners

whether facts found by can be re-opened *McCall (deceased) v Commissioners of Inland Revenue* Vol I p 28

Sports

club, whether set up for tax avoidance or *bona fide* purposes *Revenue v ORMG* Vol III p 28

Stallion fees

profits from, whether liable to tax under Schedule B or Schedule D income tax paid, whether further balance due *Cloghran Stud Farm v AG Birch (Inspector of Taxes)* Vol I p 496

Stamp duties

agreement for sale granting immediate possession on payment of deposit followed by agreement for sale of residual interest, whether the transfer of the residual interest stampable on the value of the residual interest or on the value of the entire property whether *Waterford Glass (Group Services) Ltd v Revenue* Vol IV p 187

charitable bequest, whether it had to be expended in Ireland for to qualify for exemption under SD (Ire) Act 1842 s 38 *The Revenue Commissioners v The Most Reverend Edward Doorley* Vol V p 539

Stamp duties (contd)

deed inadvertently stamped, whether repayment due, *Terence Byrne v The Revenue Commissioners* Vol V p 560

instruments relating to the internal affairs of a society were exempt from stamp duty, whether this exemption extended to a transfer of a premises to a society to conduct its business *Irish Nationwide Building Society v Revenue Commissioners* Vol IV p 296

new interest and penalty provisions introduced by FA 1991 s 100 came into effect on 1 November 1991 and previous provision for interest and penalties under Stamp Act 1891 s 15 were repealed on 29 May 1991, the date of the passing of FA 1991, whether interest and penalties applied between 29 May 1991 and 1 November 1991 *Edward O'Leary v The Revenue Commissioners* Vol IV p 357

substance of transactions, amount chargeable on a deed of transfer, contracts and consideration structured to minimise stamp duty *VIEK Investments Ltd v The Revenue Commissioners* Vol IV p 367

whether doubt in a Stamp Act construed in favour of the taxpayer, whether a lease as a conveyance for sale, *JF O'Sullivan v The Revenue Commissioners* Vol V p 570

whether deeds not properly stamped were admissible in evidence *AIB plc v James Bolger & Joan Bolger* Vol V p 1; *Kenny, J v Revenue Commissioners, Goodman & Gemon Ltd (Notice Parties)* Vol V p 362

Statutory body

whether carrying on a trade *The Exported Live Stock (Insurance) Board v TJ Carroll (Inspector of Taxes)* Vol II p 211

Stock

IN TRADE

building contractors, whether lands the subject matter of a contract for sale entered into during an accounting period constitute trading stock for the year ending in that accounting period, whether inclusion of the lands in the accounts in accordance with good accounting procedure was evidence of the commercial reality of the transaction, whether absence of possession, conveyance of legal estate and planning permission relevant to taxpayer's claim for relief *Murnaghan Brothers Ltd v S O'Maoldhomhnaigh* Vol IV p 304

cost of, development company *O'Connlain (Inspector of Taxes) v Belvedere Estates Ltd* Vol III p 271

notional loss from decrease in value of goods before delivery *The Revenue Commissioners v Latchford & Sons Ltd* Vol I p 240

trading property company, farm land, letting to partners on conacre, area zoned for development, land transferred to new company, whether land trading stock of company *L O hArgain (Inspector of Taxes) v B Ltd* Vol III p 9

Stock relief

building contractors, whether lands the subject matter of a contract for sale entered into during an accounting period constitute trading stock for the year ending in that accounting period, whether inclusion of the lands in the accounts in accordance with good accounting procedure was evidence of the commercial reality of the transaction, whether absence of possession, conveyance of legal estate and planning permission relevant to taxpayer's claim for relief *Murnaghan Brothers Ltd v S O'Maoldhomhnaigh* Vol IV p 304

Stock relief (contd)

company engaged in manufacture and erection of prefabricated buildings deposit of 15 per cent of total cost paid on execution of contract, whether payment on account of trading stock or security for contracts, whether deposit should be deducted from value of stock for stock relief purposes *O'Laoghaire (Inspector of Taxes) v CD Ltd* Vol III p 51

definition of trading stock in hand *Green & Co (Cork) Ltd v The Revenue Commissioners* Vol I p 130

under FA 1975 s 31, sales must be direct to farmers, assembly not understood as manufacturing by well informed laymen *Irish Agricultural Machinery Ltd v S O'Culachain (Inspector of Taxes)* Vol III p 611

Stocks

change therein, causing reduction in value, whether trading profit *Davis (Inspector of Taxes) v Hibernian Bank Ltd* Vol I p 503

finance company, dealing in stocks and shares, whether investments should be valued at cost or market value *AB Ltd v Mac Giolla Riogh (Inspector of Taxes)* Vol II p 419

Shares

change therein, causing reduction in value, whether trading profit *Davis (Inspector of Taxes) v Hibernian Bank Ltd* Vol I p 503

Subrogation agreements

whether third party bound by terms of original agreement *The Companies Act 1963-1983 v MFN Construction Co Ltd (in liquidation) on the application of Patrick Tuffy (liquidator)* Vol IV p 82

Subcontractors

whether lorry owners carrying sand and gravel were engaged as subcontractors under a construction contract, whether the lorry owners became the proprietors of the quarry materials *O'Grady v Laragan Quarries Ltd* Vol IV p 269

Subsidiary

whether a "post-appointed day company" was a subsidiary of the appellant company *Associated Properties Ltd v The Revenue Commissioners* Vol II p 175

Substance of transactions

stamp duties, amount chargeable on a deed of transfer, contracts and consideration structured to minimise stamp duty *VIEK Investments Ltd v The Revenue Commissioners* Vol IV p 367

Succession

joint ownership whether survivor entitled, whether resulting trust *M Lynch v M Burke & AIB plc* Vol V p 271

whether surviving spouse must exercise right under Succession Act *In the Matter of the Estates of Cummins (Decd): O'Dwyer & Ors v Keegan & Ors* Vol V p 367

Summons

served in respect of tax liabilities the subject matter of earlier appeals whether Circuit Court judge has discretion to accept late filing of notice and fee, whether dissatisfaction expressed at the Circuit Court appeal hearings, whether dissatisfaction must be expressed immediately after determination by the Circuit Court, whether notice to county registrar must be lodged within 21 days together with the £20 fee, whether payment of tax denies access to the courts, whether requirements are directory or mandatory, whether tax must be paid before the case stated is determined, whether time lapse after expression of dissatisfaction is fatal *Michael A Bairead v Martin C Carr* Vol IV p 505

Superannuation scheme

whether trustees have absolute discretion on the distribution of the fund following the death of a member, whether a separated wife, a common law wife and children are entitled to be considered as beneficiaries, whether renunciation under a separation deed rules out entitlement, whether trustees are bound by a direction in the member's will *Crowe Engineering Ltd v Phyllis Lynch & Others* Vol IV p 340

Surety

whether creditor to resort to securities received from principal before proceeding against surety *AG v Sun Alliance & London Insurance Ltd* Vol III p 265

Surcharge

corporation tax, advertising agency, whether a profession for the purposes of corporation tax surcharge *Mac Giolla Mhaith (Inspector of Taxes) v Cronin & Associates Ltd* Vol III p 211

undistributed income of close company *Rahinstown Estates Co v M Hughes (Inspector of Taxes)* Vol III p 517

T

Tax amnesty

inducement to evade tax *Beverly Cooper-Flynn v RTE, Charlie Bird and James Howard* 2001 p 97

Tax avoidance

dealing in and developing land *O'Connlain (Inspector of Taxes) v Belvedere Estates Ltd* Vol III p 271

no general anti-avoidance legislation, allowable losses for capital gains tax used for avoidance of tax, whether allowable *Patrick McGrath & Others v JE McDermott (Inspector of Taxes)* Vol III p 683

patent rights paid to non-residents, scheme within *Furniss v Dawson* principle *Pandion Haliaetus Ltd, Ospreycare Ltd, Osprey Systems Design Ltd v The Revenue Commissioners* Vol III p 670

premium on lease payable by instalments, whether allowable under ITA 1967 s 91 or whether tax avoidance scheme *The Hammond Lane Metal Co Ltd v S O'Culachain (Inspector of Taxes)* Vol IV p 187

sports club, whether set up for tax avoidance or bona fide purposes *Revenue v ORMG* Vol III p 28

stamp duties, substance of transactions, amount chargeable on a deed of transfer, contracts and consideration structured to minimise stamp duty *VIEK Investments Ltd v The Revenue Commissioners* Vol IV p 367

Tax avoidance (contd)

transfer of assets to offshore tax havens, whether accountants could be requested to furnish relevant particulars in respect of all their clients *Warnock & Others practising as Stokes Kennedy Crowley and Co v The Revenue Commissioners* Vol III p 356

whether tax avoidance scheme under ITA 1967 Ch VI effective *The Hammond Lane Metal Co Ltd v S O'Culachain (Inspector of Taxes)* Vol IV p 187

whether a tax avoidance scheme *Airspace Investments Ltd v M Moore (Inspector of Taxes)* Vol V p 3

whether a tax avoidance scheme valid *Revenue Commissioners v Henry Young* Vol V p 295

Tax clearance certificate

capital gains tax, on sale of bonds, whether applicant ordinarily resident in the state is entitled to a clearance certificate *The State (FIC Ltd) v O'Ceallaigh* Vol III p 124

for Government contracts, whether Revenue Commissioners can have regard to tax default of previous "connected" company *The State (Melbarian Enterprises Ltd) v The Revenue Commissioners* Vol III p 290

whether absence of a clearance certificate prohibited the Revenue Commissioners from repaying tax deducted by purchaser *Bank of Ireland Finance Ltd v The Revenue Commissioners* Vol IV p 217

Tax deducted from Annuity

payable under a trust, where such tax is refunded by the Revenue Commissioners to the annuitant, is the annuitant accountable to the trust for the tax so refunded *In re Swan, Deceased; The Hibernian Bank Ltd v Munro & Ors* Vol V p 565

Tax havens

transfer of assets to offshore tax havens, whether accountants could be requested to furnish relevant particulars in respect of all their clients *Warnock & Others practising as Stokes Kennedy Crowley and Co v The Revenue Commissioners* Vol III p 356

Tax evasion

Inducement to evade tax *Beverly Cooper-Flynn v RTE, Charlie Bird and James Howard* 2001 p 97

Tax returns

return of income, what constitutes a proper return of income for the assessment of income tax *MA Bairead v M McDonald* Vol IV p 475

Technical information

payments made under an agreement for the supply of *S Ltd v O'Sullivan* Vol II p 602

Temporary employee

engaged through employment agency *The Minister for Labour v PMPA Insurance Co Ltd (under administration)* Vol III p 505

Time limit

for claiming repayment of stamp duty, whether expired, *Terence Byrne v The Revenue Commissioners* Vol V p 560

Toll Roads

whether VAT should be charged on tolls for use of roads and bridges *Case C-358/97 Commission of the European Communities v Ireland* 2000 p287

Total income

payment for maintenance and upkeep of residence not part of total income *The Most Honourable Frances Elizabeth Sarah Marchioness Conyngham v The Revenue Commissioners* Vol I p 231

whether the expression "total income means income before or after the deduction of group relief *Cronin (Inspector of Taxes) v Youghal Carpets Ltd* Vol III p 229

Trade

bad debts recovered, liability to tax *Bourke (Inspector of Taxes) v Lyster and Sons Ltd* Vol II p 374

brewery, whether liability in respect of transactions under DORA requisition orders *Arthur Guinness Son & Co Ltd v CIR*

carried on *Arthur Guinness Son & Co Ltd v CIR* Vol I p 1

carried on wholly in England *O'Conaill (Inspector of Taxes) v R* Vol II p 304

collection of rents and dividends and distribution of dividends, whether constituted trading *The Commissioners of Inland Revenue and The Dublin and Kingstown Railway Co* Vol I p 119

collection of, debts whether constituted trading *The City of Dublin Steampacket Co v Revenue Commissioners* Vol I p 108

executor carrying on trade, recovery by executor of debts allowed as bad debts in lifetime of deceased, whether a trading receipt *CD v JM O'Sullivan (Inspector of Taxes)* Vol II p 140

exercised in the State *The Cunard Steam Ship Co Ltd v Herlihy (Inspector of Taxes), and The Cunard Steam Ship Co Ltd v Revenue Commissioners* Vol I p 330

formation expenses, whether allowable against trading profits *JB Kealy (Inspector of Taxes) v O'Mara (Limerick) Ltd* Vol I p 642

income from the leasing of premises, whether leasing constitutes trading whether earned income *Pairceir (Inspector of Taxes) v EM* Vol II p 596

income school and exam fees whether trading income *The Pharmaceutical Society of Ireland v The Revenue Commissioners* Vol I p 542

Industrial and Provident Societies, trading with both members and non-members, investments and property purchased out of trading profits, whether the dividends and rents form part of the profits of the trade *The Revenue Commissioners v Y Ltd* Vol II p 195

levies on course betting, whether taxable a income or profits of a trade *The Racing Board v S O'Culachain* Vol IV p 73

payments on foot of earlier debt where profit arose, whether constituted trading *The City of Dublin Steampacket Co v Revenue Commissioners* Vol I p 108

profits/receipts *O'Dwyer (Inspector of Taxes) and the Revenue Commissioners v Irish Exporters and Importers Ltd (In Liquidation)* Vol I p 629

sale at cost plus interest, whether constituted trading *McCall (deceased) v Commissioners of Inland Revenue* Vol I p 28

statutory body, whether carrying on a trade *The Exported Live Stock (Insurance) Board v T J Carroll (Inspector of Taxes)* Vol II p 211

Trade (contd)

surplus of co-op from dealing with members, whether trading profits, whether exempt *Kennedy (Inspector of Taxes) v The Rattoo Co-op Dairy Society Ltd* Vol I p 315

trade consisting of the manufacturing of goods or sale of machinery or plant to farmers *Irish Agricultural Machinery Ltd v S O'Culachain (Inspector of Taxes)* Vol III p 611

whether a sum which arose to the company on the liquidation of a wholly owned subsidiary was part of its trading profits *Guinness & Mahon Ltd v Browne (Inspector of Taxes)* Vol III p 373

whiskey in bond sold by publican, whether trading transaction *McCall (deceased) v Commissioners of Inland Revenue* Vol I p 28

Trading stock

building contractors, whether lands the subject matter of a contract for sale entered into during an accounting period constitute trading stock for the year ending in that accounting period, whether inclusion of the lands in the accounts in accordance with good accounting procedure was evidence of the commercial reality of the transaction, whether absence of possession, conveyance of legal estate and planning permission relevant to taxpayer's claim for relief *Murnaghan Brothers Ltd v S O'Maoldhomhnaigh* Vol IV p 304

in hand, definition, for stock relief purposes *Green & Co (Cork) Ltd v The Revenue Commissioners* Vol I p 130

property company, farm land, letting to partners on conacre, area zoned for development, land transferred to new company, whether land trading stock of company *L O hArgain (Inspector of Taxes) v B Ltd* Vol III p 9

Training grants

whether capital or revenue receipt *O'Cleirigh (Inspector of Taxes) v Jacobs International Ltd Incorporated* Vol III p 165

Transfer

of assets to offshore tax havens *Warnock & Others practising as Stokes Kennedy Crowley and Co v The Revenue Commissioners* Vol III p 356

of land property company, farm land, letting to partners on conacre, area zoned for development, land transferred to new company, whether land trading stock of company *L O hArgain (Inspector of Taxes) v B Ltd* Vol III p 9

Travelling expenses

Schedule E deductions *Phillips (Inspector of Taxes) v Keane* Vol I p 64

Trees

whether purchasing and planting of trees is allowable deduction from farming profits *Connolly (Inspector of Taxes) v WW* Vol II p 657

Tribunal

of inquiry, whether Tribunal of Inquiry Evidence Act 1921 applies, whether a Tribunal constitutionally valid *Charles Haughey & Other v Attorney General and Others* 1998 p 119

Trusts

business carried on abroad controlled by resident trustees *The Executors and Trustees of A C Ferguson (deceased) v Donovan (Inspector of Taxes)* Vol I p 183

joint ownership whether survivor entitled, whether resulting trust *M Lynch v M Burke & AIB plc* Vol V p 271

payment under, for maintenance of residence not part of total income *The Most Hon Frances Elizabeth Sarah Marchioness Conyngham v The Revenue Commissioners* Vol I p 231

trust in favour of charitable objects with provision for re-vestment of income in settlor in certain contingencies whether income of settlor or trustees *HPC Hughes (Inspector of Taxes) v Miss Gretta Smyth (Sister Mary Bernard) & Others* Vol I p 411

Trustees

powers of, superannuation scheme whether trustees have absolute discretion on the distribution of the fund following the death of a member, whether a separated wife, a common law wife and children are entitled to be considered as beneficiaries, whether renunciation under a separation deed rules out entitlement, whether trustees are bound by a direction in the member's will *Crowe Engineering Ltd v Phyllis Lynch & Others* Vol IV p 340

under Succession Act 1965 *Moloney (Inspector of Taxes) v Allied Irish Banks Ltd as executors of the estate of Francis J Doherty deceased* Vol III p 477

U

Unconstitutional

aggregation of earned income of married persons unconstitutional *Bernard Muckley and Anne Muckley v Ireland, The Attorney General and The Revenue Commissioners* Vol III p 188

bookmaker convicted and fined in the District Court of offences under the Betting Acts penal warrant for imprisonment, whether constitutional *John B Murphy v District Justice Brendan Wallace & Others* Vol IV p 278

residential property tax, whether unconstitutional *PJ Madigan & p Madigan v The Attorney General, The Revenue Commissioners & Others* Vol III p 127

whether penalties for failure to make returns are unconstitutional *Edward McLoughlin and Thomas Marie Tuite v The Revenue Commissioners and The Attorney General* Vol III p 387

whether unconstitutional for applicant to be convicted and fined for keeping hydrocarbon oil in his motor vehicle on which custom and excise duty had not been paid, whether delegation of powers under Imposition of Duties Act 1957 is permissible *Charles McDaid v His Honour Judge David Sheehy, the Director of Public Prosecutions & Others* Vol IV p 162, Vol V p 696

Unjust enrichment of the State

whether a common law right to restitution *O'Rourke v Revenue Commissioners* Vol V p 321

V

Valuation

agreement for sale granting immediate possession on payment of deposit followed by agreement for sale of residual interest, whether the transfer of the residual interest stampable on the value of the residual interest or on the value of the entire property whether *Waterford Glass (Group Services) Ltd v The Revenue Commissioners* Vol IV p 187

agricultural land, appeal against market value at 6 April 1974 as determined by Circuit Court, whether agricultural value the sole determining factor, whether development potential attached on 6 April 1974, whether subsequent planning permission for milk processing plant relevant *J McMahon (Inspector of Taxes) v Albert Noel Murphy* Vol IV p 125

of land under F(MP)A 1968 s 18, development company *O'Connlain (Inspector of Taxes) v Belvedere Estates Ltd* Vol III p 271

of land occupied for market gardening *L v McGarry (Inspector of Taxes)* Vol II p 241

of shares in a private trading company, *E A Smyth v Revenue Commissioners* Vol V p 532, *In the estate of Thomas McNAmee & Other v The Revenue Commissioners* Vol V p 577

of shares in a private non-trading company *Revenue Commissioners v Henry Young* Vol V p 294

finance company, dealing in stocks and shares, whether investments should be valued at cost or market value *AB Ltd v Mac Giolla Riogh (Inspector of Taxes)* Vol II p 419

Value added tax

cable television system whether liable to value added tax on sales to customers *TJ Brosnan (Inspector of Taxes) v Cork Communications Ltd* Vol IV p 349

excise duty, whether zero rated *DH Burke & Sons Ltd v The Revenue Commissioners, Ireland and The Attorney General* Vol V p 418

installation of fixtures subject to low rate of value added tax, whether or not television aerials attached to roof of a house are fixtures *John Maye v The Revenue Commissioners* Vol III p 332

interpretation of when a transaction involves the sale of a business *Cyril Forbes v John Tobin And Janet Tobin* 2001 p 71

meaning of development property *Cyril Forbes v John Tobin And Janet Tobin* 2001 p 71

Property Unit Trust - whether VAT credits allowable on all expenses at pre lease and post lease stages - special VAT provisions *Erin Executor and Trustee Co Ltd v The Revenue Commissioners* Vol V p 76

refunds to non-EU residents, whether refunds obtainable through refunding agencies, whether revenue justified in withholding repayments, *Taxback Limited v The Revenue Commissioners* Vol V p 412

scheme for retailers, interpretation of, whether based on purchases or sales, *DH Burke & Sons Ltd v The Revenue Commissioners, Ireland and The Attorney General* Vol V p 418

Value added tax (contd)

supply of services by a solicitor to a non resident, not established in the state but resident in EU, where services deemed to be *supplied JJ Bourke (Inspector of Taxes) v WG Bradley & Sons* Vol IV p 117

whether chargeable on tolls for use of roads and bridges *Commission of the European Communities v Ireland* 2000 p 287

whether non resident company registered in the State entitled to be registered for value added tax *WLD Worldwide Leather Diffusion Ltd v The Revenue Commissioners* Vol V p 61

whether corporate body exploiting copyrights supplying service within meaning of VATA - Copyright Act 1963 *Phonographic Performance (Ireland) Ltd v J Somers (Inspector of Taxes)* Vol IV p 314

whether input credit available on sale of business premises has ceased *BD O'Shea (Inspector of Taxes) v Coole Park View Service Station Limited* 2000 p 247

whether value added tax is subject to laws of the European Union *Governor & Co of the Bank of Ireland v Michael John Meeneghan & Ors* Vol V p 44

Veterinary

body corporate performing statutory functions whether profits liable to tax *The Veterinary Council v F Corr (Inspector of Taxes)* Vol II p 204

Vocation

professional jockey *Wing v O'Connell (Inspector of Taxes)* Vol I p 155

Voluntary liquidator

whether liability of voluntary liquidator is different than that of court liquidator *A Noyek & Sons Ltd (in voluntary liquidation), Alex Burns v EN Hearne* Vol III p 523

W

Widows

contributory pension and children contributory pensions granted pension payable to the widow whereas children's pension payable to widow for children *E O'Coindealbhain (Inspector of Taxes) v Breda O'Carroll* Vol IV p 221

whether increases in widow's contributory social welfare pension by resson of dependent children constitutes taxable income received by and assessable on the widow *Sean O'Siochain (Inspector of Taxes) v Bridget Neenan* 1998 p 111

Wife

separate domicile *JW v JW* Vol IV p 437

Winding up

deferred by reason of scheme of arrangement approved by High Court *The Companies Act 1963-1983 and MFN Construction Co Ltd (in liquidation) on the application of Patrick Tuffy (liquidator)* Vol IV p 82

preferential payments, whether employee engaged under a contract of service or contract for services *In the matter of The Sunday Tribune Limited (in Liquidation)* 1998 p 177

shorter period allowed for making distributions of share capital in a winding up *Rahinstown Estates Co v M Hughes (Inspector of Taxes)* Vol III p 517

Winding up (contd)

whether assessments of PRSI entitled to super preferential priority *Re Coombe Importers Ltd (In Liq) and Re the Companies Acts 1963-1990* 1998 p 59

Winding Up Petition

Meaning of substantial and reasonable defence to Revenue petition to wind up company for unpaid taxes *In the Matter of Millhouse Taverns Ltd and the Companies Act 1963-1999* 2001 p 77

Withholding tax

on professional services, whether method of granting credit for same is constitutional *Michael Daly v The Revenue Commissioners* Vol V p 213

Woodlands

whether purchasing and planting of trees is allowable deduction from farming profits *Connolly (Inspector of Taxes) v WW* Vol II p 657